# Lecture Notes in Computer Science   9972

Commenced Publication in 1973
Founding and Former Series Editors:
Gerhard Goos, Juris Hartmanis, and Jan van Leeuwen

More information about this series at http://www.springer.com/series/7412

Leszek J. Chmielewski · Amitava Datta
Ryszard Kozera · Konrad Wojciechowski (Eds.)

# Computer Vision and Graphics

International Conference, ICCVG 2016
Warsaw, Poland, September 19–21, 2016
Proceedings

 Springer

*Editors*

Leszek J. Chmielewski
Faculty of Applied Informatics and
  Mathematics
Warsaw University of Life Sciences –
  SGGW
Warsaw
Poland

Amitava Datta
School of Computer Science and Software
  Engineering
The University of Western Australia
Perth
Australia

Ryszard Kozera
Faculty of Applied Informatics and
  Mathematics
Warsaw University of Life Sciences –
  SGGW
Warsaw
Poland

Konrad Wojciechowski
Institute of Computer Science
Silesian University of Technology
Gliwice
Poland

ISSN 0302-9743 .                      ISSN 1611-3349   (electronic)
Lecture Notes in Computer Science
ISBN 978-3-319-46417-6        ISBN 978-3-319-46418-3   (eBook)
DOI 10.1007/978-3-319-46418-3

Library of Congress Control Number: 2016952504

LNCS Sublibrary: SL6 – Image Processing, Computer Vision, Pattern Recognition, and Graphics

Printed on acid-free paper

This Springer imprint is published by Springer Nature
The registered company is Springer International Publishing AG
The registered company address is: Gewerbestrasse 11, 6330 Cham, Switzerland

# Preface

The International Conference on Computer Vision and Graphics, organized since 2002, is the continuation of The International Conferences on Computer Graphics and Image Processing, GKPO, held in Poland every second year from 1990 to 2000. The founder and organizer of these conferences was Prof. Wojciech Mokrzycki. The main objective of ICCVG is to provide an environment for the exchange of ideas between researchers in the closely related domains of computer vision and computer graphics.

ICCVG 2016 brought together about 80 authors. The proceedings contain 68 papers, each accepted on the grounds of three independent reviews.

ICCVG 2016 was organized by the Association for Image Processing, Poland, (Towarzystwo Przetwarzania Obrazów – TPO), the Faculty of Applied Informatics and Mathematics, Warsaw University of Life Sciences (WZIM SGGW), together with the supporting organizers: the Faculty of Information Science, West Pomeranian University of Technology (WI ZUT), Szczecin, and the Polish-Japanese Academy of Information Technology (PJATK).

The Association for Image Processing integrates the Polish community working on the theory and applications of computer vision and graphics. It was formed between 1989 and 1991.

The Faculty of Applied Informatics and Mathematics, established in 2008 at the Warsaw University of Life Sciences – SGGW, offers programs of study in informatics as well as in informatics and econometrics. Its location at the leading life sciences university in Poland, which celebrated its 200 years recently, is the source of opportunities for valuable research at the border of applied information sciences, agribusiness, veterinary medicine, and the broadly understood domains of biology and economy.

We would like to thank all the members of the Scientific Committee, as well as the additional reviewers, for their help in ensuring the high quality of the papers. We would also like to thank Grażyna Domańska-Żurek for her excellent work on technically editing the proceedings, and Dariusz Frejlichowski, Bartosz Świderski, Luiza Ochnio, Dominika Rządkowska, and Henryk Palus for their engagement in the conference organization and administration.

September 2016

Leszek J. Chmielewski
Amitava Datta
Ryszard Kozera
Konrad Wojciechowski

# Organization

- Association for Image Processing (TPO)
- Faculty of Applied Informatics and Mathematics, Warsaw University of Life Sciences (WZIM SGGW)
- Polish-Japanese Academy of Information Technology (PJATK)
- Faculty of Information Science, West Pomeranian University of Technology (WI ZUT), Szczecin
- Springer *Lecture Notes in Computer Science* (LNCS)

## Conference General Chairs

Leszek J. Chmielewski, Poland
Ryszard Kozera, Poland
Konrad Wojciechowski, Poland

## Scientific Committee

Ivan Bajla, Slovakia
Prabir Bhattacharya, USA
Gunilla Borgefors, Sweden
Nadia Brancati, Italy
M. Emre Celebi, USA
Leszek Chmielewski, Poland
Dmitry Chetverikov, Hungary
Piotr Czapiewski, Poland
László Czúni, Hungary
Silvana Dellepiane, Italy
Marek Domański, Poland
Mariusz Flasiński, Poland
Paweł Forczmański, Poland
Dariusz Frejlichowski, Poland
Maria Frucci, Italy
André Gagalowicz, France
Duncan Gillies, UK
Samuel Morillas Gómez, Spain
Ewa Grabska, Poland
Diego Gragnaniello, Italy
Marcin Iwanowski, Poland
Adam Jóźwik, Poland
Heikki Kälviäinen, Finland

Andrzej Kasiński, Poland
Włodzimierz Kasprzak, Poland
Bertrand Kerautret, France
Nahum Kiryati, Israel
Reinhard Klette, New Zealand
Przemysław Klęsk, Poland
Józef Korbicz, Poland
Marcin Korzeń, Poland
Ryszard Kozera, Poland
Hans-Jörg Kreowski, Germany
Adam Krzyżak, Canada
Juliusz L. Kulikowski, Poland
Marek Kurzyński, Poland
Bogdan Kwolek, Poland
Y.B. Kwon, South Korea
Bart Lamiroy, France
Piotr Lech, Poland
Anna Lewandowska, Poland
Dongwei Liu, New Zealand
Vladimir Lukin, Russia
Wojciech Maleika, Poland
Witold Malina, Poland
Krzysztof Małecki, Poland

# Contents

# Human Face and Silhouette Recognition and Analysis

# Medical Image Analysis

## Motion Analysis, Tracking and Surveillance

## Security and Protection

## Applications

## Mathematical Analysis, Estimation and Approximation

# Computer Graphics, Perception and Image Quality

# Generation of Complex Underground Systems for Application in Computer Games with Schematic Maps and L-Systems

Izabella Antoniuk$^{(\boxtimes)}$ and Przemyslaw Rokita

Institute of Computer Science, Warsaw University of Technology,
Nowowiejska 15/19, Warsaw, Poland
I.Antoniuk@stud.elka.pw.edu.pl, P.Rokita@ii.pw.edu.pl

**Abstract.** This paper presents a method for procedural generation of complex underground systems, by processing set of schematic input maps and incorporating L-system and cellular automata. Existing solutions usually focus only on generation of 2D maps. 3D procedures tend to require large amount of input data or complex computation, rarely providing user with considerable level of control over shape of generated system. For applications such as computer games, most of existing algorithms are not acceptable. We present our solution, that allows controlled generation of complex, underground systems, based on simplified input. Final objects produced by presented algorithm can be further edited and are represented as meshes in 3D space. We allow evaluation at every key step, ensuring high level of controllability and proximity of final object to user specifications. Results we obtain can be used in computer games or similar applications.

## 1 Introduction

Procedural content generation algorithms, especially those used in computer games provides designer with variety of challenges. Each created object needs to meet series of specific constraints as well as satisfy different requirements. Especially in recent years amount of content in video games is growing awfully fast, increasing production costs and amount of time designer needs to spend modeling each element. Procedural algorithms are largely discarded in such applications, since they usually provide low level of control over shape of final object. Those problems are addressed in numerous works, by using simplified input as a base for generation [15], describing shape of desired terrain through constraints and properties [14] or even using genetic algorithms to evolve final terrain as close to user specifications as possible [7]. Existing algorithms also tend to vary, depending from type of terrain that is generated [10–12, 16].

Common problem with most of existing algorithms is that they are largely based on height maps or their variations, as a terrain data representation. Such approach prevents generation of terrain features with overhangs or such areas as caves or dungeons. Structures like that are integral part of numerous computer

© Springer International Publishing AG 2016
L.J. Chmielewski et al. (Eds.): ICCVG 2016, LNCS 9972, pp. 3–16, 2016.
DOI: 10.1007/978-3-319-46418-3_1

games, varying from classic dungeon crawlers like Dungeon Master or Legend of Grimrock, to recent productions like The Elder Scrolls: Skyrim, Dragon Age and Witcher series, as well as many others. Underground systems especially provide interesting and specific challenges for the player. At the same time such structures need to meet series of properties to remain believable, as well as show consistent and interesting content. Taking all that constraints into account, underground shape generation in itself is a challenging and interesting topic, also addressed in numerous works. Main problem with existing solutions is that they mostly represent created systems only in two-dimensional space [20–22]. Those algorithms that consider three-dimensional solutions often require large amount of input data or long computation. At the same time, user rarely has any control over general shape of generated system, while created objects are not easily modified [19,24,25].

Caves and dungeons, both from real world, as well as those created by designers for various computer games, usually can be divided into few basic elements: open spaces of different sizes, passages and terrains blocked by various obstacles. Defining such elements is much easier and will require fewer constraints than representing entire dungeon. In our approach we propose a method for generation of underground systems, by processing set of schematic maps. By defining basic terrain types, that are used to generate content in each section of final terrain we ensure, that overall shape of final system will follow user specifications. At the same time terrain representation we use permits overlapping structures, as well as spaces or corridors placed directly above one another. To ensure that created structures look as naturally as possible, we use L-System to generate basic shape in each tile further extending it with cellular automata and ensuring accessibility of each part of generated system. Since we permit modifications introduced by user at every key step of generation process, our approach can produce playable terrain from simple input, with well-defined overall shape. Furthermore final terrain can be easily adjusted and modified by designer.

The rest of this paper is organized as follows. In Sect. 2 we review some of existing works, related to our area of research. Section 3 contains overview of our approach, along with some initial assumptions. In Sect. 4 we discuss obtained results as well as some areas of future work. Finally we conclude our work in Sect. 5.

## 2   Related Work

Procedural content generation for computer games and other, similar applications is very popular and widely addressed topic, offering different challenges and interesting problems. Existing procedures vary, from ones producing very specific content, like vegetation [28], roads [5] or rivers [6], to more complex methodologies producing chosen type of terrain [7–9], or diverse worlds, with different properties describing their shape [10–12].

Although in most cases generated content is interesting visually, controllability over its final shape is another issue. Existing solutions if they allow user any amount of control, can vary greatly in that aspect. Starting from procedures with only basic level of control over shape of final object [13], to methods requiring that final terrain model meets series of strict properties [14]. Control user has over shape of terrain can also be provided in different ways: controlling parameters that define shape of object [9,12], using simplified shapes as input for method [7,15], incorporating story to guide generation process [16], or using schematic maps to assign different properties to final terrain [17,18].

Procedural underground generation is yet another area of research, with specific constraints and problems. While dungeons are man-made structures, with easily defined properties, caves tend to be more random, and therefore more difficult to model accurately. In real world, such structures are usually formed when rock is dissolved by acidic water and then removed by water flow [2]. By definition, caves are big enough for person to enter, and can contain different passages and spaces with characteristic structures, often placed directly below one another. Because of that property, terrain data cannot be stored in height maps in their basic form, and most procedural algorithms require additional changes before they are applied to underground generation.

First group of algorithms considers generation of various structures and features characteristic for underground environments, such as overhangs [8], stalactites, stalagmites and columns [19]. Although such structures are interesting visually, when it comes to generation of larger systems, presented algorithms can only be considered as part of larger solution. Second set of procedures focuses on generating entire systems in two-dimensional space, using different methods for defining system shape, such as: cellular automata [20], fitness function and predefined shapes [21] or fitness function and checkpoints defined by user [22]. Main problem with presented approaches is that they are mainly two-dimensional. Adapting resulting maps to 3D space would present user with repeatable shapes, and can produce areas that are not connected to main system. At the same time neither approach gives considerable level of control over general shape of generated system.

Final group of algorithms applies procedural methods to generation of three-dimensional shapes with different properties of final object as their main focus:

- Creating systems with geologically correct shapes [24,25].
- Obtaining caves with realistic features [23].
- Providing easy way to define shape of final cave [27].
- Generating playable terrain with well-defined properties [26].
- Generating vast and playable systems [1].

Although algorithms in that group produce interesting and diverse content, they still have some drawbacks. Results obtained in [24,25] despite their geological correctness can be difficult to modify or incorporate in computer game. Caves generated in [23] are very interesting, especially from gameplay point of view. Unfortunately mesh of final objects is very complex, and shows some remnants of used voxel representation, despite smoothing procedure. In [27] authors achieve very high level of control over layout of final cave, by allowing user to design it with simple shapes. At the same time representing more complex systems might require large amount of work. Also no terrain properties crucial to computer games are considered. In [26] authors take those constraints into account, making sure that cave system created by their procedure is playable. In their approach user can define most properties of desired terrain, such as size of generated spaces, number of branches or relationships between all structures. Unfortunately, since authors use volumetric terrain representation, incorporating such objects into most computer games would require additional work. Another disadvantage is that although user can define some key structures, layout of entire system is mostly random. Authors also point out, that it is sometime difficult to predict how long the generation process will take, especially with more complex systems. Another method, also focusing on playability of generated cave systems, takes slightly different approach [1]. Authors first define overall layout of underground terrain by using L-system to generate structural points. After that, they generate tunnels by wrapping meta-ball around defined path, shaping entire cave system. In next step mesh data is extracted from voxel representation of space and obtained results are rendered with textures and shaders. Terrain created by presented procedure is interesting, although covering large spaces with same texture gives impression, that entire system is repeatable. Authors also do not define overall shape of created terrain, relying only on data obtained from L-system in that aspect.

Procedural content generation allows creation of different terrains, with diverse content. For detailed study of existing algorithms see [3,4,28–31].

## 3 Algorithm Overview

In this section we would like to first present assumptions that led to design of our procedure. After initial introduction to chosen methodology and constraints, we proceed to overview of our procedural underground generation algorithm.

### 3.1 Initial Assumptions

Procedures used in content generation can vary greatly, regarding both type of data that is needed for algorithm to work and manner in which obtained information is processed. In our work we assumed, that designer should be able to incorporate objects generated by our procedure in computer game or other, similar application. Therefore we wanted to achieve high level of control over shape of generated underground system, with possibility to check algorithm progress at different stages of generation. With such approach we can avoid propagation of early errors from basic maps describing system shape to 3D object. In our previous work [32] we generated terrain, also designed for usage in computer games, by processing set of schematic maps. Terrain in computer games is usually represented by a map, that player can refer to, even if described areas are not strictly two-dimensional (i.e. underground maps in Dragon Age: Inquisition were represented as series of 2D outlines of cave shape at different levels). Taking that into account we decided to use similar approach:

- Cave system is represented with set of schematic maps.
- Each pixel in input maps represents properties of single tile from final object.

Constraints defining underground system often need to be more demanding, than those describing surface terrain. For example, we might need spaces of certain sizes, and some features can occur above each other. We chose definitions of our input maps (currently we use three types of maps), taking those constraints into account.

- System generated by our procedure is divided into levels and tiles.
- Levels contain tiles with same height dispersion, that are not overlapping.
- Tile contains fragment of generated system with properties that are either defined by user, or obtained from input maps.
- Since tiles represent pixels from input maps, we define them as squares to simplify calculations without limiting possible shapes that can be generated.
- Tile size defines number of pixels in 2D map and vertices in 3D object.
- Terrain map, stored in RGB image, contains definition of terrain type.
- Height map, stored in grey-scale image, defines relative height of tiles inside single level.
- Connection maps, separate for connections inside level and between them and stored in text file, define transitions between tiles.
- We represent multilevel data in single file (see Fig. 1).

Each map we use is independent from others, therefore providing user with easy way to modify different data, without the need to change many parameters. We can also easily obtain different versions of our layout, since basic shape generation in our procedure is seed-based. After generation process each pixel in input terrain map is represented by single region in final object, with properties and placement defined by presented input files. Each object can be modified and adjusted separately, without the need to regenerate entire cave system, preventing situations when one incorrect region disqualifies entire result.

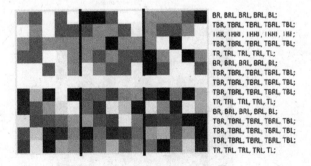

**Fig. 1.** Terrain map (top left), height map (bottom left), and all possible connections (T - Top, B - Bottom, R - Right and L - Left) between tiles defined for given set of data (right). Vertical lines mark transitions between following levels data.

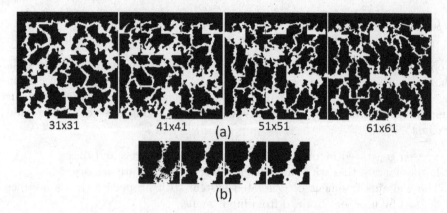

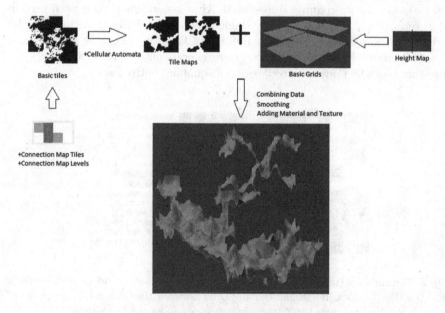

**Fig. 2.** Generated 2D tile maps: (a) Tiles generated for single 5 × 5 level, with different tile sizes. (b) Evolution of single tile. Starting from left: L-System generation, cellular automata, connecting regions and final smoothing of cave shape.

## 3.2 Method Overview

In this section we present algorithm for generation of multilevel, underground systems. Data we use in this process can be either generated automatically or provided by user. Apart from input files we also use some predefined properties, that mostly depend from type of terrain in currently processed tile. For overview of our procedure see Fig. 3. As a test platform for out method we use Blender

**Fig. 3.** Algorithm overview.

application (version 2.76). We use this 3D modeling environment, because it contains complete python interpreter, providing access to program functionality as well as easy way to both implement and visualize our procedure. Chosen application was also proven sufficient to visualization and testing purposes in our previous experiments [32]. For Blender documentation see [33]. Presented procedure consists of two main steps:

– Processing input data files and generating basic maps.
– Generating 3D objects from obtained information and input files.

**Basic Maps with L-System and Cellular Automata.**

Terrain shape generation can be performed by different methods, some complex [7,10–12,15], while other will require only simple input [13,17,18]. We decided to use L-System for basic shape generation and cellular automata, for filing operations. L-systems usually produce output, that looks naturally, therefore such algorithm adds to our final system believability. Cellular automata on the other hand can be easily adjusted, to further increase desired shape properties.

Since we use schematic maps as a base for our procedure, in first step we process them, assigning terrain properties and parameters. First map we check is terrain map. Each pixel in this file defines basic properties for tile, that will be further used in generation process. Depending from terrain type in each tile, such parameters as L-system or cellular automata iterations will differ, with highest values assigned for large space, and smallest for passages, set at one-tenth of tile size. Rules for L-system are generated randomly, from basic set of keys: T: go to top cell, B: go to bottom cell, R: go to right cell, L: go to left cell, I: increase cell height, D: decrease cell height, R: reset cell height, S: create space.

First operation we perform is creating set of tile images of given size, and filling them with evolved L-systems. Size of single tile is an user-specified parameter. We place starting points for L-system operations at each side connected to another tile (we obtain that information from both connection maps), and at the middle. After generated rule is processed, basic shape of tile can be seen (see Fig. 2(b)). At this point tile presents ragged and inconsistent appearance. We then use cellular automata to fill holes and smooth transitions inside tile. Finally we connect cave regions in generated tile and perform additional smoothing, to further increase system appearance. Resulting tile map of single level, for different tile sizes are presented at Fig. 2(a). As can be seen, sometimes tile borders are visible, especially when L-system circulates local minimum close to tile edge. Despite that generated shapes are interesting, and often quite close in their layout to real world caves (see [2]).

At this point our approach has following advantages:

– All spaces produced by our procedure are connected.
– We are not using predefined shapes.
– With our input maps we can define overall shape of underground system.
– Our data representation is fully three-dimensional.

**3D Shape Generation.**

After maps for all tiles in every level are generated and processed, we used obtained data along with information from input files, to generate 3D shape of entire system. Since our framework is Blender, that usually operates on square faces, not triangular ones, we define our map tiles as grids with given size, where number of pixels in single tile image translates directly to number of vertices in final object.

In first step of this part of our procedure, we generate planes representing each tile from terrain map (if they are not empty tiles), and place them in 3D space, according to data obtained from height map. At this point we have series of planes, that can provide quite good impression about general system layout.

After placing grids, we proceed to assigning cave shapes and height values. To achieve that, we use tile maps, generated with L-system and cellular automata, as well as set of heights for cave tiles, generated by first algorithm. For visualization purposes we then remove all wall cells and vertices that correspond to them, leaving only final cave shape. Since after this operation terrain model shows jagged appearance, we then run simple procedure, to fill those gaps, ensuring smooth edge transitions.

After assigning data from tile maps, to 3D grids we have a set of objects representing final system shapes, that are placed across the scene, but are not yet connected. Similarly as in our terrain generation method [32], we start by connecting edges of neighboring tiles (if such connection is defined). Simultaneously, we proceed with smoothing transition, starting from edge and proceeding further into region. Since L-system sometimes produce heights that are very distant, resulting in sharp transitions between cell tiles, we also run procedure to average those values. Finally we assign simple texture, to further improve our final object appearance. Figure 4, shows example elements generated by our method.

At this point we obtain complex system, where each tile of input terrain map is represented as editable Blender object. Using schematic maps as a basis for generation process proves to be quite sufficient in defining overall system layout,

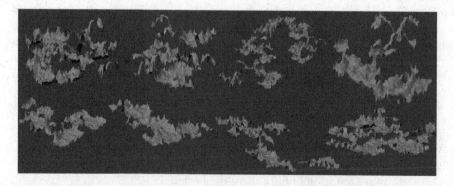

**Fig. 4.** Example terrain shapes created by our procedure.

---

**Algorithm 1.** Multilevel underground system generation

---

**procedure** CAVEGENERATION(*TileSize*, , *Size*, *HeightMap*, *ConnectionsTiles*,
    *ConnectionsLevels*, *TerrainMap*, *NumberOfLevels*)
    **for all** Tiles in TerrainMap **do**
        UpdateTileWithLSystem(TileMap)
        UpdateTileWithCellularAutomata(TileMap)
        SmoothMaps(TileMap)
    **end for**
    PlaceBasicGrids(HeightMap)
    **for all** Grids **do**
        UpdateGridData(TileMap, VertexHeights)
        AllignSmoothAndAddTexture(TileHeights,TileMaps,TileConnections,Depth,
Name)
    **end for**
**end procedure**

---

although we do not have much control over system shape in final tile, besides
defining starting points for L-system to work with. On the other hand, entire
generated system can be easily modified and adjusted, either insider Blender, or
after converting objects to other environments. For overview of entire procedure
see Algorithm 1. To summarize, proposed procedure has following advantages:

- We can define general system layout with easy to create input files.
- Mesh of our final object is not very complex, allowing incorporation in com-
  puter games or similar applications without the need for optimization.
- Although designer cannot get results at interactive rate, times required to
  produce final output are acceptable and mostly constant (see Table 1).
- Obtained system can be modified without additional operations.

**Table 1.** Rendering of example terrain[s]. System is set at 3 levels with size $5 \times 5$ tiles.

| Tile size | L-system iterations | Map generation | 3D operations | Total time |
|---|---|---|---|---|
| $21 \times 21$ | 2 | 14,425 | 4,225 | 18.650 |
| $31 \times 31$ | 3 | 59,151 | 9,042 | 68.193 |
| $41 \times 41$ | 4 | 147,929 | 22,116 | 192.161 |
| $51 \times 51$ | 5 | 424,044 | 49,135 | 473.179 |
| $61 \times 61$ | 6 | 909,183 | 71,330 | 980,513 |

## 4    Results and Future Work

Algorithm presented in this paper was implemented using in-built python interpreter in Blender application. Created program can generate underground systems and then represent them as mesh objects. Experiments were performed on

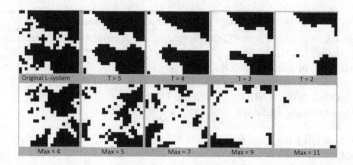

**Fig. 5.** Tile maps expanded using cellular automata with different threshold value (Top) and L-systems evolved with different maximal length of starting rules (Bottom). Tile size is set at 21.

**Table 2.** Rendering times for different number of L-system iterations. Single tile size is set at 21, and scene is set at single level with $3 \times 3$ tiles.

| L-system iterations | Map generation | 3D operations | Total time |
| --- | --- | --- | --- |
| 2 | 1,715 | 0,337 | 2,052 |
| 4 | 1,915 | 0,371 | 2,286 |
| 7 | 3,614 | 0,397 | 4,011 |
| 8 | 5,981 | 0,407 | 6,388 |
| 9 | 13,967 | 0,422 | 14,389 |

a PC with AMD Radeon HD 6650 M graphic card, Intel Core i5-2430M processor (2,4 GHz per core), and 4 GB of ram.

During our experiments we tested different values of input parameters, defining properties of used procedures. First tested value defined maximum length of transition rules for L-system. To small values resulted in repeatable shapes, while too long rules often filled entire tile. Optimal values we found usually were smaller than half of the tile size, and higher than one-fourth of this parameter (see Fig. 5, bottom).

Second value we tested, also related to L-system procedure, defines number of evolutions applied to starting word. To small values resulted in clusters, that usually stuck to starting cell and its surroundings, while to high values greatly increased computation costs (see Table 2), and quickly fills out processed tile. During experiments we discovered, that this value as well should be based on tile size. Results that were interesting and acceptable, without too great increase in computation cost were obtained by taking floor from dividing tile size by ten (see Fig. 6).

Third tested factor is related to cellular automata procedure and defines threshold for its expansion rule. We use this procedure to give underground system some volume and fill unnecessary spaces, but we wanted to avoid situations, when it would blur shape generated by L-system. We noticed that values above or equal to half of total cell neighbors number work best for this purpose (see Fig. 5, top).

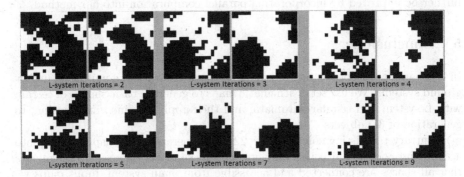

**Fig. 6.** L-system evolved with different number of iterations and resulting tile map. Tile size is set at 21.

We also consider amount of work required to create input files and control user has over shape of final object. Small maps can be drawn quickly, often taking only few minutes to create, while larger maps can better define different properties and transitions of final object. Usually maps with $5 \times 5$ tiles in each level could be completed relatively quickly and were sufficient to represent most of desired shapes.

Main application we see for models generated by our procedure concern computer games and other similar applications, therefore controllability and generation rate seem to be most important part. Our implementation provides example terrains based on simple input maps relatively quickly, especially for smaller tiles with less L-system evolutions. Generated shapes are interesting, and although sometimes tile structures are visible, such problems can be easily adjusted. One issue we encounter is directly connected to properties of L-systems. Since we use random generation rules, sometimes algorithm can produce repeatable structures, caves that stick to tile edges or clusters of connected cells. Fortunately this problem can be easily resolved by changing seed base for generation rules. Obtained terrain is divided into separate objects, each of them representing single tile. Such objects can be easily adjusted, and at the same time one faulty part does not disqualify entire result. Generated terrains are still rather simple, but they show interesting shapes, and can be easily used as base for further work or as a terrain in simple game. Another possible application is providing visualization during design process.

Presented approach still has some drawbacks, that we would like to address in the future. Firstly, we would like to add more details to terrain, either by incorporating different textures (currently we use one of in-built Blender textures), or by placing some objects across entire system. Since created spaces are mostly cave-like, we would also like to add separate procedure for generating dungeons, as well as improve current algorithm, to decrease visibility of tile borders in cases when L-system generates shapes along tile border. We would also like to add generation of different cave features. As for our performance it can further be improved by incorporating parallel computation into our method.

## 5   Conclusions

In this paper we propose a method for procedural generation of multilevel underground systems. We use set of schematic maps to generate basic shapes of terrain with L-system and cellular automata, and then apply obtained information, to generation of 3D objects.

Contrary to existing solutions [20–22], we generate basic shapes taking into account properties and constraints specific to computer games. We make sure that all spaces are connected and accessible from main system. Input maps we use ensure, that generated objects will be as close to designer specifications as possible, providing large amount of control over system layout. We also do not use predefined shapes, therefore not limiting possible outcomes inside each tile. Our maps are also designed to represent 3D terrain. Contrary to previous works in that field [1, 23–27], we avoid generation of overly complex meshes. Since our approach is seed-based, we can quickly obtain variations of final object for given set of data. User can also evaluate procedures work at each key step.

Although our approach has some drawbacks it still can produce usable terrains, that are interesting visually and from gameplay point of view. Main issues we encounter are directly connected with L-system specific properties, such as circulating local minima or to slow computation wit longer rules or greater number of evolve iterations. We plan to address this and other problems in future work. Objects generated by our procedure can represent complex systems, and as such can be used either as a base for model of terrain in computer games and similar applications or during design process, as a visualization of such elements.

## References

1. Mark, B., Berechet, T., Mahlmann, T., Togelius, J.: Procedural generation of 3D caves for games on the GPU. In: Foundations of Digital Games (2015)
2. Palmer, A.N.: Origin and morphology of limestone caves. Geol. Soc. Am. Bull. **103**(1), 1–21 (1991)
3. Shaker, N., Liapis, A., Togelius, J., Lopes, R., Bidara, R.: Constructive generation methods for dungeons and levels (DRAFT). In: Procedural Content Generation in Games, pp. 31–55 (2015)
4. van der Linden, R., Lopes, R., Bidarra, R.: Procedural generation of dungeons. IEEE Trans. Comput. Intell. AI Games **6**(1), 78–89 (2014)
5. Galin, E., Peytavie, A., Marchal, N., Gurin, E.: Procedural generation of roads. Comput. Graph. Forum **29**(2), 429–438 (2010). Blackwell Publishing Ltd
6. Huijser, R., Dobbe, J., Bronsvoort, W.F., Bidarra, R.: Procedural natural systems for game level design. In: SBGAMES, pp. 189–198. IEEE (2010)

7. Kamal, K.R., Kaykobad, M.: Generation of mountain ranges by modifying a controlled terrain generation approach. In: 11th International Conference on Computer and Information Technology, pp. 527–532. IEEE, December 2008
8. Gamito, M.N., Musgrave, F.K.: Procedural landscapes with overhangs. In: 10th Portuguese Computer Graphics Meeting, vol. 2, p. 3 (2001)
9. Michelon de Carli, D., Pozzer, C.T., Bevilacqua, F., Schetinger, V.: Procedural generation of 3D canyons. In: SIBGRAPI, pp. 103–110. IEEE (2014)
10. Peytavie, A., Galin, E., Grosjean, J., Merillou, S.: Arches: a framework for modeling complex terrains. Comput. Graph. Forum **28**(2), 457–467 (2009). Blackwell Publishing Ltd
11. Smelik, R.M., Tutenel, T., de Kraker, K.J., Bidarra, R.: A declarative approach to procedural modeling of virtual worlds. Comput. Graph. **35**(2), 352–363 (2011)
12. Smelik, R., Galka, K., de Kraker, K.J., Kuijper, F., Bidarra, R.: Semantic constraints for procedural generation of virtual worlds. In: Proceedings of the 2nd International Workshop on Procedural Content Generation in Games, p. 9. ACM (2011)
13. Prusinkiewicz, P., Hammel, M.: A fractal model of mountains with rivers. Graph. Interface **93**, 174–180 (1993). Canadian Information Processing Society
14. Tutenel, T., Bidarra, R., Smelik, R.M., De Kraker, K.J.: Rule-based layout solving and its application to procedural interior generation. In: CASA Workshop on 3D Advanced Media in Gaming and Simulation (2009)
15. Merrell, P., Manocha, D.: Model synthesis: a general procedural modeling algorithm. IEEE Trans. Visual Comput. Graphics **17**(6), 715–728 (2011)
16. Matthews, E., Malloy, B.: Procedural generation of story-driven maps. In: CGAMES, pp. 107–112. IEEE (2011)
17. Smelik, R.M., Tutenel, T., de Kraker, K.J., Bidarra, R.: A proposal for a procedural terrain modelling framework. In: EGVE, pp. 39–42 (2008)
18. Smelik, R.M., Tutenel, T., de Kraker, K.J., Bidarra, R.: Declarative terrain modeling for military training games. Int. J. Comput. Games Technol. **2010** (2010). Article no: 2
19. Raz Tortelli, D.M., Walter, M.: Modeling and rendering the growth of speleothems in real-time. In: GRAPP, pp. 27–35 (2009)
20. Johnson, L., Yannakakis, G.N., Togelius, J.: Cellular automata for real-time generation of infinite cave levels. In: Proceedings of the 2010 Workshop on Procedural Content Generation in Games, p. 10. ACM (2010)
21. Valtchanov, V., Brown, J.A.: Evolving dungeon crawler levels with relative placement. In: Proceedings of the 5th International C* Conference on Computer Science and Software Engineering, pp. 27–35. ACM (2012)
22. Ashlock, D., Lee, C., McGuinness, C.: Search-based procedural generation of maze-like levels. IEEE Trans. Comput. Intell. AI Games **3**(3), 260–273 (2011)
23. Cui, J., Chow, Y.W., Zhang, M.: Procedural generation of 3D cave models with stalactites and stalagmites (2011)
24. Boggus, M., Crawfis, R.: Explicit generation of 3D models of solution caves for virtual environments. In: CGVR, pp. 85–90 (2009)
25. Boggus, M., Crawfis, R.: Procedural creation of 3D solution cave models. In: Proceedings of IASTED, pp. 180–186 (2009)
26. Santamaria-Ibirika, A., Cantero, X., Huerta, S., Santos, I., Bringas, P.G.: Procedural playable cave systems based on voronoi diagram and delaunay triangulation. In: International Conference on Cyberworlds, pp. 15–22. IEEE (2014)

27. Boggus, M., Crawfis, R.: Prismfields: a framework for interactive modeling of three dimensional caves. In: Bebis, G., Boyle, R., Parvin, B., Koracin, D., Chung, R., Hammound, R., Hussain, M., Kar-Han, T., Crawfis, R., Thalmann, D., Kao, D., Avila, L. (eds.) ISVC 2010. LNCS, vol. 6454, pp. 213–221. Springer, Heidelberg (2010). doi:10.1007/978-3-642-17274-8_21

28. Prusinkiewicz, P., Lindenmayer, A.: The Algorithmic Beauty of Plants. Springer Science & Business Media, New York (2012)

29. Hendrikx, M., Meijer, S., Van Der Velden, J., Iosup, A.: Procedural content generation for games: a survey. ACM TOMM **9**(1), 1 (2013)

30. Smelik, R.M., Tutenel, T., Bidarra, R., Benes, B.: A survey on procedural modelling for virtual worlds. Comput. Graph. Forum **33**(6), 31–50 (2014)

31. Ebert, D.S.: Texturing & Modeling: A Procedural Approach. Morgan Kaufmann, Burlington (2003)

32. Antoniuk, I., Rokita, P.: Procedural generation of adjustable terrain for application in computer games using 2D maps. In: Kryszkiewicz, M., Bandyopadhyay, S., Rybinski, H., Pal, S.K. (eds.) PReMI 2015. LNCS, vol. 9124, pp. 75–84. Springer, Heidelberg (2015). doi:10.1007/978-3-319-19941-2_8

33. Blender application home page. https://www.blender.org/. Accesed 14 Jan 2016

# Texture Based Quality Assessment of 3D Prints for Different Lighting Conditions

Jarosław Fastowicz and Krzysztof Okarma[✉]

Department of Signal Processing and Multimedia Engineering,
Faculty of Electrical Engineering,
West Pomeranian University of Technology, Szczecin,
26. Kwietnia 10, 71-126 Szczecin, Poland
{jaroslaw.fastowicz,krzysztof.okarma}@zut.edu.pl

**Abstract.** In the paper the method of "blind" quality assessment of 3D prints based on texture analysis using the GLCM and chosen Haralick features is discussed. As the proposed approach has been verified using the images obtained by scanning the 3D printed plates, some dependencies related to the transparency of filaments may be noticed. Furthermore, considering the influence of lighting conditions, some other experiments have been made using the images acquired by a camera mounted on a 3D printer. Due to the influence of lighting conditions on the obtained images in comparison to the results of scanning, some modifications of the method have also been proposed leading to promising results allowing further extensions of our approach to no-reference quality assessment of 3D prints. Achieved results confirm the usefulness of the proposed approach for live monitoring of the progress of 3D printing process and the quality of 3D prints.

**Keywords:** 3D prints · Image analysis · GLCM · Image quality assessment

## 1 Introduction

Growing popularity of the 3D printing technologies causes a great interest in applications of the 3D prints in various areas of science and technology. In various industrial applications four main types of technologies are utilized [9], namely inkjet printing, stereolithography, selective laser sintering and Fused Deposition Modelling (FDM) considered in this paper.

Observing growing interest in machine vision and image analysis applications for various areas of automation, robotics, mechatronics and other areas of industry, one of natural directions of their development is the visual feedback in the CNC machines [6] and 3D printers. An exemplary solution [3] used for the online defect detection in fused deposition of ceramics utilizes the comparison of process signatures for the captured images and the reference ones. Another vision based method [2], used for nondestructive monitoring the top surface of

© Springer International Publishing AG 2016
L.J. Chmielewski et al. (Eds.): ICCVG 2016, LNCS 9972, pp. 17–28, 2016.
DOI: 10.1007/978-3-319-46418-3_2

the 3D print during printing, is based on the fuzzy model used for comparison of adjacent layers in order to identify the over- and under-filling.

In the paper [9] a monitoring system for 3D inkjet printer has been proposed which utilizes the neural networks for quality prediction of thin film electronic structures. The whole system is based on the measurement of resistivity without the direct use of cameras and comparison with a reference model is based on shape and geometrical properties.

Some other applications for vision based fault detection have also been provided by Szkilnyk [8] whereas the comparison of many other similar methods has been presented recently by Chauhan [1].

An initial study on the use of image analysis for automatic correction of detected errors in desktop 3D printers has been published by Straub [7]. The proposed system is based in five cameras and Raspberry Pi processing units and the images subjected to analysis are captured during numerous printing stops slowing the printing process. Unfortunately, this approach requires a precise calibration and is very sensitive to any disturbances including the camera motion and changes of lighting conditions. It allows the detection of "dry printing" caused by the lack of filament and premature termination of printing. The method utilize the comparison of the actual state of printing with the expected stage of the process and therefore can be considered as full-reference method.

A reliable quality assessment of images and textures is usually based on the comparison of some local features between two images. Recently, some interesting full-reference methods of texture similarity evaluation have been proposed [10, 11] which can be potentially useful also for evaluation of 3D prints. Nevertheless, the direct use of such methods would require the knowledge of the reference image and the perfect quality 3D print may be unavailable.

A still challenging problem is the automatic no-reference ("blind") quality assessment of 3D prints based on the detection of structural faults, preferably in a continuous mode, and therefore such a need may be considered as the main motivation of this paper.

## 2   Proposed Method for Scanned 3D Prints

### 2.1   GLCM Analysis

Quality evaluation of scanned 3D prints should be based on the analysis of textures by means of their consistency. The reason for this assumption is that, following from the principle of operation of the 3D printers, the visible patterns generated by a 3D printer should be repetitive.

One of the most popular statistical approaches to texture analysis is the use of Haralick features [4] based on the Gray-Level Co-occurrence Matrix (GLCM). Such a matrix illustrates the spatial relations between the pixels in the specified neighborhood defined by the offset $(\Delta x, \Delta y)$ and can be determined as:

$$C(i,j) = \sum_{p=1}^{P} \sum_{q=1}^{Q} \begin{cases} 1 & \text{if } A(p,q) = i \text{ and } A(p + \Delta x, q + \Delta y) = j \\ 0 & \text{otherwise} \end{cases} \quad (1)$$

where $P = M - \Delta x$ and $Q = N - \Delta y$.

Each element of the GLCM ($C(i,j)$) is calculated as the number of occurrences of pixels having the luminance level $i$ in the specified neighborhood, defined by the offset ($\Delta x, \Delta y$), with pixels of the luminance level $j$. In general four directions can be considered for each image: horizontal, vertical as well as 45° and 135° angles. Therefore 4 different matrices can be calculated for each specified distance (equal to one or more pixels).

Assuming the symmetrical definition of neighborhood, the luminance level $i$ of a pixel above $j$ is considered equally as $i$ below $j$ for the vertical GLCM. It leads to symmetrical GLCM, having even or zero values on its diagonal, used typically as the input data for the calculation of Haralick features [4]. For many natural images, as well as 3D prints considered in our paper, one may expect relatively high values near the diagonal of the GLCM due to anticipated high similarity of neighboring pixels.

Conducting the normalization of the GLCM by dividing of its elements by their sum, a convenient comparison of GLCM properties can be made, regardless of image resolution. The sum of elements can be easily predicted as for $M$ rows and $N$ columns, the sum of GLCM calculated for 45° and 135° angles is equal to $(M - \Delta x) \cdot (N - \Delta y)$ whereas for the horizontal and vertical GLCM we obtain $M \cdot (N - \Delta y)$ and $(M - \Delta x) \cdot N$ respectively.

For the maximum dynamic luminance range of $K$ levels, the GLCM matrix consisting of $K \times K$ elements is obtained. For a typical 8-bit image with $K = 256$ gray levels a reasonable compromise between the accuracy and the memory occupation, related also with computational complexity, seems to be the choice of $K = 64$ levels as it has been assumed in further part of the paper. The experiments and calculations conducted using available 3D prints have confirmed the validity of such assumption as the use of $K = 256$ levels has led to the same conclusions and obtained results are nearly identical.

## 2.2 Proposed Approach

As the GLCM is typically calculated for grayscale images and the distortions of 3D prints influence mainly the structural information, the typical color to grayscale conversion according to popular ITU recommendation BT.601-7 [5] has been assumed as the first preprocessing step. For such obtained grayscale image the vertical GLCM is calculated in order to check the repeatability of horizontal patterns which can be noticed in Fig. 1 illustrating exemplary test images used during experiments which have been obtained by scanning high quality 3D prints. The same calculations have been made for the images of distorted 3D prints as well (exemplary images are shown in Fig. 2). As mentioned above, all co-occurrence matrices have been calculated for $K = 64$ levels and then chosen Haralick features have been determined. All the 3D prints have been obtained using two available 3D printers (RepRap Pro Ormerod 2 and Prusa i3) shown in Fig. 3.

In order to verify the experimental results several 3D prints have been prepared with some of them containing visible contaminations caused mainly by

**Fig. 1.** Exemplary images obtained as scanned high quality 3D prints for different filaments

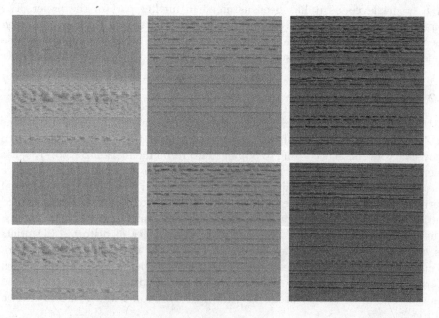

**Fig. 2.** Exemplary images obtained as scanned distorted 3D prints for different filaments (with partially high quality image on the left)

**Fig. 3.** Two FDM 3D printers used in experiments

the lack of filament. The presence of these distortions has been forced by manual change of the speed of filament's providing (slowing the feeder's drive) and simulation of clogged extruder.

However, due to the presence of some small distortions which in fact do not affect the quality of the 3D print, the results obtained for the GLCM calculated using the neighborhood defined by the offset equal to $\Delta y = 1$ pixel are unsatisfactory and do not allow a proper estimation of 3D prints quality. Therefore, the proposed extension of such approach is based on the calculation of series of co-occurrence matrices and chosen Haralick features for different values of offset $\Delta y$. Analyzing the amplitude (regarded further as peak to peak value) and oscillating character of some features in dependence on the offset, a reliable classification of images representing higher and lower quality 3D scans can be made.

The most accurate results have been obtained using the homogeneity, measuring the closeness of the distribution of normalized symmetrical GLCM elements to its diagonal, which is defined as:

$$H = \sum_{i=1}^{K}\sum_{j=1}^{K}\frac{C_{i,j}}{1 + |i - j|} \tag{2}$$

according to documentation of MATLAB Image Processing Toolbox. It is closely related to Haralick's Inverse Difference Moment and the only difference is the definition of weights $(1 + (i - j)^2$ is used in the denominator of the IDM instead

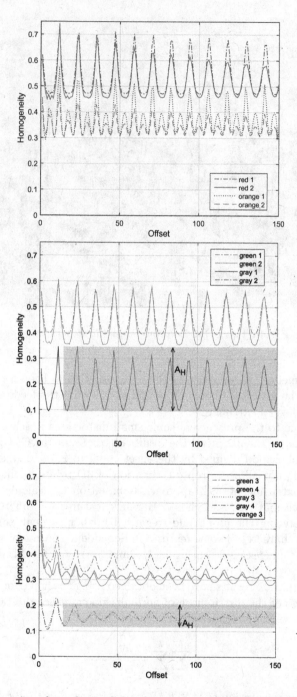

**Fig. 4.** Homogeneity plots obtained for the scanned different high quality (top and middle plots) and low quality 3D prints (bottom plots) with marked peak to peak homogeneity amplitude $A_H$ for exemplary 3D prints

of $1 + |i - j|$ used in homogeneity). Nevertheless, the obtained results are similar and do not affect the final conclusions.

### 2.3 Discussion of Experimental Results

Exemplary results of the vertical GLCM based homogeneity obtained for different 3D prints depending on the offset are shown in Fig. 4. Analyzing the plots presented in the same axis scales, it may be easily noticed that the amplitudes of oscillations of homogeneity $A_H$ for low quality 3D prints are significantly lower, especially considering the offsets larger than 15 pixels in order to eliminate the influence of some minor distortions introduced during image acquisition. The peak to peak amplitude obtained for an exemplary image "orange 3" representing the low quality 3D print is equal to 0.0522 and the values of such amplitudes for the other scanned images are presented in Table 1.

**Table 1.** Peak to peak homogeneity amplitudes $A_H$ calculated for the offsets greater than 15 pixels (as marked in Fig. 4) obtained for exemplary scans of 3D prints

| High quality 3D prints | | | | | | | |
|---|---|---|---|---|---|---|---|
| Image | $A_H$ | Image | $A_H$ | Image | $A_H$ | Image | $A_H$ |
| red 1 | 0.2421 | red 2 | 0.2407 | orange 1 | 0.2226 | orange 2 | 0.1288 |
| green 1 | 0.1982 | green 2 | 0.2429 | gray 1 | 0.2498 | gray 2 | 0.2436 |
| Low quality 3D prints | | | | | | | |
| Image | $A_H$ | Image | $A_H$ | Image | $A_H$ | Image | $A_H$ |
| green 3 | 0.0855 | green 4 | 0.0848 | gray 3 | 0.0530 | gray 4 | 0.0837 |

Lower absolute homogeneity values of orange prints as well as slightly lower oscillations both for high and low quality samples are caused by the semi-transparency of this filament illustrated in Fig. 5 where smartphone's flashlight has been used as a light source. Lower absolute values of homogeneity, although still with relatively high oscillations for high quality 3D print, observed for gray samples result from some low frequency changes of brightness well visible in the upper right part of Fig. 1.

## 3   Application for Images Captured by the Camera

In practical applications, considering various shapes of 3D prints their scanning may be troublesome and much more desired solution would be a similar method based on the analysis of images captured by a camera, preferably even during the printing process. Such an approach could be useful for monitoring purposes allowing to stop the printing in case of presence of visible distortions on the surface of a 3D print. In more advanced version assuming fully visual feedback some detected distortions may be corrected during the printing process.

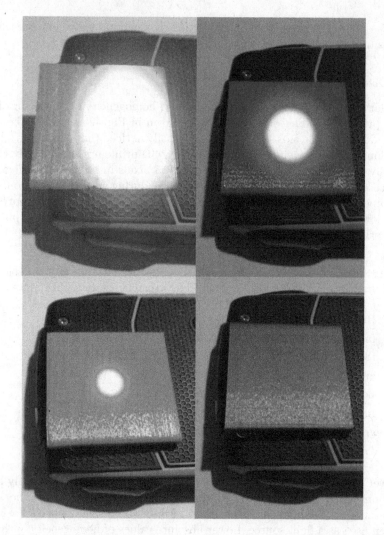

**Fig. 5.** Illustration of semi-transparency of some 3D prints for different types of PLA filaments illuminated from back side (orange, red, green and non-transparent gray). (Color figure online)

The application of the same procedure for the images captured by a camera illustrating the same 3D prints as in earlier experiments leads to the results presented in Fig. 6 and Table 2.

As can be easily noticed, the method proposed for the scanned images not always leads to satisfactory results since homogeneity amplitudes obtained for images acquired by a camera are usually lower both for high and low quality 3D prints. Their separation may be troublesome e.g. analyzing the homogeneity

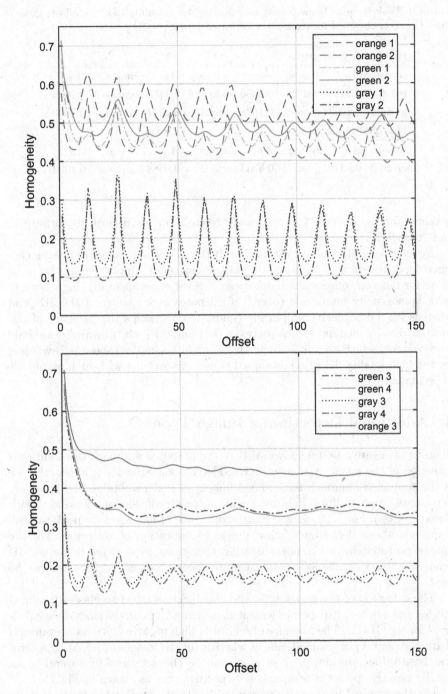

**Fig. 6.** Homogeneity plots obtained for selected high quality (upper plots) and low quality 3D prints (lower plots) captured by a camera

**Table 2.** Peak to peak homogeneity amplitudes $A_H$ calculated for the offsets greater than 15 pixels obtained for exemplary captured images of 3D prints

| High quality 3D prints | | | | | | | |
|---|---|---|---|---|---|---|---|
| Image | $A_H$ | Image | $A_H$ | Image | $A_H$ | Image | $A_H$ |
| red 1 | 0.2126 | red 2 | 0.2400 | orange 1 | 0.1308 | orange 2 | 0.1605 |
| green 1 | 0.1093 | green 2 | 0.1038 | gray 1 | 0.2304 | gray 2 | 0.2633 |
| Low quality 3D prints | | | | | | | |
| Image | $A_H$ | Image | $A_H$ | Image | $A_H$ | Image | $A_H$ |
| green 3 | 0.0340 | green 4 | 0.0363 | gray 3 | 0.0588 | gray 4 | 0.1023 |

obtained for the images "green 1" and "green 2" in comparison to "orange 1" and "orange 2".

Nevertheless, the quality estimation of the 3D prints based on images captured by a camera may be based on both homogeneity amplitude and its mean value for different offsets. As it has been verified experimentally, high peak to peak homogeneity amplitude (over 0.15) denotes high quality of the 3D print whereas low homogeneity amplitude (under 0.07) denotes the presence of distortions. For its medium values (between 0.07 and 0.15) the mean values should be considered which are much lower for low quality samples (about 0.2) whereas for the high quality 3D prints obtained values are over 0.4 with high amplitude of oscillations.

## 4    Additional Detection of Image Type

In order to ensure a better universality of the proposed approach the additional detection of the image type may be considered. Consequently it allows the use of the simplified approach for scanned images or images obtained by a camera in relatively more uniform lighting conditions (e.g. professional 3D printers with closed casings). For such images a threshold value of homogeneity peak to peak amplitude about 0.12 should allow proper classification of 3D prints. For the images captured in non-uniform lighting conditions, typical for home use 3D printers, a lower threshold dependent on the average homogeneity value can be used.

The detection of the image type and classification into two classes (scanned images and photos) can be implemented utilizing the correlation values calculated for the GLCM. The presence of relatively high negative correlation values is characteristic for the scanned images whereas for the images acquired by a camera those values are always positive or can be characterized by several times smaller negative peaks in comparison to positive ones as shown in Fig. 7.

For the scanned images the average values of the correlation for the offsets greater than 15 pixels are either negative or very small positive values (below 0.1) whereas for images acquired by a camera those values are much higher (over 0.1)

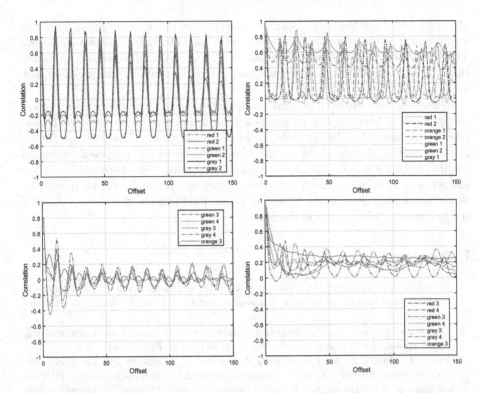

**Fig. 7.** Correlation plots obtained for selected scanned images (left plots) and photos acquired by a camera (right plots) captured by a camera (images obtained for high quality 3D prints in the top row)

and always positive. As can be observed such approach is generally valid both for high quality 3D prints as well as in the presence of distortions lowering the quality.

## 5    Conclusions

Presented results confirm the usefulness of the proposed method of quality evaluation of 3D prints based on scanned images or photos captured by cameras. For all tested samples the proposed metric based on the amplitude of homogeneity calculated for vertical GLCM, together with its mean value for images acquired by cameras, has led to very promising results. Proposed method of determining the image type, based on the correlation calculated for the vertical GLCM as well, allows the choice of the proper version of the method in the second stage.

Comparing the results obtained for high and low quality 3D prints made from the same filament, lowering the mean values and the amplitude of homogeneity can be noticed. Nevertheless, in practical applications related to live monitoring of the 3D printing, a comparison of parameters with previously made high quality

3D print based on the same filament may be troublesome and would require a calibration of the system's parameters after each change of the filament type. Therefore, such a method can be considered rather as a full-reference approach than a "blind" quality evaluation without comparison to any images of perfect quality 3D prints.

Observing the influence of semi-transparency of different filaments an interesting relation between the transparency level and the mean value of homogeneity calculated for the vertical GLCM may be noticed. Therefore, our future research will be concentrated on the improvements of the proposed approach towards fully automated no-reference quality assessment of 3D prints for different types of filaments. Another direction of future research will be related to experiments with some other shapes of printed 3D objects in order to improve the universality of the proposed method.

# References

1. Chauhan, V., Surgenor, B.: A comparative study of machine vision based methods for fault detection in an automated assembly machine. Procedia Manufact. **1**, 416–428 (2015)
2. Cheng, Y., Jafari, M.A.: Vision-based online process control in manufacturing applications. IEEE Trans. Autom. Sci. Eng. **5**(1), 140–153 (2008)
3. Fang, T., Jafari, M.A., Bakhadyrov, I., Safari, A., Danforth, S., Langrana, N.: Online defect detection in layered manufacturing using process signature. In: Proceedings of IEEE International Conference on Systems, Man and Cybernetics, San Diego, California, USA, vol. 5, pp. 4373–4378, October 1998
4. Haralick, R.M., Shanmugam, K., Dinstein, I.: Textural features for image classification. IEEE Trans. Syst. Man Cybern. **3**(6), 610–621 (1973)
5. ITU-T: Recommendation BT.601-7 - Studio encoding parameters of digital television for standard 4: 3 and wide-screen 16: 9 aspect ratios (2011)
6. Okarma, K., Grudziński, M.: The 3D scanning system for the machine vision based positioning of workpieces on the CNC machine tools. In: Proceedings of 17th International Conference Methods and Models in Automation and Robotics (MMAR), Międzyzdroje, Poland, pp. 85–90, August 2012
7. Straub, J.: Initial work on the characterization of additive manufacturing (3D printing) using software image analysis. Machines **3**(2), 55–71 (2015)
8. Szkilnyk, G., Hughes, K., Surgenor, B.: Vision based fault detection of automated assembly equipment. In: Proceedings of ASME/IEEE International Conference on Mechatronic and Embedded Systems and Applications, Parts A and B, Washington, DC, USA, vol. 3, pp. 691–697, August 2011
9. Tourloukis, G., Stoyanov, S., Tilford, T., Bailey, C.: Data driven approach to quality assessment of 3D printed electronic products. In: Proceedings of 38th International Spring Seminar on Electronics Technology (ISSE), Eger, Hungary, pp. 300–305, May 2015
10. Žujović, J., Pappas, T.N., Neuhoff, D.L.: Structural similarity metrics for texture analysis and retrieval. In: Proceedings of 16th IEEE International Conference on Image Processing (ICIP), Cairo, Egypt, pp. 2225–2228, November 2009
11. Žujović, J., Pappas, T.N., Neuhoff, D.L.: Structural texture similarity metrics for image analysis and retrieval. IEEE Trans. Image Process. **22**(7), 2545–2558 (2013)

# Pseudoinversion Fractals

Krzysztof Gdawiec[(✉)]

Institute of Computer Science, University of Silesia,
Będzińska 39, 41-200 Sosnowiec, Poland
kgdawiec@ux2.math.us.edu.pl

**Abstract.** In this paper, we present some modifications of inversion fractals. The first modification is based on the use of different metrics in the inversion transformation. Moreover, we propose a switching process between different metric spaces. All the proposed modifications allowed us to obtain new and diverse fractal patterns that differ from the original inversion fractals.

**Keywords:** Fractal · Pseudoinversion · Computer art

## 1 Introduction

Fractals discovered by Mandelbrot in 1970s are used to model complex shapes such as clouds, plants, mountains, sea-shores. They are also applied in the field of art and computer graphics. Many different methods of obtaining fractal patterns were proposed in the literature, e.g., dynamical systems [4], hyperbolic geometry [6], complex numbers [5] or iterated function systems [9]. One of the recent methods is the use of inversion transformation of the star-shaped sets [2,3]. This type of fractals are called inversion fractals. In this paper we propose some modifications of the inversion transformation that lead to new fractal patterns.

The paper is organized as follows. In Sect. 2, we briefly introduce the inversion fractals and the algorithm to generate them. Next, in Sect. 3, we introduce some modifications of inversion fractals. The first modification is based on the use of pair of metrics in the inversion transformation and the second modification uses switching process between pairs of metrics. Some examples of fractal patterns obtained with the proposed modifications are presented in Sect. 4. Finally, in Sect. 5, we give some concluding remarks.

## 2 Inversion Fractals

To introduce the psuedoinversion fractals firstly we must know what the inversion fractals are. The first fractals of this type appeared about 2000 in [1]. They were based on circle inversion. Later in [2] a generalization from circles to the star-shaped sets was introduced. Some further generalizations, namely the use of iteration process from fixed-point theory and the use of $q$-systems, were presented in [3].

Following [3] let us start with some definitions.

© Springer International Publishing AG 2016
L.J. Chmielewski et al. (Eds.): ICCVG 2016, LNCS 9972, pp. 29–36, 2016.
DOI: 10.1007/978-3-319-46418-3_3

**Definition 1.** *A set $S$ in a metric space $(\mathbb{R}^2, d_e)$, where $d_e$ is the Euclidean distance, is* star-shaped *if there exists a point $z \in int\ S$ (int $S$ means the interior of $S$) such that for all points $p \in S$ the line segment $\overline{zp}$ lies entirely within $S$. The locus of the points $z$ having the above property is the* kernel *of $S$ and is denoted by* ker $S$.

Let us assume that we have a star-shaped set $S$, some point $o \in$ ker $S$ and point $p \neq o$ for which we want to calculate the inversion. We start by shooting a ray $r$ from $o$ in the direction $p - o$, i.e., $r(t) = o + t(p - o)$, where $t \in [0, \infty)$. Then, we find the intersection point $b$ of $r$ and the boundary of $S$.

**Definition 2.** *Point $p'$ is said to be the* inverse *of $p$ with respect to $S$ if it satisfies the following equation:*

$$d_e(o, p) \cdot d_e(o, p') = [d_e(o, b)]^2. \tag{1}$$

*Point $o$ is called the* centre of inversion. *The transformation that takes $p$ and transforms it into $p'$ is called the* star-shaped set inversion transformation *and it is denoted by $I_S$.*

The inversion transformation can be extended also to $o$ in a following way: $I_S(o) = \infty$ and $I_S(\infty) = o$. Relation (1) is uncomfortable in implementation, so after some derivations we can obtain a better formula:

$$p' = I_S(p) = o + \left[ \frac{d_e(o, b)}{d_e(o, p)} \right]^2 (p - o). \tag{2}$$

Now, having a set of $k$ star shaped sets that define star-shaped set inversion transformations we are able to generate an inversion fractal. For this purpose we can use algorithm presented in Algorithm 1. The $P_v$ in the algorithm is an iteration process: iteration from fixed point theory or switching process [3]. In the examples presented later in Sect. 4 we will use only the standard Picard iteration, i.e., iteration process of the form:

$$p_{i+1} = I_S(p_i). \tag{3}$$

## 3   Pseudoinversion Fractals

In the definition of inversion transformation (circle or star-shaped set) we use the Euclidean metric. In [8] Ramírez et al. have changed the metric to the metrics:

$$d_q(a, b) = (|a_x - b_x|^q + |a_y - b_y|^q)^{\frac{1}{q}}, \tag{4}$$

where $a, b \in \mathbb{R}^2$ and $q \in [1, \infty)$. So, using this modification the inversion transformation has the following form:

$$I_{S,q}(p) = o + \left[ \frac{d_q(o, b)}{d_q(o, p)} \right]^2 (p - o), \tag{5}$$

where $q \in [1, \infty)$.

---

**Algorithm 1.** Extended random inversion algorithm with colouring [3]

---

**Input:** $S_1, \ldots, S_k$ – star-shaped sets with chosen centres of inversion, $c_1, \ldots, c_k$
– colours of the transformations, $p_0$ – starting point external to
$S_1, \ldots, S_k$, $n > 20$ – number of iterations, $P_v$ – iteration with
parameters $v$, $W$, $H$ – image dimensions, $\gamma \in \mathbb{R}_+$

**Output:** Image $I$ with an approximation of a star-shaped set inversion fractal

1  **for** $(x,y) \in \{0,1,\ldots,W-1\} \times \{0,1,\ldots,H-1\}$ **do**
2  $\quad$ $I(x,y) = $ black
3  $\quad$ $\mathcal{H}(x,y) = 0$

4  $c = $ random colour
5  $j = $ random number from $\{1,\ldots,k\}$
6  $p = P_v(I_{S_j}, p_0)$
7  **for** $i = 2$ **to** $n$ **do**
8  $\quad$ $l = $ random number from $\{1,\ldots,k\}$
9  $\quad$ **while** $j = l$ **or** $inSet(S_l, p)$ **do**
10 $\quad\quad$ $l = $ random number from $\{1,\ldots,k\}$
11 $\quad$ $j = l$
12 $\quad$ $p = P_v(I_{S_j}, p)$
13 $\quad$ **if** $i > 20$ **then**
14 $\quad\quad$ $x = \lfloor x_p \rfloor$
15 $\quad\quad$ $y = \lfloor y_p \rfloor$
16 $\quad\quad$ $\mathcal{H}(x,y) = \mathcal{H}(x,y) + 1$
17 $\quad\quad$ $c = \frac{c+c_j}{2}$
18 $\quad\quad$ $I(x,y) = c$

19 $m_{\mathcal{H}} = \max_{(x,y)} \mathcal{H}(x,y)$
20 **for** $(x,y) \in \{0,1,\ldots,W-1\} \times \{0,1,\ldots,H-1\}$ **do**
21 $\quad$ **if** $\mathcal{H}(x,y) > 0$ **then**
22 $\quad\quad$ $I(x,y) = \left( \frac{\log_2(1+\mathcal{H}(x,y))}{\log_2(1+m_{\mathcal{H}})} \right)^{1/\gamma} I(x,y)$

---

In the case of circle inversion together with the change of the metric the shape of the circle also changes, so the value of the inversion is different in different metric spaces. But, in the case of the star-shaped sets the shape of the set remains unchanged and it is easy to prove the following theorem.

**Theorem 1.** *Let $S$ be a star-shaped set, $o \in \ker S$ be a centre of inversion and $p$ point for which we want to calculate the inverse. Assume that $b$ is the point of intersection of $r(t) = o + t(p - o)$, where $t \in [0, \infty)$ with the boundary of $S$. Then, for any $q_1, q_2 \in [1, \infty)$:*

$$\frac{d_{q_1}(o,b)}{d_{q_1}(o,p)} = \frac{d_{q_2}(o,b)}{d_{q_2}(o,p)}. \tag{6}$$

From Theorem 1 we can conclude that for a fixed star shaped set $S$ and any $q_1, q_2 \in [1, \infty)$ the following equality is true:

$$\forall_{p \in \mathbb{R}^2} \quad I_{S,q_1}(p) = I_{S,q_2}(p). \tag{7}$$

So, the use of different metrics of the form (4) does not change the value of the star shaped inversion transformation and thus the inversion fractal remains the same.

From mathematical analysis we know that for any $q_1, q_2 \in [1, \infty)$ such that $q_1 \leq q_2$ we have [7]:

$$d_{q_2}(a, b) \leq d_{q_1}(a, b). \tag{8}$$

From this fact we can conclude that for $q_1 \neq q_2$ $(q_1, q_2 \in [1, \infty))$ and for a fixed $q \in \{q_1, q_2\}$ we have:

$$\frac{d_q(o, b)}{d_q(o, p)} \leq \frac{d_{q_1}(o, b)}{d_{q_2}(o, p)} \quad \text{or} \quad \frac{d_q(o, b)}{d_q(o, p)} \geq \frac{d_{q_1}(o, b)}{d_{q_2}(o, p)}. \tag{9}$$

In the inversion transformation we can use a pair of metrics for $q_1$ and $q_2$ $(q_1 \neq q_2)$ instead of one metric for $q$. In this way, following (9), we change the value of the inversion transformation. The obtained point will be laying (on the ray) closer or further from the centre of inversion. This modification of inversion transformation causes that we loose some of the properties of the inversion. Because of that the modified inversion transformation will be called pseudoinversion transformation.

Replacing the inversion transformations with pseudoinversions will change the shape of the original inversion fractal. This type of fractal will be called pseudoinversion fractal.

If we look at the set of inversion transformations as the transformations in separate metric spaces, then for each of the transformations we can use a different pair of metrics $(q_1, q_2)$. This will allow us to modify the shape of the fractal in a local manner.

Moreover, we can introduce a switching process of the metric spaces. Let us assume that we have $M$ pairs of numbers defining metrics of the form (4), i.e., $(q_1^0, q_2^0), (q_1^1, q_2^1), \ldots, (q_1^{M-1}, q_2^{M-1})$. Now, in the $m$-th iteration of the iteration process we use $m \mod M$ pair of metric spaces, i.e., $(q_1^{m \mod M}, q_2^{m \mod M})$.

## 4    Examples

In this section, we present some examples of pseudoinversion fractals obtained with the proposed methods. The first example is presenting the use of pseudoinversion transformation using one pair $(q_1, q_2) \in [1, \infty)^2$ of parameters defining metrics for all the transformations. Figure 1 presents the star-shaped sets defining the transformations and the inversion fractal generated using the inversion transformations of the sets. Examples of pseudoinversion fractals generated with the same star-shaped sets are presented in Fig. 2. The parameters used to generate these images were the following (from left): $(3, 7), (2, 1), (10, 3)$. From the

**Fig. 1.** Star-shaped sets defining the transformations (left) and original inversion fractal (right)

**Fig. 2.** Pseudoinversion fractals obtained with the use of different metrics

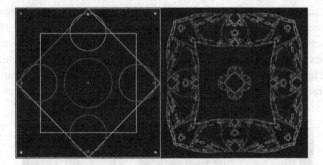

**Fig. 3.** Star-shaped sets defining the transformations (left) and original inversion fractal (right)

images we see that using different pairs of metrics we are able to obtain new fractal shapes that are different from the original inversion fractal.

In the second example we will use the same star-shaped sets and different pairs of metrics for different sets. Star-shaped sets defining the transformations and original inversion fractal are presented in Fig. 3. Figure 4 presents examples of psuedoinversion fractals. The pairs of metrics for the individual sets are

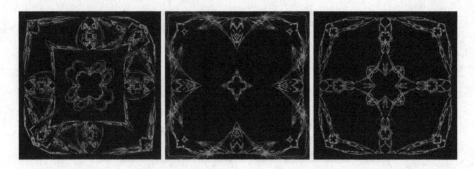

**Fig. 4.** Pseudoinversion fractals obtained with the use of various metrics for different transformations

**Table 1.** Parameters used to generate fractals from Fig. 4, T – triangle, Sq – square, C – circle, N – North, S – South, E – East, W – West, M – middle

| Image | NWT | NET | SET | SWT | Sq | NC | EC | SC | WC | MC |
|---|---|---|---|---|---|---|---|---|---|---|
| Left | $(2,1)$ | $(2,3)$ | $(2,1)$ | $(2,3)$ | $(2,2)$ | $(2,2)$ | $(2,2)$ | $(2,2)$ | $(2,2)$ | $(1.1,3)$ |
| Middle | $(2,2)$ | $(2,2)$ | $(2,2)$ | $(2,2)$ | $(1,2.3)$ | $(2,2)$ | $(2,2)$ | $(2,2)$ | $(2,2)$ | $(2,2)$ |
| Right | $(2,2)$ | $(2,2)$ | $(2,2)$ | $(2,2)$ | $(5,1)$ | $(2,2)$ | $(2,2)$ | $(2,2)$ | $(2,2)$ | $(1,5)$ |

gathered in Table 1. From the figure we can observe that the use of different pairs of metrics for different transformations changes the shape of the fractal. In this way we can place the sets in a symmetrical way and the shape of the fractal can loose its symmetry, e.g., left image in Fig. 4. Moreover, we can observe that the shapes of pseudoinversion fractals differ in a significant way from the original inversion fractal.

The last example present fractal shapes obtained with the switching process of metrics. Figure 5 presents star-shaped sets defining the transformations and original inversion fractal. In the first example of switching we will use two pairs

**Fig. 5.** Star-shaped sets defining the transformations (left) and original inversion fractal (right)

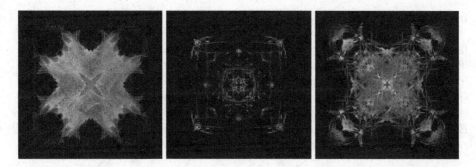

**Fig. 6.** Original pseudoinversion fractals (left, middle) and the result of switching their metric spaces (right)

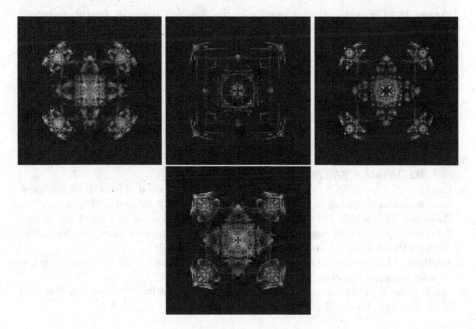

**Fig. 7.** Original pseudoinversion fractals (top) and the result of switching their metric spaces (bottom)

of metrics. Images on the left and in the middle of Fig. 6 present pseudoinversion fractals obtained with the pairs: $(1, 3)$, $(2, 1)$, respectively. Fractal pattern obtained using switching process of these two pairs of metrics is presented on the right of Fig. 6.

The second example of switching metric spaces in presented in Fig. 7. This time we switch between three different pairs of metric spaces. The patterns at the top of this figure were obtained using the following pairs: $(2, 3)$, $(3, 1)$, $(5, 3)$. The result of switching between these three pairs of metric spaces is presented in the bottom part of Fig. 7.

# 5    Conclusions

In this paper, we presented modification of inversion fractals. The proposed modification was based on the use of different metrics in the inversion transformation formula. Moreover, we proposed a switching process between different metric spaces. Patterns which were obtained with the proposed modification differ in a significant way from the original inversion fractals and form new fractal shapes. Because of the interesting and aesthetic structure the pseudoinversion fractals can be used among other things as textile, wallpaper or ceramics patterns.

# References

1. Frame, M., Cogevina, T.: An infinite circle inversion limit set fractal. Comput. Graph. **24**(5), 797–804 (2000)
2. Gdawiec, K.: Star-shaped set inversion fractals. Fractals **22**(4), 1450009, 7 pages (2014)
3. Gdawiec, K.: Inversion fractals and iteration processes in the generation of aesthetic patterns. Comput. Graph. Forum. (in press). doi:10.1111/cgf.12783
4. Lu, J., Zou, Y., Tu, G., Wu, H.: A family of functions for generating colorful patterns with mixed symmetries from dynamical systems. In: Wang, W. (ed.) Mechatronics and Automatic Control Systems. LNEE, vol. 237, pp. 883–890. Springer, Heidelberg (2014). doi:10.1007/978-3-319-01273-5_99
5. Mitchell, K.: Fun with chaotic orbits in the Mandelbrot set. In: Bridges 2012, pp. 389–392. Towson, USA (2012)
6. Ouyang, P., Cheng, D., Cao, Y., Zhan, X.: The visualization of hyperbolic patterns from invariant mapping method. Comput. Graph. **36**(2), 92–100 (2012)
7. Raïssouli, M., Jebril, I.H.: Various proofs for the decrease monotonicity of the Schatten's power norm, various families of $\mathbb{R}^n$-norms and some open problems. Int. J. Open Probl. Comput. Sci. Math. **3**(2), 164–174 (2010)
8. Ramírez, J.L., Rubiano, G.N., Zlobec, B.J.: Generating fractal patterns by using $p$-circle inversion. Fractals **23**(4), 1550047, 13 pages (2015)
9. van Loocke, P.: Polygon-based fractals from compressed iterated function systems. IEEE Comput. Grap. Appl. **30**(2), 34–44 (2010)

# Easing Functions in the New Form Based on Bézier Curves

Łukasz Izdebski and Dariusz Sawicki(✉)

Warsaw University of Technology, Pl. Politechniki 1, 00-661 Warsaw, Poland
jurgus007@gmail.com, dasa@iem.pw.edu.pl

**Abstract.** The transition problem is one of the important problems of animation. The Penners easing functions solve this successfully. There are some well known and widely used approximations of these functions where Bézier curves have been used. However, the transition functions, obtained by such approximation differ substantially from the original. We proposed new form of approximation in the paper. Two class of easing functions are discussed. In first simple approximation allows obtaining sufficient effects. In the second the easing function is divided into two symmetric parts where the approximation is done. For every approximation the root mean square error (RMSE) has been determined and the animated transition using new solution is analyzed. The new approximation allows obtaining better RMSE as well as better visual effects in animation.

**Keywords:** Easing function · Tweening function · Transition · Keyframing · CSS

## 1 Introduction

The word tween can be treated as an abbreviation or simplification of between. In traditional animation one of the most important tasks was to complete the movement between keyframes. This means also a problem how to combine certain states and positions by sequence (known number) of frames. Proper selection of animation elements enables developers to make a more attractive appearance and behavior of the various elements on the screen. This applies to games, websites and advertisings. However, it is worth to look at this subject from the wider perspective. The transition problem is one of the most important problems of animation [1]. It is worth noting that an observer can accept conventionality, simplification of drawing and schematic character, but will not accept movement of this character that is unnatural or simply, diverges from expectations significantly. Disney cartoons have achieved great success, mainly because the authors have taken care of movement of created characters and shoved it in outstanding, natural way.

The change of position between points $P_{start}$ and $P_{stop}$ determines the fluidity of movement. The easiest way is a linear tween which connects $P_{start}$ and $P_{stop}$

© Springer International Publishing AG 2016
L.J. Chmielewski et al. (Eds.): ICCVG 2016, LNCS 9972, pp. 37–48, 2016.
DOI: 10.1007/978-3-319-46418-3_4

by line segment and constant movement speed. This is the simplest solution but in most cases the most unnatural. On the other hand we can consider dynamic tweening with adding acceleration depending of the expected animation effect [2].

Robert Penner is the Author of the widely used solution [2, 3] of the transition problem. Most practical applications of transition in animation are based on his easing functions. Penner in his book [2] distinguishes two types of transition functions.

**Tweening functions** which describe a position for a specific time, depending on starting position, ending position and duration.

**Easing functions** concerning to acceleration. These functions allow changing speed and are connected to the transition between the states of moving and notmoving.

Authors of publications and documents in Internet use interchangeably both terms. The second of them seems to be used much more often and therefore in our work we used the term easing functions.

In computer animation easing functions allow describing transitions in movement of cartoon characters especially when the appearance of the character can be separated from its movement [4]. In the computer animation easing is often associated with morphing, forming combined tools for creating movement and possible shape changes in shape for the connections between frames [5]. Easing allows also increasing frame rates for animation created at very low frame rates [6].

Today the term easing refers primarily to animation made for games and HTMLs applications [7, 8]. Implementation of transition functions appear also in libraries Qt [9], jQuery [10], and .NET Framework ver. 4 [11]. On the Action-Script and Adobe Flash platform [12]. Because Web applications are important and frequently occurring application, so in Internet we can find many tutorials and tips. There are general presentation [13], as well as concerning on selected environments and platforms: ActionScript [14], Adobe Flash [15].

Easing functions are widely applied in Cascading Style Sheets (CSS) [16]. CSS is a specific language, which helps describing pictures and animations for documents prepared in markup languages. CSS was introduced by Håkon Wium Lie in 1994 [17]. Easing with CSS allows enhance visual style of web pages, user interface, web applications and also mobile applications. There is only one problem. The standard descriptions of easing functions is made using very simple formulas. But different mathematical functions are used (polynomial, trigonometric, exponential etc.). CSS support only Bézier form of curves. On the other hand, the development of a good approximation for easing functions would allow using this mechanism in environments for animation modeling such as Blender and commercial solutions.

There are several easing functions approximation by Bézier curves. The solution [18] is commonly used. However, none of these solutions is a good approximation of easing functions. This means that the transition functions, obtained by approximation differs substantially from the original. The aim of this paper is to propose a new version of the easing functions in the form of Bézier cubic curves. Version that approximates the original function much better than existing solutions and thus has great practical importance.

## 2    Original Penners Functions

There are many commercial or open tools where the source code and mathematical description of transition functions are available [19–21]. In a modified version also [22].

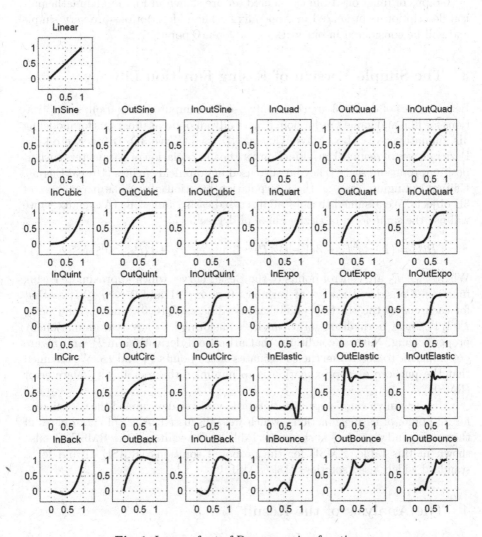

**Fig. 1.** Image of set of Penners easing functions

As a basis for analysis in our article we considered the original (Penners) form of the function [3]. Unfortunately it is very difficult to find a publication where their mathematical forms are given. Instead, we can reconstruct these descriptions based on source program given as additions to the Author's library [3]. We assumed that all discussed functions are in form: $y = TweenFun(x)$, and the ranges of $x$ and $y$ are normalized. I.e. $0 \leq x \leq 1$ and $0 \leq y \leq 1$. This normalization helped simplify the mathematical description, without limitation for practical applications. On the other hand simple scaling allows adjusting it to the respective range of time or variables.

Graphs of functions from considered set are shown in Fig. 1. The mathematical description is presented in Appendix A. These descriptions are very simple and will be considered in our work as a reference point.

## 3    The Simple Version of Easing Function Library

Bézier curves of degree 3 are commonly used in computer animation; in applications for film and game production. Practically all popular programs for modeling 3D animation (3ds Max, Maya, Cinema 4D, LightWave 3D, Blender, etc.) use Bézier curves of degree 3 as a function for the interpolation of parameters such as position, rotation, scale. They are also used in graphical engines (Unreal Engine, Unity, CryEngine, etc.) as the interpolation function of various parameters of 3D objects. We assumed that for all discussed easing functions (Appendix A) we will use the same form of Bézier curve of degree 3 (1).

$$B(t) = (1 - t)^3 P_0 + 3(1 - t)^2 t P_1 + 3(1 - t)t^2 P_2 + t^3 P_3, \quad 0 \leq t \leq 1. \quad (1)$$

Where $P_0 - P_3$ are control points of the Bézier curve, which approximate easing function. Considered ranges of variables $0 \leq x \leq 1$ and $0 \leq y \leq 1$, so that for each curve, the starting point has coordinates $P_0(0,0)$, and the end point $P_3(1,1)$. Such normalized form can be transformed to any real animation by proper scaling. Natural conditions that arise from derivatives in $P_0$ and $P_3$ are not sufficient to determine the coordinates of the points $P_1$ and $P_2$. We assumed that the purpose of approximation is to minimize the root mean square error (RMSE).

After solving a simple optimization task, we have determined the coordinates for all points of easing functions, which were discussed. A set of coordinates of the corresponding points is shown in Table 1. The values of the RMSE are also shown in this table. RMSE for the proposed solutions (RMSE 1) and for a standard widely used solutions [18] (RMSE 0).

## 4    The Analysis of the Result

Analysis of Table 1 shows that the resulting RMSE of the proposed solution are smaller (in some cases much) than the known solution. Thus, the proposed

**Table 1.** Coordinates of control points $P_1, P_2$ for proposed approximation of easing functions, $P_0(0,0), P_3(1,1)$. RMSE 0 of standard approximation [18], RMSE 1 of our approximation

|  | $P_1$ | $P_2$ | RMSE 0 | RMSE 1 |
|---|---|---|---|---|
| Linear | (0.33333333, 0.33333333) | (0.66666667, 0.66666667) | $2.83942e^{-16}$ | 0.00000000 |
| InQuad | (0.33333333, 0.00000000) | (0.66666667, 0.33333333) | 0.02081546 | 0.00000000 |
| OutQuad | (0.33333333, 0.66666667) | (0.66666667, 1.00000000) | 0.01362409 | 0.00000000 |
| InOutQuad | (0.47646877, 0.03576543) | (0.52353123, 0.96423457) | 0.00821011 | 0.00203389 |
| InCubic | (0.33333333, 0.00000000) | (0.66666667, 0.00000000) | 0.02141739 | 0.00000000 |
| OutCubic | (0.33333333, 1.00000000) | (0.66666667, 1.00000000) | 0.01080029 | 0.00000000 |
| InOutCubic | (0.61870333, −0.04796333) | (0.38129667, 1.04796333) | 0.01438956 | 0.00146290 |
| InQuart | (0.43478863, 0.0060621) | (0.73090123, −0.07258137) | 0.02824949 | 0.00020596 |
| OutQuart | (0.26909877, 1.07258137) | (0.56521137, 0.9939379) | 0.02092234 | 0.00020596 |
| InOutQuart | (0.7085679, −0.09626) | (0.2914321, 1.09626) | 0.03240890 | 0.00342290 |
| InQuint | (0.5195679, 0.01253123) | (0.77403667, −0.11892667) | 0.04253327 | 0.00051938 |
| OutQuint | (0.22596333, 1.11926) | (0.48109877, 0.98746877) | 0.00672244 | 0.00051928 |
| InOutQuint | (0.77029667, −0.12850543) | (0.22970333, 1.12850543) | 0.04841866 | 0.00610494 |
| InSine | (0.36078017, −0.00043597) | (0.67348626, 0.48655350) | 0.01455569 | 0.00046963 |
| OutSine | (0.33093073, 0.5207369) | (0.6413116, 1.00033333) | 0.01739439 | 0.00004824 |
| InOutSine | (0.36303667, −0.0011979) | (0.63696333, 1.0011979) | 0.00927085 | 0.00006930 |
| InExpo | (0.63696333, 0.01990123) | (0.84433333, −0.0609379) | 0.02708955 | 0.00053018 |
| OutExpo | (0.15566667, 1.0609379) | (0.36303667, 0.98009877) | 0.01333120 | 0.00053018 |
| InOutExpo | (0.84433333, −0.11616123) | (0.15566667, 1.11616123) | 0.03861114 | 0.00753976 |
| InCirc | (0.55402543, 0.0011979) | (0.9988021, 0.44680173) | 0.02450023 | 0.00014209 |
| OutCirc | (0.0011979, 0.55319827) | (0.44597457, 0.9988021) | 0.10986799 | 0.00014209 |
| InOutCirc | (0.87766667, 0.13090123) | (0.12233333, 0.86909877) | 0.03884565 | 0.00885744 |
| InBack | (0.33333333, 0.00000000) | (0.66666667, −0.56719333) | 0.03817577 | 0.00000000 |
| OutBack | (0.33333333, 1.56719333) | (0.66666667, 1.0000000) | 0.02245829 | 0.00000000 |
| InOutBack | (0.72113543, −0.54672913) | (0.27886457, 1.54672913) | 0.04187979 | 0.01439023 |

**Fig. 2.** Three frames as an example of a bad approximation for the new solution. Function = InOutQuint, solid line - original Penner's function, dashed line - standard approximation [18], dotted line - new proposition

curves should better approximate the easing functions. But it is worth to analyze the object motion in an animation using these functions. Experiments were carried out for all cases. We can identify a number of easing functions for which the developed solution provides the ability to control movement in a way that is not different from the original Penner function. Unfortunately, there are some cases where an improvement is negligible (Fig. 2). Small reducing of the RMSE does not mean visible improvement of the object motion control. Despite a better approximation it is still a problem with the practical application of easing functions and replacement by Bézier curves. Our aim was not to look for the right measure of error, but to solve the practical task - to find the proper interpolation. However, right measure of error could be analyzed in the future as the different problem.

## 5   The Advanced Version of Easing Library

The set of functions that despite the improvement approximation still show a visible difference to the original Penner functions includes: InOutQuad, InOutCubic, InOutQuart, InOutQuint, InOutSine, InOutExpo, InOutCirc, InOutBack. Is worth noting, that all the curves described by these functions have a future of point symmetry. To solve the problem for these functions we suggested dividing functions into two ranges respectively for $0 \leq x \leq 0.5$ and $0.5 \leq x \leq 1$. Therefore, the control points are determined only for the range $0 \leq x \leq 0.5$. For the remaining range of $x$, the coordinates of the control points can be determined on the basis of point symmetry. In Table 2 we presented the second version of a set of control points for discussed here functions. Just like before, for all of them, we analyzed motion of the object in an animation using proposed functions. We can notice a significant improvement in approximation. Comparison of frames for particular cases confirms the correctness of this solution (Fig. 3).

**Table 2.** Coordinates of control points for improved approximation of easing functions. Rows of the table have been grouped in order to select parts of the same function. Each part of function has independent control points $P_0 - P_3$

| | $P_0$ | $P_1$ | $P_2$ | $P_3$ |
|---|---|---|---|---|
| InOutQuad | (0.0, 0.0) | (0.1666666667, 0.0000000000) | (0.3333333333, 0.1666666667) | (0.5, 0.5) |
| InOutQuad | (0.5, 0.5) | (0.6666666667, 0.8333333333) | (0.8333333333, 1.0000000000) | (1.0, 1.0) |
| InOutCubic | (0.0, 0.0) | (0.1666666667, 0.0000000000) | (0.3333333333, 0.0000000000) | (0.5, 0.5) |
| InOutCubic | (0.5, 0.5) | (0.6666666667, 1.0000000000) | (0.8333333333, 1.0000000000) | (1.0, 1.0) |
| InOutQuart | (0.0, 0.0) | (0.2173943150, 0.0030310500) | (0.3654506150, −0.036290685) | (0.5, 0.5) |
| InOutQuart | (0.5, 0.5) | (0.6345493850, 1.0362906850) | (0.7826056850, 0.9969689500) | (1.0, 1.0) |
| InOutQuint | (0.0, 0.0) | (0.2597839500, 0.0062656150) | (0.3870183350, −0.059463335) | (0.5, 0.5) |
| InOutQuint | (0.5, 0.5) | (0.6129816650, 1.0596300000) | (0.7405493850, 0.9937343850) | (1.0, 1.0) |
| InOutSine | (0.0, 0.0) | (0.1803900850, −0.000217985) | (0.3367431300, 0.2432767500) | (0.5, 0.5) |
| InOutSine | (0.5, 0.5) | (0.6654653650, 0.7603684500) | (0.8206558000, 1.0001666650) | (1.0, 1.0) |
| InOutExpo | (0.0, 0.0) | (0.3184816650, 0.0099506150) | (0.4221666650, −0.030468950) | (0.5, 0.5) |
| InOutExpo | (0.5, 0.5) | (0.5778333350, 1.0304689500) | (0.6815183350, 0.9900493850) | (1.0, 1.0) |
| InOutCirc | (0.0, 0.0) | (0.2770127150, 0.0005989500) | (0.4994010500, 0.2234008650) | (0.5, 0.5) |
| InOutCirc | (0.5, 0.5) | (0.5005989500, 0.7765991350) | (0.7229872850, 0.9994010500) | (1.0, 1.0) |
| InOutBack | (0.0, 0.0) | (0.1666666667, 0.0000000000) | (0.3333333333, −0.4324849167) | (0.5, 0.5) |
| InOutBack | (0.5, 0.5) | (0.6666666667, 1.4324849167) | (0.8333333333, 1.0000000000) | (1.0, 1.0) |

**Table 3.** Coordinates of control points for additional set of InOut functions. Rows of the table have been grouped in order to select parts of the same function. Each part of function has independent control points $P_0 - P_3$

|  | $P_0$ | $P_1$ | $P_2$ | $P_3$ |
|---|---|---|---|---|
| InElastic | (0.0000, 0.0) | (0.17500000, 0.00250747) | (0.17354200, 0.00000000) | (0.1750, 0.0) |
| InElastic | (0.1750, 0.0) | (0.44250000, −0.0184028) | (0.35250000, 0.05000000) | (0.4750, 0.0) |
| InElastic | (0.4750, 0.0) | (0.73500000, −0.1430950) | (0.65750000, 0.38333300) | (0.7750, 0.0) |
| InElastic | (0.7750, 0.0) | (0.90812500, −0.5861390) | (0.86687500, −0.6666670) | (1.0000, 1.0) |
| OutElastic | (0.0000, 0.0) | (0.13312500, 1.66666700) | (0.09187500, 1.58613900) | (0.2250, 1.0) |
| OutElastic | (0.2250, 1.0) | (0.34250000, 0.61666700) | (0.26500000, 1.14309500) | (0.5250, 1.0) |
| OutElastic | (0.5250, 1.0) | (0.64750000, 0.95000000) | (0.55750000, 1.01840280) | (0.8250, 1.0) |
| OutElastic | (0.8250, 1.0) | (0.82645800, 1.00000000) | (0.82500000, 0.99749253) | (1.0000, 1.0) |
| InOutElastic | (0.0000, 0.0) | (0.08750000, 0.00125373) | (0.08677100, 0.00000000) | (0.0875, 0.0) |
| InOutElastic | (0.0875, 0.0) | (0.22125000, −0.0092014) | (0.17625000, 0.02500000) | (0.2375, 0.0) |
| InOutElastic | (0.2375, 0.0) | (0.36750000, −0.0715475) | (0.32875000, 0.19166650) | (0.3875, 0.0) |
| InOutElastic | (0.3875, 0.0) | (0.45406250, −0.2930695) | (0.43343750, −0.3333335) | (0.5000, 0.5) |
| InOutElastic | (0.5000, 0.5) | (0.56656250, 1.33333350) | (0.54593750, 1.29306950) | (0.6125, 1.0) |
| InOutElastic | (0.6125, 1.0) | (0.67125000, 0.80833350) | (0.63250000, 1.07154750) | (0.7625, 1.0) |
| InOutElastic | (0.7625, 1.0) | (0.82375000, 0.97500000) | (0.77875000, 1.00920140) | (0.9125, 1.0) |
| InOutElastic | (0.9125, 1.0) | (0.91322900, 1.00000000) | (0.91250000, 0.99874626) | (1.0000, 1.0) |
| InBouce | (0.0000, 0.0) | (0.03030303, 0.02083333) | (0.06060606, 0.02083333) | (0.0909, 0.0) |
| InBouce | (0.0909, 0.0) | (0.15151515, 0.08333333) | (0.21212121, 0.08333333) | (0.2727, 0.0) |
| InBouce | (0.2727, 0.0) | (0.39393939, 0.33333333) | (0.51515152, 0.33333333) | (0.6364, 0.0) |
| InBouce | (0.6364, 0.0) | (0.75757576, 0.66666667) | (0.87878788, 1.00000000) | (1.0000, 1.0) |
| OutBounce | (0.0000, 0.0) | (0.12121212, 0.00000000) | (0.24242424, 0.33333333) | (0.3636, 1.0) |
| OutBounce | (0.3636, 1.0) | (0.48484848, 0.66666667) | (0.60606061, 0.66666667) | (0.7273, 1.0) |
| OutBounce | (0.7273, 1.0) | (0.78787879, 0.91666667) | (0.84848485, 0.91666667) | (0.9091, 1.0) |
| OutBounce | (0.9091, 1.0) | (0.93939394, 0.97916667) | (0.96969697, 0.97916667) | (1.0000, 1.0) |
| InOutBounce | (0.0000, 0.0) | (0.01515152, 0.01041667) | (0.03030303, 0.01041667) | (0.0455, 0.0) |
| InOutBounce | (0.0455, 0.0) | (0.07575758, 0.04166667) | (0.10606061, 0.04166667) | (0.1364, 0.0) |
| InOutBounce | (0.1364, 0.0) | (0.19696970, 0.16666667) | (0.25757576, 0.16666667) | (0.3182, 0.0) |
| InOutBounce | (0.3182, 0.0) | (0.37878788, 0.33333333) | (0.43939394, 0.50000000) | (0.5000, 0.5) |
| InOutBounce | (0.5000, 0.5) | (0.56060606, 0.50000000) | (0.62121212, 0.66666667) | (0.6818, 1.0) |
| InOutBounce | (0.6818, 1.0) | (0.74242424, 0.83333333) | (0.80303030, 0.83333333) | (0.8636, 1.0) |
| InOutBounce | (0.8636, 1.0) | (0.89393939, 0.95833333) | (0.92424242, 0.95833333) | (0.9550, 1.0) |
| InOutBounce | (0.9545, 1.0) | (0.96969697, 0.98958333) | (0.98484848, 0.98958333) | (1.0000, 1.0) |

In addition, in Table 3 we present the set of functions that previously were not approximated by cubic Bézier curves. In order to get a good approximation quality (comparable to the functions that have been discussed earlier), we divided these functions into more than two parts.

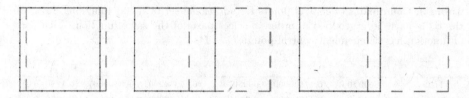

**Fig. 3.** An example of good approximation for the improved solution the same set of frames as in Fig. 2. Function = InOutQuint, solid line - original Penner's function, dashed line - standard approximation [18], dotted line - new proposition

## 6    Summary

In this paper the new version of approximation for Penner's easing functions has been introduced. The proposed solution based on the cubic Bézier curve.

The new propositions have been compared to original Penner's easing functions and to one of the well known and widely used example of approximation. The root mean square error (RMSE) was lower than for known solution. However, experiments with animation shown that evaluation based only on a numerical measure of error, is not a good option. The new approximations have been used as a transition function in a simple animation. The comparison with original easing function shown, that in some cases there is no possibility obtaining good approximation using cubic Bézier curve. For such functions the different form has been proposed. Function has been divided into two symmetric parts where the approximation has been done.

As the result of the study good approximation for all discussed easing functions have been reach. The result is concerning also to the visual effect of animation. The new form of easing function could be widely applied in Cascading Style Sheets (CSS). From the practical point of view new approximation could be useful for movement prototyping in application for animation. Additionally in some cases there is a need to convert animation from the program which supports the easing functions to the program which not support. Perhaps not the only one, but a good solution, would be using Bézier curves and proposed here approximations.

# A    Formulas of the Penner's Easing Functions

| | |
|---|---|
| Linear | $y = x \quad x \in [0,1]$ |
| InQuad | $y = x^2 \quad x \in [0,1]$ |
| OutQuad | $y = 1 - (x-1)^2 \quad x \in [0,1]$ |
| InOutQuad | $y = \begin{cases} 2x^2 & x \in [0, \frac{1}{2}) \\ 1 - 2(x-1)^2 & x \in [\frac{1}{2}, 1] \end{cases}$ |
| InCubic | $y = x^3 \quad x \in [0,1]$ |
| OutCubic | $y = 1 + (x-1)^3 \quad x \in [0,1]$ |
| InOutCubic | $y = \begin{cases} 4x^3 & x \in [0, \frac{1}{2}) \\ 1 + 4(x-1)^3 & x \in [\frac{1}{2}, 1] \end{cases}$ |
| InQuart | $y = x^4 \quad x \in [0,1]$ |
| OutQuart | $y = 1 - (x-1)^4 \quad x \in [0,1]$ |
| InOutQuart | $y = \begin{cases} 8x^4 & x \in [0, \frac{1}{2}) \\ 1 - 8(x-1)^4 & x \in [\frac{1}{2}, 1] \end{cases}$ |
| InQuint | $y = x^5 \quad x \in [0,1]$ |
| OutQuint | $y = 1 + (x-1)^5 \quad x \in [0,1]$ |
| InOutQuint | $y = \begin{cases} 16x^5 & x \in [0, \frac{1}{2}) \\ 1 + 16(x-1)^5 & x \in [\frac{1}{2}, 1] \end{cases}$ |
| InSine | $y = 1 - \cos(x \frac{\pi}{2}) \quad x \in [0,1]$ |
| OutSine | $y = \sin(x \frac{\pi}{2}) \quad x \in [0,1]$ |
| InOutSine | $y = \frac{1}{2} - \frac{1}{2}\cos(x\pi)$ |
| InExpo | $y = \begin{cases} 0 & x = 0 \\ 2^{10x-10} & (0,1] \end{cases}$ |
| OutExpo | $y = \begin{cases} -2^{-10x} + 1 & [0,1) \\ 1 & x = 1 \end{cases}$ |
| InOutExpo | $y = \begin{cases} 0 & x = 0 \\ 2^{20x-11} & (0, \frac{1}{2}] \\ 1 - 2^{-20x+9} & (\frac{1}{2}, 1) \\ 1 & x = 1 \end{cases}$ |

| InCirc | $y = 1 - \sqrt{1 - x^2} \quad x \in [0, 1]$ |
|---|---|
| OutCirc | $y = \sqrt{1 - (x - 1)^2} \quad x \in [0, 1]$ |
| InOutCirc | $y = \begin{cases} \frac{1}{2} - \frac{1}{2}\sqrt{1 - 4x^2} & x \in [0, \frac{1}{2}) \\ \frac{1}{2} + \frac{1}{2}\sqrt{1 - 4(x - 1)^2} & x \in [\frac{1}{2}, 1] \end{cases}$ |
| InBack | $y = x^2(2.70158x - 1.70158) \quad x \in [0, 1]$ |
| OutBack | $y = (x - 1)^2(2.70158x - 1) + 1 \quad x \in [0, 1]$ |
| InOutBack | $y = \begin{cases} 2x^2(7.189819x - 2.5949095) & x \in [0, \frac{1}{2}) \\ 2(x - 1)^2(7.189819x - 4.5949095) + 1 & x \in [\frac{1}{2}, 1] \end{cases}$ |
| InElastic | $y = \begin{cases} 0 & x = 0 \\ -2^{10x-10}\sin(\frac{20}{3}\pi(x - \frac{43}{40})) & x \in (0, 1) \\ 1 & x = 1 \end{cases}$ |
| OutElastic | $y = \begin{cases} 0 & x = 0 \\ 2^{-10x}\sin(\frac{20}{3}\pi(x - \frac{3}{40})) + 1 & x \in (0, 1) \\ 1 & x = 1 \end{cases}$ |
| InOutElastic | $y = \begin{cases} 0 & x = 0 \\ -2^{20x-11}\sin(\frac{40}{9}\pi(2x - \frac{89}{80})) & x \in (0, \frac{1}{2}] \\ 2^{9-20x}\sin(\frac{40}{9}\pi(2x - \frac{89}{80})) + 1 & x \in (\frac{1}{2}, 1) \\ 1 & x = 1 \end{cases}$ |
| InBounce | $y = \begin{cases} \frac{1}{64} - \frac{121}{16}(\frac{1}{22} - x)^2 & x \in (0, \frac{1}{11}] \\ \frac{1}{16} - \frac{121}{16}(\frac{2}{11} - x)^2 & x \in (\frac{1}{11}, \frac{3}{11}] \\ \frac{1}{4} - \frac{121}{16}(\frac{5}{11} - x)^2 & x \in (\frac{3}{11}, \frac{7}{11}] \\ 1 - \frac{121}{16}(1 - x)^2 & x \in (\frac{7}{11}, 1] \end{cases}$ |
| OutBounce | $y = \begin{cases} \frac{121}{16}x^2 & x \in [0, \frac{4}{11}) \\ \frac{121}{16}(x - \frac{6}{11})^2 + \frac{3}{4} & x \in [\frac{4}{11}, \frac{8}{11}) \\ \frac{121}{16}(x - \frac{9}{11})^2 + \frac{15}{16} & x \in [\frac{8}{11}, \frac{10}{11}) \\ \frac{121}{16}(x - \frac{21}{22})^2 + \frac{63}{64} & x \in [\frac{10}{11}, 1] \end{cases}$ |

| | |
|---|---|
| InOutBounce | $y = \begin{cases} \frac{1}{128} - \frac{121}{32}\left(\frac{1}{22} - 2x\right)^2 & x \in [0, \frac{1}{22}] \\[6pt] \frac{1}{32} - \frac{121}{32}\left(\frac{2}{11} - 2x\right)^2 & x \in (\frac{1}{22}, \frac{3}{22}] \\[6pt] \frac{1}{8} - \frac{121}{32}\left(\frac{5}{11} - 2x\right)^2 & x \in (\frac{3}{22}, \frac{7}{22}] \\[6pt] \frac{1}{2} - \frac{121}{32}(1 - 2x)^2 & x \in (\frac{7}{22}, \frac{1}{2}] \\[6pt] \frac{1}{2} + \frac{121}{32}(2x - 1)^2 & x \in (\frac{1}{2}, \frac{15}{22}] \\[6pt] \frac{7}{8} + \frac{121}{32}\left(2x - \frac{17}{11}\right)^2 & x \in (\frac{15}{22}, \frac{19}{22}] \\[6pt] \frac{31}{32} + \frac{121}{32}\left(2x - \frac{20}{11}\right)^2 & x \in (\frac{19}{22}, \frac{21}{22}] \\[6pt] \frac{127}{128} + \frac{121}{32}\left(2x - \frac{43}{22}\right)^2 & x \in (\frac{21}{22}, 1] \end{cases}$ |

# References

1. Parent, R.: Computer Animation, 3rd edn. Morgan Kaufmann, Burlington (2012)
2. Penner, R.: Motion, tweening, and easing. In: Programming Macromedia Flash MX, chap. 7, pp. 191–240. McGraw-Hill/OsborneMedia (2002). http://www.robertpenner.com/easing/penner_chapter7_tweening.pdf. Accessed 10 Mar 2016
3. Robert Penner's Easing Functions. http://robertpenner.com/easing/. Accessed 10 Mar 2016
4. Owen, M., Willis, P.: Modelling and interpolating cartoon characters. In: Proceedings of the Computer Animation 1994, Geneva, 25–28 May 1994, pp. 148–155. http://ieeexplore.ieee.org/iel2/987/7718/00323996.pdf. Accessed 10 Mar 2016
5. Melikhov, K., Tian, F., Seah, H.S., Chen, Q., Qiu, J.: Frame skeleton based auto-inbetweening in computer assisted cel animation. In: Proceedings of the 2004 International Conference on Cyberworlds (CW 2004), 18–20 November 2004, Tokyo, Japan, pp. 216–223 (2004)
6. Sakchaicharoenkul, T.: MCFI-based animation tweening algorithm for 2D parametric motion flow/optical flow. Mach. Graph. Vis. Int. J. **15**(1), 29–49 (2006)
7. van der Spuy, R.: Tweening. In: van der Spuy, R. (ed.) Advanced Game Design with HTML5 and JavaScript, chap. 10, pp. 369–406. Apress/Springer, New York (2015)
8. Peters, K.: Tween Engines. In: Peters, K. (ed.) Advanced ActionScript 3.0 Animation, chap. 10. Apress/Springer, New York (2009)
9. EasingCurve Class. In: Qt Documentation. http://doc.qt.io/qt-4.8/qeasingcurve.html. Accessed 10 Mar 2016
10. jQuery user interface, Easing. https://jqueryui.com/easing/. Accessed 10 Mar 2016
11. Easing Functions. In: .NET Framework v4 Documentation, https://msdn.microsoft.com/en-us/library/ee308751%28v=vs.100%29.aspx. Accessed 10 Mar 2016
12. Tweener (ActionScript) at GoogleCode. https://code.google.com/archive/p/tweener/. Accessed 10 Mar 2016
13. The secret of tweening: when and when not to. Broder Jakobs Flash. http://www.broderjakob.se/2007/09/07/the-secret-of-tweening-using-it-when-you-need-it/. Accessed 10 Mar 2016

14. Apt, D.: An Introduction to Tweening with ActionScript 3.0. (2009). http://code.tutsplus.com/tutorials/an-introduction-to-tweening-with-actionscript-30--active-2022. Accessed 10 Mar 2016
15. Smith, J., Smith, C., Gerantabee, F.: How to Create a Motion Tween in Adobe Flash CS6. http://www.dummies.com/how-to/content/how-to-create-a-motion-tween-in-adobe-flash-cs6.html. Accessed 10 Mar 2016
16. Cascading Style Sheets (CSS). The Official Definition, W3C Working Group Note, 13 October 2015. https://www.w3.org/TR/CSS/#css. Accessed 10 Mar 2016
17. Lie, H.W.: Cascading HTML Style Sheets a Proposal. https://www.w3.org/People/howcome/p/cascade.html. Accessed 10 Mar 2016
18. Ceaser CSS Easing Animation Tool. https://matthewlein.com/ceaser/. Accessed 10 Mar 2016
19. Tween Class. http://www.createjs.com/docs/tweenjs/classes/Tween.html. Accessed 10 Mar 2016
20. AHEasing. A library of easing functions for C, C++ and Objective-C. https://github.com/warrenm/AHEasing. Accessed 10 Mar 2016
21. Easing Equation by Robert Penner. http://gizma.com/easing/. Accessed 10 Mar 2016
22. Tween-functions. Robert Penner's easing functions, slightly modified. https://www.npmjs.com/package/tween-functions. Accessed 10 Mar 2016

# Perceptual Experiments Optimisation by Initial Database Reduction

Anna Lewandowska (Tomaszewska)[(⊠)]

Faculty of Computer Science and Information Technology,
West Pomeranian University of Technology,
Zolnierska 49, 71-210 Szczecin, Poland
atomaszewska@wi.zut.edu.pl

**Abstract.** Image quality plays important role in many image processing applications. For assessing perceptual image quality, there is need
to quantify the visibility of differences between a distorted image and
a reference image using a variety of known properties of the human
visual system. Also to provide a convincing proof that a new method is
better than the state-of-the-art the image quality assessment should be
employed. Therefore image based projects are often accompanied by user
studies, in which a group of observers rank or rate results of several algorithms. Unfortunately the problem posed by subjective experiments is
their time-consuming and expensive nature. Huge size of input databases
is crucial in that situation. This paper is intended to reduce the database
size and made the subjective experiments less expensive and therefore
more usable. To achieve it we employ a clustering technique and human
visual system based objective metrics.

## 1 Introduction

When developing a new imaging or algorithm with visual results, there is often
a need to compare them with the state-of-the-art methods. Comparison via several examples included in the paper and carefully inspected with the results of
competitive algorithms is an effective method, but only if the visual difference
is unquestionably large. If the differences are subtle, such informal comparison
is often disputable. The most reliable way of assessing the quality of an image
is by subjective evaluation. Indeed, the mean opinion score (MOS), a subjective quality measure requiring the services of a number of human observers, has
been long regarded as the best method of image quality measurement. However,
the MOS method is expensive, and time-consuming.

The scene reduction may be useful to solve the problem especially when it
gives reliable results. The selection of the right set of images, as well as their
number, is a non-trivial problem. Ideally, we should consider as many images as
possible for the most representative sample of possible scenes. However, for practical reasons testing large image sets is often not feasible, especially in academic
projects. Even when considering much smaller image sets, we need to decide
whether it is more desirable to collect fewer measurements for a larger number

© Springer International Publishing AG 2016
L.J. Chmielewski et al. (Eds.): ICCVG 2016, LNCS 9972, pp. 49–60, 2016.
DOI: 10.1007/978-3-319-46418-3_5

of images, so that the sample is more representative, or rather collect more measurements for fewer images, so that the measurements are more accurate and their statistical power is higher.

In this work that complements our approach presented in [15], we address the problem of reducing the number of total scenes for effective subjective quality assessment experiments. Our approach enables balance between high experiment cost and the approximation of the received results. It gives the opportunity to reduce the database size, and thus decrease in the experiment cost. The problem with subjective metrics is that they are only some approximation of the whole population feeling. As well the full experiment is only some measure of human perception. Reduced database is an approximation of the full database, and therefore still approximation of the whole population feeling. The key is how close the approximation is. The correlation gives us the answer.

To check practical usage of the approach we verified a method on a standard well-known databases: LIVE [9], IVC_SubQualityDB [13], TID2008 [10] and CISQ [12].

The problem is that before starting the procedure of the scene reduction we do not have knowledge about database redundancy. Therefore there is a question if the procedure of scene preselection makes sense. Gathering the opinion of some observers by means of a subjective experiment is obviously time consuming and expensive, even for the pilot stage. Moreover we can not guarantee that the procedure will be finished successfully. For this reason we changed the approach presented in [15], and introduced additional stage before the procedure of scene pre-selection started. This step we called database redundancy checking. We used the fact that the objective metrics aim to predict subjective visibility and/or quality and therefore we employed the perceptually based objective metrics known as MS-SSIM to estimate the database redundancy.

The paper is organized as follows. In Sect. 2, previous works are discussed. Experiment design is described in Sect. 3. Analysis of databases redundancy and usability of the approach tested on the well-known databases are presented in Sect. 4. The last section presents conclusions and suggestions for possible future work.

## 2    Previous Work

The subjective quality assessment are used practically in different applications [4–8]. However the problem posed by subjective experiments is their time consuming and expensive nature. Time compensation through the reduction of trial or scene numbers may be a solution to the problem. The number of trials in pair-comparisons methods can be limited using balanced incomplete block designs [11] in which all possible paired comparisons are indirectly inferred. As reported in [8,14], when the reduced design with sorting algorithm is used for the forced choice technique, the method is even faster than the single stimulus. However, the number of images selected for the experiment still influences the reduced number of trials. If the number is high, the experiments remain time-consuming.

Therefore, the scene pre-selection is not an uncommon practice, and was proposed to measure quality scales (quality rulers) for the ISO 20462 standard [1]. Nonetheless, the methodology of this process is not well explained and analyzed.

In [16] to decrease the number of required sessions per observer, a semi-manual selection process was used. Nevertheless, it is not a common and practical solution, as taking manually into account all the parameters expected to have an influence on the quality might become very complex and unreliable. The use of adapted objective quality metrics to estimate the quality of data before the test may be a promising alternative. Such an approach was proposed in [17,18], where the problem of decreasing the number of video sequences was analyzed. Naturally, this raises questions about the reliability of the measure. The scene preselection was examined also in [15], where a method of limiting the number of scenes that need to be tested, by employing a clustering technique and evaluated it on the basis of compactness and separation criteria is proposed. As we reported a correlation analysis between the full and reduced experiments indicated that the method was most suitable for the forced choice and double stimulus metrics. The problem is that before starting the procedure of the scene reduction we do not have knowledge about database redundancy. In the paper that complements the approach, we introduced database redundancy estimation computed via human visual system based objective metrics - MS-SSIM.

## 2.1   Experiment Design

For experiments we selected 10 images from the Kodak Photo CD photo sampler collection, as shown in Fig. 1. This is the subset of images used to collect data for the LIVE quality database [9]. They contain a broad range of content type, including faces, animals, manmade objects, and nature. We selected JPEG 2000 (JP2K) compression distortions and unsharp masking based on the bilateral filter ($\varsigma_s = 8$, $\varsigma_r = 50$) as the two evaluated algorithms, both at three levels of either distortion (JP2K) or enhancement (unsharp masking). The JP2K test images are the same as in the LIVE quality database [9] while unsharp masking is a new algorithm that we decided to include in our study. Unlike JP2K, unsharp masking can potentially improve image quality, though the quality will degrade if the filter is applied in excessive amounts. Because of this, unsharp masking is a very difficult case for computational (objective) quality metrics, which rely on the difference between test and reference images. Unsharp masking is also a common component of many computer graphics algorithms, such as tone mapping. We intentionally selected two well-known and understood algorithms, which are not comparable, so that we could focus on the scene reduction problem rather than on finding a better algorithm.

In our experiment we used the following conditions.

**Observers.** The images were assessed by naïve observers who were confirmed to have normal or corrected to normal vision. The age varied between 22 and 43. 11 observers completed the two pairwise comparison experiments. For additional reliability, all observers repeated each experiment three times, but no two repetitions took place on the same day in order to reduce the learning effect.

**Fig. 1.** The reference images (scenes) from the public domain Kodak photo CD used in the experiments.

**Display Conditions.** The experiments were run in two separate laboratories on two different displays: 26" NEC SpectraView 2690 and 24" HP LP2480zx. Both are high quality, 1920 × 1200 pixel resolution, LCD displays offering very good color reproduction. The display responses were measured with the Minolta CS-200 colorimeter and Specbos 1201 spectroradiometer. The measurements were used to calibrate the displays and ensure that all images were reproduced in the sRGB colour space.

**Experimental Procedure.** The observers were asked to read a written instruction before the experiment. Following [2,3] the recommendation, the experiment started with a training session in which the observers could familiarize themselves with the task, interface, and typical images. After that session, they could ask questions or start the main experiment. To ensure that the observers fully attend the experiment, three random trials were shown at the beginning of the main session without recording the results. The images were displayed in a random order and with a different randomization for each session. Two consecutive trials showing the same scene were avoided if possible. No session took longer than 30 min to avoid fatigue.

## 2.2   The Most Prominent Experimental Method for Scene Preselection

Deeply analyzed in [15] subjective metrics indicated two methods as the most prominent for initial scene reduction: the Double Stimulus and the Forced Choice metrics illustrated in Fig. 2.

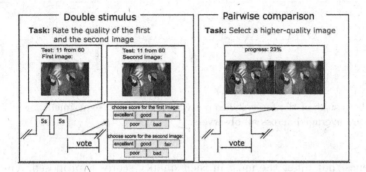

**Fig. 2.** Overview of the double stimulus and forced choice subjective quality assessment methods we investigate in this work. The diagram shows the timeline of each method and the corresponding screens.

**Double stimulus categorical rating** is analogous to the single-stimulus method, but a reference image and a test image are presented one after another for 3 s each (see Fig. 2: Left). Following that, a voting screen is displayed on which both images are assessed separately using the same scale as for the single stimulus method. The method requires $n$ trials to assess $n$ conditions.

**Ordering by Force-Choice Pairwise Comparison.** The observers are shown a pair of images (of the same scene) corresponding to different conditions and asked to indicate an image of higher quality (see Fig. 2: Right). Observers are always forced to choose one image, even if they see no difference between them (thus a forced-choice design). There is no time limit or minimum time to make the choice. The method is straightforward and thus expected to be more accurate than rating methods. But it also requires more trials to compare each possible pair of conditions: $0.5\,(n \cdot (n-1))$ for $n$ conditions. The number of trials can be limited using balanced incomplete block designs [11] in which all possible paired comparisons are indirectly inferred. But even more effective reduction of trials can be achieved if a sorting algorithm is used to choose pairs to compare [20].

## 3   Scene Pre-selection Method

The experimental results concerning many cases and conducted in different sessions are often noisy and their proper analysis and interpretation is not trivial. Instead of studying a large number of scenes, focusing the measurement on

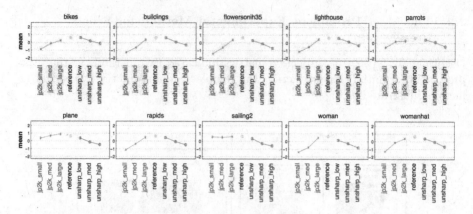

**Fig. 3.** The results of the force-choice pairwise comparison experiment for all images. The data are averaged across all observers.

a few scenes that differ the most in their quality scores is proposed. The rationale is that measuring two scenes that result in very similar quality scores does not contribute to better understanding of how image content affects quality. For example, after inspecting forced choice results (the *mean* row in Fig. 3), it can be noticed that the scenes *lighthouse*, *buildings* and *rapids* give very similar average quality scores and there is probably no need to measure the quality for both of them together. But the scene *sailing2* differs significantly from the rest, especially for the J2PK distortions. In this particular case, the undistorted image is inspected and noticed that it contains a high amount of noise. We suspect that no effect of JP2K compression on quality is mostly due to blurring introduced by the compression, which also happens to remove noise and thus improves the overall image quality. This shows that measuring individual scenes can reveal important insights into the algorithm performance, which would be lost if the measurements were averaged across the scenes. Our main intention is to reduce the effort in algorithm evaluation by selecting only the representative scenes and running the full experiment on them. But to decide on the representative scenes, their quality should be known, which makes it necessary to run the experiment on all images.

**Pilot Stage.** The image selection, however, can be relatively efficient if the decision can be based on a small sample collected for all images in a pilot experiment. By the pilot experiment, the first phase of experiment to choose representative images is understood. In the practical application, the subjective results to make the Pilot stage are unknown. Therefore to verify the procedure, the Pilot stage was computed parallel with two different data: subjective results and objective metrics MS-SSIM. Subjective data were clustered and then values of images from the cluster were replaced with the value of the representative image, as our method suggested. Then the Pearson correlation was computed (see Fig. 6). In second path, the objective metrics values to cluster database are used.

Then in reduced database, subjective results instead of objective metrics values are replaced. In other words in second path, the pilot stage from experimental procedure is replaced by the automatic procedure with objective metrics. The rest of the rules stayed the same. The difference between the approaches is shown in Figs. 6, 8 and 9.

**Redundancy.** Before the scene pre-selection starts, there is the question if the database is redundant and the procedure of scene preselection makes sense. Gathering the opinion of some observers by mean of a subjective experiment is obviously time consuming and expensive, even for the pilot stage, especially if we do not know if the procedure will be finished successfully. Therefore, the fact that objective metrics aim to predict subjective visibility and/or quality and employed the perceptually based objective metrics to estimate the database redundancy is used. Our choice was multi-scale structural similarity index (MS-SSIM) [19] However, it can be changed for other objective metrics if it better fits on analyzed database. We chose the MS-SSIM metrics as it is based on the assumption that the human visual system is highly adapted for extracting structural information from the scene. Therefore, it can provide a good approximation to perceived image quality. Moreover, the multiscale approach is reported as flexibility in incorporating the variations of viewing conditions [19].

**Number of Representatives.** Another important question is how many representative images (or clusters) should be selected for further analysis. During experiments the hierarchical algorithm (AHC) is found as the most stable and producing the best (smallest) partition index, especially when given a small number of samples. Therefore the AHC algorithm for further analysis is employed. It is available as *clusterdata* function in the MATLAB statistical toolbox.

In the nest step, the correlations between full and reduced databases is analyzed, according to different samples and clusters number. Details are described in [15]. We found that the best results, stable with an increasing cluster numbers (starting from 3 clusters), and sample numbers (starting from 12 samples), were received for the forced choice method that, as reported in [4], resulted in

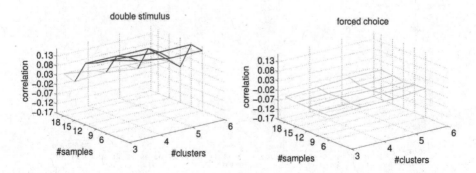

**Fig. 4.** The error between full and reduced versions of the experiment with LIVE databases, computed for all metrics, cluster and sample numbers.

the smallest measurement variance and thus produced the most accurate results. Promising results were obtained for the double stimulus technique, too. Their correlation level was higher than 90 %.

The correctness of results was verified by the correlation between a reduced our database with the LIVE database [9]. The comparison of the error values was computed as the difference between the correlation for full and reduced experiments (Fig. 4). The best results evidenced by the smallest error values (error of 2–3%) were received for the forced choice method. For double stimulus, the error was about 5 % to 6 %.

After the Pilot stage and the database reduction there is a question how to determine if a reduced-size database can replace the original database with the same functions in the IQA field? Determination if the reduced database can be replaced with the original is performed by the Pearson correlation between full and reduced databases. The acceptable level of correlation depends on the research destination. It may differ between applications, e.g. lower for task of choosing images to the fotoalbum, higher for application looking for specific features in the images. However since objective metrics is not ideal approximation of human perception, starting reduction no less than 60 % of whole database (in the case from 8 clusters) is suggested.

## 4    Approach Verification for a Well-Known Databases

For practical test of the approach the experiments are performed and analyzed not only on LIVE database [9], but also on the other standard well-known databases: TID2008 [10], CISQ [12] and IVC_SubQualityDB [13].

**TID2008 database** includes 25 reference images × 17 types of distortions × 4 levels of distortions. First the database redundancy is checked Fig. 5. As the correlation level was high we assume that the database was redundant. Then the pilot stage is executed. For pilot stage (see Fig. 6) we used also MS-SSIM objective metrics, especially that the authors of TID2008 database reported that it characterizes with maximal Pearson and Kendall correlation with subjective

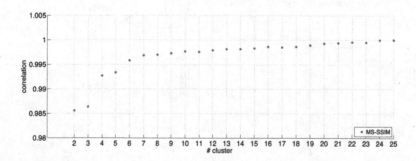

**Fig. 5.** Correlation between original and reduced TID2008 databases [10] based on objective results.

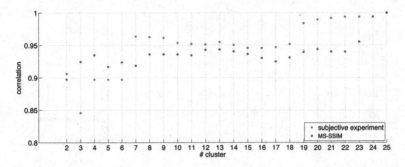

**Fig. 6.** The results of input TID2008 [10] dataset redundancy estimation. 'MS-SSIM' denotes the correlation between full and reduced data, where quality is evaluated by MS-SSIM metrics. Subjective experiment means the correlation between full and reduced data, where quality is acquired throughout subjective experiment - forced choice.

results between other objective metrics. In pilot stage it can be noticed a correlation level higher than 90 % starting from 3 clusters, however real results confirm the correlation level starting from 7 clusters.

For small cluster number the MS-SSIM metrics gave higher correlation level, then subjective results were more accurate. It is worth to mention that in special situation, when the pilot stage is to expensive, objective metrics could be used. However it is only the approximation of the subjective results and could be prone to errors. In case of TID2008 database, the MS-SSIM metrics quite correctly reflects the subjective results.

**CISQ database** consists of 30 original images, each is distorted using six different types of distortions at four to five different levels of distortion. CSIQ images are subjectively rated base on a linear displacement of the images across four calibrated LCD monitors placed side by side with equal viewing distance to the observer. The database contains 5000 subjective ratings from 35 different observers, and ratings are reported in the form of DMOS. Results of the

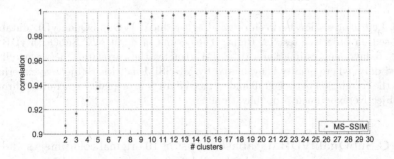

**Fig. 7.** Correlation between original and reduced CISQ databases [12] based on objective results.

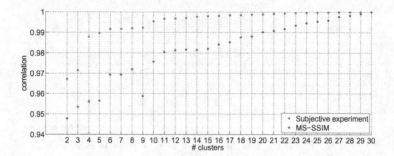

**Fig. 8.** The results of input CISQ [12] dataset redundancy estimation. 'MS-SSIM' denotes the correlation between full and reduced data, where quality is evaluated by MS-SSIM metrics. Subjective experiment means the correlation between full and reduced data, where quality is acquired throughout subjective experiment - forced choice.

redundancy checking depicted Fig. 7. As the correlation level was high we assume that the database was redundant. Then executed pilot stage (see Fig. 8). In pilot stage it can be noticed correlation level higher than 90 % starting from 2 clusters. In case of CISQ database, the MS-SSIM metrics quite correctly reflects the subjective results as well.

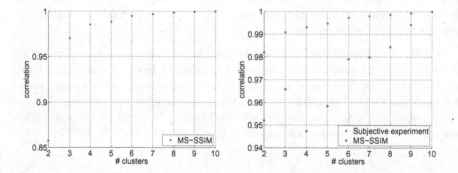

**Fig. 9.** Left: Correlation between original and reduced IVC_SubQualityDB databases [13] based on objective results. Right: The results of input IVC_SubQualityDB [13] dataset redundancy estimation. 'MS-SSIM' denotes the correlation between full and reduced data, where quality is evaluated by MS-SSIM metrics. Subjective experiment means the correlation between full and reduced data, where quality is acquired throughout subjective experiment - double stimulus.

**IVC_SubQualityDB database** consist of 10 original color images and 120 distorted images were generated from 3 different processing, and 5 compression rates. Subjective evaluations were made at viewing distance of 6 times the screen height using a DSIS (Double Stimulus Impairment Scale) method with 5 categories and 20 observers. Distortions for each processing and each image have been optimised in order to uniformly cover the subjective scale. As before, first the database redundancy is checked (see Fig. 9 Left). As the correlation level was high we assume that the database was redundant. After that, the Pilot stage was executed (see Fig. 9 Right). In pilot stage it can be noticed correlation level higher than 90 % starting from 2 clusters. In case of IVC_SubQualityDB database, the MS-SSIM metrics quite correctly reflects the subjective results as well.

We suggest above, the acceptable level of the correlation depends on the user approach, on the database usage destiny. If the lower cost of the experiment is preferable, more than a level of the results approximation then our approach should be used. Since objective metrics is not ideal approximation of human perception, starting reduction no less than 60 % of whole database (in the case from 8 clusters) is suggested.

## 5    Conclusions and Future Work

In the paper the results of a modification of the earlier approach [15], for a scene-preselection is presented. The approach is used to reduce the database size used in subjective experiments and makes it less expensive and therefore more usable. As before starting the procedure of the scene reduction there is lack of knowledge about database redundancy, therefore checking it by human visual system based objective metrics - MS-SSIM was introduced. The second problem is that in the practical application, we do not know the subjective results to make the Pilot stage. Therefore to verify the procedure, the Pilot stage was computed parallely with two different data: subjective results and objective metrics MS-SSIM. We check successfully our approach on the well-known databases LIVE [9], IVC_SubQualityDB [13], TID2008 [10] and CISQ [12].

## References

1. Keelan, B.W.: A psychophysical image quality measurement standard. SPIE **5294**, 181–189 (2003)
2. ITU-R.Rec.BT.500-11, Methodology for the Subjective Assessment of the Quality for Television Pictures (2002)
3. ITU-T.Rec.P.910, Subjective audiovisual quality assessment methods for multimedia applications (2008)
4. Mantiuk, R., Tomaszewska, A., Mantiuk, R.: Comparison of four subjective methods for image quality assessment. Comput. Graph. Forum **31**, 2478–2491 (2012)
5. Tomaszewska, A.: Blind noise level detection. In: Kamel, M., Campilho, A. (eds.) ICIAR 2012, Part I. LNCS, vol. 7324, pp. 107–114. Springer, Heidelberg (2012)
6. Tomaszewska, A., Stefanowski, K.: Real-time spherical harmonics based subsurface scattering. In: Campilho, A., Kamel, M. (eds.) ICIAR 2012, Part I. LNCS, vol. 7324, pp. 402–409. Springer, Heidelberg (2012)

7. Tomaszewska, A.: User study in non-static HDR scenes acquisition. In: Bolc, L., Tadeusiewicz, R., Chmielewski, L.J., Wojciechowski, K. (eds.) ICCVG 2012. LNCS, vol. 7594, pp. 245–252. Springer, Heidelberg (2012)

8. Mantiuk, R., Mantiuk, R., Tomaszewska, A., Heidrich, W.: Color correction for tone mapping. Comput. Graph. Forum **28**, 193–202 (2009)

9. Sheikh, H.R., Sabir, M.F., Bovik, A.C.: A statistical evaluation of recent full reference image quality assessment algorithms. IEEE Trans. Image Process. **15**(11), 3441–3452 (2006)

10. Ponomarenko, N., Lukin, V., Zelensky, A., Egiazarian, K., Carli, M., Battisti, F.: TID2008 - a database for evaluation of full-reference visual quality assessment metrics. Adv. Mod. Radioelectron. **10**, 30–45 (2009)

11. Gulliksen, H., Tucker, L.R.: A general procedure for obtaining paired comparisons from multiple rank orders. Psychometrika **26**, 173–184 (1961)

12. Larson, E.C., Chandler, D.M.: Most apparent distortion: full-reference image quality assessment and the role of strategy. J. Electron. Imaging **19**(1), 1–21 (2010)

13. Strauss, C., Pasteau, F., Autrusseau, F., Babel, M., Bedat, L., Deforges, O.: Subjective and objective quality evaluation of LAR coded art images. In: IEEE International Conference on Multimedia and Expo, ICME 2009, New York, USA (2009)

14. Lewandowska (Tomaszewska), A.: Time compensation in perceptual experiments. In: Chmielewski, L.J., Kozera, R., Shin, B.-S., Wojciechowski, K. (eds.) ICCVG 2014. LNCS, vol. 8671, pp. 33–40. Springer, Heidelberg (2014)

15. Lewandowska (Tomaszewska), A.: Scene reduction for subjective image quality assessment. J. Electron. Imaging **25**(1), 221–226 (2016). doi:10.1117/1.JEI.25.1.013015

16. Pitrey, Y., Barkowsky, M., Pepion, R., Le Callet, P., Hlavacs, H.: Influence of the source content and encoding configuration on the perceived quality for scalable video coding. In: Proceedings of SPIE, vol. 8291, pp. 82911K–82911K-8 (2012)

17. Pinson, M., Wolf, S.: Techniques for evaluating objective video quality models using overlapping subjective data sets [electronic resource]/Pinson, M.H., Wolf, S., U.S. Deptartment of Commerce, National Telecommunications and Information Administration, 1 online resource, United States (2008)

18. Pitrey, Y., Robitza, W., Hlavacs, H.: Instance selection techniques for subjective quality of experience evaluation. In: QoEMCS, Part of the EuroITV conference (2012). http://dcti.iscte.pt/events/qoemcs/

19. Wang, Z., Simoncelli, E.P., Bovik, A.C.: Multi-scale structural similarity for image quality assessment, In: Proceedings of IEEE Asilomar Conference on Signals, Systems, and Computers, (Asilomar), pp. 1398–1402 (2003)

20. Silverstein, D.A., Farrell, J.E.: Efficient method for paired comparison. J. Electron. Imaging **10**, 394–398 (2001)

# Decoupling Rendering and Display Using Fast Depth Image Based Rendering on the GPU

Julian Meder[1,2(✉)] and Beat Brüderlin[1]

[1] TU Ilmenau, Helmholtzplatz 5, 98693 Ilmenau, Germany
{Julian.Meder,Beat.Bruederlin}@tu-ilmenau.de
[2] 3DInteractive GmbH, Am Vogelherd 10, 98693 Ilmenau, Germany

**Abstract.** Feasible rendering of massive scenes with hardware capabilities and scene data size concurrently growing has been an active subject of research in recent decades. While past attempts showed realtime rendering on basic consumer workstations, frame rates can still be too low for the growing demand in the professional CAD industry and sectors like entertainment for stable high frame rates. The work described in this paper focuses on fulfilling this demand in the context of CAD software. A fast custom application of the Depth Image Based Rendering (DIBR) technique is used to construct a view synthesis system generating the required rate using past frames of a classical parallel renderer. Artifacts associated with this technique are addressed in a cost-effective manner.

## 1 Introduction

In the past decade great advances have been made in the field of culling and out-of-core techniques, enabling the interactive display of massive scenes with acceptable quality [1,9] on standard workstation hardware. Still, view dependent scene complexity combined with insufficient hardware capabilities result in frequently changing frame rates, often below the acceptable. This creates two main problems:

- **Bad viewing comfort:** A stable high frame rate is needed (60 Hz and above)
- **Input lag:** Ensuring a low user input delay prevents user irritation

Failing to comply with these requirements can have a profound impact on usability and productivity, for example motion sickness with virtual reality.

The main target applications for this paper are renderers of professional CAD. Based on the insufficient image sequence of a slow CAD renderer we generate a new one at the required frame rate. For this, Depth Image Based Rendering (DIBR) is adapted as a novel fast GPU application.

The following Sect. 2 briefly summarizes DIBR while the rest of this paper is organized as follows: Sect. 2.1 gives previous work in the field of DIBR. Section 2.2 describes possible and previously implemented DIBR applications on the GPU. Following a general description of our system in Sect. 3, the projection method and its' GPU implementation is detailed in Sect. 4. Section 5 shows the solutions to reduce artifacts. Finally, an empirical analysis is given in Sect. 6 and conclusions in Sect. 7.

© Springer International Publishing AG 2016
L.J. Chmielewski et al. (Eds.): ICCVG 2016, LNCS 9972, pp. 61–72, 2016.
DOI: 10.1007/978-3-319-46418-3_6

## 2   Depth Image Based Rendering

The first appearance of the DIBR term can be found in the work of C. Fehn [7], while the previous common designation was 3D image warping [13, 18]. It involves the following pixel transformation:

$$p_t = P_t R_t T_t T_s^{-1} R_s^{-1} P_s^{-1} p_s$$
$$p_t = M_t M_s^{-1} p_s \tag{1}$$

A pixel $p_s$ is transformed from the source image to a target view screen space position $p_t$ by inverting the source view camera's projection $P_s$, view rotation $R_s$ and translation $T_s$ and applying the transformations of the target view's camera.

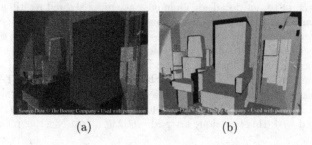

(a)                              (b)

**Fig. 1.** Naive DIBR projections show artifacts: (a) The forward mapping problem and (b) information gaps (black)

DIBR suffers from a problem known as holes [17, 22], of which Fig. 1 shows two distinctions. The first results due to texture mapping from source to target space, which is not necessarily surjective, while the second occurs when scene geometry visible from the target view is occluded in the source view.

### 2.1   Related Work

One popular field of applications of DIBR has been pseudo stereoscopic image generation. The work of Fehn included a simplified version of the general 3D warp by formulating the projection only in x-direction of the screen space [7] and a gaussian source depth blur to avoid holes. Zhang et al. proposed an asymmetrical gaussian filter creating fewer distortions in the target image [22], which Horng et al. improved by additionally rotating the kernel by local depth edge directions and constricting the filter to hole regions [11].

Since these filling methods proved to be unsuitable for the general projection case, Ndjiki-Nya et al. [16] and Xi et al. [21] employed a more complex method via Inpainting combined with a background model, except the approaches were not real time capable. The latter used a higher quality projection method involving a forward projection to target space of the source depth buffer, subsequent depth hole filling and finally a backward projection to sample the color image. This idea has also been used by Oh et al. [17] and Zinger et al. [23]. Zinger et al. additionally accelerated the forward-backward projection by only backprojecting pixels which needed to be filled in the target depth image.

Image space triangulation for general warping was used by Fu et al., who constructed a topological ordering of the generated triangles to render without a z-buffer [8]. Mark et al. proposed an online method for free camera movement, which renders necessary reference frames from predicted future viewpoints [13]. Ghiletiuc et al. applied a cube map technique in an online variant, continually creating small cube map meshes based on the last known client camera on a server and sending them to a mobile client for conventional rendering [10]. Another mesh rendering variant was proposed by Didyk et al. who use a multi pass mesh refinement through a geometry shader to create pseudo stereo images [5].

## 2.2 GPU-Suitable DIBR

A straightforward way of implementing DIBR on a GPU is point rendering. Every pixel of the source image is assigned a vertex with a position derived from the pixel's texture coordinates and the corresponding depth value, which is transformed by Eq. (1) in the vertex shader. Chang et al. utilize such a simple point rendering [2]. This method clearly shows the forward mapping problem, which may be reduced by employing splatting [20]. However, only quadratic and circular reconstruction kernels are currently directly hardware-supported, which either introduces new artifacts, due to inaccurate splatting forms, or decreased performance, when implementing more complex kernels.

A second GPU-adaptable DIBR method was introduced by Morvan et al. [15], who separated the projection (1). His first step, a source space homogeneous translation, is done first line- and then column-wise for easy neighbor interpolation, solving the forward mapping problem. However, this step can have a large memory footprint and needs to write an arbitrary amount of pixels, requiring implementation through GPGPU. In contrast, the second step, a perspective texture mapping, is directly supported by the traditional GPU-pipeline [15].

GPU DIBR projection can also be implemented by using triangle meshes. The method creating the basis for this paper has been used for example by Mark et al. [13]. Vertices are placed in the center of each pixel, with each quadruple of neighboring vertices being connected via two triangles. This avoids holes caused by forward mapping, but new problems are introduced as the assumption of one continuous surface over the whole image does not hold in general (see Sect. 5). The constructed mesh is rendered conventionally as a textured model (the texture being the source color image). Some publications therefore call these meshes impostors [4, 10].

## 3   General System Overview

Figure 2 depicts the two parallel independent processes resident on the same hardware: the classic renderer and the DIBR projector. View camera changes

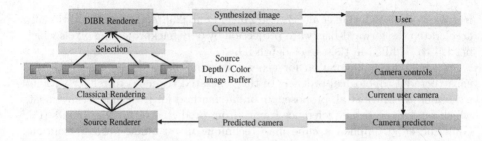

**Fig. 2.** The constructed system

are not directly reflected in the source renderer, but rather evaluated by a prediction algorithm generating the final cameras used for source rendering (Sect. 5.1). Rendered source frames are buffered for asynchronous retrieval by the DIBR target renderer, which uses a subset of buffered frames and the current view camera to synthesize an expected view image for the user. Consequently, the user input and the frame display are decoupled from the original renderer, ensuring low input delay and hiding varying frame rates of the source renderer.

## 4    On-the-Fly Tessellation Reprojection

One critical observation about the triangle mesh method of Mark et al. [13] is its' high rendering cost. Given the pixel width $m$ and height $n$ of a source image, the amount of triangles needed is $2(m-1)(n-1)$. We reduce this cost by dynamically tessellating the source image space for every DIBR projection. The higher efficiency of this method is shown in Sect. 6.1.

Contrary to the geometry shader method of Didyk et al. [5] a single pass tessellation shader is used. It carries more potential for concurrency, as generated vertices are processed in parallel after fixed-function tessellation, which is not possible in a geometry shader. Also, the multi-pass transform feedback has a higher performance and memory access overhead than using hardware-accelerated single pass tessellation.

### 4.1    Mesh Layout Considerations

The original mesh structure used by Mark et al. [13] exhibited the problem of deleting a half-pixel edge at the image's border and on edges between surfaces of different depth (see Sect. 6.2 for a comparison). To avoid this problem, every source pixel is treated as a small surface by placing the vertices on the pixel edges instead of the center. The starting mesh before tessellation however is a coarse set of $\lceil \frac{m \times n}{t_{max}^2} \rceil$ patches, $m \times n$ being the source image resolution and $t_{max}$ the tessellation factor used.

As our approach is single pass, a binary decision whether to tessellate a patch is made. When tessellated, a coarse starting mesh with few large patches could

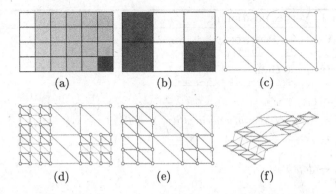

**Fig. 3.** (a) Edge regions of the depth map are (b) queried from the edge mipmap of a level corresponding to the (c) patch size. (d) Intermediate triangles are (e) quasi degenerated through vertex positioning. (f) A resulting projection

introduce many unnecessary triangles. Contrarily, many small patches are costly. We empirically chose a tessellation factor $t_{max}$ of 16 for our target hardware (listed in Sect. 6).

Surfaces with largely differing source depth values need to be disjoint in the generated mesh to avoid artifacts (see Sect. 5). Hardware tessellation however produces connected triangle grids from patches. For a quasi-separation, further rows and columns of intermediate triangles are introduced, which are discarded later, modifying the required tessellation factor to $2t_{max} - 1$.

## 4.2   Depth Guided Subdivision

For reduced memory bandwidth usage the coarse starting mesh is stored only as an indexed quad set in GPU memory, while the source image space positions are generated during vertex processing (vertex shader) from the vertex ids.

To decide on patch subdivision Didyk et al. [5] use a disparity measure trivially calculated from the depth image, as their stereoscopic projection case only involves camera translation on the local x-axis. Such a measure is however not trivial to calculate for free camera movement, as the whole pixel region in question would need to be fully projected first to evaluate the pixel displacement.

Instead, we create a simple impostor by tessellating regions of high depth variance. We precalculate an edge image via a thresholded laplace operator on the depth image and use its' mipmap level corresponding to the coarse mesh ($\lceil \log_2 t_{max} \rceil$) to evaluate a present edge in a patch's image region (see Fig. 3).

Vertex Image space positions after fixed function tessellation are assigned

$$v_{ij} = v_{00} + \left( \frac{\lceil 0.5\,i \rceil}{m}, \frac{\lceil 0.5\,j \rceil}{n} \right), \tag{2}$$

with $v_{00}$ being the lower left edge vertex of the patch, $i, j \in [0; 2\,t_{max} - 1]$ the vertices' relative ids in the patch and $m, n$ the width and height of the source image. This quasi degenerates the intermediate triangles (Fig. 3(e)).

---

**Algorithm 1.** Vertex positioning

---

**function** VERTEX $-$ POSITION($v_{00}, i, j, m, n, T$)

    $v_{ij} \leftarrow v_{00} + \left( \frac{\lceil 0.5\,i \rceil}{m}, \frac{\lceil 0.5\,j \rceil}{n} \right)$

    **if** $edge(v_{ij}) > 0$ **then**

        $v'_{ij} \leftarrow v_{ij} + \left( \frac{0.5 - i \bmod 2}{m}, \frac{0.5 - j \bmod 2}{n} \right)$

        $N \leftarrow \left\{ v_{ij} + w | w = (x,y), x \in \left\{ -\frac{1}{2m}, \frac{1}{2m} \right\}, y \in \left\{ -\frac{1}{2n}, \frac{1}{2n} \right\} \right\}$

        $N' \leftarrow \left\{ w \in N \, \big| \, |depth(w) - depth(v'_{ij})| < T \right\}$

        $d_{ij} \leftarrow \frac{\sum_{w \in N'} depth(w)}{|N'|}$

    **else**

        $d_{ij} \leftarrow depth(v_{ij})$

    **end if**

    **return** $(v_{ij}, d_{ij})$

**end function**

---

Vertices not residing on depth edges are assigned linearly interpolated depth values fetched directly at their image position. For edge vertices this would create invalid depth values [10] and thus a simple reconstruction similar to [21] is employed by averaging all neighboring pixel depths that are closer than a threshold $T$ to the depth of the reference pixel, given by

$$v'_{ij} = v_{ij} + \left( \frac{0.5 - i \bmod 2}{m}, \frac{0.5 - j \bmod 2}{n} \right). \tag{3}$$

The full vertex positioning is summarized in Algorithm 1. Resulting vertices are transformed using Eq. (1) to finally obtain the desired reprojection.

## 4.3   Mesh Reduction

To lower the cost of the added intermediary triangles in Sect. 4.1 the global tessellation amount can be reduced. To exploit present edge mipmaps the amount of subdivisions and the assumed source image size during vertex positioning is simply decreased by a power of two, i.e. $t'_{max} = \lfloor \frac{t_{max}}{2^i} \rfloor$ and $(m', n') = (\lfloor \frac{m}{2^i} \rfloor, \lfloor \frac{n}{2^i} \rfloor)$ and the initial coarse mesh constructed accordingly.

The results of this procedure are exemplified by the reprojections in Fig. 4. A color bleeding effect can be seen on some object boundaries, which is induced

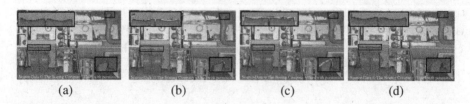

     (a)             (b)             (c)             (d)

**Fig. 4.** Downsampling levels (a) 0, (b) 1, (c) 2, and (d) 1 with artifact suppression (artifacts in enlarged frames) (Color figure online)

through a mismatch between the real source pixel depth and the mipmapped depth of the impostor geometry. This effect can be suppressed by slightly shifting the texture coordinates away from an edge (see Fig. 4(d)). General image quality is preserved by still accessing the full resolution source color image.

# 5   Artifacts

Artifacts typically occurring in mesh based DIBR applications are so called skins [10] or rubber-sheets [4,13], which are triangles spanning depth edge regions, creating false surfaces. The projection method of Sect. 4 already removes them implicitly by discarding the intermediate triangles, creating holes. Additional holes can occur on edges between patches of different tessellation strength (the T-Junction problem [5]). Other artifacts are created by dynamic lighting.

## 5.1   Hole Filling Through Multi-camera Look-Ahead-Rendering

Different methods for hole filling have already been proposed in literature: Pseudo stereo synthesizers like [7,11,21,22] rely on some form of Inpainting approach, which are either clearly noticeable when applied to larger hole areas or too costly for interactive display. Other works use a combination of multiple sources from either different views (multi-camera composition) [2,3,6] or layered images from the same view (depth peeling) [14,18].

To avoid increasing time differences between consecutive source frames, we did not use depth peeling. Rather, a cost-efficient multi-camera composition is achieved by buffering and projecting a set of past source frames.

For the buffering to be effective, predicted source cameras are used rather than the current user camera. Mark et al. already experimented with a similar setup using simulated prediction through random jittering of a known camera path [13]. The prediction is based on a simple linear extrapolation shown in Fig. 5, evidently not accurately reflecting a possible non-linear camera path, but sufficient if the time distance between cameras is small [13].

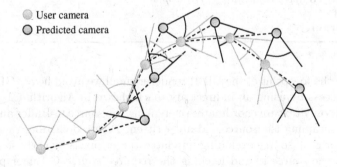

**Fig. 5.** Linear camera prediction

## 5.2  Additional Redundancy

Projecting all buffered source images for one synthetic frame is not cost-efficient, due to increasingly distant views carrying decreasingly useful information. For quick selection of a meaningful subset the following distance measure is applied:

$$dist(c_s, c_t, r_s, r_t) = \frac{1 + \|c_s - c_t\|^2}{0.5(r_s \circ r_t + 1)} - 1, \tag{4}$$

the conservative assumption being decreasing image quality with increasing square euclidean distance of source and target camera positions $c_i$ (pixel areas change proportionally) and with increasing divergence of the cameras' normalized view directions $r_i$ ($\circ$ being the dot product).

In addition, the source frames are rendered with a larger field of view (FOV) compared to the target camera's, providing interception of holes caused by camera rotation. As a consequence, the source frames need to have a higher resolution to avoid blur in the projections.

## 5.3  Avoiding Lighting Artifacts

Time-varying lighting like specularities or from animated lights can also cause artifacts: Already shaded scene portions from different source images create noticable wrong shading in the synthesized image (see Sect. 6.2 for an example). Deferred shading via G-Buffer rendering [19] was implemented as a remedy.

---

**Algorithm 2.** Deferred lighting of a target pixel

> **function** INDIRECT _ GBUFFER _ LIGHTING($p_{xy}, sid, light$)
>     **if** $stencil(p_{xy}) \neq sid$ **then**
>         **return**                                 ▷ pixel unwritten or belonging to different source
>     **else**
>         $p'_{xy} \leftarrow target(p_{xy})$                         ▷ coordinates from DIBR pass
>         $f_{gbuffer} \leftarrow source[sid](p'_{xy})$                         ▷ source G-Buffer pixel
>         **return** $apply\_lighting(f_{gbuffer}, light)$
>     **end if**
> **end function**

---

To keep the footprint of the DIBR renderer small we avoid heavy GPU memory write access by using an indirect approach shown in Algorithm 2: For each target pixel, only texture coordinates referencing the source G-Buffer and a stencil buffer containing the source's id are written. Deferred shading then applies each light for each source excluding unrelated target pixels by early stencil testing against the source id and fetching the required source G-Buffer pixels via the texture coordinates.

# 6 Analysis

The method described previously has been implemented on a Windows $7 \times 64$ platform in C++ and OpenGL, with the executing hardware including an Intel Core i7-3820 CPU and a NVIDIA GeForce GTX 650 GPU. Two CAD scenes where used for evaluation: a 777 plane model with approx. 300 million triangles of The Boeing Company and an $8 \times 8 \times 8$ replicated Powerplant model of the University of North Carolina yielding approx. 6.5 billion triangles. 3DInteractive's VGR renderer [1] was used as the source renderer.

## 6.1 Rendering Time

Both renderers were executed simultaneously during scene flythrough. Two sources were used for each synthesis with a source FOV of 110°and a target FOV of 90°(the source images were approx. 1.43× the target image size), with 1× mesh downsampling enabled. Methods described in Sect. 2.2 were also implemented on the GPU for comparison.

Table 1 shows Morvan's method to be unsuitable for this paper's target application. It cannot leverage part of the GPU's units, as the GPGPU execution is confined to the shaders and every pixel is projected individually. The highly tessellated triangle net of Mark et al. also suffers from the latter problem, making it unsuitable for high resolutions. In contrast, the point rendering fares better due to a very simple pipeline (no skin detection and removal, no interpolation), but its' complexity is also directly influenced by the source pixel count.

Our method leverages more GPU functionality through tessellation and has a lower overhead in image regions of low depth variance. As a consequence the frame computation times are lower than all other methods on the test hardware.

**Table 1.** Flythrough average frame times (in ms), with the results of this paper's method marked in bold

| Scene | Renderer | Target resolution | | | |
|---|---|---|---|---|---|
| | | $1280 \times 720$ | $1366 \times 768$ | $1600 \times 900$ | $1920 \times 1080$ |
| 777 | Morvan et al. | 34.2 | 38.5 | 53.1 | 76.6 |
| | Point | 8.7 | 10.2 | 13.4 | 16.3 |
| | Mark et al. | 11.8 | 14.0 | 19.6 | 30.2 |
| | **Proposed** | **4.5** | **5.0** | **6.7** | **9.3** |
| | Source | 27.7 | 33.8 | 37.8 | 40.0 |
| Powerplant | Morvan et al. | 36.5 | 40.7 | 55.3 | 79.0 |
| | Point | 9.3 | 11.1 | 14.1 | 16.3 |
| | Mark et al. | 23.1 | 27.6 | 43.2 | 84.2 |
| | **Proposed** | **8.2** | **9.2** | **11.8** | **15.5** |
| | Source | 36.4 | 41.1 | 48.6 | 56.1 |

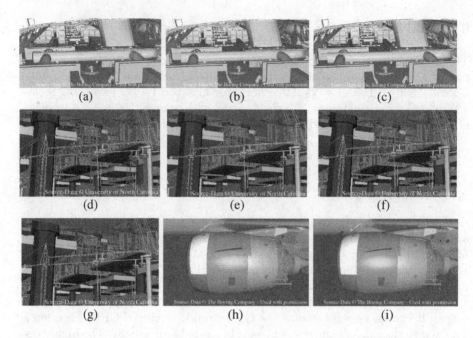

**Fig. 6.** Image quality during a camera flight through the (a, b, c) 777 Boeing and the (d, e, f, g) Powerplant scene. (a, d) Without hole filling, noticable information gaps occur, while (b, f) being greatly reduced with one additional projection. Contrary to (e) [13], edge regions are not diminished. Plausible reconstructions are reached in comparison with the (c, g) ground truth. (h) Artifacts from view-dependent shading of multiple different sources are (i) removed when using the proposed deferred shading approach

However, the per-primitive complexity is higher compared to the point rendering resulting in roughly the same frame times when the whole image shows high depth variance, which is largely the case for the Powerplant scene.

## 6.2    Image Quality

As can be seen from Fig. 6(a) and (d), a single DIBR projection does not suffice for an acceptable synthesis, even when using the predictor. In contrast, the proposed hole filling already shows great improvement when using two projections. Also, the method does not exhibit the diminished borders of Mark et al.s' original full triangle mesh technique and thus retains small pixel regions.

Figures 6(h) and (i) show an example of the approach of Sect. 5.3. Artifacts can be seen when combining view-dependent shading from multiple different sources, while the deferred shaded approach shows plausible results.

### 6.3   Drawbacks and Remaining Problems

A significant downside to the new method is the source buffers' GPU memory consumption: Ten buffered G-Buffers (each with a layout of three 8bit RGBA, one 16bit RGB and one 24bit depth buffer) take around 420 MB at $1920 \times 1080$. We aim to use compression and material tables in the future.

For acceptable results a minimum source frame rate is required. 15 Hz or above seemed sufficient to produce little to no remaining holes in the synthetic images. The results were still acceptable around 5 to 10 Hz, while 5 Hz and below showed too sparse updates and many information gaps in the perceived scene.

Only static scenes are currently supported. Animated parts need to be rendered separately for correct display. An additional step in the DIBR projection equation handling the animation transformations could be a solution.

## 7   Conclusion and Future Work

During the course of this paper it has been shown, that DIBR can be efficiently implemented via the modern standard GPU pipeline using a novel implementation by adaptive hardware accelerated tessellation. The system design decoupling the user input and display from the source renderer proved to be a viable solution for the high frame rate and responsiveness problems listed in Sect. 1.

Subsequent work will focus on improving the method: The simple predictor will be replaced by a more sophisticated approach realizing a non linear prediction. Providing more redundancy via depth peeling will be tested, as there exist efficient one pass techniques [12]. Applying the static mesh downsampling of Sect. 4.3 dynamically promises further performance.

Other endeavors will include porting the described system to mobile devices. The main challenge will be the significantly lower graphic capabilities or the lack of support of required features used in this paper.

## References

1. Brüderlin, B., Heyer, M., Pfützner, S.: Interviews3D: a platform for interactive handling of massive data sets. IEEE Comput. Graph. Appl. **27**(6), 48–59 (2007)
2. Chang, C.-F., Ger, S.-H.: Enhancing 3D graphics on mobile devices by image-based rendering. In: Chen, Y.-C., Chang, L.-W., Hsu, C.-T. (eds.) PCM 2002. LNCS, vol. 2532, pp. 1105–1111. Springer, Heidelberg (2002). doi:10.1007/3-540-36228-2_137
3. Darsa, L., Costa Silva, B., Varshney, A.: Navigating static environments using image-space simplification and morphing. In: Proceedings of the 1997 Symposium on Interactive 3D Graphics. I3D 1997, pp. 25-ff. ACM, New York (1997)
4. Decoret, X., Schaufler, G., Sillion, F., Dorsey, J.: Multi-layered impostors for accelerated rendering. In: EUROGRAPHICS 1999, vol. 18 (1999)
5. Didyk, P., Ritschel, T., Eisemann, E., Myszkowski, K., Seidel, H.P.: Adaptive image-space stereo view synthesis. In: Vision, Modeling and Visualization Workshop, pp. 299–306, Siegen, Germany (2010)

6. Do, L., Zinger, S., Morvan, Y., de With, P.: Quality improving techniques in DIBR for free-viewpoint video. In: 3DTV Conference: The True Vision - Capture, Transmission and Display of 3D Video, 2009, pp. 1–4, May 2009

7. Fehn, C.: A 3D-TV approach using depth-image-based rendering (DIBR). In: Proceedings of Visualization, Imaging and Image Processing, pp. 482–487 (2003)

8. Fu, C., Wong, T., Heng, P.: Triangle-based view interpolation without depth-buffering. J. Graph. Tools 3, 13–31 (1998)

9. Funkhouser, T.A., Séquin, C.H.: Adaptive display algorithm for interactive frame rates during visualization of complex virtual environments. In: Proceedings of the 20th Annual Conference on Computer Graphics and Interactive Techniques. SIGGRAPH 1993, pp. 247–254. ACM, New York (1993)

10. Ghiletiuc, J., Färber, M., Brüderlin, B.: Real-time remote rendering of large 3D models on smartphones using multi-layered impostors. In: Proceedings of the 6th International Conference on Computer Vision/Computer Graphics Collaboration Techniques and Applications. MIRAGE 2013, pp. 14: 1–14: 8. ACM, New York (2013)

11. Horng, Y.R., Tseng, Y.C., Chang, T.S.: Stereoscopic images generation with directional Gaussian filter. In: Proceedings of 2010 IEEE International Symposium on Circuits and Systems (ISCAS), pp. 2650–2653 (2010)

12. Liu, F., Huang, M.C., Liu, X.H., Wu, E.H.: Single pass depth peeling via CUDA rasterizer. In: SIGGRAPH 2009: Talks. SIGGRAPH 2009, p. 79: 1. ACM, New York (2009)

13. Mark, W.R., McMillan, L., Bishop, G.: Post-rendering 3D warping. In: Proceedings of the 1997 Symposium on Interactive 3D Graphics. I3D 1997, pp. 7-ff. ACM, New York (1997)

14. Max, N., Ohsaki, K.: Rendering trees from precomputed z-buffer views. In: Eurographics Rendering Workshop, pp. 45–54 (1995)

15. Morvan, Y., Farin, D., de With, P.: System architecture for free-viewpoint video and 3D-TV. IEEE Trans. Consum. Electron. 54(2), 925–932 (2008)

16. Ndjiki-Nya, P., Koppel, M., Doshkov, D., Lakshman, H., Merkle, P., Muller, K., Wiegand, T.: Depth image-based rendering with advanced texture synthesis for 3-D video. IEEE Trans. Multimedia 13(3), 453–465 (2011)

17. Oh, K.J., Yea, S., Ho, Y.S.: Hole filling method using depth based in-painting for view synthesis in free viewpoint television and 3-D video. In: Picture Coding Symposium, 2009. PCS 2009, pp. 1–4, May 2009

18. Popescu, V., Lastra, A., Aliaga, D., Neto, M.D.O.: Efficient warping for architectural walkthroughs using layered depth images. In: IEEE Visualization, pp. 211–215 (1998)

19. Saito, T., Takahashi, T.: Comprehensible rendering of 3-D shapes. In: Proceedings of the 17th Annual Conference on Computer Graphics and Interactive Techniques. SIGGRAPH 1990, pp. 197–206. ACM, New York (1990)

20. Westover, L.: Footprint evaluation for volume rendering. In: Proceedings of the 17th Annual Conference on Computer Graphics and Interactive Techniques. SIGGRAPH 1990, pp. 367–376. ACM, New York (1990)

21. Xi, M., Wang, L.H., Yang, Q.Q., Li, D.X., Zhang, M.: Depth-image-based rendering with spatial and temporal texture synthesis for 3DTV. EURASIP J. Image Video Process. 2013(1), 1–18 (2013)

22. Zhang, L., Tam, W.J.: Stereoscopic image generation based on depth images for 3D TV. IEEE Trans. Broadcast. 51(2), 191–199 (2005)

23. Zinger, S., Do, L., de With, P.H.N.: Free-viewpoint depth image based rendering. J. Vis. Commun. Image Represent. 21(5–6), 533–541 (2010)

# Physically Based Area Lighting Model for Real-Time Animation

Michał Olejnik, Dominik Szajerman, and Piotr Napieralski[⊠]

Institute of Information Technology, Łódź University of Technology, Łódź, Poland
{piotr.napieralski,dominik.szajerman}@p.lodz.pl

**Abstract.** Physically based rendering is not a new concept and it has been pursued in the scientific fields for a long time. However, it has not been until recently that the new generation of game consoles allowed more expensive algorithms to be adapted and computed in real-time constraints. In this paper, we analyse methods of approximating the lighting received from geometrical emitters (area lights) and compare them to the ground truth reference model computed through the Monte Carlo numerical integration algorithm.

## 1 Introduction

Ever since first 3D games emerged, real-time computer graphics have been simulating lighting by using non-physically based light sources such as point lights, spot lights and directional lights. This simplification allowed solving the rendering equation for only one direction per light, which was a huge advantage in terms of computational complexity. While this simplification is reasonable for very distant light sources, real world light sources are not infinitely small.

Although physically based rendering is not a new concept and it has been pursued in the scientific fields for a long time, it has not been until recently that the new generation of game consoles allowed for more expensive algorithms to be adapted and computed in real-time constraints.

The computation of incoming radiance for an emitter of an arbitrary shape and size is a difficult task as it involves a real-time evaluation of the rendering equation's integral. It has not been until recently that the first games implementing those algorithms were released.

There are several downsides to using infinitely small light sources. They cannot simulate light 'wrapping' around an object, which is common when the object is much smaller than the light. Lighting artists tend to compensate for the lack of area lights by placing several point emitters. Moreover, if an object is extremely glossy, the infinitely small light source will have an infinitely small specular reflection. Several sources [12,14] have noted that this limitation often makes texture artists avoid painting low roughness values on materials, which is more of a workaround than an actual solution and violates physically based rendering principle of creating art content that looks correct under a variety of lighting conditions.

© Springer International Publishing AG 2016
L.J. Chmielewski et al. (Eds.): ICCVG 2016, LNCS 9972, pp. 73–85, 2016.
DOI: 10.1007/978-3-319-46418-3_7

Simulation of the phenomena associated with the light has become feasible with programmable graphics hardware. Often natural approximation of the direct light use some approaches at indirect illumination, placing Virtual Point Lights (VPLs) in an area light. Segovia et al. [9] proposed interleaved sampling of VPLs (Virtual Point Lights) with graphics hardware for conservative extension of deferred shading.

An early effort to include area lights in real-time rendering was made by Snyder [6]. His work presents analytical formulae for the local reflection integral of some combinations of area light sources and BRDFs. Although this approach has a small run-time overhead, it has not been used widely, because of the restrictions it imposes on light shape and BRDF. Dachsbacher and Stamminger [7] use an efficient importance sampling technique and even include an approximation of visibility. Oat [8] proposed volume textures of spherical harmonics coefficients with GPU-based rasterisation formulation of irradiance for real-time rendering. Precomputed irradiance has been used in many games and virtual-reality applications.

Some techniques like the point approach [15] made some accuracy trade-off to achieve real-time performance. Lecocq et al. [16] introduced some analytic approximations with simple peak functions for accurate real-time rendering of specular surfaces illuminated by polygonal light sources.

Our work provides robust Physically Based Area lighting model for real-time animation. Presented methods approximate lighting received from geometrical emitters (area lights) and compares them to the ground truth reference model computed through the Monte Carlo numerical integration algorithm.

## 2   Real-Time Rendering

In order to calculate outgoing radiance for a point $p$ being illuminated by an area light we have to solve the rendering equation:

$$L(p, \omega_o) = \int_{\Omega(n)} f_r(p, \omega_o, \omega_i) L(p, \omega_i) cos\theta_i d\omega_i, \tag{1}$$

where the incoming radiance $L(p, \omega_i)$ is dependent on the radiant flux emitted by an area light from a point $q$ in the direction $-\omega_i$. Point $q$ can be found by finding the intersection of light shape with direction $\omega_i$. For simplicity, we will assume that area lights emit the same flux from all points $q$ belonging to the emitter's surface and in all directions (but they still obey Lambert's law). $L(p, \omega_i)$ is assumed to be 0 for all directions that do not intersect the light's shape.

Solving this integral analytically is not feasible for real-time graphics. It can be approximated using numerical integration methods. Monte Carlo integration is that its convergence rate is independent of dimensionality of the integrand, making it perfect for evaluating the shading equations and light transport algorithms. MC uses randomness to evaluate integrals. Its error is dependent on the number of samples used – the more samples, the more it resembles the correct solution. The error manifests itself as a noise.

The most basic evaluation of Monte Carlo estimator for the rendering equation is to find a uniform distribution of directions on the unit sphere.

MC method for area lights is extremely expensive when compared to computing illumination from directional and point lights. Nevertheless, it is important to have a physically correct reference model before trying to find less expensive approximations.

Numerical integration methods require high quality random numbers. When working with real-time constraints we would ideally like an even distribution of random values over the domain regardless of the samples count. Such numbers are called quasi-random (or sub-random) and one of the most common methods to obtain them is the Hammersley sequence [1].

The numbers obtained from the Hammersley sequence are only dependent on the samples count. In order to force usage of different samples on different pixels being shaded we can introduce an offset. However, an offset based on some simple value like screen space UV coordinates might be not random enough. To improve randomness, we can pass the UV values to some random number generator. TEA (Tiny Encryption Algorithm) [4] provides an inexpensive way to do so and simultaneously enables an adjustment of the quality of the generated random numbers by changing the number of iterations.

## 3    Area Lights Importance Sampling

Ray and light shapes intersection algorithms are necessary when working with area lights. We will consider four types of emitters:

- spheres,
- disks,
- rectangles,
- tubes (capsules – cylinders with spherical caps).

Ray-shape intersections is to put the mathematical equation for the ray into the parametric equation of the shape and determine if there is a real solution, under the assumption that all shaded points lie outside of the light geometry, which means that we will ignore cases when the origin of the ray lies inside the light.

The probability density function (PDF) is used to define the optimal directions for such sampling. The PDF is a normalized function, where the integral over the entire domain of the function is 1 and the peaks represent important regions for sampling. Usually, the most important samples are those that have the biggest values. Basing on this conclusion we can devise a non-constant PDF that will assign bigger probabilities to those values.

The most obvious conclusion when analysing uniform sampling approach for area lights is that most samples will never hit the actual emitter and effectively will have no contribution to the final result. To eliminate that shortcoming, we can generate points on the emitter's geometry and by using the position of the point being shaded we can determine the final sampling direction vector. Then, the contribution must be normalized by calculating the PDF for this direction.

## 4 BRDF Importance Sampling for Area Lights

Light shape importance sampling greatly reduces variance. However it still fails to capture faithfully the reflections from very glossy surfaces. For such materials the specular peak is extremely narrow, making it very difficult to capture for bigger light sources. In that case, it might be preferable to devise a probabilistic distribution based on the shape of a specular lobe. As the Monte Carlo estimator converges the quickest when the PDF is very similar to the integrand, we could devise a distribution based on the BRDF. Unfortunately, the whole Torrance-Sparrow BRDF is very complicated and creating distribution for the entire BRDF is very hard and computationally expensive. In practice, sampling through the microfacet distribution alone gives great improvements and also allows the use of importance sampling with different geometry factors and Fresnel approximations.

Normal distribution function is used to describe the probability that a microfacet has normal $\omega_h$. NDFs must be normalized similarly to BRDFs. However, instead of normalizing hemispherical-directional reflectance, we have to normalize the projected area of all facets, so that it will be equal to the area of macroscopic surface they represent:

$$\int_{\Omega(n)} D(\omega_h) \cos\theta d\omega_h = 1. \tag{2}$$

Additionally, instead of normalizing the projected area, we want the percentages of well-oriented facets to sum up to $100\%$ after evaluating all possible directions $\omega_h$ on the hemisphere:

$$\int_{\Omega(n)} D_{\omega_o}(\omega_h) d\omega_h = 1. \tag{3}$$

We can use that to devise the PDF for Blinn [3]:

$$p_h(\theta) = \frac{(n+2)\cos\theta^n}{2\pi} \cos\theta. \tag{4}$$

After computing the half-angle vector we can compute the sampling vector from Snell's law. The PDF was computed by evaluating the integral with respect to $\omega_h$, but the reflection integral considers direction $\omega_i$ (sampling vector). We must convert the PDF representing the density in terms of $\omega_h$ to the PDF representing the density in terms of $\omega_i$.

Most materials have much longer specular "tail", which means that specular response does not approach zero as quickly as the previously mentioned NDFs would suggest. Walter et al. [10] introduced an NDF called GGX that fixed those shortcomings (although it was quite similar – different constant factor – to the one introduced by Trowbridge and Reitz [2]):

$$p_h(\theta) = \frac{m^2}{\pi(\cos\theta_h{}^2(m^2-1)+1)^2}\cos\theta$$

$$p(\theta) = \frac{m^2}{4\pi\cos\theta_h(\cos\theta^2(m^2-1)+1)^2}\cos\theta \quad (5)$$

$$\cos\theta = \sqrt{\frac{1-\xi_1}{(m^2-1)\xi_1+1}}$$

$$\phi = 2\pi\xi_2.$$

where $\pi$ in the denominator is the normalization factor.

Importance sampling of Lambert BRDF can be done by using cosine weighted hemisphere sampling [11]. However in practice the difference between this approach and uniform sampling of hemisphere is negligible.

When dealing with diffuse and specular BRDF, we have to combine the importance sampling strategies. [11] suggested introducing third canonical uniform random variable $\xi_3$, which can be used to choose which BRDF's distribution to sample, compute the lighting with sampled vector for all BRDFs and normalize the result by dividing by the average of all PDFs (assuming that all distributions have equal chance to be chosen). This may be problematic for GPU importance sampling because of the lack of quality random numbers. We could mitigate this problem by using the Hammersley sequence for $\xi_1$ and $\xi_2$, but the third random variable has to be independent from the previous two. We can try using fractals to produce such variable, but it is easier to evaluate diffuse and specular components separately (compute the diffuse lighting contribution for directions sampled from diffuse component distribution and vice-versa). In fact, based on empirical observations, the second approach provides less variance (Fig. 1).

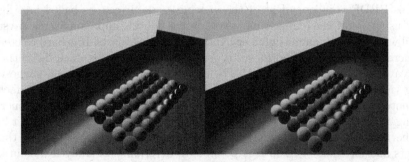

**Fig. 1.** Comparison of BRDF importance sampling with choosing random distribution from BRDFs (left) and separate evaluation of diffuse and specular components (right) for 256 samples.

Light shape importance sampling fails to capture narrow specular peak for glossy materials, while using BRDF importance sampling may cause many sampled vectors to miss the light's geometry. Veach [5] introduced a technique called multiple importance sampling (MIS) that made it possible to balance between several importance sampling strategies. The Monte Carlo estimator for $\int f(x)g(x)dx$ given by MIS for two distributions $p_f$ and $g_f$ is:

$$\frac{1}{n_f}\sum_{i=1}^{n_f}\frac{f(X_i)g(X_i)w_f(X_i)}{p_f(X_i)} + \frac{1}{n_g}\sum_{j=1}^{n_g}\frac{f(Y_j)g(Y_j)w_g(Y_j)}{p_g(Y_j)}, \tag{6}$$

where $n_x$ is the number of samples taken from distribution $p_x$ and $w_x$ is a weighting function.

Weighting function is the most important part of MIS estimator. It reduces variance for cases when for sample $X$ drawn from distribution $p_f$ value of corresponding function $f(X)$ is small but the other function $g(X)$ returns a high value. Veach proved that the estimator was correct when the values returned by the weighting function $w_i$ summed up to 1 for all samples and suggested using the balance heuristic:

$$w_s(x) = \frac{n_s p_s(x)}{\sum_i n_i p_i(x)} \tag{7}$$

## 5   Area Lighting Approximations

Faithful evaluation of the rendering equation is an extremely expensive process, so we may expect any devised cheap approximations to be crude. The most important phenomenon to capture is the soft wrapping of lighting around the object as it is the most visually noticeable feature of area lighting. On the other hand, the overall attenuation of light and any other discrepancies with the reference model should not be distinguishable for user as long as there are no discontinuities and major artifacts.

In this section, we will consider only the Lambertian diffuse for simplicity. As this BRDF is independent of the viewing angle, it can be baked into light maps using an off-line renderer; however, diffuse lighting approximations are still useful when using dynamic lights or lighting dynamic objects. It is hard to create a generalized approximation for all types of the primitives, so each light has to be treated as a special case [13–15, 17]. Lagarde and de Rousiers [14] suggested using view factors for computing sphere and disk light sources. The view factor originates from the field of radiative transfer and describes the fraction of energy exiting an isothermal, opaque and diffuse surface (in our case the light) that hits another surface. View factors are dependent solely on the geometry of those objects and for some of them it is possible to determine an analytical solution, which guarantees a physically correct solution.

The implementation is straightforward: the computed factor is multiplied by the diffuse colour to obtain final lighting. Note that $\pi$ from Lambert BRDF's denominator is already included in the view factor.

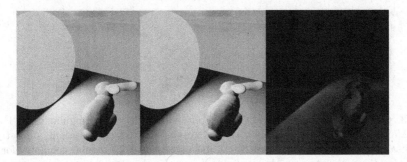

**Fig. 2.** Diffuse lighting approximation for a disk. View factor approximation (right) introduces a substantial error, but it is unnoticeable without knowing the reference lighting.

A view factor for an oriented disk is much harder to calculate, but it can be approximated with a similar one. Lagarde suggested using a factor for differential tilted planar patch and disk from [14]. Unfortunately, this factor is correct only for elements lying on the normal vector of the disk originating from its centre (Fig. 2).

To compensate for the fact that this factor considers a not oriented disk, Lagarde suggests multiplying the factor by the cosine of angle between the light's normal vector and the vector from the light's centre to the shaded point. The approximation causes a visible error, but produces no artifacts and the wrapped lighting scales nicely with the radius of the light source.

Finding a view factor for an oriented rectangle is extremely hard. Drobot [15] devised an alternative method called the most representative point (MRP). The core idea is to find a single point on a light source (a direction) that provides the best fit for the entire rendering integral and normalizes its contribution with the solid angle subtended by the light. Drobot found a good approximation experimentally and did not provide his methodology. The most representative point for a rectangular emitter can be found using the following steps:

- calculate point $p'$ by intersecting a ray from shading point $p$ in direction $\omega_n$ with the light plane,
- calculate point $p''$ by finding the closest point on the light plane from point $p$,
- calculate points $p'_r$ and $p''_r$ by finding the closest points on the rectangle to points $p'$ and $p''$,
- calculate a half-vector $\omega_p$ from the vectors $p''_r - p$ and $p'_r - p$,
- evaluate the rendering equation for $\omega_p$ and multiply the lighting by the solid angle subtended by the rectangle.

Additionally, to find a correct point $p'$ the ray must be skewed towards the light plane in cases when the ray would not hit the plane (it does not matter how much the ray is skewed, $p'_r$ will always be the same) and for point $p''$ the ray must be limited to the hemisphere oriented around $\omega_n$.

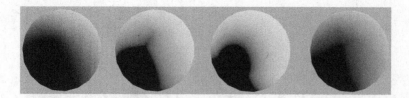

**Fig. 3.** Comparison of all diffuse lighting approximations for rectangular light. From left: Monte Carlo reference, Drobot MRP, Drobot MRP (cheaper variant) and structured sampling. Wrapping artifacts are visible on objects with regular geometry for all approximations, the structured sampling seams to be the closest to the reference.

To optimize this process further, Drobot suggested skipping the computation of points $p'_r$ and $p''_r$, using a half-vector for vectors $p''-p$ and $p'-p$, computing the intersection with the light plane and finding the closest point on the rectangle to use as the most representative point. This solution yields bigger error and produces different kind of wrapping of diffuse lighting (Fig. 3).

Calculating the solid angle subtended by an oriented rectangle is a complex task. Drobot suggested approximating it with a solid angle subtended by a right pyramid (a pyramid that has its apex directly above the centre of its base) of height equal to the distance between MRP and shading point and base of the size of the rectangle. Lagarde suggested using more correct and complex solution from [13] which computes the solid angle for a rectangle but without handling the horizon case (a case when not the entire light shape is above the plane defined by the shading point and its normal vector).

Lagarde proposed approximation called structured sampling, which computes diffuse BRDF for several fixed points at the rectangle. He suggested using all corners and the middle, computing the average and normalizing it by the solid angle subtended by the light. This approach produces a different kind of artifacts than Drobot's approach, so the choice between those approximations is a purely artistic one. However, Lagarde's solution seems to produce much softer falloff of wrapped lighting, which matches the reference much better (Fig. 4).

**Fig. 4.** Comparison of MRP approximation (left) and structured sampling (right). Falloff of lighting when crossing the light's horizon is much gentler for the second approach.

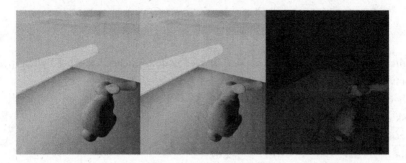

**Fig. 5.** Comparison of Monte Carlo reference (left) and approximated solution (right) for a short tube light.

A capsule is a complex shape; obtaining a view factor analytically is not feasible and MRP will not capture all characteristics of a three dimensional emitter. Lagarde suggested representing a tube light by a mix of sphere and rectangle lights and using their corresponding approximations. For the sphere part, we can find the point closest to the shading point on the tube's axis and place a sphere of the same radius on it. The rectangle is placed on the same axis and is always oriented towards the shading point, while its dimensions are defined by the length of the axis and the tube's radius (Fig. 5).

Approximating specular lighting is much harder than Lambertian, as the domain of possible inputs is bigger ($\omega_o$, roughness). Dependence on the viewing angle also means that it is impossible to bake it into light maps. Note that usage of view factors is impossible, as they are correct only for Lambertian surfaces.

The most important feature of specular approximation is the preservation of the overall shape of specular reflection, especially for glossier materials. This includes stretching of reflections at grazing angles. As with diffuse lighting, all light shapes must be considered separately [12]. Karis [12] devised a method of approximating specular lighting for sphere and tube lights with the most representative point algorithm. For specular reflection the MRP is a point on the light's surface which gives the smallest angle between the view direction reflection ray $\omega_r$ and vector from shading point to the MRP. This point can be approximated as a point on the light that is the closest to $\omega_r$:

$$\omega_l = \left| \omega_i + \omega_c \, saturate\left(\frac{r}{|\omega_c|}\right) \right|, \tag{8}$$

where $r$ is the radius of the sphere, $\omega_c$ is a vector from the light's center to the ray and $\omega_l$ is the direction vector to the MRP. Note that $\omega_i$ is unnormalized in this equation.

This approach has the effect of widening the specular distribution of the NDF, causing a surplus of received energy which has to be compensated for. Karis suggested an approximate normalization term for GGX NDF to fix this shortcoming. Karis' approximation scales well with light's radius, but is not physically correct and suffers from visual artifacts at grazing angles. Moreover,

**Table 1.** Rendering time of a single frame for various lighting setups.

| Light | Frame time (ms) | |
|---|---|---|
| | Code with all branches | Removed code branches for other light types |
| Point | 2.01 | 1.57 |
| Sphere | 2.11 | 1.63 |
| Disk | 2.14 | 1.77 |
| Rectangle | 2.33 | 1.88 |
| Tube | 2.34 | 2.07 |

the energy conservation adjustment term $E$ almost nullifies the long tail of GGX distribution. Karis also asserted that irradiance received from a sphere light is the same as from evenly distant point light if the light is above the surface's horizon, so by ignoring the horizon case we can compute irradiance from inverse square law. This resembles the view factor for a sphere. However, the view factors are computed for Lambertian surfaces, so this assertion is not correct. Karis extended his approach to tube lights by using approximation of irradiance for line segment above the horizon for Tube light. We can extend Karis' approach to other primitives. For a disk light we can determine the MRP using a similar approach as with the rectangular diffuse algorithm. The reflection vector is skewed in case it points away from the light's surface and the closest position on the light's shape is determined by computing ray-plane intersection and trimming the $p' - p_c$ vector to the light's radius. Energy balance is applied analogically to the previous algorithms and irradiance is approximated in the same way as with diffuse lighting calculations for disk light.

Drobot approximated specular lighting from a rectangular light by finding the geometric center of a common area between the light's shape and cone of importance sampling and using it as MRP. The result was normalized by the subtended angle of the area found. Unfortunately, this algorithm works only for BRDFs with symmetrical specular distribution (e.g., Phong), making this approach impractical for half-vector based NDFs.

Implementation of Karis' algorithm for a rectangular light is very similar to the disk's one, but instead of using a view factor we normalize irradiance contribution with the solid angle subtended by the rectangle.

## 6    Conclusion and Future Work

The presented algorithms are useful in approximating real-time lighting from area emitters. The Monte Carlo estimator was discussed in order to provide means of verifying the results with a ground truth reference model. Importance sampling strategies were addressed to allow a real-time evaluation of Monte Carlo algorithm on modern GPUs.

In order to discern the overall performance hit caused by analysed algorithms a test scene was rendered in $1920 \times 1080$ resolution using an NVIDIA GTX 970.

Frame rendering times were analysed for a lighting setup with one area light and skybox lighting using a tiled deferred renderer with the following G-buffer formats: R32G32B32A32 (normal and roughness), R8G8B8A8 (base colour and specular intensity) and R8 (metallic value). No anti-aliasing was used. Using a deferred renderer guarantees that lighting will be evaluated only once for each pixel. This approach decouples the performance hit caused by advanced lighting techniques from geometrical complexity of the scene. In other words the render time differences between any two analysed approaches should be the same as when rendering an extremely complex scene in a shipped game.

Table 1 underlines the problem that comes when working with multiple light shapes. Theoretically, modern GPUs support dynamic branching that is needed for handling multiple light shapes in the shader code, but if only one thread (pixel kernel) in a scheduling unit (called warp for NVIDIA GPUs or wavefront for AMD GPUs) takes a divergent branch, all other threads in the unit have to wait for it. For a tiled based deferred renderer it should not be a problem as long as the tile size is a multiple of the scheduling unit's size (64 for wavefronts, 32 for warps), especially in the analysed test case where there is only one light. Nevertheless, the results are unambiguous - using a codebase with branches between different light shapes introduces a performance hit. As expected, the tube light is the most expensive one, followed by a rectangle, a disk and a sphere. Depending on the requirements of the application it might be preferable to choose only some of the light shapes. While the tube light is the most expensive one, it can can be also simplified to a sphere light, effectively handling two light sources simultaneously. Using a tube light without other light sources is still quicker then computing lighting from a sphere light in a complete model, so it may be reasonable to limit the model to the tube light alone.

Evaluated approximations satisfy the posed requirements. Diffuse algorithms enable visually plausible wrapping of lighting around objects and specular approximations preserve the overall shape of the reflected emitters. Tests show that the overall complexity of those algorithms is much lower than the evaluation of dozen of samples for Monte Carlo estimator that would be required to reach a similar quality of the image. Simultaneously, those approximations do not experience the noise that is unavoidable when using numerical integration methods.

Despite those benefits, the area lighting approximations provide results that are far from ideal. Most steps depend on very crude simplifications necessitated by the lack of proper mathematical tools. The error is usually unpredictable and varies depending on light's orientation, distance and dimensions. Most specular approximations suffer from noticeable artifacts at grazing angles. Diffuse lighting wrapping has a visible error on geometrically flat, regular shapes and the lighting falloff is sometimes too sudden.

Regardless of all the defects, the availability of area lighting algorithms that are feasible for real-time constraints is a big improvement over standard point and directional lights.

The presented algorithms proved to be efficient and visually appealing, while also demonstrating good scalability. Every rendering engine can benefit from energy conserving BRDFs, although switching to metallic workflow and microfacet-based BRDFs is a process that necessitates reexamination of existing graphics pipeline, tools and content. Nevertheless, the improvement that can be gained by adapting a physically based shading model cannot be denied.

Area lights are the topic that requires the most research, as the existing methods introduce a substantial error and some of the shapes display artifacts at certain angles.

# References

1. Hammersley, J.M., Handscomb, D.C.: Monte Carlo Methods. Methuen, London (1964)
2. Trowbridge, T.S., Reitz, K.P.: Average irregularity representation of a rough surface for ray reflection. J. Opt. Soc. Am. **65**(5) (1975)
3. Blinn, J.F.: Models of light reflection for computer synthesized pictures. In: Proceedings of the 4th Annual Conference on Computer Graphics and Interactive Techniques (1977)
4. Wheeler, D.J., Needham, R.M.: TEA, a tiny encryption algorithm. In: Preneel, B. (ed.) Fast Software Encryption. LNCS, vol. 1008, pp. 363–366. Springer, Heidelberg (1995)
5. Veach, E.: Robust Monte Carlo methods for light transport simulation. Ph.D. thesis, Stanford University, Stanford, CA, USA (1998)
6. Hasenfratz, J.-M., Lapierre, M., Holzschuch, N., Sillion, F.: A survey of real-time soft shadows algorithms. Comput. Graph. Forum **22**(4) (2003)
7. Dachsbacher, C., Stamminger, M.: Splatting indirect illumination. In: SI3D 2006 (2006)
8. Oat, C.: Irradiance volumes for real-time rendering. In: ShaderX5: Advanced Rendering Techniques (2006)
9. Segovia, B., Iehl, J.C., Mitanchey, R., Péroche, B.: Non-interleaved Deferred Shading of Interleaved Sample Patterns. The Eurographics Association (2006)
10. Walter, B., Marschner, S.R., Li, H., Torrance, K.E.: Microfacet models for refraction through rough surfaces. In: Proceedings of Eurographics Symposium on Rendering (2007)
11. Pharr, M., Humphreys, G.: Physically Based Rendering: From Theory to Implementation, 2nd edn. Morgan Kaufmann Publishers Inc., San Francisco (2010)
12. Karis, B.: Real shading in unreal engine 4. In: Proceedings of SIGGRAPH, Physically Based Shading in Theory and Practice (2013). http://blog.selfshadow.com/publications/s2013-shading-course/. Accessed 14 Jan 2015
13. Ureña, C., Fajardo, M., King, A.: An area-preserving parametrization for spherical rectangles. Comput. Graph. Forum **32**(4) (2013). https://www.solidangle.com/arnold/research/. Accessed 15 Feb 2015
14. Lagarde, S., de Rousiers, C.: Moving Frostbite to PBR. In: Proceedings of SIGGRAPH, Physically Based Shading in Theory and Practice (2014). http://blog.selfshadow.com/publications/s2014-shading-course/. Accessed 14 Jan 2015
15. Drobot, M.: Physically based area lights. In: Engel, W. (ed.) GPU Pro 5, pp. 67–100. A K Peters, Natick (2014)

16. Lecocq, P., Dufay, A., Sourimant, G., Marvie, J.-E.: Accurate analytic approximations for real-time specular area lighting. In: SIGGRAPH 2015 Talks. Lieu Los Angeles, August 2015

17. Martínez I.: Radiative view factors. http://webserver.dmt.upm.es/~isidoro/tc3/Radiation%20View%20factors.pdf. Accessed 15 Feb 2015

# Calibration of Structural Similarity Index Metric to Detect Artefacts in Game Engines

Rafał Piórkowski and Radosław Mantiuk[✉]

Faculty of Computer Science and Information Technology, West–Pomeranian University of Technology, Żołnierska Str. 49, 71–210 Szczecin, Poland
{rpiorkowski,rmantiuk}@wi.zut.edu.pl

**Abstract.** Previous studies reveal that Image Quality Metics (IQMs) can be efficiently used to automatically detect perceptual visibility of artefacts in the game engines. Very good matching was achieved for shadow acne, peter panning, and Z-fighting deteriorations, while IQM with the best detection rate proved to be the Structural Similarity Index Metric (SSIM). However, this metric generates noticeably worse results for the aliasing. Using SSIM, the artefacts are identified as differences in intensity, contrast, and structure between an image with deterioration and the corresponding reference. In this work we calibrate SSIM to improve matching for aliasing artefacts. We compare results generated by SSIM with the reference data created during subjective experiments in which people manually mark the visible local artefacts in the screenshots from game engines. In other words, we maximise convergence in the detection between the maps created by humans and computed by SSIM. The results of the cross-validation performed on a large collection of examples revealed that AUC (area under curve) in the receiver-operator analysis can be improved from 0.92 for default SSIM parameters to 0.97 for optimised parameters.

## 1 Introduction

*Graphics artefacts* are anomalies found in rendered images. They can significantly degrade an image perception and reduce the overall quality of graphics. Interestingly, even professional game engines are not free from presence of the visually confusing artefacts. Computer games developers seek a trade-off between quality of graphics and the rendering performance. Therefore, they often tolerate a kind of visual artefacts to save the game engine resources.

The most prominent artefact in game engines is *aliasing* manifested as the jagged edges of objects, or in the most extreme cases the disappearance of objects. This artefact is clearly visible even when advanced antialiasing techniques are used (see examples in Fig. 1). A good example of artefact is *shadow acne* caused by limited resolution of the depth maps used in the shadow maps technique [1]. This artefact can be reduced by applying the bias shift to the depth computation. However, too excessive displacement can cause the discontinuity of shadows, also called the *peter panning* deterioration. This latter artefact

© Springer International Publishing AG 2016
L.J. Chmielewski et al. (Eds.): ICCVG 2016, LNCS 9972, pp. 86–94, 2016.
DOI: 10.1007/978-3-319-46418-3_8

does not degrade the graphics quality directly but can be perceived by humans as something unnatural. Another artefact is *Z-fighting* caused by the incorrect order of drawing polygons due to the limited precision of the Z-buffer or placing two polygons in exactly the same distance from the camera.

In this work we look for the best methods for detection of the game engine artifacts. We argue that some of the deterioration must be avoided because they are highly annoying for game players. Our goal is to deliver a technique, which would automatically detect artefacts perceivable for human observers and skip the invisible deteriorations. We believe that this techniques will be useful for the game developers to find significant graphics artefacts in their engines.

In Piorkowski and Mantiuk [2] a framework for detection of the game engine artefacts based on the *image quality metrics* (IQMs) has been proposed. IQM is an algorithm, which compares two images: reference image without deteriorations and test image degraded by the shadow acne, peter panning, Z-fighting, or aliasing. The resulting distortion map shows areas in the test image that are identified as artefacts by the average human observer. In the mentioned work the Structural Similarity Index Metric (SSIM) [3] was indicated as the best method for detection of the game engine artefacts. This metric surpasses other advanced objective metrics like HDR-VDP-2 [4], S-CIELAB [5], and generates similar results to more complex MS-SSIM [6]. However, SSIM efficiency is different for different artifacts [2]. Very good matching was achieved for shadow acne, peter panning, and Z-fighting deteriorations, while SSIM generates noticeably worse results for the aliasing (see details in Sect. 4). The main goal of this work is to calibrate SSIM to improve matching for aliasing artefacts.

SSIM detects changes in luminance, contrast, and structure of the image (see Sect. 4.1 for details). In [2] these three components were treated in the same way, i.e. affect in the same way the final result. The main focus of our work is to investigate, which component has crucial impact on correct detection. We formulate the objective function, which minimizes the detection error by varying the impact of the individual components. The calculations are performed on a large dataset of the examples of the game engine artefacts (see Sect. 3). This dataset consists of the reference images without deteriorations and their equivalents with artefacts. We compare distortion maps generated by SSIM with the reference maps created during subjective experiments in which people manually mark the visible local artefacts. In other words, we maximise convergence in the detection between the maps computed by SSIM and created by humans. The results of the optimisation reveal that calibration of SSIM significantly improves detection of the aliasing deteriorations (see Sect. 4).

## 2   Background

### 2.1   Objective Image Quality Metrics

A human observer can easily choose which one of the two images looks better. However, running an extensive user study for numerous possible images and algorithm parameter variations is often impractical [7]. Therefore, there is a need for computational metrics that could predict a visually significant difference between a test image and its reference. The goal of this metric is to replace user studies or perceptual experiments. Such metric is especially practical for game engines, in which artefacts can occur in individual frames of the real time animation consisting of thousands of images.

There are a number of IQMs that prove their effectiveness (we refer the reader to the textbooks [8,9], and survey papers [10–12]). In this section we focus on presentation of the SSIM metric, which is favoured in the recent work and has been successfully used for detection of the game engine artefacts [2].

## 2.2 Aliasing Artefacts in Computer Games

The rendering is the process of sampling three-dimensional scene in order to obtain colours for each pixel in the raster image. A three-dimensional scene is never bandlimited because no matter how closely packed the samples are, objects can still be small enough that they do not get sampled at all [13, Sect. 5.6.1]. Common examples of aliasing are the jaggies of polygon edge or lines in the textures. The most popular antialiasing strategy in contemporary GPUs is called multisample antialiasing technique (MSAA). In MSAA, two, four, or eight samples per pixel are used to compute the coverage of a pixel by the triangle. The colours computed for different triangles that cover the same pixel are blended to produce the final pixel colour. This technique reduces aliasing, but at the same time decreases rendering performance.

In Fig. 1 we present examples of the aliasing artefacts. For a detailed description of other artefacts we refer the reader to paper [2].

**Fig. 1.** Left: reference image without deteriorations. Middle: image with aliasing artefacts, the inset shows magnified picture frame with visible jaggies. There are the same jaggies at the edges of other objects. The right column shows a reference distortion map (see Sect. 3.2 for details).

## 3  Experimental Dataset

### 3.1  Images with Artefacts

We built a database consisting of the images with artefacts and related references. These images were generated in three different graphics engines that deliver development environments for the independent developers: Unity 3D, CryEngine 3, and Unreal Engine 4. We modeled 27 custom 3D scenes (see Fig. 2) using example objects delivered with the engines but also external objects imported to the development environments. The scenes were used to prepare 36 pairs of images for testing aliasing artefacts. To avoid motions, all scenes were static without any object or camera movements. The scenes were rendered using the graphics engines and the images were captured as screenshots with the resolution of 800 × 600 pixels (using FRAPS (www.fraps.com)).

To test aliasing we used the GPU based 8× MSAA technique to render the reference images. These images were compared to deteriorated images without antialiasing, and to images processed using the 2× and 4× MSAA technique delivered by the Unity 3D game engine. For the remaining engines we applied the antialiasing setting corresponding to the MSAA technique.

**Fig. 2.** Example images from our dataset showing variation of the modelled scenes.

### 3.2 Reference Distortion Maps

For each pair of the test-reference image, the database contains the reference distortion map. Following the methodology presented in [14,15], this map was created by manually marking visible differences between image by human observers. The maps were averaged over a number of observers and binarised with a 0.5

threshold, i.e. the pixels marked by 50 % of observers were set to 1 and remaining pixels to 0. This thresholding gives reliable result during further statistical analysis, because it eliminates strong deviations in markings. Experimental procedure used to generate the reference maps is described in [2]. Example reference distortion map is presented in Fig. 1 (right).

## 4    SSIM Calibration

The goal of the SSIM calibration is to improve the efficiency of this metric for detection of the game engine artefacts. We optimise the SSIM parameters based on the dataset of images with typical artefacts.

### 4.1    SSIM Metric

SSIM detects difference in the mean of the intensity and contrast but the main factors are structural changes in the image. Local correlation of pixels (or more precisely windows surrounding these pixels) are analysed to find information about the structure of the image content. The similarity measure between windows $x$ and $y$ is defined as:

$$SSIM(x,y) = [l(x,y)]^{\alpha} \cdot [c(x,y)]^{\beta} \cdot [s(x,y)]^{\gamma}, \tag{1}$$

where $l(x,y)$, $c(x,y)$, and $s(x,y)$ denote intensity, contrast and structure, respectively. $\alpha$, $\beta$, and $\gamma$ are parameters used to adjust the relative importance of the three components. These components are equal to:

$$l(x,y) = \frac{2\mu_x\mu_y + c_1}{(\mu_x^2 + \mu_y^2 + c_1)}, \tag{2}$$

$$c(x,y) = \frac{2\sigma_x\sigma_y + c_2}{(\sigma_x^2 + \sigma_y^2 + c_2)}, \tag{3}$$

$$s(x,y) = \frac{\sigma_{xy} + c_3}{(\sigma_x\sigma_y + c_3)}. \tag{4}$$

For each pixel, the SSIM value is computed as a measure of difference between two windows $x$ and $y$ of size $N \times N$ pixels ($8 \times 8$ as proposed in [8]) surrounding the pixel. $\mu_x$ and $\mu_y$ are mean intensities, and $\sigma_x$ and $\sigma_y$ are standard deviations of $x$ and $y$ windows, respectively. $\sigma_{xy}$ is a covariance of $x$ and $y$. The $c_1$ and $c_2$ variables stabilise the division with weak denominator and are equal to $c_1 = (k_1L)^2$, $c_2 = (k_2L)^2$ for $k_1 = 0.01$ and $k_2 = 0.03$, $c_3 = c_2/2$. $L$ denotes the dynamic range of pixel values ($L = 2^{number\ of\ bits\ per\ pixel} - 1$). SSIM generates the distortion map consisting of the $SSIM(x,y)$ values computed for individual windows. It also returns the SSIM index, which is an average value of the distortion map.

## 4.2   ROC Analysis

The intensity, contrast, and structural components of the SSIM metric can have varying impact on its efficiency. Changing values of the $\alpha$, $\beta$, and $\gamma$ parameters, one can calibrate the metric for an arbitrary type of artefacts.

The key question is whether any set of the $\alpha$, $\beta$, and $\gamma$ parameters performs significantly better than the others in terms of detecting the aliasing artefacts. As we generated the reference distortion maps with binary classified pixels that contained artefacts (see Sect. 3.2), this maps can be compared to the distortion maps produced by SSIM. The performance of such classification can be analysed using the receiver-operator-characteristic (ROC) [16]. ROC captures the relation between the size of artefacts that were correctly marked by a SSIM (true positives), and the regions that do not contain artefacts but were still marked (false positives). Set of the $\alpha$, $\beta$, and $\gamma$ parameters that produces a larger *area under the ROC curve* (AUC) is assumed to perform better.

The ROC plots for individual artefacts are presented in Fig. 3. In this plot we assumed equal influence of the intensity, contrast, and structure components ($\alpha = \beta = \gamma = 1$) as it was proposed in the source SSIM paper [3]. AUC values for shadow acne, peter panning, and Z-fighting are close to 1, which indicates almost perfect match. The calibration procedure would not improve significantly results for these deterioration. Therefore, we limit this procedure to aliasing, for which AUC $= 0.9236$ can be further improved.

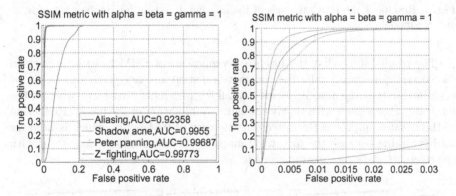

**Fig. 3.** Left: results of the ROC analysis for aliasing, shadow acne, peter panning, and Z-fighting artefacts for $\alpha = \beta = \gamma = 1$. Right: the inset of the plot from the left side, depicting differences between ROC curves for the analysed artefacts.

## 4.3   Calibration

To fairly test the SSIM efficiency, it is necessary to find the best set of $\alpha$, $\beta$, and $\gamma$ parameters. We activated the optimisation procedure, which generated the SSIM distortion maps for these parameters ranging from 0 to 3. These maps were compared to the reference distortion maps using the ROC analysis. The highest AUC value indicated the best set of parameters.

To avoid overfitting, we performed cross-validation with a random 50 %/50 % division of the our artefact dataset into training and testing sets. The downhill simplex method with multiple starting points was used for a derivative-free optimisation of the parameters, which avoided local minima.

The results are presented in Fig. 4. We randomly chose a 50 % subset from 36 pairs of images generated for aliasing. AUC was optimised for this subset. We repeated the computation 3 times and the resulting $\alpha$, $\beta$, and $\gamma$ were averaged. We obtained the AUC value for $\alpha$, $\beta$, and $\gamma$ computed for all 36 pairs of images equals to 0.5950, 2.6061, 2.5288 respectively.

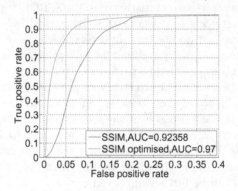

**Fig. 4.** Results of the ROC analysis of the aliasing detection for the best set of $\alpha$, $\beta$, and $\gamma$ parameters.

The results show that the intensity component of SSIM has less impact on the correct detection, while the contrast and structure are preferred. It can be explained in that the aliasing forms a small high-frequency artifacts, whereas the intensity is correlated with slowly changing illumination in the image. Reduction of the $\alpha$ value improves the detection intensity of 0.5 % only, which is however intrinsic value because the distortion maps are noticeably more consistent with the reference data (see example in Fig. 5).

**Fig. 5.** Left column: reference distortion map. Middle: SSIM map computed for default parameters. Right: SSIM map computed for the optimised parameters. To improve the readability we binarised the SSIM maps with threshold of 0.75.

# 5    Conclusions and Future Work

In this work we demonstrated that the SSIM image quality metric based on the well calibrated parameters can reliably predict visibility of the aliasing artefacts in game engines. The prediction for the tested dataset was improved from $AUC = 0.92$ for the default set of the $\alpha$, $\beta$, and $\gamma$ parameters to $AUC = 0.97$ for $\alpha = 0.5950$, $\beta = 2.6061$, and $\gamma = 2.5288$. This improvement significantly increases the efficiency of the metric for the high frequency aliasing artefacts, because the $\alpha$ parameter is correlated with slowly changing brightness in the image.

In future work we plan to analyse visibility of the temporal aliasing. This type of deterioration is even more prominent than the static aliasing, because it causes strongly noticeable flickering. Analysis of the temporal artefacts requires different quality metrics and building a dataset of the reference animations.

**Acknowledgement.** The project was partially funded by the Polish National Science Centre (grant number DEC-2013/09/B/ST6/02270).

# References

1. Williams, L.: Casting curved shadows on curved surfaces. ACM SIGGRAPH Comput. Graph. **12**, 270–274 (1978)
2. Piórkowski, R., Mantiuk, R.: Using full reference image quality metrics to detect game engine artefacts. In: Proceedings of the ACM SIGGRAPH Symposium on Applied Perception, pp. 83–90. ACM (2015)
3. Wang, Z., Bovik, A., Sheikh, H., Simoncelli, E.: Image quality assessment: from error visibility to structural similarity. IEEE Trans. Image Process. **13**, 600–612 (2004)
4. Mantiuk, R., Kim, K.J., Rempel, A.G., Heidrich, W.: HDR-VDP-2: a calibrated visual metric for visibility and quality predictions in all luminance conditions. ACM Trans. Graph. **30**, 40:1–40:14 (2011)
5. Zhang, X.M., Wandell, B.A.: A spatial extension to CIELAB for digital color image reproduction. In: Proceedings of the SID Symposiums, pp. 731–734 (1996)
6. Wang, Z., Simoncelli, E.P., Bovik, A.C.: Multiscale structural similarity for image quality assessment. In: Conference Record of the Thirty-Seventh Asilomar Conference on Signals, Systems and Computers, 2004, vol. 2, pp. 1398–1402. IEEE (2003)
7. Mantiuk, R., Tomaszewska, A.M., Mantiuk, R.: Comparison of four subjective methods for image quality assessment. Comput. Graph. Forum **31**, 2478–2491 (2012)
8. Wang, Z., Bovik, A.: Modern Image Quality Assessment. Morgan & Claypool Publishers, San Rafael (2006)
9. Wu, H., Rao, K.: Digital Video Image Quality and Perceptual Coding. CRC Press, Boca Raton (2005)
10. Lin, W., Kuo, C.C.J.: Perceptual visual quality metrics: a survey. J. Vis. Commun. Image Represent. **22**, 297–312 (2011)
11. Pedersen, M., Hardeberg, J.Y.: Full-reference image quality metrics: classification and evaluation. Found. Trends® Comput. Graph. Vis. **7**, 1–80 (2012)

12. Čadík, M., Herzog, R., Mantiuk, R., Mantiuk, R., Myszkowski, K., Seidel, H.P.: Learning to predict localized distortions in rendered images. Comput. Graph. Forum **32**, 401–410 (2013)
13. Akenine-Möller, T., Haines, E., Hoffman, N.: Real-Time Rendering, 3rd edn. A K Peters Ltd., Wallesley (2008)
14. Čadík, M., Herzog, R., Mantiuk, R., Myszkowski, K., Seidel, H.P.: New measurements reveal weaknesses of image quality metrics in evaluating graphics artifacts. ACM Trans. Graph. (TOG) **31**, 147 (2012)
15. Sergej, T., Mantiuk, R.: Perceptual evaluation of demosaicing artefacts. In: Campilho, A., Kamel, M. (eds.) ICIAR 2014, Part I. LNCS, vol. 8814, pp. 38–45. Springer, Heidelberg (2014)
16. Baldi, P., Brunak, S., Chauvin, Y., Anderson, C.A.F., Nielsen, H.: Assessing the accuracy of prediction algorithms for classification: an overview. Bioinformatics **16**, 640–648 (2000)

# Generalized Depth-of-Field
# Light-Field Rendering

David C. Schedl, Clemens Birklbauer, Johann Gschnaller,
and Oliver Bimber[⊠]

Institute of Computer Graphics, Johannes Kepler University, Linz, Austria
gschnaller.j@gmail.com,
{david.schedl,clemens.birklbauer,oliver.bimber}@jku.at

**Abstract.** Typical light-field rendering uses a single focal plane to define
the depth at which objects should appear sharp. This emulates the
behavior of classical cameras. However, plenoptic cameras together with
advanced light-field rendering enable depth-of-field effects that go far
beyond the capabilities of conventional imaging. We present a generalized
depth-of-field light-field rendering method that allows arbitrarily shaped
objects to be all in focus while the surrounding fore- and background
is consistently rendered out of focus based on user-defined focal plane
and aperture settings. Our approach generates soft occlusion boundaries
with a natural appearance which is not possible with existing techniques.
It furthermore does not rely on dense depth estimation and thus allows
presenting complex scenes with non-physical visual effects.

## 1 Introduction

With the availability of consumer light-field cameras (Raytrix and Lytro), light
fields [8,16] are slowly gaining popularity. Their processing, however, still lacks
novel tools that go beyond classical light-field rendering. Existing methods are
mainly limited to simple aperture and focus control during rendering. For conventional light-field rendering, a synthetic focal plane—usually parallel to the
image plane of the rendering camera—defines the depth at which objects appear
sharp [10]. As for physical cameras, focus is set by the focal plane while depth
of field is controlled by the aperture diameter.

In photography and cinematography depth of field is often used to guide
the audience's attention to objects in focus, while deemphasizing the fore- and
the background. For virtual scenes depth-of-field effects going beyond physical
constraints have been presented [15]. Such effects can not be achieved with conventional imaging systems. Plenoptic cameras together with advanced light-field
rendering, however, enable such non-physical depth-of-field effects. We present

**Electronic supplementary material** The online version of this chapter (doi:10.
1007/978-3-319-46418-3_9) contains supplementary material, which is available to
authorized users.

© Springer International Publishing AG 2016
L.J. Chmielewski et al. (Eds.): ICCVG 2016, LNCS 9972, pp. 95–105, 2016.
DOI: 10.1007/978-3-319-46418-3_9

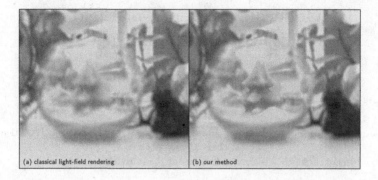

**Fig. 1.** The *x-mas* scene rendered with classical light-field rendering (a) and our generalized depth-of-field light-field rendering (b). With our method the tree in the glass is rendered all in focus, while the remaining scene is rendered out of focus.

a generalized depth-of-field light-field rendering method that allows arbitrarily shaped objects—independent from their physical depth or shape in the scene—to be all in focus, while the surrounding fore- and background is consistently rendered out of focus based on user-defined focal plane and aperture settings. Thus, our method allows to emphasize objects of interest by keeping them in focus, while the remaining scene is defocused (i.e., varying the depth of field on an object basis). Although our approach presents a non-physical effect, it preserves a natural image appearance (i.e., occlusions of in-focus objects produce soft borders to support natural depth perception). Thereby, it generates consistent occlusion boundaries that cannot be achieved with existing techniques (Fig. 1) and avoids halo artifacts by rendering in-focus and out-of-focus objects separately. Our approach requires the depth of an object for rendering it in focus. Precise depth reconstruction, however, is not possible for complex scenes (i.e., transparent objects, non-Lambertian surfaces) and often fails at occlusion boundaries, where accurate depth is important for segmentation. Therefore, we only sparsely estimate the depth of object contours and support fast and simple interactive corrections in our editor. We allow presenting complex scenes with non-physical visual effects and demonstrate our algorithm by means of five exemplary light fields.

Our key contributions are:

- an interactive editor for 4D object segmentation, that does not rely on dense depth reconstruction, to select all-in-focus objects;
- artifact free generalized depth-of-field effects achieved by rendering the all-in-focus objects and the remaining scene separately with subsequent blending;
- an advanced blending approach to generate occlusion boundaries for occluded all-in-focus objects.

## 2   Related Work

A thorough discussion of light fields is beyond the scope of this article and we refer interested readers to [26]. We mainly focus on related light-field rendering, editing and segmentation techniques. Classical light-field rendering with a single focal plane and specific aperture settings has been shown in [8,16]. The possibility of an arbitrary parameterizable focal surface was theoretically discussed in [10], which is also the basis for our generalized depth-of-field rendering. Rendering with the scene depth as focal surface has been used in various works for reducing aliasing [2,3,21]. Accurate dense depth reconstruction, however, is not possible for complex scenes (i.e., transparent objects, non-Lambertian surfaces) and often fails at occlusion boundaries [5]. To allow material editing and relighting, surface light fields [27,28] parameterize the plenoptic function directly based on the detailed geometry of the scene. However, complex acquisition steps are required to gather surface light fields in adequate quality. While we also define 3D geometry for all-in-focus objects, we only sparsely estimate depth for object contours and support fast and simple manual corrections.

Other methods approximate the scene as planar layers. Such layers can be computed from stereo pairs, as shown in [1]. In [23] light fields are split into multiple 2D layers by manual selection. We use similar methods for segmentation but produce non-physical depth-of-field effects and support arbitrary surfaces, while the layers in [23] are rendered completely in focus and are only planar.

Our editor applies semi-automatic image segmentation tools, such as lasso selection or GrabCut [20], for easy interaction. However, most 2D algorithms can not be directly applied to multi-view data, because selections need to be consistent across views. Such tools for stereo image pairs are proposed in [17, 19], but require dense depth estimations for transferring segmentations from one view to the other. In the context of light-field segmentation or editing, few works have been presented. One of the first methods is [22], which also supports painting and cutting out scene parts. The interactive deformation of light fields based on coarse bounding boxes was proposed in [4]. Jarabo et al. explored the propagation of edits across all light-field views in [12]. In [29] morphing between two light fields, with user-marked features was shown. Similar to our polygonal selection, 3D polygons for guiding the morphing process are manually defined across multiple views. Recently, a survey on user interfaces for consistent light-field editing has been presented in [11]. Although we use segmentation instead of editing, we apply some of their findings, such as multi-view editing along epipolar lines and disparity editing while rendering. Overall, none of these light-field editing approaches allows non-physical rendering of objects.

Non-physical depth of field has been explored in the context of information visualization [13] to depict relevance as focus and irrelevance as blur. Generalized depth of field has been shown for 3D rendering of virtual scenes: as post process via heat diffusion [14]; or during rendering via ray tracing [15]. While the later methods support the generation of non-physical depth-of-field effects, they require complete knowledge of the scene's geometry, which is only practical for virtual scenes. Lightshop [9] describes a shader language for light fields that would support the composition of non-physical focus effects. However, they do not address the related segmentation and occlusion problems.

While we incorporate ideas and methods from previous work, our approach is a first full system for practical generalized depth-of-field light-field rendering.

# 3   Method

The goal of our approach is to render multiple and arbitrary-shaped objects in focus—independent from their physical depth or shape in the scene. The remaining area is rendered with classical light-field rendering using a single user-defined focal plane. Our approach can be outlined as follows (Fig. 2): After loading a light field into our editor (step 1), the all-in-focus objects are segmented (steps 2–3; see Sect. 3.1). The all-in-focus objects and the remaining scene are masked and rendered, resulting in two subimages that are blended (steps 4–6; Sect. 3.2). If necessary, additional disparity samples inside the all-in-focus objects can be defined to correct focus issues (step 7). Potential occlusions of all-in-focus with foreground objects can be identified with our editor and are consequently rendered with soft borders for a natural appearance (step 8).

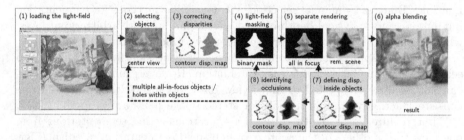

**Fig. 2.** Steps of our method: (1) loading the light field into our editor; (2) selecting an all-in-focus object in the central perspective and (3) correcting automatically estimated contour disparities if necessary; (4) light fields are masked and (5) rendered two times: for the all-in-focus objects and for the remaining scene; (6) the resulting subimages are alpha blended to an artifact-free image; (7) additional disparity samples inside objects can be defined for correcting focus issues during rendering; (8) occlusions of the all-in-focus object can be identified for improving the binary masks and blending. For selecting multiple all-in-focus objects or holes in objects, the process restarts with step 2. Gray boxes denote optional steps.

## 3.1   Segmentation (steps 2–3)

For segmentation, we follow the multi-view editing guidelines presented in [11]. Our editor supports the selection of multiple all-in-focus objects with arbitrary polygonal shapes. We offer GrabCut [20] and a lasso selection [18] for identifying objects in the central perspective. The GrabCut algorithm performs semi-automatic segmentation using an optimization on color and edge information. The user draws a coarse outline around the desired all-in-focus object and if needed further constrains the automatic segmentation by marking image parts as all-in-focus or background. With the lasso tool the user roughly traces the all-in-focus object's boundary with the mouse, while the algorithm chooses a minimum cost contour based on edges. In comparison to GrabCut the lasso tool typically requires elongated interaction times. Its outcome however is more predictive and therefore desired in situations where GrabCut does not produce the favored segmentation (See Supplementary Video).

The segmentation leads to a polygonal contour line of the all-in-focus object, which we reduce to a sparse number of contour points using the Ramer-Douglas-Peucker algorithm [7] for efficiency reasons. The contour polygon has to be propagated from the central perspective to all other views of the light field. Therefore, we compute a disparity for each contour point by matching a local 2D block along the corresponding epipolar line of each point within the other perspectives. For performance reasons, we only use a subset of the light-field views. From these we calculate the median disparity for each contour point, allowing us to compute its position in all light-field perspectives. We manually correct disparities, where the automatic block matching fails. They can be identified when the automatically propagated contour does not fit the corresponding object in other perspectives. We carry out manual corrections of disparities in off-center perspectives by moving contour points along the epipolar line, similar to [11]. Holes within all-in-focus objects are segmented like the all-in-focus objects themselves, but are explicitly marked as background and excluded from rendering.

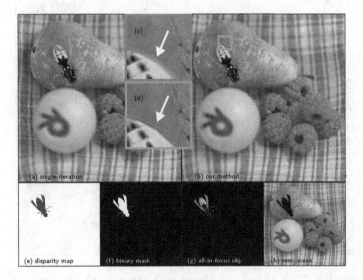

**Fig. 3.** Single-iteration rendering of the *still life* scene causes halo artifacts around the all-in-focus objects (a,c). Separate rendering and subsequent blending avoids these artifacts (b,d). Insets (c,d) show details of (a,b) and clearly depict the halo artifact. The disparity map used for rendering is shown in (e). Binary masks (f) used to render the all-in-focus objects (g), and the remaining scene (h) separately.

## 3.2 Rendering (steps 4–6)

For rendering, a dense disparity map (Fig. 3e) is computed by interpolating the original disparity values of the contour points within the areas of the contour polygons. The remaining scene is set to a user-defined uniform disparity. However, single-iteration light-field rendering with this disparity map causes halo-like artifacts, caused by contributions of the all-in-focus objects to the remaining out-of-focus scene. With our method, we avoid those artifacts by rendering the light field separately for the all-in-focus objects and for the out-of-focus scene (Fig. 3a, b).

As a preparation step, the contour polygons are warped to each light-field perspective, resulting in a 4D binary mask (Fig. 3f) that we apply for separation. Then the scene is rendered two times: We first mask the all-in-focus objects and use the computed disparity map as focal surface. In the second pass, we mask the remaining scene and use a user-defined focal plane. This results in two subimages, with corresponding alpha values, that need to be blended (Fig. 3g, h). Blending these subimages with the all-in-focus alpha map ($\alpha$) generates artifact-free results.

**Disparities Inside Objects (step 7).** For objects with large depth variances, linear interpolation of contour disparities (Fig. 4a, b) is not sufficient for enabling

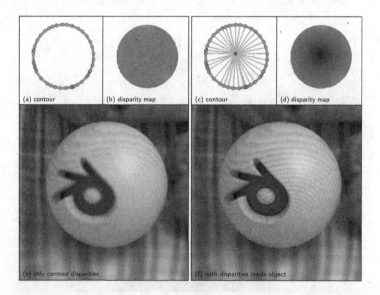

**Fig. 4.** Rendering of an all-in-focus object with large depth variance (i.e. wooden sphere) might cause defocus (e), if the dense disparity map is only computed from contour disparities (a,b). Additional disparity samples within the all-in-focus object (c) and re-interpolation of the dense disparity map (d), allow a sharp rendering (f). Note that contour disparities are marked in green, while disparities inside objects are marked in red (Color figure online).

all-in-focus rendering (Fig. 4e). Therefore, we allow additional disparity samples to be defined within the all-in-focus polygon. Their positions are selected by mouse clicks within the rendering view of our editor. The disparity values are manually adjusted until the area around the new sample appears all in focus in the light-field rendering. The additional samples lead to a re-triangulation of the polygons and to a re-interpolation of the dense disparity map (Fig. 4c, d). Improved focus is clearly visible in Fig. 4f.

**Identifying Occlusions (step 8).** Contour points of occluded all-in-focus objects contain disparities of the occluding foreground object. This results in wrong disparities when interpolating the disparity map, causing visual artifacts during rendering. Therefore, if an all-in-focus object is occluded by the remaining scene, we need to distinguish between two different occlusion boundary types for each contour point: the ones that border on the background and the ones that border on the foreground scenery (occluded). Our editor assumes background borders (not occluded) as default and requires foreground occlusions to be identified with the lasso selection. Contour points that border on the foreground (occluded) are excluded from the disparity map interpolation (Fig. 5a–d). Hard boundaries, as generated by alpha blending without occlusion handling (using $\alpha$), appear unrealistic at occluded object boundaries (Fig. 5e).

Object edges are a visual cue for relative depth perception: objects with hard edges on top of a blurred scene appear in front, while soft boundaries indicate the occlusion by a foreground object. Thus, for a natural appearance of occlusion boundaries, the alpha map should contain soft borders matching the blur of the remaining scene (i.e., the rendered alpha mask ($\beta$) of the remaining scene, shown in Fig. 5j). Therefore, our desired alpha map for blending contains the hard edges from $\alpha$ at background borders and the soft edges from $\beta$ at foreground borders of the all-in-focus contour (Fig. 5k). We compute this combined alpha mask by changing the disparities of contour points that border on the background scenery (not occluded) to the uniform disparity of the remaining scene. With these updated contour disparities, we recompute the binary masks and then light-field render the masks like the remaining scene with the uniform disparity. This results in an alpha map ($\gamma$) with hard edges at not-occluded and soft borders at occluded contour points (Fig. 5k). However, blending with $\gamma$ would result in missing data within the rendered all-in-focus subimage along the soft borders (dark areas in Fig. 5g). Therefore, $\gamma$ has to be reduced in size to not extend $\alpha$, resulting in $\gamma' = \min(\alpha, s(\gamma))$. To avoid reintroducing hard blending edges, we scale the alpha values in $\gamma$ by the heuristic function $s(\gamma) = \max(2\gamma - 1, 0)$ before computing the minimum of $\alpha$ and $\gamma$. Blending the two subimages with the alpha mask $\gamma'$ (Fig. 5l) leads to soft borders at occlusions (Fig. 5h).

## 4   Results

Figure 6 shows various results rendered with our generalized depth-of-field light-field rendering. We compare our method to classical light-field rendering

(Fig. 6 center). We apply our method to scenes captured with a hand-held Lytro light-field camera (*balcony* and *x-mas*), to scenes recorded with a camera gantry (*chess*), and to synthetically rendered scenes (*buddha* and *still life*).

Our Supplementary Video presents user interactions and focal stacks for the light-field recordings of Fig. 6. Editing times varied from 50 s, for simple scenes (e.g., *balcony*), to 5 min, for complex settings, such as fine structures, holes, and multiple objects (e.g., *still life* and *buddha*).

## 5   Implementation

The editor and all algorithms are implemented in MATLAB. To achieve interactive rates, we employ the GPU using NVIDIA's CUDA for light-field rendering. For our experiments linearly interpolating the dense disparity map was sufficient and very efficient. The contour line simplification with the Ramers-Douglas-Peucker algorithm uses a tolerance of 1 pixel as the maximal euclidean

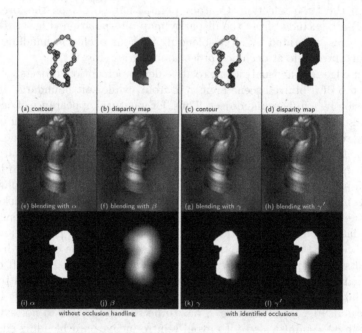

**Fig. 5.** Occluded contour points contain disparities of the occluding foreground object resulting in wrong disparity maps (a,b). Identifying occlusions with the lasso selection (c) and excluding them from the disparity-map interpolation leads to correct disparity maps (d). Blending the *chess* scene with $\alpha$ (e), $\beta$ (f), $\gamma$ (g) and $\gamma'$ (h). Note that blending with $\beta$ and $\gamma$ produces darkening artifacts due to missing data. The alpha map $\alpha$ from the all-in-focus subimage has hard edges (i), while the inverted alpha map $\beta$ from the remaining scene has soft borders (j). For our occlusion handling an alpha map $\gamma$ (k) is generated by combining $\alpha$ and $\beta$. It has to be rescaled to $\gamma'$ (l) before it is used for blending (h). The full *chess* scene is shown in Fig. 6.

**Fig. 6.** Five light-field recordings: the center perspectives (left), renderings with classical light-field rendering (center), and our generalized depth-of-field light-field rendering (right). The scenes *balcony* and *x-mas* are captured with a Lytro light-field camera and decoded with [6], whereas *chess* is recorded by a camera gantry [24]. Scenes *buddha* and *still life* are synthetic scenes [25]. Our method allows arbitrarily shaped objects to be all in focus while the remaining scene is consistently rendered out of focus based on a user-defined focal plane.

distance between the new simplified contour and existing contour points. For our experiments, we applied the automatic disparity estimation to a subset of five perspectives, using a block size of $21 \times 21$ pixels for spatial light-field resolutions between $700 \times 400$ and $768 \times 768$ pixels.

## 6  Conclusion and Future Work

Our method allows multiple arbitrarily shaped objects to be all in focus while the remaining scene is consistently rendered out of focus based on user-defined focal plane and aperture settings. The editor supports the selection of objects without dense depth reconstruction and allows fast corrections where our sparse automatic disparity estimations fail. We achieve artifact-free generalized depth-of-field light-field renderings by processing the all-in-focus objects and the remaining scene separately. Objects with large depth variances can be handled by user-defined disparity samples inside objects. Furthermore, we present a method for manually specifying occlusions of the all-in-focus object and rendering them naturally (i.e., with soft borders). Besides focus and aperture control, other processing techniques have to be offered for making light-field photography truly applicable. Our approach presents one step in this direction.

In the future, we intend to incorporate better matting techniques for sub-pixel accurate masking to reduce wrong color contributions in the subimages. Single pixels at occlusion boundaries can contain contributions from all-in-focus objects and the remaining scene, caused by the camera's PSF, interpolation, fuzzy (e.g., furry or cloudy), and transparent objects. Figure 3h illustrates these artifact, where the legs of the wasp (all-in-focus object) contribute to the subimage of the remaining scene.

## References

1. Baker, S., Szeliski, R., Anandan, P.: A layered approach to stereo reconstruction. In: CVPR, pp. 434–441 (1998)
2. Buehler, C., Bosse, M., McMillan, L., Gortler, S., Cohen, M.: Unstructured lumigraph rendering. In: SIGGRAPH, pp. 425–432 (2001)
3. Chai, J.X., Tong, X., Chan, S.C., Shum, H.Y.: Plenoptic sampling. In: SIGGRAPH, pp. 307–318 (2000)
4. Chen, B., Ofek, E., Shum, H.Y., Levoy, M.: Interactive deformation of light fields. In: I3D, pp. 139–146 (2005)
5. Chen, C., Lin, H., Yu, Z., Kang, S.B., Yu, J.: Light field stereo matching using bilateral statistics of surface cameras. In: CVPR, pp. 1518–1525 (2014)
6. Dansereau, D.G., Pizarro, O., Williams, S.B.: Decoding, calibration and rectification for lenselet-based plenoptic cameras. In: CVPR, pp. 1027–1034 (2013)
7. Douglas, D.H., Peucker, T.K.: Algorithms for the reduction of the number of points required to represent a digitized line or its caricature. Cartographica **10**(2), 112–122 (1973)
8. Gortler, S.J., Grzeszczuk, R., Szeliski, R., Cohen, M.F.: The lumigraph. In: SIGGRAPH, pp. 43–54 (1996)

9. Horn, D.R., Chen, B.: Lightshop: interactive light field manipulation and rendering. In: I3D, pp. 121–128 (2007)
10. Isaksen, A., McMillan, L., Gortler, S.J.: Dynamically reparameterized light fields. In: SIGGRAPH, pp. 297–306 (2000)
11. Jarabo, A., Masia, B., Bousseau, A., Pellacini, F., Gutierrez, D.: How do people edit light fields? TOG **33**(4), 146:1–146:10 (2014)
12. Jarabo, A., Masia, B., Gutierrez, D.: Efficient propagation of light field edits. In: SIACG, pp. 75–80 (2011)
13. Kosara, R., Miksch, S., Hauser, H.: Semantic depth of field. In: InfoVis, p. 97 (2001)
14. Kosloff, T.J., Barsky, B.A.: An algorithm for rendering generalized depth of field effects based on simulated heat diffusion. In: ICCSA, pp. 1124–1140 (2007)
15. Kosloff, T.J., Barsky, B.A.: Three techniques for rendering generalized depth of field effects. In: SIAM, pp. 42–48 (2009)
16. Levoy, M., Hanrahan, P.: Light field rendering. In: SIGGRAPH, pp. 31–42 (1996)
17. Lo, W.Y., van Baar, J., Knaus, C., Zwicker, M., Gross, M.: Stereoscopic 3D copy & paste. TOG **29**(6), 147:1–147:10 (2010)
18. Mortensen, E.N., Barrett, W.A.: Intelligent scissors for image composition. In: SIGGRAPH, pp. 191–198 (1995)
19. Price, B.L., Cohen, S.: Stereocut: Consistent interactive object selection in stereo image pairs. In: ICCV, pp. 1148–1155 (2011)
20. Rother, C., Kolmogorov, V., Blake, A.: "Grabcut": interactive foreground extraction using iterated graph cuts. TOG **23**(3), 309–314 (2004)
21. Schirmacher, H., Heidrich, W., Seidel, H.P.: High-quality interactive lumigraph rendering through warping. In: GI, pp. 87–94 (2000)
22. Seitz, S.M., Kutulakos, K.N.: Plenoptic image editing. IJCV **48**(2), 115–129 (2002)
23. Shum, H.Y., Sun, J., Yamazaki, S., Li, Y., Tang, C.K.: Pop-up light field: an interactive image-based modeling and rendering system. TOG **23**(2), 143–162 (2004)
24. Vaish, V., Adams, A.: The (new) stanford light field archive (2008). http://lightfield.stanford.edu
25. Wanner, S., Meister, S., Goldluecke, B.: Datasets and benchmarks for densely sampled 4D light fields. In: VMV, pp. 225–226 (2013)
26. Wetzstein, G., Ihrke, I., Lanman, D., Heidrich, W.: Computational plenoptic imaging. Comput. Graph. Forum. **30**, 2397–2426 (2011)
27. Weyrich, T., Pfister, H., Gross, M.: Rendering deformable surface reflectance fields. TVCG **11**(1), 48–58 (2005)
28. Wood, D.N., Azuma, D.I., Aldinger, K., Curless, B., Duchamp, T., Salesin, D.H., Stuetzle, W.: Surface light fields for 3D photography. In: SIGGRAPH, pp. 287–296 (2000)
29. Zhang, Z., Wang, L., Guo, B., Shum, H.Y.: Feature-based light field morphing. TOG **21**(3), 457–464 (2002)

# Low-Level and Middle-Level
Image Processing

# Anisotropic Diffusion for Smoothing:
# A Comparative Study

César Bustacara[1], Miller Gómez-Mora[1,2], and Leonardo Flórez-Valencia[1(✉)]

[1] Pontificia Universidad Javeriana, Bogotá D.C., Colombia
{cbustaca,miller.gomez,florez-l}@javeriana.edu.co,
mgomezm@udistrital.edu.co
[2] Universidad Distrital Francisco José de Caldas, Bogotá D.C., Colombia

**Abstract.** Anisotropic diffusion is a powerful image processing technique, which allows simultaneously to remove noise and to enhance sharp features in two and three dimensional images. Anisotropic diffusion filtering concentrates on preservation of important surface features, such as sharp edges and corners, by applying direction dependent smoothing. This feature is very important in image smoothing, edge detection, image segmentation and image enhancement. For instance, in the image segmentation case, it is necessary to smooth images as accurately as possible in order to use gradient-based segmentation methods. If image edges are seriously polluted by noise, these methods would not be able to detect them, so edge features cannot be retained. The aim of this paper is to present a comparative study of three methods that have been used for smoothing using anisotropic diffusion techniques. These methods have been compared using the root mean square error (RMSE) and the Nash-Sutcliffe error. Numerical results are presented for both artificial data and real data.

## 1 Introduction

Edge preserving filters are used to smooth an image, while reducing edge blurring effects across edge like halos, phantom etc. To introduce the concept of edge preserving we begin with the nonlinear diffusion technique proposed by Perona and Malik [10]. They proposed a nonlinear diffusion method for avoiding blurring and localization problems caused by linear diffusion filtering. Based on the importance of image scale-space representation, introduced by Witkin [18], Perona and Malik suggested a new definition of scale-space through Anisotropic diffusion (AD), a non-linear partial differential equation-based diffusion process [10]. Anisotropic diffusion has become a very useful tool in image smoothing, edge detection, image segmentation and image enhancement.

Anisotropic diffusion aims at reducing image noise without removing significant parts of the image content, typically lines, edges or other details that are important for image interpretation, in our case, image segmentation [4]. Many papers have appeared proposing different models, investigating their theoretical foundations, and describing interesting applications [15]. For example, Gerig et al.

© Springer International Publishing AG 2016
L.J. Chmielewski et al. (Eds.): ICCVG 2016, LNCS 9972, pp. 109–120, 2016.
DOI: 10.1007/978-3-319-46418-3_10

used such filters to enhance magnetic resonance images [3]. Olver, Sapiro and Tannenbaum used a similar technique to perform edge preserving smoothing of such images [8]. In the extreme case, this smoothing might produce a profile of radio frequency inhomogeneity in the images. Others have shown that diffusion filters can be used to enhance and detect object edges within images [1,7].

However, Anisotropic diffusion filtering is highly dependent on some crucial parameters, such as the conductance function, the gradient threshold parameter and the stopping time of the iterative process. Overestimating one of those parameters may lead to an oversmoothed blurry result, while underestimating them may leave noise in the image unfiltered. Therefore, it is crucial that all parameters are determined in an optimal and automatic way in every step of the iterative process, by evaluating the denoising needed and the edge quality of the given image.

Tsiotsios and Petrou [14] proposed an automatic stopping criterion, that takes into consideration quality of preserved edges as opposed to just the level of smoothing achieved. One recent contribution, using AD is presented by Mirebeau et al. [6]. They used the approximation proposed by Weickert [15], understanding that diffusion tensors are anisotropic and reflect the local orientation of image features. This is in contrast with the non-linear diffusion filter of Perona and Malik, which only involves scalar diffusion coefficients, in other words isotropic diffusion tensors [2,6].

The paper is organized as follows: Sect. 2 reviews principal aspects behind the anisotropic diffusion process. Test data and accuracy metrics are described in Sect. 3. Results for the implementation of the methods are given in Sect. 4, and finally, in Sect. 5 some conclusions are given.

## 2    Anisotropic Diffusion Process

In general, an image can be interpreted as an initial concentration distribution:

$$u(x, y, t = 0) = I(x, y) \tag{1}$$

This image is changed (in time) according to:

$$\frac{\partial u}{\partial t} = div(D \cdot \nabla u) \tag{2}$$

where the diffusion tensor $D$ controls the diffusion process. Equation 2 is called the *diffusion equation*. This equation appears in many physical transport processes. To use it in image processing we need to associate the concentration distribution with the grey value at a certain location.

The type of difussion process depend directly on the type of filter, and on the diffusion tensor $D$ used. If the diffusion tensor $D$ is constant over the whole image domain, one speaks of homogeneous diffusion, and a space-dependent filtering is called inhomogeneous. Often the diffusion tensor $D$ is a function of the differential structure of the evolving image itself. Such a feedback leads to nonlinear diffusion filters. Diffusion which does not depend on the evolving image is called linear [15].

The linear diffusion equation is the oldest and best investigated partial differential equation (PDE) method in image processing. Let $f(x)$ denote a grayscale (noisy) input image, and let $u(x, t)$ be initialized with $u(x, 0) = u^0(x) = f(x)$. Then, the linear diffusion process can be defined by the equation

$$\frac{\partial u}{\partial t} = \nabla \cdot (\nabla u) = \nabla^2 u \tag{3}$$

where $\nabla\cdot$ denotes the divergence operator. Thus, the equation is:

$$\frac{\partial u}{\partial t} = \frac{\partial^2 u}{\partial x^2} + \frac{\partial^2 u}{\partial y^2} \tag{4}$$

The diffusion process can be seen as an evolution process with an artificial time variable $t$, denoting the diffusion time where the input image is smoothed at a constant rate in all directions. Starting from the initial image $u^0(x)$, evolving images $u(x, t)$ under the governed equation represent the successively smoothed versions of the initial input image $f(x)$, and thus create a scale space representation of the given image $f$, with $t > 0$ being the scale [13,15].

Nonlinear diffusion has attracted much attention in the field of image processing for its ability to reduce noise while preserving or even enhancing important features of the image, such as edges or discontinuities [15]. To alleviate the problem of isotropic diffusion, which is similar to Gaussian blurring, Perona and Malik [10] proposed an anisotropic diffusion scheme, which we will refer to as the PM model for brevity. They apply an inhomogeneous process that reduces diffusivity at those locations which have a larger likelihood to be edges. This likelihood is measured by $|\nabla u|^2$. The PM filter is based on the equation

$$\frac{\partial u}{\partial t} = div\left(g\left(|\nabla u|^2\right) \cdot \nabla u\right) \tag{5}$$

and it uses diffusivities such as

$$g\left(s^2\right) = \frac{1}{1 + \frac{s^2}{\lambda^2}} \quad (\lambda > 0) \tag{6}$$

Mirebeau et al. [6] indicated that, although PM diffusion has been the subject of considerable academic and industrial interest, it is mathematically ill-posed, unstable, often leads to unsightly staircasing visual artifacts, and is not adequate for oscillating patterns. To overcome these issues, an anisotropic difussion filter is preferable which uses diffusion along edges instead of diffusion perpendicular to them. According to Weickert [15] many papers have appeared proposing different anisotropic diffusion filters, investigating their theoretical foundations, and describing interesting applications. For example, Gerig et al. [3] used anisotropic diffusion filters to enhance MR images. Olver, Sapiro and Tannenbaum [8] used a similar technique to perform edge preserving smoothing of MR images. Others have shown that diffusion filters can be used to enhance and detect object edges within images [1,7].

All linear and nonlinear diffusion filters mentioned above use a scalar-valued diffusivity $g$ which is adapted to the underlying image structure. Therefore, they are isotropic and the flux $j = -g\nabla u$ is always parallel to $\nabla u$. However, in certain applications it would be desirable to bias the flux towards the orientation of interesting features. These requirements cannot be satisfied by a scalar diffusivity, a diffusion tensor leading to anisotropic diffusion filters has to be introduced instead.

Anisotropic models do not only take into account the modulus of the edge detector $\nabla u_\sigma$, but also its direction. Suppose an orthonormal system of eigenvectors $v_1$, $v_2$ of the diffusion tensor $D$ is constructed in such way, that they reflect the estimated edge structure [16]:

$$v_1 \parallel \nabla u_\sigma, \qquad v_2 \perp \nabla u_\sigma \tag{7}$$

In order to prefer smoothing along the edge to smoothing across it, Weickert [15] proposed to choose the corresponding eigenvalues $\lambda_1$ and $\lambda_2$ as

$$\begin{aligned} \lambda_1(\nabla u_\sigma) &:= g(|\nabla u|^2) \\ \lambda_2(\nabla u_\sigma) &:= 1 \end{aligned} \tag{8}$$

As $\nabla u$ does not coincide with one of the eigenvectors of $D$ as long as $\sigma > 0$.

In this paper, anisotropic diffusion is understood in the sense of Weickert, meaning that diffusion tensors are anisotropic and reflect the local orientation of image features. This is in contrast with the non-linear diffusion filter of Perona and Malik, which only involves scalar diffusion coefficients, in other words isotropic diffusion tensors [6].

Below three representatives of anisotropic diffusion processes are considered. The first offers advantages at noisy edges, the second is well-adapted for denoising images that are approximately piecewise constant, whereas the third relies on Lattice Basis Reduction, a tool from discrete mathematics which has recently shown its relevance for the discretization on grids of strongly anisotropic PDE.

### 2.1   Anisotropic Gradient Diffusion

The first inhomogeneous diffusion model was introduced by Perona and Malik [10]. The idea was to vary the conduction spatially to favor noise removal in nearly homogeneous regions while avoiding any alteration of the signal along significant discontinuities. The change in intensity $u$ over time was defined as:

$$\frac{\partial u}{\partial t} = div\left(g\left(|\nabla u|\right) \cdot \nabla u\right) \tag{9}$$

$$g\left(|\nabla u|\right) = \frac{1}{1 + \frac{|\nabla u|^2}{K^2}} \quad (K > 0) \tag{10}$$

Perona and Malik indicated that, the constant K is fixed either by hand at some fixed value, or using the "noise estimator" [10].

## 2.2  Anisotropic Curvature Diffusion

Whitaker and Xue [17] presented a variation on the classic Perona-Malik equation. This variation is a level-set analog of that equation and they called as modified curvature diffusion equation (MCDE) [17]. MCDE does not exhibit edge enhancing properties of classic anisotropic diffusion, which can under certain conditions undergo a negative diffusion, which enhances edge contrast. Equations of the form of MCDE always undergo positive diffusion, with the conductance term only varying the strength of that diffusion.

Qualitatively, MCDE compares well with other non-linear diffusion techniques. It is less sensitive to contrast than PM, and preserves finer detailed structures in images. There is a potential speed trade-off for using this function in place of classic PM. Each iteration of the solution takes roughly twice as long. Fewer iterations, however, may be required to reach an acceptable solution.

The MCDE equation is given as:

$$f_t = |\nabla f| \nabla \cdot c(|\nabla f|) \frac{\nabla f}{|\nabla f|} \tag{11}$$

where the conductance modified curvature term is

$$\nabla \cdot \frac{\nabla f}{|\nabla f|} \tag{12}$$

## 2.3  Anisotropic Diffusion Using Lattice Basis Reduction

Mirebeau et al. [6] described two anisotropic non-linear diffusion techniques based on a recent adaptive scheme making the diffusion stable and requiring limited numerical resources. These techniques are called Coherence Enhancing Diffusion (CED) and Edge Enhancing Diffusion (EED), which are based on more complex tensor constructions introduced by Weickert [15,16].

Weickert's diffusion tensors $D = D_u(x,t)$, are defined in terms of this eigenanalysis of the structure tensor $S = S_u(x,t)$ as:

$$D = \sum_{1 \leq i \leq d} \mu_i e_i \otimes e_i \tag{13}$$

where

$$S = \sum_{1 \leq i \leq d} \lambda_i e_i \otimes e_i \tag{14}$$

Smoothing is promoted in direction $e_i$ if $\mu_i$ is large, and prevented if $\mu_i$ is small, for any $1 \leq i \leq d$.

Mirebeau et al. proposed an Edge Enhancing Diffusion (EED) technique. EED aims to avoid significant diffusion across the set $\Gamma$ of image contours, but to allow it anywhere else. According to Mirebeau et al. [6], the first diffusion tensor eigenvalue is $\mu_1 = 1$, because the eigenvector $e_1$ is orthogonal to the image (approximate) gradient direction $e_d$, hence never transverse to $\Gamma$. Additional conditions are presented in the original paper to obtain the equation for $\mu_i$ as:

$$\mu_i = 1 - (1 - \alpha) \exp\left(-\left(\frac{\lambda}{\lambda_i - \lambda_1}\right)^m\right) \tag{15}$$

But, this choice to set $\mu_1 = 1$, may lead to undesired effects, for this reason, Mirebeau et al., proposed introduce a Conservative variant of EED (cEED) for which $\mu_1$ can be small, when appropriate, so as to prevent diffusion around angles of $\Gamma$. The final equation is:

$$\mu_i = 1 - (1 - \alpha) \exp\left(-\left(\frac{\lambda}{\lambda_i}\right)^m\right) \tag{16}$$

## 3    Test Images Used

We compare selected methods by three examples, one using numerical data and other using experimental data: (1) the arctan function, (2) standard test image (lena), and (3) data from computed tomography (CT):

1. numerical data (synthetic image) is generated using the arctan function:

$$f(x, y) = arctan(10x(1 + y))$$

   with thin image spacing $(0.04 \times 0.08)$ mm (see Table 1). It contains an edge of varying steepness, ideal for studying how processing methods handle the delineation of objects.
2. Standard Lena image, shown in Table 1 (third column), with resolution $(512 \times 512)$ and spacing of 1 in both directions.
3. Coronal nasal cavity plane of a head-neck CT, with image acquisition resolution $(0.46 \times 0.46)$ mm) (see Table 1). The medical image is cropped to focus in detail on desired features and facilitate presentation of results.

Furthermore, Gaussian noise was added to the synthetic image in order to observe the behavior of smoothing methods in noisy images. We choose a Gaussian noise with mean value zero and with a standard deviation equal to $\sigma = 2$, $5$ and $10$ (see Table 2).

We quantify our results by two error measures: the root mean square error (RMSE) and Nash-Sutcliffe error.

**Table 1.** Synthetic and CT test images

| Synthetic image Normalized [0, 255] | Topographic primal sketch | Lena | CTA image | ROI CTA image |
|---|---|---|---|---|

**Table 2.** Synthetic images with Gaussian noise (noisy images)

| Gaussian Noise | Noisy image | Primal sketch |
|:---:|:---:|:---:|
| (2%) | | |
| (5%) | | |
| (10%) | | |

## 4 Numerical Results

Parameters for anisotropic gradient filters and curvature filters are the number of iterations, the time step, and the conductance. The appropriate number of iterations depend on applications and images being processed. As a general rule, the more iterations performed, the more diffused images will become. The time step is constrained at run-time to keep the solution stable. In general, the time step should be at or below $(PixelSpacing)/2^{N+1}$, where $N$ is the dimensionality of the image. The conductance parameter controls the sensitivity of the conductance term in the basic anisotropic diffusion equation. It affects the conductance term in different ways depending on the particular variation on the basic equation. As a general rule, the lower the value, the more strongly the diffusion equation preserves image features (such as high gradients or curvature). A high value for conductance will cause the filter to diffuse image features more readily.

According to above conditions, first tests were carried out to see the behavior of conductance for anisotropic filters based on gradient and curvature. For this, the number of iterations was fixed at 5, time step was fixed at 0.005, and the independent parameter (conductance) was varied between 0.1 and 1.9.

The results for the synthetic image are presented in Table 3, in which can be seen that the smallest error for anisotropic diffusion based on gradient is achieved with a conductance value of 1.0. Similarly for anisotropic diffusion based on curvature, the best value for the conductance was 0.9.

**Table 3.** Gradient and curvature anisotropic diffusion varying conductance (c)

| c | RMSE | Nash | c | RMSE | Nash |
|---|------|------|---|------|------|
| 0.1 | 1.97322 | 0.999608 | 1.1 | 1.34215 | 0.999818 |
| 0.2 | 1.76341 | 0.999687 | 1.2 | 1.35322 | 0.999815 |
| 0.3 | 1.61686 | 0.999736 | 1.3 | 1.36879 | 0.99981 |
| 0.4 | 1.53844 | 0.999761 | 1.4 | 1.3893 | 0.999805 |
| 0.5 | 1.48225 | 0.999778 | 1.5 | 1.41515 | 0.999797 |
| 0.6 | 1.43279 | 0.999793 | 1.6 | 1.44588 | 0.999788 |
| 0.7 | 1.38847 | 0.999805 | 1.7 | 1.48019 | 0.999778 |
| 0.8 | 1.35575 | 0.999814 | 1.8 | 1.51622 | 0.999767 |
| 0.9 | 1.33919 | 0.999819 | 1.9 | 1.55207 | 0.999756 |
| 1.0 | 1.33636 | 0.99982 | | | |

| c | RMSE | Nash | c | RMSE | Nash |
|---|------|------|---|------|------|
| 0.1 | 1.83697 | 0.99966 | 1.1 | 1.55247 | 0.999757 |
| 0.2 | 1.6157 | 0.999737 | 1.2 | 1.56575 | 0.999753 |
| 0.3 | 1.57057 | 0.999751 | 1.3 | 1.58178 | 0.999748 |
| 0.4 | 1.55997 | 0.999755 | 1.4 | 1.60108 | 0.999742 |
| 0.5 | 1.55387 | 0.999757 | 1.5 | 1.62352 | 0.999734 |
| 0.6 | 1.55181 | 0.999757 | 1.6 | 1.64866 | 0.999726 |
| 0.7 | 1.5462 | 0.999759 | 1.7 | 1.67508 | 0.999717 |
| 0.8 | 1.53913 | 0.999761 | 1.8 | 1.70237 | 0.999708 |
| **0.9** | **1.53718** | **0.999762** | 1.9 | 1.72958 | 0.999698 |
| 1.0 | 1.54247 | 0.99976 | | | |

The second test is performed for the anisotropic filter based on lattice basis reduction. Parameters of diffusion time, lambda, noise scale and feature scale were considered as follows: diffusion time was set at 0.004, noise scale at 1, feature scale at 2 and lambda was varied in the interval [0.001, 0.09]. The results for the synthetic image are presented in Table 4, in which can be seen that the smallest error is achieved with a lambda value of 0.001 for EED and 0.002 for cEED.

Based on previous two tests, we proceeded to evaluate different methods using noisy images (Gaussian noise 2 %, 5 % and 10 %). For this, we proceeded in similar way as in previous tests, and finally we selected the best result for each method (see Table 5).

In Table 6 we present visual results (only for image with 5 % of Gaussian noise) using a topographic primal sketch representation according to results presented in Table 5. In these images the quality achieved for each method can be seen.

**Table 4.** Edge enhancing diffusion and conservative variant of EED varying lambda

| λ | RMSE | Nash | λ | RMSE | Nash |
|---|------|------|---|------|------|
| **0.001** | **0.848186** | **0.999927** | 0.01 | 1.16145 | 0.999864 |
| 0.002 | 0.8581 | 0.999926 | 0.02 | 1.57394 | 0.999749 |
| 0.003 | 0.884603 | 0.999921 | 0.03 | 1.94815 | 0.999615 |
| 0.004 | 0.923592 | 0.999914 | 0.04 | 2.24432 | 0.999488 |
| 0.005 | 0.963368 | 0.999906 | 0.05 | 2.48529 | 0.99937 |
| 0.006 | 1.00226 | 0.999898 | 0.06 | 2.72387 | 0.999242 |
| 0.007 | 1.04136 | 0.99989 | 0.07 | 2.98617 | 0.999087 |
| 0.008 | 1.08092 | 0.999882 | 0.08 | 3.26649 | 0.998906 |
| 0.009 | 1.12096 | 0.999873 | 0.09 | 3.54988 | 0.998706 |

| λ | RMSE | Nash | λ | RMSE | Nash |
|---|------|------|---|------|------|
| 0.001 | 0.880427 | 0.999922 | 0.01 | 1.15116 | 0.999866 |
| **0.002** | **0.867581** | **0.999924** | 0.02 | 1.55818 | 0.999754 |
| 0.003 | 0.89122 | 0.99992 | 0.03 | 1.93358 | 0.999621 |
| 0.004 | 0.927137 | 0.999913 | 0.04 | 2.23199 | 0.999493 |
| 0.005 | 0.963529 | 0.999906 | 0.05 | 2.47426 | 0.999376 |
| 0.006 | 0.998744 | 0.999899 | 0.06 | 2.71266 | 0.999249 |
| 0.007 | 1.0348 | 0.999892 | 0.07 | 2.97404 | 0.999095 |
| 0.008 | 1.07262 | 0.999884 | 0.08 | 3.25397 | 0.998914 |
| 0.009 | 1.11159 | 0.999875 | 0.09 | 3.53769 | 0.998715 |

**Table 5.** Smoothing error comparison

| Method | 5-Iterations | | | | | | | | |
|---|---|---|---|---|---|---|---|---|---|
| | 2 % | | | 5 % | | | 10 % | | |
| | | RMSE | Nash | | RMSE | Nash | | RMSE | Nash |
| GD | c=1.0 | 1.33636 | 0.99982 | c=1.9 | 2.67889 | 0.99927 | c=1.9 | 4.9809 | 0.99747 |
| CD | c=0.9 | 1.53718 | 0.999762 | c=1.9 | 2.97282 | 0.999104 | c=1.9 | 4.90073 | 0.997551 |
| EED | $\lambda = 0.001$ | **0.848186** | **0.999927** | $\lambda = 0.007$ | 1.68657 | 0.999712 | $\lambda = 0.01$ | 2.80065 | 0.999201 |
| cEED | $\lambda = 0.002$ | 0.867581 | 0.999924 | $\lambda = 0.007$ | **1.68004** | **0.999714** | $\lambda = 0.02$ | **2.78606** | **0.999208** |

**Table 6.** Topographic primal sketch for smoothing results (image with 5 % of Gaussian noise)

| Noisy image | GD | CD | EED | cEED |
|---|---|---|---|---|

Finally for synthetic images, we vary the number of iterations to determine their influence on the smoothing quality. For this reason, tests were performed using 10 and 20 iterations (see Tables 7 and 8). Conductance and lambda were varied according to the methods.

In summary, comparing Tables 5, 7 and 8, we can see that the EED method produces best results compared to methods based on gradient and curvature. Visually this is reflected in Table 6.

**Table 7.** Smoothing error using 10 iterations

| Method | Noisy images | | | | | | | | |
|---|---|---|---|---|---|---|---|---|---|
| | 2 % | | | 5 % | | | 10 % | | |
| | | RMSE | Nash | | RMSE | Nash | | RMSE | Nash |
| GD | c=0.7 | 1.6336 | 0.999731 | c=1.4 | 2.9489 | 0.999114 | c=1.9 | 4.5406 | 0.997885 |
| CD | c=0.2 | 1.67313 | 0.999718 | c=0.9 | 3.41067 | 0.998822 | c=1.9 | 5.06651 | 0.99738 |
| EED | $\lambda = 0.001$ | **1.55132** | **0.999756** | $\lambda = 0.002$ | **1.56787** | **0.99975** | $\lambda = 0.006$ | **2.5611** | **0.999331** |
| cEED | $\lambda = 0.001$ | 1.58706 | 0.999745 | $\lambda = 0.003$ | 1.63234 | 0.99973 | $\lambda = 0.007$ | 2.57334 | 0.999324 |

**Table 8.** Smoothing error using 20 iterations

| Method | 20-Iterations | | | | | | | | |
|---|---|---|---|---|---|---|---|---|---|
| | 2 % | | | 5 % | | | 10 % | | |
| | | RMSE | Nash | | RMSE | Nash | | RMSE | Nash |
| GD | c=0.2 | 1.6336 | 0.999731 | c=0.7 | 3.56251 | 0.998711 | c=1.1 | 5.06153 | 0.997373 |
| CD | c=0.2 | 1.67313 | 0.999718 | c=0.3 | 3.57919 | 0.998704 | c=1.1 | 5.78947 | 0.996586 |
| EED | $\lambda = 0.001$ | **1.55132** | **0.999756** | $\lambda = 0.001$ | **1.76858** | **0.999682** | $\lambda = 0.003$ | **2.65759** | **0.999278** |
| cEED | $\lambda = 0.001$ | 1.58706 | 0.999745 | $\lambda = 0.001$ | 1.82193 | 0.999662 | $\lambda = 0.004$ | 2.73952 | 0.999232 |

**Table 9.** Smoothing of CT image

| | PM | CADF | EED | cEED |
|---|---|---|---|---|
| Lena | 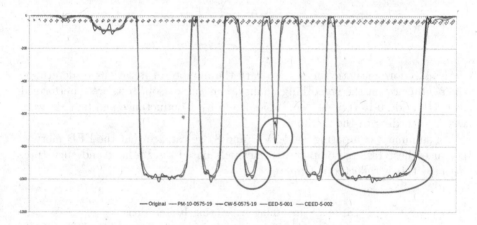 | | | |
| | GD-5-0125-19 | CD-5-0125-19 | EED-5-001 | cEED-5-001 |
| CT | | | | |
| | GD-5-0575-19 | CD-5-0575-19 | EED-5-001 | cEED-5-002 |

—Original —PM-10-0575-19 —CW-5-0575-19 —EED-5-001 —CEED-5-002

**Fig. 1.** Intensity profile of CT image (Color figure online)

Using these results, we compute smoothing methods for real image (lena and CT). The results are shown in Table 9. A visual analysis presents a great similarity between the results obtained using gradient and curvature techniques with 5 iterations. The EED and cEED methods have better results than first two methods.

To observe in detail the accuracy of the implemented methods a row image was selected to analyze the profile obtained by applying each of them with respect to the original image. To select the row of interest, a scan of the original image was made and row 84 was chosen, which crosses areas with low contrast and which are fundamental in the segmentation of nasal cavities (see bottom row in Table 1). With respect to the lena image, we select the row 256, the results were very similar to those obtained with the CT image.

In general, the anisotropic gradient diffusion method (Perona-Malik) attenuates image intensity in thin regions, and does not maintain image edges. This can be seen in regions enclosed by circles in Fig. 1, the green curve represents obtained results. Anisotropic curvature diffusion method (Whitaker et al.) presents a lower attenuation of intensities in homogeneous regions and preserves edges in a better way that the anisotropic gradient diffusion (magenta curve in Fig. 1), but in thin regions, both gradient filters and curvature filters attenuate region intensity. These drawbacks can be solved using anisotropic diffusion based on lattice basis reduction (EED and cEED), which allows smooth homogeneous regions preserving edges and maintain intensity in thin regions (red and orange curves in Fig. 1).

## 5    Conclusions

In this paper, a comparative study on anisotropic diffusion for smoothing has been presented. To compare the methods, the root mean square error (RMSE) and the Nash-Sutcliffe error have been used. Numerical results for two 2D images have demostrated that anisotropic diffusion using lattice basis reduction preserves more image information than the anisotropic gradient diffusion and the anisotropic curvature diffusion. Filters were tested on three images with different conditions and the results show that, in the low noise case, the anisotropic method based on lattice basis reduction performs much better than the anisotropic gradient and anisotropic curvature filters. EED and cEED smooth out the noise in homogeneous areas while still maintaining edge strengths with minimum blurring across edges. Furthermore, anisotropic filtering based on lattice basis reduction maintains intensity values in thin regions, while the other two filters significantly attenuate it. In general, anisotropic diffusion methods based on gradient and curvature have drawbacks when regions are thin. In addition, edge accuracy is lost, resulting in increase of miscalculations by filters applied after the smoothing.

## References

1. Alvarez, L., Lions, P.-L., Morel, J.-M.: Image selective smoothing and edge detection by nonlinear diffusion. II. SIAM J. Numer. Anal. **29**, 845–866 (1992)
2. Fehrenbach, J., Mirebeau, J.-M.: Sparse non-negative stencils for anisotropic diffusion. J. Math. Imaging Vis. **49**, 1–25 (2013)
3. Gerig, G., Kubler, O., Kikinis, R., Jolesz, F.A.: Nonlinear anisotrophic filtering of MRI data. IEEE Trans. Med. Imaging **11**, 221–232 (1992)
4. Gómez-Mora, M., Flórez-Valencia, L.: Surface reconstruction from three-dimensional segmentations using implicit functions. In: Computing Colombian Conference (10 CCC), pp. 317–323. IEEE (2015)
5. Hosssain, Z., Möller, T.: Edge aware anisotropic diffusion for 3D scalar data. IEEE Trans. Vis. Comput. Graph. **16**, 1376–1385 (2010)
6. Mirebeau, J.-M., Fehrenbach, J., Risser, L., Tobji, S.: Anisotropic diffusion in ITK. Insight J. 1–9 (2014)

7. Nordstrom, K.N.: Biased anisotropic diffusion - a unified regularization and diffusion approach to edge detection. In: Faugeras, O. (ed.) ECCV 1990. LNCS, vol. 427, pp. 18–27. Springer, Heidelberg (1990). **8**, 318-327 (1990)

8. Olver, P.J., Sapiro, G., Tannenbaum, A.: Affine invariant detection: Edge maps, anisotropic diffusion and active contours. Acta Appl. Math. **59**, 45–77 (1999)

9. Pal, C., Chakrabarti, A., Ghosh, R.: A brief survey of recent edge-preserving smoothing algorithms on digital images. Procedia Comput. Sci. 1–40 (2015)

10. Perona, P., Malik, J.: Scale-space and edge detection using anisotropic diffusion. IEEE Trans. Pattern Anal. Mach. Intell. **12**, 629–639 (1990)

11. Press, W., Teukolsky, S., Vetterling, W., Flannery, B.: Numerical Recipesin C: The Art of Scientific Computing. Cambridge University Press, Cambridge (2002)

12. Staggs, J.E.J.: Savitzky-Golay smoothing and numerical differentiation of cone calorimeter mass data. Fire Saf. J. **40**, 493–505 (2005)

13. ter Haar Romeny, B.M., Florack, L.M.J.: Front-end vision: a multiscale geometry engine. In: Bülthoff, H.H., Poggio, T.A., Lee, S.-W. (eds.) BMCV 2000. LNCS, vol. 1811, pp. 297–307. Springer, Heidelberg (2000)

14. Tsiotsios, C., Petrou, M.: On the choice of the parameters for anisotropic diffusion in image processing. Pattern Recognit. **46**, 1369–1381 (2013)

15. Weickert, J.: A review of nonlinear diffusion filtering. In: ter Haar Romeny, B.M., Florack, L.M.J., Viergever, M.A. (eds.) Scale-Space 1997. LNCS, vol. 1252, pp. 3–28. Springer, Heidelberg (1997)

16. Weickert, J.: Anisotropic Diffusion in Image Processing. B.G. Teubner, Stuttgart (1998)

17. Whitaker, R.T., Xue, X.: Variable-conductance, level-set curvature for image denoising. In: Proceedings 2001 International Conference on Image Processing, pp. 142–145 (2001)

18. Witkin, A.P.: Scale-space filtering. Int. Jt. Conf. Artif. Intell. **2**, 1019–1022 (1983)

# Comparison and Evaluation
# of First Derivatives Estimation

César Bustacara-Medina$^{(\boxtimes)}$ and Leonardo Flórez-Valencia

Pontificia Universidad Javeriana, Bogotá, DC, Colombia
{cbustaca,florez-l}@javeriana.edu.co

**Abstract.** Computing derivatives from observed integral data is known
as an ill-posed inverse problem. The ill-posed qualifier refers to the noise
amplification that can occur in the numerical solution if appropriate
measures are not taken (small errors for measurement values on specified
points may induce large errors in the derivatives). For example, the accurate computation of the derivatives is often hampered in medical images
by the presence of noise and a limited resolution, affecting the accuracy
of segmentation methods. In our case, we want to obtain an upper airways segmentation, so it is necessary to compute the first derivatives as
accurately as possible, in order to use gradient-based segmentation techniques. For this reason, the aim of this paper is to present a comparative
analysis of several methods (finite differences, interpolation, operators
and regularization), that have been developed for numerical differentiation. Numerical results are presented for artificial and real data sets.

## 1 Introduction

The problem of approximating a derivative of a function defined by error contaminated data points arises in several scientific computing and engineering dis-
ciplines. Computation of local image derivatives is an important operation in
many image processing tasks that involve feature detection and extraction, such
as edges, corners or more complicated features. Additionally, the spatial derivatives of the image intensity provide topographic information that may be used
to identify and segment objects.

However, derivative computation in discrete images is an ill-posed problem
and derivative operators without any prior smoothing are known to enhance
noise (see [8,15,23,26,27]). Poggio et al. [27] indicated that the problem is ill-
posed because the solution does not depend continuously on the data. The problem is to find the solution $z$ to $y = Az$ with $(Az)(x) = \int_0^x z(s)\,ds$. Thus, $z$ is the
derivative of the data $y$.

According to the literature, the algorithms based on first derivatives studied
in this paper share a common structure, and only differ in the type of filtering
used to compute those derivatives. The input image is filtered using an approximation of first derivative and then is computed the gradient magnitude. The
usual tool to find the magnitude of the intensity changes of an image $f$ is the
gradient operator (denoted as $\nabla$), defined as the vector

© Springer International Publishing AG 2016
L.J. Chmielewski et al. (Eds.): ICCVG 2016, LNCS 9972, pp. 121–133, 2016.
DOI: 10.1007/978-3-319-46418-3_11

$$\nabla f = \begin{bmatrix} f_x \\ f_y \end{bmatrix} = \begin{bmatrix} \frac{\partial f}{\partial x} \\ \frac{\partial f}{\partial y} \end{bmatrix} \tag{1}$$

To obtain the gradient, the partial derivatives $\partial f/\partial x$ and $\partial f/\partial y$ need to be computed at every pixel of the image. When dealing with digital images, numerical approximations of these derivatives are computed in a neighborhood of each point. In general, the gradient computations form the basis for most problems in numerical analysis and simulation of physical systems. Specifically in image processing and computer vision, gradient operators are widely used as a substrate for the detection of edges and estimation of their local orientation. In medical imaging, they are commonly used to estimate the direction of surface normals when processing volumetric data [7].

A number of different techniques have been developed to construct useful formulas for numerical derivatives. Several categories have been defined to classify these techniques, for example Knowles et al. [19], Ramm et al. [29], Li [21], Jauberteau et al. [13] indicated three categories: difference methods, interpolation methods and regularization methods. According to Li in [21], exists five categories: finite difference type [3,15–18,20], polynomial interpolation type [3–5], operator type [5,30], lozenge diagrams [9], and undetermined coefficients [9,12].

Other numerical differentiation methods, which do not aim at developing difference formulas of derivatives but evaluating numerical derivatives by use of data or given analytical forms of functions, include: Richardson extrapolation [3,5], spline numerical differentiation [13,33,34], regularization method [4,23], and automatic differentiation (AD) [11].

According to Ramm et al. [29], finite differences and interpolation methods have the advantage of simplicity. In addition, these methods are considered by many authors to be the ones which yield satisfactory results when the function to be differentiated is given very precisely and noise-free [1,4,19,29].

This paper focuses on accurate computation of spatial derivatives and their subsequent use to process an image gradient field directly, from which an image with improved characteristics can be segmented. We compare four different techniques: central finite differences, Savitzky–Golay, Gaussian filters (discrete and recursive) and Sobel kernel. The paper is organized as follows: In Sect. 2, we give a brief overview of the selected derivatives methods. Test data and accuracy metrics are described in Sect. 3. Relevant results for the different methods implemented are presented in Sect. 4, and finally, in Sect. 5 some conclusions are given.

## 2    First Derivatives Estimation

In this section, the following techniques are briefly reviewed to compute the first derivatives: finite differences, polynomial interpolation, Sobel operators and Gaussian operators (discrete and recursive).

## 2.1  Finite Difference Type

The approximation of derivatives by finite differences plays a central role in finite difference methods for the numerical solution of differential equations, especially boundary value problems [11,12,17].

Finite differences which were introduced by Sir Isaac Newton, deal with the changes that take place in the value of a function $f(x)$ due to finite changes in $x$. Finite difference operators include, forward difference, backward difference, shift operator, central difference, divided difference and mean operator. Central difference was only considered.

**Central difference:** Using Taylor series, a $f$ function can be expanded to calculate a next value on the basis of a present value [3,15–18,20]. Differentiating with respect to $x$, at $x = x_0$ , and truncating this equation after the first derivative and rearranging yields, we obtain the approximation to the derivative $f'(x)$ with step size $h$ as

$$f'(x_k) = \frac{1}{2h}\left[f(x_{k+1}) - f(x_{k-1})\right] - O\left(h^2\right) \tag{2}$$

where the error is $O\left(h^2\right)$.

If we truncate to two term after derivative, we get

$$f'(x_k) = \frac{1}{12h}\left[-f(x_{k+2}) + 8f(x_{k+1}) - 8f(x_{k-1}) + f(x_{k-2})\right] - O\left(h^4\right) \tag{3}$$

where the error is $O\left(h^4\right)$.

Notice that in the first approximation, the truncation error is of the order of $h^2$ in contrast to the forward and backward approximations that are of the order of $h$ [1,4,11]. Consequently, the Taylor series analysis yields the practical information that the central difference is a more accurate representation of the derivative. Formulas for $N = 3, 5, 7, 9$ are listed in Table 1.

**Table 1.** Central differences approximations with different width (N)

| N | N-point stencil central differences |
|---|---|
| 3 | $\dfrac{f_1 - f_{-1}}{2h}$ |
| 5 | $\dfrac{f_{-2} - 8f_{-1} + 8f_1 - f_2}{12h}$ |
| 7 | $\dfrac{-f_{-3} + 9f_{-2} - 45f_{-1} + 45f_1 - 9f_2 + f_3}{60h}$ |
| 9 | $\dfrac{3f_{-4} - 32f_{-3} + 168f_{-2} - 672f_{-1} + 672f_1 - 168f_2 + 32f_3 - 3f_4}{840h}$ |

## 2.2 Polynomial Interpolation Type

The first stage is to construct an interpolating polynomial from the data, then an approximation of the derivative at any point can be obtained by a direct differentiation of the interpolant. Numerical differentiation formulas based on interpolating polynomials (e.g., Lagrangian, Newton, Chebyshev, Hermite, Gauss, Bessel, etc.) may be found in many literatures [3,5].

The advantages of the methods are that they do not require that the data be equispaced, and some specific difference formulas deduced from the methods can be used to estimate the derivative anywhere within the range prescribed by the known points. Unfortunately, the methods are generally implicit. In this differentiation type, the Savitzky-Golay method was considered.

**Savitzky-Golay (SG):** The procedure is to perform a least squares fit of a small set of consecutive data points to a polynomial and take the calculated central point of the fitted polynomial curve as the new smoothed data point.

Savitzky and Golay [24,25,28] showed that a set of integers

$$\left( A_{-n}, A_{-(n-1)}, \cdots, A_{n-1}, A_n \right)$$

could be derived and used as weighting coefficients to carry out the smoothing operation. The use of these weighting coefficients, known as convolution integers, turns out to be exactly equivalent to fitting the data to a polynomial, as just described and it is computationally more effective and much faster. Therefore, the smoothed data point $(y_k)_s$ by the Savitzky-Golay algorithm is given by the following equation:

$$(y_k)_s = \frac{\sum_{i=-n}^n A_i y_{k+1}}{\sum_{i=-n}^n A_i} \tag{4}$$

Many sets of convolution integers can be used depending on the filter width and the polynomial degree. The coefficients are equivalent to least squares fitting a high order polynomial to the data. To achieve the derivatives is necessary to derive the smooth representation (Eq. 4) and compute the new coefficients using least squares fitting. For example, coefficients for quadratic order with different width ($N = 3, 5, 7, 9$) are listed in Table 2.

**Table 2.** SG coefficients for first-derivative quadratic fit with different width

| pos/width | -4 | -3 | -2 | -1 | 0 | 1 | 2 | 3 | 4 |
|---|---|---|---|---|---|---|---|---|---|
| 3 | | | | -0.5 | 0 | 0.5 | | | |
| 5 | | | -0.20 | -0.10 | 0 | 0.10 | 0.20 | | |
| 7 | | -0.1071 | -0.0714 | -0.0357 | 0 | 0.0357 | 0.0714 | 0.1071 | |
| 9 | -0.0667 | -0.0500 | -0.0333 | -0.0250 | 0 | 0.0250 | 0.0333 | 0.0500 | 0.0667 |

Savitzky-Golay algorithm is very useful for calculating the derivatives of noisy signals consisting of discrete and equidistant points [24,25,28].

## 2.3   Operator Type

Many operators have been proposed to compute the derivative in an image (e.g., Roberts, Prewitt and Sobel operators). However, they do not compute the derivative without adding extra blur and they are very inaccurate [2,20].

**Sobel Operators:** The Sobel operators are discrete differential operators. According to the literature [3–5,11,13,21,31], Sobel is less sensitive to noise present in images, but cannot produce accurate edge detection with thin and smooth edge. Corresponds to the convolution of the image with: $[1\ 2\ 1]\star[-1\ 0\ 1]$.

In this case, Sobel mask can be seen as the convolution of a vertical derivation mask $[-1\ 0\ 1]^T$ with an horizontal smoothing filter $[1\ 2\ 1]$, for this reason, we must consider this situation in the result analysis phase (other techniques don't include smoothing – If we do not include smoothing filter, Sobel kernel has the same coefficients that central finite differences kernel for window size equal to 3, see first row in Table 1).

**Gaussian Operators:** The Gaussian derivatives are often applied in the fields of image processing and computer vision as differential operators [2,32], and used to implement differential invariant operators. Bouma et al. [2], indicated that in the medical field, the Gaussian derivatives are used to compute features in huge multi-dimensional images for a computer-aided interpretation of the data, sometimes even at multiple scales. This processing requires an efficient and accurate implementation of the Gaussian derivatives. Bouma et al. [2], shown four ways to obtain the derivative of an image. The first way is computes one convolution with the derivative of a Gaussian. The second and third way convolve the image with a Gaussian and then with a smaller derivative of a Gaussian or a B-Spline derivative. The last way convolves the image with a Gaussian and then with the derivative of an interpolator.

Robust measurement of image derivatives is obtained by convolution with Gaussian derivative filters, a well known result from scale-space theory [22]. Additionally, research on recursive Gaussian filtering has given rise to three main techniques [6,14,35]. These techniques were derived using different methods. Deriche [6] approximates the Gaussian function in the space domain, Jin et al. [14] in the z domain and Vliet et al. [35] in the Fourier domain. They all use different optimisation techniques. To maintain shift invariance (or zero phase), the filter is implemented as a cascade of forward and backward difference equations with real-valued coefficients $b$ how is shown in the Eqs. 5 and 6, respectively.

$$v[n] = \alpha x[n] - \sum_{i=1}^{N} b_i v[n-i], \quad with\ \alpha = 1 + \sum_{i=1}^{N} b_i \tag{5}$$

$$y[n] = \alpha v[n] - \sum_{i=1}^{N} b_i y[n+i], \quad with\ \alpha = 1 + \sum_{i=1}^{N} b_i \tag{6}$$

An interesting property of recursive filters is that the number of operations is independent of the variance of the filter [10].

Macia [26] provides an implementation using ITK[1] of a separable discrete Gaussian derivative kernel, which uses two approaches to generate the filter coefficients. The first approach calculates the coefficients of a polynomial that is multiplied by the Gaussian kernel, thus calculating the final derivative Gaussian kernel the same way we would calculate analytically the derivatives of a Gaussian function. This is possible because the discrete Gaussian kernel represents an analogue of the continuous Gaussian kernel and the linear properties are kept. The second approach calculates the convolution of an Gaussian operator with a Derivative operator to set up the final Gaussian derivative operator.

## 3    Test Images Used

We compare the selected methods by two examples, one using numerical data and one using experimental data: (1) the arctan function, and (2) data from computed tomography (CT):

1. Numerical data (synthetic image) is generated using the arctan function presented in Eq. 7 (see first column in Table 3).

$$f(x,y) = arctan(10x(1+y)) \qquad (7)$$

   It contains an edge of varying steepness, ideal for studying how the processing methods handle the delineation of objects [8], with thin image spacing $(0.04 \times 0.04)$ mm. The gradient and its magnitude was computed using analytic formulas for partial derivatives presented in Eq. 8 (see second column in Table 3).

$$\frac{\partial f}{\partial x} = \frac{10(1+y)}{1 + (10x + 10xy)^2}, \quad \frac{\partial f}{\partial y} = \frac{10x}{1 + (10x + 10xy)^2} \qquad (8)$$

   Furthermore, in order to observe the behavior of the differentiation methods in noisy images, Gaussian noise in the synthetic image was added. We choose a Gaussian noise with mean value zero and with a standard deviation equal to $\sigma = 0.05$, $0.1$ and $0.2$ (see last three columns in Table 3).
2. CT of head-neck, specifically, the coronal plane to identify the nasal cavity (often in respiratory airways study): the thin scroll-like structure suffers from inadequate resolution (image acquisition resolution $(0.46 \times 0.46)$ mm). The medical image is cropped to focus in detail on desired features and facilitate the results presentation (see Fig. 1).

We quantify our results using two error measures: the root mean square error (RMSE) and Nash-Sutcliffe error.

## 4    Numerical Results

In this section we present numerical results obtained by the numerical algorithms described in Sect. 2, and we make a comparison between them. These approaches

---

[1] Insight Segmentation and Registration Toolkit, http://www.itk.org/.

**Table 3.** Synthetic and noisy test images

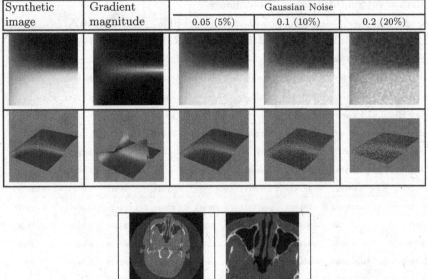

**Fig. 1.** CT test images (left: coronal plane and right: Region of Interest-ROI)

are Central Finite Differences (CFD) with window size equals to $[3 \times 3]$, $[5 \times 5]$, $[7 \times 7]$ and $[9 \times 9]$, Sobel kernel, Discrete Gaussian Derivatives (DGDO) with kernel size equals to $[3 \times 3]$, $[5 \times 5]$, $[7 \times 7]$ and $[9 \times 9]$, Recursive Gaussian Derivatives (RGIF) with sigma values equals to $\sigma = 0.01$, $0.02$ *and* $0.03$ and finally, Savitzky-Golay (SG) with window size equals to $[3 \times 3]$, $[5 \times 5]$ and $[7 \times 7]$ with order according to the window size.

In order to quantify the accuracy, we first observe results on the arctan image. For this, the different techniques to calculate the first derivatives were applied

**Table 4.** Gradient magnitude for synthetic images (best case)

**Table 5.** Derivative error

| Method | Synthetic image | | Noisy image | | | | | |
|---|---|---|---|---|---|---|---|---|
| | | | 5% | | 10% | | 20% | |
| | RMSE | Nash | RMSE | Nash | RMSE | Nash | RMSE | Nash |
| CFD [3 × 3] | 0.460953 | 0.964363 | 1.05467 | 0.792608 | 2.01243 | 0.257005 | 4.22195 | −1.14731 |
| CFD [5 × 5] | 0.42777 | 0.971107 | 1.35829 | 0.675299 | 2.71013 | −0.152187 | 5.76685 | −1.68169 |
| CFD [7 × 7] | 0.427716 | 0.971403 | 1.53389 | 0.592442 | 3.10467 | −0.392349 | 6.62379 | −1.89561 |
| CFD [9 × 9] | 0.429954 | 0.971206 | 1.64976 | 0.533261 | 3.36382 | −0.54593 | 7.18777 | −2.01212 |
| Sobel | 0.461401 | 0.964239 | **0.729335** | **0.903742** | 1.27478 | 0.687727 | 2.49112 | −0.11016 |
| DGDO [3 × 3] | 0.460954 | 0.964362 | 1.05467 | 0.792608 | 2.01242 | 0.257005 | 4.22194 | −1.14731 |
| DGDO [5 × 5] | 0.461994 | 0.964159 | 1.04952 | 0.794433 | 2.00000 | 0.264303 | 4.19371 | −1.13505 |
| DGDO [7 × 7] | 0.471546 | 0.962290 | 1.00671 | 0.809389 | 1.89529 | 0.325511 | 3.95436 | −1.02635 |
| DGDO [9 × 9] | 0.500212 | 0.956456 | 0.914832 | 0.839613 | 1.65827 | 0.45982 | 3.40103 | −0.742927 |
| RGIF-0.01 | 0.458648 | 0.964809 | 1.06671 | 0.788291 | 2.04133 | 0.239905 | 4.2875 | −1.17549 |
| RGIF-0.02 | 0.461143 | 0.964351 | 1.04706 | 0.795755 | 1.99431 | 0.269159 | 4.1814 | −1.12806 |
| RGIF-0.03 | 0.502988 | 0.955981 | 0.896721 | 0.846199 | 1.61192 | 0.488179 | 3.29395 | −0.67691 |
| SG-1-1 | 0.460953 | 0.964363 | 1.05467 | 0.792608 | 2.01243 | 0.257005 | 4.22195 | −1.14731 |
| SG-2-1 | 0.666264 | 0.915154 | 0.77940 | 0.876599 | 1.09425 | 0.739348 | 1.92484 | 0.204102 |
| SG-2-3 | 0.427769 | 0.971107 | 1.35829 | 0.675299 | 2.71014 | −0.152187 | 5.76686 | −1.68169 |
| SG-3-1 | 0.897471 | 0.823441 | 0.925962 | 0.805696 | 1.04425 | 0.73501 | 1.39764 | 0.50843 |
| SG-3-3 | 0.500062 | 0.958771 | 0.844683 | 0.871176 | 1.47820 | 0.589369 | 3.01959 | −0.45357 |
| SG-3-5 | 0.427716 | 0.971403 | 1.53389 | 0.592442 | 3.10467 | −0.392349 | 6.62379 | −1.89561 |

to noiseless and noisy images. Based on the results the gradient for each case was calculated (see the best result for each method in Table 4) and the error value according to the methods mentioned in Sect. 3 (RMSE and Nash-Sutcliffe) is shown in Table 5. This error is computed between the analytic function and discrete approximations, averaged over the entire image.

Similarly, we selected two regions in the image (column 20 (L1) and column 40 (L2)) that have smooth and strong changes in the gradient. The error was evaluated in L1 and L2, obtaining the same trend over entire image.

For the central finite difference method, we varied the width between 3 and 9. The optimal width was 7 for the original image. With noisy images, CFD results in larger fluctuations, whereas an increasing noise will not approximate the desired derivative. Finite differences show the strongest fluctuations among all considered techniques (see Table 5). In practice CFD should not be the first choice, although it showed the best results for the noiseless image.

For the Discrete Gaussian Derivatives, the window size was varied between 3 and 9. It is important to mention that to determine kernel coefficients, we seek the best gaussian function to be adjusted to the window size to reduce the approximation errors. Error values shown by DGDO technique for noiseless

**Table 6.** Techniques classification according to Nash-Sutcliffe Error

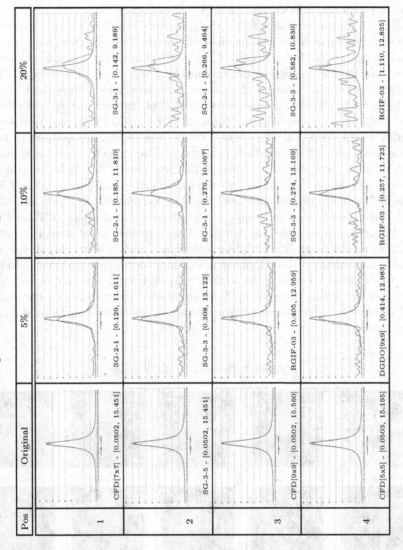

| Pos | Original | 5% | 10% | 20% |
|-----|----------|-----|------|------|
| 1 | CFD[7x7] - [0.0502, 15.451] | SG-2-1 - [0.129, 11.611] | SG-2-1 - [0.185, 11.810] | SG-3-1 - [0.142, 9.189] |
| 2 | SG-3-5 - [0.0502, 15.451] | SG-3-3 - [0.308, 13.122] | SG-3-1 - [0.276, 10.067] | SG-2-1 - [0.266, 9.464] |
| 3 | CFD[9x9] - [0.0502, 15.560] | RGIF-03 - [0.405, 12.959] | SG-3-3 - [0.274, 13.169] | SG-3-3 - [0.582, 10.830] |
| 4 | CFD[5x5] - [0.0503, 15.195] | DGDO[9x9] - [0.414, 12.983] | RGIF-03 - [0.257, 11.723] | RGIF-03 - [1.110, 12.835] |

image indicates that as the kernel size increases, the error increases. However, this behavior is opposite for noisy images (see Table 5) since the error is reduced as the window size increases.

To Recursive Gaussian Derivatives (RGIF), using the noiseless image and sigma values varying between 0.01 and 0.03, errors are increased, but are lower than the DGDO. In the case of noisy images, its accuracy is less than that achieved with the DGDO (see Table 5).

Finally, for the Savitzky– Golay (SG), we varied the window size and order to find an optimum at 3 and 5 respectively, for original image. This result is exactly equal to the result obtained using CFD (see Table 5). For a larger window, SG filter smooths the image too much, and the result tends to a constant. For a smaller window the influence of noise becomes locally more important.

In summary, Table 6 shows the profile (L2) of different images (noiseless and noisy) obtained by the 4 best techniques (CFD, SG, RGIF and DGDO) and conditions for each. For the original image, the results are quite close to the theoretical value of the gradient magnitude. The expected maximum value is 16.0, resulting in a loss of precision in the best case of 3.43 % for central finite difference technique and 5.03 % for Savitzky-Golay with window size of 5 and order 3. For noisy images, the loss of precision varies between 13.8 % and 42.5 %.

Using these results, we compute derivatives for real image (CT) and some results are shown in Table 7. A visual analysis presents a great similarity between obtained results using differentiation techniques considered in this paper. For this reason, an analysis of the CT image profile in a specific row was made. To select the row of interest, a scan of the original image was made and row 84 was chosen. This row was selected because it has important features such as: low contrast and thin tissue, which are crucial in derivatives estimation and in nasal cavity segmentation.

**Table 7.** Derivatives of CT image

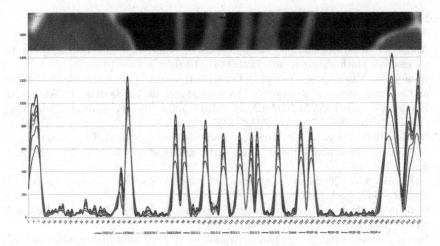

**Fig. 2.** Gradient magnitude profile of CT image

Figure 2 shows the result for the different techniques of differentiation, in which the same trend that for the original arctan image is observed. This implies that the best results are obtained using CDF [7 × 7] and SG-3-5. The errors varies between 5.6 % and 32 %, representing a loss of accuracy between 64 and 374 points in the gradient magnitude with respect to the value obtained using the above techniques.

## 5   Conclusions

We presented a quantitative comparison of methods for the numerical estimation of derivatives. To compare the methods, the dependence on parameters has been investigated and optimal parameters were determined in an experimental way. The noise dependence has been studied and we found some similarities in the methods, for example, the results obtained with CFD (width of 7) are the same than using SG (width of 7 and order 5) in original image and in CT image. In the same way, use central differences with width 5 is equal to use Savitzky-Golay with width 5 and order 3. In general, we found that polynomial interpolation approach (Savitzky-Golay) for computing the spatial derivatives gives more accurate results when compared with existing popular methods. An important benefit of using the SG approach is the possibility of maintaining high accuracy for a small computational mask size (5 or 7). This can mean that the use of SG approach to calculate derivatives by itself improves the quality of results for current image processing methods.

# References

1. Anderssen, R.S., Hegland, M.: For numerical differentiation, dimensionality can be a blessing!. Math. Comput. **68**, 1121–1141 (1999)
2. Bouma, H., Vilanova, A., Bescós, J.O., Haar Romeny, B.M., Gerritsen, F.A.: Fast and accurate gaussian derivatives based on B-splines. In: Sgallari, F., Murli, A., Paragios, N. (eds.) SSVM 2007. LNCS, vol. 4485, pp. 406–417. Springer, Heidelberg (2007). doi:10.1007/978-3-540-72823-8_35
3. Burden, R.L., Faires, J.D.: Numerical Analysis. Brooks Colem, USA (2011)
4. Cullum, J.: Numerical differentiation and regularization. SIAM J. Numer. Anal. **8**, 254–265 (1971)
5. Dahlquist, G., Björck, Å.: Numerical Methodsin Scientific Computing, vol. I. Prentice-Hall, USA (2007)
6. Deriche, R.: Recursively implementating the gaussian and its derivatives. Research report 1893, INRIA, France (1993)
7. Farid, H., Simoncelli, E.P.: Differentiation of discrete multidimensional signals. IEEE Trans. Image Process. **13**, 496–508 (2004)
8. Gambaruto, A.M.: Processing the image gradient field using a topographic primal sketch approach. Int. J. Numer. Methods Biomed. Eng. **28**, 72–86 (2015)
9. Gerald, C.F., Wheatley, P.O.: Applied Numerical Analysis. Pearson, USA (2004)
10. Getreuer, P.: A survey of gaussian convolution algorithms. Image Process. Line **3**, 276–300 (2013)
11. Griewank, A., Walther, A.: Evaluating derivatives: principles and techniques of algorithmic differentiation. Society for Industrial and Applied Mathematics, Philadelphia (2008)
12. Hamming, R.W.: Numerical Methods for Scientists and Engineers. Dover Publications Inc., New York (1986)
13. Jauberteau, F., Jauberteau, J.L.: Numerical differentiation with noisy signal. Appl. Math. Comput. **215**, 2283–2297 (2009)
14. Jin, J.S., Gao, Y.: Recursive implementation of LoG filtering. Real-Time Imaging **3**, 59–65 (1997)
15. Khan, I.R., Ohba, R., Hozumi, N.: Mathematical proof of closed form expressions for finite difference approximations based on Taylor series. J. Comput. Appl. Math. **150**, 303–309 (2003)
16. Khan, I.R., Ohba, R.: Closed-form expressions for the finite difference approximations of first and higher derivatives based on Taylor series. J. Comput. Appl. Math. **107**, 179–193 (1999)
17. Khan, I.R., Ohba, R.: Digital differentiators based on Taylor series. IEICE Trans. Fundam. Electron. Commun. Comput. Sci. **E82–A**, 2822–2824 (1999)
18. Khan, I.R., Ohba, R.: Taylor series based finite difference approximations of higher-degree derivatives. J. Comput. Appl. Math. **154**, 115–124 (2003)
19. Knowles, I., Wallace, R.: A variational method for numerical differentiation. Numer. Math. **70**, 91–111 (1995)
20. Krueger, W.M., Phillips, K.: The geometry of differential operators with application to image processing. IEEE Trans. Pattern Anal. Mach. Intell. **11**, 1252–1264 (1989)
21. Li, J.: General explicit difference formulas for numerical differentiation. J. Comput. Appl. Math. **183**, 29–52 (2005)
22. Lindeberg, T.: Scale-space: a framework for handling image structures at multiple scales. Cern Eur. Organ. Nucl. Res. **96**, 1–12 (1996)

23. Lu, S., Pereverzev, S.V.: Numerical differentiation from a viewpoint of regularization theory. Math. Comput. **75**, 1853–1870 (2006)
24. Luo, J., Ying, K., He, P., Bai, J.: Properties of Savitzky-Golay digital differentiators. Digit. Signal Process. A Rev. J. **15**, 122–136 (2005)
25. Luo, J., Ying, K., Bai, J.: Savitzky-Golay smoothing and differentiation filter for even number data. Signal Process. **85**, 1429–1434 (2005)
26. Macia, I.: Generalized computation of gaussian derivatives using ITK. Insight J. 1–14 (2007)
27. Poggio, T., Koch, C.: Ill-Posed problems in early vision: from computational theory to analogue networks. In: Proceedings of the Royal Society of London. Series B, Biological Sciences, pp. 303–323 (1985)
28. Press, W., Teukolsky, S., Vetterling, W., Flannery, B.: Numerical Recipesin C: The Art of Scientific Computing. Cambridge University Press, Cambridge (2002)
29. Ramm, A.G., Smirnova, A.B.: On stable numerical differentiation. Math. Comput. **70**, 1131–1153 (2001)
30. Silvester, P.: Numerical formation of finite-difference operators. IEEE Trans. Microwave Theory Tech. **18**, 740–743 (1970)
31. Spontón, H., Cardelino, J.: A review of classic edge detectors. Image Process. Line. **5**, 90–123 (2015)
32. ter Haar Romeny, B.M., Florack, L.M.J.: Front end vision: a multiscale geometry engine. In: Lee, S.-W., Bülthoff, H.H., Poggio, T. (eds.) BMCV 2000. LNCS, vol. 1811, pp. 297–307. Springer, Heidelberg (2000)
33. Unser, M.: Splines: a perfect fit for medical imaging. Med. Imaging Process. Proc. Spie. **4684**, 225–236 (2002)
34. Unser, M.: Splines: a perfect fit for signal and image processing. IEEE Signal Process. Mag. **16**, 22–38 (1999)
35. van Vliet, L.J., Young, I.T., Verbeek, P.W.: Recursive gaussian derivative filters. In: Proceedings of Fourteenth International Conference Pattern Recognition, pp. 509–514 (1998)

# Linear Spectral Mixture Analysis
# of Hyperspectral Images
# with Atmospheric Distortions

Anna Denisova[✉], Yuliya Juravel, and Vladislav Myasnikov

Samara National Research University,
34 Moskovskoe Shosse, Samara 443086, Russian Federation
{denisova_ay,vmyas}@geosamara.ru, julita66@mail.ru
http://ssau.ru

**Abstract.** In this paper a novel method of linear spectral mixture parameters estimation for hyperspectral images is proposed. This method
allows to omit preliminary atmospheric correction of input image. To provide a solution to mixture problem different models of radiation transmission in atmosphere are considered. An evaluation of effect of noise, number
of input pixels and number of signatories on accuracy of restored linear
mixture coefficients and input pixel representation error is provided.

**Keywords:** Hyperspectral images · Linear spectral mixture analysis ·
Atmospheric correction

## 1 Introduction

Hyperspectral images, acquired by space and aviation remote sensing systems,
contain significant amount of information about physical and chemical properties of the underlying objects and can be widely used for various applications. In
contrast to the laboratory and ground measurements, spectra of different materials jointly compose resulting hyperspectral image pixel because of finite spatial
resolution of space and aerial images. The fractions of constituent spectra correspond to abundances of materials. To provide subpixel analysis of hyperspectral
data mixing process should be reconstructed.

The atmosphere influences significantly to reflected light, which leads to con-
founding of pixel values. Usually atmospheric effects are removed during preprocessing step referred to as atmospheric correction (AC). AC requires information about quantitative and qualitative spatial distribution of gases and aerosols
at the moment of observation. But it is impossible to measure atmospheric parameters for each image directly. For this purpose several models of radiation
transmission in optical spectral band has been developed [1–3]. These models
have been implemented in commercial software products such as MODTRAN,
FLAASH, ATCOR and etc. However, consumers of remote sensing data often
face the problem of absence of necessary initial data such as weather conditions
or observation parameters (azimuth, line-of-sight distance and etc.)

© Springer International Publishing AG 2016
L.J. Chmielewski et al. (Eds.): ICCVG 2016, LNCS 9972, pp. 134–141, 2016.
DOI: 10.1007/978-3-319-46418-3_12

In this paper the methods of spectral mixture parameters estimation for hyperspectral images without atmospheric correction are introduced. Proposed methods do not require special software for modeling atmospheric effects and can be applied to images directly.

The paper is structured as follows. The first section includes unmixing problem statement and describes models of atmospheric distortion in common use. In the second section the solution to unmixing problem is suggested. The next section contains the results of experimental research. At the end of the work there are conclusions about proposed algorithms.

## 2    Related Works

There are two common approaches to spectral mixture modeling. First of them is a linear spectral mixture model (LSMM) [4] in which hyperspectral pixel is presented as linear combination of spectral signatories corresponding to spectra of particular materials. In the second one, intimate spectral mixture model, pixel is assumed to be a nonlinear combination of spectral signatories. This model can be linearized and methods of linear spectral mixture analysis (LSMA) can be applied to it.

A detailed classification of LSMA methods is given in monograph of Chein-I. Chang [4]. According it all methods are classified as supervised (SLSMA) and unsupervised (ULSMA) methods. In SLSMA methods, signatories are supposed to be known and a predefined list of signatories is used. ULSMA methods allow to obtain endmember spectra from input pixels and then SLSMA algorithms can be applied. According to another classification [5] linear spectral unmixing methods are grouped by optimization criterion (quadratic or another one) and by coefficients constraints.

Among commonly used linear spectral unmixing methods nonstatistical methods with quadratic optimization criteria should be specially mentioned. These methods differs from each other in statement of spectral mixture problem depending on various constraints on coefficients. The first group of methods does not incorporate any constraints, e.g., orthogonal subspace projection (OSP) and least square projection classifier [4]. The second group includes methods with partially constrained least square optimization, e.g., sum-to-one constrained linear square (SCLS) and nonnegativity constrained linear square (NCLS) [5]. The third group takes into account both constraints simultaneously and they are called fully constrained linear square (FCLS) methods [6]. Type of constraints defines computational complexity of the algorithms and implies diverse interpretation of results.

Methods proposed in this paper methods combine the model of atmospheric effects for each image component and LSMM with fully constraints for a particular pixel into one complex observation model. To obtain spectral mixture coefficients least square problem is solved. Models and approaches analyzed in this article show the possibility of linear unmixing in case of atmospheric distortions to the image. Coefficients of AC can be obtained as optional product of the same unmixing process.

## 3  Problem Statement

LSMM assumes that each image pixel is a linear combination of several spectral signatories $\{\bar{s}_l\}_{l=0}^{L-1}$, where $\bar{s}_l = \left(s_{l0}, s_{l1}, \ldots, s_{l(J-1)}\right)^T$ and $J$ is a number of spectral components of image (dimension of signatory vector). It is expressed as:

$$\bar{v} = \sum_{l=0}^{L-1} \alpha_l \bar{s}_l, \alpha_l \geq 0, \sum_{l=0}^{L-1} \alpha_l = 1. \tag{1}$$

where $\alpha_l$ represents the coefficients of the model. Standard expression of spectral radiance for the top layers of atmosphere for Lambert surface is written as [7]:

$$L = \frac{A\rho}{1 - \tilde{\rho}S} + \frac{B\tilde{\rho}}{1 - \tilde{\rho}S} + C, \tag{2}$$

where $\rho$ is the reflectance coefficient for projection of pixel to the ground, $\tilde{\rho}$ is the average reflectance coefficient for projection of pixel to the ground and its neighborhood, $S$ is spectral albedo of the atmosphere, $C$ is the radiance of cloud, $A$ and $B$ are the coefficients depending on the state of the atmosphere and on geometrical parameters of observation and independent from properties of underling surface.

In our notation an expression for spectral radiance for j component takes the form:

$$x_j(n) = \frac{A_j v_j(n)}{1 - S_j \tilde{v}_j(n)} + \frac{B \tilde{v}_j(n)}{1 - S_j \tilde{v}_j(n)} + C_j, \tag{3}$$

where $\tilde{v}_j(n)$ is a function of undistorted neighbor pixels $v_j(n+m)$, $-M \leq m \leq M$.

In this study four models are considered, that are obtained from Eq. (3) by different assumptions. Model 1 corresponds to $S_j = B_j = C_j = 0$. Model 2 is formulated in case of $B_j = S_j = 0$ and $\tilde{v}_j(n) = const$. Model 3 is used in case of $S_j = 0$. And the last Model 4 is a general model expressed as (3).

Unmixing problem in presence of atmospheric effects implies restoring unknown coefficients of spectral mixture $\alpha_l(n), 0 \leq l \leq L-1, 0 \leq n \leq N-1$ and unknown coefficients of atmospheric correction $A_j, B_j, C_j, S_j$ in accordance with accepted suppositions for each particular model. Mixture coefficients must be subject to constraints from (1). The initial set of signatories is supposed to be known.

## 4  Proposed Solutions

In this section an examples of typical solutions to unmixing problem in each particular case are given. For Model 1 an approach based on standard methods of quadratic programming is proposed. The other three models can be evaluated by means of gradient algorithm. A detailed description and experimental results of gradient method is provided only for model 2 due to page limit. Solutions to other models can be obtained similarly.

## 4.1   Solution to Model 1

In order to construct a system of linear equations, normalized observed pixels $y_j(n) = x_j(n)/\tilde{x}_j$ are used, where $\tilde{x}_j$ is an average value for the image component j. Evaluation of coefficients is provided by solving the system of linear equations

$$\begin{cases} \sum_{m=0}^{N-1} \sum_{l=0}^{L-1} \alpha_l(m) z_{lj}^{mn} = 0, 0 \leq n \leq N-1, 0 \leq j \leq J-1; \\ \sum_{l=0}^{L-1} \alpha_l(n) = 1, \alpha_l(n) \geq 0. \end{cases} \quad (4)$$

where coefficients of the system are

$$z_{lj}^{mn} = \begin{cases} \frac{1}{N} s_{lj} y_j(n), m \neq n, \\ s_{lj}\left(\frac{y_j(n)}{N} - 1\right), m = n, \end{cases} \quad 0 \leq l \leq, 0 \leq j \leq J-1. \quad (5)$$

It is impossible to find a precise solution to (4) under constraints. Therefore instead of system (4) it is offered to find a solution to the optimization task (6), which can be done with the help of standard methods of quadratic programming:

$$\begin{cases} \left(\sum_{m=0}^{N-1} \sum_{l=0}^{L-1} \alpha_l(m) z_{lj}^{mn}\right)^2 \to min_{\alpha_l(m)}; \\ \sum_{l=0}^{L-1} \alpha_l(n) = 1, \alpha_l(n) \geq 0. \end{cases} \quad (6)$$

## 4.2   Solution to Model 2–4

Solutions to the unmixing problem for the rest models can be found as a result of minimization of square error of observed pixels $x_j(n)$ and pixels $\hat{x}_j(n)$ reconstructed by Eqs. (3) and (1):

$$\varepsilon^2 = \sum_{n=0}^{N-1} \sum_{j=0}^{J-1} (x_j(n) - \hat{x}_j(n))^2 \to min_{A_j, B_j, C_j, S_j, \alpha_l(n)}, \quad (7)$$

$$\alpha_l(n) \geq 0, 0 \leq n \leq N-1, 0 \leq l \leq L-1. \quad (8)$$

To include sum-to-one constraint into task (7) the substitution $\alpha_0(n) = 1 - \sum_{l=0}^{L-1} \alpha_l(n)$ is used. Gradient method is proposed to solve the problem (7) and to find the coefficients, because it cannot be solved in the same way as in case of Model 1.

A general form of the gradient algorithm is written as follows:

1. Initialize vectors of unknown coefficients: $\alpha_t(n), A_j, Bj, C_j, S_j$.
2. On every iteration do:
   (a) Calculate the derivatives of optimization criteria by unknown coefficients.
   (b) Change values of coefficients using expressions below
       $\alpha_t(n) \leftarrow \alpha_t(n) + \psi \frac{\partial \varepsilon^2}{\partial \alpha_t(n)}, Q_j \leftarrow Q_j + \psi \frac{\partial \varepsilon^2}{\partial Q_j}, Q_j \in \{A_j, B_j, C_j, S_j\}$.
   (c) Check constraints for $\alpha_t(n)$ and correct values if coefficients do not comply with the conditions.

(d) Calculate current estimations for $\hat{x}_j(n)$ and $\hat{v}_j(n)$ using expressions (3) and (1) respectively.

(e) Calculate current value of criteria (7).

(f) Check stop condition.

For every particular model 2–4 described above the algorithm is the same. All we should do is to calculate appropriate derivatives for every model. Parameter $\psi$ defines a step of gradient optimization process and regulates the speed and accuracy of the solution.

## 5    Experimental Research

### 5.1    Description of Input Data and Experiments

Experimental research was implemented in MATLAB for simulated hyperspectral data samples. To create a sample set of $N$ pixels with $J$ components, a number of random spectral signatories and coefficients were used. $L$ is the total amount of signatories used in the experiment. The number of unknown mixture coefficients equals to $N \times L$. All pixels were synthesized according to the linear mixture model (1).

Coefficients, describing atmospheric effects, were also generated as random numbers: $A_j, B_j, S_j \in [0,1]$, $C_j > 0$, $0 \le j \le J - 1$. Distorted pixels were modeled according to a particular model and represented input data for the experiments. For models 3 and 4 weight average of pixels were used as a value of $\tilde{v}_j(n) = \sum_{m=-M}^{M} \rho_m^n v_j(n+m)$, $\rho_m^n = \frac{1}{3}, \forall n$, $m = -1, 0, 1$.

In order to estimate accuracy of the derived solution root mean square errors for coefficients and image pixels were used

$$
\begin{aligned}
\varepsilon_\alpha &= \sqrt{\frac{1}{NL} \sum_{n=0}^{N-1} \sum_{l=0}^{L-1} \left(\alpha_l(n) - \hat{\alpha}_l(n)\right)^2}, \\
\varepsilon_{X_i} &= \sqrt{\frac{1}{NJ} \sum_{n=0}^{N-1} \sum_{j=0}^{J-1} \left(x_j(n) - \hat{x}_j(n)\right)^2}, \quad i = 1, 2, 3,
\end{aligned}
\tag{9}
$$

where $\hat{\alpha}$ is a solution to the unmixing problem, $x(n)$ is observed pixel and pixel $\hat{x}(n)$ is modeled with restored coefficients, $i$ is a number of model.

Number of pixels used in experiments was chosen to evaluate coefficients quickly enough. Every experiment was made $K$ times and all results illustrate average values of chosen quality measures. In case of model 2–4 100000 iterations with step $\psi = 0.0001$ were used to obtain the results for gradient methods.

The aim of experiments was to determine the influence of noise, number of input pixels $N$ and degree of signatories list overdetermination on restoring spectral unmixing coefficients error and pixel representation error. Because of the lack of space experimental results are presented only for Model 1 and Model 2 as an example of gradient approach to the solution. Model 3 and Model 4 have shown behavior similar to Model 2 and will be presented in the report.

## 5.2    Experimental Results

In experiments with noise data additive independent white gauss noise with given signal to noise ratio (SNR) was used. The results of experiments are shown in Fig. 1. As it can be seen from charts, proposed methods provide high quality of solution if SNR is more than 15. Hyperspectral images [8] actually have SNR values higher than 15. This means that proposed method can be successfully applied to real data. So it can be concluded that described methods are noise stable with quadratic programming allowing for providing a more precise coefficients evaluation. It is seen that $\varepsilon_{X2}$ continues to fall down even when $\varepsilon_{\alpha}$ achieves stable value. It means that further increase of accuracy deals with the decrease of restoration error of atmospheric model coefficients.

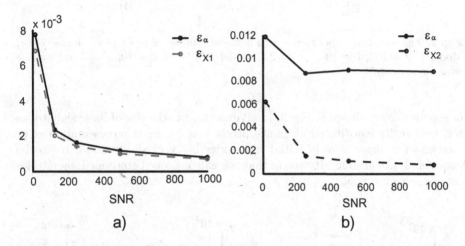

**Fig. 1.** The results of experiments with different SNR in case of (a) Model 1 ($J = 100$, $L = 10$, $K = 5$) (b) Model 2 ($J = 50$, $L = 10$, $K = 5$)

The results of experiment with different number of pixels are presented in Fig. 2. There was no noise on input images in this experiment. In both cases errors can be regarded as constant. This experiment shows that input data can be divided into several blocks each being evaluated independently. Thus, the algorithms proposed can be easily parallelized.

To investigate the impact of predefined signatories set size, input pixels were generated with $L$ basic signatories. The parameters estimation was performed for a lager set of signatories, that included all signatories from basic set and some extra random signatories. The size of signatories list, used for coefficients evaluation, is denoted $Lbig$. Coefficients of extra signatories in final results must be equal to zero. This experiment shows a possibility to use entire spectral libraries to unmix hyperspectral data. The results of experiment with different number

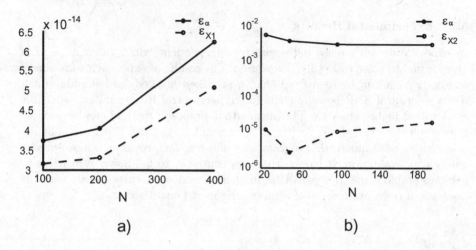

a)                                    b)

**Fig. 2.** The results of experiments with different number of input pixels in case of (a) Model 1 ($J = 100$, $L = 10$, $K = 5$), (b) Model 2 ($J = 50$, $L = 10$, $K = 5$ (log scale is used for ordinate))

of signatories are shown in Fig. 3. In all experiments the size of basic signatories set, that really constituted all image pixels, was 10. Pixel representation error increases for larger sizes of initial signatories list very slowly and can also be considered as constant. It means that we can use overdetermined signatories lists to solve the task.

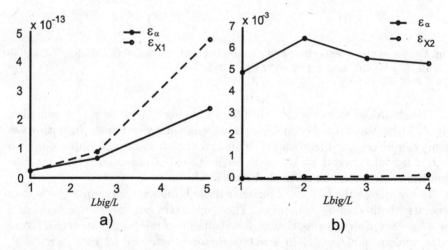

a)                                    b)

**Fig. 3.** The results of experiments with different number of input signatories in case of (a) Model 1 ($J = 100$, $N = 100$, $K = 5$), (b) Model 2 ($J = 50$, $N = 50$, $K = 5$)

# 6    Conclusion

In this article linear spectral unmixing tasks were considered for hyperspectral images without atmospheric correction. Three observation models were described and methods of their parameters estimation were proposed. Experimental research showed that coefficients of linear spectral mixture can be retrieved for a little portion of observed pixels independently. Proposed methods performs well for noised images, when SNR is more than 15, and provide accurate results in case of overdetermined list of signatories.

This study aims to show possibility of solving linear unmixing task without atmospheric correction. Questions of computational effective realizations are left for future work.

**Acknowledgements.** This work was financially supported by the Russian Science Foundation (RSF), grant no. 14-31-00014 Establishment of a Laboratory of Advanced Technology for Earth Remote Sensing.

# References

1. Matthew, M.V., Adler-Golden, S.M., Berk, A., Felde, G., Anderson, G.P., Gorodetzky, D., Paswaters, S., Shippert, M.: Atmospheric correction of spectral imagery: evaluation of the FLAASH algorithm with AVIRIS data. In: Applied Imagery Pattern Recognition Workshop, 2002, AIPR, 31 February 2002, pp. 157–163. IEEE (2002)

2. Kruse, F.A.: Comparison of ATREM, ACORN, and FLAASH atmospheric corrections using low-altitude AVIRIS data of Boulder, CO. In: Summaries of 13th JPL Airborne Geoscience Workshop, Jet Propulsion Lab, Pasadena, CA (2004)

3. Belov, A.M., Myasnikov, V.V.: Atmospheric correction of hyperspectral images based on approximate solution of transmittance equation. In: 7th International Conference on Machine Vision (ICMV 2014), pp. 94450S–94450S5. International Society for Optics and Photonics (2015)

4. Chang, C.I.: Hyperspectral Data Processing: Algorithm Design and Analysis. Wiley, Hoboken (2013)

5. Keshara, N.A.: Survey of spectral unmixing algorithms. Lincoln Lab. J. **14**(1), 55–78 (2003)

6. Denisova, A., Myasnikov, V.: Fully constrained linear spectral unmixing algorithm for hyperspectral image analysis. Comput. Opt. **38**(4), 782–789 (2014)

7. Yuanliu, X., Runsheng, W., Shengwei, L., Suming, Y., Bokun, Y.: Atmospheric correction of hyperspectral data using MODTRAN model. Proc. SPIE Int. Soc. Opt. Eng. **7123**, 7123061–7123067 (2003)

8. Kruse, F.A., Boardman, J.W., Huntington, J.F.: Comparison of airborne hyperspectral data and EO-1 Hyperion for mineral mapping. IEEE Trans. Geosci. Remote Sens. **41**(6), 1388–1400 (2003)

# Simple and Efficient Method of Low-Contrast Grayscale Image Binarization

Kamil Ekštein[(✉)]

Department of Computer Science and Engineering, Faculty of Applied Sciences,
University of West Bohemia, Pilsen, Czech Republic
kekstein@kiv.zcu.cz

**Abstract.** This paper describes a simple analytic method for determining an optimal threshold position during low-contrast grayscale image binarization. The described method uses no tunable or user-set parameters and is invariant to both image size and pixel intensity value range. It uses both the pixel intensity histogram of the analysed image and its first-order derivative to estimate the threshold position. There is an assumption that the histogram is bimodal by its nature, however, the method can cope with the histograms where the peaks are very close or even overlapping due to low contrast. The method performance is comparable with the traditionally used Otsu's method [1] on unproblematic images, however, it significantly outperforms Otsu's on specific images, like e.g. electron microscopy of composite material fibres or x-ray mammography, where the bimodal histogram is almost (but not entirely) collapsed into unimodal.

**Keywords:** Low-contrast image segmentation · Binarization · Thresholding · Threshold estimation

## 1 Introduction

One of the most crucial operations in the process of image analysis is to separate the objects of further interest from the background. There has been developed a large number of methods to achive this, i.e. to *binarize* the input image, or to *classify its pixels into two classes*: OBJECT and BACKGROUND, or—in the simplest words—to "repaint" the pixels so that the white (value 1) pixels pertain to objects of interest and the black ones (value 0) to background.

This work was motivated by the need of researchers in material engineering: They wanted to count carbon fibres on photographs of orthogonal cuts of a composite material obtained from an electron microscope (see an example on Fig. 1) and compute the ratio between the área occupied by the fibres and the area filled with the resin (matrix). Unfortunately, the Otsu's method—as implemented e.g. in MATLAB's function graythresh(·) which was used by the material engineers—failed completely on most of these images. Figure 3 shows the estimated threshold position (red dotted line): It is clear that such threshold position leads to an unusable, all-white binary image (see Fig. 2(c)).

© Springer International Publishing AG 2016
L.J. Chmielewski et al. (Eds.): ICCVG 2016, LNCS 9972, pp. 142–150, 2016.
DOI: 10.1007/978-3-319-46418-3_13

Thus, an effort was made to develop a threshold estimation method that would be robust enough to find a usable threshold position even on images with such intensity histograms where there is bimodality present, however, the "valley" between the two peaks (classes) is very narrow or nearly dissolved in the (almost) overlapping peaks.

The methods based upon investigations of statistical properties of histograms may easily lead towards inaccurate threshold settings when assumptions are not met as hinted in [2]. Therefore, focus was put on developing a purely analytical approach with the goal to find a local minimum in the histogram in such position that it corresponds to the actual boundary between the background and the object class projection.

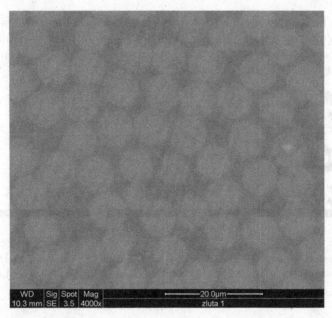

**Fig. 1.** Typical problematic low-contrast image: Electron microscopy image of a composite material section with fibres (circular objects) and matrix. *Image courtesy of Dept. of Mechanics, Faculty of Applied Science, University of West Bohemia.*

## 1.1 Current State-of-the-art in Image Binarization

Over the years, the Otsu's method [1] published in 1979, became a de facto standard in many computer vision applications. In majority of cases, it provides the most satisfactory results and is implemented in many widely used computer vision packages (like e.g. OpenCV, MATLAB Image Processing Toolbox, etc.). However, it calculates the optimal threshold position by maximizing the inter-class variance of the two classes. Thus, it fails in such cases where the intra-class variances of the object and background pixel intensities are larger than the inter-class variance.

However, the Otsu's method is—due to its statistical preconditions—highly sensitive to situations when the pixels do not form disjoint sets. Thus, few adaptive methods have been developed to cope with such situations. Among them, the AdOtsu [3] method—an adaptive parameterless evolution of the original idea— stands out with its performance and ability to estimate not only the threshold position but also some other features useful for further image processing. Nonetheless, it is less general than its spiritual ancestor and designed to perform best in the OCR task of separating text characters from a document background.

Alongside, there exist a number of complex binarization techniques targeting specific input images (e.g. historic manuscripts, etc.) such as Sauvola's method [5] and Lu's method [6]. These techniques gain accuracy of over 90 % on these specific tasks.

Another interesting method that performs well is the integral image adaptive thresholding method by Bradley and Roth [4] which has used the integral image approach for the first time in the binarization task and is general enough (therefore, it was chosen for comparison, see 3).

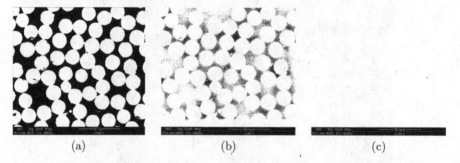

(a)                          (b)                          (c)

**Fig. 2.** The results of processing of the input image from Fig. 1 as binarized by (a) the described method, (b) the Bradley's and Roth's integral image adaptive thresholding method, and (c) the Otsu's method.

## 2    Thresholding Method Description

The following section describes step-by-step the proposed analytic method. Generally, it consists of the image preprocessing stage (accomplished by common techniques) and the innovative threshold estimation stage.

### 2.1    Image Preprocessing

Before computing the threshold estimate, it is advisable to *reduce the image noise*. It does not actually matter which de-noising procedure is used, however, "less precise" methods are favoured like e.g. plain averaging or median filtering. It ensures that the pixel intensity histogram of the input image is clear of disproportionate step changes and is generally smoother. This smoothness allows easy and precise numeric differentiation needed during the further processing.

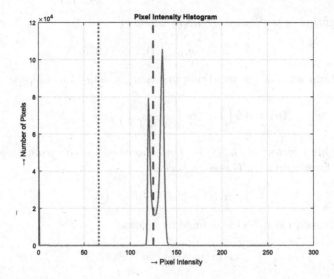

**Fig. 3.** Comparison of binarization threshold estimates (by Otsu—red dotted line, by the described method—green dashed line). The depicted histogram (blue curve) belongs to the image from Fig. 1. (Color figure online)

Thus, the whole processed image is filtered by a convolutional *median filter*:

$$f(x, y) = T_{Med}\big(f_{inp}(x, y), w\big), \tag{1}$$

where $f_{inp}(x, y)$ is the input digital image function of pixel intensities (grayscale) and $T_{Med}$ is a non-linear function performing median filtering over a $w \times w$ neighbourhood. Median filtering over a 0.33 %-neighbourhood[1] was tested and proven suitable during the experiments.

## 2.2   Threshold Position Estimation

**Histogram Preprocessing** — At first, a histogram of pixel intensities $h(i)$, $i \in \langle 0, M \rangle$ is computed. The histogram resolution does not play an important role as long as it is reasonably fine. In the experiments, the traditional 8-bit grayscale depth was used, and thus the histogram had 256 discrete values, $i \in \langle 0, 255 \rangle$, $M = 255$.

Usually, it is convenient to apply weighting on the obtained histogram before further processing as it might contain rather extreme values at both ends, i.e. both very low and very high intensities are extensively present in the image (mostly due to the black-and-white state information added e.g. by the electron microscope or the mammogram-processing software).

---

[1] Rounded 0.33 % of the input image width was taken as the width $w$ of the reference pixel neighbourhood, i.e. as the size of the convolution filter kernel. For majority of the testing images, this resulted in a 3-pixel neighbourhood.

The weighting is performed by *Hann window*:

$$h_w(i) = h(i) \cdot w_{Hann}(i), i \in \langle 0, 255 \rangle, \tag{2}$$

where the Hann window (or weighting function) is defined as follows:

$$w_{Hann}(n) = 0.5 \left( 1 - \cos \left( \frac{2\pi n}{N-1} \right) \right), n \in \langle 0, N-1 \rangle. \tag{3}$$

The weighted histogram $h_w(i)$ is then smoothed by *Gaussian smoothing*, a convolution filtering with a Gaussian kernel:

$$h_s(i) = (h_w * G)(i), \tag{4}$$

where the Gaussian kernel $G$ is defined as follows:

$$G(x) = \frac{1}{\sqrt{2\pi}\sigma} \cdot e^{-\frac{x^2}{2\sigma^2}}. \tag{5}$$

The neighbourhood used for the numerical (i.e. "finite") convolution is odd ceiling of 2.5 % of the whole histogram length, thus, for the 256-bin histogram 7 neighbouring values are used. The value of variance $\sigma$ is set to 1.

**Histogram Processing** — The weighted smoothed histogram $h_s(i)$ is numerically differentiated in order to get an estimate of the first-order derivative with respect to $i$: $h'_s(i)$. The derivative is smoothed by Gaussian smoothing with the same parameters as above.

In the next step, the histogram derivative $h'_s(i)$ is *gated*, i.e. a gating function $g(x)$ is applied:

$$h'_g(i) = g\left(h'_s(i)\right), \tag{6}$$

where the gating function is defined as follows:

$$g(x) = \begin{cases} 0 : x < \varepsilon \\ x : x \geq \varepsilon, \end{cases} \tag{7}$$

the value of $\varepsilon$ used for gating is 2.5 % of the gated function maximum (i.e. of the maximum value of the histogram derivative, $h'_s(i)$).

**Threshold Estimation** — A list of threshold position candidates $i$ is assembled by putting $h'_g(i) = 0$, see Fig. 4. As the function $h'_g(i)$ is practically discrete, a non-trivial *zero-crossing detection* algorithm must be applied. The positions where the derivative $h'_g(i)$ leaves off the zero value (the leftmost and the rightmost, marked with green ray-decorated dots in Fig. 4) are also put into the candidate list. The candidate list is then sorted by position (i.e. intensity value) in ascending order.

Depending on the character of the input image, the candidate list should have at least 3 items—it indicates a unimodal histogram—and optimally 5 items (although under real conditions, it has usually more than 5 and the algorithm is robust to such case). One of the candidate items is always equal to the position of the global maximum value in the histogram $h_s(i)$. Then, the **threshold position is set to the next immediately neighbouring candidate** in the direction towards the side where there are more remaining candidates (in the case that there are 5 or more candidates in the list).

If there are only 3 candidates, the histogram is purely unimodal (or the bimodality traits are way below the smoothing and gating resolution) and the middle candidate corresponds to the global histogram maximum. In such case, an extra computation must be performed: There are two marginal regions of the histogram where the gated derivative is equal to zero. By numerical integration of these regions two marginal weights are obtained:

$$w_L = \int_0^a h(i)\mathrm{d}i, \;\; w_R = \int_b^M h(i)\mathrm{d}i, \tag{8}$$

where for the integration bounds, $a$ and $b$, hold that:

$$a = \max \left\{ i \in \langle 0, M \rangle : h'_g(i) = 0 \wedge \forall k \in \langle 0, a) : h'_g(k) = 0 \right\}, \tag{9}$$

$$b = \min \left\{ i \in \langle 0, M \rangle : h'_g(i) = 0 \wedge \forall k \in (b, M] : h'_g(k) = 0 \right\}. \tag{10}$$

These values, $a$ and $b$, correspond to the positions of the leftmost and the rightmost candidate as depicted in Fig. 4, respectively.

The threshold position is then set to the candidate **not equal** to the maximum position, i.e. to the leftmost or the rightmost candidate according to which marginal weight is higher, whether the left $w_L$ or the right $w_R$.

## 3   Results and Performance Analysis

The method performance[2] was evaluated using two sets of images: (i) **electron microscopy** images of composite material cuts—83 grayscale images, 1024×943 px, 8 bpp; and (ii) **x-ray mammography** images—100 grayscale images, 2184×4840 px, 8 bpp.

The method was compared with (i) the MATLAB implementation of the **Otsu's method** (function graythresh( · )) and (ii) the OpenCV-based implementation of the **integral image adaptive thresholding** by Bradley and Roth [4]. The results obtained using an Intel® Core™ i7 workstation[3] are summarised in Table 1 below.

A fair direct comparison with the recently introduced **AdOtsu** method [3] was not feasible as the MATLAB implementation of the AdOtsu needed 812.38 s (over 12 min) to binarize one 1024×943 image on the testing workstation.

---

[2] The described method was implemented in Free Pascal using the in-house image processing library IASON.

[3] The testing workstation configuration was: Intel® Core™ i7-4790S 3.2 GHz 4-core CPU, 8 GB RAM, no GPU acceleration used.

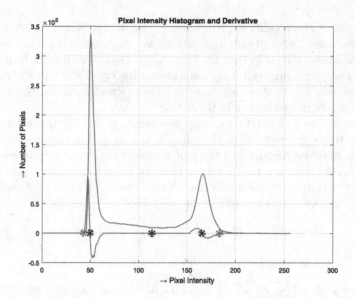

**Fig. 4.** Smoothed pixel intensity histogram (blue) and its gated first-order derivative (red) corresponding to the x-ray mammography image from Fig. 5 (a). The detected threshold candidates are marked with ray-decorated dots. (Color figure online)

Moreverover, the AdOtsu method failed (binarized image assessed as INCORRECT) on 5 randomly selected images from the testing set.

There were only two possible assessments of the binarization threshold estimate considered during the evaluation: CORRECT and INCORRECT. The CORRECT class represents those estimates that are in accord with the manual threshold setting (done by an expert) and that label correctly the actual objects of interest in the images, i.e. the binarized image is usable for further processing. The INCORRECT class is the complement, i.e. those estimates that lead to incorrect image segmentation and that are positioned elsewhere than an expert would set them.

**Table 1.** Performance comparison of the method on two datasets

|  | Electron microscopy | | X-ray mammography | |
|---|---|---|---|---|
|  | CORRECT | time/img | CORRECT | time/img |
| Described method | 72.29 % | 0.36 s | 89.0 % | 1.37 s |
| Otsu | 01.20 % | 0.07 s | 86.0 % | 3.48 s |
| Bradley & Roth | 32.53 % | 0.51 s | N/A[a] | N/A[a] |

([a]) The available OpenCV-based implementation of the Bradley's and Roth's method was not able to process the x-ray mammographic images properly due to their size.

An altogether unwelcome situation in the mammographic image analysis can occur as the Otsu's method sets the threshold in such a way that considerable part of the x-rayed tissue is marked as background and thus not analysed during the consequent steps although it may contain traits of tumours. It was obviously placed into the INCORRECT class during the evaluation.

It can be seen from the results in Table 1 that the newly developed method is less prone to set the threshold in a way that *parts* of objects are missed, especially on the mammographic images. The performance on the electron microscopy dataset is slightly worse than on the x-ray mammography, however, the Otsu's failed completely on the microscopy (most of the images repainted to all-white or all-black).

Moreover, the described method demonstrated a convenient behaviour during the testing that may facilitate any further processing of the binarized images: It fails in an identifiable way, i.e. repaints the image to all-white or all-black, instead of selecting only few pixels out of the objects of interest.

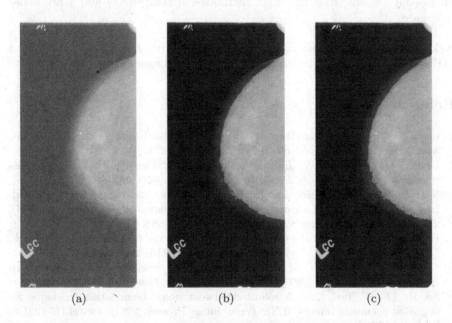

(a)                              (b)                              (c)

**Fig. 5.** Method performance comparison on an unproblematic x-ray mammography image: (a) original scan, (b) the described method, (c) Otsu's method. The red channel is used to highlight the detected object region. The green and blue channels copy the values from the original grayscale image. (Color figure online)

The computational complexity of the threshold-setting algorithm itself (i.e. without the preprocessing stage where the used algorithms have their own respective complexities) is linearly dependent on the total dynamic range of the binarized image, $O(n)$, where $n$ is the dynamic range or simply the number of discrete values on the x-axis of the histogram.

# 4  Conclusion

A simple analytic method for estimating the binarization threshold position was introduced and described. It has two main advantages: Firstly, there are no parameters to be fine-tuned and the method is very easy to implement and has modest computational demands. Secondly, this method (especially compared to the current mainstream binarization method, Otsu's) offers significantly higher robustness and finds a usable threshold position even in case of low-contrast images with intensity histograms where bimodality is rather latent than actually present. Thus, it happens more seldom that a substantial part of an object of interest is missed because of incorrectly set binarization threshold.

The method was tested on a representative set of low-contrast grayscale images and demonstrated a competitive performance, closely comparable to the state-of-the-art methods (see Fig. 5 and Table 1). Moreover, it provides satisfactory results on problematic low-contrast images originating from electron microscopy (where Otsu and other methods fail completely) and x-ray mammography.

**Acknowledgement.** This research work has been partly supported by the project LO1506 of the Czech Ministry of Education, Youth and Sports.

# References

1. Otsu, N.: A threshold selection method from gray-level histograms. IEEE Trans. Syst. Man Cybern. **9**(1), 62–66 (1979). ISSN 0018–9472
2. Li, H., Lai, Z.A., Lei, J.W.: Image threshold segmentation algorithm based on histogram statistical property. Appl. Mech. Mater. **644–650**, 4027–4030 (2014)
3. Moghaddam, R.F., Cheriet, M.: AdOtsu an adaptive and parameterless generalization of otsu's method for document image binarization. Pattern Recogn. **45**(6), 2419–2431 (2012). Elsevier Science Inc., New York. ISSN 0031–3203
4. Bradley, D., Roth, G.: Adaptive thresholding using the integral image. J. Graph. GPU Game Tools **12**(2), 13–21 (2011). doi:10.1080/2151237X.2007.10129236
5. Sauvola, J., Pietikainen, M.: Adaptive document image binarization. Pattern Recogn. **33**(2), 225–236 (2000). Elsevier Science Inc., New York. ISSN 0031–3203
6. Su, B., Lu, S., Tan, C.L.: A robust document image binarization technique for degraded document images. IEEE Trans. Image Process. **22**(4), 1408–1417 (2013). ISSN 1057-7149
7. Hlaváč, V., Šonka, M.: Počítačové vidění. Grada, Prague (1992). ISBN 80-85424-67-3
8. Rektorys, K., et al.: Přehled užité matematiky. Prometheus, Prague (2000). ISBN 80-7196-179-5

# Single Image Haze Removal Using Single Pixel Approach Based on Dark Channel Prior with Fast Filtering

Sung Yong Jo$^{(\boxtimes)}$, Jeongmok Ha, and Hong Jeong

Department of Electrical Engineering, Pohang University of Science and Technology,
77 Cheongam-Ro, Nam-Gu, Pohang, Gyeongbuk, South Korea
{sungyongjo,jmokha,hjeong}@postech.ac.kr

**Abstract.** We propose a fast image-dehazing method that uses a *pixelwise dark channel prior* (PDCP). We argue that the neighbor minimum filter in the *dark channel prior* (DCP) is not crucial in image dehazing. We prove this assertion in experiments that compare dehazed images and histograms of dark channel images obtained using PDCP and DCP. To refine the transmission map in the Koschmieder model of the degradation of a hazy image, we use a fast guided filter to replace the *soft matting* (SM) used in DCP, because SM is the main reason for the slowness of DCP. The proposed algorithm is faster than existing methods, but achieves similar dehazing. This new method is useful for applications that require fast dehazing.

## 1 Introduction

Outdoor computer vision has many applications such as object detection and surveillance [13]. In outdoor scenes, haze is a crucial problem, because generally, computer vision algorithms are based on the assumption that input image from the camera is clear enough for the algorithm to work. However, when the input includes haze, the detection accuracy of the application is degraded.

To solve this problem, various approaches have achieved satisfactory results. However, these methods generally did not consider computation speed; they focused on only increasing the visibility of a hazy image. These methods tend to be computationally complex and therefore slow. The most effective algorithm was proposed by He et al. [5], who proposed the use of a *dark channel prior* (DCP) to estimate the haze transmission. It is also too slow because of the *soft matting* (SM) [9] in refinement of transmission map. Then various methods, based on the DCP framework, proposed to speed up the refinement of transmission map.

Subsequently, many authors have tried to reduce the complexity, but all methods are slow. If this complexity can be reduced in outdoor applications, dehazing methods can be widely used. In this paper, we propose a fast dehazing algorithm that uses a *pixelwise DCP* (PDCP) and a *fast guided filter* (FGF) [3].

We prove that dark channel images from DCP and from PDCP give similar results if refinement is used. Whereas DCP chooses a minimum value in a patch,

© Springer International Publishing AG 2016
L.J. Chmielewski et al. (Eds.): ICCVG 2016, LNCS 9972, pp. 151–162, 2016.
DOI: 10.1007/978-3-319-46418-3_14

PDCP chooses a minimum value in a pixel. The difference is that when DCP is used, the minimum operator of neighboring pixels does not have a significant effect on quality. We demonstrate this effect on various hazy images with proof and evaluations.

The SM used in He's method is the main cause of its computational complexity. Later methods used filters such as *joint bilateral filter* (JBF) [6] or *guided filter* (GF) [4], but the algorithms are still too slow. So we use a dehazing algorithm based on FGF [3] instead of on SM. Also we prove that our method is faster than other methods, but provides similar image quality.

## 2    Related Work

Because of the importance of haze removal, numerous attempts have been made to increase the visibility of a hazy input image. The classical methods of image enhancement such as histogram equalization and linear mapping can be used to increase image contrast. However, these methods do not utilize that the distribution of haze is proportional to the distance of an object. Thus, these methods cannot restore appropriately the visibility degradation of a hazy image.

More advanced dehazing algorithms first estimate object depths using the mathematical model of the degradation of a hazy image. Several dehazing algorithms have been proposed to estimate object depths from using additional depth information or multiple images. Polarization-based methods [14,15] remove the haze effect by comparing two or more images taken with different degrees of polarization. The dehazed image is obtained from multiple images of the same scene under different weather conditions [10,11,13]. Depth-based methods [7,12] require rough depth information either from user interactions or from known 3D models.

Recently, single-image dehazing methods have been significantly improved. Researchers have suggested different prior constraints to solve the model-based imaging formula to alleviate the requirements for scene depth. Fattal [1] provided an approach that estimates transmission map by assuming that the shading and transmission functions are locally independent. However, this method may fail when processing heavily-hazed images. Tan [16] argued that a haze-free image has stronger contrast than a hazy one, and gave a method to enhance hazy images by maximizing their local contrast. This method successfully dehazed very densely hazed image, but can produce over-saturated results. He et al. [5], called as He's method, proposed a DCP method based on a statistical observation that most local patches in haze-free images contain some low-intensity pixels. In most haze images, DCP can recover high-quality haze-free images, but refinement of the transmission map using the SM [9] takes a long time.

Several methods have been proposed to improve the efficiency of image dehazing. He et al. proposed the GF [4], and found that the output of the GF could be an approximate solution of the Laplacian matting optimization [9]. This method greatly reduced the time complexity, however, as it is not considered to be enough for application.

Tarel [17] proposed a fast dehazing algorithm using median filter, but it does not preserve the depth information of the scene. JBF [6] is used to dehaze images by calculating weights based on spatial and range filter kernels in [18], but the method is still too slow.

## 3   Problem Statement

Dehazing as visibility restoration is an ill-posed problem. The Koschmieder model [8], i.e., the mathematical model of the degradation of a hazy image, is represented as:

$$I(\mathbf{x}) = J(\mathbf{x})t(\mathbf{x}) + A(1 - t(\mathbf{x})), \tag{1}$$

where $\mathbf{x}$ denotes the pixel location, $I(\mathbf{x})$ is the observed haze image, $J(\mathbf{x})$ is the dehazed image that we want to obtain, $A$ is the global atmospheric light, and $t(\mathbf{x})$ is the transmission map that represents hazy elements in the image. The purpose of dehazing is to recover $J(\mathbf{x})$ by estimating $t(\mathbf{x})$ and $A$ in $I(\mathbf{x})$.

The haze removal, i.e., recovering the radiance of scene $J(\mathbf{x})$ for each pixel of the input image $I(\mathbf{x})$, is estimated using $t(\mathbf{x})$ and $A$:

$$J(\mathbf{x}) = \frac{I(\mathbf{x}) - A}{\max{(t(\mathbf{x}), t_0)}}, \tag{2}$$

where $t_0$ is a lower bound of denominator and a typical value of $t_0$ is 0.1.

Among the existing methods that calculate $t(\mathbf{x})$ and $A$, He's method [5] that uses DCP is simple and powerful. It is based on the observation that in most non-sky patches, at least one color channel of the patch is close to zero. Based on the DCP, the transmission map $t(\mathbf{x})$ is computed as:

$$t(\mathbf{x}) = 1 - \min_{\mathbf{y} \in \Omega(\mathbf{x})} \left( \min_{c \in \{R,G,B\}} \frac{I^c(\mathbf{y})}{A^c} \right), \tag{3}$$

where $\mathbf{y}$ represents a neighbor pixel of $\mathbf{x}$, $\Omega(\mathbf{x})$ represents local patch centered at $\mathbf{x}$, $I^c(\mathbf{y})$ is one color channel of $I(\mathbf{y})$, and $A^c$ is one color channel of $A$. Atmospheric $A$ is determined by selecting the brightest pixel in input image among 0.1% brightest pixels in the dark channel image.

However, the assumption that the transmission map is always constant in small area is not satisfied because the neighbor minimum operator blurs the transmission map. For this reason, a filter, e.g., GF, SM, or JBF, is used to refine the transmission map [5].

Although DCP is simple and achieves good accuracy, we find two problems. First, when the $t(\mathbf{x})$ is estimated, patchwise minimum filtering is unnecessary when the refinement is used after the transmission map is estimated; i.e., we assert that DCP with pixelwise minimum operation is sufficient to attain a good dehazing result if the refinement is used. Second, most of the complexity in He's method is the calculation of SM. Although many authors have recently proposed other filtering methods instead of the SM, they are still too slow (Fig. 1).

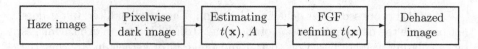

**Fig. 1.** A block diagram of proposed algorithm

## 4   Pixelwise Dark Channel Prior

The DCP is based on the observation in haze-free image that at least one color channel of pixel in a patch is close to zero [5]. The DCP consists of two minimum operators:

$$\min_{\mathbf{y} \in \Omega(\mathbf{x})} \left( \min_{c \in \{R,G,B\}} J^c(\mathbf{y}) \right) \approx 0, \tag{4}$$

one to filter neighbors, and the other one to filter RGB channels. When DCP is applied in haze-free images, $\geq 95\%$ of the pixels have values close to zero. The image that is obtained after applying the two minimum operators in an input image is called a dark channel image. Usually, a large window size is recommended because the possibility that an area has a value close to zero increases as the window size increases.

However, the DCP has the limitation that the use of neighbor minimum filter can sometimes distort the color in the dehazed image. This effect occurs because white components are considered as haze components, so a few color elements in a white object may be emphasized. The neighbor filter can also cause a halo effect. Previous work uses the refinement to weaken these effects.

In this paper, we claim that the dark channel image and transmission map can be obtained without using neighbor minimum filtering.

*Claim. A dark channel image obtained using both minimum operators with respect to neighbor and channel filtering (Eq. (4)) is proportional to the dark channel image obtained using only minimum operator with respect to channel filtering if the refinement $\mathcal{F}(\cdot)$ is applied after the dark channel image was obtained.*

$$\mathcal{F} \left( \min_{\mathbf{y} \in \Omega(\mathbf{x})} \left( \min_{c \in \{R,G,B\}} J(\mathbf{y}) \right) \right) = \omega \cdot \mathcal{F} \left( \min_{c \in \{R,G,B\}} J(\mathbf{y}) \right), \tag{5}$$

*where $\omega$ is a constant that is used to adjust the intensity scale.*

*Proof.* In He's method, DCP was applied to the patch. Without using neighbor minimum filtering, we find that DCP applied to the pixel is sufficient to estimate the atmospheric light and transmission map. We call this pixelwise DCP (PDCP).

When the refinement is used, the neighbor operation has no meaning, because of the refinement using pixelwise channel space when refining the dark channel image. The blurred dark channel image is re-computed to be a sharp image. The only difference is the intensity scaling. Because the minimum neighbor operation of larger patch size choose a minimum value in more pixels, the dark channel image obtained by our PDCP is not as dark as that obtained by the patch-based approach.

We can estimate the transmission map $t(\mathbf{x})$ without using a neighbor minimum operator.

$$t(\mathbf{x}) = 1 - \omega \left( \min_{c \in \{R,G,B\}} \frac{I^c(\mathbf{y})}{A^c} \right), \tag{6}$$

where $\omega$ is a constant. However, because of difference in intensity scale between the neighbor minimum operation and the pixelwise minimum operation, the result will look dim and regions on white objects or surfaces will be too dark. With the PDCP in which the above claim is correct, we can adjust $\omega$ to remove the haze component naturally. To avoid over-saturation, we choose the value of $\omega$ experimentally by considering the characteristics of an input hazy image as a parameter. We will demonstrate that the neighbor filtering is useless when the refinement is applied; dark channel images and histograms of those computed from original DCP and PDCP will be compared to each other.      □

## 5   Comparison of PDCP and DCP

In this section, we experimentally compare PDCP with DCP [5]. We show that our *Claim* is valid by comparing histograms of dark channel images obtained using PDCP and DCP respectively. We also present the dehazed result images which demonstrate that the neighbor minimum filter is not crucial to dehaze an image.

### 5.1   Observation of PDCP

From haze-free images obtained from a free photo website[1], refined dark channel images can be attained using PDCP and DCP with the SM. Then we observe histograms of the refined dark channel images. In this observation, we use refined dark channel images because we will finally use the refined transmission map; this map is computed using dark channel image of a normalized form to recover a haze image. To ensure objective comparison of the effect of the neighbor minimum filter, we did not replace the SM with the DCP.

PDCP and DCP were both applied with 5×5 patches in input images (Fig. 2a) into refined dark channel images (Fig. 2b,c), then to obtain histograms of the refined dark channel images (Fig. 2d,e). In each images, the histograms of refined dark channel images were similarly distributed but had slightly different scaling; this observation demonstrates that dehazing does not require the neighbor minimum filter. Although the dark channel images of PDCP are brighter than those of DCP, the dehazed images can be obtained similarly by adjusting $\omega$.

---

[1] https://pixabay.com/.

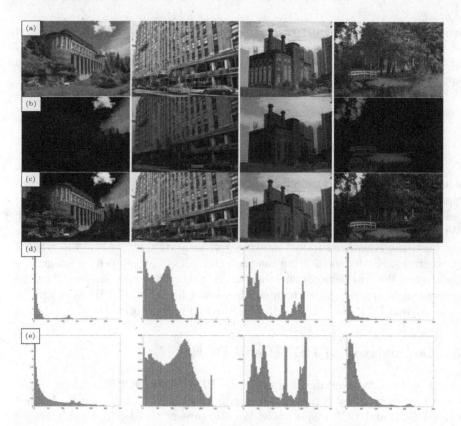

**Fig. 2.** Some examples of histogram comparisons between DCP and PDCP. (a) Input images. (b) Refined dark channel images using PDCP. (c) Refined dark channel images using DCP with 5×5 patch. (d) Histograms of refined dark channel images using PDCP. (e) Histograms of refined dark channel images using DCP with 5×5 patch.

## 5.2    Comparison of Results Between PDCP and DCP

To test the assertion that PDCP can yield dehazed results that are comparable to those of DCP, new input images (Fig. 3a) were obtained, then DCP and PDCP were used to generate refined transmission maps (Fig. 3b,c), and then to obtain dehazed images (Fig. 3d,e). Images recovered using DCP were similar to those recovered using PDCP; i.e., PDCP is sufficient to dehaze input images, if $\omega$ is set appropriately; in these images, the $\omega$ values were form 0.7 to 0.9.

In specific local regions, PDCP obtained better detail than did DCP. Result images of DCP show some block artifacts with yellowish color distortion in the sky (Image 2 of Fig. 3); this problem is a result of over-saturation of the neighbor minimum filter. Also the refined transmission map of PDCP shows that it is more accurate than DCP between the leaves in the foreground (Image 3 of Fig. 3).

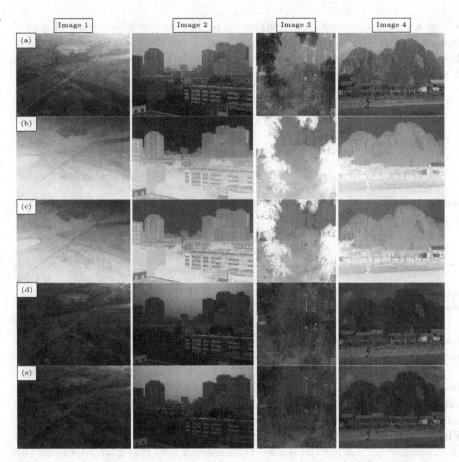

**Fig. 3.** Some examples of dehazed results from PDCP and DCP. (a) Input images. (b) Refined transmission maps using DCP ($\omega = 0.9$ for all images). (c) Refined transmission maps using PDCP (from left to right, $\omega = 0.9, 0.7, 0.8,$ and $0.8$, respectively). (d) Dehazed images using DCP. (e) Dehazed images using PDCP.

## 6   Refinement Using Fast Guided Filter

He's method uses the SM [9] to refine $t(\mathbf{x})$, but this approach uses a massive amount of computation; this is one of the biggest causes of slow speed in the existing methods. Instead of the SM, this paper exploit the FGF [3], which is an edge-aware filter that was proposed recently to improve the speed of the GF [4].

First, we define the notations of GF and introduce the FGF. In GF, guidance, filtering input and output images can be considered as the input hazy image $I(\mathbf{x})$, the transmission map $t(\mathbf{x})$, and the refined transmission map $\tilde{t}(\mathbf{x})$, respectively. This images are related using a local linear model. So the GF is:

$$\tilde{t}(\mathbf{x}) = a_{\mathbf{y}}I(\mathbf{x}) + b_{\mathbf{y}}, \forall \mathbf{x} \in \omega_k, \tag{7}$$

where $\mathbf{x}$ denotes the pixel location, and $\mathbf{y}$ represents a neighbor pixel of a local square window $\Omega(\mathbf{x})$ with a radius $r$. $a_k$ and $b_k$ are the parameters of the local linear model. Given the image $t(\mathbf{x})$, we minimize the reconstruction error between $t(\mathbf{x})$ and $\tilde{t}(\mathbf{x})$. This is described as:

$$a_{\mathbf{y}} = \frac{\frac{1}{|\Omega(\mathbf{x})|} \sum_{\mathbf{x} \in \Omega(\mathbf{x})} I(\mathbf{x})p(\mathbf{x}) - \mu_{\mathbf{y}}\bar{p}(\mathbf{y})}{\sigma_{\mathbf{y}}^2 + \epsilon} \tag{8}$$

$$b_{\mathbf{y}} = \bar{p}(\mathbf{y}) - a_{\mathbf{y}}\mu_{\mathbf{y}} \tag{9}$$

where $\mu_{\mathbf{y}}$ and $\sigma_{\mathbf{y}}$ are the mean and variance of $I(\mathbf{x})$ in the window $\Omega(\mathbf{x})$, $\epsilon$ is a smoothing parameter.

In the GF, the output is obtained as:

$$\tilde{t}(\mathbf{x}) = \bar{a}_{\mathbf{x}}I(\mathbf{x}) + \bar{b}(\mathbf{x}), \tag{10}$$

where $\bar{a}_{\mathbf{x}}$ and $\bar{b}_{\mathbf{x}}$ are the mean of a and b of the window $\Omega(\mathbf{x})$ centered at $\mathbf{x}$, respectively.

As in FGF, we subsample the input transmission map $t(\mathbf{x})$ and the input hazy image as guidance $I(\mathbf{x})$ by a ratio $s$. Any method can be used for this purpose.

Using the subsampled images, all of the box filters are performed on the low-resolution maps. Computation of these box filters is the major reason for the slowness of the algorithm, so a large speed-up is achieved by computing them on subsampled images. Then, the two coefficient maps $\bar{a}$ and $\bar{b}$ are upsampled. Finally, the refined transmission map $\tilde{t}(\mathbf{x})$ can be attained using (10).

Therefore we can get the refined transmission map $t(\mathbf{x})$ from FGF, and can estimate $A$ simply by selecting the brightest pixel; this process is reasonable in a hazy image. After obtaining all unknowns from $I(\mathbf{x})$, we can generate the dehazed image using (2).

# 7    Comparison of FGF and Other Refinement Methods

In this section, we compare speed and accuracy of the proposed algorithm with those of SM [9] in He's method [5], GF [4], and JBF [6] at various patch sizes. The major parameters of the compared algorithms are empirically determined. In FGF and GF, the radius of local square window is fixed at 30. The scale of sampling in FGF is fixed at 4. In JBF, the standard variations of spatial-domain and intensity-domain of the bilateral filter are fixed 3 and 0.1 respectively and the half-size of the Gaussian bilateral filter window is fixed at 5. The test data set consists of 33 images of a variety of scenes. The experiments were run on a desktop computer with an Intel quad core 3.4-GHz CPU using MATLAB R2015b with academic license.

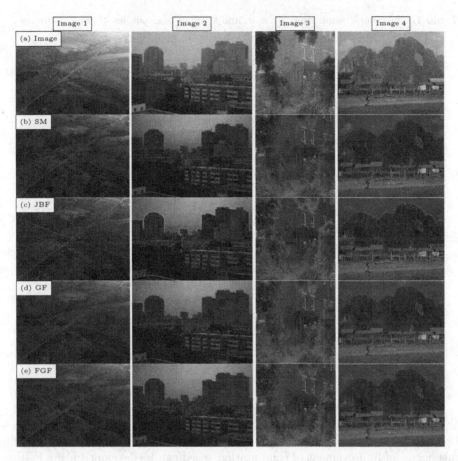

**Fig. 4.** Some examples of dehazed results from (b) *soft matting* (SM), (c) *joint bilateral filter* (JBF), (d) *guided filter* (GF), and (e) *fast guided filter* (FGF). 5×5 patch and $\omega = 0.9$ were used.

## 7.1   Qualitative Evaluation

FGF was much faster than the other algorithms (Table 1), but produced results that were the same or better in quality than those of SM, GF, and JBF (Fig. 4). To demonstrate objectively the effect of the FGF, the experiment was repeated with patch size fixed at 5, and $\omega$ fixed at 0.9.

All refinement methods in all images show a similar haze removal capacity, but the important differences occur in detailed areas. JBF commits halo artifacts at the boundaries surrounding all objects that have a significant depth difference from their surroundings (Fig. 4c). The algorithms remove haze well in most images, except the image 3 of Fig. 4; in this case, FGF and GF did not eliminate haze between the leaves in the foreground. All algorithms except JBF gave similar overall results, and SM was slightly better than the others.

**Table 1.** The computation time (s), $e$, $\sigma$, and $\bar{r}$ values of examples of dehazed images.

| Image | Filter | Time (s) | $e$ | | | $\bar{r}$ | | | $\sigma$ | | |
|---|---|---|---|---|---|---|---|---|---|---|---|
| | | | 1×1 | 5×5 | 9×9 | 1×1 | 5×5 | 9×9 | 1×1 | 5×5 | 9×9 |
| 1 | SM | 20.73 | 0.82 | 0.66 | 0.59 | 0.91 | 0.96 | 0.98 | 0.060 | 0.013 | 0.007 |
| | JBF | 2.80 | 0.93 | 1.02 | 0.95 | 1.27 | 1.39 | 1.41 | 0.060 | 0.013 | 0.007 |
| | GF | 4.32 | 0.40 | 0.33 | 0.31 | 0.80 | 0.76 | 0.82 | 0 | 0.007 | 0.005 |
| | FGF | **0.28** | 0.39 | 0.33 | 0.30 | 0.80 | 0.76 | 0.82 | 0 | 0.004 | 0.004 |
| 2 | SM | 17.98 | 0.12 | 0.08 | 0.07 | 0.60 | 0.85 | 0.93 | 2.970 | 0.257 | 0.116 |
| | JBF | 2.48 | 0.06 | 0.12 | 0.13 | 1.11 | 1.33 | 1.37 | 2.970 | 0.257 | 0.116 |
| | GF | 3.83 | 3.83 | 0.13 | 0.11 | 0.59 | 0.89 | 1.04 | 0 | 0.055 | 0.115 |
| | FGF | **0.25** | 0.12 | 0.12 | 0.13 | 0.59 | 0.88 | 1.07 | 0 | 0.051 | 0.117 |
| 3 | SM | 14.68 | 0.10 | 0.10 | 0.09 | 0.78 | 0.97 | 0.99 | 0 | 0 | 0 |
| | JBF | 2.10 | 0.14 | 0.14 | 0.13 | 1.14 | 1.31 | 1.31 | 0 | 0 | 0 |
| | GF | 3.17 | 0.07 | 0.12 | 0.12 | 0.82 | 1.20 | 1.23 | 0 | 0 | 0 |
| | FGF | **0.21** | 0.07 | 0.12 | 0.12 | 0.83 | 1.20 | 1.23 | 0 | 0 | 0 |
| 4 | SM | 14.63 | 0.15 | 0.14 | 0.13 | 0.81 | 0.92 | 0.95 | 0.013 | 0.018 | 0.023 |
| | JBF | 2.04 | 0.16 | 0.19 | 0.17 | 1.13 | 1.25 | 1.26 | 0.013 | 0.018 | 0.023 |
| | GF | 3.14 | 0.06 | 0.19 | 0.11 | 0.75 | 0.91 | 1.00 | 0.008 | 0.031 | 0.054 |
| | FGF | **0.20** | 0.06 | 0.11 | 0.11 | 0.75 | 0.90 | 1.00 | 0.009 | 0.028 | 0.05 |

However, SM was by far the slowest algorithm (Table 1). In average for all 33 input images, FGF was significantly faster than the other algorithms: 70 times faster than the SM, 15 times faster than GF, and 10 times faster than JBF. If this degree of improvement of computation speed can be developed using FGF, our method will be useful in many application that require fast dehazing.

## 7.2 Quantitative Evaluation

Three indices [2] was used to assess the results obtained using a variety of refinement algorithms at various patch sizes. Index $e$ represents the rate of edges newly visible after restoration; a high value is good. Index $\sigma$ evaluates the level of over-saturation; specifically, the percentage of pixels that are completely white or completely black in the result image; a low value is good. Index $\bar{r}$ measures the increase in contrast restoration; a high value is good. The values of the indices did not seem to be affected by patch size and refinement algorithm (Table 1). Regardless of patch size, FGF has a slightly lower value than SM in $e$. However, because SM sometimes judges noise to be an edge, this apparent superiority of SM over FGF may not be real. Also patch size did not uniformly affect the result image.

# 8  Conclusion

We proposed a fast algorithm to dehaze images. First, we demonstrated that the neighbor minimum filter used in the DCP increases its computational complexity. Then we proposed the pixelwise DCP (PDCP) that uses the minimum operator in pixel itself to remove a redundant minimum operator. Second, we tried to replace SM, which is the most significant reason for the slowness of DCP. We used FGF to refine the transmission map. Because of these changes, our method is an order of magnitude faster than existing methods, but achieve comparable dehazing results, and is therefore the most appropriate method for fast haze removal. However, the new method can still be improved. Our method fails when the model of the degradation of a hazy image is invalid; the limitation is the same as in other existing methods. In the future, we will seek to address this problem.

**Acknowledgement.** This work was supported by the Human Resource Training Program for Regional Innovation and Creativity through the Ministry of Education and National Research Foundation of Korea (NRF-2014H1C1A1073141).

# References

1. Fattal, R.: Single image dehazing. ACM Trans. Graph. (TOG) **27**(3), 72 (2008). ACM
2. Hautiere, N., Tarel, J.P., Aubert, D., Dumont, E., et al.: Blind contrast enhancement assessment by gradient ratioing at visible edges. Image Anal. Stereology J. **27**(2), 87–95 (2008)
3. He, K., Sun, J.: Fast guided filter. CoRR abs/1505.00996 (2015). http://arxiv.org/abs/1505.00996
4. He, K., Sun, J., Tang, X.: Guided image filtering. In: Daniilidis, K., Maragos, P., Paragios, N. (eds.) ECCV 2010. LNCS, vol. 6311, pp. 1–14. Springer, Heidelberg (2010). doi:10.1007/978-3-642-15549-9_1
5. He, K., Sun, J., Tang, X.: Single image haze removal using dark channel prior. IEEE Trans. Pattern Anal. Mach. Intell. **33**(12), 2341–2353 (2011)
6. Kopf, J., Cohen, M.F., Lischinski, D., Uyttendaele, M.: Joint bilateral upsampling. ACM Trans. Graph. (TOG) **26**(3), 96 (2007)
7. Kopf, J., Neubert, B., Chen, B., Cohen, M., Cohen-Or, D., Deussen, O., Uyttendaele, M., Lischinski, D.: Deep photo model-based photograph enhancement and viewing. ACM Trans. Graph. **27**, 116 (2008). ACM
8. Koschmieder, H.: Theorie der horizontalen sichtweite: kontrast und sichtweite. Keim & Nemnich (1925)
9. Levin, A., Lischinski, D., Weiss, Y.: A closed-form solution to natural image matting. IEEE Trans. Pattern Anal. Mach. Intell. **30**(2), 228–242 (2008)
10. Narasimhan, S.G., Nayar, S.K.: Chromatic framework for vision in bad weather. In: 2000 Proceedings of the IEEE Conference on Computer Vision and Pattern Recognition, vol. 1, pp. 598–605. IEEE (2000)
11. Narasimhan, S.G., Nayar, S.K.: Contrast restoration of weather degraded images. IEEE Trans. Pattern Anal. Mach. Intell. **25**(6), 713–724 (2003)

12. Narasimhan, S.G., Nayar, S.K.: Interactive (de) weathering of an image using physical models. In: IEEE Workshop on Color and Photometric Methods in Computer Vision, vol. 6, p. 1. France (2003)
13. Nayar, S.K., Narasimhan, S.G.: Vision in bad weather. In: Proceedings 1999 of the Seventh IEEE International Conference on Computer Vision, vol. 2, pp. 820–827. IEEE (1999)
14. Schechner, Y.Y., Narasimhan, S.G., Nayar, S.K.: Instant dehazing of images using polarization. In: 2001 Proceedings of the IEEE Computer Society Conference on Computer Vision and Pattern Recognition, CVPR 2001, vol. 1, p. I-325. IEEE (2001)
15. Shwartz, S., Namer, E., Schechner, Y.Y.: Blind haze separation. In: 2006 IEEE Computer Society Conference on Computer Vision and Pattern Recognition, vol. 2, pp. 1984–1991. IEEE (2006)
16. Tan, R.T.: Visibility in bad weather from a single image. In: 2008 IEEE Conference on Computer Vision and Pattern Recognition, CVPR 2008. pp. 1–8. IEEE (2008)
17. Tarel, J.P., Hautiere, N.: Fast visibility restoration from a single color or gray level image. In: 2009 12th IEEE International Conference on Computer Vision, pp. 2201–2208. IEEE (2009)
18. Xu, H., Guo, J., Liu, Q., Ye, L.: Fast image dehazing using improved dark channel prior. In: 2012 International Conference on Information Science and Technology (ICIST), pp. 663–667. IEEE (2012)

# Deep Neural Image Denoising

Michał Koziarski[1](✉) and Bogusław Cyganek[2]

[1] Wrocław University of Science and Technology, Wrocław, Poland
michalkoziarski@gmail.com
[2] AGH University of Science and Technology, Kraków, Poland
cyganek@agh.edu.pl

**Abstract.** Presence of noise poses a common problem in image recognition tasks. In this paper we propose and analyse architecture of convolutional neural network capable of image denoising. We evaluate its performance with various types of artificial distortions present, with both known and unknown noise conditions. Finally, we measure how including denoising procedure in image recognition pipeline influences classification accuracy.

## 1 Introduction

Presence of unwanted distortions poses a common problem in the field of computer vision. Noise can affect not only human perception of images but also performance of algorithms in tasks such as image recognition. Especially unknown noise conditions, often occurring in practice, pose significant threat of negatively altering results. Therefore, having well-performing denoising methods at our disposal might be essential to ensure proper function of image processing pipelines.

In this paper we evaluate performance of deep convolutional neural network [3] used for image denoising. Convolutional neural networks (CNNs) achieve state-of-the-art results in many image processing tasks, including image recognition [6,14,17,18] and denoising [2,5,10–12,21]. We propose architecture of convolutional network capable of removing distortions from images and evaluate it on chosen dataset. We also include denoising network as part of image recognition pipeline, trained using high amount of unlabeled data. Finally, we evaluate its influence on classification accuracy in image recognition task.

The rest of the paper is organized as follows. In Sect. 2 we discuss related work in image denoising with neural networks. Section 3 gives a brief overview of different types of noise models used throughout the experiments. In Sect. 4 we describe neural architecture and training procedure used during denoising. We also present an alternate view on denoising as a form of pretraining neural network during image recognition task. In Sect. 5 we describe conducted experiments. We present our experimental setup, implementation, used dataset and discuss obtained results. Finally, Sect. 6 presents our conclusions.

© Springer International Publishing AG 2016
L.J. Chmielewski et al. (Eds.): ICCVG 2016, LNCS 9972, pp. 163–173, 2016.
DOI: 10.1007/978-3-319-46418-3_15

## 2   Related Work

Neural networks have previously been explored in context of signal denoising task. Various different approaches were evaluated, including plain neural networks [5], convolutional neural networks [11] and stacked sparse denoising autoencoders [2]. Examples in literature are not limited to image denoising either and include tasks such as speech denoising [12], in which convolutional autoencoders are being used. Several related tasks were examined as well, prime example being [21], in which image inpainting is considered.

Closely related to our work are [10], in which convolutional architecture is used in task of removal of localized rain and dirt artifacts, and [11], in which presented model is being evaluated under varying noise conditions. We extend approach presented in above papers by considering different types of artificial distortions and adapting architecture of the network to the dataset considered. We also evaluate the impact of denoising on image recognition task.

## 3   Mathematical Noise Models

Noise is an additional component interfering with a pure signal, occurring in images due to various physical phenomena [4,8]. High amounts of noise might not only influence human perception of images, but also worsen performance of image recognition algorithms. In this section we describe noise models used throughout the experiments.

### 3.1   Gaussian Noise

Gaussian noise is likely the most popular type of noise model, used often to represent thermal distortions. Probability density of Gaussian noise is defined as

$$p(x) = \frac{1}{\sigma\sqrt{2\pi}}e^{-\frac{(x-\mu)^2}{2\sigma^2}}, \tag{1}$$

with $\mu$ being the mean of distribution, $\sigma^2$ its variance, and $-\infty < x < \infty$.

### 3.2   Quantization Noise

Quantization noise is most often associated with quality drop occurring due to converting continuous signal into digital format. It can be modeled as a noise sampled uniformly from distribution with specified range from 0 to $q$.

### 3.3   Salt and Pepper Noise

Salt & pepper noise can be used to model distortions introduced while transmitting data through noisy channel, resulting in loss of information in a number of pixels. We can model salt & pepper noise by altering $n$-th pixel with probability specified as

$$P(X_n = x_n) = 1 - p, \tag{2}$$

$$P(X_n = max) = \frac{p}{2}, \tag{3}$$

$$P(X_n = min) = \frac{p}{2}, \tag{4}$$

with $max$ and $min$ being, respectively, maximum and minimum pixel values, and $p$ being the probability of alteration.

## 4 Image Denosing with Convolutional Neural Networks

In this section we present proposed neural networks architecture together with employed training procedure. We also present different view at image recognition pipeline with denoising network involved.

### 4.1 Network Architecture

Architecture used throughout the experiments consists exclusively of convolutional layers. The network has 6 hidden layers with 64 $5 \times 5$ filters in each layer and an output layer consisting of single $5 \times 5$ filter, introduced to preserve the shape of images after forward pass through the network. Additionally, padding was used in each layer for the same reason. Size of filters was fine-tuned to accommodate specific size of images in dataset used throughout the experiment ($96 \times 96$ pixels), and was reduced in favor of increasing the depth of architecture. Hyperbolic tangent was used as an activation function in every layer but last, in which rectified linear unit (ReLU) [15] was used.

### 4.2 Training

Proposed network was trained to reconstruct original images given their distorted version. At every iteration artificial noise of specified type was randomly generated and applied to the original image. The sum of mean squared error between the two and L2 norm of the weights was then minimized using momentum optimizer.

### 4.3 Denoising as a Form of Unsupervised Pretraining

It was shown that presence of noise in images might have significant impact on image classification task [13]. Ideally, we would like our model to learn to recognize images despite introduced distortions. In practice, however, the amount of labeled data might be scarce, not sufficient to train large models able to adapt to noisy representations. In these cases we may take advantage of unlabeled data at our disposal and train larger network solely to denoise images. This can be viewed as a form of pretraining, after which we can add additional layers and either freeze the front part of the network obtained during pretraining, or finetune whole network to image recognition task.

# 5  Experimental Study

In this section we present setup of conducted experiments. We describe details of implementation, dataset used, baseline denoising methods and parameters of denoising procedure. After that, we propose denoising as part of preprocessing during image classification. Finally, we present results of the experiments.

## 5.1  Implementation

All the conducted experiments were implemented in Python programming language and were using TensorFlow [1] software library. Due to the length of training procedure, Graphics Processing Unit was used to speed up the computation, specifically NVIDIA Tesla K40 XL. Training single denoising model lasted approximately 24 h, it should however be noted that achieving highest possible training speed was not the main consideration and computation speed was lowered due to frequent evaluation.

## 5.2  Dataset

Throughout the experiments, STL-10 dataset [7] was used. It is an image recognition dataset, divided into three distinct parts: train and test sets, consisting of 5000 and 8000 images, respectively, with each image assigned to one of 10 classes; and unlabeled pretrain set, consisting of 100000 images taken from a similar but broader distribution (containing additional classes in addition to the ones in the labeled set).

Every image has size of $96 \times 96$ pixels. All images were converted to grayscale, and their pixels were normalized to range from 0 to 1.

During the experiments, denoising networks were trained using pretrain set and evaluated on train set. Networks used for classification, on the other hand, were trained on training set and evaluated on test set.

## 5.3  Baseline Methods

Performance of presented denoising approach was compared against three baseline methods: median filtering, bilateral filtering [16,20] and BM3D [9]. Parameters of every baseline method were tuned for different types of noise conditions. Only the best result was reported in each case.

For median filtering, $3 \times 3$, $5 \times 5$, $7 \times 7$ and $9 \times 9$ windows were tested. For bilateral filtering, parameters $\sigma_s \in \{0.2, 0.3, 0.4\}$ and $\sigma_r \in \{2, 3, 4\}$. And for BM3D method, $\sigma \in \{0.1, 0.15, 0.2, 0.25\}$.

## 5.4  Denoising with Known Noise Conditions

In this task we trained neural network to denoise images with known noise conditions. Different noise models with various parameters were used. Specifically, Gaussian noise with standard deviation $\sigma$, quantization noise with range of distortion $q$, and salt & pepper noise with probability of flipping pixel $p$. All types of noise were tested with corresponding parameters taking values from set $\{0.05, 0.1, 0.2, 0.5\}$.

Weights were initialized randomly with values sampled from normal distribution with standard deviation of 0.01, whereas biases were all set to 0. Training lasted 20 epochs. Constant learning rate of 0.000001 was used, together with weight decay of 0.0002 and momentum of 0.9. Training was performed in stochastic mode, which turned out to be crucial for correct learning.

### 5.5 Blind Denoising

In blind denoising task specific parameters of noise models were not known a priori. Instead, they were sampled uniformly from range from 0 to 0.5 at every iteration. Additionally, more extreme case was tested, with noise model being chosen randomly as well.

Training parameters used were the same as during denoising with known noise conditions.

### 5.6 Classification of Distorted Images

Presence of noise in images can have significant impact on classification accuracy during image recognition task. In [13] we examined amount of drop in correct classification rate (CCR) due to various types of artificial distortion present in test images. We also compared it to the case in which data used to train our model had similar corruption present.

We conducted similar experiment with STL-10 dataset and compared the results with alternative approach of dealing with noise in image classification: training classification model on data without distortions and classifying test images denoised with previously trained model.

**Table 1.** Architecture of CNN used during classification task.

| Layer | Type | Size |
|---|---|---|
| 0 | input | $96 \times 96 \times 1$ |
| 1 | convolutional | $7 \times 7 \times 32$ |
| 2 | max pooling | $2 \times 2$ |
| 3 | convolutional | $5 \times 5 \times 64$ |
| 4 | max pooling | $2 \times 2$ |
| 5 | convolutional | $3 \times 3 \times 128$ |
| 6 | max pooling | $2 \times 2$ |
| 7 | fully connected | 1024 |
| 8 | fully connected | 1024 |
| 9 | softmax | 10 |

Due to low number of images available for training in STL-10 dataset, neural network architecture used was fairly shallow. Architecture summary was presented in Table 1. Activation function was set to ReLU in all hidden layers. Model was trained for 100 epochs, using learning rate of 0.01, momentum of 0.9 and batch size of 50. Additionally, dropout [19] with probability of 0.5 was applied after both fully connected layers as a form of regularization.

## 5.7    Results and Discussion

Results of denoising with known noise conditions were presented in Table 2, and sample denoised images were presented on Fig. 1. Denoising using CNN outperforms baseline methods in every case except one. Gain in PSNR is especially significant, compared to baseline methods, when dealing with high amounts of distortion. Proposed method also works well with different models of noise, which may suggest its adaptability to less popular types of distortions that might be encountered in practical applications.

**Table 2.** Average values of PSNR for different denoising methods with known noise conditions.

| Type of noise | Input | CNN | BM3D | Bilateral | Median |
|---|---|---|---|---|---|
| Gaussian (0.05) | 24.50 | **27.11** | 25.58 | 25.42 | 23.98 |
| Gaussian (0.10) | 19.71 | 24.70 | **24.97** | 23.85 | 22.43 |
| Gaussian (0.20) | 14.69 | **22.76** | 22.27 | 20.73 | 19.55 |
| Gaussian (0.50) | 9.17 | **18.91** | 16.25 | 13.36 | 15.77 |
| Quantization (0.05) | 28.29 | **27.78** | 24.74 | 24.90 | 24.00 |
| Quantization (0.10) | 23.81 | **27.40** | 22.83 | 23.03 | 22.25 |
| Quantization (0.20) | 18.55 | **26.73** | 19.08 | 19.20 | 18.64 |
| Quantization (0.50) | 11.48 | **23.99** | 12.37 | 12.43 | 11.95 |
| Salt & Pepper (0.05) | 17.52 | **25.89** | 23.56 | 21.17 | 24.34 |
| Salt & Pepper (0.10) | 14.73 | **28.44** | 22.43 | 19.48 | 23.58 |
| Salt & Pepper (0.20) | 11.86 | **27.57** | 20.62 | 16.59 | 21.66 |
| Salt & Pepper (0.50) | 7.98 | **24.09** | 13.59 | 10.89 | 16.77 |

**Table 3.** Average values of PSNR for different denoising methods with unknown noise conditions.

| Type of noise | Input | CNN | BM3D | Bilateral | Median |
|---|---|---|---|---|---|
| Gaussian | 15.36 | **21.65** | 20.77 | 18.96 | 18.89 |
| Quantization | 18.77 | **24.67** | 18.25 | 18.36 | 17.82 |
| Salt & Pepper | 12.19 | **26.54** | 19.10 | 15.87 | 20.08 |
| Mixture | 15.32 | **22.27** | 19.03 | 17.42 | 18.85 |

**Fig. 1.** Sample images from STL-10 dataset, with different types of noise applied. Top row: original images, middle row: images with artificial distortion applied, bottom row: images denoised using CNN. Left column: Gaussian noise with $\sigma = 0.1$, middle column: quantization noise with $q = 0.2$, right column: salt & pepper noise with $p = 0.5$.

Results of blind denoising were presented in Table 3. Denoising with proposed CNN once again outperforms baseline methods. This results may indicate robustness to variance in noise parameters.

Results of classification with different noise conditions were presented in Fig. 2. Four different cases were considered: baseline, in which no artificial noise was imposed (C2C); case, in which distortions were present in test data, but were unavailable during training (C2N); case, in which distortions were introduced in both train and test data (N2N); and finally the case, in which train data had no distortions, and noise present in test data was removed using previously trained model (C2D).

As expected, applying noise results in CCR drop proportional to the amount of distortion and dependent on specific type of noise model used. This is partially remedied if similar distortions are present in train data as well. However, higher gain was observed when images were denoised prior to classification. Summary of CCR over all types of distortions was presented in Table 4. Detailed values of CCR for different types of noise was presented in Table 5.

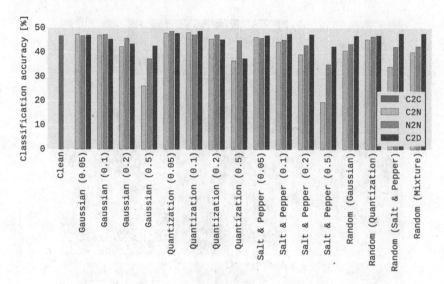

**Fig. 2.** Classification accuracy depending on type of artificial distortion applied, in four cases: with no artificial noise (C2C), with only test set distorted (C2N), with both training and test sets distorted (N2N) and with test set distorted and denoised (C2D). If applies, values of noise parameters where specified in parentheses, namely: standard deviation for Gaussian noise, probability of flipping pixel for salt & pepper noise and range of distortion for quantization noise.

**Table 4.** Average classification accuracy for different approaches of dealing with distortions in data.

| Method | Accuracy |
|--------|----------|
| C2C    | 46.72 %  |
| C2N    | 40.58 %  |
| N2N    | 44.22 %  |
| C2D    | 45.61 %  |

## 6   Conclusions and Future Works

During the experiments we evaluated performance of proposed neural architecture in image denoising task. We obtained significant improvement in image quality after denoising compared to baseline methods on STL-10 dataset, especially when significant distortions were present. Improvements were observed in denoising with known noise conditions and blind denoising, for various types and parameters of distortion. Overall, proposed method yielded high quality image denoising while remaining robust to variance in noise parameters.

Furthermore, we investigated influence of various noise conditions on classification accuracy during image recognition task. Two approaches of dealing with noise were evaluated: training on distorted data and denoising images prior

**Table 5.** Detailed classification accuracy for different types of noise and different approaches of dealing with distortions in data.

| Type of noise | C2N | N2N | C2D |
|---|---|---|---|
| Gaussian (0.05) | **47.26** | 46.72 | 46.97 |
| Gaussian (0.10) | 46.94 | **47.20** | 45.32 |
| Gaussian (0.20) | 42.24 | **45.68** | 43.30 |
| Gaussian (0.50) | 26.16 | 37.30 | **42.62** |
| Quantization (0.05) | 47.90 | **48.60** | 47.73 |
| Quantization (0.10) | 47.99 | 47.15 | **48.67** |
| Quantization (0.20) | 45.47 | **47.12** | 45.15 |
| Quantization (0.50) | 36.50 | **44.79** | 37.39 |
| Salt & Pepper (0.05) | 46.19 | 45.75 | **46.81** |
| Salt & Pepper (0.10) | 44.27 | 45.05 | **47.48** |
| Salt & Pepper (0.20) | 39.04 | 42.80 | **47.30** |
| Salt & Pepper (0.50) | 19.45 | 34.94 | **42.35** |
| Random (Gaussian) | 40.62 | 43.33 | **46.67** |
| Random (Quantization) | 45.23 | 46.42 | **46.85** |
| Random (Salt & Pepper) | 34.02 | 42.23 | **47.65** |
| Random (Mixture) | 40.03 | 42.40 | **47.59** |

to classification. The second method yielded better results during experiments, close to baseline accuracy, when no distortions were present. This suggests that training separate network exclusively for image denoising might be preferred approach, especially in situation when labeled data is scarce but we posses high amount of unlabeled examples.

Relatively small images were used during the experiments, enabling processing whole images during training. This might turn out to be inefficient for larger images, requiring adjusting proposed architecture and training procedure. More thorough experiments on additional datasets would be required to establish influence of various hyperparameters and architecture choices on denoising quality. Larger models would also have to be evaluated during classification to test the limits of training on distorted data. This is left for further research.

**Acknowledgement.** This research was supported in part by PLGrid Infrastructure. This work was supported by the Polish National Science Centre under the grant no. DEC-2014/15/B/ST6/00609.

# References

1. Abadi, M., Agarwal, A., Barham, P., Brevdo, E., Chen, Z., Citro, C., Ghemawat, S., et al.: TensorFlow: Large-Scale Machine Learning on Heterogeneous Distributed Systems (2016). arXiv preprint arXiv:1603.04467

2. Agostinelli, F., Anderson, M.R., Lee, H.: Adaptive multi-column deep neural networks with application to robust image denoising. In: Advances in Neural Information Processing Systems, pp. 1493–1501 (2013)
3. Bengio, Y., Goodfellow, I.J., Courville, A.: Deep Learning. An MIT Press Book in Preparation. MIT Press, Cambridge (2015)
4. Bovik, A.C.: Handbook of Image and Video Processing. Academic press, Orlando (2010)
5. Burger, H.C., Schuler, C.J., Harmeling, S.: Image denoising: can plain neural networks compete with BM3D? In: 2012 IEEE Conference on Computer Vision and Pattern Recognition (CVPR), pp. 2392–2399. IEEE, June 2012
6. Cireşan, D., Meier, U., Masci, J., Schmidhuber, J.: Multi-column deep neural network for traffic sign classification. Neural Netw. **32**, 333–338 (2012)
7. Coates, A., Ng, A.Y., Lee, H.: An analysis of single-layer networks in unsupervised feature learning. In: International Conference on Artificial Intelligence and Statistics, pp. 215–223 (2011)
8. Cyganek, B., Siebert, J.P.: An Introduction to 3D Computer Vision Techniques and Algorithms. Wiley, Hoboken (2011)
9. Dabov, K., Foi, A., Katkovnik, V., Egiazarian, K.: Image denoising with block-matching and 3D filtering. In: Electronic Imaging 2006, pp. 606414–606414. International Society for Optics and Photonics, February 2006
10. Eigen, D., Krishnan, D., Fergus, R.: Restoring an image taken through a window covered with dirt or rain. In: Proceedings of the IEEE International Conference on Computer Vision, pp. 633–640 (2013)
11. Jain, V., Seung, S.: Natural image denoising with convolutional networks. In: Advances in Neural Information Processing Systems, pp. 769–776 (2009)
12. Kayser, M., Zhong, V.: Denoising Convolutional Autoencoders for Noisy Speech Recognition
13. Koziarski, M., Cyganek, B.: Examination of the deep neural networks in classification of distorted signals. In: Rutkowski, L., Korytkowski, M., Scherer, R., Tadeusiewicz, R., Zadeh, L.A., Zurada, J.M. (eds.) ICAISC 2016. LNCS (LNAI), vol. 9693, pp. 680–688. Springer, Heidelberg (2016). doi:10.1007/978-3-319-39384-1_60
14. Krizhevsky, A., Sutskever, I., Hinton, G.E.: Imagenet classification with deep convolutional neural networks. In: Advances in Neural Information Processing Systems, pp. 1097–1105 (2012)
15. Nair, V., Hinton, G.E. Rectified linear units improve restricted Boltzmann machines. In: Proceedings of the 27th International Conference on Machine Learning (ICML-10), pp. 807–814 (2010)
16. Paris, S., Durand, F.: A fast approximation of the bilateral filter using a signal processing approach. In: Leonardis, A., Bischof, H., Pinz, A. (eds.) ECCV 2006. LNCS, vol. 3954, pp. 568–580. Springer, Heidelberg (2006). doi:10.1007/11744085_44
17. Sermanet, P., LeCun, Y.: Traffic sign recognition with multi-scale convolutional networks. In: The 2011 International Joint Conference on Neural Networks (IJCNN), pp. 2809–2813. IEEE, July 2011
18. Simonyan, K., Zisserman, A.: Very deep convolutional networks for large-scale image recognition (2014). arXiv preprint arXiv:1409.1556
19. Srivastava, N., Hinton, G., Krizhevsky, A., Sutskever, I., Salakhutdinov, R.: Dropout: a simple way to prevent neural networks from overfitting. J. Mach. Learn. Res. **15**(1), 1929–1958 (2014)

20. Tomasi, C., Manduchi, R.: Bilateral filtering for gray and color images. In: Sixth International Conference on Computer Vision, 1998, pp. 839–846. IEEE, January 1998
21. Xie, J., Xu, L., Chen, E.: Image denoising and inpainting with deep neural networks. In: Advances in Neural Information Processing Systems, pp. 341–349 (2012)

# Multi–layer Lacunarity for Texture Recognition

Przemysław Mazurek[1(✉)] and Dorota Oszutowska–Mazurek[2]

[1] Department of Signal Processing and Multimedia Engineering, West–Pomeranian University of Technology, 26. Kwietnia 10 Street, 71126 Szczecin, Poland
przemyslaw.mazurek@zut.edu.pl
[2] Faculty of Motor Transport, Higher School of Technology and Economics in Szczecin, Klonowica 14 Street, 71244 Szczecin, Poland
adorotta@op.pl

**Abstract.** Lacunarity could be applied for the analysis of different types of textures. Application of binary lacunarity for the analysis of grayscale images is proposed in this paper. Input image is thresholded using predefined set of values and every binary image is processed using lacunarity for the selected scale. Obtained vector could be used for the analysis and segmentation purposes. Achieved probability of identification is 30 % for ideal detection and more then 60 % for 10 % acceptance margin.

**Keywords:** Lacunarity · Image analysis · Image binarization

## 1 Introduction

Texture analysis and recognition are essential in low–level image processing and could be applied in numerous applications. There are numerous techniques for the texture description and the most important classification uses random, fractal and repetitive subclasses. Natural and artificial (man–made) textures could be assigned to all mentioned subclasses. The most important algorithms approaches are based on multiscale analysis, because numerous image properties depend the on texture scale [1–3]. Spatial descriptors that support textures are especially important, because non–spatial analysis, e.g. using histogram looses important information. It is difficult to find entire texture descriptor, because full information is included in texture image only, and a single or a few parameters are very often is not sufficient. Adequate descriptor or descriptors allow the discrimination between different textures according to application requirements [4,5].

Fractal descriptors are useful, because they support all mentioned subclasses of textures [6–8]. Random and periodic textures are not fractal, but obtained parameters could be applied [9,10].

### 1.1 Related Works

Grayscale image could be processed using Triangular Prism Method (TPM) [11], Tiled TPM [12] and variogram [13] directly. Layered approach is possible using

© Springer International Publishing AG 2016
L.J. Chmielewski et al. (Eds.): ICCVG 2016, LNCS 9972, pp. 174–183, 2016.
DOI: 10.1007/978-3-319-46418-3_16

Slit Island Method [14] and Area–Perimeter Method [15]. Some of mentioned algorithms, like variogram, allow the processing of irregular texture area also. The rectangular areas of analysis is assumed in this paper. Grayscale image processing with the use of lacunarity is considered in [16].

### 1.2   Content and Contribution of the Paper

Novel technique for the grayscale texture analysis is proposed in this paper, and is based on lacunarity. The binary lacunarity is applied for an image with predefined threshold set in this paper. Lacunarity for binary images is briefly presented in Sect. 2. Proposed texture analysis is considered in Sect. 3. Example analysis for Brodatz textures and discussion are presented in Sect. 4. Final conclusions and further works are considered in Sect. 5.

## 2   Lacunarity for Binary Images

Lacunarity for binary images in this section is briefly presented. More details are available in [16,17]. Lacunarity supports multifractal analysis, because properties of the texture are scale variable. The output of the lacunarity is not single value but a vector of values, related to different scales. Object pixels are ones (1's) and holes are zeros (0's). The input image could be processed using small tiles (non overlapped) or using sliding (moving) window ($R \times R$ size). The sliding window requires much more computations, but gives less noise in output vector values. There are $R^2$ of pixels inside of particular window $W$ position and the number of ones (pixels assigned to object) are counted:

$$s_i = \sum_i W_i, \tag{1}$$

where $i$ is the index related to unique 2D position of the window.

The frequency of the occurrence of $s$–value for particular $r$ is calculated successively using the following update formula:

$$n(s,r) \leftarrow n(s,r) + 1, \tag{2}$$

and the following starting condition are used:

$$n(s,r) = 0. \tag{3}$$

The probability table $Q$ is computed using the following normalization formula:

$$Q(.,r) = \frac{n(.,r)}{\sum n(.,r)}, \tag{4}$$

so proper distribution is obtained. The calculation of lacunarity is based on the computation of two first moments for the distribution $Q$. The first moment is defined as:

$$Z_1(r) = \sum_i s_i Q(s_i, r), \tag{5}$$

and the second moment is:

$$Z_2(r) = \sum_i s_i^2 Q(s_i, r), \tag{6}$$

so lacunarity $\Lambda(r)$ for the window is defined as:

$$\Lambda(r) = \frac{Z_2(r)}{[Z_1(r)]^2}. \tag{7}$$

Lacunarity output vector is obtained by the testing of different window sizes depending on the application, but large windows gives noisy results because the number of large windows is smaller comparing to smaller windows.

Proper lacunarity is normalized $\Lambda_{norm}(r)$ and presented on double logarithmic plot (log10–log10):

$$\Lambda_{norm}(r) = \frac{\Lambda(r)}{\Lambda(1)} \tag{8}$$

## 3 Proposed Estimator

Example Brodatz textures are shown in Fig. 1. Brodatz textures are grayscale so binary threshold is applied at different levels after the image normalization (contrast/brightness).

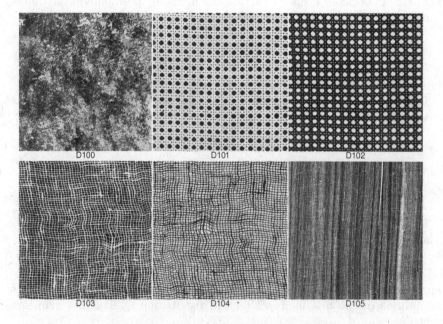

**Fig. 1.** Example of grayscale Brodatz images.

The process of binary layers extraction from grayscale image is depicted in Fig. 2. There are assumed nine threshold $T_i$ values: $0.1, 0.2, 0.3, \cdots, 0.9$. Some Brodatz textures are high contrast so intermediate values of the threshold do not add important information if two high contrast textures are compared. The input image $X$ could be converted to the set of binary images $X^i$ using the following formula:

$$X^i(x,y) = \begin{cases} 1 & : X(x,y) > T_i \\ 0 & : X(x,y) \leq T_i \end{cases} \tag{9}$$

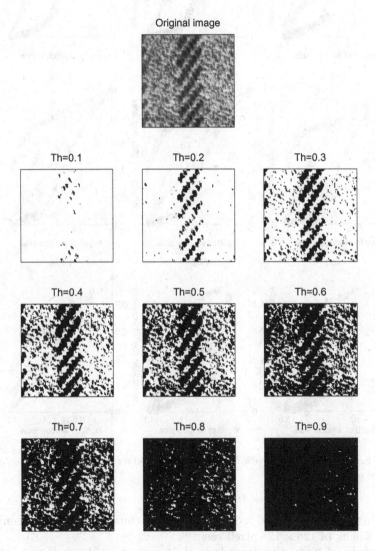

**Fig. 2.** Example binary layer obtained from the input image.

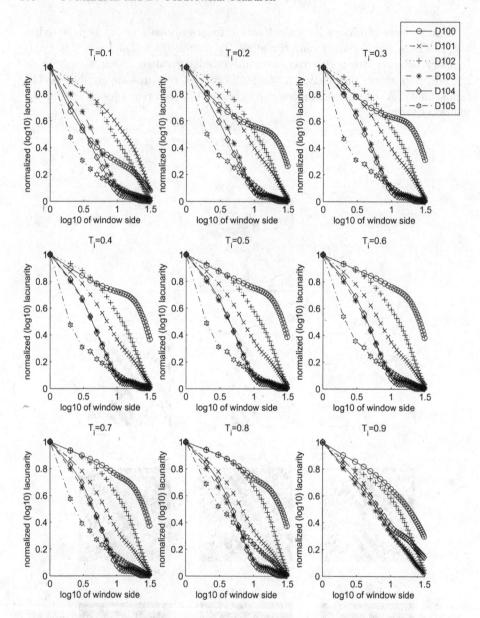

**Fig. 3.** Lacunarity vectors for example grayscale Brodatz images. Different threshold values are applied.

Original images have $640 \times 640$ resolution. Lacunarity is computed only for left–top square of $128 \times 128$ pixels size.

The shape of lacunarity depends on the texture type [16], and texture scale influences the shape left–right position. The shape of lacunarity vector values is typically smooth so many windows sizes could be omitted. Such approach reduces computation cost.

Lacunarity vectors $\Lambda^i_{norm}(r)$ are obtained for all binary images. In numerous application single scale $(r)$ is sufficient: $\Lambda^i_{norm}(r = const)$ and this is the output of the proposed multi–layer lacunarity estimator.

Example lacunarity vectors are shown in Fig. 3 related to images shown in Fig. 1.

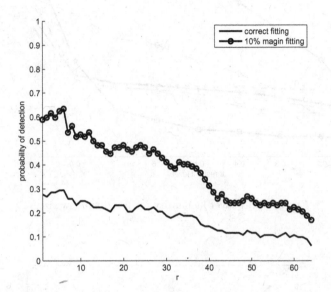

**Fig. 4.** Example of texture identification based on single sample.

The testing of the identification of texture uses the following metric:

$$E_{nm}(r) = \sum_i |\Lambda^n_{norm}(r) - \Lambda^m_{norm}(r)|, \tag{10}$$

where $n$ and $m$ are indexes of pair consisting reference and tested texture. The probability of correct detection is depicted in Fig. 4 as a function of window side. Assuming 10 % margin, related to minimal $E$ value, allows multiple reference textures assignment to the particular texture. The correct texture could be in this set and such identification results are shown in Fig. 4 also.

Example vectors of lacunarity for selected 6 × 6 window size are shown in Fig. 5 for two different non–overlapping regions. This window size is selected for due to results obtained from Fig. 4.

The correct detection cases as function of image number is shown in Fig. 6. The false and correct detections, including multiple assignments due to 10 % margin, are shown in Fig. 7.

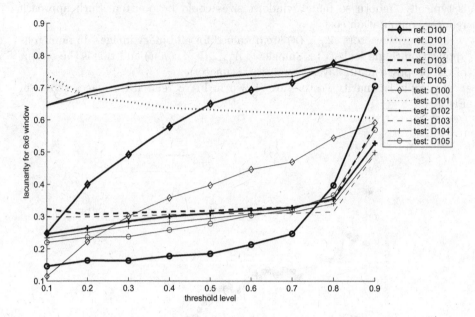

**Fig. 5.** Multi–layer lacunarity for $6 \times 6$ window size

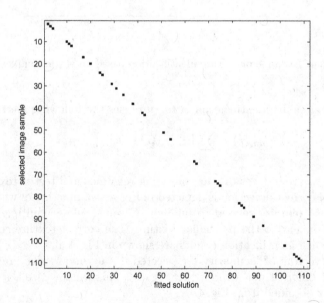

**Fig. 6.** Example of texture correct identification based on single sample ($6 \times 6$ window size).

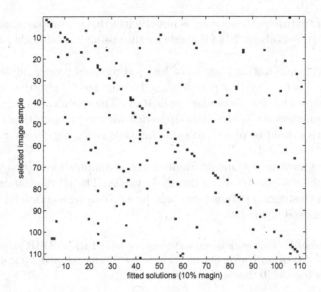

**Fig. 7.** Example of identification texture based on single sample - assumed 10 % margin acceptance related to minimal value ($6 \times 6$ window size).

## 4    Results and Discussion

Binary lacunarity depends on the threshold and image type. It is well visible for 'D100' texture, where for $T_i = 0.1$ is observed fractal texture. Grouped texture [16] is observed for higher threshold values.

The results depend on data set, so they should be verified for final application. Highest probability of detection is obtained for $6 \times 6$ window size (Fig. 4). The implementation of margin e.g. 10 % improves this probability from 0.3 to more then 0.6. The assignment of tested texture to more reference textures could be accepted by some applications. Additional texture descriptors may improve general results also.

The selection of small window size ($6 \times 6$) is related to the properties of database. The database considered in this paper contains numerous textures of different sizes. Small patterns are typical, but large patterns are also available. Typical tests of segmentation algorithms are based on only small patterns, so subset of Brodatz database is preferred by many researchers.

It is important that the identification is based only on 9 parameters only for single window size. Some of the parameters (obtained for intermediate threshold level) could be redundant for high contrast images.

## 5    Conclusions

The proposed multi–layer approach for lacunarity estimation of grayscale image is interesting way for the texture analysis, but for some databases with very wide range of texture patterns sizes is not efficient due to computation cost. The computation time is about 10 s for single texture using Matlab code and 2.4 GHz processor.

Lacunarity computation cost is not low and requires proper implementation of algorithm. There are many possibilities, but the most important is the optimization of algorithm for particular application. The specification of parameters range or parameters set is the main approach for the computation cost reduction. Lacunarity could be processed using multiple processor cores for improving performance, fortunately.

One of the most important problems is the normalization of image, because binary images are obtained using threshold values. The normalization of image based on some histogram parameters could be a promising solution for improving results of proposed algorithm.

**Acknowledgment.** This work is supported by the UE EFRR ZPORR project Z/2.32/ I/1.3.1/267/05 "Szczecin University of Technology – Research and Education Center of Modern Multimedia Technologies" (Poland).

# References

1. Wornell, G.: Signal Processing with Fractals: A Wavelet-Based Approach. Prentice Hall, Newjersy (1996)
2. Williams, G.: Chaos Theory Tamed. Joseph Henry Press, Washington (1999)
3. Seuront, L.: Fractals and Multifractals in Ecology and Aquatic Science. CRC Press, Boca Raton (2010)
4. Engler, O., Randle, V.: Introduction to Texture Analysis: Macrotexture, Microtexture, and Orientation Mapping. CRC Press, Boca Raton (2010)
5. Blackledge, J., Dubovitskiy, D.: Texture classification using fractal geometry for the diagnosis of skin cancers. In: Tang, W., Collomosse, J.P. (eds.) TPCG. Eurographics Association, pp. 41–48 (2009)
6. Mandelbrot, B.: The Fractal Geometry of the Nature. W.H. Freeman and Company, New York (1983)
7. Voss, R.: Fractals in nature: from characterization to simulation. In: Peitgen, H.-O., Saupe, D. (eds.) The Science of Fractal Images, pp. 21–70. Springer, Heidelberg (1988)
8. Turner, M., Blackledge, J., Andrews, P.: Fractal Geometry in Digital Imaging. Academic Press, New York (1998)
9. Stoyan, D., Stoyan, H.: Fractals, Random Shapes and Point Fields. Methods of Geometrical Statistics. Willey, Chichester (1994)
10. Peitgen, H., Jürgens, H., Saupe, D.: Fractals for the Classrooms, vol. 2. Springer-Verlag, Heidelberg (1992)
11. Oszutowska-Mazurek, D., Mazurek, P., Sycz, K., Waker-Wójciuk, G.: Estimation of fractal dimension according to optical density of cell nuclei in papanicolaou smears. In: Piętka, E., Kawa, J. (eds.) ITIB 2012. LNCS, vol. 7339, pp. 456–463. Springer, Heidelberg (2012). doi:10.1007/978-3-642-31196-3_46
12. Oszutowska, D., Purczyński, J.: Estimation of the fractal dimension using tiled triangular prism method for biological non-rectangular objects. Electr. Rev. **R.88**(10b), 261–263 (2012)

13. Oszutowska-Mazurek, D., Mazurek, P., Sycz, K., Wójciuk, G.W.: Variogram based estimator of fractal dimension for the analysis of cell nuclei from the papanicolaou smears. In: Choraś, R.S. (ed.) Image Processing and Communications Challenges 4. AISC, vol. 184, pp. 47–54. Springer, Heidelberg (2013). doi:10.1007/978-3-642-32384-3_7

14. Mandelbrot, B., Passoja, D., Paullay, A.: Fractal character of fracture surfaces of metals. Nature **308**, 721–722 (1984)

15. Mazurek, P., Oszutowska-Mazurek, D.: From slit-island method to ising model - analysis of grayscale images. Int. J. Appl. Math. Comput. Sci. **24**(1), 49–63 (2014)

16. Plotnick, R., Gardner, R., Hargrove, W., Prestegaard, K., Perlmutter, M.: Lacunarity analysis: a general technique for the analysis of spatial patterns. Phys. Rev. E **53**(5), 5461–5468 (1996)

17. Oszutowska-Mazurek, D., Mazurek, P., Sycz, K., Waker-Wójciuk, G.: Lacunarity based estimator for the analysis of cell nuclei from the papanicolaou smears. In: Chmielewski, L.J., Kozera, R., Shin, B.-S., Wojciechowski, K. (eds.) ICCVG 2014. LNCS, vol. 8671, pp. 486–493. Springer, Heidelberg (2014). doi:10.1007/978-3-319-11331-9_58

# Saliency Enhanced Decolorization

Michal Zemko and Elena Sikudova[✉]

Faculty of Mathematics, Physics and Informatics
Comenius University, Bratislava, Slovakia
zemko10@uniba.sk, sikudova@sccg.sk

**Abstract.** Color-to-grayscale conversion methods are widely used in the field of computer vision and image processing. The importance of preserving the source color image details is really high, because only correctly converted images can be used in real world applications (e.g. a colorblind version of a webpage, etc.). The lack of some image details can cause misunderstandings and incorrect data evaluation. Saliency maps help us identify areas of the image that attract the visual attention of users. In this paper we propose a new method for color-to-grayscale conversion based on preserving image saliency.

**Keywords:** Saliency map · Decolorize · Grayscale · Color-to-grayscale conversion

## 1 Introduction

Medicine, robotics, industry and many more possible applications can profit from perfect color-to-grayscale transformations. A grayscale image is often a better alternative to a colored one. Less processing operations, faster visualization and computations, lower power consumption – all that can be achieved by using a single-channel data information. Many practical applications of image processing as a part of the computer vision pipeline can benefit from these advantages. Finally, grayscale photography is becoming popular again, also as a part of the advertisement design business.

Unfortunately, in the real world it is impossible to make the color-to-grayscale transformation perfect without errors. At first, we need to define what a perfect transformation means. Enhance contrast, preserve chromatic differences or preserve saliency? The best approach would involve all of them, since the human visual system is very complex. Based on the signals gathered from rods and cones, the brain interprets the scene. Contrast, color, intensity changes, lines and/or orientation attract the low level attention. Figure 1 shows a color image transformed to grayscale with three different methods.

In this paper we propose a saliency enhancement of the Decolorize method by Grundland and Dodgson [10]. Their random based bivariate Gaussian distribution pixel pairing system does not take the saliency potential of an image into account. We emphasize the importance of image saliency maps in color-to-grayscale conversion methods.

© Springer International Publishing AG 2016
L.J. Chmielewski et al. (Eds.): ICCVG 2016, LNCS 9972, pp. 184–193, 2016.
DOI: 10.1007/978-3-319-46418-3_17

**Fig. 1.** Different color-to-grayscale methods. From left: input RGB image, Apparent Grayscale [19], Decolorize [10] and our Saliency Enhanced Decolorization.

## 2    Related Work

The simplest approach to color-to-grayscale transformation is to use the Y channel of CIE XYZ color space [8]. In many cases, taking only the luminance channel and neglecting the chrominance channels produces satisfactory results fast and efficiently. On the other side, in case of isoluminant input this method fails.

Bala and Eschbach [2] proposed to improve the negative results of the CIE Y method by adding high-frequency chrominance information into the luminance channel. This spatial approach preserves chrominant edges. The weighted output of a spatial high-pass filter of chromatic channels is added to the luminance channel.

Grundland and Dodgson [10] proposed the contrast enhancing Decolorize algorithm for color-to-grayscale conversion. The method consists of (1) global conversion to a linear color space analogous to human visual processing (2) Gaussian pairing based image sampling (3) dimensionality reduction by predominant component analysis and (4) image fusion of luminance and chrominance. Finally, the algorithm adjusts the dynamic range of the output.

Gooch et al. [9] proposed the local saliency preserving Color2Gray algorithm. In the CIE Lab space they calculated the differences in chroma and luminance for nearby pixels. The last step of their method is a selective modulation of the luminance difference by the least square optimization methods. Optimized brightness and color values are combined into a final output.

A different approach was proposed by Rasche et al. [18]. Their method aims at preserving contrast and maintaining the luminance consistency. These two goals are expressed in the form of a constrained, multidimensional scaling problem.

Neumann et al. [16] proposed a local method based on their newly created Coloroid color system. This method is divided into three main parts. First, they create the gradient field from CIE Lab and Coloroid equations. Then, they use orthogonal projections to correct errors in the gradient field. This approach is computationally faster than Poisson solver or other computationally intensive algorithms. Finally, output image is constructed via simple 2D integration.

The global and local conversion method proposed by Smith et al. [19] belongs to the most efficient color-to-grayscale algorithms. A two-step approach at first globally assigns gray values based in Helmholtz-Kohlrausch effect and determine color ordering. Second, it locally enhances the output by weighted multiscale unsharp masking to reproduce the original contrast.

## 3    Algorithm

Our approach focuses on preserving the saliency of the color image in the transformed image.

Analyzing the results of perceptual evaluation of color-to-grayscale image conversions [5], where the algorithms mentioned in Sect. 2 were compared, we decided to modify the Decolorize algorithm [10] in order to use the saliency information for preserving contrast in the image. The Decolorize algorithm together with the Apparent Grayscale method [19] performed the best. Decolorize is used in our method, since it can benefit more from adding the saliency information. The algorithm is efficient at enhancing image contrast. Its main features are: preservation of global image consistency, grayscale preservation and fast performance. For common test image resolution it reaches real-time performance. In contrast with other methods, Decolorize avoids the image noise, contouring and hallo artifacts. The original algorithm consist of five easily replaceable parts:

1. Color representation using the YPQ color space
2. Image sampling by Gaussian pairing
3. Dimensionality reduction by predominant component analysis
4. Image fusion of luminance and chrominance
5. Saturation dependent dynamic range adjustment

RGB input is converted to the YPQ linear color space. YPQ color channels are analogous to human visual processing. Its advantage is easy linear transformation and well defined calculation of hue and saturation values. Image sampling by Gaussian pairing is used to find image pixel pairs. Pixels to be paired are chosen randomly according to a displacement vector from an isotropic bivariate Gaussian distribution. Grundland and Dodgson introduced a new dimensionality reduction strategy to find the color axis that best represents chromatic contrast loss – predominant component analysis. The next step consists of luminance and chrominance information fusion. Finally, saturation is used to calibrate luminance while adjusting its dynamic range and image noise compensation.

### 3.1    Decolorization Enhancement

From our investigation, the second step of the Decolorize algorithm – image sampling by Gaussian pairing – is the best place to incorporate the saliency information to enhance the results. In the original method, pairing pixels are taken randomly from the pixels neighborhood according to a displacement vector. The displacements in $x$ and $y$ axes are each drawn from a univariate Gaussian distribution $N(0, \frac{2}{\pi}\sigma^2)$.

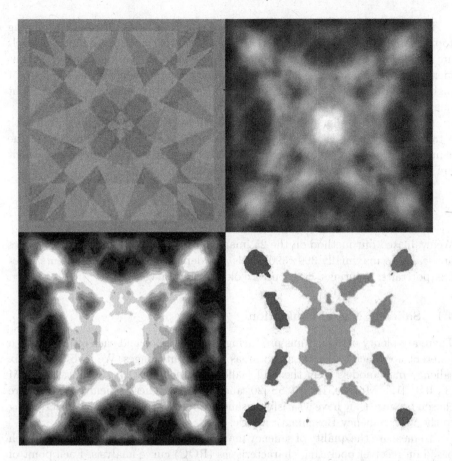

**Fig. 2.** Saliency map segmentation: (top left) input image, (top right) Murray saliency map, (bottom left) non uniform quantized saliency map, (bottom right) segmented different areas in one saliency map level.

Our saliency based pairing constraints the pairing pixels to have the same saliency level as the investigated pixel. This ensures that the pair of pixels will belong to a visually similar area.

The process is illustrated in Fig. 2. On the top left, the original color image is shown. The top right part shows the computed saliency map of the color image. This saliency map is quantized in the next step (bottom left). The easiest way is to use a uniform quantization with a selected number of levels. This approach gives fast results, but produces relatively large errors, because uniform quantization applies regular partitioning of the image histogram, which can end up mixing up different salient areas together. Hence, we use a non-uniform quantization based on finding local maxima in the image histogram. Figure 2 shows the non-uniform quantization.

Finally, the bottom right part of the image identifies all pixels belonging to the same saliency level as the chosen investigated pixel. All quantized levels are divided to 8-connected components. Each pixel in the input image is thus identified by its saliency level and the connected component in this level. Color highlighted different components of one saliency level are shown at bottom-right image in Fig. 2.

Finally, in the saliency based pairing, each source image pixel is paired with a target image pixel that is randomly chosen from the same component of the same saliency level as the source pixel. Image pixel pairs from our enhancement are processed at step 3 of the Decolorize algorithm.

# 4   Evaluation

We evaluated our method on the 25 image dataset used in [5]. All of the images are scaled to maximally 390×390 pixels and depict various motifs - plants, photos, portraits, paintings, cartoons or color testing images.

## 4.1   Saliency Model Evaluation

There are plenty of algorithms producing saliency maps and each of them uses a different approach to select salient areas from input images. We investigated six saliency map models from the MIT Saliency Benchmark [4]: Achanta [1], AIM [3], Itti[1] [12], Murray [15], RCSS [20] and SWD [7]. These saliency models were chosen because they have a satisfying saliency output and performance according to the MIT Saliency Benchmark metric.

To measure the quality of saliency maps, we employed a widely used approach based on receiver operating characteristics (ROC) curve analysis. Each point of the ROC curve is a pair of the true positive rate (TPR) and the false positive rate (FPR), where

$$TPR = \frac{\text{nr. of pixels correctly classified as salient}}{\text{total nr. of salient pixels}}$$

and

$$FPR = \frac{\text{nr. of pixels falsely classified as salient}}{\text{total nr. of non-salient pixels}}.$$

These rate are obtained by comparing a thresholded saliency map (SM) to a ground truth saliency map (GT). Both maps are obtained by using Itti saliency model [12], but for the grayscale image the color information is neglected. GT is a binary map of top 20 % [13] salient pixels in the color image. The thresholded SM is obtained by binarizing the SM with a varying threshold. For each level of the threshold we obtain one point of the ROC curve. Figure 3 shows the ROC curves for SWD (left) and Achanta (right) saliency maps of all 25 images.

---

[1] Implemented in GBVS [11].

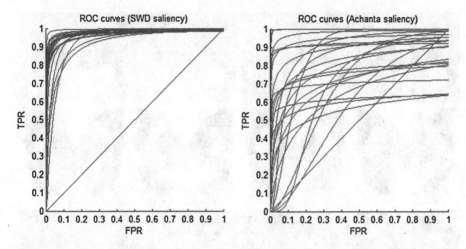

**Fig. 3.** The best and the worst saliency maps by plotted ROC curves for each image.

The ROC curves can be compared by computing the areas under the curves (AUC). The higher the AUC value, the better the classification. A perfect ROC curve has AUC=1. The average AUC values together with the standard deviation values for all investigated saliency map methods are summarized in Table 1. The best average AUC rate has SWD, AIM and RCSS, respectively. Unambiguously, the worst one is Achanta.

**Table 1.** Average AUC and Std for each saliency map

| Saliency map | Achanta | AIM | Itti | Murray | RCSS | SWD |
|---|---|---|---|---|---|---|
| Avg. AUC | *0.7932* | 0.9355 | 0.8916 | 0.8536 | 0.9174 | **0.9707** |
| Std | 0.1445 | 0.0430 | 0.0611 | 0.0985 | 0.0734 | **0.0178** |

The best saliency map model generates the largest AUC. However, if two ROC curves intersect we cannot use a simple comparative metric, because we do not know which of them performs better. The significance of the difference between two ROC curves can be calculated as a critical ratio test – Z-score [17]

$$Z - score = \frac{AUC_1 - AUC_2}{\sqrt{SE^2(AUC_1) + SE^2(AUC)}},$$

where $AUC_i$ is the area under the ROC $i$ and $SE(AUC_i)$ is the standard error of the computed area. Our $H0$ hypothesis is that the difference between the two areas is zero. The critical ratio has the asymptotic Gaussian(0,1) distribution.

For all 25 images we calculated the statistical significance of the pairwise differences in 6 saliency maps ROC curves. The ROC curves, AUC values and standard errors were obtained using the code in [6]. In only 5 cases we could not reject the $H0$ hypothesis.

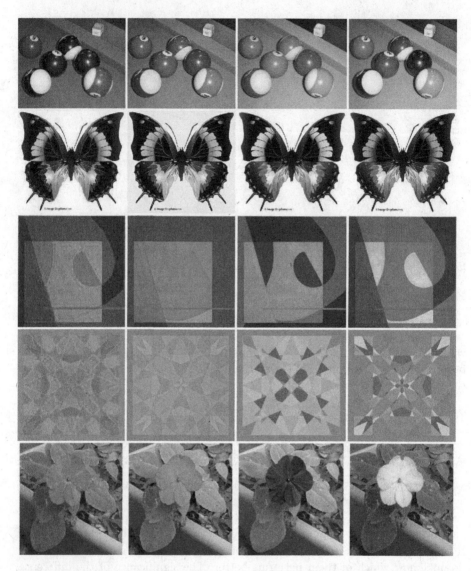

**Fig. 4.** Results. From left: input RGB image, Apparent Grayscale [19], Decolorize [10] and our Saliency Enhanced Decolorization using SWD saliency map. (Color figure online)

## 5    Results and Discussion

Figure 4 compares our method to the Apparent Grayscale method and to the Decolorize method on a wide variety of images. In the left column the original color picture is shown in order to compare the image details preservation in grayscale versions. In the "pool balls" image we can see the enhanced contrast

**Table 2.** Experiment results

| Image number | User preferred our method | Quality score | |
|---|---|---|---|
| | | Decolorize | Our method |
| 1 | 11,76 % | 0,842904 | 0,690803 |
| 2 | 64,71 % | 0,951664 | 0,951371 |
| 3 | 47,06 % | 0,83521 | 0,832587 |
| 4 | 94,12 % | 0,946204 | 0,953081 |
| 5 | 82,35 % | 0,855092 | 0,890217 |
| 6 | 52,94 % | 0,899429 | 0,888166 |
| 7 | 58,82 % | 0,9599 | 0,949037 |
| 8 | 5,88 % | 0,864202 | 0,664077 |
| 9 | 76,47 % | 0,876419 | 0,88083 |
| 10 | 70,59 % | 0,692302 | 0,694057 |
| 11 | 76,47 % | 0,869917 | 0,871951 |
| 12 | 29,41 % | 0,903007 | 0,842666 |
| 13 | 70,59 % | 0,84091 | 0,841955 |
| 14 | 82,35 % | 0,734117 | 0,719028 |
| 15 | 52,94 % | 0,949161 | 0,939466 |
| 16 | 76,47 % | 0,824522 | 0,828213 |
| 17 | 35,29 % | 0,926812 | 0,924398 |
| 18 | 64,71 % | 0,974702 | 0,974638 |
| 19 | 41,18 % | 0,721443 | 0,734115 |
| 20 | 64,71 % | 0,785748 | 0,787549 |
| 21 | 64,71 % | 0,871361 | 0,871381 |
| 22 | 0,00 % | 0,969352 | 0,966908 |
| 23 | 41,18 % | 0,685882 | 0,682481 |
| 24 | 70,59 % | 0,623736 | 0,626921 |
| 25 | 23,53 % | 0,951963 | 0,917019 |

on violet and blue balls. The "butterfly" image seems quite similar to Decolorize, but there is one main difference. The upper part of the butterfly's wings is missing the pattern in the Decolorize version. Our output contains the pattern due to its saliency potential. The next two images are synthetic, mainly used for isoluminant testing. More details are visible in the "kaleidoscope" image, especially in the corners. The "flower" photo looks different at leaves and flower petals. The leaves are darker in our method and the petals are brighter in contrast with the dark Decolorize output. Our algorithm performs better than the Apparent Grayscale method because of the predominant component analysis used in the Decolorize algorithm. The main question is, if it is better than the original Decolorize algorithm.

In order to determine, if our proposed modification is better than the original method we conducted a user study experiment. The experiment was a paired-comparison experiment with a reference image. The observers were presented a reference color image and two grayscale images. They were asked to identify the grayscale image, which in their opinion approximated the color image better. The experiment was randomized, that is the order of images and the position (left or right) of the grayscale images were varying. We tested 25 images dataset [5] with a group of 17 naive participants between 18 and 47 years old with normal or corrected to normal vision. We also used an objective quality measure [14]. The results of the experiment and the quality scores are shown in Table 2. The analysis has shown that the difference between the original method and the saliency enhanced method is not statistically significant.

## 6    Conclusion

In this paper we presented Saliency Enhanced Decolorization method, which is based on the Decolorize algorithm [10]. On a small 25 diverse image dataset our method produces visually plausible grayscale image outputs, although the statistical analysis did not show statistically significant differences in user preferences. On the other side, the saliency of the color image preserved in our decolorization method was statistically different than the saliency preserved in the original method.

**Acknowledgment.** The authors wish to thank Dr. Martin Ilcik for the proof-reading of the manuscript.

## References

1. Achanta, R., Hemami, S., Estrada, F., Susstrunk, S.: Frequency-tuned salient region detection. In: IEEE Conference on Computer Vision and Pattern Recognition, CVPR 2009, pp. 1597–1604, June 2009
2. Bala, R., Eschbach, R.: Spatial color-to-grayscale transform preserving chrominance edge information. In: Color Imaging Conference, pp. 82–86. IS & T - The Society for Imaging Science and Technology (2004)
3. Bruce, N., Tsotsos, J.: Attention based on information maximization. J. Vis. **7**(9), 950 (2007)
4. Bylinskii, Z., Judd, T., Borji, A., Itti, L., Durand, F., Oliva, A., Torralba, A.: Mit saliency benchmark (2015). http://saliency.mit.edu/
5. Čadík, M.: Perceptual evaluation of color-to-grayscale image conversions. Comput. Graph. Forum **27**(7), 1745–1754 (2008)
6. Cardillo, G.: Roc curve: compute a receiver operating characteristics curve (2015). http://www.mathworks.com/matlabcentral/fileexchange/19950
7. Duan, L., Wu, C., Miao, J., Qing, L., Fu, Y.: Visual saliency detection by spatially weighted dissimilarity. In: 2011 IEEE Conference on Computer Vision and Pattern Recognition (CVPR), pp. 473–480, June 2011
8. Fairchild, M.: Color Appearance Models. The Wiley-IS & T Series in Imaging Science and Technology. Wiley, USA (2005)

9. Gooch, A.A., Olsen, S.C., Tumblin, J., Gooch, B.: Color2gray: salience-preserving color removal. ACM Trans. Graph. **24**(3), 634–639 (2005)

10. Grundland, M., Dodgson, N.A.: Decolorize: fast, contrast enhancing, color to grayscale conversion. Pattern Recogn. **40**(11), 2891–2896 (2007)

11. Harel, J.: A saliency implementation in matlab (2015). http://www.vision.caltech.edu/~harel/share/gbvs.php

12. Itti, L., Koch, C., Niebur, E.: A model of saliency-based visual attention for rapid scene analysis. IEEE Trans. Pattern Anal. Mach. Intell. **20**(11), 1254–1259 (1998)

13. Judd, T., Ehinger, K., Durand, F., Torralba, A.: Learning to predict where humans look. In: 2009 IEEE 12th International Conference on Computer Vision, pp. 2106–2113, September 2009

14. Ma, K., Zhao, T., Zeng, K., Wang, Z.: Objective quality assessment for color-to-gray image conversion. IEEE Trans. Image Process. **24**(12), 4673–4685 (2015)

15. Murray, N., Vanrell, M., Otazu, X., Parraga, C.A.: Saliency estimation using a non-parametric low-level vision model. In: 2011 IEEE Conference on Computer Vision and Pattern Recognition (CVPR), pp. 433–440, June 2011

16. Neumann, L., Čadík, M., Nemcsics, A.: An efficient perception-based adaptive color to gray transformation. In: Proceedings of the Third Eurographics Conference on Computational Aesthetics in Graphics, Visualization and Imaging, Computational Aesthetics 2007, pp. 73–80. Eurographics Association, Aire-la-Ville, Switzerland (2007)

17. Pearce, J., Ferrier, S.: Evaluating the predictive performance of habitat models developed using logistic regression. Ecol. Model. **133**(3), 225–245 (2000)

18. Rasche, K., Geist, R., Westall, J.: Re-coloring images for gamuts of lower dimension. Comput. Graph. Forum **24**(3), 423–432 (2005)

19. Smith, K., Landes, P.E., Thollot, J., Myszkowski, K.: Apparent greyscale: a simple and fast conversion to perceptually accurate images and video. Comput. Graph. Forum **27**(2), 193–200 (2008). Special issue: Proceedings of Eurographics 2008

20. Vikram, T.N., Tscherepanow, M., Wrede, B.: A saliency map based on sampling an image into random rectangular regions of interest. Pattern Recogn. **45**(9), 3114–3124 (2012)

# 3D and Stereo Image Processing

# Depth Guided Detection of Salient Objects

Łukasz Dąbała[✉] and Przemysław Rokita

Institute of Computer Science, Warsaw University of Technology,
Nowowiejska 15/19 00-665, Warsaw, Poland
L.Dabala@stud.elka.pw.edu.pl, pro@ii.pw.edu.pl

**Abstract.** Saliency estimation is a complex problem of computer vision area, which results can enhance many tools or applications. In most of existing solutions, data that comes from stereopsis was not involved. We propose an algorithm, that adds depth information to detection of important objects in the scene. We show and confirm, that the whole problem of salient objects detection can be decomposed into series of simple image processing operations. To verify functioning and performance of the method, we test it on available RGBD datasets.

## 1 Introduction

One of many complex multidisciplinary problems is image saliency, which refers to finding image elements, that stands out from its surrounding and catch user's attention [1]. This problem was analyzed in psychology [2] or vision perception [3]. Most of existing solutions use 2D information, such as color, texture, or edge [4]. This assumption is valid only, when at least one feature is present and can be disinguished. In other cases, this can lead to not marking salient objects, even if they are clearly visible for people. Additional cue, which is independent from others, is depth. What speaks for depth usage is functioning of human visual system, because it uses 3D information for environment understanding.

Depth information has been successfully used in many applications [5,6], but previously only a couple [7,8] considered it in detection of salient objects. In this work we propose an algorithm, which uses contrast measures in color and depth, but in comparison to [9], where they base on the observation, that the image content can be decomposed into basic, structurally meaningful elements, we do not need such assumption.

In this work our first contribution is course-to-fine uniqueness measurement. In addition to involving depth into this computation, this approach also speed up the whole operation, by going from global to local contrast measurement.

Another thing, that was considered in this paper, involves distribution of objects in terms of luminance and depth change. By taking into consideration such component, it is possible to get rid of erroneously detected salient regions.

Our method, is a simple composition of many image processing operations, what will be described in the Sect. 3. We check our method on existing RGBD datasets [8,10] and the results are shown in Sect. 4.

© Springer International Publishing AG 2016
L.J. Chmielewski et al. (Eds.): ICCVG 2016, LNCS 9972, pp. 197–205, 2016.
DOI: 10.1007/978-3-319-46418-3_18

# 2    Background and Previous Work

In this section we provide a short explanation of existing methods for detecting salient objects, as well as functioning of human visual system in terms of depth.

## 2.1    Image Saliency

There were already several methods, that tried to compute saliency. Authors tried different approaches, which can be divided into two categories: biological inspired and computationaly oriented. One of the most known papers inspired by the first class work by Itti [11]. In this work authors takes into consideration several features from input image, such as color, intensity and orientation. They are computed by Differences of Gaussians and combined into feature maps, from which the final saliency map is computed by using winner-take-all strategy. The problem with this method is, that it can overemphasize small local features, what can be less effective in using such maps in applications.

Another approach for saliency estimation is taking all computations into frequency domain [12], which represents second category. Such approaches can better preserve image structure, but they tend to highlight edges instead of whole objects.

Image estimation methods can be divided into local and global ones. Methods used in the first case involve per pixel comparisons in the neighbourhood [13] or histogram usage [14]. Global methods compute saliency using image patches such as work by [15,16]. They can find salient object, but tend to omit local features. The method by [9] is using Gaussians to determine important objects in the image. Currently, this is one of the best methods, that is using only color information for computation. They decomposed saliency estimation into four steps involving abstraction, uniqueness, distribution and combination of all into single map.

There were also more complicated approaches, such as work by Liu [16], which uses conditional random fields or [14] where they tried to use 3D histograms.

Recently, because of growing popularity of stereoscopy, there were approaches, that tried to involve depth and comfort into saliency estimation. In work by Niu [7] they showed possibility of accomodation-vergance conflict usage. They showed, that salient objects tend to be in comfort zone. In the work by Cheng [8] they use depth contrast as one of the factors, as well as the center bias (because people tend to look at the center of the image). Final disparity achieved in their work, gives too much weight to background and tends to be segmented into large patches.

## 2.2    Human Visual System

Stereopsis [17,18] is one of the most influential cues, that has strong impact on viewing experience. Binocular vision is one of the most important attributes of the human organism, which allows to see surrounding from slightly different points. The difference between retinal images is used to estimate the depth in the scene. Information, that comes from the depth, helps people to identify background objects from foreground ones. The most challenging task, is distinguishing objects with similar visual attributes. Then without depth information is nearly impossible to estimate, which objects are salient. Usually people tend to consider closer objects as more salient than the further ones.

# 3   Our Method

Our method is modifying the algorithm of [9], by adding depth, multiscale approach and rejection map. At the same time we resigned from distribution maps, and usage of Superpixels [19].

Proposed method can be decomposed into several steps:

1. Applying bilateral Gaussian blur into the input image
2. Decomposition into multiresolution input
3. Computation of outstanding regions
4. Creation of rejection maps out of color and depth
5. Combination of uniqueness measurement and rejection maps into final saliency.

## 3.1   Preprocessing

In our method we omit the step of decomposing the image into basic elements, as many other methods do. Instead of simple division of an image, we blur it with bilateral filter. Such operation removes noise and because of the edge preserving operation it performs in nearly the same way as decomposition into homogenous regions. Everything depends on the kernel size of the blur operation. If we use too small value, noise will be present in the image. If we use too high value, there is a possibility that we will lose some features. On the other hand, because of edges and information, that they provide, this is not likely to happen.

After blur operation we want to turn color space into more perceptually meaningful one, to be as close to human vision as possible. For this operation we change the RGB color space into CIELAB, what allows us to say, that when the color changes, also the importance changes.

## 3.2   Creation of Multiresolution Input

Next step in our algorithm is creation of pyramid of images and its usage in uniqueness computation. Let us denote $L_i$ as a level in the pyramid of images, as it is presented in Fig. 1. Each of the images in pyramid is build with $3 \times 3$ Gaussian kernel and has half of the resolution of the previous level.

**Fig. 1.** Different levels on pyramid of images, used in measurement of how much pixel is unique from others.

### 3.3 Finding Outstanding Regions

Next, we can assign, the value telling how much pixel differ from others at every level of the pyramid, which can be denoted as in Eq. 1.

$$U_{L_i}(x,y) = \overline{W}U_{L_{i-1}} + (1 - \overline{W})Uc_{L_i} \tag{1}$$

The value $W$ tells how much previous level should be taken into consideration, when calculating new value of uniqueness on current level. The $U_{i-1}$ is weighted sum of all pixels from previous level in window around the pixel for which we compute the previous value of uniqueness. The weight for pixels above is a difference in colors (in YCbCr color space) and depth, so the bigger difference, the less weight it will have. That will assure, that we do not make objects unique out of no where. Current level can be computed as in Eq. 2.

$$Uc_{L_i}(x,y) = \frac{1}{Z} \sum_{\substack{-W_s \leq k \leq W_s \\ -W_s \leq l \leq W_s}} e^{\frac{-1}{2\sigma^2}(P(x,y)-P(k,l))^2} * (\overline{W_c}(C(x,y) - C(k,l)))^2 \tag{2}$$

In Eq. 2 functions $P$ and $C$ are responsible for reading position and color with depth respectively. To assure, that we do not pollute final result with taking too much information from luminance or depth, we choose to weight the difference of functions $C$. What speaks for such weighting is that human vision is much more sensitive to color changes than luminance. If it comes to depth, it can easily overwhelm other sources of data. That can lead to avoidance of regions, that are standing out from background, but their depth is nearly the same. In Eq. 2 $Z$ is the normalization factor, which takes all of the weighting of all pixels from the neighbourhood of $(x,y)$. $W_s$ is responsible for size of the area, that will be taken into consideration during measurement of uniqueness. That parameter is scaled differently at different levels, what allows us to minimize the number of pixels that should be checked. Such scaling, gives our algorithm ability to be global and local at the same time. At higher levels of pyramid, algorithm works globally, because windows size is big enough to consider whole image for every pixel. With every step, window size is getting smaller and smaller, and algorithm refines the result from earlier levels.

### 3.4    Rejection Map Creation

Next step in our pipeline is creating maps, that will be responsible for removal of objects that are false positives, because of for example repetetive pattern or gradient in color. To handle such cases we perform two sets of operations on luminance and depth separately. First step is gradient calculation for which we use Sobel's operator. Next we get statistics around the pixel $(x, y)$, to be more precise - variance, which tells us how much given pixel is different from its surrounding. Using this map without further processing, will result in noisy map, because even small variance will result in pixel acceptance. To get rid of noisy variance map, we threshold the result and blur it with bilateral Gaussian filter to propagate it to neighbours. The same operations are performed for luminance and for depth. This will result in two maps, where first will handle gradients in color, second - repetetive patterns. Combination of both is used to create rejection map $R$.

### 3.5    Final Saliency

To create final saliency $S$, we use previously created maps of uniqueness and rejection. They are combined according to Eq. 3.

$$S(x,y) = U(x,y)e^{-kR(x,y)} \tag{3}$$

To be sure, that every pixel is showed correctly after saliency assignment, we rescale the map to interval $[0, 1]$. Symbol $k$ is responsible for strengthen the influence of the rejection map $R$.

## 4    Discussion and Result

In our algorithm we can change weights of the input data, as well as we can just switch off completely depth or color gradient, what influences final saliency map. As a test input we take an image as it is in Fig. 2a. If we take a look at different weighting in our algorithm, it can be clearly seen, that depth information has big influence on its work, that is seen on uniqueness maps, during changing $\overline{W}$. What is important using different rejection maps $R$, changes final saliency map. The depth removes that homogenous regions, that are impossible to remove by color rejection map only and vice versa. It also highlights regions that are closer, because this regions are more probably the ones, that will catch user's attention.

Problem with performance testing, is that our algorithm uses depth. There are not many RGBD datasets for saliency measurement. In sets that we used [10], [8], all of the images are in low resolution ($640 \times 480$), because both of them were captured with kinect camera. The results, that we achieved are presented on Fig. 3. For this comparison we use the same parameters for every input data, as well as the data provided by Borji in [20].

We compare to several algorithms, even if they use only color images. The first one $DES$ [8] is using depth for calculations. The others: $Saliency Filters$ [9],

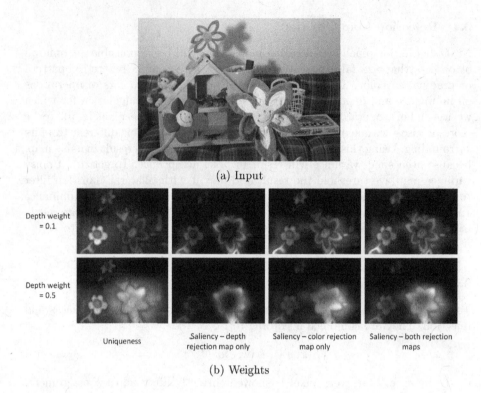

(a) Input

Depth weight = 0.1

Depth weight = 0.5

Uniqueness    Saliency – depth rejection map only    Saliency – color rejection map only    Saliency – both rejection maps

(b) Weights

**Fig. 2.** (a) Input image for weighting comparisons. (b) Different weights in algorithm and its influence on final result.

$FT$ [21], $MSS$ [22], $GMR$ [23], $GU$ [14], $GC$ [24] are using color information only as an input. Column, that is signed as 'Ours' shows results achieved by algorithm presented in this paper. Images in the last column present segmented input and mark objects that should be identified as salient. This input also comes from the datasets. If we compare the outputs of different methods to the segmented images, it is really hard for every of them to get only the salient objects out of the input. Instead of concentrating on trying to get whole objects, we should try to identify parts of the image, that really will catch attention of the user's eye like outstanding colors, highlights, or objects much different in depth. Examples for this are red rose, vase or fire extinguisher, which are different in color, or toy if it comes to depth. Many algorithms, identify too much as salient, for example on the image on the wall, where everything has nearly the same color or depth. The same applies to the green plant.

As it can be seen, our method resolves problems, that were described in Sect. 3, as it can be seen for couch and toy on repetetive background. The problem will be for the green plant, where everything has nearly the same depth, and the color information gives not much information. In this case, the algorithm seems to fail, when it will be compared to others like [9].

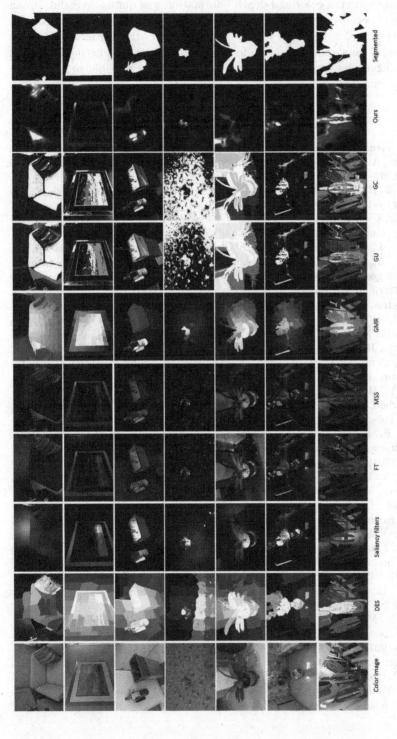

**Fig. 3.** Comparison with different algorithms: DES [8], Saliency Filters [9], FT [21], MSS [22], GMR [23], GU [14], GC [24]. Column annotated by 'Ours' represents output of the algorithm presented in this paper. Last column is segmented output, which is shows objects that should be identified as salient.

Our combination of color and depth information was quite successful. It can handle some special cases, where other methods seems to be unconfident. To make it better, it is worth to try some methods from artificial intelligence, for example neural networks or random forests. By voting or predicting the result from many examples from many methods, it should be possible to achive the ultimate saliency map.

# References

1. Itti, L.: Visual salience. Scholarpedia **2**(9), 3327 (2007)
2. Treisman, A.M., Gelade, G.: A feature-integration theory of attention. Cogn. Psychol. **12**, 97–136 (1980)
3. Nothdurft, H.-C.: Salience from feature contrast: additivity across dimensions. Vis. Res. **40**(10–12), 1183–1201 (2000)
4. Koch, C., Ullman, S.: Shifts in selective attention: towards the underlying neural circuitry. Hum. Neurobiol. **4**, 219–227 (1985)
5. Shotton, J., Fitzgibbon, A., Cook, M., Sharp, T., Finocchio, M., Moore, R., Kipman, A., Blake, A.: Real-time human pose recognition in parts from single depth images. In: Proceedings of the 2011 IEEE Conference on Computer Vision and Pattern Recognition, CVPR 2011, pp. 1297–1304. IEEE Computer Society, Washington, DC, USA (2011)
6. Hadfield, S., Bowden, R.: Kinecting the dots: particle based scene flow from depth sensors. In: Metaxas, D., Quan, L., Sanfeliu, A., Van Gool, L. (eds.) ICCV, pp. 2290–2295. IEEE Computer Society (2011)
7. Niu, Y., Geng, Y., Li, X., Liu, F.: Leveraging stereopsis for saliency analysis. In: CVPR, pp. 454–461. IEEE Computer Society (2012)
8. Cheng, Y., Huazhu, F., Wei, X., Xiao, J., Cao, X.: Depth enhanced saliency detection method. In: Wang, H., Davis, L., Zhu, W., Kopf, S., Qu, Y., Yu, J., Sang, J., Mei, T. (eds.) ICIMCS, p. 23. ACM (2014)
9. Perazzi, F., Kraehenbuehl, P., Pritch, Y., Hornung, A.: Saliency filters: contrast based filtering for salient region detection. In: CVPR, pp. 733–740. IEEE Computer Society (2012)
10. Ciptadi, A., Hermans, T., Rehg, J.M.: An in depth view of saliency. In: Burghardt, T., Damen, D., Mayol-Cuevas, W.W., Mirmehdi, M. (eds.) BMVC. BMVA Press, Guildford (2013)
11. Itti, L., Koch, C., Niebur, E.: A model of saliency-based visual attention for rapid scene analysis. IEEE Trans. on PAMI **20**(11), 1254–1259 (1998)
12. Guo, C., Ma, Q., Zhang, L.: Spatio-temporal saliency detection using phase spectrum of quaternion fourier transform. In: CVPR. IEEE Computer Society (2008)
13. Ma, Y.-F., Zhang, H.: Contrast-based image attention analysis by using fuzzy growing. In: Rowe, L.A., Vin, H.M., Plagemann, T., Shenoy, P.J., Smith, J.R. (eds.) ACM Multimedia, pp. 374–381. ACM (2003)
14. Cheng, M.-M., Mitra, N.J., Huang, X., Torr, P.H.S., Hu, S.-M.: Global contrast based salient region detection. IEEE Trans. Pattern Anal. Mach. Intell. **37**(3), 569–582 (2015)
15. Goferman, S., Zelnik-Manor, L., Tal, A.: Context-aware saliency detection. IEEE Trans. Pattern Anal. Mach. Intell. **34**(10), 1915–1926 (2012)
16. Liu, T., Yuan, Z., Sun, J., Wang, J., Zheng, N., Tang, X., Shum, H.-Y.: Learning to detect a salient object. IEEE Trans. Pattern Anal. Mach. Intell. **33**(2), 353–367 (2011)

17. Palmer, S.E.: Vision Science: Photons to Phenomenology. The MIT Press, Cambridge (1999)
18. Howard, I.P., Rogers, B.J.: Perceiving in Depth. Stereoscopic Vision, vol. 2. OUP, USA (2012)
19. Achanta, R., Shaji, A., Smith, K., Lucchi, A., Fua, P., Suesstrunk, S.: SLIC superpixels. Technical report, EPFL (2010)
20. Borji, A., Sihite, D.N., Itti, L.: Salient object detection: a benchmark. In: Fitzgibbon, A., Lazebnik, S., Perona, P., Sato, Y., Schmid, C. (eds.) ECCV 2012, vol. 7573, pp. 414–429. Springer, Heidelberg (2012)
21. Achanta, R., Hemami, S.S., Estrada, F.J., Suesstrunk, S.: Frequency-tuned salient region detection. In: CVPR, pp. 1597–1604. IEEE Computer Society (2009)
22. Achanta, R., Suesstrunk, S.: Saliency detection using maximum symmetric surround. In: ICIP, pp. 2653–2656. IEEE (2010)
23. Yang, C., Zhang, L., Huchuan, L., Ruan, X., Yang, M.-H.: Saliency detection via graph-based manifold ranking. In: CVPR, pp. 3166–3173. IEEE (2013)
24. Cheng, M.-M., Warrell, J., Lin, W.-Y., Zheng, S., Vineet, V., Crook, N.: Efficient salient region detection with soft image abstraction. In: ICCV, pp. 1529–1536. IEEE Computer Society (2013)

# Fast Extraction of 3D Fourier Moments via Multiple Integral Images: An Application to Antitank Mine Detection in GPR C-Scans

Przemysław Klęsk$^{(\boxtimes)}$, Mariusz Kapruziak, and Bogdan Olech

Faculty of Computer Science and Information Technology,
West Pomeranian University of Technology, ul. Żołnierska 49,
71-210 Szczecin, Poland
{pklesk,mkapruziak,bolech}@wi.zut.edu.pl

**Abstract.** Automatic landmine detection is a challenging problem in post-conflict areas. This paper demonstrates experiments on antitank mine detection in subsurface 3D images generated by Ground Penetrating Radar. In the algorithmic part, we study *piecewise Fourier approximations of low orders* which are applied to successive 3D windows of an image. We take coefficients — moments — of these approximations as features for machine learning. The main contribution of the paper is a technique to calculate the moments fast. We construct a *set* of suitable integral images, which allows later to calculate each moment in constant time. The technique is akin to, but significantly different from the known idea of Viola and Jones, namely: we calculate Fourier moments rather than simple differential features; secondly, we use multiple integral images, not a single one; thirdly, our integral images are cumulative inner products between input image and suitable trigonometric terms. Conducted tests involve boosted decision trees as detectors.

## 1 Introduction

In the field of computer vision, in the last decade, the ideas of *Haar-like features* and *classifiers cascade* due to Viola and Jones [12] have led to a significant progress in detection tasks. One should realize that the efficiency of Haar-like features is not owed to the nature of these features as such, but rather to a computational trick called *integral image*. A simple integral image is a cumulative function of pixel intensities. Once it is calculated, sums of intensities over any rectangular image region can be calculated in constant time — $O(1)$ — by means of the integral image growth[1]. Note that a dense detection procedure may involve even hundreds of thousands of windows to be analyzed per image.

Surveying recent literature proves that Haar-like features are widely applied in detection frameworks [1,5,11], and integral images, in their simplest form, are

---

This work was partially financed by the Ministry of Science and Higher Education in Poland (R&D project no. 0 R00 0091 12, agreement signed on 30.11.2010).

[1] For 2D images the growth operation boils down to 2 subtractions and 1 addition on only 4 points read from the integral image array.

L.J. Chmielewski et al. (Eds.): ICCVG 2016, LNCS 9972, pp. 206–220, 2016.
DOI: 10.1007/978-3-319-46418-3_19

also ubiquitous. They accelarate calculations related not only to features extraction but also e.g. to region splicing, noise estimation, or median and bileteral filtering [13]. However, we dare noticing that the core of the Viola and Jones's idea remains essentially the same. Little has been done to exploit this idea further in the mathematical sense.

Potentially, one might consider other types of features — not only Haar-like — and try to couple them with some sort of integral images to speed up the extraction. For example, Doretto and Yao [2] have managed to express statistical moments by integral images and applied them for vehicle detection in aerial videos. In our previous work (Klęsk et al. 2015) [7, Appendix B], we have suggested an integral image related modification for the HOG descriptor. Yet, similar approaches can rarely be met.

It should also be explained that in the mentioned approaches, the proposed integral images are no longer simple cumulants of pixel intensities. Possibly, they can be defined as cumulative inner products between input image and some other function related to the given type of features. In this paper we demonstrate a construction of that kind, suited for three-dimensional Fourier moments. The moments are calculated with just a few arithmetic and trigonometric operations, regardless of the number of pixels in the scanning window and its position. Such a computational saving is important in practice, especially when one performs a dense detection procedure over 3D radar images.

## 1.1 Ground Penetrating Radar: Image Types, Hyperbolic Patterns

Ground Penetrating Radar (GPR) and its applications have become a popular research subject in recent years [6,14]. There are three main variants of GPR images researchers can work with. The most simple radagram is an A-scan. It is a one-dimensional signal defined over an axis directed inwards the ground (depth or time axis). A linear collection of A-scans forms a B-scan — a 2D image. And finally, a collection of successive B-scans forms a C-scan — a 3D image. Commonly, the coordinate system for C-scans is defined as: across track × along track × depth/time. Objects non-transparent to GPR waves are *not* seen in their natural shapes in the images. Instead, in C-scans, they produce patterns consisting of *hyperboloids* (shapes resembling bowls). In B-scans hyperboloids reduce to hyperbolas, and if time slices are considered hyperboloids reduce to ellipses. Therefore, the detection task is in fact about distinguishing hyperboloids, or their projections, characteristic for landmines from other hyperboloids.

Typically, GPR images are not clear and strongly corrupted with noise. In case of landmine detection, researches struggle with false alarms induced by: cans, boxes, stones, bottles, roots; i.e. objects with some resemblance to mines in terms of their hyperbolic patterns seen in images. For example, Kovalenko et al. [8] worked on 1D echos from a video-impulse GPR (A-scans within a C-scan). The discrimination was based on similarity measures between an input waveform and a reference (ideal) waveform. ROCs obtained from three geographical sites indicate that 100 % sensitivities (i.e. detection rates for positive targets) were achieved at the cost of the following false alarm rates (FAR): 1.1 FA/m$^2$ (sand 1),

2.8 FA/m$^2$ (sand 2) and 1.0 FA/m$^2$ (grass). In a more advanced GPR research project, Torrione et al. [10] applied the HOG descriptor and Random Forest as the learning algorithm. Features (216 in total) were extracted from two middle B-scans, accross and along track. Reported results come from a large U.S. test site of approximately 200 000 m$^2$ area. The data included 2 960 target encounters over 740 unique targets (vehicle was driven four times over the same roads). The authors obtained a small FAR: 0.0048 FA/m$^2$, but simultaneously a moderately high sensitivity of 95 %.

For more thorough reading on GPR and more mine detection results we address the reader also e.g. to [4,9,14].

### 1.2   Motivation

Our motivation is twofold. The purely algorithmic motivation is to demonstrate a fast — constant-time — technique, based on multiple integral images, suited for extraction of Fourier moments. The technique, as such, is general and can be used in many computer vision problems. We use 3D moments (due to our application context) but reductions or extensions to other dimensionalities are straightforward.

Our engineering motivation is to solve the task of antitank (AT) mine detection better than we did previously in [7]. The main goal is to improve the accuracy and simultaneously not to deteriorate significantly the computation time. In [7] we were generating 17 000 3D Haar-like features (via one integral image), from which a subset of about 1 400 features was selected by a boosting algorithm. Achieved was a good average time of analysis per window (sequential: 0.8 ms, parallel: 0.3 ms)$^2$, but there was room for accuracy improvement. Sensitivities in our experimental conditions$^3$ were: 95.71 % for metal AT mines and 92.83 % for plastic AT mines; and about 20 false alarms over 210 m$^2$ were registered. AUC measures calculated at the windows level-of-detail were: 98.89 % (metal mines) and 95.74 % (plastic mines).

We also explain that we purposely do not apply the cascade of classifiers due to the characteristic of our application, and we ignore this topic in the paper.

## 2   Calculation of 3D Fourier Moments via Integral Images

Let $i(x, y, t)$ denote the image function of a C-scan (accross track $\times$ along track $\times$ time coordinates). Consider the following 3D approximation (inverse FT) of an image fragment restricted to a cuboid spanning from $(x_1, y_1, t_1)$ to $(x_2, y_2, t_2)$:

$$i(x,y,t) \approx \sum_{-n \leq k_x \leq n} \sum_{-n \leq k_y \leq n} \sum_{-n \leq k_t \leq n} c_{\substack{x_1,y_1,t_1 \\ x_2,y_2,t_2}}^{k_x,k_y,k_t} e^{2\pi i \left( k_x \frac{x-x_1}{N_x} + k_y \frac{y-y_1}{N_y} + k_t \frac{t-t_1}{N_t} \right)}, \quad (1)$$

---

$^2$ Intel Core i7 1.6 GHz CPU; application written in C# language.

$^3$ Garden soil, in-door laboratory test stand, strong clutter, variations on mine placements, lean angles, multiple disruptive objects (cans, discs, cables, bricks, etc.).

where: $n$ is the harmonic order of approximation variable-wise, $i = \sqrt{-1}$ is the imaginary unit (please note the calligraphic difference from $i$ denoting the image), the coefficients $c$ are complex numbers, and $N_x = x_2 - x_1 + 1$, $N_y = y_2 - y_1 + 1$, $N_t = t_2 - t_1 + 1$ are cuboid widths in pixels. The superscripts $k_x, k_y, k_t$ of $c$ coefficients indicate the particular harmonic indexes. The subscripts represent the boundaries of the cuboid. In the current context the boundaries are constant, but will vary later when partitioning of the detection window becomes involved. To avoid confusion, we explain that throughout the paper $N_x$, $k_x$ and similar subscript notations should *not* be treated as functions of the specific subscript value, but as indicating the coordinate the quantity is associated with.

It is easy to check that the optimal complex coefficients from (1) are

$$
c_{\substack{x_1,y_1,t_1 \\ x_2,y_2,t_2}}^{k_x,k_y,k_t} = \frac{1}{N_x N_y N_t} \sum_{x=x_1}^{x_2} \sum_{y=y_1}^{y_2} \sum_{t=t_1}^{t_2} i(x,y,t) e^{-2\pi i \left( k_x \frac{x-x_1}{N_x} + k_y \frac{y-y_1}{N_y} + k_t \frac{t-t_1}{N_t} \right)}. \quad (2)
$$

From now on, we shall refer to the coefficients as Fourier moments, and we intend to use their real and imaginary parts as features for learning and detection.

Now, let us introduce **two sets** of **integral images**: $\{ii_{\cos}\}$, $\{ii_{\sin}\}$, related to cosine and sine functions respectively. We construct them as follows:

$$
ii_{\substack{\cos \\ N_x,N_y,N_t}}^{k_x,k_y,k_t}(x,y,t) = \sum_{j_x=1}^{x} \sum_{j_y=1}^{y} \sum_{j_t=1}^{t} i(j_x,j_y,j_t) \cos\left( -2\pi \left( \frac{k_x j_x}{N_x} + \frac{k_y j_y}{N_y} + \frac{k_t j_t}{N_t} \right) \right), \quad (3)
$$

$$
ii_{\substack{\sin \\ N_x,N_y,N_t}}^{k_x,k_y,k_t}(x,y,t) = \sum_{j_x=1}^{x} \sum_{j_y=1}^{y} \sum_{j_t=1}^{t} i(j_x,j_y,j_t) \sin\left( -2\pi \left( \frac{k_x j_x}{N_x} + \frac{k_y j_y}{N_y} + \frac{k_t j_t}{N_t} \right) \right). \quad (4)
$$

For simplicity, one can now assume that the $k_x, k_y, k_t$ indexes iterate over all the integers within the maximum harmonic order, i.e.: $-n \le k_x, k_y, k_t \le n$; thereby generating two sets of integral images, each of size $(2n + 1)^3$. Later, we shall remark that a smaller set of indexes is sufficient due to the properties of Fourier transform. The $N_x$, $N_y$, $N_t$ denominators in (3) and (4) should be treated as constants. They shall be determined by the window partitioning into cuboids (explained in in the next section). We should also remark that a single integral image of form (3) or (4) can be calculated by induction in linear time with respect to the total number of pixels in the input image (i.e. with one pass).

Let us now define the **growth operator** for any integral image $ii$ taken from either of the sets $\{ii_{\cos}\}$, $\{ii_{\sin}\}$:

$$
\underset{\substack{x_1,y_1,t_1 \\ x_2,y_2,t_2}}{\Delta}(ii) = ii(x_2,y_2,t_2) - ii(x_1{-}1,y_2,t_2) - ii(x_2,y_1{-}1,t_2) + ii(x_1{-}1,y_1{-}1,t_2)
$$

$$
- \Big( ii(x_2,y_2,t_1{-}1) - ii(x_1{-}1,y_2,t_1{-}1) - ii(x_2,y_1{-}1,t_1{-}1) + ii(x_1{-}1,y_1{-}1,t_1{-}1) \Big). \quad (5)
$$

Note that $\Delta$ returns a subsum over given cuboid in constant time using just 2 additions and 5 subtractions, instead of $O(N_x N_y N_t)$ operations.

The following proposition constitutes the main contribution of the paper.

**Proposition 1.** *Suppose the two sets of integral images:*

$$\left\{ ii_{\cos \, N_x,N_y,N_t}^{\cdot \cdot k_x,k_y,k_t} \right\}, \quad \left\{ ii_{\sin \, N_x,N_y,N_t}^{\cdot \cdot k_x,k_y,k_t} \right\},$$

*defined as in (3) and (4), respectively, have been calculated prior to the detection procedure. Then, for any cuboid of widths $N_x$, $N_y$, $N_t$ in the image, the real and imaginary parts of each of its Fourier moments can be calculated in constant time — $O(1)$ — as follows:*

$$Re\left( c_{\substack{x_1,y_1,t_1 \\ x_2,y_2,t_2}}^{k_x,k_y,k_t} \right) = \frac{1}{N_x N_y N_t} \left( \cos\left( 2\pi \left( \frac{k_x x_1}{N_x} + \frac{k_y y_1}{N_y} + \frac{k_t t_1}{N_t} \right) \right) \cdot \underset{\substack{x_1,y_1,t_1 \\ x_2,y_2,t_2}}{\Delta} \left( ii_{\cos \, N_x,N_y,N_t}^{\cdot \cdot k_x,k_y,k_t} \right) \right.$$

$$\left. - \sin\left( 2\pi \left( \frac{k_x x_1}{N_x} + \frac{k_y y_1}{N_y} + \frac{k_t t_1}{N_t} \right) \right) \cdot \underset{\substack{x_1,y_1,t_1 \\ x_2,y_2,t_2}}{\Delta} \left( ii_{\sin \, N_x,N_y,N_t}^{\cdot \cdot k_x,k_y,k_t} \right) \right), \quad (6)$$

$$Im\left( c_{\substack{x_1,y_1,t_1 \\ x_2,y_2,t_2}}^{k_x,k_y,k_t} \right) = \frac{1}{N_x N_y N_t} \left( \sin\left( 2\pi \left( \frac{k_x x_1}{N_x} + \frac{k_y y_1}{N_y} + \frac{k_t t_1}{N_t} \right) \right) \cdot \underset{\substack{x_1,y_1,t_1 \\ x_2,y_2,t_2}}{\Delta} \left( ii_{\cos \, N_x,N_y,N_t}^{\cdot \cdot k_x,k_y,k_t} \right) \right.$$

$$\left. + \cos\left( 2\pi \left( \frac{k_x x_1}{N_x} + \frac{k_y y_1}{N_y} + \frac{k_t t_1}{N_t} \right) \right) \cdot \underset{\substack{x_1,y_1,t_1 \\ x_2,y_2,t_2}}{\Delta} \left( ii_{\sin \, N_x,N_y,N_t}^{\cdot \cdot k_x,k_y,k_t} \right) \right). \quad (7)$$

As one can see, both parts, real (6) and imaginary (7), require two growth operations and two trigonometric functions. It is easy check that this comprises the total of: 17 additions (or subtractions), 10 multiplications, 4 divisions, and 2 trigonometric functions for either of the two formulas. Note that it is sufficient to calculate the argument under trigonometric functions only once. Also, it is worth noting that this argument depends on the offset $(x_1, y_1, t_1)$ of the cuboid, but does *not* depend on the cuboid's contents — pixels intensities, thereby making the overall calculation a constant-time calculation. The proof of the proposition is a straightforward derivation.

*Proof.* Rewriting the moments from (2) using Euler's identity leads to:

$$c_{\substack{x_1,y_1,t_1 \\ x_2,y_2,t_2}}^{k_x,k_y,k_t} = \frac{1}{N_x N_y N_t} \sum_{x=x_1}^{x_2} \sum_{y=y_1}^{y_2} \sum_{t=t_1}^{t_2} i(x,y,t) \left( \cos\left( -2\pi \left( k_x \frac{x-x_1}{N_x} + k_y \frac{y-y_1}{N_y} + k_t \frac{t-t_1}{N_t} \right) \right) \right.$$

$$\left. + i \sin\left( -2\pi \left( k_x \frac{x-x_1}{N_x} + k_y \frac{y-y_1}{N_y} + k_t \frac{t-t_1}{N_t} \right) \right) \right). \quad (8)$$

The argument of the trigonometric functions can be parted into a group of terms independent from the pixel index $(x, y, t)$ and a group dependent on it as follows:

$$\alpha = 2\pi \left( k_x x_1/N_x + k_y y_1/N_y + k_t t_1/N_t \right),$$
$$\beta(x,y,t) = -2\pi \left( k_x x/N_x + k_y y/N_y + k_t t/N_t \right).$$

Now, one can apply in (8) the trigonometric identities for $\cos(\alpha + \beta)$ and $\sin(\alpha + \beta)$. Simultaneously, the $\cos\alpha$ and $\sin\alpha$ terms can be pulled as factors in front of the summations as they are independent of the pixel index $(x, y, t)$. Finally, by splitting the expression into real and imaginary parts one obtains:

$$\text{Re}\left(c_{\substack{x_1,y_1,t_1\\x_2,y_2,t_2}}^{k_x,k_y,k_t}\right) = \frac{1}{N_x N_y N_t} \cdot$$

$$\left(\cos\alpha \underbrace{\sum_{x=x_1}^{x_2}\sum_{y=y_1}^{y_2}\sum_{t=t_1}^{t_2} i(x,y,t)\cos\beta(x,y,t)}_{\substack{\Delta\\x_1,y_1,t_1\\x_2,y_2,t_2}\left(ii_{\cos}^{k_x,k_y,k_t}{}_{N_x,N_y,N_t}\right)} - \sin\alpha \underbrace{\sum_{x=x_1}^{x_2}\sum_{y=y_1}^{y_2}\sum_{t=t_1}^{t_2} i(x,y,t)\sin\beta(x,y,t)}_{\substack{\Delta\\x_1,y_1,t_1\\x_2,y_2,t_2}\left(ii_{\sin}^{k_x,k_y,k_t}{}_{N_x,N_y,N_t}\right)}\right),$$

$$\text{Im}\left(c_{\substack{x_1,y_1,t_1\\x_2,y_2,t_2}}^{k_x,k_y,k_t}\right) = \frac{1}{N_x N_y N_t} \cdot$$

$$\left(\sin\alpha \underbrace{\sum_{x=x_1}^{x_2}\sum_{y=y_1}^{y_2}\sum_{t=t_1}^{t_2} i(x,y,t)\cos\beta(x,y,t)}_{\substack{\Delta\\x_1,y_1,t_1\\x_2,y_2,t_2}\left(ii_{\cos}^{k_x,k_y,k_t}{}_{N_x,N_y,N_t}\right)} + \cos\alpha \underbrace{\sum_{x=x_1}^{x_2}\sum_{y=y_1}^{y_2}\sum_{t=t_1}^{t_2} i(x,y,t)\sin\beta(x,y,t)}_{\substack{\Delta\\x_1,y_1,t_1\\x_2,y_2,t_2}\left(ii_{\sin}^{k_x,k_y,k_t}{}_{N_x,N_y,N_t}\right)}\right).$$

The undebraces indicate how the expensive summations over pixels get replaced by cheap (constant-time) growths of integral images, yielding formulas (6), (7). □

## 3 Fourier Moments as Features

### 3.1 Number of Distinct Moments

Due to the symmetry property (complex conjugacy of opposed coefficients):

$$\text{Re}\left(c_{\substack{x_1,y_1,t_1\\x_2,y_2,t_2}}^{-k_x,-k_y,-k_t}\right) = \text{Re}\left(c_{\substack{x_1,y_1,t_1\\x_2,y_2,t_2}}^{k_x,k_y,k_t}\right), \quad \text{Im}\left(c_{\substack{x_1,y_1,t_1\\x_2,y_2,t_2}}^{-k_x,-k_y,-k_t}\right) = -\text{Im}\left(c_{\substack{x_1,y_1,t_1\\x_2,y_2,t_2}}^{k_x,k_y,k_t}\right), \quad (9)$$

and due to the fact that the zeroth order moment is a real number, $\text{Im}(c^{0,0,0}) = 0$, it suffices to calculate roughly only a half of all moments; more precisely:

$$1/2\left((2n+1)^3 - 1\right) + 1, \tag{10}$$

which yields $4n^3 + 6n^2 + 3n + 1$. Algorithmically, this corresponds to iterating over, for example, the following set of indexes:

$$\left\{(k_x, k_y, k_t): -n \le k_x \le -1, -n \le k_y \le n, -n \le k_t \le n\right\} \cup \left\{(0, k_y, k_t):\right.$$
$$\left. -n \le k_y \le -1, -n \le k_t \le n\right\} \cup \left\{(0, 0, k_t): -n \le k_t \le -1\right\} \cup \left\{(0, 0, 0)\right\}. \tag{11}$$

In fact, any set of $4n^3 + 6n^2 + 3n + 1$ coefficients will do to uniquely reconstruct the remaining coefficients if need be.

As regards the needed number of integral images, it is equal to the double of (10), i.e. $(2n + 1)^3 + 1$, since both $ii_{\cos}$ and $ii_{\sin}$ images are required for each $k_x, k_y, k_t$ triplet. Hence, the calculation of all integral images is potentially expensive. That is why one should impose fairly low harmonic orders in practice.

## 3.2   Window Partitioning (Piecewise Approximations) and Features

Apart from harmonic order $n$, we introduce an integer parameter $p > 0$ responsible for the window partitioning and affecting the final number of features. We partition the window into a regular grid of $p^3$ cuboids, as illustrated in Fig. 1. The moments are then extracted from each of them. This approach may be viewed as a piecewise Fourier approximation of the current window under detection.

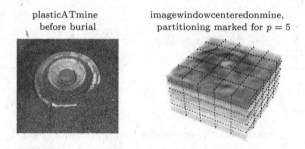

plasticATmine
before burial

imagewindowcenteredonmine,
partitioning marked for $p = 5$

**Fig. 1.** Illustration of the partitioning parameter $p$.

For a single image pass with detection window of size $w_x \times w_y \times w_t$ let the widths of cuboids implied by the partitioning be $N_x = \lfloor w_x/p \rfloor$, $N_y = \lfloor w_y/p \rfloor$, $N_t = \lfloor w_t/p \rfloor$. We denote the corresponding division remainders as: $m_x = w_x \bmod p$, $m_y = w_y \bmod p$, $m_t = w_t \bmod p$. Now, for a window spanning from pixel $(x_1, y_1, t_1)$ and for fixed numbers $N_x, N_y, N_t$, we define the collection of features, $\{f(\cdots)\}$, as:

$$
f(k_x, k_y, k_t, p_x, p_y, p_t, r) = \begin{cases} \mathrm{Re}\left(c^{k_x, k_y, k_t}_{\substack{x'_1 + p_x N_x, y'_1 + p_y N_y, t'_1 + p_t N_t \\ x'_1 + (p_x+1)N_x - 1, y'_1 + (p_y+1)N_y - 1, t'_1 + (p_t+1)N_t - 1}}\right), & r = 1; \\[2em] \mathrm{Im}\left(c^{k_x, k_y, k_t}_{\substack{x'_1 + p_x N_x, y'_1 + p_y N_y, t'_1 + p_t N_t \\ x'_1 + (p_x+1)N_x - 1, y'_1 + (p_y+1)N_y - 1, t'_1 + (p_t+1)N_t - 1}}\right), & r = 0; \end{cases}
\tag{12}
$$

where: $(x'_1, y'_1, t'_1) = (x_1 + \lfloor m_x/2 \rfloor, y_1 + \lfloor m_y/2 \rfloor, t_1 + \lfloor m_t/2 \rfloor)$ is a shifted starting point, taking into account small corrections arose due to the partitioning remainders[4]; indexes $k_x$, $k_y$, $k_t$ iterate over the set defined in (11); $0 \le p_x, p_y, p_t \le p-1$

---

[4] This operation is meant to center the grid of cuboids within the scanning window.

represent the index (and hence the offset) of a particular cuboid; and $r$ is a flag switching between real and imaginary parts. Since $\text{Im}(c^{0,0,0}_{\cdot}) = 0$, then $f(0,0,0,p_x,p_y,p_t,0)$ is also zero for any $p_x,p_y,p_t$, and therefore should not be taken as an actual feature. Hence finally, the total number of features is:

$$d(n,p) = (2n+1)^3 p^3. \tag{13}$$

Since, we aim at low harmonic orders $n$, the increase of the parameter $p$ lets us generate more features for a window, without additional integral images. Obviously, $p$ should still be selected reasonably small. A large value could result in too small cuboidal pieces of little informative relevance and prone to noises.

### 3.3  Image Reconstructions from Features

To give an idea on the descriptive capability of the features, in this section we demonstrate some reconstructions, using formula (1) with respect to cuboids, for different setups of $n$ and $p$ parameters. We report ratios of the number of features to the number of pixels in the window ($67 \times 67 \times 35$ containing $157\,115$ pixels) together with mean absolute errors (MAE) between reconstructions and originals. Figures 2, 3, 4 and 5 depict reconstructions of metal AT mine and metal shaft images for increasing values of, respectively, $n$ and $p$ with the other parameter held constant. In particular, reconstructions for $n = 0$ are simply

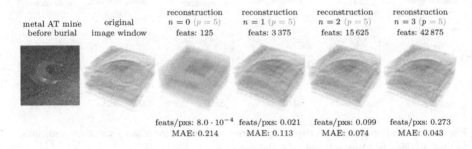

| | | reconstruction $n=0$ $(p=5)$ | reconstruction $n=1$ $(p=5)$ | reconstruction $n=2$ $(p=5)$ | reconstruction $n=3$ $(p=5)$ |
|---|---|---|---|---|---|
| metal AT mine before burial | original image window | feats: 125 | feats: 3 375 | feats: 15 625 | feats: 42 875 |
| | | feats/pxs: $8.0 \cdot 10^{-4}$ MAE: 0.214 | feats/pxs: 0.021 MAE: 0.113 | feats/pxs: 0.099 MAE: 0.074 | feats/pxs: 0.273 MAE: 0.043 |

**Fig. 2.** Reconstructions of metal mine image for successive orders $n$ (fixed $p = 5$).

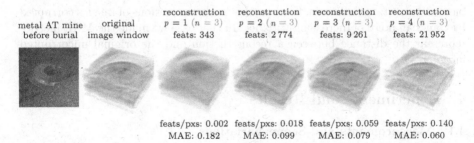

| | | reconstruction $p=1$ $(n=3)$ | reconstruction $p=2$ $(n=3)$ | reconstruction $p=3$ $(n=3)$ | reconstruction $p=4$ $(n=3)$ |
|---|---|---|---|---|---|
| metal AT mine before burial | original image window | feats: 343 | feats: 2 774 | feats: 9 261 | feats: 21 952 |
| | | feats/pxs: 0.002 MAE: 0.182 | feats/pxs: 0.018 MAE: 0.099 | feats/pxs: 0.059 MAE: 0.079 | feats/pxs: 0.140 MAE: 0.060 |

**Fig. 3.** Reconstructions of metal mine image for successive $p$ values (fixed $n = 3$).

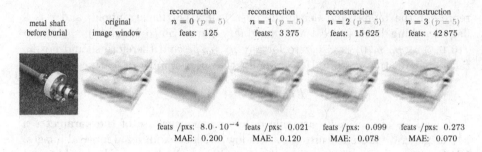

metal shaft before burial | original image window | reconstruction $n = 0\ (p = 5)$ feats: 125 | reconstruction $n = 1\ (p = 5)$ feats: 3 375 | reconstruction $n = 2\ (p = 5)$ feats: 15 625 | reconstruction $n = 3\ (p = 5)$ feats: 42 875

feats /pxs: $8.0 \cdot 10^{-4}$    feats /pxs: 0.021    feats /pxs: 0.099    feats /pxs: 0.273
MAE: 0.200        MAE: 0.120        MAE: 0.078        MAE: 0.070

**Fig. 4.** Reconstructions of a metal shaft image for successive orders $n$ (fixed $p = 5$).

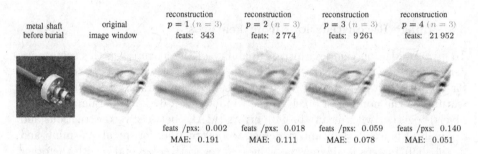

metal shaft before burial | original image window | reconstruction $p = 1\ (n = 3)$ feats: 343 | reconstruction $p = 2\ (n = 3)$ feats: 2 774 | reconstruction $p = 3\ (n = 3)$ feats: 9 261 | reconstruction $p = 4\ (n = 3)$ feats: 21 952

feats /pxs: 0.002    feats /pxs: 0.018    feats /pxs: 0.059    feats /pxs: 0.140
MAE: 0.191       MAE: 0.111       MAE: 0.078       MAE: 0.051

**Fig. 5.** Reconstructions of a metal shaft image for successive $p$ values (fixed $n = 3$).

noised original $\sim \mathcal{N}(0, 0.1)$ | reconstruction $n = 2,\ p = 5$ | noised original $\sim \mathcal{N}(0, 0.25)$ | reconstruction $n = 2,\ p = 5$ | noised original $\sim \mathcal{N}(0, 0.5)$ | reconstruction $n = 2,\ p = 5$

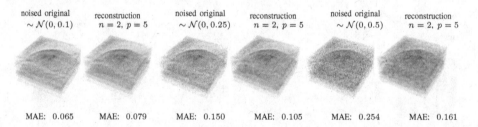

MAE: 0.065    MAE: 0.079    MAE: 0.150    MAE: 0.105    MAE: 0.254    MAE: 0.161

**Fig. 6.** Metal mine images corrupted by Gaussian noise of increasing variance and their reconstructions filtering out some of the noise.

piecewise constant functions. Figure 6 shows reconstructions of images corrupted by Gaussian noise of increasing variance. In that case we made the MAE metrics represent the distance between a reconstruction and the original uncorrupted image.

## 4    Experiments and Results

### 4.1    Measurements and Scene Variations

We have built a remotely (WiFi) controlled prototype vehicle equipped with a SFCW GPR (Stepped Frequency Continuous Wave), see Fig. 7. It is based

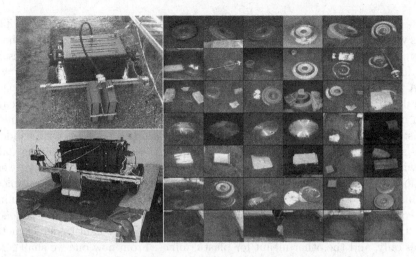

**Fig. 7.** Left: GPR prototype vehicle — on outdoor test lane (top) and indoor laboratory test stand (bottom). Right: examples of scanning scenarios and scene variations.

on a standard VNA (Agilent E5071C) and a light antenna system of our own construction (Vivaldi + shielded loop). The system generates microwaves with an effective bandwith of 12.7 GHz. All the software for control, imaging, learning and detection has been written in C# programming language.

For convenience reasons the learning material was collected on a laboratory test stand from a container of approximately $1\,m^2$ area filled with garden soil. We gathered a set of 210 C-scans with the physical resolution of 1 cm (distance between successive A-scans). The image resolution was $92 \times 91 \times 512$ (across track $\times$ along track $\times$ time). Our main objects of interest were two antitank mine models — a metal one (TM-62M, height 128 mm, diameter 320 mm) and a plastic one (PT-Mi-Ba III, height 110 mm, diameter 330 mm). We have introduced a variety of scanning scenarios: changes of mine placement and inclination angles, groups of overlapping objects, soil surface variations, puddle imitations; and a variety of disruptive non-mine objects: metal and plastic cans and boxes, cables, bricks, rods, shafts, discs, trays. Some scenes were purposely arranged in a way to resemble mines in the generated image. Examples are depicted in Fig. 7.

Our collection of scans (210 in total) was divided into three main groups:

- metal mine and possibly other objects (70 scans),
- plastic mine and possibly other objects (70 scans),
- non-mine objects only (70 scans).

## 4.2  Learning Algorithm, Cross-Validation Scheme and Results

As the learning algorithm we have implemented **boosted decision trees** with real-valued responses (logit transform). We have applied the *weight trimming* technique [3] to shorten the training time. Trees were grown using Gini index as the impurity function and a binning mechanism for splits selection [7]. The trees were shallow — of depth 2, i.e. with 4 terminals at most. Experiments have shown that ensembles of 600 led to satisfactory accuracy and AUC measures on our data[5].

A **10-fold cross-validation** scheme was set up. In each fold the testing pack included: 7 scans with a metal mine, 7 scans with a plastic mine, and 7 scans with non-mine objects. The training packs consisted therefore of 189 remaining scans. Each scan was traversed by a scanning 3D window (2 passes with window sizes suitable for mines: $67 \times 67 \times 35$ and $77 \times 77 \times 40$), and a training data set with positive and negative window examples was thus produced. We were memorizing all positive windows[6], whereas negatives had to be undersampled. We imposed 0.5 % as the sampling probability. Such a procedure led to training sets containing approximately $7 \cdot 10^4$ **negatives** and $2 \cdot 10^3$ **positives**[7] per each fold. Using the data, we always trained two detectors: one meant to detect metal mines only, and the other meant for plastic mines. From now one we shall refer to them in short as "metal detector" and "plastic detector" respectively. With weight trimming, the learning procedures were $\approx 2.5\,\mathrm{h}$ long (without it: $\approx 50\,\mathrm{h}$).

After preliminary experimentations, we chose $n = 2$ and $p = 5$ as the final parametrization. This resulted in a space consisting of **15 625 features** in total. The above choice was as a trade-off between the computation time invested in integral images (see Table 1a) and richness of description. Since our ensembles consisted of 600 trees with at most 4 terminals, then while learning, a classifier was potentially able to select at most 1 800 features out of total of 15 625 features.

Table 1b reports detailed cross-validation results obtained by our "metal" and "plastic" detectors. In the table, beside the sensitivity rate ('sens.'), we report false alarms ('FAR') and we distinguish two categories of them: alarms on wrong type of object and side alarms (on ground clutter or 'echo' traces). As one can see both detectors achieved high **sensitivities: 97.14% ("metal detector")** and **98.57% ("plastic detector")**. As regards false alarms, there were only 5/210 registered in total for the **"metal detector"** yielding the **2.38% FAR**. In particular, this detector never mistook a plastic mine for a metal one, and alarmed falsely only 4/70 times on non-mine objects. A slightly worse **5.24% FAR** was registered for the **"plastic detector"** due to 11/210 false alarms. Figure 8 depicts ROC curves obtained for our detectors, calculated at the windows level-of-detail[8]. The **AUC measures** obtained from the mean ROCs were: **99.57% ("metal detector")** and **99.45% ("plastic detector")**.

To give the reader an idea on how single detections look like we show some examples in Fig. 9. In particular, scene no. 3 (a, b) is worth attention — it

---

[5] In fact, already about 300 trees were leading to good accuracy and the improvement in AUC was minor from thereafter (smaller than 0.5 %).

[6] According to the typical supervised learning scenario — mine positions in images had to be visually determined and registered by human prior to the learning stage.

[7] A single positive target was represented by a cluster of approximately 32 windows on average, differing by small pixel shifts along each axis (an imposed tolerance).

[8] This means that all single 3D windows from the scanning procedure were treated separately as objects under classification (rather than the whole images).

**Table 1.** (a) Preliminary tests on computation time (Intel Core i7 1.6 GHz CPU) required for all integral images and low harmonic orders; (b) Final results of 10-fold cross-validation for detectors trained on 3D Fourier moments with $n = 2$, $p = 5$.

| (a) computation of all integral images (1.1 megapixel each): $x = 1, \ldots, 92$ (accross track) $y = 1, \ldots, 91$ (along track) $t = 374, \ldots, 512$ (subsurface) | | | | (b) cross-validation results "metal detector" | | | | cross-validation results "plastic detector" | | | |
|---|---|---|---|---|---|---|---|---|---|---|---|
| | | | | object type | no. of scans | detected as metal mine | side false alarms | object type | no. of scans | detected as plastic mine | side false alarms |
| $n$ | no. of integral images | sequential | parallel | metal mine | 70 | 68/70 **97.14%** **(sens.)** | 0/70 0.00% (FAR) | metal mine | 70 | 1/70 1.43% (FAR) | 4/70 5.71% (FAR) |
| 0 | 1 | 0.05 s | n.a. | plastic mine | 70 | 0/70 0.00% (FAR) | 0/70 0.00% (FAR) | plastic mine | 70 | 69/70 **98.57%** **(sens.)** | 0/70 0.00% (FAR) |
| 1 | 28 | 1.46 s | 0.63 s | | | | | | | | |
| 2 | 126 | 6.55 s | 2.72 s | other | 70 | 4/70 5.71% (FAR) | 1/70 1.43% (FAR) | other | 70 | 4/70 5.71% (FAR) | 2/70 2.86% (FAR) |
| 3 | 344 | 17.41 s | 7.36 s | total FAR: 5/210 ≈ **2.38%** | | | | total FAR: 11/210 ≈ **5.24%** | | | |

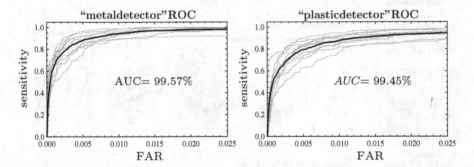

**Fig. 8.** Mean ROC curves (black) and AUC measures for "metal" and "plastic" detectors at the windows level-of-detail. ROCs from particular CV folds plotted in gray. FAR axis purposely narrowed down to $[0, 0.025]$ for better visibility.

represents a situation with a plastic mine lying on top of a metal mine, with both detectors returning correct indications. Scene no. 4 is an example of a false alarm, where a metal disc with a can on top (purposely arranged to resemble a mine) is mistaken for the metal mine by the detector.

Finally, we would like to report on time performance. With only subsurface time slices analyzed ($t = 374, \ldots, 512$), the detection procedure was testing about $2.1 \cdot 10^4$ 3D windows in an image. Then, the total time of parallel computations (including: $2 \cdot 126$ integral images, features extractions and classifications for all windows) took on average 9.8 s. Dividing the time by the number of windows yields **0.47** ms as the **mean time of analysis per single 3D window**.

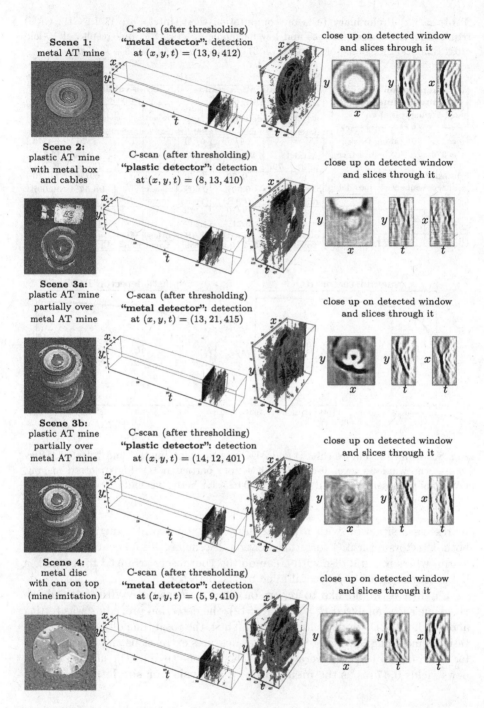

**Fig. 9.** Exemplary single detections by our AT mine detectors. Examples no. 1–3b are correct positive indications, example 4 is a false alarm.

# 5    Conclusions

We have derived a computational technique, based on a construction of multiple integral images, suited for extraction of low order Fourier moments from image windows. The moments can be used as features in detection tasks, especially when a dense scanning procedure is involved. Owing to the technique each moment is calculated fast — in constant time. Constructed integral images are inner products of image and suitable trigonometric terms. Additional time that has to be invested in the calculation of these integral images depends on: dimensionality and size of input images, and the wanted harmonic order of moments. Depending on an application, that additional time may or may not allow for real-time processing. Yet, the method is for certain competitive to Viola and Jones' idea in terms of accuracy. In many applications the approximation properties of Fourier moments outperform Haar-like features (which in fact are rough contours). In the algorithmic sense, our proposition takes the idea due to Viola and Jones one step 'ahead', possibly indicating still new developments to come.

We have shown a possible application for the proposed technique, namely, detection of AT landmines in GPR 3D images known as C-scans.

# References

1. Charles, J., et al.: Automatic and efficient human pose estimation for sign language videos. Int. J. Comput. Vis. **110**(1), 70–90 (2014)
2. Doretto, G., Yao, Y.: Region moments: fast invariant descriptors for detecting small image structures. In: Computer Vision and Pattern Recognition (CVPR), pp. 3019–3026. IEEE (2010)
3. Friedman, J., Hastie, T., Tibshirani, R.: Additive logistic regression: a statistical view of boosting. Ann. Stat. **28**(2), 337–407 (2000)
4. Frigui, H., Zhang, L., Gader, P.D.: Context-dependent multisensor fusion and its application to land mine detection. IEEE Trans. Geosci. Remote Sens. **48**(6), 2528–2543 (2010)
5. Islam, S.M.S., et al.: Efficient detection and recognition of 3D ears. Int. J. Comput. Vis. **95**(1), 52–73 (2011)
6. Jol, H.M.: Ground Penetrating Radar: Theory and Applications. Elsevier, Oxford (2009)
7. Klęsk, P., Godziuk, A., Kapruziak, M., Olech, B.: Fast analysis of C-scans from ground penetrating radar via 3D haar-like features with application to landmine detection. IEEE Trans. Geosci. Remote Sens. **53**(7), 3996–4009 (2015)
8. Kovalenko, V., Yarovoy, A.G., Ligthart, L.P.: A novel clutter suppression algorithm for landmine detection with GPR. IEEE Trans. Geosci. Remote Sens. **45**(11), 3740–3751 (2007)
9. Torrione, P., Collins, L.M.: Texture features for antitank landmine detection using ground penetrating radar. IEEE Trans. Geosci. Remote Sens. **45**(7), 2374–2382 (2007)
10. Torrione, P.A., Morton, K.D., Collins, J.: Histogram of oriented gradients for landmine detection in ground-penetrating radar data. IEEE Trans. Geosci. Remote Sens. **32**(3), 1539–1550 (2014)

11. Tresadern, P.A., Ionita, M.C., Cootes, T.F.: Real-time facial feature tracking on a mobile device. Int. J. Comput. Vis. **96**(3), 280–289 (2012)

12. Viola, P., Jones, M.: Robust real-time face detection. Int. J. Comput. Vis. **57**(2), 137–154 (2004)

13. Yang, Q., Ahuja, N., Tan, K.H.: Constant time median and bilateral filtering. Int. J. Comput. Vis. **112**(3), 307–317 (2015)

14. Yarovoy, A.: Landmine and unexploded ordnance detection and classification with ground penetrating radar. In: Jol, H.M. (ed.) Ground Penetrating Radar: Theory and Applications, pp. 445–478. Elsevier, Oxford (2009)

# Achieving Flexible 3D Reconstruction Volumes for RGB-D and RGB Camera Based Approaches

Sebastian Mock[1]([✉]), Philipp Lensing[2], and Wolfgang Broll[3]

[1] fayteq AG, Erfurt, Germany
sebastian.mock@fayteq.com
[2] Osnabrück University of Applied Science, Osnabrück, Germany
p.lensing@hs-osnabrueck.de
[3] Ilmenau University of Technology, Ilmenau, Germany
wolfgang.broll@tu-ilmenau.de

**Abstract.** Recently, quite a number of approaches came up to reconstruct 3D volumes from RGB or RGBD camera input. However, most of these approaches are rather inflexible regarding the initial camera position with respect of the reconstruction volume and the overall size of the area to be reconstructed. This severly limits the usability of those approaches. In this work we present a flexible approach to store and dynamically extend the reconstruction volume overcoming those problems. We show that our approach additionally requires significantly less memory due to a pyramid-based data storage. We demonstrate that our approach is real-time capable when implemented using the GPU and by that provides a flexible alternative to data structures used in previous approaches.

## 1 Introduction

Camera-based real-time scene analysis and reconstruction offers many new opportunities in particular for augmented and mixed reality applications. In order to accurately register virtual objects in their real environment and to allow for interaction between real and virtual content, it is essential to have a precise geometrical representation of the environment. Further, a segmentation of reconstructed objects can be computed like shown by Newcombe et al. [4].

Realization of such a system requires an accurate 3D map. Several approaches exist for extracting and storing surface information. Approaches previously used include point clouds [6] or voxel structures [11].

Allowing for an interaction with large scale environments requires the storage and management of a huge amount of data in real-time. While previous work such as KinectFusion [11] describe techniques to handle depth data from an active sensor in real-time, they also introduce severe limitations with respect to the space to be reconstructed.

One of the limitations many large scale reconstruction algorithms such as [13, 14,16] come along with is, that for achieving compact data structures the initial camera position with respect to the entire volume to be reconstructed must be

© Springer International Publishing AG 2016
L.J. Chmielewski et al. (Eds.): ICCVG 2016, LNCS 9972, pp. 221–232, 2016.
DOI: 10.1007/978-3-319-46418-3_20

known in advance. This limitation is twofold: first, one needs to know the overall size of the volume to be reconstructed and second, one needs to know the exact camera pose with respect to this volume. Both is fine for sculptures or other well defined spaces, allowing for easily adjusting those parameters in advance. However, when starting to scan and reconstruct an arbitrary environment e.g. a room, this typically turns out to be rather difficult. Thus, in order to overcome these limitations, more efficient techniques are required here.

Our approach introduces a much more flexible data structure for storing and managing the data captured. In contrast to previous approaches, our approach is independent of the initial camera position as the data structure allows for dynamic adaptation to the volume reconstructed.

Our current system is based on the Kinect camera for the depth input and applies an approach similar to KinectFusion for the preprocessing of the noisy depth data (bilateral filtering, vertex and normal map creation) and the camera tracking. However, our approach is independent of any specific dense tracking or reconstruction approach, i.e. it could also be applied to more recent approaches using a single RGB camera (rather than an RGBD sensor).

Our approach is based on a highly parallelized general purpose GPU (GPGPU) technique to achieve real-time capability.

In this paper we will present our approach to flexible and efficient data storage and management for camera based dense 3D scene reconstruction. The overall structure of this paper is as follows: In Sect. 2 we will review related work with respect to 3D scene reconstruction. In the third section we will introduce our approach to flexible data storage. Section 4 contains some insights on the actual GPU implementation, before discussing and comparing our results in Sect. 5. Finally, we will conclude and provide a look into future work.

## 2    Related Work

The 3D reconstruction of a real world scene requires the extraction of the surface information of its objects. There are several approaches for capturing and processing this data. In this section we will review common approaches for 3D reconstruction using cameras with an emphasis on their flexibility with respect to the overall reconstruction volume and the initial camera pose.

Newcombe et al. [11] presented KinectFusion, which is based on a 3D voxel grid structure to store the surface information. This technique provides a good reconstruction quality using low cost depth sensors but has limitations in the reconstruction area. The volume holding the 3D data has a fixed size, typically including large areas without any surface information. In addition the initial camera position has to be specified with respect to the 3D volume. If this pose is not accurately selected with respect to the space that shall be reconstructed, a reasonable amount of memory allocated for data storage will actually not be used.

Steinbrücker et al. presented a large scale approach from RGB-D sequences [14]. They fuse the depth maps in a multi-scale octree representation to reduce the memory usage and apply a signed distance function for the stored values (similar to the KinectFusion approach). By using octrees, the amount of memory required to store the 3D volume data could be reduced significantly compared to the approach used by KinectFusion. Thus, e.g. an entire office room could be reconstructed. However, the overall data structure is restricted to a cuboid to avoid an unbalanced octree. Further, the initial camera position with respect to the cuboid must be known in advance. Zeng et al. [17] introduced another approach based on an octree. This octrees is subdivided in four semantical layers with several levels of detail. That offers a memory efficient storage of surface informations but is also limited to the cuboid structure and initial camera pose. Furthermore the finest layer that contains the data must be preallocated by a user defined coefficient.

Kintinuous [16] is an extension of the KinectFusion approach using a point cloud. Whelan et al. introduce a 3D data structure consisting of voxels. As soon as the camera is moving outside the volume, the existing voxel grid is converted to a point cloud and moved from the graphics card to the main memory to allow for large scale reconstructions. At the current camera position a new voxel grid is generated in the GPU memory. The more recent approach by Whelan et al. [15] improves the creation of new volumes. Instead of creating whole grid data structures, the existing volume is modified when the camera is moving outside. Voxels which are not visible from the current viewpoint are removed from the graphics card and new voxels are added at the current position. This is achieved applying a modulo addressing of each voxel. The major challenge and drawback when converting the grid structure into a point cloud and streaming it to the main memory, is the fusion of the surface informations in regions that were already converted. An accurate fusion of the stored point cloud with the current grid structure is quite difficult. Furthermore, streaming data between the GPU and CPU reduces the overall performance significantly. Our approach avoids streaming any data to the CPU side to allow a dynamic and simple fusion of surface modifications at pre-captured regions.

Niessner et al. proposed in [13] the use of voxel hashing to receive large scale reconstruction volumes. Their approach uses a simple spatial hashing scheme instead of a regular or hierarchical grid to compress the data. Surface data is only stored densely in a hash table if actual measurements are observed. Additionally, the data is streamed from the GPU to the CPU and vive versa to achieve the ability to reconstruct large scenes. Again, it is rather difficult to fuse depth data from those regions which were already transferred to the CPU side respectively to the hash table. Additionally, an unbalanced hashing of incoming data may also become a problem, resulting in an inefficient data storage.

For image based modeling Loop et al. presented a high resolution sparse voxel-based approach [8] using multiple calibrated RGB cameras. KinectDeform [1] demonstrated an algorithm to reconstruct scenes containing non-rigidly deforming objects. It combines an octree based data representation and hierarchical voxel association with a recursive filtering mechanism. Also Newcombe et al. released DynamicFusion [9] to reconstruct non-rigidly deforming scenes by fusing RGB-D scans captured from commodity sensors. As these approaches are construed and demonstrated for non-rigid objects, they are not suitable for room reconstructions with most rigid objects.

With Klein and Murray's Parallel Tracking and Mapping system (PTAM) [7] small areas can be reconstructed baseed on hundreds of features per frame from a single monocular camera. Newcombe et al. also showed a reconstruction using a monecular camera [10]. The real world scene is reconstructed using point-based structure from motion (SFM). The novel contribution was the use of an approximate but smooth base mesh and warping this mesh into a highly accurate depth map. Newcombe et al. presented with Dense Tracking and Mapping (DTAM) [12] another approach for a reconstruction with a single RGB camera. The results of both approaches are only shown for the reconstruction of rather small areas. Further the reconstruction quality is by far not as good as using active depth sensors.

While the data structures provided might be quite efficient, the major drawback of most previous approaches is the necessity to know the initial camera position in relation to the area to be reconstructed in advance.

Further many works achieve a large scale reconstruction by streaming the data between the GPU and CPU side. Our approach offers a large scale reconstruction applying the graphic cards memory only and without the need to know or restrict the initial camera pose.

## 3   Data Structures for Flexible Reconstruction Volumes

In this section we describe the underlaying components we use in order to make 3D reconstruction more flexible and efficient. We describe how the surface information from an active depth sensor is processed and stored in our novel designed data structure. This data structure consists of several partial data structures representing individual levels of detail. The arrangement of these structures is explained in the following subsections.

### 3.1   Data Structure

In order to allow for a much larger reconstruction volume we increase the efficiency of the data storage. Within a typical large 3D volume, there are rather plenty of areas, without any surface information. Consistently, no surfaces can be extracted in those areas. Thus, the approach aims for reducing the large amount of storage typically used up for actually empty space.

Similar to previous approaches, we use a three dimensional voxel structure as basis. However, instead of using a single voxel grid representing all surface information we subdivide the data structure in $k+1$ hierarchical levels achieving voxel pyramids similar to the approach from Chen $et$ $al.$ [2]. See Fig. 1 showing an example of surface information stored in several levels.

Each level $l_i$ has a predefined voxel resolution of $n_i \times n_i \times n_i$. The first (most coarse) level $l_0$, defines a root grid (see also below). Each voxel $v$ inside the root

Level $l_0$
Level $l_1$
Level $l_{k-1}$
Level $l_k$
$n_0$
$n_1$
$n_{k-1}$
$n_k$
$n_0$
$n_1$
$n_{k-1}$
$n_k$

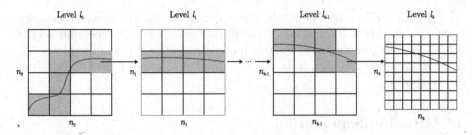

**Fig. 1.** Schematic representation of the data structure. The red line represents the actual surface and the green squares are the voxels containing the surface. (Color figure online)

grid may have one of two states. Either it contains valid surface information $s$ or not. If a voxel $v_{i,j}$ of level $l_i$ contains a surface $s$, this voxel is refined by an additional voxel grid of level $l_{i+1}$. Thus the following refinement exist:

$$\forall v_{i,j} \in l_i, i \in [0, k-1], j \in [0, n_i^3] : \{l_{i+1,j} | s \in v_{i,j}\} \tag{1}$$

This procedure is iterated until level $l_{k-1}$. If a voxel at this level still contains surface information a final level $l_k$ is generated. This final voxel grid is built similar to the one used by KinectFusion [11] to apply a fast data fusion. Thus we apply a 3D voxel grid with a resolution of $n_k \times n_k \times n_k$ where each voxel contains a truncated signed distance function (TSDF) value and a weight.

### 3.2 Arrangement of Root Grids

If we had only a single root grid we would also have the problem of having to define the initial camera position in advance, which could lead to an unbalanced hierarchical grid structure. This can be solved by using several root grids. Those are arranged in a grid structure themselves where the position $p_r$ of a root grid $r$ is

$$p_r = (x, y, z)^T | x, y, z \in \mathbb{Z} \tag{2}$$

This position is the upper left corner of a voxel cuboid and is used to unanimously identify each root grid. Grids are aligned to a 3D raster where each raster unit corresponds to the size of a root grid. We create an unique ID for each root grid based on this position. A 64 bit value is used to store the position information (see Fig. 2).

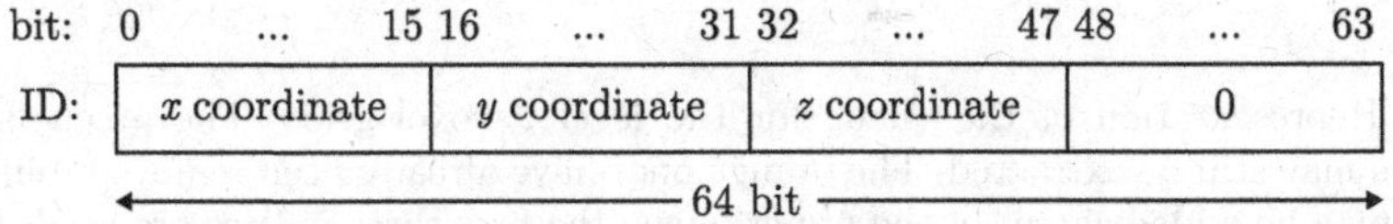

bit: 0 ... 15 16 ... 31 32 ... 47 48 ... 63
ID:
$x$ coordinate
$y$ coordinate
$z$ coordinate
0
64 bit

**Fig. 2.** Structure of the unique ID of a root grid. The first 48 bit are used for the upper corner position of the grid.

Thus, we create a root grid only, if it is within the camera view and actually contains any surface information. Actually, root grids are built depending on the camera position, so the initial camera pose is irrelevant. At the initial iteration of our system, the first root grids will be created at locations based on the initial camera position.

# 4  GPU Implementation

We implemented the data structures allowing for size and initial view independence on the GPU using CUDA. This section describes how this implementation works and how the volumetric integration as well as the ray casting were adapted to deal with the novel data structure.

Our empirical tests showed that a reasonable size for a root grid in 3D space for a Kinect 2 sensor is $1\,m \times 1\,m \times 1\,m$ to obtain a good overhead vs. information ratio. Thereby, a root grid has a size, so that only a few voxels do not refer to a finer grid. Further we not have too much overhead for the root grid management. Our tests revealed that three grid levels are typically sufficient even for complex volumes. In our implementation we therefore used a resolution of $4 \times 4 \times 4$ for the first two levels. For the finest grid level, containing the actual TSDF values, we applied a resolution depending on the desired real world voxel size. For a size of $2\,mm \rightarrow 32 \times 32 \times 32$, $4\,mm \rightarrow 16 \times 16 \times 16$ and $8\,mm \rightarrow 8 \times 8 \times 8$. Thus, a node of the last level encompasses a total space of $64\,mm \times 64\,mm \times 64\,mm$.

## 4.1  Storage of the Data Structure

Each time we have to create a root grid we fully allocate the first two levels of it on the graphic cards memory. For each voxel we store an integer referring to the grid's next level. Hence, we get $64 \times 64 \times 64$ integer values. Each is initialized by $-1$ to indicate there is no surface stored in it. The full allocation of all possible

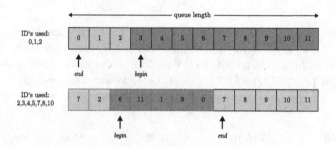

**Fig. 3.** Representation of the queue for the level 2 voxel grids. The green labeled elements may still be extracted. The orange ones have already been removed, but their indices may be added again. In the upper queue the first three indices are used. In the bottom one all indices were removed once and seven elements inserted again (marked by a red border). Furthermore two indices from the re-inserted elements were already removed. (Color figure online)

level 1 grids turned out to be useful as it avoids post-allocation costs when integrating the sensor data.

The grids of the final level are pre-allocated on the GPU. Their number depends on the available memory size of the GPU. For these grids a queue is generated to store their indices (see Fig. 3). Each time a grid is needed, the corresponding index is obtained from the queue and can be re-inserted if it is not needed anymore. In addition to the grid pointers the unique id is stored for each root grid.

## 4.2 Volumetric Integration

At the beginning of each integration it has to be determined which root grids are actually needed, i.e. in which root grids the surfaces lie. In order to do this we create a vertex map from the raw depth map and determine the root grid where a vertex lies in. This can easily be achieved using the unique IDs. Each vertex is assigned to a separate CUDA thread. Hence, we compute the corresponding ID by the vertex position $p$

$$uid_x = \left\lfloor \frac{p_x}{w} \right\rfloor \tag{3}$$

$$uid_y = \left\lfloor \frac{p_y}{w} \right\rfloor \tag{4}$$

$$uid_z = \left\lfloor \frac{p_z}{w} \right\rfloor \tag{5}$$

where $w$ is the length of a root grid in each dimension. Based on these values the unique ID can be created. All IDs required are stored in a list.

Based on this list one can easily determine on the CPU which root grid must be allocated. Further, we can now step through all these root grids to determine the TSDF values. We do this for each root grid separately. For the first level, we assign a voxel to each CUDA block (see Fig. 4). Like the approach of a voxel projection from Chen *et al.* [2], each block first determines the bounding box of the voxel on the camera image plane. Thus, only the pixels inside this bounding box have to be checked rather than the entire image. Now for each pixel assigned to a single thread, we extract the corresponding vertex and check if the truncated region around this vertex lies inside the voxel. For achieving an efficient processing we approximate the spherical region by a cube. Thus, we can determine a collision of this cube and the voxel cube simply by applying an axis aligned bounding box collision test. If a collision is detected, we store a 1 in a shared array, 0 otherwise, for each pixel. Using a parallel tree-based reduction [3] we receive the sum for each voxel. For any value larger than 0 voxels contain some surface information.

Whenever there is some voxel information within the first level grid, we evaluate the corresponding second level grids. Further, we assign one voxel to each CUDA block. This allows us to calculate the voxels of all level 1 grids of the root grid containing any surface information in parallel. If a voxel does not (yet) have a child grid, again a bounding box of the voxel on the camera image plane

**for all** voxel $v \in l_0$ **do in parallel**
    $tid \leftarrow$ thread index
    $bb \leftarrow$ bounding box of $v$ at camera image plane
    **for all** pixel $c \in bb$ **do in parallel**
        $p \leftarrow$ vertex of $c$
        **if** collision of $v$ with $p$ **then**
            $sharedData[tid] \leftarrow 1$
        **else**
            $sharedData[tid] \leftarrow 0$
        **end if**
    **end for**
    $sum \leftarrow$ tree-based reduction of $sharedData$
    **if** $tid = 0$ and $sum > 0$ **then**
        set child index of $v$
    **end if**
**end for**

**Fig. 4.** Depth integration of Level 0 grids

is calculated to verify whether any vertex lies within. In this case, a level 3 grid index is extracted from the queue and assigned to the voxel. Finally, for these voxels holding a valid child, the TSDF values and weights are calculated using the corresponding voxels of the third level. This step is similar to the calculation used by the KinectFusion algorithm [11].

In addition to their algorithm we determine the average TSDF value ($tsdf_{avg}$) of each grid. If $tsdf_{avg} > 1 - \varepsilon$ we know that all voxels inside have approximately a TSDF value of 1. Thus, there is no surface inside this grid. Thus, we can clear that grid by setting all TSDF values to $-1$ and all weights to 0. Additionally, we re-insert the index of the grid into the queue and remove the link between this grid and its parent voxel.

Finally, we have to pass through all level 1 grids and check if any voxel has a child grid. If no level 2 grids are used, we set the child index of the voxel to $-1$.

## 4.3   Ray Casting

In addition to the volumetric integration, the ray casting has to be adopted to the new data structure as well.

We determine the vertex and normal maps of the current reconstruction volume. We start with a ray length of 1 mm, which is the smallest measurable value in our hardware setup. We determine the root grid which is associated to the ray position $p$. This is computed similar to the first step of the depth integration process. Next we use the list of root grid ids as obtained from the integration step to check if the calculated root grid actually exists. Iterating over all root grids would be rather costly. Experiments revealed that the list of allocated root grids typically is almost identical the list of all root grid ids within the current camera view.

If the current root grid id is not yet in the list, we increase its length of the ray. Thus, the ray intersects the next available root grid in this direction. Otherwise, if the root grid id is already in the list, we extract the TSDF value from the level 2 grid at $p$. Thus, we need the indices $idx$ of the voxel $v$ at levels 1 and 2. We achieve this by applying the following Eqs. 6–10.

We subtract the offset $o$ from $p$ where $o$ is the metric value of the root grid position (multiplying the root grid size of one dimension with the actual position values). The $x$, $y$ and $z$ coordinates of the desired voxel are determined by the floor value of $\hat{p}$ and a modulo operation with the voxel resolution of the corresponding level. Because the resolution of each grid level is a power of 2, the modulo operation can be very efficiently calculated by a bitwise AND operation.

$$\hat{p} = p - o \tag{6}$$

$$v_{i_x} = \left\lfloor \frac{\hat{p}_x}{s_i} \right\rfloor \; mod \; r_i \tag{7}$$

$$v_{i_y} = \left\lfloor \frac{\hat{p}_y}{s_i} \right\rfloor \; mod \; r_i \tag{8}$$

$$v_{i_z} = \left\lfloor \frac{\hat{p}_z}{s_i} \right\rfloor \; mod \; r_i \tag{9}$$

$$idx_i = r_i \cdot r_i \cdot v_{i_z} + r_i \cdot v_{i_y} + v_{i_x} \tag{10}$$

If the TSDF value from the previous iteration is above 0 and the current value is below 0, we can determine a vertex and normal as described in the original KinectFusion work [11]. The length of the ray is increased by the truncated distance, if the TSDF value is above 0. Otherwise, there is no voxel at $p$. Thus, we increase the length by the size of the level 2 grid.

## 5   Results

In this section we present the results of our approach with respect to performance, memory consumption, and reconstruction quality. The following results apply to a Kinect 2 sensor. All tests were performed on the following system: Intel® Xeon® E5-2687W v2 - 3.4 GHz, Nvidia® Quadro® K6000.

Figure 5 shows the results of the performance analysis. The figures represent average values of several scenes. As the figures show, the approach achieves real-time performance, in particular when using a voxel size of 4 mm or 8 mm at the final grid level. The time for the volumetric integration is drastically reduced by increasing the voxel size. This is due to less voxels requiring to be processed in the integration step.

Finally, we want to examine the memory consumption of our system. At first, we examine a rather small scene containing a fan, which we also use for the evaluation of the reconstruction quality (see below). This scene has a size of 2 m × 2 m × 1.6 m. The memory consumption of our approach applied to this scene is approximately 20 percent below that of our own implementation of the KinectFusion algorithm [11].

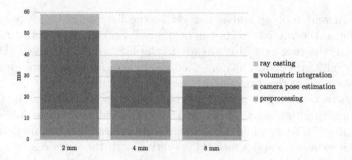

**Fig. 5.** Illustration of the performance measurements of our system using different voxel sizes for the finest grid level. From bottom to top: preprocessing, camera pose estimation, volumetric integration, ray casting.

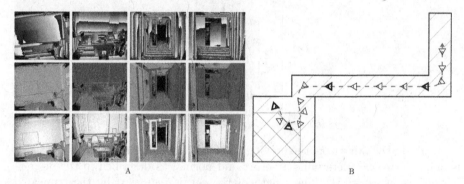

**Fig. 6.** A: Illustration of sample shots from a large area reconstruction. The first row shows the filtered input depth map, the second row our determined normal map and the third row the resulting ray casted image. B: Illustration of the tracking shot for a the reconstruction. The bold camera symbols represent the sample shots of B. The red hatched area indicates the space which could be reconstructed by the KinectFusion approach with a similar memory consumption to that used by our system for the entire area.

For a full size room reconstruction, applying an overall volume of 3.75 m × 5.90 m × 2.60 m, our approach already requires 60 percent less memory compared to the volume required by the KinectFusion approach.

Furthermore we performed a tracking shot of a rather large indoor area including the entire room and the adjacent corridor (see Fig. 6). That entire area had a size of approximately 63 square meters. With the memory consumed by our system, the KinectFusion approach would only be able to handle approximately 17 square meters of that scene as roughly illustrated in Fig. 6 by the red hatched area. Please note, that the actual KinectFusion approach would not be able to handle such large volumes. An advantage of our system is the dynamic adaptation to the layout of the reconstruction area. As most other approaches are based on a cuboid data structure, they need to define a much larger area than the actual scene in case of a non cuboid reconstruction volume as common for most spacious areas as illustrated by our example.

Compared to other systems, our approach does not require the initial camera pose to be known in advance. The data structure will adapt to the actual real world scene. We do not need any information of the scene for the initialization of our algorithm. Further, it is flexible regarding the overall extension and shape of the reconstruction area. Thus, even when used for non rectangular room shapes, it can apply an efficient memory allocation. For rooms of rather irregular shapes, which are quite common in many buildings, other approaches would need significantly more memory or even may not be able to handle the amount of data due to their cuboid reconstruction areas. Our system offers a memory efficient reconstruction especially for sparsely populated scenes.

## 6   Conclusion

In this paper we presented a flexible and memory efficient data management for camera based 3D scene reconstruction. We implemented our approach and showed that it operates in real-time. Based on a flexible arrangement of root grids, we reach a dynamically adaption to the extensions of a scene, especially for non cuboid areas. This in particular renders the initial camera position irrelevant. Due to the hierarchical storage model our approach allows for rather large environments. Furthermore we demonstrated how our approach can be used as part of a highly parallelized GPU based computation.

The general approach can easily be applied to other camera based dense reconstruction systems. This includes other sensors for depth map generation as well as other techniques for camera pose estimation.

In our future work we expect to further elaborate the mechanisms developed. Dynamic parallelism as provided by CUDA was not used in our system due to the limitation of the graphics hardware available for development. We expect the performance of our system to be further improved when applying this feature. Furthermore the approach of Kähler *et al.* [5] especially with respect to the camera tracking could be used to speed up our system.

By moving the stored data from the GPU to the CPU and vice versa the reconstruction area could be further increased. Regions which are no longer in the current camera view may be transferred to RAM and moved back when the camera observes the same region again.

Another area for future investigations is the realization of a robust mechanism for the integration of color values into the memory structure.

## References

1. Afzal, H., Ismaeil, K.A., Aouda, D., Destelle, F., Mirbach, B., Ottersten, B.: KinectDeform: enhanced 3D reconstruction of non-rigidly deforming objects. In: 3DV Workshop on Dynamic Shape Measurement and Analysis (2014)

2. Chen, J., Bautembach, D., Izadi, S.: Scalable real-time volumetric surface reconstruction. ACM Trans. Graph. **32**(4), 113: 1–113: 16 (2013)
3. Harris, M., Sengupta, S., Owens, J.D.: Parralel prefix sum (scan) with CUDA. In: Nguyen, H. (ed.) GPU Gems 3, Chap. 39, pp. 851–876. Addison Wesley (2007)
4. Izadi, S., Kim, D., Hilliges, O., Molyneaux, D., Newcombe, R., Kohli, P., Shotton, J., Hodges, S., Freeman, D., Davison, A., Fitzgibbon, A.: KinectFusion: real-time 3D reconstruction and interaction using a moving depth camera. In: Symposium on User Interface Software and Technology (UIST) (2011)
5. Kahler, O., Prisacariu, V.A., Ren, C.Y., Sun, X., Torr, P.H.S., Murray, D.W.: Very High frame rate volumetric integration of depth images on mobile device. IEEE Trans. Vis. Comput. Graph. (Proceedings International Symposium on Mixed and Augmented Reality) 22(11) (2015)
6. Keller, M., Lefloch, D., Lambers, M., Izadi, S., Weyrich, T., Kolb, A.: Real-time 3D reconstruction in dynamic scenes using point-based fusion. In: Proceedings of the 2013 International Conference on 3D Vision, pp. 1–8 (2013)
7. Klein, G., Murray, D.W.: Parallel tracking and mapping for small AR workspaces. In: Proceedings of the International Symposium on Mixed and Augmented Reality (ISMAR) (2007)
8. Loop, C., Zhang, C., Zhang, Z.: Real-time high-resolution sparse voxelization with application to image-based modeling. In: Proceedings of the 5th High-Performance Graphics Conference, HPG 2013, pp. 73–79 (2013)
9. Newcombe, R., Fox, D., Seitz, S.: DynamicFusion: reconstruction and tracking of non-rigid scenes in real-time. In: IEEE International Conference on Computer Vision and Pattern Recognition (CVPR), pp. 343–352 (2015)
10. Newcombe, R.A., Davison, A.J.: Live dense reconstruction with a single moving camera. In: Proceedings of the IEEE Conference on Computer Vision and Pattern Recognition (CVPR) (2010)
11. Newcombe, R.A., Izadi, S., Hilliges, O., Molyneaux, D., Kim, D., Davison, A.J., Kohli, P., Shotton, J., Hodges, S., Fitzgibbon, A.: KinectFusion: real-time dense surface mapping and tracking. In: ISMAR, pp. 127–136. IEEE (2011)
12. Newcombe, R.A., Lovegrove, S.J., Davison, A.J.: Dtam: dense tracking and mapping in real-time. In: Proceedings of the 2011 International Conference on Computer Vision, pp. 2320–2327 (2011)
13. Niessner, M., Zollhöfer, M., Izadi, S., Stamminger, M.: Real-time 3D reconstruction at scale using voxel hashing. ACM Trans. Graph. **32**(6), 169:1–169:11 (2013)
14. Steinbrücker, F., Kerl, C., Sturm, J., Cremers, D.: Large-scale multi-resolution surface reconstruction from RGB-D sequences. In: International Conference on Computer Vision, pp. 4321–4328 (2013)
15. Whelan, T., Kaess, M., Johannsson, H., Fallon, M., Leonard, J., McDonald, J.: Real-time large scale dense RGB-D SLAM with volumetric fusion. International Journal of Robotics Research (2014)
16. Whelan, T., McDonald, J., Kaess, M., Fallon, M., Johannsson, H., Leonard, J.J.: Kintinuous: spatially extended KinectFusion. In: RSS Workshop on RGB-D: Advanced Reasoning with Depth Cameras (2012)
17. Zeng, M., Zhao, F., Zheng, J., Liu, X.: Octree-based fusion for realtime 3D reconstruction. Graph. Models **75**(3), 126–136 (2013)

# Minimal Interaction Touchless Text Input with Head Movements and Stereo Vision

Adam Nowosielski[✉]

Faculty of Computer Science and Information Technology, West Pomeranian
University of Technology, Żołnierska 52, 71-210 Szczecin, Poland
anowosielski@wi.zut.edu.pl

**Abstract.** Many modern interfaces for human-computer interaction are
based on some kind of visual system and offer touchless and convenient
medium for communication for the user. These non-contact interfaces
predominantly limit their operations to gesture recognition or a pointer
manipulation in a graphical user interface. The problem of typing in
most cases is omitted since touchless interfaces are not designed for text
entry purposes. There is, however, a great number of people who suffer
from some form of disability. They are unable to use standard input
devices (mouse and keyboard) or modern touchless interfaces. For those
physically challenged people a minimal interaction interface for text entry
operated with head movements is proposed in the paper. It is based on
processing video streams from a stereo webcam, uses only directional
head movements and a dictionary support.

## 1 Introduction

Many new electronic devices are equipped with touchscreens which serve for
convenient interaction. Created interfaces are minimalistic and limit the user to
a few available options. The typing, when needed, is provided by different touch
or gesture (swipe) keyboards. These form of interaction seems to be perfect and
might be one of the reason of great popularity of modern equipment (e.g. tablets).
On the other hand, contemporary research on new interfaces also focuses on
computer vision and pattern recognition approaches. Natural User Interfaces
(NUIs) operated with gestures are gaining more and more attention. There are,
however, over 1 billion people in the world who have some form of disability
(according to *World report on disability* [1]). Almost one fifth of them encounter
significant difficulties in their daily lives. To increase their independence and
provide the access to digital world new assistive technologies are introduced.
The control/input devices and interfaces play the key role here.

Touchless interaction enables users to operate without additional medium
and intermediate equipment. This is of particular interest with large-display
environments and intermittent or casual interaction. The touchless interaction
is particularly suitable for the following scenarios [2–6]: public spaces, clinical
environments, consumer electronics, brainstorming, visualization, vision-based

L.J. Chmielewski et al. (Eds.): ICCVG 2016, LNCS 9972, pp. 233–243, 2016.
DOI: 10.1007/978-3-319-46418-3_21

augmented reality, 3D CAD modeling, sign language recognition, robot control etc. It is natural and convenient to interact with gestures with limited and adapted menus but all touchless interfaces encounter problems when the user have to type even a simple text. For example, the user can select the content by gesture on new smart TVs but on entering the web address a form of physical keyboard is needed. A conversion from the gesture to a different method of communication is the current standard. Casual short writing as one of the many elements of the touchless interface should be considered and addressed. Moreover, the interface for touchless typing is of particular necessity for physically challenged people who are unable to operate the standard devices.

In this paper we focus on the solution for text entry using only head movements. The assumed interaction is minimal and uncomplicated. The user is provided with the dictionary support. The proposed solution operates on the basis of stereo vision and computer vision approaches.

The rest of the article is structured as follows. In Sect. 2 touchless approaches to typing are presented and discussed. Section 3 introduces the solution for touchless text input with head movements and stereo vision. Its details are provided in Sect. 4. Final conclusions and a summary are provided in Sect. 5.

## 2    Touchless Approaches to Typing

Computer vision approaches are an excellent basis to create new natural interfaces. They have great potential and applicability and can provide complete information of human body arrangements for steering purposes. There are also several alternative techniques for touchless interfaces and most popular of these include: brain computer interfaces, speech recognition, eyetracking. The current price level of some of these solutions is far too high for many individuals. The use of other is not possible for some people due to their disabilities.

The obvious solution for the touchless typing is speech recognition. The technology has been a topic of research since the 1950s and now is considered mature [7]. Apart from dictation the speech recognition has a great potential in dialogue systems and device control. The main drawback of these solution is a lack of privacy and silence. A solution for those problems exists in the form of silent speech [8]. Most importantly the silent speech technology can be used as an aid for the speech-handicapped [8].

Another solution for touchless typing is offered by eyetracking which provides sophisticated methods for capturing the humans gaze direction. The eye movements can replace traditional control devices: the mouse and the keyboard [9]. The Dasher project [10] is a good example here. It is the system of text entry by continuous pointing gestures. The eyetracking as one mode of steering is reported to achieve typing speed comparable to normal handwriting by experienced users (29 words per minute) [10].

Touchless text entry is also possible with the hand movement and some approaches have already been reported in the literature. The scientific literature devoted to the problem of hand gesture recognition is abundant and good surveys can be found in [5,6,11]. In [12] two interfaces for touchless text input have been proposed and compared. The first one uses standard onscreen QWERTY keyboard operated with hand movements in front of the camera. The second solution is the adaptation of the *8pen* [13] stroke-based technique to the touchless environment. An interesting solution have been presented in [14] where the user's hand and fingers are tracked. The separation of words is achieved with a pinch gesture. Consecutive words are typed using the continuous gesture (swipe) technique with hand movements in the air. Such an approach requires strong dictionary support. A similar solution have been proposed in [15] where typing the letters have been substituted with swipe word patterns.

Finally, the problem of touchless text input have also been considered with the help of head movements. In the QVirtboard [16,17] the interface of the onscreen keyboard can be operated (among others) with directional or rotary head movements. In [18] head movements for touchless typing are supported with three face gestures chosen for a key selection: mouth open, brows up and brows down. Most head (also face or facial features) operated interfaces focus, however, on conventional mouse replacement and the pointer manipulation in the graphical user interface (e.g. [19,20]).

Researchers are actively engaged in the development of touchless interaction. Text input and mouse control are the two most important tasks in human-computer interaction. However, the problem of touchless typing is neglected in the contemporary research. The touchless interaction generally focus on some sort of selections and gestures. The text entry in touchless environment is considered as a novel issue [12,14] and vision-based text entry interfaces are still rare and insufficiently studied [18].

## 3   Proposition of the Interface

Natural User Interface (NUI) have to be imperceptible and should base on nature or natural elements [21]. The user is expected to interact with electronic devices in a natural way. These principles have been a determinant of the proposed text-entry interface operated with head movements. Head movements are assumed to be simple and straightforward, easy to understand, learn and operate by new users. The interface is expected to be minimalistic in the operation and in the form (without any additional distracting elements). To achieve all the above goals the appropriate onscreen layout and adequate techniques to capture user movements are required.

### 3.1   The Onscreen Keyboard

The first issue for consideration about the interface is the layout of the onscreen keyboard. Most often modern keyboards are based on the QWERTY key arrangement designed in the 19th century. More efficient and ergonomic new alternatives have been introduced with the aim to minimize finger path distances and make heavy use of the home row (the Dvorak and the Colemak are best examples). Unfortunately, despite the improved performance, they didn't gained sufficient interest and popularity. Users are reluctant to learn new key arrangements and even the latest innovations (like e.g. *8pen* [13]) based on new concepts are unwillingly received.

More frequently the QWERTY keyboard is substituted with alphabetically arranged layouts (e.g. in smart TVs). The alphabetical order of keys have also been used in the 12-keys mobile phone keypad and 5-keys pagers. After our previous experience with the touchless typing [12,15,17,22] we decided to base our new interface for text input with head movement on a single row alphabetical keyboard for the following reasons:

– the QWERTY layout requires movement in four directions,
– with the letter selection through four directional movements another mode for the touchless key press is required in the QWERTY layout,
– the alphabetical order is intuitive and easily operable,
– with a single row layout the selection of a letter requires only moves to the left and right with the up and down movements available for other actions (e.g. pressing),
– the speed of the movement in the letter selection process can be a function of the head shift.

Considering the users habits the first choice solution should be the QWERTY keyboard. With head movements transferred to the letter selection the problem with the process of pressing occurs. It can be solved with the controlled eye blink like in many alternatives for human computer interaction (e.g. [20]). Another solution is the division of the process of letter selection on QWERTY keyboard into two stages as proposed in [17] where the user first selects the column and then the row. The referred solution, however, turned out to be slow for spontaneous casual writing [12,22]. Contrary, on the one row keyboard with left and right directional movements the selection of a letter can be easily obtained. The keypress can be simulated with the movement in the downward direction. The up direction can be arranged for the backspace (letter deletion). Such proposition is very straightforward: 4 directional head movements are required for the text entry.

### 3.2   The Interface

The whole concept of the interface is shown in the Fig. 1. The proposed interface consists of two rows with the upper one composed of alphabet letters and the bottom one composed of suggested dictionary words. Individual letters and words are treated as keys, one of which is always active (i.e. highlighted). The typing starts with the head movements in horizontal directions (left or right). The head shift moves the active letter to the neighbor. While remaining in the shifted position consecutive letters are periodically activated (the speed of the change is a function of the range of the head shift). On the return to the central position the last activated letter remains active and with the nod gesture can be typed.

To improve the speed of typing - suggestions of words are provided as in most new solutions. With the new letter typed the dictionary is used for suggestions

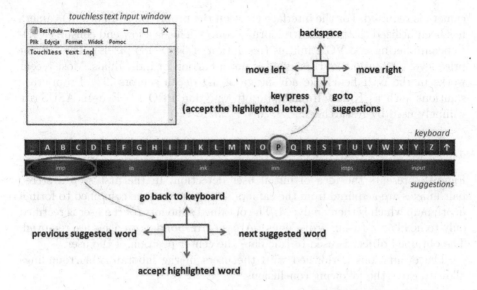

**Fig. 1.** The concept of the operation of the interface

which are displayed in the lower row. The contents of this line is dynamic. The suggestions are accessible with the double nod gesture. The double nod moves the selection to the lower row. Here, the left and right directions move through the individual words. The pressing (acceptance of the word) is achieved with the nod gesture after which the steering returns to the upper row. The withdrawal from the line of suggested words is available with the head up gesture - the list of suggested words remains, nothing is typed, the steering returns to the character selection.

The last note regards the feedback for the user. In our earlier approach, the QVirtboard [16,17], we mapped all users actions into the marker plane. The marker plane consisted of five sectors (four directional and the central one called the dead zone). The marker representing the user motion moved above the marker plane. Additionally, it had a form of animated circle shape presenting the lapse of time. Such feedback turned out to be helpful for new users in the learning stage or during the calibration. In the interface proposed in this paper we resigned from any additional previews. In a minimalistic solution any form of supplementary information makes the interface overgrowth. What is more, in the proposed solution only four directional movements are used. Motions in each direction have the predefined effect in the interface, visible to the user, so additional feedback mechanism can be omitted thoroughly.

## 4   Mechanisms Used in the Interface

The technique used to capture the user's head movements in the proposed solution is based on stereo vision. A pair of calibrated cameras or a single stereoscopic camera is required. For the interface creation the proprietary Minoru 3D camera has been utilized (http://www.minoru3d.com/). This is a low-end consumer 3D-webcam offering two VGA images (resolution of 640 × 480 pixels). The current price level of solutions of these kind is not a barrier for individuals. Most recent works in the NUI field take advantage of 3D depth sensors [23]. Proprietary solutions such as Kinect from Microsoft or Xtion PRO LIVE from ASUS are willingly used by researchers.

## 4.1 Stereo Vision

Figure 2 presents the idea of initial user detection. In the first step a stereo pair images are acquired from the camera. Those images are combined to form a depth map which is then analyzed. The obtained silhouette of the user is rectified only to head area (using projections). Areas corresponding to arms are removed. The obtained object is used to calculate the center position of the user.

The evaluations performed with the users in the laboratory surroundings allow to draw the following conclusions:

- head movements in horizontal directions are easy to make for the user and very well detectable,
- the offset distance of the head can be directly transformed to the speed in key selection procedure (the greater the distance the faster the movement),
- head movements in the vertical direction, despite easy to detect, are difficult or inconvenient for the user to perform,
- the interface is operable but not comfortable for the user considering the up and down head movements.

To make the interface more user friendly it was crucial to provide the user a better solution for vertical operations. The choice was the head rotary movements (tilt of the head up and down). These actions are natural and easy to perform. They have, however, a minimal effect in the vertical coordinate of the calculated user position (see the examples in Fig. 3). The calculated center remains roughly unchanged. The stereo vision used alone for the head movement detection in the task of touchless text input is not sufficient.

## 4.2 Eye Line

Figure 4 presents masked face images that correspond to those depicted in Fig. 3. The changes are clearly visible in the localization of face features against the body contour. Tilt of the head down (the nod gesture) and the opposite upward gesture can be detected through those changes. We based our approach on the position of eyes.

Since the individual locations of both eyes are not required the eye line have been adopted for the vertical coordinate of the head position. The eye line detection algorithm is based on the combination of well known and widely used Viola and Jones approach [24] and the method of projections. Projections

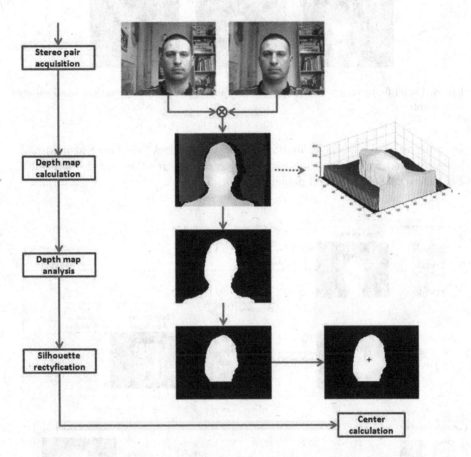

**Fig. 2.** Initial calculation of the user position

**Fig. 3.** Limited change of the ordinate position during head rotary movements

**Fig. 4.** Facial features against calculated silhouette center during vertical head rotary movements

are powerful and efficient in finding distinctive features (like face features) [25]. Supplemented by guiding functions [26] can provide reliable and stable results. The entire process has been depicted in Fig. 5.

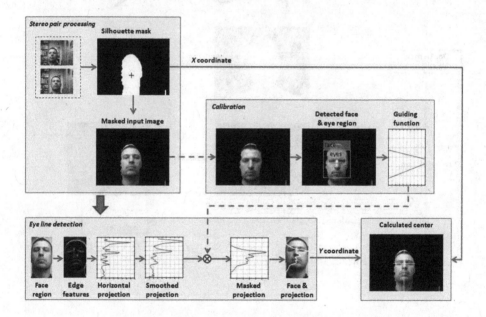

**Fig. 5.** Calculation of the head position

The $X$ coordinate of the user head position is calculated from the silhouette mask. The $Y$ coordinate is based on the eye line calculated as follows. First, the face region is extracted and edge features are calculated. Then, the horizontal projection for edge features is computed, smoothed and masked using the guiding function. Position of the maximum in the horizontal projection indicates the localization of the eye line. The process is based on algorithms presented in [25, 26]. Here, however, the guiding function is created dynamically in the calibration step on the base of face and eye regions found by the Viola and Jones method.

With the presented approach stable and reliable head position is acquired. User movements to the left and to the right are transformed to shifts on the keyboard. Tilt of the head down (the nod gesture used for the key press or dictionary word affirmation) and the opposite upward gesture (used for backspace or leaving the dictionary suggestions row) are very well detectable. The double nod (used for the shift to the dictionary row) is detected through subsequent two quick nods.

After the calibration the initial head center is stored as the reference point. Coordinates of the reference point are updated with involuntary natural user movements in front of the computer monitor (adaptation). Changes exceeding preset thresholds do not update the reference position but recognized as directional movements provide a basis for interaction in the interface. Moreover, the motion detection in a given direction automatically locks the perpendicular direction. This procedure prevents the accidental transitions between letters or the accidental pressing. During horizontal head movements users tend to tilt their heads sideways causing the eye line to decrease. As the result the accidental press may occur. Similarly, without the locking procedure, during vertical head movements, shifts to an adjacent characters also occurred.

## 5 Conclusions

In the paper, the problem of text entry using head movements have been addressed. The interface of touchless text entry is of particular importance for physically challenged people who are unable to operate the standard computer input devices. Since most non-contact interfaces for typing focus on conventional mouse replacement the touchless text entry still remains a challenge.

The interface proposed in this paper is minimalistic. It has a form of single row alphabetical keyboard accompanied with the row presenting suggested words (dictionary matched with each new letter typed). The interactions are performed through head left and right directional movements and up and down head rotary movements. These movements are detected respectively using stereo vision and face features (position of the eye line). The speed of processing on contemporary standard PC is sufficient for the real-time interaction.

Experiments conducted among 18 participants (mostly computer science students, aged 22–23 years), for whom the interface was a novelty and who used it for the first time, provided the average performance rate of 11.08 cpm (chars per minute) with the standard deviation of 2.08. With more trials the best participants were able to achieve typing speed of approx. 15 cpm. These results are slower compared to other computer vision approaches to the touchless typing (eyetracking, hand gesture) but the solution using head movements might be the only choice for some people with physical disabilities.

## References

1. World Health Organization: The World Bank: World Report on Disability. WHO Press, World Health Organization, Switzerland (2011)

2. Chattopadhyay, D., Bolchini, D.: Understanding visual feedback in large-display touchless interactions: an exploratory study. Research report, IUPUI Scholar Works, Indiana University (2014)
3. Johnson, R., O'Hara, K., Sellen, A., Cousins, C., Criminisi, A.: Exploring the potential for touchless interaction in image-guided interventional radiology. In: ACM Conference on Computer-Human Interaction (CHI 2011), pp. 3323–3332 (2011)
4. Dostal, J., Hinrichs, U., Kristensson, P.O., Quigley, A.: SpiderEyes: designing attention- and proximity-aware collaborative interfaces for wall-sized displays. In: Proceedings of the 19th International Conference on Intelligent User Interfaces, IUI 2014, pp. 143–152, Haifa, Israel (2014)
5. Sarkar, A.R., Sanyal, G., Majumder, S.: Hand gesture recognition systems: a survey. Int. J. Comput. Appl. **71**(15), 25–37 (2013)
6. Mitra, S., Acharya, T.: Gesture recognition: a survey. IEEE Trans. Syst. Man Cybern. Part C Appl. Rev. **37**(3), 311–324 (2007)
7. Rebman, C.M., Aiken, M.W., Cegielski, C.G.: Speech recognition in the human computer interface. Inform. Manage. **40**(6), 509–519 (2003)
8. Denby, B., Schultz, T., Honda, K., Hueber, T., Gilbert, J.M., Brumberg, J.S.: Silent speech interfaces. Speech Commun. **52**(4), 270–287 (2010)
9. Jacob, R.J.K., Karn, K.S.: Eye tracking in human-computer interaction and usability research: ready to deliver the promises. In: The Minds Eye: Cognitive and Applied Aspects of Eye Movement Research. Elsevier Science, Oxford (2003)
10. Dasher Project (2016). http://www.inference.phy.cam.ac.uk/dasher/
11. Ibraheem, N.A., Khan, R.Z.: Survey on various gesture recognition technologies and techniques. Int. J. Comput. Appl. **50**(7), 38–44 (2012)
12. Nowosielski, A.: QWERTY- and *8pen*- based touchless text input with hand movement. In: Chmielewski, L.J., Kozera, R., Shin, B.-S., Wojciechowski, K. (eds.) ICCVG 2014. LNCS, vol. 8671, pp. 470–477. Springer, Heidelberg (2014). doi:10.1007/978-3-319-11331-9_56
13. 8pen (2016). http://www.the8pen.com/
14. Markussen, A., Jakobsen, M.R., Hornbk, K.: Vulture: a mid-air word-gesture keyboard. In: Proceedings of the SIGCHI Conference on Human Factors in Computing Systems CHI 2014, pp. 1073–1082 (2014)
15. Wierzchowski, M., Nowosielski, A.: Swipe text input for touchless interfaces. In: Burduk, R., Jackowski, K., Kurzyński, M., Woźniak, M., Żołnierek, A. (eds.) Proceedings of the 9th International Conference on Computer Recognition Systems CORES 2015. AISC, vol. 403, pp. 619–629. Springer, Heidelberg (2016). doi:10.1007/978-3-319-26227-7_58
16. QVirtboard (2016). http://qvirtboard.sourceforge.net/
17. Nowosielski, A., Chodyła, Ł.: Touchless input interface for disabled. In: Burduk, R., Jackowski, K., Kurzynski, M., Wozniak, M., Zolnierek, A. (eds.) CORES 2013. AISC, vol. 226, pp. 701–709. Springer, Heidelberg (2013). doi:10.1007/978-3-319-00969-8_69
18. Gizatdinova, Y., Spakov, O., Surakka, V.: Face typing: vision-based perceptual interface for hands-free text entry with a scrollable virtual keyboard. In: IEEE Workshop on Applications of Computer Vision 2012, Breckenridge, CO, USA, pp. 81–87 (2012)
19. Morris, T., Chauhan, V.: Facial feature tracking for cursor control. J. Netw. Comput. Appl. **29**(2006), 62–80 (2006)
20. Varona, J., Manresa-Yee, C., Perales, F.J.: Hands-free vision-based interface for computer accessibility. J. Netw. Comput. Appl. **31**(4), 357–374 (2008)

21. Giorio, C., Fascinari, M.: Kinect in Motion Audio and Visual Tracking by Example Starting. Packt Publishing, Birmingham (2013)
22. Nowosielski, A.: Evaluation of touchless typing techniques with hand movement. In: Burduk, R., Jackowski, K., Kurzyński, M., Woźniak, M., Żołnierek, A. (eds.) Proceedings of the 9th International Conference on Computer Recognition Systems CORES 2015. AISC, vol. 403, pp. 441–449. Springer, Heidelberg (2016). doi:10.1007/978-3-319-26227-7_41
23. Placitelli, A.P.: Toward a framework for rapid prototyping of touchless user interfaces. In: 2012 Sixth International Conference on Complex, Intelligent, and Software Intensive Systems, pp. 539–543 (2012)
24. Viola, P., Jones, M.: Robust real-time face detection. Int. J. Comput. Vis. **57**(2), 137–154 (2004)
25. Kukharev, G., Nowosielski, A.: Fast and efficient algorithm for face detection in colour images. Mach. Graph. Vis. **13**(4), 377–399 (2004)
26. Kukharev, G., Kumiski, A.: Biometric Techniques Part I. Face Recognition Methods (in Polish). Szczecin University of Technology Press, Szczecin (2003)

# Application of Structural Similarity Based Metrics for Quality Assessment of 3D Prints

Krzysztof Okarma$^{(\boxtimes)}$, Jarosław Fastowicz, and Mateusz Tecław

Faculty of Electrical Engineering, Department of Signal Processing
and Multimedia Engineering,
West Pomeranian University of Technology, Szczecin,
26. Kwietnia 10, 71-126 Szczecin, Poland
{krzysztof.okarma,jaroslaw.fastowicz,mateusz.teclaw}@zut.edu.pl

**Abstract.** The paper is related to the verification of the usefulness of some metrics, typically used for image quality assessment and texture similarity evaluation, for no-reference quality assessment of 3D prints. The proposed approach is based on the assumption that a surface of high quality 3D print should be homogeneous and therefore some parts of it should be self-similar. Considering the local similarity of some fragments of 3D prints, some distortions can be detected which lower the overall quality of the 3D print. Since many image quality assessment methods, as well as texture similarity metrics, are based on the comparison of fragments of two images, a modification of such approach has been proposed which allows the no-reference evaluation without any information about the reference image or model.

**Keywords:** 3D prints · Texture analysis · SSIM · STSIM · Image quality assessment

## 1 Introduction

Development of modern 3D printing technologies causes the increase of popularity and availability of 3D printers which can be distinguished as four major groups based on different printing technologies. They can be divided into [10] inkjet printing, selective laser sintering, stereolithography and Fused Deposition Modelling (FDM). The latter one is the basic technology considered in this paper.

Although some machine vision solutions, related e.g. to visual feedback for detection of defects [4] or monitoring of top surface of the print [3] based on fuzzy logic, have already been proposed, there is still an open challenge related to reliable quality assessment of 3D prints. Some other methods are related to monitoring of the process and fault detection [1,9,10] although on some recent papers the application of image analysis has also been considered e.g. in Straub's paper [8]. His system based on Raspberry Pi units and five cameras is able to detect the lack of filament and unexpected stops of the printing process but is

© Springer International Publishing AG 2016
L.J. Chmielewski et al. (Eds.): ICCVG 2016, LNCS 9972, pp. 244–252, 2016.
DOI: 10.1007/978-3-319-46418-3_22

very sensitive to lighting conditions as well as camera motions and therefore its precise calibration is required.

In this paper an application of some metrics based on the well-known idea of Structural Similarity (SSIM) [14,15] is considered together with its application for a no-reference quality evaluation of 3D prints. As the "pure" SSIM metric is not expected to lead to satisfactory results, some its modifications have been analyzed and two of them, leading to promising results, namely Complex Wavelet SSIM [7] and Structural Texture Similarity (STSIM) [11,12,16], have been investigated in this paper.

## 2    Selected SSIM Based Metrics and Proposed Approach

The idea of Structural Similarity (SSIM) applied for image quality assessment task has been proposed at first as so called Universal Image Quality Index [13] calculated as the mean value of the local indexes obtained by the comparison of luminance ($l$), structure ($s$) and contrast ($c$) information between two fragments of images (the distorted image and the reference one without any distortions). The default size of those fragments has been defined as the $8 \times 8$ pixels and the sliding window approach has been used for the calculation of the overall index. Due to potential instability of results obtained for flat and/or dark areas of images, some modifications have been proposed by the same authors leading to the widely known SSIM metric utilizing $11 \times 11$ pixels Gaussian windows with additional constants preventing the possible division by zero. The local value of the SSIM index is calculated as:

$$ SSIM = l(x,y) \cdot c(x,y) \cdot s(x,y) = \frac{2\bar{x}\bar{y} + C_1}{\bar{x}^2 + \bar{y}^2 + C_1} \cdot \frac{2\sigma_x\sigma_y + C_2}{\sigma_x^2 + \sigma_y^2 + C_2} \cdot \frac{\sigma_{xy} + C_3}{\sigma_x\sigma_y + C_3}, \quad (1) $$

where $C_1$, $C_2$ and $C_3$ are small values used for preventing the potential division by zero. The default values are $C_1 = (0.01 \times 255)^2$, $C_2 = (0.03 \times 255)^2$ and $C_3 = C_2/2$ for 8-bit grayscale images. The symbols $\bar{x}$ and $\bar{y}$ are the mean values of the original and distorted image respectively, $\sigma_x^2$, $\sigma_y^2$ and $\sigma_{xy}$ denote the respective variances and the covariance inside the current position of the sliding window.

In recent years some other modifications and extensions of the SSIM metric have also been proposed e.g. gradient based SSIM (G-SSIM) [2], Complex-Wavelet SSIM [7], Multi-Scale SSIM [15] or 3-Component Weighted SSIM [6]. The most useful for texture analysis seems to be the Complex-Wavelet SSIM which has been used also in this paper for comparison purposes. The main advantage of such wavelet based approach seems to be much less sensitivity to typical geometrical operations such as translation, scaling and rotation of images in comparison to the "classical" SSIM. In consequence, the CW-SSIM metric is more sensitive to structural distortions which are much more important in 3D prints. Three major features of the CW-SSIM metric distinguished by its inventors [7] are:

– separation of measurements of magnitude and phase distortions,

**Fig. 1.** Scanned images used in experiments

– higher sensitivity to phase than magnitude distortions,
– insensitivity to consistent relative phase distortions.

Using the symmetric complex wavelets the quality index can be defined as:

$$\hat{S}(c_x, c_y) = \frac{2\left|\sum_{i=1}^{N} c_{x,i} c_{y,i}^*\right| + K}{\sum_{i=1}^{N} \left|c_{x,i}^2\right| + \sum_{i=1}^{N} \left|c_{y,i}^2\right| + K} \tag{2}$$

where $K$ is a small constant value preventing the possible division by zero for small local signal to noise ratios and $c^*$ is the complex conjugate of $c$.

**Fig. 2.** Images used in experiments obtained by a camera

The above formula can also be rewritten as:

$$\hat{S}(c_x, c_y) = \frac{2\sum\limits_{i=1}^{N}|c_{x,i}|\,|c_{y,i}| + K}{\sum\limits_{i=1}^{N}|c_{x,i}|^2 + \sum\limits_{i=1}^{N}|c_{y,i}|^2 + K} \cdot \frac{2\left|\sum\limits_{i=1}^{N} c_{x,i}c_{y,i}^*\right| + K}{2\sum\limits_{i=1}^{N}\left|c_{x,i}c_{y,i}^*\right| + K} \qquad (3)$$

where the two distinguished components are sensitive to magnitude of coefficients and the second one depends on the consistency of phase differences.

Another interesting extension of the SSIM metric, considered in this paper has been discussed and verified by Zhao, Reyes, Pappas and Neuhoff [16] and further extended by Žujović, Pappas and Neuhoff [11,12] and is known as Structural Texture Similarity (STSIM). It has two versions and is generally based on intra- and inter-subband correlations calculated utilizing the multiscale frequency decomposition. As the metric has been proposed initially for the natural textures with potential applications mainly for image retrieval, verification of its usefulness for the evaluation of 3D prints quality seems to be an interesting new area of its applications.

## 3   Experiments

In our experiments an extension towards a no-reference 3D prints quality metric has been considered. Since an image of the 3D print can be obtained by a camera in unknown lighting conditions and in some applications, depending on the shape

**Table 1.** Experimental results obtained using different metrics for mutual comparisons of 4 and 16 blocks obtained by division of scanned images presented in Fig. 1 (bold numbers for high quality 3D prints)

| 4 blocks | | | 16 blocks | | |
|---|---|---|---|---|---|
| SSIM | CW-SSIM | STSIM | SSIM | CW-SSIM | STSIM |
| 0.3030 | 0.2980 | 0.6492 | 0.3029 | 0.3050 | 0.6460 |
| 0.1453 | 0.4132 | 0.7068 | 0.1105 | 0.4014 | 0.6766 |
| 0.0622 | 0.4378 | 0.6948 | 0.0439 | 0.4507 | 0.6917 |
| **0.0438** | **0.6316** | **0.7390** | **0.0323** | **0.6362** | **0.7589** |
| **0.0080** | **0.6323** | **0.7518** | **0.0267** | **0.6295** | **0.7674** |
| **0.3062** | **0.6010** | **0.7228** | **0.3141** | **0.5999** | **0.7162** |
| **0.2551** | **0.6300** | **0.7451** | **0.2550** | **0.6222** | **0.7231** |
| 0.3268 | 0.4380 | 0.7115 | 0.3026 | 0.4426 | 0.6826 |
| 0.2397 | 0.4283 | 0.6918 | 0.2501 | 0.4235 | 0.6763 |
| **0.2270** | **0.6139** | **0.7341** | **0.2383** | **0.6159** | **0.7367** |
| **0.2293** | **0.5837** | **0.6996** | **0.2562** | **0.5941** | **0.7145** |
| **0.9818** | **0.3944** | **0.7666** | **0.9820** | **0.4008** | **0.7443** |
| **0.9837** | **0.4248** | **0.7841** | **0.9839** | **0.4316** | **0.7558** |
| 0.9161 | 0.3155 | 0.7235 | 0.9166 | 0.3023 | 0.7080 |
| 0.8379 | 0.3231 | 0.6975 | 0.8408 | 0.2938 | 0.6791 |
| 0.2463 | 0.4198 | 0.6920 | 0.2592 | 0.4157 | 0.6839 |
| 0.2622 | 0.4688 | 0.7053 | 0.2622 | 0.4689 | 0.6946 |

**Table 2.** Experimental results obtained using different metrics for mutual comparisons of 4 and 16 blocks obtained by division of images acquired by a camera presented in Fig. 2 (bold numbers for high quality 3D prints)

| 4 blocks | | | 16 blocks | | |
|---|---|---|---|---|---|
| SSIM | CW-SSIM | STSIM | SSIM | CW-SSIM | STSIM |
| **0.6019** | **0.4140** | **0.7136** | **0.6061** | **0.3985** | **0.6714** |
| **0.6922** | **0.3764** | **0.7180** | **0.6884** | **0.3645** | **0.6861** |
| **0.2962** | **0.3392** | **0.6462** | **0.3104** | **0.3418** | **0.6411** |
| 0.5460 | 0.3172 | 0.6905 | 0.5460 | 0.3090 | 0.6716 |
| 0.5538 | 0.3219 | 0.6873 | 0.5507 | 0.2967 | 0.6658 |
| **0.0854** | **0.5229** | **0.7312** | **0.0465** | **0.5331** | **0.7248** |
| **0.0771** | **0.5993** | **0.7280** | **0.0401** | **0.5921** | **0.7489** |
| **0.0054** | **0.5810** | **0.7457** | **0.0604** | **0.5783** | **0.7457** |
| 0.0613 | 0.3507 | 0.6690 | 0.0788 | 0.3668 | 0.6706 |
| 0.0756 | 0.4272 | 0.6984 | 0.1150 | 0.4246 | 0.6977 |
| **0.6922** | **0.4620** | **0.7528** | **0.6733** | **0.4346** | **0.6898** |
| **0.3009** | **0.2877** | **0.6108** | **0.3319** | **0.3238** | **0.6205** |
| 0.7846 | 0.3788 | 0.7639 | 0.7832 | 0.3244 | 0.6834 |
| 0.6002 | 0.2484 | 0.6604 | 0.6031 | 0.2455 | 0.6451 |
| 0.2804 | 0.3632 | 0.7141 | 0.2921 | 0.3571 | 0.6863 |
| **0.2011** | **0.5419** | **0.7640** | **0.2522** | **0.5469** | **0.7293** |
| **0.3111** | **0.4291** | **0.6650** | **0.3450** | **0.4406** | **0.6481** |
| **0.4270** | **0.4614** | **0.6821** | **0.4674** | **0.4851** | **0.6829** |
| 0.5664 | 0.3013 | 0.7057 | 0.5700 | 0.3075 | 0.6816 |
| 0.4393 | 0.3973 | 0.6718 | 0.4493 | 0.4032 | 0.6685 |
| **0.7272** | **0.5722** | **0.7183** | **0.7335** | **0.5715** | **0.6894** |
| **0.7972** | **0.5304** | **0.6973** | **0.7908** | **0.5467** | **0.6769** |
| 0.7668 | 0.4463 | 0.7260 | 0.7656 | 0.4339 | 0.6905 |
| 0.7437 | 0.4599 | 0.6973 | 0.7449 | 0.4567 | 0.6761 |

of the 3D print, scanning process can also be used for relatively flat objects, the experimental verification has been made using a set of 41 images of printed 3D plates of the same size using different filaments. In some of the 3D prints some typical distortions, e.g. caused by the lack of filament, have been introduced during the printing process. Most of the images have been obtained in two ways: using the digital camera and with the use of high resolution 2D scanner. The scanned images used in our experiments have been shown if Fig. 1 (except two scans obtained for high quality 3D prints using the white filament) whereas the images obtained by a camera are presented in Fig. 2. As can be seen the distortions in the 3D prints from white filament are hardly visible due to the limited resolution of presented images.

As all three metrics investigated in the paper are based on the comparison of two images, their application for the no-reference assessment of 3D prints requires some modifications based on the division of the whole assessed image into block. In order to verify the validity of such idea the divisions into 4 and 16 blocks have been assumed. For such obtained 4 sub-blocks the SSIM, CW-SSIM and STSIM values have been calculated between each sub-block leading to the similarity matrix of 16 elements (4 × 4) for each metric. As the values on its diagonal are always equal to 1 due to the comparison of each block to itself, they have been removed from the matrix and the remaining values have been averaged. The same procedure has been conducted also for the division into 16 blocks leading to the matrix of 256 elements for each metric (with 16 removed "ones" from its diagonal).

Obtained average values for each of three metrics for scanned images as well as those obtained by a camera are presented in Tables 1 and 2 respectively. Bold numbers indicate the values obtained for the images of high quality 3D prints.

As can be noticed, the application of SSIM index does not lead to satisfactory results neither for scans nor the images obtained by a camera. The values of this metric vary from very low values to relatively high ones independently on the quality of the 3D print. Such a phenomenon is the result of its sensitivity to structural mismatching of patterns visible on each part of the compared images (sub-blocks). The use of the Complex Wavelet SSIM allows a significant reduction of this influence so that the results obtained for scanned images assuming the division into 4 blocks are highly consistent with the quality of the 3D prints. Nevertheless for the values of CW-SSIM between 0.39 and 0.47 an unambiguous quality assessment of the 3D prints cannot be made. A similar situation occurs for the division into 16 sub-blocks.

The use of the STSIM metric [16] for scanned images allows proper separation of high and low quality 3D prints using the threshold value 0.71 assuming the division into 16 sub-blocks. Using only 4 sub-blocks some ambiguities may occur for the STSIM values between 0.69 and 0.73 and therefore the combination of CW-SSIM and STSIM should be used. For those images the additional calculation of the CW-SSIM metric allows proper classification assuming that the CW-SSIM values higher than 0.5 denote high quality of 3D prints.

Unfortunately, due to non-uniform illumination in images acquired by cameras a proper classification of images is not an easy task. Nevertheless, for most of those images the application of the CW-SSIM metric leads to better results than STSIM. In both cases the use of "classical" SSIM index does not lead to satisfactory results.

## 4   Conclusions

Application of modified metrics based on the Structural Similarity approach for the quality estimation of the 3D prints leads to promising results. Although the classification of images into two sets representing high and low quality 3D prints is not always correct, preliminary results are enocuraging for further research towards the application of some combined metrics. Due to the presence of horizontal lines visible in each 3D print some other combined methods utilizing line detection algorithms [5] can also be considered in future work. Another possible idea is the combination of the approach investigated in the paper with some statistical texture analysis methods e.g. based on Haralick features.

# References

1. Chauhan, V., Surgenor, B.: A comparative study of machine vision based methods for fault detection in an automated assembly machine. Procedia Manuf. **1**, 416–428 (2015)
2. Chen, G.H., Yang, C.L., Xie, S.L.: Gradient-based structural similarity for image quality assessment. In: Proceedings of the IEEE International Conference on Image Processing (ICIP), Atlanta, Georgia, pp. 2929–2932, October 2006
3. Cheng, Y., Jafari, M.A.: Vision-based online process control in manufacturing applications. IEEE Trans. Autom. Sci. Eng. **5**(1), 140–153 (2008)
4. Fang, T., Jafari, M.A., Bakhadyrov, I., Safari, A., Danforth, S., Langrana, N.: Online defect detection in layered manufacturing using process signature. In: Proceedings of the IEEE International Conference on Systems, Man and Cybernetics, San Diego, California, USA, vol. 5, pp. 4373–4378, October 1998
5. Lech, P.: The detection of horizontal lines based on the monte carlo reduced resolution images. In: Chmielewski, L.J., Kozera, R., Shin, B.-S., Wojciechowski, K. (eds.) ICCVG 2014. LNCS, vol. 8671, pp. 374–381. Springer, Heidelberg (2014). doi:10.1007/978-3-319-11331-9_45
6. Li, C., Bovik, A.: Three-component weighted structural similarity index. In: Proceedings of SPIE - Image Quality and System Performance VI, San Jose, California, vol. 7242, p. 72420Q, January 2009
7. Sampat, M., Wang, Z., Gupta, S., Bovik, A., Markey, M.: Complex wavelet structural similarity: A new image similarity index. IEEE Trans. Image Process. **18**(11), 2385–2401 (2009)
8. Straub, J.: Initial work on the characterization of additive manufacturing (3D printing) using software image analysis. Machines **3**(2), 55–71 (2015)
9. Szkilnyk, G., Hughes, K., Surgenor, B.: Vision based fault detection ofautomated assembly equipment. In: Proceedings of the ASME/IEEE International Conference on Mechatronic and Embedded Systems and Applications, Parts A and B, Washington, DC, USA, vol. 3, pp. 691–697, August 2011
10. Tourloukis, G., Stoyanov, S., Tilford, T., Bailey, C.: Data driven approach to quality assessment of 3D printed electronic products. In: Proceedings of the 38th International Spring Seminar on Electronics Technology (ISSE), Eger, Hungary, pp. 300–305, May 2015
11. Žujović, J., Pappas, T.N., Neuhoff, D.L.: Structural similarity metrics for texture analysis and retrieval. In: Proceedings of the 16th IEEE International Conference on Image Processing (ICIP), Cairo, Egypt, pp. 2225–2228, November 2009
12. Žujović, J., Pappas, T.N., Neuhoff, D.L.: Structural texture similarity metrics for image analysis and retrieval. IEEE Trans. Image Process. **22**(7), 2545–2558 (2013)
13. Wang, Z., Bovik, A.: A universal image quality index. IEEE Signal Process. Lett. **9**(3), 81–84 (2002)

14. Wang, Z., Bovik, A.C., Sheikh, H., Simoncelli, E.: Image quality assessment: From error measurement to structural similarity. IEEE Trans. Image Process. **13**(4), 600–612 (2004)
15. Wang, Z., Simoncelli, E., Bovik, A.C.: Multi-scale structural similarity for image quality assessment. In: Proceedings of the 37th IEEE Asilomar Conference on Signals, Systems and Computers, Pacific Grove, California (2003)
16. Zhao, X., Reyes, M.G., Pappas, T.N., Neuhoff, D.L.: Structural texture similarity metrics for retrieval applications. In: Proceedings of the 15th IEEE International Conference on Image Processing (ICIP), San Diego, California, pp. 1196–1199, October 2008

# Depth Estimation Based on Maximization of a Posteriori Probability

Olgierd Stankiewicz(✉), Krzysztof Wegner, and Marek Domanski

Chair of Multimedia Telecommunications and Microelectronics,
Poznań University of Technology, Poznań, Poland
ostank@multimedia.edu.pl

**Abstract.** This paper presents a proposal of depth estimation method which employs empirical modeling of cost function based on Maximization of A posteriori Probability (MAP) rule. The proposed method allows for unsupervised depth estimation without a need for usage of arbitrary settings or control parameters, like Smoothing Coefficient in Depth Estimation Reference Software (DERS), which was used as a reference. The attained quality of generated depth maps is comparable to a case when supervised depth estimation is used, and such parameters are manually optimized. In the case when sub-optimal settings of control parameters in supervised depth estimation with DERS is used, the proposed method provides gains of about 2.8dB measured in average PSNR quality of virtual views synthesized with the use of estimated depth maps in the tested sequence set.

## 1 Introduction

Depth map is a practical format of 3D representation of a scene [1]. A common method to obtain depth maps is to estimate them algorithmically from a video. Although the first works on depth estimation go back to 1950's, the current state of the art is still far away from satisfying level in many applications, especially in case of new generation of 3D video systems [2].

The basic principle of algorithmic depth estimation is finding correspondence between features in two (or more) views of the same 3D scene [1]. Estimation of depth map requires finding correspondence (disparity) between all pixels in one view and pixels in other views. This problem is computationally expensive and is typically solved by employing generic optimization algorithms [4] like Belief Propagation or Graph Cuts. In order to do so, a cost function over a depth map is formulated. Such function is often related to as "energy", "goal function" or "performance index" in other optimization applications.

In this paper we present a novel, theoretically founded approach to depth estimation which employs Maximum A posteriori Probability (MAP) rule for modeling of the cost function used in optimization algorithms. The proposal is presented along with a method for estimation of parameters of such model.

© Springer International Publishing AG 2016
L.J. Chmielewski et al. (Eds.): ICCVG 2016, LNCS 9972, pp. 253–265, 2016.
DOI: 10.1007/978-3-319-46418-3_23

## 2   State of the Art

In depth estimation, typically the cost function (denoted $Fitness$) is modeled as a sum of two sub-functions: $DataCost$ and $TransitionCost$ for each pixel:

$$Fitness = \sum_{p} DataCost_p\,(d_q) + \sum_{q \in (neighborhood\ of\ p)} TransitionCost_{p \rightarrow q}\,(d_p, d_q) \quad (1)$$

where $p$ is a particular pixel in the considered depth map, $q$ is some pixel (point) in the neighborhood of pixel $p$ in the same view, $d_p$ and $d_q$ are assumed depth values for pixels $p$ and $q$ respectively. The terms $DataCost_p\,(d_q)$ and $TransitionCost_{p \rightarrow q}\,(d_p, d_q)$ are functions described below.

$DataCost_p\,(d_q)$ models the direct correspondence between pixels and expresses how given pixel $p$ is similar to pixel in one of other images pointed by its depth $d_p$. The higher is the difference between those pixels, the higher is the value of $DataCost_p\,(d_q)$. The most commonly $DataCost$ is defined in terms of energy related to similarity metrics between fragments of images, calculated in pixels or blocks. Typically, Sum of Absolute Differences (SAD) [5] or Sum of Squared Differences (SSD) [6,7] metrics are used. Some state-of-the-art works which relate to $DataCost$ function propose usage of "rank" or "census" [8] for calculation of better similarity metric. Work [9] proposes a more advanced approach, where mixture of various similarity metrics is incorporated in order to attain better quality in depth estimation but theoretical foundations are missing. In paper [7] authors provide a derivation of $FitCost$ function based on MAP assumptions. Unfortunately, the work omits the consequences of this derivation related to $DataCost$ which limited the work to consideration of gaussian model (corresponding to Sum of Squared differences energy formulation). No verification is provided, whether such assumptions are correct. Similarly, work [10] employs posteriori probability for modeling of $Fitness$. Authors consider a more advanced model for $DataCost$ which incorporates Generalized gaussian-like model with arbitrary power exponent. Also this work does not provide any verification of whether taken assumptions are correct, apart from theoretical considerations. In work [11] authors have proposed usage of truncated-linear $DataCost$ function which actually corresponds to Absolute Difference similarity metric, additionally saturated, so that it does not exceed some given maximal level. Apart from the concept being very scientifically interesting and giving promising results, the authors have not supported their proposal with empirical data verifying their assumptions. In work [12] authors thoughtfully analyze probabilistic model of correspondence in 3D space. Instead of MAP rule, a different approach for evaluating entropy and mutual information, called EMMA, is proposed. Unfortunately, the method is presented in context of 3D modeling and not depth map estimation itself which disallows comparison with other state-of-the-art methods.

The second component of $Fitness$ function, $TransitionCost_{p \rightarrow q}\,(d_p, d_q)$, penalizes depth maps that are not smooth. Its role is regularization of the resultant depth map. The higher are the differences between depth $d_p$ of pixel $p$ and depth values $d_q$ of all neighboring pixels $q$, the higher is the value of $TransitionCost_{p \to q}(d_p, d_q)$. Typically, $TransitionCost_{p \to q}(d_p, d_q)$ is defined independently from particular pixel positions $p$ and $q$ and thus can be simplified to $TransitionCost(d_p, d_q)$. Also, very often, $TransitionCost$ is not defined as a function of $d_p$ and $d_q$ independently, but as a function of their absolute difference $|d_p - d_q|$ only: $TransitionCost(|d_p - d_q|)$. Among the most commonly known models for $TransitionCost$ function of this type there are Potts model [13], Linear model [14,15] and Truncated-linear model [11].

In general, $TransitionCost$ functions incorporate some sort of constant parameters, like the penalty value in Potts Model or the slope of penalty segment in Linear Model. The main purpose of such constant parameters is to provide weighting of $TransitionCost$ related to $DataCost$ function (to which it is added to formulate $Fitness$ function (1)). The most commonly, such a weight is called "Smoothing Coefficient" as its value sets how much depth maps that are not smooth are penalized by $Fitness$ function. The use of small values of Smoothing Coefficient results in sharp but noisy depth maps. The use of large values results in very smooth, even blurred depth maps. The selection of particulac value is typically done manually (the depth estimation is thus supervised) which is an important problem in practical use of depth estimation methods in applications, where unsupervised operation is expected.

All of the mentioned models (Potts, linear and truncated-linear) are widely used because they are simple and can be efficiently implemented in optimization algorithms like BP of GC algorithms. Unfortunately, the use of a specific model is rarely justified by scientific reasons. E.g. in work [11], authors have proposed usage of truncated-linear-shaped $TransitionCost$ function for depth estimation and have compared it against other state-of-the-art techniques. Although the results are promising, the foundations of the proposal are not given. In papers [7,10] authors consider derivation of $TransitionCost$ function based on MAP rule, similar to the approach in this paper. Markov Random Field model for stereoscopic depth estimation is formulated by means of BP algorithm. Unfortunately, the work proposes only an approximation of $TransitionCost$ function.

To summarize, there is lack of works which provide theoretical analysis of application of Maximum A posteriori Probability (MAP) optimization rule to formulate $DataCost$ and $TransitionCost$ functions for depth estimation, along with empirical experimentation which would support formulation of such theoretical models. This lack is a motivation of this work.

## 3   Proposed Cost Function Derivation Based on MAP

Below we provide derivation of $Fitness$ function based on Maximum A posteriori Probability rule. First, a theoretical formulation for depth map estimation based on Maximum A posteriori Probability (MAP) optimization rule is presented. It is shown what are the assumptions required in order to attain classically used Absolute Differences [5] or Squared Differences [6,7] pixel similarity metrics in formulation of $DataCost$ function. Then, similarly, a formulation of $TransitionCost$ function is proposed on the basis of a probabilistic model.

## 3.1  DataCost Component

Let us consider depth estimation in a case of two identical cameras which are perfectly horizontally aligned with parallel optical axes. The views are rectified and the distortions are assumed to be removed [16]. Therefore, epipolar lines (along which correspondence search is performed) are aligned with horizontal rows in the images. Images from the left view $L_{x,y}$ and from the right view $R_{x,y}$ have the same widths $W$ and the same heights $H$.

For given row $y$ of pixels in both views, observed are pixel luminance values in the left view $(L_{1,y}, \cdots, L_{W,y})$ and in the right view $(R_{1,y}, \cdots, R_{W,y})$, both indexed from row 1 to row $H$. All of these are random variables are considered to have been observed and thus they constitute our a posteriori observation set.

We search for depth value $d_{x,y}$ for each pixel at coordinates $x, y$ (in the right view) which would maximize probability $p(d_{x,y})$ under the condition of a posteriori observations of luminance values in both views. This probability will be demarked as $p_{x,y,d}$:

$$p_{x,y,d} \equiv p\left(d_{x,y} \mid (L_{1,y}, \cdots, L_{W,y}, R_{1,y}, \cdots, R_{W,y})\right) \tag{2}$$

where $\mid (L_{1,y}, \cdots, R_{W,y})$ is overall conditional expression of observation of luminance values. Therefore MAP rule for selecting optimal depth value $d_{x,y}^*$ is:

$$d_{x,y}^* = max_{arg\ d}\left(p_{x,y,d}\right) \tag{3}$$

In order to allow the depth estimation algorithm to use the MAP rule (3), the term $p_{x,y,d}$ has to be modeled basing solely on values that are known after the observation (a posteriori), e.g. luminance values in both of the views $L_{1\cdots W,y}$ and $R_{1\cdots W,y}$. Thus, with the use of the Bayes rule we will transform equation (2). Then, by rearrangement of $(L_{1,y}, \cdots, L_{W,y}, R_{1,y}, \cdots, R_{W,y}) \mid d_{x,y}$ term for each luminance variable separately (e.g. $L_{1,y}$), we get:

$$p_{x,y,d} = \frac{p\left(L_{1,y} \mid d_{x,y}, \cdots, L_{W,y} \mid d_{x,y}, R_{1,y} \mid d_{x,y}, \cdots, R_{W,y} \mid d_{x,y}\right) \cdot p\left(d_{x,y}\right)}{p\left(L_{1,y}, \cdots, L_{W,y}, R_{1,y}, \cdots, R_{W,y}\right)} \tag{4}$$

Assumed is presence of noise which has independent realizations in each of the views. Thus, pixel luminance values in the left view $L_{1,y}, \cdots, L_{W,y}$ are independent from each other and the same in the right view. This holds true for all terms in the denominator of (4), specifically also for the sought pair of pixels matched by depth $d_{x,y}$, as the denominator does not consider any specific matching or correspondence of pixels, as those probabilities are not conditional with respect to $d_{x,y}$. Therefore, we can simplify the denominator of (4) as $\prod_{l=1..W} p\left(L_{l,y}\right) \cdot \prod_{r=1..W} p\left(R_{r,y}\right)$. A similar simplification could be done in the case of the nominator of (4), but here, on the contrary, probabilities are conditional because they are considered under the condition of occurrence of $d_{x,y}$. Such condition of $d_{x,y}$ means that in the given pixel $(x, y)$, for which we calculate $p_{x,y,d}$, a depth value $d_{x,y}$ is assumed, so that two pixels, with coordinates $l$ in the left and $r$ in the right view, correspond to each other through depth $d_{x,y}$. For the sake of brevity lets assume that $x + d_{x,y}$ operation will represent corresponding coordinate (just like $d_{x,y}$ would be direct disparity value), thus:

$$r = x, \; l = x + d_{x,y} \tag{5}$$

$x$ expresses the coordinate in the right view for which $d_{x,y}$ is considered. Such pair of pixels is not independent, and therefore probabilities of their luminance values $p\left(L_{l,y}\right)$ and $p\left(R_{r,y}\right)$ cannot be simplified. For other pairs of pixels (not corresponding to each other) random variables describing their luminance values are independent. Therefore, we can express $p_{x,y,d}$ from (4) as:

$$p_{x,y,d} = \frac{\prod\limits_{\substack{l=1..W, \\ l \neq x+d_{x,y}}} p\left(L_{l,y}\mid d_{x,y}\right) \cdot \prod\limits_{\substack{r=1..W, \\ r \neq x}} p\left(R_{r,y}\mid d_{x,y}\right)}{\prod_{l=1..W} p\left(L_{l,y}\right) \cdot \prod_{r=1..W} p\left(R_{r,y}\right)} \cdot p\left(\left(L_{x+d_{x,y},y}, R_{x,y}\right) \mid d_{x,y}\right) \cdot p\left(d_{x,y}\right) \tag{6}$$

Also, with the exception for the mentioned case (5), the probability distributions related to $p\left(L_{l,y} \mid d_{x,y}\right)$ and $p\left(R_{r,y} \mid d_{x,y}\right)$ are independent from $d_{x,y}$ and thus can be reduced with the denominator:

$$p_{x,y,d} = \frac{1}{p\left(L_{x+d_{x,y},y}\right) \cdot p\left(R_{x,y}\right)} \cdot p\left(\left(L_{x+d_{x,y},y}, R_{x,y}\right) \mid d_{x,y}\right) \cdot p\left(d_{x,y}\right) \tag{7}$$

It can be further seen that term $p\left(L_{x+d_{x,y},y}\right)$ is probability distribution of luminance values in the left view (which is independent of particular pixel position) and can be expressed as $p\left(L_{x,y}\right)$. We finally get:

$$p_{x,y,d} = \frac{1}{p\left(L_{x,y}\right) \cdot p\left(R_{x,y}\right)} \cdot p\left(\left(L_{x+d_{x,y},y}, R_{x,y}\right) \mid d_{x,y}\right) \cdot p\left(d_{x,y}\right) \tag{8}$$

Further in the paper this formula will be used to propose a novel depth estimation method with the use of Maximum A posteriori Probability (MAP) rule (3) but, in the meanwhile, we can notice it can be simplified in order to attain classical SSD and SAD pixel similarity metrics that are commonly used in depth estimation algorithms. The term $p\left(\left(L_{x+d_{x,y},y}, R_{x,y}\right) \mid d_{x,y}\right)$ is a joint probability that luminance value $L_{x+d_{x,y},y}$ of pixel in the left view and luminance value $R_{x,y}$ of pixel in the right view will occur, on the condition that those pixels are corresponding to each other under depth $d_{x,y}$. Again, according to Bayes rule, it can be expressed as $p\left(R_{x,y}\right) \cdot p\left(L_{x+d_{x,y},y} \mid \left(R_{x,y}, d_{x,y}\right)\right)$. Therefore, the term $p\left(R_{x,y}\right)$ simplifies with the term in the denominator of (8):

$$p_{x,y,d} = \frac{p\left(d_{x,y}\right)}{p\left(L_{x,y}\right)} \cdot p\left(L_{x+d_{x,y},y} \mid \left(R_{x,y}, d_{x,y}\right)\right) \tag{9}$$

Let's assume the following:

A1. The presence of additive noise, the same in both of the views (in particular, with equal standard deviation $\sigma$).

A2. Lambertian model of reflectance in the scene, which means that the observed light intensity of given point in the scene is independent from the angle of viewing, and thus is equal amongst the views.

A3. Color correspondence between the views, which means that color profiles of the cameras are compatible, so that given light intensity is represented as the same luminance value $\mu$ among the views (in the consideration, for given pair of corresponding pixels $L_{l,y}$ in the left view and $R_{r,y}$ in the right view).

If we consider gaussian distribution of the noise, with mean value $\mu$ and standard deviation $\sigma$, then $L_{l,y} \sim Gaussian_{(\mu,\sigma)}$, and $R_{r,y} \sim Gaussian_{(\mu,\sigma)}$. In the term $p\left(L_{x+d_{x,y},y} \mid R_{x,y}, d_{x,y}\right)$ random variable $R_{x,y}$ is assumed to be a posteriori observation with given, specific value (also as $d_{x,y}$ is considered conditionally too), therefore $\mu = R_{x,y}$. Thus, the pixels are assumed to correspond to each other and thus both random variables have the same expected value $\mu_{x,y}$. Moreover, the difference in luminance between $L_{x+d_{x,y},y}$ and $R_{x,y}$ results only from the probability distribution $Gaussian_{(R_{x,y},\sigma)}\left(L_{x+d_{x,y},y}\right)$ of the noise, where both $R_{x,y}$ and $L_{x+d_{x,y},y}$ are our a posteriori observations:

$$p\left(L_{x+d_{x,y},y} \mid R_{x,y}, d_{x,y}\right) = \frac{1}{\sigma\sqrt{2\pi}} \cdot \exp\left(-\frac{1}{2\sigma^2}\left(L_{x+d_{x,y},y} - R_{x,y}\right)^2\right) \quad (10)$$

therefore we get:

$$p_{x,y,d} = \frac{p\left(d_{x,y}\right)}{p\left(L_{x,y}\right)}\frac{1}{\sigma\sqrt{2\pi}} \cdot \exp\left(-\frac{1}{2\sigma^2}\left(L_{x+d_{x,y},y} - R_{x,y}\right)^2\right) \quad (11)$$

We are looking for depth with Maximum A posteriori Probability and thus we search for the best matching depth $d^*$ which has the highest (maximal) probability $p_{x,y,d}$. It is equivalent to finding $d$ with minimal $-\log\left(p_{x,y,d}\right)$. After natural logarithm on both sides of the Eq. (11) is taken we get:

$$-\log\left(p_{x,y,d}\right) = -\log\left(p\left(d_{x,y}\right)\right) + \log\left(p\left(L_{x,y}\right)\right) + \log\left(\sigma\sqrt{2\pi}\right) + \frac{1}{2\sigma^2}\left(L_{x+d_{x,y},y} - R_{x,y}\right)^2 \quad (12)$$

It can be noticed that if all terms except the last one (on the right) are omitted, the Eq. (12) simplifies to SSD formula for pixel similarity metric:

$$-\log\left(p_{x,y,d}\right) = \left(L_{x+d_{x,y},y} - R_{x,y}\right)^2 \quad (13)$$

The omitted terms $p\left(d_{x,y}\right)$ and $p\left(L_{x,y}\right)$, $\log\left(\sigma\sqrt{2\pi}\right)$ and $\frac{1}{2\sigma^2}$ correspond to: probability distribution of depth values, probability distribution of luminance values in the left view, constant offset and constant scaling factor, respectively. Such omission could be justified if all of those terms were constants which would be true if we add two more assumptions to our considerations:

A4. Distribution of $p\left(d_{x,y}\right)$ is uniform.

A5. Distribution of $p\left(L_{x,y}\right)$ is uniform.

Analogous reasoning can be performed for the presence of Laplace distribution of the noise $L_{l,y}, R_{r,y} \sim Laplace_{(\mu,b)}$. In such a case we get:

$$-\log\left(p_{x,y,d}\right) = -\log\left(p\left(d_{x,y}\right)\right) + \log\left(p\left(L_{x,y}\right)\right) + \log\left(2b\right) + \frac{1}{b}\left|L_{x+d_{x,y},y} - R_{x,y}\right| \quad (14)$$

Here, we can see that if all terms except the last one (on the right) are omitted, the Eq. (14) simplifies to SAD formula for pixel similarity metric:

$$- \log\left(p_{x,y,d}\right) = \left|L_{x+d_{x,y},y} - R_{x,y}\right| \tag{15}$$

Again, the omitted terms, $p\left(d_{x,y}\right)$, $p\left(L_{x,y}\right)$, $\log\left(2b\right)$ and $\frac{1}{b}$ correspond to: probability distribution of depth values, probability distribution of luminance values in the left view, constant offset and constant scaling factor, respectively. Such omission could be justified if all of those terms were constants which would be true if both of the mentioned probability distributions (A4 and A5) were uniform.

We can thus conclude, that usage of SSD (Sum of Squared Differences)/SAD (Sum of Absolute Differences) metric is optimal (from Maximum A posteriori Probability point of view) for the case of presence of additive (assumption A1) gaussian (SSD)/Laplace (SAD) noise, independent between the views, Lambertian model of reflectance (A2), color correspondence (A3), uniformity of distributions of possible disparities (A4) and luminance (A5) values.

For the sake of brevity we omit verification of these assumptions, which can be found in [3,17]. Here we only conclude that in most of the cases, the assumptions are not true for the tested sequence data set. The probability distributions of luminance (A4) and depth (A5) values for the tested sequences are clearly not uniform. For an another example, in Fig. 1 (left) we can see that measured distribution of noise in exemplary *Poznan Carpark* sequence [16] is similar to gaussian but it is slightly skewed in such a way, that the maximum of the distribution is at position of about 0.4. In Fig. 1 (right) we can see that also there is evidence that either or both assumptions A2 or A3 are not true, because the relation between luminance vales of pixels corresponding in two views (denoted X and Y) is not linear. In the tested set ([3], Table 1) only synthetic *Undo Dancer* [23] sequence conforms the assumptions.

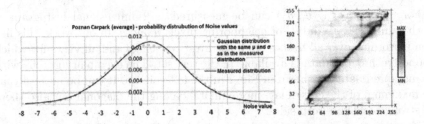

**Fig. 1.** Measured probability distribution of noise values [3], averaged over all views (left) and 2-dimensional histogram of luminance values (in logarithmic gray-level scale) of corresponding pixels in the views $X = 4$ and $Y = 3$ (right) of *Poznan Carpark* sequence [16].

As mentioned above, the simplifications leading to simplification of (8) to SAD or SSD are not justified in the case of the tested set. Therefore we propose to use formula (8). We express it in a logarithmic scale in decibels (thus 10 scaling factor) which is a common trick used in formulation of energy cost and probability functions for optimization algorithms [3]:

$$DataCost_{x,y}(d_{x,y}) = -10 \cdot \log(p_{x,y,d}) \tag{16}$$

For an practical application, all of the terms of probability in (8) have to been modeled. Therefore, we have empirically measured distributions of $p(L_{x,y})$ and $p(R_{x,y})$ as histograms of the input pictures, as those terms do not depend on pixel correspondence related to depth $d_{x,y}$. On the other hand, probability distribution of depth $p(d_{(}x,y))$, and probability of corresponding luminance values in the left and the right view $p((L_{x+d_{x,y},y}, R_{x,y}) \mid d_{x,y})$ depend on depth $d_{x,y}$. Having a ground truth depth map for a given scene, both of those terms can be directly modeled. $p(d_{x,y})$, which is probability distribution of depth $d_{x,y}$, has been estimated as a histogram of the given ground truth depth map. $p((L_{x+d_{x,y},y}, R_{x,y}) \mid d_{x,y})$ is a 2-dimensional probability distribution that has been estimated as a 2-dimensional histogram of luminance values $L_{x+d_{x,y},y}$ and $R_{x,y}$ of pixel pairs, which are known to correspond to each other, basing on given depth value $d_{x,y}$ from the ground truth depth map (example of such histogram is presented in Fig. 1 right).

## 3.2   TransitionCost Component

Similarly to previous section, we propose a probabilistic model for *Transition Cost*. We assume that $TransitionCost_{p,q}(d_p, d_q)$ can be modeled basing on probability that given two neighboring pixels $p$ and $q$ have depths $d_p$ and $d_q$ respectively. Just like before, we use logarithmic decibel scale, so that it could be used directly inside of state-of-the-art depth estimation algorithms [14]:

$$TransitionCost_{p,q}(d_p, d_q) = -10 \cdot \log(p_{2D}(d_p, d_q)) \tag{17}$$

For real data $p_{2D}(d_p, d_q)$ can be measured as 2-dimensional histogram of depth value pairs $d_p$ and $d_q$ of neighboring pixels $p$ and $q$. In our work, this has been performed over all frames of all used test sequences and all views for which ground truth depth data is available in the test set. The exemplary graphs with the measured data are shown in Fig. 2 in the left column. It can be noticed that the maximum of the curves lay approximately along the diagonal but also there are strong bands on both sides.

Because often TransitionCost is expressed as a function of a single argument $|d_p - d_q|$, instead of two independent arguments, it is interesting to also see whether such formulation is justified. In order to do that, apart from figures presenting $p_{2D}(d_p, d_q)$ as 2-dimensional plots, also 1 dimensional plots of probability of given disparity difference $d_p - d_q$, $p_{1D}(d_p - d_q)$, have been visualized see Fig. 2 in the right column. The plots are firstly falling approximately linearly and then they reach plateau until the limits of the histogram plot. Such curves resemble the shapes of linear model and truncated-linear model of $TransitionCost$. Therefore we can conclude that those classical models (linear and truncated-linear) may be adequate for the case, when the *TransitionCost* express probability in a logarithmic scale (in which *TransitionCost* has been depicted in figures). What is important in case of each sequence, *TransitionCost* has different scale (slope of the curve). Without the knowledge coming from empirical analysis of the *TransitionCost*, performed likewise as in the work, this scale would have to be calibrated manually of experimentally (e.g. with use of Smoothing Coefficient in DERS [14]). This is an important advantage of the proposal.

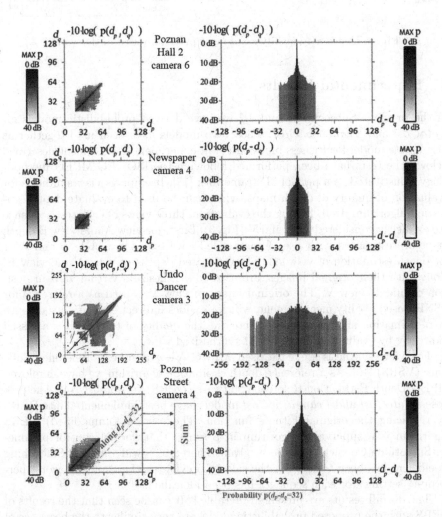

**Fig. 2.** Distributions of probability that neighboring pixels $p$ and $q$ in the ground truth depth map have depth (disparity) values $d_p$ and $d_q$. Measured as 2-dimensional histograms $p_{2D}(d_p, d_q)$ (on the left) and 1-dimensional histograms $p_{1D}(d_p - d_q)$ (on the right). Exemplary calculation of $p_{1D}(d_p - d_q = 32)$ from $p_{2D}(d_p, d_q)$ has been shown in red. All plots are in logarithmic scale (Color figure online)

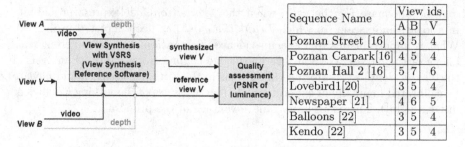

**Fig. 3.** Depth map quality assessment procedure used in the work.

## 4   Experimental Results

In the previous Subsects. 3.1 and 3.2 we have derived probabilistic models for *DataCost* and *TransitionCost*. Those two models have been used together as a complete model for Fitness function (1) in experimental assessment described below. The tests have been performed following the ISO/IEC MPEG methodology, constituted as a part of 3D framework [18]. It employs view synthesis for evaluation of quality of depth maps, which can be used to evaluate depth estimation algorithm itself. During the evaluation, three views of each test sequence are explicitly considered A, B and V (Fig. 3). First, for view A and view B depth maps are estimated with use of some side views (e.g. views A-1, A and A+1 for depth estimation of view A). The estimated depths of view A and view B, along with their original images, are used to synthesize a virtual view in position of middle view V. The original image of view V is used as a reference for PSNR-based quality measurement, which provides indirect evaluation the depth map estimation algorithm used. Therefore, the quality of the depth is assessed indirectly by evaluation of quality of synthesized view.

For view synthesis we have used MPEG View Synthesis Reference Software (VSRS) [19]. As a reference depth estimation algorithm we have employed MPEG Depth Estimation Reference Software (DERS) version 5.1 [14]. The proposed *DataCost* and *TransitionCost* models have been implemented into DERS by replacing the original Fitness function. The original (unmodified) DERS algorithm is a supervised algorithm in a sense, that special control parameter Smoothing Coefficient has to be given. Therefore, a wide range of Smoothing Coefficient has been tested. For the sake of brevity, the best and the worst performing settings for each sequence has been identified.

The overall results are presented in Table 1. It can be seen that the results of DERS with the proposed probabilistic model are very similar to the best case of the original (unmodified) DERS in most of the cases and are very little better in some cases. In average over the tested sequences, the proposed method provides about 0.08 dB gain over the best identified case generated with the original, unmodified DERS (with manually crafted Smoothing Coefficient per sequence) and about 2.79 dB gain over the worst case generated by DERS.

**Table 1.** Gains attained with joint usage of the proposed *DataCost* and *TransitionCost* models, related to the best and the worst results attained by the original (unmodified) DERS, depending on Smoothing Coefficient parameter setting

| Sequence name | PSNR [dB] virtual view versus the original view | | |
| | DERS - the worst[1] | DERS - the best[2] | Proposed[3] |
| --- | --- | --- | --- |
| Poznan street [16] | 27.56 | 31.98 | 32.02 |
| Poznan carpark [16] | 29.05 | 30.71 | 30.95 |
| Poznan hall 2 [16] | 32.17 | 32.85 | 32.81 |
| Lovebird1 [20] | 27.09 | 29.80 | 29.83 |
| Newspaper [21] | 27.86 | 31.91 | 31.95 |
| Balloons [22] | 29.95 | 32.94 | 32.98 |
| Kendo [22] | 33.02 | 35.46 | 35.69 |
| Average | 29.53 | 32.24 | 32.32 |
| Average gain of the proposal | +2.79 | +0.08 | - |

[1] Original (unmodified) DERS - the worst setting of Smoothing Coefficient.
[2] Original (unmodified) DERS - the best setting of Smoothing Coefficient.

[3] Proposed probability-based model implemented in DERS.

The most important thing to notice is that the proposed depth estimation technique does not require any manual settings (usage of such depth estimation is thus unsupervised). The employed Fitness function model, based on Maximum A Posteriori rule is inhered from the knowledge coming from analysis of the *TransitionCost*. Therefore, the proposed depth map estimation method has been tested only once in one configuration.

## 5   Conclusions

A derivation of *DataCost* based on Maximum A posteriori Probability (MAP) rule has been presented. It has been shown that some of the conditions needed for simplification to SSD or SAD forms are not met and basing on that an improved depth estimation technique has been proposed. A method for estimation of parameters of this model has been shown on an example of the test sequences. Next, a probabilistic model for *TransitionCost* has been proposed also with a method for estimation of parameters of this model. In the end experimental verification has been conducted. The attained results show average gain of about 0.08dB to 2.8dB, calculated with respect to PSNR of virtual views, synthesized with use of depth maps generated with the proposed method, over the reference. As a reference, original unmodified MPEG Depth Estimation Reference Software has been used with manual calibration of Smoothing Coefficient per sequence. For the case of selection of the worst checked Smoothing Coefficient value for the original DERS, the gain is about 2.8dB of PSNR, averaged over all of the tested sequences. For the case of selection of the best found Smoothing Coefficient in original DERS software, the average gain is only about 0.08dB of PSNR, but it can be noted that the proposed technique attained that without manual calibration of such coefficient. This constitutes one of the biggest advantages of the proposed depth estimation method it does not require arbitrary manual calibration of parameters like Smoothing Coefficient. All required model parameters can be algorithmically estimated.

**Acknowledgement.** This work has been supported by the public funds as a DS research project.

# References

1. Müller, K., Merkle, P., Wiegand, T.: 3-D video representation using depth maps. Proc. IEEE **99**(4), 643–656 (2011)
2. Domański, M., Klimaszewski, K., Konieczny, J., Kurc, M., Łuczak, A., Stankiewicz, O., Wegner, K.: An experimental free-view television system. In: Choraś, R., Zabłudowski, A. (eds.) Image Processing and Communications Challenges, Academy Publishing House EXIT Warsaw, pp. 169–176 (2009)
3. Stankiewicz, O.: Stereoscopic depth map estimation and coding techniques for multiview video systems. Ph.D. dissertaation, Faculty of Electronics and Telecommunications, Poznan University of Technology, Poznań (2014)
4. Tappen, M.F., et al.: Comparison of graph cuts with belief propagation for stereo, using identical MRF parameters. In: IEEE International Conference on Computer Vision (2003)
5. Kanade, T., Okutomi, M.: A stereo matching algorithm with an adaptive window: theory and experiment. IEEE Trans. Pattern Anal. Mach. Intell. **16**(9), 920–932 (1994)
6. Boykov, Y., et al.: A variable window approach to early vision. IEEE Trans. Pattern Anal. Mach. Intell. **20**(12), 1283–1294 (1998)
7. Sun, J., et al.: Stereo matching using belief propagation. IEEE Trans. Pattern Anal. Mach. Intell. **25**(7), 787–800 (2003)
8. Zabih, R., Woodfill, J.: Non-parametric local transforms for computing visual correspondence. In: Proceedings of European Conference on Computer Vision (1994)
9. Wegner, K., Stankiewicz, O.: Similiarity measures for depth estimation. In: 3DTV-Conference 2009 The True Vision Capture, Potsdam, Germany, 4-6 May 2009
10. Cheng, L., Caelli, T.: Bayesian stereo matching. In: Proceedings of the Conference Computer Vision and Pattern Recognition Workshop, pp. 192–192 (2004)
11. Zhang, L., Seitz, S.M.: Estimating optimal parameters for MRF stereo from a single image pair. IEEE Trans. Pattern Anal. Mach. Intell. **29**(2), 331–342 (2007)
12. Viola, P., Wells, W.: Alignment by maximization of mutual information. In: Proceedings of Fifth International Conference on Computer Vision, Cambridge, MA, USA, pp. 16–23, 20–23 June 1995
13. Geman, S., Geman, G.: Stochastic relaxation, gibbs distribuition and the bayesian restoration of images. IEEE Trans. Pattern Anal. Mach. Intell. **6**, 721–741 (1984)
14. Tanimoto, M., Fujii, T., Suzuki, K.: Video depth estimation reference software (DERS) with image segmentation and block matching. ISO/IEC MPEG M16092, Lausanne, Switzerland, February 2009
15. Greig, D.M., et al.: Exact maximum a posteriori estimation for binary images. J. Royal Stat. Soc. Series B **51**, 271–279 (1989)

16. Stankowski, J., Klimaszewski, K., Stankiewicz, O., Wegner, K., Domański, M.: Preprocessing methods used for Poznan 3D/FTV test sequences. ISO/IEC JTC1/SC29/WG11 MPEG 2010/M17174, m17174, Kyoto, Japan, January 2010

17. Stankiewicz, O., Domański, M., Wegner, K.: Analysis of noise in multi-camera systems. 3DTV Conference 2014, Budapest, Hungary, 2-4 July 2014

18. "Overview of 3D video coding", ISO/IEC JTC1/SC29/WG11, Doc. N9784, Archamps, France, May 2008

19. "View synthesis algorithm in view synthesis reference software 3.0 (VSRS3.0)", ISO/IEC JTC1/SC29/WG11 Doc. M16090, February 2009

20. Um, Gi-M., Ban, G., Ho, Yo-S., et al.: Video Test Material of Outdoor Scene. ISO/IEC JTC1/SC29/WG11, MPEG/ M15371, Archamps, France, April 2008

21. Ho, Y.-S., Lee, E.-K., Lee, C.: Video Test Sequence and Camera Parameters. ISO/IEC MPEG M15419, Archamps, France, April 2008

22. Tanimoto, M., Fujii, T., Fukushima, N.: 1D Parallel Test Sequences for MPEG-FTV. MPEG M15378, Archamps, France, April 2008

23. Rusanovskyy, D., Aflaki, P., Hannuksela, M.M.: Undo Dancer 3DV sequence for purposes of 3DV standardization. ISO/IEC JTC1/SC29/WG11, Doc. M20028, Geneva, Switzerland, March 2011

# 3D Reconstruction of Ultrasonic B-Scans for Nondestructive Testing of Composites

Angelika Wronkowicz[1]($\boxtimes$), Krzysztof Dragan[2], Michał Dziendzikowski[2],
Marek Chalimoniuk[3], and Claudio Sbarufatti[4]

[1] Institute of Fundamentals of Machinery Design,
Silesian University of Technology, Gliwice, Poland
angelika.wronkowicz@polsl.pl
[2] Laboratory of Non-Destructive Testing,
Air Force Institute of Technology, Warsaw, Poland
{krzysztof.dragan,michal.dziendzikowski}@itwl.pl
[3] Engine Division, Air Force Institute of Technology, Warsaw, Poland
marek.chalimoniuk@itwl.pl
[4] Mechanical Department, Politecnico di Milano, Milan, Italy
claudio.sbarufatti@polimi.it

**Abstract.** The paper presents an approach to 3D reconstruction of a sequence of ultrasonic B-Scans for the purpose of facilitating nondestructive testing of composites. The results of ultrasonic testing of a carbon fiber reinforced polymer specimen with barely visible impact damage was used for algorithm testing. 3D visualisation of damage based on image thresholding, contour extraction and volume rendering facilitates interpretation of ultrasonic data and can be useful in the assessment of a flaw size and location, including its depth. Accuracy of the 3D reconstruction of the internal damage of the tested specimen was verified on the basis of reference data acquired with the X-ray computed tomography. Owing to the low computational complexity of the proposed algorithm it could be applied during ultrasonic inspections of composite structures.

## 1 Introduction

Composite structures, owing to their numerous advantages, are nowadays widely used in many branches of industry. Their relatively low weight in relation to the strength and the possibility of obtaining a surface with a complex geometrical shape enables applying them to, among others, aerospace components (tails, wings, fuselages, propellers), boat and scull hulls, bicycle frames and car bodies.

However, composite structures are susceptible to damage both during their manufacturing as well as during operation. The most common types of manufacturing defects are porosity, foreign object inclusions, delaminations, defective bonding, fibre or ply misalignment, and ply cracking. To the in-service defects one can include cracks, delaminations, ingress of moisture, failures of bond, buckling or fracture of fibres and failure of the interface between matrix and fibres [1]. Major conditions that contribute to damaging processes are impacts, fatigue,

© Springer International Publishing AG 2016
L.J. Chmielewski et al. (Eds.): ICCVG 2016, LNCS 9972, pp. 266–277, 2016.
DOI: 10.1007/978-3-319-46418-3_24

static overloads, overheating and hydrothermal effects. Low energy impacts are the source of most concern since they may cause remarkable internal damage with simultaneous very limited visible marks on the impacted surface [2], often referred to as Barely Visible Impact Damage (BVID).

Because composite structures are very often an integral part of structural aircraft elements, carrying significant loads (e.g. an aircraft skin), they are required to be diagnosed regularly. According to the commonly respected damage tolerance philosophy, a composite structure with a flaw is permitted to be operated if it does not weaken structural integrity. For this reason, a maintenance program is required to ensure a flaw or a damage is detected before it reduces the residual strength of the structure below an acceptable limit. This approach makes the identification of the damage type and its size very important.

## 1.1   Ultrasonic Testing

Among numerous nondestructive testing (NDT) methods used for inspections of composite structures, one of the most universal is ultrasonic testing (UT) [3]. This is due to volumetric nature and high sensitivity of this method to the types of flaws which may occur in such structures during manufacturing and in operation.

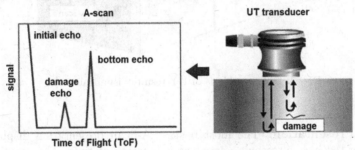

**Fig. 1.** General idea of UT method [4]

UT consists in transmission of ultrasonic waves into a tested material and observation of the received echo. Ultrasonic transducers excite elastic waves, which can interact with any type of structural damage, e.g. they can be scattered on or reflected from structure discontinuities. Usually, in the so called *pulse-echo* testing, a material is tested through its cross-section under the location of a probe, using longitudinal waves within the frequency range of 1–5 MHz (especially for composites). For an undamaged structure, there are essentially two main signal components on the so called A-Scan (Fig. 1), i.e. the first one comes from the surface on which the ultrasound probe is placed, and the second one is the resultant echo of elastic wave reflected from the bottom surface of the examined structure. All of the wave scatterings coming from other possible boundaries can be easily extracted since they appear later in the probe. If a structure is damaged, e.g. delaminated, an additional signal component is present between the described ones (Fig. 1).

If damage causes significant changes of local mechanical properties of the structure, then the echo from the bottom boundary may disappear. Ultrasonic devices typically record two fundamental parameters of received energy: the relative amount (amplitude), and where it occurs in time with respect to a zero point (ToF – Time-of-Flight).

There are different types of visualization of UT results. The three basic and most common of them are called A-Scan, B-Scan and C-Scan presentations (see example in Fig. 2).

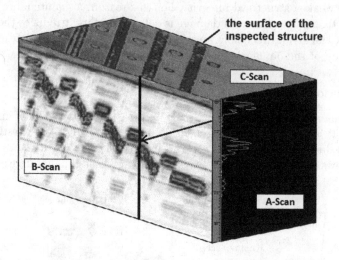

**Fig. 2.** Different kinds of UT results visualization [5]

**A-Scan Presentation.** The most basic – A-Scan presentation displays the amount of received ultrasonic energy as a function of time. The amplitude is plotted along the vertical axis whereas the elapsed time is displayed along the horizontal axis.

**B-Scan Presentation.** By merging the A-Scans acquired along a path followed by the UT transducer, it is possible to visualize the cross section of the inspected structure along this path in the form of B-Scan (Fig. 2). The B-Scan carries complete information about the signal, i.e. it is possible to reconstruct A-Scans for any point on a path of scanning. If B-Scans are acquired for various scanning paths covering the surface of the structure, it is possible to represent the damage located at a given depth, by restricting B-Scans to a proper ToF (see Fig. 1).

**C-Scan Presentation.** Usually damage is visualized in the form of C-Scans (Fig. 2), which are obtained by extracting some limited information from all of the B-Scans. For a given point of the surface (Fig. 2), the amplitude C-Scan carries the information about the maximum value of signal amplitude acquired at this point (Fig. 1). This allows examining homogeneity of acoustic impedance of the structure. The ToF C-Scan represents ToF (Fig. 1) of the signal component with the highest amplitude. It usually corresponds to damage located the closest to the surface of the inspected structure, thus it is possible to obtain at least partial 3D reconstruction of damage.

## 1.2   Related Works

In the literature, various approaches aimed at 3D reconstruction based on 2D ultrasonic data can be found. Osman et al. [6] proposed an algorithm based on image segmentation and classification procedure, applied on a C-scan of a carbon fibre composite. Another method used for inspection of composite structures was presented in the study of Li and Chu [7], where a 3D view was generated by means of a rule and thresholding based algorithm applied to a region of interest (ROI) in B-scan data sets. In the paper of Yeh and Liu [8], the surface rendering technique, after use of a frequency-depth transform and wavelet marginal spectrum as a band-pass filter, was introduced in order to reconstruct internal defects in concrete structures.

Other examples of performing 3D reconstruction have been proposed for medical applications. Migeon and Marché [9] presented a 3D reconstruction of long bones of a newborn, based on image segmentation and contour interpolation method. Further example is a study of Qiu et al. [10], introducing a hole-filling algorithm using Distance Weight interpolation applied to ultrasound data of chicken kidney.

The preliminary study of Wronkowicz et al. on 3D reconstruction of C-Scans, based on the multilevel Otsu thresholding and morphological processing, can be found in [11]. These results showed a great potential in 3D visualisation of UT results for the NDT purposes. However, there is a loss of information in a C-Scan due to covering of damage located below damage being the closest to the surface of the structure. For this reason, the authors decided to study the accuracy of 3D reconstruction of a series of B-Scans compared to reconstruction of a C-Scan.

## 1.3   Motivation

The aim of this study was to develop a method for 3D reconstruction and visualisation of ultrasonic B-Scans in order to facilitate the NDT procedures. Since interpretation of ultrasonic scans is often difficult due to the presence of noise or due to the complexity of the structure geometry (e.g. including the presence of embedded elements, bolt connections, etc.), its 3D visualisation could significantly facilitate the diagnostic inference procedure. Another advantage is a reconstruction of the internal design of a structure, which would be useful for a precise assessment of a flaw location (e.g. with respect to composite layers) as well as to determine the true size of damage. To verify the obtained results, they were compared to two reference data, including (i) a 3D reconstruction of C-Scan, based on a previous work by some of the authors and (ii) the 3D specimen representation based on the X-ray computed tomography (CT).

## 2   Testing Methodology (UT)

**Specimen.** The carbon fiber reinforced polymer (CFRP) specimen consists of I7 carbon fibers and MTM45-1 epoxy matrix. The laminate has a balanced stacking sequence of $[0, 45, 90, -45]_S$ and 32 plies are superposed to obtain 4 mm thickness. The planar dimensions are $100 \times 150$ mm. The fabrication process consisted of debulking, vacuum bagging and curing. The specimen was cured at 180°C for 3 h under 6 bar pressure. The views of the specimen are depicted in Fig. 3.

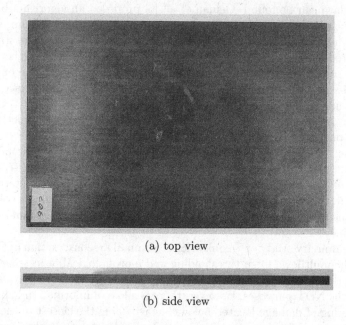

(a) top view

(b) side view

**Fig. 3.** Views of the CFRP specimen

The specimen underwent impact test, which has been performed by means of a drop test apparatus. The experimental set-up consisted of a Plexiglas tube to guide the impactor toward the specimen, which was grounded using steel frames in order to assure proper boundary conditions. The speed of the impactor was measured by laser acquisition, thus allowing to estimate the impact energy, resulting in 30 J. The impact caused BVID with a global dimension of $50.3 \times 64.5$ mm (Fig. 4), as measured by means of the ultrasonic tests described below.

**Ultrasonic Testing.** UT of the described above specimen was performed with use of FlawInspecta® scanner. Signal amplifier enables data generation within the 1–15 MHz with Phased Array transducer containing 128 independent active elements. For the purpose of the inspection 5 MHz frequency and radio frequency (RF) data capturing were used. The results of ultrasonic testing are depicted in Figs. 4(C-Scans) and 6 (selected sequence of B-Scans).

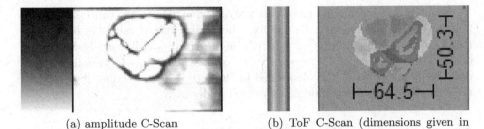

(a) amplitude C-Scan

(b) ToF C-Scan (dimensions given in millimiters)

**Fig. 4.** The results of ultrasonic testing of the specimen (C-Scans)

# 3    3D Visualisation of Damage in Ultrasonic Scans

## 3.1    3D Reconstruction of a C-Scan

The algorithms described in this paper were implemented in Matlab® with use of the Image Processing Toolbox. Firstly, the C-Scan of the tested structure was reconstructed into 3D array and visualised (Fig. 5).

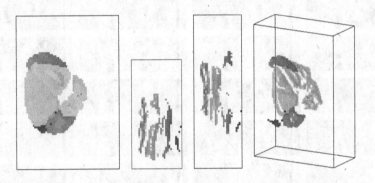

**Fig. 5.** Data presentation after 3D reconstruction of the C-scan (ToF)

A ToF C-Scan map, in the form of 8-bit matrices, was loaded into the workspace as an image. Then, global thresholding was performed in order to display only the regions presenting damage, namely to remove pixels of undamaged areas. It was performed in such a way that the pixels of the image $I$ which values are higher than given threshold value $T$ become zeros and the lower or equal remains unchanged. Such operation can be expressed by:

$$J_{i,j} = \begin{cases} 0 & \text{for } I_{i,j} > T, \\ I_{i,j} & \text{for } I_{i,j} \leq T, \end{cases} \tag{1}$$

where $i, j$ denote coordinates of the image, i.e. the ordinal number of a row and a column, respectively.

Finally, the resulting image was reconstructed in 3D, i.e. the values of the 2D image were distributed to a 3D matrix, where each unique value lies on a level (layer) corresponding to this value. Analysing the results visible in Fig. 5 one can observe that the simple 3D reconstruction of C-Scans improves visualisation of damage, however, as it was mentioned in the introduction section, flaws which are closest to the surface hide flaws located underneath.

## 3.2    3D Reconstruction of a Series of B-Scans

A series of B-Scan maps, recorded in the form of a video, was converted into a sequence of images, presenting the consecutive cross sections of the structure (selected sections are presented in Fig. 6).

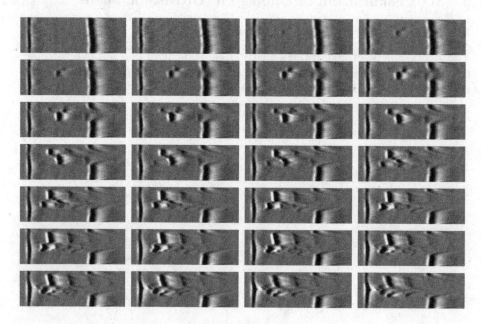

**Fig. 6.** Selected sequence of ultrasonic B-Scans (sections no. 18–45)

Then, all of these images were converted into a 3D matrix, i.e. stacked sequentially according to the order of the ultrasonic scanning path. Visualisation of such input matrix is presented in Fig. 7a as well as with a transparency in Fig. 7b, where one can clearly notice the existence of an internal damage.

The next step was the global thresholding in order to obtain two matrices, namely the first one with voxels representing only damaged regions of the inspected specimen, and the second one with the voxels of undamaged regions. The threshold value $T$ for (1) was selected manually. Three versions of 3D visualisation of damage were proposed. Firstly, both matrices (damage with healthy regions of the structure) were displayed simultaneously with a selected transparency, where the values of voxels in the matrix representing damage were emphasized in a resulting image (Fig. 7c). The second version is the display of only the matrix representing damage without any transparency (Fig. 7d). Figure 7e is the visualisation of damage (with transparency setting) after changing the terms in the matrix by means of a linear ascending scaling along the specimen thickness, thus distinguishing with individual colors composite delaminations at different depths.

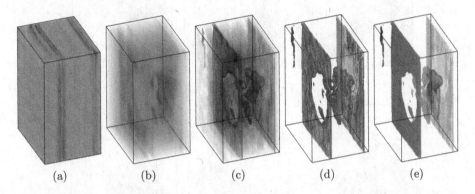

(a)          (b)          (c)          (d)          (e)

**Fig. 7.** Input 3D matrix of a series of B-Scans (without and with a transparency) and three different versions of their initial processing

As can be observed in Fig. 7, not only damage is visible but also the surface of the specimen and its bottom wall. In order to obtain better visualisation results, the matrix was cut by limiting the number of its columns. Final visualisations in three versions analogously to the above described ones are depicted in Fig. 8. It can be noticed that damage is very well visible on the resulting visualisations and reconstruction of B-Scans provides more details than a C-Scan reconstruction. Additionally, in Figs. 8c–d, some of the layers of the structure are distinguishable, which can be useful in assessment of damage location. The last step was the extraction of a contour around the damage obtained after binarization of the image and calculation of its surface area, which reached 2219.1 mm$^2$ for the considered specimen.

## 4    CT Based Verification of the Results

### 4.1    Testing Methodology (CT)

The specimen used in this study was investigated using the X-ray CT system – GE phoenix v|tome|x m with 300 kV tube and a detector array. The tests were carried out under the following conditions: voltage 120 kV, current intensity 120 μA and timing 330 ms. The sample was located 80–100 mm from the radiation source, determining a voxel size around 20–50 μm. The sample was

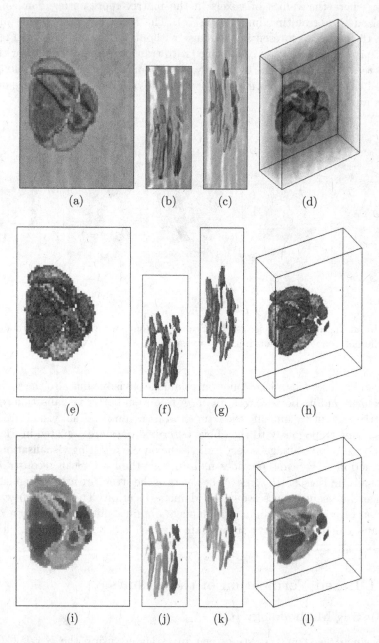

**Fig. 8.** 3D reconstruction of a series of B-Scans (a–d – with emphasized damage, e–h – after thresholding, i–l – with changed color map) (Color figure online)

installed on a rotating holder at an angle of 30 degrees with respect to the beam, in order to have a uniform illumination. The rotation step was 0.25°. The image was reconstructed using a graphical station with Phoenix Datosx 2 program. Then, VG Studio Max 2.2 software was used for initial processing of the images. Selected slices of tomograms from the top view are presented in Fig. 9.

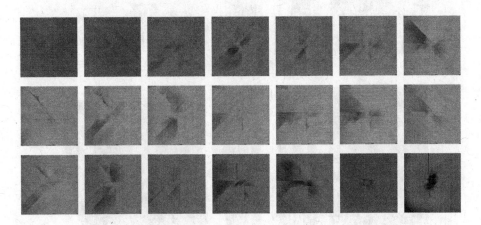

**Fig. 9.** Selected tomograms (no. of slices between 80–820)

## 4.2  3D Reconstruction of Tomograms

The tomograms were processed using the same algorithms as for processing of B-Scans. The 3D reconstructed and visualised image before thresholding and with no transparency can be seen in Figs. 10a–d, where the crack at the top of the structure is very well noticeable.

The 3D visualisation of the specimen after emphasizing the regions below the chosen threshold and adding a transparency for the rest voxels is presented in Figs. 10e–h. In this case, the crack at the top is well visible as well as the delaminated areas inside the structure. After limiting the range of displayed slices of the 3D matrix to the internal ones where delaminations are visible, as well as changing the color map, the results depicted in Figs. 10i–l were obtained. When comparing the results of 3D reconstruction of B-Scans and tomograms one can notice that there is a correlation between the delaminated areas (compare Figs. 10i–l with Figs. 8i–l). It can also be seen that the delaminated areas are more widespred in case of the results obtained from CT, however, their location and general form are comparable. This is due to a higher sensitivity of CT method and necessity of applying additional operations for the purpose of removing artefacts [12] from tomograms, which was not included in this study. Based on these initial results, 3D reconstruction of B-Scans seems to be a very helpful tool and alternative to CT, thus further studies in this area are planned to be performed.

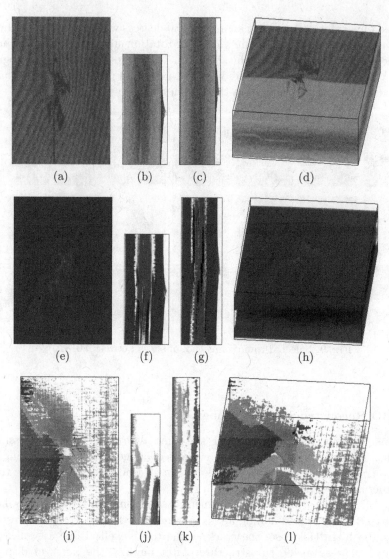

**Fig. 10.** 3D matrix of tomograms and visualisation of damage

## 5   Conclusions

In this paper, the authors presented an approach to 3D reconstruction of ultra-sonic B-Scans for the purpose of facilitating inspections of composite structures. The results of ultrasonic testing of CFRP specimen with BVID was used. The proposed approach is based on (i) image thresholding, to highlight the damage shape, and (ii) boundary tracing in order to exactly calculate damage extent. Volume rendering was used for the aim of visualization of a 3D matrix. 3D reconstruction of a sequence of B-Scans significantly facilitates interpretation of ultrasonic data and can be useful in assessment of a flaw size and location, including its depth. Accuracy of the 3D reconstruction of delaminated areas inside the tested structure was verified on the basis of reference data acquired with CT method. CT was chosen since it is considered the most sensitive and precise method for the purpose of analysing the inner and outer geometry of various types of objects. However, extensive dimensions of elements made of composite materials such as aerospace components disqualify them from inspections with use of CT. Moreover, a very high price of this method, time-consuming scanning and no possibility of performing field research make UT still the most universal method of diagnostics of composite elements. From the obtained results one can notice a correlation between damage detected in reconstructed B-Scans and tomograms, especially its shape and location. However, damage is more widespread in case of reconstruction from CT, which may result from a higher sensitivity of this method and not removed artefacts from the obtained data. The low computational complexity of the algorithm enables using it during UT of composites.

**Acknowledgements.** The publication is financed from the statutory funds of the Faculty of Mechanical Engineering of the Silesian University of Technology in 2016.

# References

1. Smith, R.A.: Composite defects and their detection. UNESCO Encyclopaedia Life Support Syst. Mater. Sci. Eng. **3**, 103–143 (2002)
2. Fanteria, D., Longo, G., Panettieri, E.: A non-linear shear damage model to reproduce permanent indentation caused by impacts in composite laminates. Compos. Struct. **111**, 111–121 (2014)
3. Davis, J.R.: ASM Handbook: Nondestructive Evaluation and Quality Control, vol. 17. ASM International, Materials Park (1989)
4. NDT Resource Center. http://www.ndt-ed.org/
5. Olympus IMS. http://www.olympus-ims.com/
6. Osman, A., Hassler, U., Kaftandjian, V., Hornegger, J.: An automated data processing method dedicated to 3D ultrasonic non destructive testing of composite pieces. In: International Symposium on Ultrasound in the Control of Industrial Processes (UCIP 2012), IOP Conference Series: Materials Science and Engineering, vol. 42, pp. 1–4 (2012)
7. Li, S., Chu, T.P.: Ultrasonic 3D reconstruction of CFRP panel delaminations. In: Fall Conference & Quality Testing Show 2012, Orlando, FL (2012)
8. Yeh, P.-L., Liu, P.-L.: Imaging of internal cracks in concrete structures using the surface rendering technique. NDT and E Int. **42**, 181–187 (2009)
9. Migeon, B., Marché, P.: In vitro 3D reconstruction of long bones using B-scan image processing. Med. Biol. Eng. Comput. **35**, 369–372 (1997)
10. Qiu, T., Wen, T., Gu, J.: Freehand 3D ultrasound reconstruction on image-guided surgery. Bulettin Adv. Technol. Res. **5**, 52–56 (2011)
11. Wronkowicz, A., Katunin, A., Dragan, K.: Ultrasonic C-scan image processing using multilevel thresholding for damage evaluation in aircraft vertical stabilizer. I.J. Image Graph. Signal Process. **11**, 1–8 (2015)
12. Barrett, J.F., Keat, N.: Artifacts in CT: recognition and avoidance. RadioGraphics **24**, 1679–1691 (2004)

# Human Face and Silhouette Recognition and Analysis

# Automatically Analyzing Interpersonal Closeness in Photo Albums

Gaocheng Bai[✉], Jiansheng Chen, Bo Huang, and Zhengqin Li

Department of Electronic Engineering, Tsinghua University, Beijing 100084, China
jschenthu@mail.tsinghua.edu.cn,
{bgc13,huangb14,li-zq12}@mails.tsinghua.edu.cn
http://jschenthu.weebly.com/projects.html

**Abstract.** We study the problem of automatically discovering the interpersonal closeness between people from a personal photo album in this
paper. The work is divided into two parts, the first part is the automatical
detection of person figures and the identity annotation, while the second
part is the analysis of the interpersonal closeness between identities. The
detection of person figures is solved by the cooperation of a face detector
and a person detector. Similarities between pairs of person figures are calculated by face verification and color descriptor matching, and a greedy
stratagem is used for identity assignment. The second part of the work is
a ranking process in which for each identity the other identities are ranked
by his(her) closeness to them. The algorithm aims at analyzing and ranking interpersonal closeness according to the image information extracted
from the album. The image information used by our method includes co-
appearing frequencies of persons, order distances between person figures
and the number of persons in each photo. We build a new database for
this work. Experiments on our database show that our method is effective
especially for finding the closest persons. The closeness rankings can be
used to do further interpersonal relationship analyses such as discovering
subgroups and finding the most active members.

**Keywords:** Identity annotation · Interpersonal closeness · Ranking

## 1 Introduction

In recent years social networks such as Facebook, WeChat have been more and
more prevalent with the rapid development of the Internet [2]. In the social networks, the relationships between people form very valuable information. Acquir-
ing interpersonal relationships is useful for advertisement recommending, mes-
sage transferring, data mining and analysis, and so on. While using the social
networks, people tend to upload a great amount of digital personal photos.
Human beings can easily analyze the relationships implied in a digital album
while browsing it.

It is usually hard to discriminate the interpersonal relationships between
people with only image information. Instead, it is more practical to estimate

© Springer International Publishing AG 2016
L.J. Chmielewski et al. (Eds.): ICCVG 2016, LNCS 9972, pp. 281–292, 2016.
DOI: 10.1007/978-3-319-46418-3_25

the closeness between people [14] which can help us analyze the connection between people. In this paper, we focus on discovering the closeness between people by using image information. Suppose we have a personal photo album, for a concerned person **h**, we are trying to rank the closeness between **h** and the other persons. For automatically solving this problem, there are two main steps required. The first is identity annotation of the person figures in the photos, and the second is ranking the identities by the calculated closeness parameters.

Identity annotation is an important step of our work. Aside from providing the users with convenience on personal album management, it can also provide an important foundation for data analysis of photo albums. Several systems of automatic or semi-automatic annotation of person identities in photo sets have been proposed [4,5,9,17]. Zhang et al. [17] proposed a typical semi-automatic identity annotation system. The system runs an accumulative process in which the user sequentially annotate the detected faces with the help of the automatically generated suggestion name list. Naaman et al. [4] proposed a semi-automatic system in which photos were partially manually annotated with person names. They studied how well the context information based on time and location can help suggest a name list for user to fully annotate the photo sets. Song et al. [9] proposed an identity clustering framework in personal photo albums. Similarities between faces and extracted clothes feature were calculated and integrated for employing spectral clustering on the identities.

For most of the previous identity annotation works, only those person figures with face detected are annotated. To avoid missing the person figures without face detected, we additionally use person detection to get the person figures. In personal albums, person figures usually have different postures and different shape completeness, which makes person detection a challenging task. To deal with these difficulties, we use the method proposed in [6] for person detection, which is a state-of-the-art object detection network capable of detecting objects with high variations.

Discovering interpersonal relationships such as spouses, parents & children, siblings from photo albums has attracted a lot of attention [1,8,13,16]. Different from directly discovering the interpersonal relationships, Wu et al. built a social imaging application [14] that can reveal closeness of people's relationship. Wu et al. proposed a method to calculate the pairwise closeness, but no numerical results of ranking were provided. In their next work [15], they used the calculated closeness to build a weighted undirected graph and then a graph clustering algorithm was applied to detect the social clusters.

As far as we know, there are no published numerical experiments for testing automatical analysis of interpersonal closeness from personal photo albums. In this paper, we try to design an automatical analyzing system to guess the subjective closeness between people. And numerical experiments on a newly established database are performed to show the effectiveness of our method.

## 2    Data Preparation

We have built a database composed of 114 photos taken in one group travel. For conciseness, we call this database $S$. Altogether there are 12 group members photographed in $S$ with totally 282 person figures. Each person figure is well annotated pixel-wisely. Three sample photos are shown in Fig. 1, the overlapping between person figures is complex that cropping rectangles may lead to ambiguity which can be avoided by pixel-wise ground-truth. The person figures are numbered according to their identities.

**Fig. 1.** Sample photos and corresponding pixel-wise labeling in $S$.

We use ranking to formulate the problem of analyzing interpersonal closeness. Select an identity as the host, and regard the others as the clients, our task is to rank the clients by the closeness between the host and the clients. Higher closeness ranking indicates closer relationship. We ask each person in $S$ to rank the other concerned persons by his(her) subjective closeness to each of them and take the subjective rankings as the ground-truths. For each pair of the ranked clients, if their order in the ranking keeps the same in both the ground-truth and the result of the algorithm, we call it a concordant pair. More concordant pairs there are, more precise the ranking algorithm is.

## 3    Methodology

### 3.1    Identity Annotation

**Person Figure Detection.** Before identity annotation, face detector and person detector are used to get candidates of person figures. Our face detector is a high-speed Viola-Jones face detector [12] cascaded with a CNN based face filter that can reduce false alarm by evaluating the qualities of the detected face rectangles. To deal with the variation of person figures in real-life photos, a so called

Faster R-CNN real-time object detector with Region Proposal Networks [6] is used and the results of person class are taken.

The outputs of the face detector and the person detector are both rectangles. Because of the high recall rate of the person detector, we regard the detected person rectangles as the basic units of automatically detected person figures. Detected faces are related to the person rectangles according to their overlapping areas. If there are two faces related to one person rectangle and the horizontal distance between the faces is large enough, we will divide the person rectangle into a left part and a right part that each of them has a related face. However, if two faces related to a person rectangles are too near in horizontal, we will abandon the upper one because it belongs to a person standing behind the person with the lower face, which means his(her) body is occluded severely. Moreover, small person rectangles that overlap greatly with some large person rectangle are omitted for promoting the precision. After the person figure detection, we can get person rectangles with or without a related face. We call the processed person rectangles as person figures. Some samples of person figures detected are shown in Fig. 2.

**Fig. 2.** Samples of detected person figures.

**Similarities Between Person Figures.** We adopted face verification technology proposed in [10] which uses a deep convolutional neural network for calculating *Facial Similarities*. The facial similarities are linearly mapped into $[0, 1]$. We denote the facial similarity between a pair of person figures as $s_f$.

To use the visual information besides faces, Harris-Laplace salient point detector [11] is used to get salient points with different scales, then color descriptors are calculated over the area around the salient points according to their scales to extract normalized constant-length features. In our experiments we use Opponent-SIFT [11] feature to describe the salient points. Suppose we are trying to calculate the similarity between person figure $f_1$ and person figure $f_2$. Firstly we calculate the Euclidean distances between salient point features of $f_1$ and salient point features of $f_2$ and use bipartite matching to select 50 best matching pairs of them. One naive method is to calculate the sum of the distances of the selected matching pairs of features and set the similarity between

$f_1$ and $f_2$ as a function of this sum. But this method will waste the geometric information contained in the positions of the salient points. For robustness we make further efforts to search the possible geometric transforms hidden in these selected salient points. Denote the set of the selected 50 salient points of $f_1$ as $P_1$, the set of the corresponding 50 salient points of $f_2$ as $P_2$. We try to find out as many as possible similarity transforms that each of them map several points in $P_1$ to their corresponding points in $P_2$. The basis of this method is that the person figures have local rigidity and global flexibility. Each similarity transform is corresponded to a rigid local part and multi-transforms imply that geometric flexibility is permitted among different parts. We use $RANSAC$ algorithm [3] to search possible similarity transforms, those with at least 3 pairs of salient points and transform residual less than a threshold are selected. Figure 3 shows three samples of person figure matching, the lines with one kind of color represent a similarity transform. Denote the similarity derived from this matching-and-selecting process of salient points as $S_m$. Suppose the total number of the salient-point-pairs related to all the selected transforms is $n$, we set $s_m = n/50$. The range of $s_m$ is also $[0, 1]$.

(a)　　　　　　　　　(b)　　　　　　　　　(c)

**Fig. 3.** Samples of similarity transforms in person figure matching. Lines of one kind of color represent a similarity transform. (Color figure online)

When calculating the similarity between two person figures, if they both have a detected face rectangle, the final similarity $s$ between a pair of person figures is calculated as $s = \sqrt{(s_f^2 + s_m^2)/2}$, otherwise let $s = s_m$.

**Identity Annotation.** We manually choose one correctly automatically detected person figure for each identity to form the confirmed sets for assigning identities to the person figures. While assigning identities to the detected person figures in a photo, we calculate the similarities between 12 confirmed sets and the person figures, and preferentially select the larger similarities for assignment. After an assignment, the selected new person figure will be included in the corresponding confirmed set, and the confirmed set will not be used again in the same photo since a person can only appear once in a photo. This is simply a greedy stratagem. For automatically abandoning the unwanted person figures, a threshold is given that only assignments with similarities higher than it are adopted. Obviously, higher similarity threshold usually implies higher precision rate and lower recall rate. While calculating the similarity between a confirmed set and a new person figure, the average or maximum of the similarities between the confirmed person figures and the new person figure is taken. We call these two options as average stratagem and maximum stratagem.

## 3.2   Closeness Ranking

We can make three speculations on interpersonal closeness. (1) **frequency speculation:** Higher co-appearing frequency indicates closer relationship. (2) **distance speculation:** For two persons both appear in one photo, being closer in location indicates being closer in relationship. (3) **co-appearing speculation:** Relationships among the persons appearing in the photo will be closer if there are fewer appearing persons in total.

We need to import a so called **"order distance"** [1] into our equation of interpersonal closeness. Order distance is more precise to evaluate interpersonal closeness than Euclidean distance. The order distance between two persons is the number of the other persons that intervene them. Before calculating the order distances, we build a graph in which the vertexes are the gravity centers of person figures and the edge weights are the Euclidean distances between the gravity centers, then find an minimum spanning tree (MST) of the graph. The order distance between two persons is the number of the other vertexes in the shortest path on the MST starting from one person to the other. Note that the order distance is counted from 0. For a host $\mathbf{h}$ and a client $\mathbf{c}$ that both appear in a photo, we denote the order distance between them as $\bar{d}(\mathbf{h}, \mathbf{c})$.

Now we denote the interpersonal closeness between $\mathbf{h}$ and $\mathbf{c}$ as $c(\mathbf{h}, \mathbf{c})$ in Eq. 1.

$$c(\mathbf{h}, \mathbf{c}) = [\frac{1}{m} \sum_{S(\mathbf{h}) \cap S(\mathbf{c})} \frac{\exp(-\bar{d}(\mathbf{h}, \mathbf{c})/(N-2))}{\sqrt{n-1}}] \times \exp(\alpha m) \qquad (1)$$

In Eq. 1, $n$ means the number of the persons in the photo while $N$ means the number of all the identities. $S(\mathbf{h})$ means the largest subset of $S$ of which each photo contains $\mathbf{h}$. The value of $m$ is the number of photos in $(S(\mathbf{h}) \cap S(\mathbf{c}))$. The fraction means the interpersonal closeness calculated from a single photo, where the numerator is corresponded to the distance speculation and the denominator is corresponded to the co-appearing speculation. The exponential term on the right is corresponded to the frequency speculation. The holistic interpersonal closeness is equal to the average single-photo interpersonal closeness multiplied with the frequency term.

With the calculated interpersonal closeness between the host **h** and the clients, we can rank the clients by the closeness to get the result of closeness ranking.

## 4  Performance Evaluation

### 4.1  Identity Annotation

Before evaluating the performance of identity annotation we should make an exclusive matching between automatically detected person figures and the manually annotated person regions. An automatically detected figure is possible to be matched with a manually annotated person region if they overlap. For exclusive principle we choose matched pairs with the largest overlapping areas among all possible candidates.

We call it a hit if an automatically detected person figure is matched with a manually annotated person figure and their identity annotations are accordant. The precision of identity annotation is defined as the ratio of the number of all hits to the number of all automatically detected person figures. The recall of identity annotation is defined as the ratio of the number of all hits to the number of all ground-truths. Note that the ground-truths only include person figures of the 12 concerned identities.

### 4.2  Closeness Ranking

For each person we are trying to deduce the ranking of the closeness between he(she) and the other persons. For **h** being the host, suppose the ground-truth ranking of the clients is $[c_1, c_2, \cdots, c_{N-1}]$. Denote the ranking result for **h** of the algorithm is $r$, the comparison value $r(c_a, c_b) = 1 (a < b)$ if the rank of $c_a$ is higher than the rank of $c_b$ in $r$, or saying $c_a$ is deduced to be closer to **h** than $c_b$ is. Otherwise $r(c_a, c_b) = 0$. For **h** we calculate a pairwise precision $Pre$ as Eq. 2 shows.

$$
\begin{aligned}
Pre &= \frac{P}{P+Q}, \\
P &= \#\{(a,b)|a < b, r(c_a, c_b) = 1\}, \\
Q &= \#\{(a,b)|a < b, r(c_a, c_b) = 0\}
\end{aligned}
\tag{2}
$$

We can discover that the scope of $Pre$ is $[0, 1]$ and $Pre$ being less than 0.5 means the ranking is too bad that even the reverse of it is more precise. $Pre$ is a global parameter that indicates the overall precision of rankings. Sometimes we focus more on the closest clients to the host especially the closest one, because that can reveal more valuable and reliable information about social relationship. Denote the top-i precision as $Pre(i)$. The definition of $Pre(i)$ is shown in Eq. 3.

$$
\begin{aligned}
Pre(i) &= \frac{P(i)}{P(i) + Q(i)}, \\
P(i) &= \#\{(a,b)|a \leq i, a < b, r(c_a, c_b) = 1\}, \\
Q(i) &= \#\{(a,b)|a \leq i, a < b, r(c_a, c_b) = 0\}
\end{aligned}
\tag{3}
$$

Top-i precision $Pre(i)$ means how precise the orders of the pairs which are related to the $i$ most closest clients are. Especially, $Pre(1)$ indicates the resulting rank of the closest client, and $Pre(N)$ is exactly the global pairwise precision. In our experiments, we take every identity as the host and calculate the precisions separately, then use the averages of them as the result to evaluate the algorithms.

# 5    Experiments

## 5.1    Identity Annotation

Figure 4 shows the results of automatical identity annotation. The average stratagem and the maximum stratagem are compared. We define $F$ value as the harmonic mean of precision and recall. The star marks represent the best $F$ values. We can see that the average stratagem is more conservative that it tends to maintain higher precision by sacrificing recall.

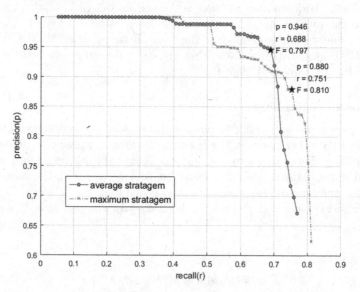

**Fig. 4.** Precision/Recall curves of identity annotation.

## 5.2    Closeness Ranking

While testing the closeness ranking methods we adopt Wu's method [14] as a competitor. While using Wu's method we substitute the pairwise face distance with pairwise person centroid distance. This is because in our database there are over 30 percents of person figures that are hard or even impossible to detect a face, and these two kinds of distances can work approximately the same way. The results of ranking by co-appearing frequency are also displayed to form a baseline. The automatical identity annotation using the average stratagem with

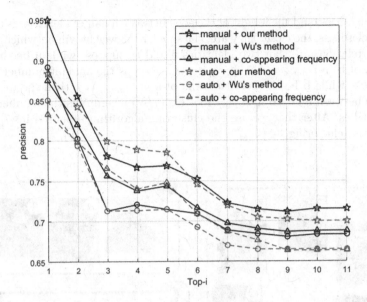

**Fig. 5.** Top-i precision curves of the ranking methods. (Color figure online)

the best $F$ value of 0.797 as well as the manual person figure annotation are adopted for the experiment.

We show the Top-i precision curves in Fig. 5. The red dashed curves are the results of methods with automatical annotation while the blue solid curves are the results of methods with manual annotation. It is obviously shown that our method is superior to Wu's method and the basic co-appearing frequency method using both two kinds of annotation. The curves also indicate that no matter which kind of annotation we take, our method is especially applicable for ranking the closest persons, which is important for real applications. The value of $Pre(1)$ approaches 95.0 % while using manual annotation. This precision still remains as high as 88.3 % with the automatical annotation which gets an $F$ value of only 0.797. The results tell us that merely weak manual labeling such as one person figure annotation for one identity can provide powerful assistance for the work of closeness ranking, especially for ranking the closest persons.

### 5.3   Analyses of Inpterpersonal Relationships

With deduced rankings of interpersonal closeness based on image information, we can do further analyses of interpersonal relationships. In the following we will show experimental results on two problems: subgroup discovering and the most active persons finding. To guarantee the reliability of the experiments, we use the rankings based on the interpersonal closeness designed by us and the manual annotation of person figures. We denote $r_{image}$ as the rankings we use.

**Discovering Subgroups.** We use clustering to discover the subgroups in the large group. Firstly we generate an undirected complete graph in which the nodes are the identities, and the weight of the edge between a pair of identities is related to their closeness, the closer they are, the smaller the weight will be(which means stronger relationship). For two identities **a** and **b**, suppose while **a** be the host the rank of **b** in $r_{image}$ is $i$ $(1 <= i <= N - 1, N$ is the amount number of the identities.), while **b** be the host the rank of **a** in $r_{image}$ is $j$, then the weight of the edge between **a** and **b** is $\exp(i/N) + \exp(j/N)$ where $N$ is the number of all the identities. After that we use the clustering algorithm proposed in [7] to do the identity clustering.

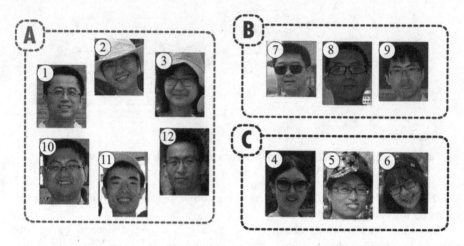

**Fig. 6.** Result of discovering subgroups.

Suppose we preset the number of clustering groups as $M$. Figure 6 shows the clustering result of M = 3. This result is concordant with the reality. In Subgroup A, Member 1, 11 and 12 belong to a laboratory $lab_a$, Member 2 is Member 1's wife. Member 3 only knew member 1 and member 2 before this travel. The members of Subgroup B and Subgroup C all belong to another laboratory $lab_b$. Although member 10 in fact belongs to $lab_b$, but he has frequent interaction with member 1 and member 11, therefore his being clustered into subgroup A is reasonable to some extent. The three members of subgroup B are old members of $lab_b$, while the three members of subgroup C are new female members of $lab_b$ that are familiar with each other.

**Finding the Most Active Members.** For an identity **a**, denote $r^a_{image}$ as all his(her) ranks in $r_{image}$, we set **a**'s activity degree as

$$\sum_{i \in r^a_{image}} \exp(i/N).$$

Then rank the identities by their activity degrees to find the most active members. In our experiment result the most active member is Member 11. Member

11 is the most senior master degree candidate of $lab_a$, he knows all the other members well except Member 3. The second active member is Member 1 who is the supervisor of $lab_a$. The most inactive member is Member 3, this is concordant with the reality that she only knew Member 1 and Member 2 before the travel.

Synthesizing the above results, we verify that our methods for analyzing interpersonal relationships based on image information are applicable.

## 6 Conclusion

In this paper we have proposed a system to automatically rank people by their closeness to the others. Face detection and person detection are used to detect person figures before face verification and color descriptor matching are used for calculating similarities between person figures. Then identity annotation is done by a greedy stratagem. Several kinds of fundamental image information such as co-appearing frequency of persons, order distances between person figures and the number of persons in each photo are extracted to calculate interpersonal closeness for ranking. Experiments have indicated that the proposed closeness measurements can effectively reflect the rankings of persons' subjective closeness. Moreover, our method is labor-saving(only need to select one person figure for each identity) and robust for unperfect annotation. Closeness rankings based on image information are also useful for doing interpersonal relationship analyses such as discovering subgroups and finding the most active persons. For further improving the reliability of interpersonal closeness analysis, the future works may try to recognize more kinds of high-level information, such as social roles of the persons, interactive actions between persons, activities the persons are participating, and so on.

This work was supported by the National Natural Science Foundation of China (61101152), the Tsinghua University Initiative Scientific Research Program (20131089382), and the Beijing Higher Education Young Elite Teacher Project (YETP0104).

## References

1. Chen, Y.Y., Hsu, W.H., Liao, H.Y.M.: Discovering informative social subgraphs and predicting pairwise relationships from group photos. In: Proceedings of the 20th ACM International Conference on Multimedia. pp. 669–678. ACM (2012)
2. Cheung, C.M., Chiu, P.Y., Lee, M.K.: Online social networks: why do students use facebook? Comput. Hum. Behav. **27**(4), 1337–1343 (2011)
3. Fischler, M.A., Bolles, R.C.: Random sample consensus: a paradigm for model fitting with applications to image analysis and automated cartography. Commun. ACM **24**(6), 381–395 (1981)
4. Naaman, M., Yeh, R.B., Garcia-Molina, H., Paepcke, A.: Leveraging context to resolve identity in photo albums. In: Proceedings of the 5th ACM/IEEE-CS Joint Conference on Digital Libraries. JCDL 2005, pp. 178–187. IEEE (2005)

5. O'Hare, N., Smeaton, A.F.: Context-aware person identification in personal photo collections. IEEE Trans. Multimedia **11**(2), 220–228 (2009)
6. Ren, S., He, K., Girshick, R., Sun, J.: Faster R-CNN: towards real-time object detection with region proposal networks. In: Advances in Neural Information Processing Systems, pp. 91–99 (2015)
7. Rodriguez, A., Laio, A.: Clustering by fast search and find of density peaks. Science **344**(6191), 1492–1496 (2014)
8. Singla, P., Kautz, H., Luo, J., Gallagher, A.: Discovery of social relationships in consumer photo collections using markov logic. In: IEEE Computer Society Conference on Computer Vision and Pattern Recognition Workshops, CVPRW 2008, pp. 1–7. IEEE (2008)
9. Song, Y., Leung, T.: Context-aided human recognition – clustering. In: Leonardis, A., Bischof, H., Pinz, A. (eds.) ECCV 2006. LNCS, vol. 3953, pp. 382–395. Springer, Heidelberg (2006). doi:10.1007/11744078_30
10. Sun, Y., Chen, Y., Wang, X., Tang, X.: Deep learning face representation by joint identification-verification. In: Advances in Neural Information Processing Systems, pp. 1988–1996 (2014)
11. Van De Sande, K.E., Gevers, T., Snoek, C.G.: Evaluating color descriptors for object and scene recognition. IEEE Trans. Pattern Anal. Mach. Intell. **32**(9), 1582–1596 (2010)
12. Viola, P., Jones, M.J.: Robust real-time face detection. Int. J. Comput. Vis. **57**(2), 137–154 (2004)
13. Wang, G., Gallagher, A., Luo, J., Forsyth, D.: Seeing people in social context: recognizing people and social relationships. In: Daniilidis, K., Maragos, P., Paragios, N. (eds.) ECCV 2010. LNCS, vol. 6315, pp. 169–182. Springer, Heidelberg (2010). doi:10.1007/978-3-642-15555-0_13
14. Wu, P., Ding, W., Mao, Z., Tretter, D.: Close & closer: discover social relationship from photo collections. In: IEEE International Conference on Multimedia and Expo. ICME 2009, pp. 1652–1655. IEEE (2009)
15. Wu, P., Tretter, D.: Close & closer: social cluster and closeness from photo collections. In: Proceedings of the 17th ACM International Conference on Multimedia, pp. 709–712. ACM (2009)
16. Xia, S., Shao, M., Luo, J., Fu, Y.: Understanding kin relationships in a photo. IEEE Trans. Multimedia **14**(4), 1046–1056 (2012)
17. Zhang, L., Chen, L., Li, M., Zhang, H.: Automated annotation of human faces in family albums. In: Proceedings of the Eleventh ACM International Conference on Multimedia, pp. 355–358. ACM (2003)

# Component-Based Ethnicity Identification from Facial Images

A. Boyseens and S. Viriri[✉]

School of Maths, Statistics and Computer Science,
University of KwaZulu-Natal, Durban, South Africa
{210501411,viriris}@ukzn.ac.za

**Abstract.** This paper presents an exhaustive component-based analysis to identify the ethnicity from facial images. The different ethnic groups identified are Asian, African, African American, Asian Middle East, Caucasian and Other. The classification techniques investigated include Decision Trees, Naïve Bayes, Random Forest and K-Nearest Neighbor. Naïve Bayes achieved 84.7 % and 85.6 % accuracy rates for African ethnicity and Asian ethnicity identification, respectively. The Decision Trees achieved 85.8 % for African American ethnicity identification rate, while K-Nearest Neighbor achieved 86.8 % for Asian Middle East ethnicity and Random Forest achieved 90.8 % for Caucasian ethnicity identification rate. This research work achieved an overall ethnicity identification rate of 86.6 %.

## 1 Introduction

This paper investigates methods of analysing and identifying ethnicity of a facial image. These ethnicities are Asian, African, African American, Asian Middle East, Caucasian and Other. The aim of this research work is to investigate a model for the efficient ethnicity identification using facial components.

Ethnicity is a socially defined category of people who are identified by each other based on the common social, cultural and ancestral backgrounds [1]. Ethnic facial recognition is an important biometric authentication technology, there are various applications of facial recognition, these include law enforcement, security systems and biometric system therefore the need for an ethnic facial recognition system is essential.

## 2 Related Work

Lu and Jain [2] described techniques, which use Nearest Neighbor (NN) and Linear Discriminant Analysis (LDA) for ethnic identification from facial images. The two classes identified are Asian and Non-Asian ethnicity. The feature extraction technique used were Hu Moment and Zernike Moments. The experimental results achieved an average accuracy rate of 86 %. The short falls experienced are that it only classified for two classes Asian and non-Asian ethnicity. Another short fall was that Product Rule was used to achieve an integrated strategy to

© Springer International Publishing AG 2016
L.J. Chmielewski et al. (Eds.): ICCVG 2016, LNCS 9972, pp. 293–303, 2016.
DOI: 10.1007/978-3-319-46418-3_26

combine outputs and the data results achieved are estimated due to the extensive cross-validation that was used.

Buchala et al. [3] discussed the effects that Principal Component Analysis (PCA) has on the identification of Gender, Ethnicity, Age and Identity of facial images. Three classes are identified these are Caucasian, African American and East Asian. The feature extractions technique were Elastic Bunchc Graph. The experimental results achieved an average accuracy for Ethnicity of 81.67%. This paper had the following short falls it only classified for three different classes Caucasian, African American and East Asian and the authors assumed that using Linear Discriminant Analysis (LDA) would achieve better results than that of PCA.

Tin and Sein [4] analysis the use of Nearest Neighbor (NN) and Principal Component Analysis (PCA) in order to achieve ethnicity identification from facial images. This paper distinguish between two classes Myanmar and Non-Myanmar ethnicities. The feature extraction technique used was Hu Moments. The experimental results obtained by the paper on average are 92% ethnic identification accuracy. The insufficiency experienced were that it only classified between two different classes Myanmar and Non-Myanmar. The authors assumed that more images are needed to achieve a better result and the system needs to be more identity-sensitive to features that are closer together.

## 3    Methods and Techniques

The component-based ethnicity identification system is depicted in Fig. 1.

### 3.1    Facial Components

The facial components are extracted using the Haar Transformation [5] which is real and orthogonal. Haar Transformation $HT^n(f)$ of an N-input function $X^n(f)$ is the $2^{nd}$ element vector as described in Eq. (1). The Haar Transformation cross multiplies a function with Haar matrix that contains Haar functions with different widths at different locations. It is calculated at two levels which decomposes the discrete signal into two components at half of the original lengths [5].

$$HT^n(f) = H^n X^n(f) \tag{1}$$

where $n$ is the number of elements in the function, $H^n$ is the element vector and $X^n(f)$ is the $2^n$ element vector. The components that are extracted are the left eye, right eye, mouth, nose, chin, forehead, left cheek and right cheek.

### 3.2    Feature Extraction

From each component a feature vector is obtained. Analysis was done on different textural and structural or geometrical feature extractions, 7 Hu Moments, Zernike Moments, Local Binary Pattern (LBP), Gabor Filter and Haralick Texture Moments, in order to obtain the correct feature extraction for that component.

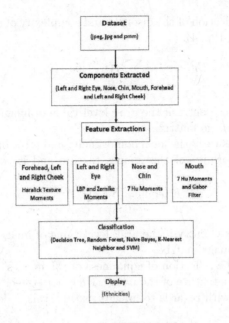

**Fig. 1.** Overview of ethnicity identification system

**The Hu Moments** are a set of invariant moments and it characterizes regardless of their scale, positions, size and orientation. These are computed by normalizing the central moments though order 3 [6] in terms of the central moments.

**The Zernike Moments** are used to overcome redundancy in which certain geometric moments obtain [6]. They are a class of orthogonal moments which are rotational invariant and effective in image representation. Zernike are a set of complex, orthogonal polynomials defined as the interior of the unit circle. The general form of the Zernike Moments is defined in Eq. (2).

$$Z_{nm}(x,y) = Z_{nm}(p,\theta) = R_{nm}(p)\epsilon^{jm\theta} \tag{2}$$

where $x$, $y$, $p$ and $\theta$ correspond to Cartesian and Polar coordinates respectively, $n \in Z^+$ and $m \in Z$, constrained to $n - m$ even, $m \leq n$

$$R_{nm}(p) = \sum_{k=0}^{\frac{n-m}{2}} \frac{(-1)^k (n-k)!}{k!(\frac{n+m}{2} - k)!(\frac{n-m}{2} - k)!} p^{n-2k} \tag{3}$$

where $R_{nm}(p)$ is a radial polynomial and $k$ is the order.

**The Haralick Texture Moments** are texture features that can be used to analyze the spatial distribution of the image's texture features [6] with different spatial positions and angles. Four of these Haralick Texture Moments are computed; Energy, Entropy, Correlation and Homogeneity.

Entropy is the reflection of the disorder and complexity of the images texture. This is defined using Eq. (4).

$$Entropy = \sum_{ij} \hat{f}(i,j) \log \hat{f}(i,j) \qquad (4)$$

where $\hat{f}(i,j)$ is the $[i,j]$ entry if the gray level value of image matrix and $i$ and $j$ are points on the image matrix.

Energy is the measure of the local homogeneity and is the opposite of Entropy. This shows the uniformity of the images texture and is computed using the Eq. (5).

$$Energy = \sum_{ij} \hat{f}(i,j)^2 \qquad (5)$$

where $\hat{f}(i,j)$ is the $[i,j]$ entry if the gray level value of image matrix and $i$ and $j$ are points on the image matrix.

Homogeneity is the reflection of equaliness of the images' textures and scale of local changes in the texture of the image. High homogeneity shows no change between the regions with regards to images texture, this is defined in Eq. (6).

$$Homogeneity = \sum_{i} \sum_{j} \frac{1}{1 + (i-j)^2} \hat{f}_{i,j} \qquad (6)$$

where $\hat{f}(i,j)$ is the $[i,j]$ entry if the gray level value of image matrix and $i$ and $j$ are points on the image matrix.

Correlation is the consistency of the images texture which is described in Eq. (7).

$$Correlation = \sum_{ij} \frac{(i-\mu_i)(j-\mu_j)\hat{f}(i,j)}{\sigma_i \sigma_j} \qquad (7)$$

In which $\mu_j$, $\mu_i$, $\sigma_i$ and $\sigma_j$ are described as:

$$\mu_i = \sum_{i=1}^{n} \sum_{j=1}^{n} i\hat{f}(i,j) \qquad \mu_j = \sum_{i=1}^{n} \sum_{j=1}^{n} j\hat{f}(i,j) \qquad (8)$$

$$\sigma_i = \sqrt{\sum_{i=1}^{n} \sum_{j=1}^{n} (i-\mu_i)^2 \hat{f}(i,j)} \qquad \sigma_j = \sqrt{\sum_{i=1}^{n} \sum_{j=1}^{n} (i-\mu_j)^2 \hat{f}(i,j)} \qquad (9)$$

**The Gabor Filters** are geometric moments which are the product between an elliptical Gaussian and a sinusoidal, [7]. Gabor elementary function can be defined as the product of the pulse with a harmonic oscillation of frequency.

$$g(t) = \epsilon^{-\alpha^2(t-t_0)^2} \epsilon^{-i2\pi(f-f_o)+\phi} \qquad (10)$$

where $\alpha$ is the time duration of the Gaussian envelope, $t_0$ denotes the centroid, $f_0$ is the frequency of the sinusoidal and $\phi$ denotes the phase shift.

**Local Binary Pattern (LBP)** is a geometric moment operator that described the surrounding of the pixels by obtaining a bit code of a pixel [8], this is defined using Eq. (11).

$$C = \sum_{k=0}^{k=7} (2^k b_k) \tag{11}$$

$$b_k = \begin{cases} 1, \sum_{k=0}^{k=7} (t_k \geq C) \\ 0, \sum_{k=0}^{k=7} (t_k < C) \end{cases}$$

where $t_k$ is the gray scale amount. $b_k$ is the binary variables between 1 and 0 and $C$ is a constant value of 0 and 1.

### 3.3  Classification

A number of different supervised and unsupervised machine learning algorithms are used in order to identify ethnicity of the facial images. The classification techniques used are Naïve Bayes, K-Nearest Neighbor and Decision Tree.

**The Decision Trees** use recursive partitioning to separate the dataset by finding the best variable [9], and using the selected variable to split the data. Then using the entropy, defined in Eqs. (12) and (13), to calculate the difference that variable would make on the results if it is chosen. If the entropy is 0 then that variable is prefect to use, else a new variable needs to be selected.

$$H(D) = - \sum_{i=1}^{k} P(C_i|D) \log_k (P(C_i|D)) \tag{12}$$

where the entropy of a sample $D$ with repest to target variable of $k$ possible classes $C_i$.

$$P(C_i|D) = \frac{number\, of\, correct\, observation\, for\, that\, class}{total\, observation\, for\, that\, class} \tag{13}$$

where the probability of class $C_i$ in $D$ is obtained directly from the dataset.

**Naïve Bayes** classify an instance by assuming the presence or absence of a particular feature and sees if it is unrelated to the presence or absence of another feature, given in the class variable [9,10]. This is done by calculating the probability for which it occurred, as defined in Eq. (14).

$$P(x_1, \ldots\ldots, x_n|y) = \frac{\prod_{i=1}^{n} P(y)P(x_n|y)}{P(x_1, \ldots\ldots, x_n)} \tag{14}$$

where case $y$ is a class value, attributes are $x_1, \ldots\ldots, x_n$ and $n$ is the sample size.

**K-Nearest Neighbor (KNN)** classifies by a majority vote of its neighbors, with the case being assigned to the class with the most common amongst its dataset. The KNN is measured by a distance function, for example Euclidean, as defined in Eq. (15).

$$d = \sqrt{\sum_{i=1}^{n}(x_i - q_i)^2} \tag{15}$$

where $n$ is the size of the data, $x_i$ is an element in the dataset and $q_i$ is a central point.

## 4    Results and Discussion

This paper used a union of four different facial image databases. The total dataset contained 1300 facial images of 900 subjects. The subjects were divided into six different ethnic groups (Asian, African, African American, Asian Middle East, Caucasian and Other). Asian dataset composed of Yale [11] and FERET [12], African dataset was composed of MUCT [13], African American was composed of Yale [11], ORL [14] and FERET [12], Caucasian dataset was composed of Yale [11], ORL [14], FERET [12] and MUCT [13], Asian Middle East was composed of ORL [14], Yale [11], FERET [12] and MUCT [13] and Other was composed of FERET [12].

Analysis was done to obtain which feature extraction technique would achieve the most accurate True Positive Rate (TPR) for ethnic identification. These analysis results were obtained by taking the feature vector for each component and classifying it using K-Nearest Neighbor, to observe which feature vector obtained the highest True Positive Rate, results obtained are shown in Table 1.

**Table 1.** Accuracy rates per component per feature extraction technique

|             | 7 Hu moments | Zernike moments | LBP   | Gabor filter | Haralick texture moments |
|-------------|--------------|-----------------|-------|--------------|--------------------------|
| Nose        | 85.0%        | 80.1%           | 62.7% | 82.5%        | 66.5%                    |
| Left eye    | 57.2%        | 76.4%           | 83.7% | 73.4%        | 77.1%                    |
| Right eye   | 62.7%        | 76.3%           | 37.6% | 71.8%        | 63.4%                    |
| Mouth       | 89.5%        | 72.1%           | 76.9% | 88.2%        | 70.1%                    |
| Forehead    | 45.2%        | 79.5%           | 81.0% | 70.6%        | 82.3%                    |
| Chin        | 80.5%        | 72.6%           | 47.5% | 66.8%        | 69.8%                    |
| Left cheek  | 60.4%        | 52.6%           | 30.5% | 66.7%        | 72.8%                    |
| Right cheek | 62.5%        | 71.5%           | 22.7% | 81.8%        | 84.2%                    |

Zernike Moments is a geometric feature extraction technique which achieved a TPR of 76.3% for the right eye. LBP is a geometric feature extraction technique it achieved a TPR of 83.7% for the left eye. These two geometric feature extraction technique achieved high results as the eyes are structurally different in size and shape between ethnic groups.

Gabor Filter, 88.2 %, and 7 Hu Moment, 89.5 %, achieved a high TPR for the mouth component. Both feature extraction techniques are textural based. These achieved high results as the mouth is different in colour, shape and coarseness for different ethnic groups.

The forehead, 82.3 % TPR, left cheek, 72.8 % TPR and right cheek, 84.2 % TPR, have different textures, colours and gradients. These achieved high results due to the fact that Haralick Texture Moments calculate the correlation and homogeneity for each pixel.

7 Hu Moments is a textural feature extraction techniques it achieved 80.5 % for the chin and 85.0 % for the nose. This is due to all components needing to be identified by using the texture of the component which 7 Hu Moments achieves.

### 4.1 African Ethnicity Results

In Buchala et al. [3] it was shown that for African ethnicity the percentage achieved was on average 80 % for the Principal Component Analysis (PCA). These results were obtained from a dataset size of 320 images from the FERET dataset. The Naïve Bayes produced the best results for the whole database. K-nearest Neighbour produced high results, shown in Fig. 2.

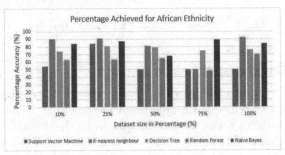

**Fig. 2.** Accuracy achieved for African ethnicity

### 4.2 African American Ethnicity Results

Buchala et al. [3] showed that for African ethnicity the percentage achieved was on average 80 % for the Principal Component Analysis (PCA). The results obtained are shown in Fig. 3. The Decision Trees achieved the best results of 85.8 %.

### 4.3 Asian Ethnicity Results

In Lu and Juain [2] obtained an average of 97 % for Nearest Neighbour and 95 % for Linear Discriminant Analysis (LDA) for Asian identification. The Naïve Bayes produced the best accuracy rate of 86 %, and the K-nearest Neighbor produced the accuracy rate of 75 % as shown in Fig. 4.

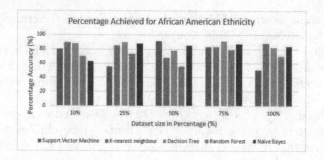

**Fig. 3.** Accuracy achieved for African American ethnicity

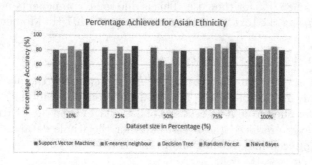

**Fig. 4.** Accuracy achieved for Asian ethnicity

## 4.4   Asian Middle East Ethnicity Results

Buchala et al. [3] results obtained for Asian Middle East ethnicity were on average 83 % for the Principal Component Analysis (PCA). These results were obtained from a dataset size of 363 images from the FERET dataset. The K-Nearest Neighbor is the best machine learning algorithm to identify the Asian Middle East ethnicity for all images, this produced 86.8 %, among other technique as shown in Fig. 5.

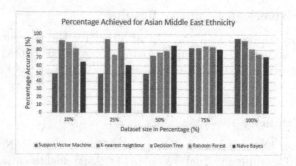

**Fig. 5.** Accuracy achieved for Asian Middle East ethnicity

## 4.5    Caucasian Ethnicity Results

In Buchala et al. [3] results showed that for Caucasian ethnicity the percentage achieved was 82 % for the Principal Component Analysis (PCA). These results were obtained by using 1758 images from the FERET dataset. The Random Forest is best used to identify the Caucasian ethnicity for all images, this produced 90.8 %. Random Forest achieved well here as most of the testing data was made up of Caucasian images and the decision rule produced easily classified the Caucasian ethnicity. After testing it was found that all datasets produced on average a 90 % for ethnic accuracy identification, as shown in Fig. 6.

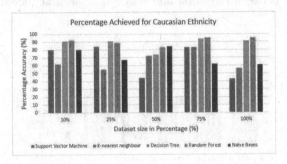

**Fig. 6.** Accuracy achieved for caucasian ethnicity

## 4.6    Other Ethnicity Results

Tin and Sein [4] achieved on average for other ethnicity was on average 93 % for Nearest Neighbour (NN) and 96 % for Principal Component Analysis (PCA). These results were obtained from a 250 images obtained from the Internet. The K-Nearest Neighbor is best accuracy rate of 80 % as shown in Fig. 7.

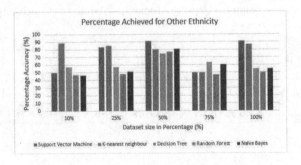

**Fig. 7.** Accuracy achieved for other ethnicity

### 4.7  Results of All Six Ethnicities

A number empirical experiments were carried out to investigate which machine learning algorithm would be suitable to determine the best results for ethnicity. The dataset testing sizes ranged from 10 % to 100 % of the original dataset and were tested against the different machine learning algorithms. These training datasets were filled with randomly chosen images from the original dataset.

The tests showed that the Decision Tree machine learning algorithm achieved 86.6 % ethnicity detection rate. The worst machine learning algorithm was Random Forest which achieved 70 % ethnic accuracy identification rate. This is a variation of 6 % between the worst and best ethnic accuracy identification rate, as shown in Fig. 8.

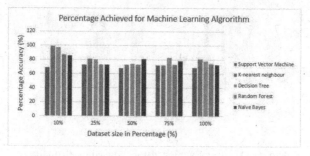

**Fig. 8.** Accuracy achieved for all six ethnicity

Table 2 shows the comparison between the results achieved by related works for ethnicity identification and our work for ethnicity identification. It is seen that the results obtained for Asian ethnicity identification were lower than that of Lu and Jain [2], possibly due the bigger size dataset used in this work.

**Table 2.** Comparison of related works results to our results for ethnicity identification

|  | Asian | African | African American | Asian Middle East | Caucasian | Other |
|---|---|---|---|---|---|---|
| Lu and Jain [2] | 97.7 % | - | - | - | - | - |
| Buchala et al. [3] | - | 80.2 % | 80.0 % | 83.1 % | 82.0 % | - |
| Tin and Sein [4] | - | - | - | - | - | 96.0 % |
| **Our Work** | **85.6 %** | **84.7 %** | **85.8 %** | **86.8 %** | **90.8 %** | **82.3 %** |

## 5  Conclusion

This paper presented a component-based ethnicity identification from facial images using machine learning algorithms. The ethnicities that were identified were Asian, African, African American, Asian Middle East, Caucasian and

Other. The feature vector that was obtained were Haralick Texture Moments for the forehead, Left cheek and right cheek. Zernike Moments was used for the right eye and LBP for the left eye. Gabor Filter for the Mouth and 7 Hu Moments for the chin, mouth and nose, which is fused and normalized to obtain results. African ethnicity identification rate achieved 84.7 % with Naïve Bayes, 85.8 % was achieved with Decision Tree achieved for African American ethnicity identification rate. Naïve Bayes achieved 85.6 % for Asian ethnicity identification rate, K-Nearest Neighbor Classification achieved 86.8 % for Asian Middle East ethnicity identification rate. 90.8 % was achieved for Caucasian ethnicity identification rate with Random Forest achieved and K-Nearest Neighbor Classification achieved a 82.3 % for Other ethnicity identification rate. This research achieved a total ethnicity identification rate of 86.6 %.

# References

1. Lu, X.: Image analysis for face recognition. Personal notes, 5 May (2003)
2. Lu, X., Jain, A.K.: Ethnicity identification from face images. In: Defense and Security, International Society for Optics and Photonics, pp. 114–123 (2004)
3. Buchala, S., Davey, N., Gale, T.M., Frank, R.J.: Principal component analysis of gender, ethnicity, age, and identity of face images. In: Proceedings of IEEE ICMI (2005)
4. Tin, H.H.K., Sein, M.M.: Race identification for face images. ACEEE Int. J. Inform. Tech. 1(02) (2011)
5. Mulcahy, C.: Image compression using the haar wavelet transform. Spelman Sci. Math. J. 1(1), 22–31 (1997)
6. Teague, M.R.: Image analysis via the general theory of moments. JOSA 70(8), 920–930 (1980)
7. Berisha, S.: Image classification using gabor filters and machine learning (2009)
8. Salah, S.H., Du, H., Al-Jawad, N.: Fusing local binary patterns with wavelet features for ethnicity identification. In: Proceedings of IEEE International Conference on Signal Image Process, vol. 21, pp. 416–422 (2013)
9. Domingos, P.: A few useful things to know about machine learning. Commun. ACM 55(10), 78–87 (2012)
10. Lowd, D., Domingos, P.: Naive bayes models for probability estimation. In: Proceedings of the 22nd International Conference on Machine Learning, pp. 529–536. ACM (2005)
11. Belhumeur, P.N., Hespanha, J.P., Kriegman, D.J.: Eigenfaces vs. fisherfaces: recognition using class specific linear projection. IEEE Trans. Pattern Anal. Mach. Intell. 19(7), 711–720 (1997)
12. Phillips, P.J., Wechsler, H., Huang, J., Rauss, P.J.: The feret database and evaluation procedure for face-recognition algorithms. Image Vis. Comput. 16(5), 295–306 (1998)
13. Milborrow, S., Morkel, J., Nicolls, F.: The MUCT landmarked face database. In: Pattern Recognition Association of South Africa (2010)
14. Samaria, F.S., Harter, A.C.: Parameterisation of a stochastic model for human face identification. In: Proceedings of the Second IEEE Workshop on Applications of Computer Vision, pp. 138–142. IEEE (1994)

# Human Detection in Low Resolution Thermal Images Based on Combined HOG Classifier

Sebastian Budzan[✉]

Institute of Automatic Control, Silesian University of Technology, Gliwice, Poland
Sebastian.Budzan@polsl.pl

**Abstract.** The human detection in real environment is important task of the computer vision, especially if we take into account thermal imagery. Most of the recent methods are based on the low-level features or body parts detection or combination. Method proposed in this paper uses combination of modified Histogram of Oriented Gradients (HOG) with detection of the human head. The minimal distance classifier has been used to improve the reduction of the human candidates process. The experiments have been performed on thermal images taken in real environment in different scenario such as missing body parts, overlapped people, different pose, far and near distance to the human, small groups of people, large groups of the people. The performance of the proposed algorithm has been evaluated using *Precision* and *Recall* quality measure with comparison to the selected reference methods.

## 1 Introduction

Human and pedestrian detection is growing part of computer vision, especially when we take into account large range of applications where the human detection can be applied. In practice human detection process is difficult due to many elements that can impact the detection result e.g. different human pose, moving peoples, size, appearance, colour, dressing style, time of day, variable lighting, different types of the cameras, camera perspective, resolution of the camera, distance to the human, fast changing background, also the environment in which a human being present. In recent years many solutions of this problem have been proposed which are based on low-level features, gradients, shape, gait analysis, geometric matching, contours, skin color, detection of the body parts. One of the most fundamental reason of growing interest in this computer vision area is a wide range of the application, due to rapid hardware evolution such as smart–phones, microprocessors, real–time boards, night vision systems, 3D cameras and thermal cameras. One of the human detection fundamental goal is recognition of pedestrians in real–time traffic. Only in 2014 year in Poland [1] 8940 peoples were hitted by a car in which 1104 peoples were killed and 8339 were injured. In the same year pedestrians were reason of 3050 accidents which in 565 of them were killed, generally accidents between drivers and pedestrians subside only to accidents between two or more cars, especially side impact.

© Springer International Publishing AG 2016
L.J. Chmielewski et al. (Eds.): ICCVG 2016, LNCS 9972, pp. 304–315, 2016.
DOI: 10.1007/978-3-319-46418-3_27

Commonly pedestrian detection systems have a few phases [2]. Generally a training phase and a classification phase. In the first phase the features of the human are extracted from reference dataset such as INRIA database for visual images. In second step the created feature vector are used to build decision function during classification process. Usually, the process of human detection is more detailed. First, the image must be acquired – with different type of the cameras with different parameters. Next, the preprocessing step should be performed which increase the quality of the image. In the next step, all of the required features of the human should be calculated and classification should be performed. On the Fig. 1 have been presented images with some of the disadvantages which should be taken into account during algorithms development.

**Fig. 1.** Images with complex foreground from INRIA dataset (top), thermal images with common situations in different scenario (bottom): many peoples in the scene (left), only top part of the body (middle), low resolution peoples (right)

Nowadays, human detection algorithms find applications in many fields [3], for example traffic systems to counting people, sport activities, rehabilitation, video games, biometrical identification systems, also give us many useful information [4], such as identification of human position, state, motion direction, gesture recognition, 3D modelling of the human body. However most important goal of the recent activities in this field is safety improvement [5]. Many of the cars manufacturers working on the pedestrian collision systems which themselves are stopping the car or warn the driver in a probable collision with a pedestrian. Some proposed solutions are also equipped with the functionality to predict collisions under the dynamic movements of passers-by and the analysis of their behavior.

This paper is organized as follows. In Sect. 2, the review of previous studies related to the human detection in visual and thermal images has been described.

In Sect. 3 the proposed method which combine HOG and human head modelling has been described. The experimental results obtained on thermal images database can be found in Sect. 4. Finally, the conclusions are presented in Sect. 5.

## 2    Related Work

There are numerous studies and approaches related to human and pedestrian detection. Most of the proposed human detection methods are developed to processing images taken by cameras working in visible spectrum. Although, they may be used with some modification to process also images taken from other modalities such as infrared or 3D cameras. Thermal images have several differences regarding to the well known visible images e.g. they include the distribution of temperatures of the human in taken picture – it can be used in the algorithm, because the distribution of the temperature on the body stands among other objects in environment, in consequence the method of detection human in infrared should based on thermal distribution, some region features, shape of the detected objects, also the difference betwen human and other objects.

In recent years numerous algorithms have been developed and proposed. Generally, methods of human detection can be also categorized into a two main groups, such as single images processing and sequence of images. In the listed method most of them are based on region of interest selection, low-level features vector, gait analysis, motion analysis, shapelet features, detection of the body parts, background modelling, Haar-like features, SVM or AdaBoost classifier. One of the most popular method is based on modelling of the human body in some of the region of interest such as body parts. The final results of the human detection depends on correct detection of the individual body parts such as head, hands, legs. Review of the existing literature in this area show, that the body part which is the most loaded with wrong identification are human legs. Segmentation of the body method is presented in [6]. Authors proposed an approach for human identification by using body prior and the generalized Earth Mover's Distance (EMD). The human body is divided into three parts: legs, trunk and head. Next, the each body parts are weighted and the distance to the middle of the body is calculated. An approach based on the assumption that an individual's walking style is unique and can be used to gait analysis has been presented in [4]. The proposed method characterizes gait in terms of a gait signature computed directly from the sequence of silhouettes. First, the background modelling is done. Next, the moving objects are segmented using the background subtraction algorithm and the morphological skeleton operator is used to track the moving silhouettes of a walking figure. Finally, the persons identity is determined by training and testing using Modified Independent Component Analysis (MICA) on the extracted feature vectors.

Feature extraction of the human body is another solution proposed in the literature. Most popular methods of detecting people on images was proposed by N. Dalal and B. Triggs [7]. Their algorithm focuses on low level features described as HOG (Histogram of Oriented Gradients) which uses the information on the intensity of the gradient for the featured nine directions (0–180°). It is possible to analyze the share of the pixels in the certain cell on the defined gradient direction. Image for the analysis is searched by the window of detection with size $64 \times 128$ pixels, which are in the next steps divided for square blocks with size 16 pixels. Next, they are divided into 4 cells in system $2 \times 2$ with size $8 \times 8$ pixels. Each cell have 9 features, which with the features calculated in the other cells create input of the Support Vector Machine (SVM) classifier. The proposed method is not very efficient in terms of processing time. This is due to the fact that each detection window of size $64 \times 128$ require 3780 pixels features to calculate the characteristics in order to classify the window to the appropriate class. To improve the processing time linear SVM classifier with e.g. cascade classifier [8] has been used. Authors developed in their paper integration the cascade–of–rejectors approach with the Histograms of Oriented Gradients features to achieve a fast and accurate human detection system. Using AdaBoost for feature selection, they identify the appropriate set of blocks, from a large set of possible blocks. Another method which based on HOG algorithm was developed by Watanabe, Ito and Yokoi [9]. The authors proposes a method for extracting feature descriptors consisting of co–occurrence histograms of oriented gradients (CoHOG). Including co–occurrence with various positional offsets, the feature descriptors can express complex shapes of objects with local and global distributions of gradient orientations. Local Binary Pattern (LBP) has been used to improve HOG in [10]. Method proposed by the authors is classic two–stage cascade, where on the first stage the features of the all regions are extracted with special consideration regions with pedestrians only. In the second stage HOG-LBP classifier is used to select some of the candidates from the first stage.

Most of the above described methods can be used only in visible range and for static 2D images. Another approach is the use of 3D information [11], RGB–D images [12] or infrared [13]. Human detection by infrared camera installed in a car as a part of a driver assistance system has been presented first time in [14]. Infrared imaging is an interesting method used in many other scientific areas such as fluid flow [15], device testing [16] or non–destructive testing [17]. Infrared human detection is based mainly on localization of warm symmetrical objects with specific aspect ratio and size. The filtering process to avoid a number of false positives is performed to select only pedestrians. Finally, validation procedure based on human morphological and thermal characteristics is performed. Another detection and tracking algorithm in real–time has been presented in [18]. The foreground segmentation with a Gaussian background model and tracking step based on connected components intersections is performed. The cascade of boosted classifiers based on Haar wavelets is used to classification. The authors of [19] identified many problems regarding to the infrared human detection such as low image resolution, low contrast and the large noises of thermal images, influence of the high temperature of backgrounds during the day [20]. The proposed algorithm consists of four main steps. First, filtering procedures based on maximum gray level, size filtering and region erasing are applied to remove the human areas from the background image. Next, the human candidate regions in the image are located, also some of the regions are merged, especially those in which are more than two human regions. Finally, the candidate human regions are removed based on ratio of the height and width of the region. Another method of night-time pedestrian detection using far–infrared camera has been presented in [21]. Proposed method consists of two main steps, regions of interest generation and pedestrian recognition in a cascade. Authors proposed pixel–gradient oriented vertical projection to estimate the input image with modified HOG for more effective pedestrian representations by capturing both the local object shape and its pyramid spatial layout.

# 3 Proposed Method

Thermal images have a few important advantages such as temperature values and its distribution or greater contrast between human and foreground than in visual images. In most traffic situations, foreground of the human will vary if we take temperature values – presented on the thermal image as lighter or darker regions. The thermal images help in human recognition with success at dark night, fog, even rain. Unfortunately, thermal images have some disadvantages such as commonly lower resolution, higher value of the noise, also the price is still much higher than visible light cameras. The presented algorithm is a part of the research focused on pedestrian detection in traffic using smartphone's thermal cameras, thus both the images database and the proposed algorithm have been created regarding to this assumption.

Generally, the novelty of the proposed method is based on the combination of two different approaches – HOG features and human body parts modelling (Fig. 2). Histogram of Oriented Gradients have some disadvantages such as rough detection of people in complex images, large computational complexity regarding to the real–time applications, on the other hand HOG produces very good results for images where people are separated from foreground. Human body parts modelling is used for high resolution images which is based on the combination of the recognized body parts such as legs and hands. Taking into account thousands of the human thermal images (Fig. 3), head is one of the distinctive

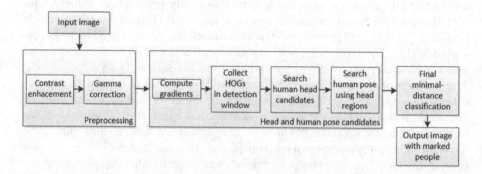

**Fig. 2.** Scheme diagram of the proposed method

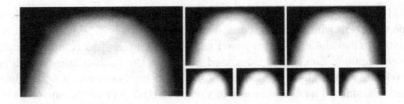

**Fig. 3.** Averaged thermal image of the human head on different scale

part of the human body, more effective than in visual images and more human position independent. The model of the head can be used on the different scales depeneding on the distance between human and the camera.

First, the preprocessing step is performed which increase the overall quality of the image. This step is based on changing the contrast and gamma correction. In cosequence, people contrast to the background will be increased and the background objects will be reduced. In second step the proposed modified HOG is performed. Commonly HOG uses 9 features representing possible gradient directions from range 0–180°, those 9 features are used to determination the cell values for HOG algorithm. One of the presented novelty of the proposed algorithm is calculation gradients with higher resolution – in the same range 0–180°, but with 1° step, what makes the algorithm more sensitive to the differences in the human pose, especially of the people near to the camera. In consequence, there is more possible directions discriminated. The cell size can be changed to the minimal squared $2 \times 2$ pixels, but for smaller cells the algorithm can produce too detailed results, which must be grouped during the classification step. Changing the cell size of HOG, will change also the sensitivity of the algorithm, because the algorithm will be sensitive to a different size of the human body regarding to the image. On the classification step both, the head and the human body candidates are examined with the rule: find the candidate head and then find possible human body candidate.

The gradient for all pixels in the image is determined, what generally lets to find similar regions in the image with similar temperature values and directions of the temperature changes, also the head and human model is recalculated into the gradient space. Gradient of the one pixel can be calculated using equation:

$$G(x,y) = \sqrt{G_x(x,y)^2 + G_y(x,y)^2} \tag{1}$$

where $G_x(x,y)$ and $G_y(x,y)$ are horizontal and vertical components of the gradient.

$$\theta = \arctan\left(\frac{G_y(x,y)}{G_x(x,y)}\right) \tag{2}$$

where $G(x,y)$ is the result gradient for pixel $(x,y)$, $\theta$ is an orientation of the gradient.

All of the detected human candidates must be classified into one of the group: pedestrian or non-pedestrian. In most recent publication authors proposes usage of SVM classifier which produces good results, but the complexity is high, e.g. for one detection window with dimensions $64 \times 128$ pixels 3780 features must be calculated. Thus the author proposed usage of the much less complex minimal distance classifier. Generally, calculated matrix of the probabilities, which contains regions with highest probability of human being is examined with minimal distance classifier. The classifier assign the detected object to the one of the predefined classes using information about distance between two sets of variables. Each of the image in the training set has been divided into cells, then gradient has been calculated in each cell, which in basic form has the same weight. If $X$ is the feature set of the detected object and $Y$ will be set of the model human being assignment X to the class k is determined as follows:

$$D(X, Y^{(k)}) = minD(X, Y^{(i)}, i = 1, ..., n) \tag{3}$$

where: $D$ – distance between $X$ and $Y$, $k$ – number of the predefined class, $n$ – number of the all defined classes ($n = 2$).

## 4    Experiments and Results

Using images in visual range there exists many of the prepared images databases such as INRIA, ETH, Daimler DB or Caltech. For thermal images well known database is an OTCBVS database with over 200 thermal images, but most of the images are taken from the far distance. For experiments presented in this paper a database of over 400 thermal images has been created. All of the images have been captured with a Wuhan-Guide TP8 IR camera. The camera is equipped with a 384–288 pixel uncooled FPA microbolometer. Its spectral range is 8–14 $\mu$m and thermal sensitivity is equal 0.08°C. The camera produces two main types of the files: temperature files and RGB files with in the selected color profile. The dataset images have been acquired generally in outdoor and indoor conditions, but for checking of the algorithm quality the images have been divided into a smaller group of images i.e. short distance between camera and human, long distance (over 10 meters), also images with least three people, at most three people, while body presented, some body parts missing, also one of the best for testing: images with people close to each other, generally, not separated. For teaching the classifier and calculation of the head model have been selected 100 thermal images with a human in frontal pose and 100 thermal images without a human.

The required thermal images are in raw format without any prior processing, in consequence thermal images contains many of the unnecessary features. Thermal cameras not register only the temperature of the examined object, but the ambient temperature, the temperature of the all objects in the scene which affect the main object, the temperature between camera lens and the examined object. The registered temperature in the pixel is a resultant of the mentioned temperatures. The dynamically changed scene also is the reason of some undesirable effects such as bluring effect, some body parts occlusion. We have possiblity to remove some of the mentioned features before registering the thermal images, e.g. the lower range value of the temperature can be set as 30°C to remove all of the objects with temperature less than assumed temperature. This method can be used for static images in stable conditions, but not for a dynamically changed scene, especially with people in traffic.

The quality of the algorithm can be evaluated using many of the quality measures, such as *missrate*, number of *FalsePositive* (*FP*), *FalseNegative* (*FN*), *TruePositive* (*TP*), also combination of last three, known as *Precision* and *Recall*, which are defined [12]. *Precision* give the information about how many of the images classified as human class contained a least one human. *Recall* estimate how many of the tested images contained at least one human have been classified as human class. The measures can be calculated as follows:

$$Precision = \frac{TP}{TP + FP} Recall = \frac{TP}{TP + FN} \tag{4}$$

where: $FP$ – False Positive, $FN$ – False Negative, $TP$ – True Positive.

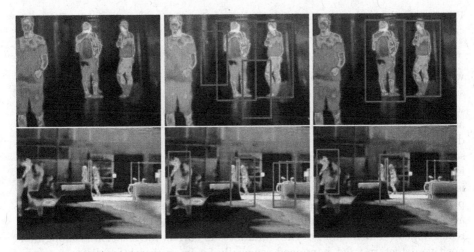

**Fig. 4.** Original thermal image (left), results image without preprocessing (middle), results image with preprocessing (right)

On the Fig. 4 have been presented result images of the human detection with and without preprocessing. The preprocessing step changes the contrast in the image, what can be seen especially on the left images where the number of the final rectangles is less than without preprocessing. Changing of the contrast using histogram alignment and gamma correction doesn't change the correct detection (true positive), but remove false positive one, true positive one are increased. The images (Fig. 4) show next advantage of the preprocessing and head classification process, namely people can be detected and localized with high accuracy, even the some body parts are missing (left–bottom image) when the people on the image take the small part referring to the entire size image.

On the Fig. 5 has been presented the main problem of all human detection algorithms with classification process. The classification procedure must deal

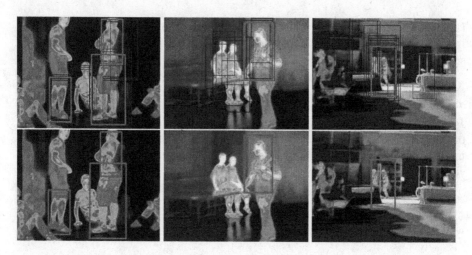

**Fig. 5.** Samples of human detection with poor localization results with all human candidates (top), after classification (bottom)

with large number of people which are on the the image - some of them are separated, also with distance between camera and human. At the first step of the most human detection algorithms the human candidates have been determined and considered at final classification step. On the presented figure the three different situations are presented and for all of them algorithm detected only some of the people, besides the localization of them are not correct, except left image, where people are smaller than on two first images. Mentioned result is caused by the detection process and the final classification. The detection process produces candidates for human – as it can be seen on left image; there are many of the possibile candidates, even in parts of the image where they do not really appear. The number of the candidates in correct localization is enough for positive detection what happened especially for images with far distance to the people. For images with people close to the camera we get only a few candidates for one human, thus even the final classification will be optimal the result will be poor. In the proposed method this problem has been taken into consideration and the minimal distance classification has been performed - this method increases the grouping of the candidates close to each other, also the preclassification process has been changed regarding to the human head assumption - of course the natural consequence of this assumption will be that the algorithm can detect only humans with head. Results can be seen on the Fig. 6, where the comparison with other methods has been presented.

Comparison to the other selected methods such as classic Histogram of Oriented Gradients or combination between HOG and LBP method is presented on the Fig. 6. On the top images have been presented final results of the detection – green rectangles for group of the people which are near distance to the camera and on the bottom the final result with marked human candidates for only one person far distance to the camera. Presented images have been selected especially

**Fig. 6.** Results images for HOG (left), HOG+LBP (middle) and Proposed (right)

to present the advantage of the proposed algorithm - one dataset with group of the people and second one with only one human. On the left images the results of the HOG have been presented. On the left–top image only the central human has been detected correctly and on the left-bottom the HOG doesn't detect the human, despite the human candidates have been detected, but for the classification step the number of detected candidates is to less for correct detection. On the middle images the results of the HOG–LBP algorithm have been presented. This algorithm have overall better quality of the detection process, what is consequence of the using LBP method for classification of the human candidates, but still some of the people are not recognized correctly on the top image. On the middle–bottom image correct detection result has been presented, but with some incorrect candidates. Results of the proposed algorithm have been preseented on the right image. The detection process at the first step produces better localized candidates what can be seen especially on the right-bottom image, at the same time the classification step produces generally greater number of the detected people.

All the results are summarized also on the Fig. 7, where the results for selected methods and proposed method have been presented. The results of the proposed method have been divided into to main groups: long distance and short distance. The results have been obtained for all of the images in the thermal dataset. The final results are better than for other methods, especially for a long distance dataset. Results for a short distance are also satisfactory. It is consequence of the combination of the head and human body model and proper classification procedure with minimal distance classifier.

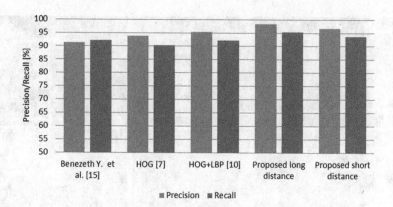

**Fig. 7.** Results for precision and recall for tested methods

## 5   Conclusions

In this paper has been presented a novel method for human detection in thermal images. Proposed method has been developed especially for thermal images registered in dynamically changed scene, e.g. for pedestrian detection. The major contribution of the proposed solution are: (1) combination of the HOG method with head modelling, (2) modification of the HOG procedure to more detailed, (3) classification with minimal distance classifier to reduce false detection. The people on the thermal images have some properties such as much more difference between human and background, better contrast to the other objects, other hand we should deal with other objects with shape similar to the human pose, overlapped people or people too far/near distance to the camera. Proposed algorithm gives good results, especially for complex images.

**Acknowledgment.** This work was supported by the Ministry of Science and Higher Education under grant BK/227/RAu1/2015 t. 7.

## References

1. Symon, E.: Road accidents in Poland 2014 (Wypadki drogowe w Polsce w 2014 roku). Polish National Police, pp. 1–86 (2015)
2. Chaquet, J.M., Carmona, E.J., Fernandez-Caballero, A.: A survey of video datasets for human action and activity recognition. Comput. Vis. Image Underst. **117**, 633–659 (2013)
3. Ouyang, Y., Zhang, S., Zhang, Y.: Based on cluster tree human action recognition algorithm for monocular video. J. Comput. Inf. Syst. **7**, 4082–4089 (2011)
4. Rani, M.P., Arumugam, G.: An efficient gait recognition system for human identification using modified ICA. Int. J. Comput. Sci. Inf. Technol. **2**, 55–67 (2010)
5. Cosma, C., Brehar, R., Nedevschi, S.: Pedestrians detection using a cascade of LBP and HOG classifiers. In: Proceedings of IEEE International Conference on ICCP, pp. 69–75 (2013)

 6. Ma, L., Yang, X., Xu, Y., Zhu, J.: Human identification using body prior and generalized EMD. In: Proceedings of 18th IEE International Conference on Image Process, pp. 1441–1444 (2011)
 7. Dalal, N., Triggs, B.: Histograms of oriented gradients for human detection. In: IEEE Computer Society Conference on Computer Vision and Pattern Recognition, pp. 1–8 (2005)
 8. Zhu, Q., Avidan, S., Yeh, M., Cheng, K.: Fast human detection using a cascade of histograms of oriented gradients. In: Proceedings of IEEE Conference on Computer Vision and Pattern Recognition (CVPR), pp. 1491–1498 (2006)
 9. Watanabe, T., Ito, S., Yokoi, K.: Co-occurrence histograms of oriented gradients for pedestrian detection. IPSJ Trans. Comput. Vis. Appl. **2**, 39–47 (2010)
10. Park, W.-J., Kim, D.-H., Lyuh, C.-G., Roh, T.M., Ko, S.-J.: Fast human detection using selective block-based HOG-LBP. In: IEEE International Conference on Image Processing, pp. 601–604 (2012)
11. Oliver, J., Albiol, A., Albiol, A.: 3D descriptor for people re-identification. In: International Conference on Pattern Recognition (ICPR), pp. 1395–1398 (2012)
12. Xia, L., Chen, C., Aggarwal, J.K.: Human detection using depth information by kinect. In: Computer Society Conference on Computer Vision and Pattern Recognition Workshops, pp. 15–22 (2011)
13. Zeng, J., Sayedelahl, A., Chouikha, M.F., Gilmore, E.T., Frazier, P.D.: Human detection in non-urban environment using infrared images. In: International Conference on Information, Communications and Signal Processing, pp. 1–4 (2007)
14. Bertozzi, M., Broggi, A., Fascioli, A., Graf, T., Meineckew, M.: Pedestrian detection for driver assistance using multiresolution infrared vision. Trans. Veh. Technol. **53**, 1666–1678 (2004)
15. Komisarczyk, A., Dziworska, G., Krucinska, I., Michalak, M., Strzembosz, W., Kaflak, A., Kaluza, M.: Visualisation of liquid flow phenomena in textiles applied as a wound dressing. Autex Res. J. **13**, 141–149 (2013)
16. Papagiannopoulos, I., Chatziathanasiou, V., Hatzopoulos, A., Kaluza, M., Wiecek, B., De Mey, G.: Thermal analysis of integrated spiral inductors. Infrared Phys. Technol. **56**, 80–84 (2013)
17. Dudzik, S.: Two-stage neural algorithm for defect detection and characterization uses an active thermography. Infrared Phys. Technol. **71**, 187–197 (2015)
18. Benezeth, Y., Emile, B., Laurent, H., Rosenberger, C.: A real time human detection system based on far infrared vision. In: Elmoataz, A., Lezoray, O., Nouboud, F., Mammass, D. (eds.) ICISP 2008. LNCS, vol. 5099, pp. 76–84. Springer, Heidelberg (2008). doi:10.1007/978-3-540-69905-7_9
19. Jeon, E.S., Choi, J.S., Lee, J.H., Shin, K.Y., Kim, Y.G., Le, T.T., Park, K.R.: Human detection based on the generation of a background image by using a far-infrared light camera. Sensors **19**, 6763–6788 (2015)
20. Budzan, S., Wyżgolik, R.: Noise reduction in thermal images. In: Chmielewski, L.J., Kozera, R., Shin, B.-S., Wojciechowski, K. (eds.) ICCVG 2014. LNCS, vol. 8671, pp. 116–123. Springer, Heidelberg (2014). doi:10.1007/978-3-319-11331-9_15
21. Liu, Q., Zhuang, J., Ma, J.: Robust and fast pedestrian detection method for far-infrared automotive driving assistance systems. Infrared Phys. Technol. **60**, 288–299 (2013)

# Kinect and IMU Sensors Imprecisions Compensation Method for Human Limbs Tracking

Grzegorz Glonek[(⊠)] and Adam Wojciechowski

Institute of Computer Science, Łódź University of Technology, Łódź, Poland
grzegorz@glonek.net.pl, adam.wojciechowski@p.lodz.pl

**Abstract.** Microsoft Kinect v.1 and inertial measurement units (IMU) became very popular and broadly available depth and inertia estimating devices, which allow home users to detect and track human limbs motion. Due to their working characteristics both of these devices are sufficient for casual scenarios, where precision is not a crucial factor. In the following paper a detailed review of their characteristics, verified by experiments of both devices, is presented, as well as the method of their imprecisions compensation. Comparing with other authors, the obtained limbs tracking accuracy improvement (by 12 %) has proved that elaborated method outperforms other solutions.

## 1 Introduction

Since Microsoft Kinect has been released in 2010 and inertial devices have become an integral and almost mandatory part of every smartphone, motion tracking and motion detection became very popular and easily available for the home usage. Kinect is mainly used in the field that it was created for games and entertainment. However, due to the limitations, mostly caused by the way it was built, only relatively simple casual games were developed for this controller. On the other hand, Microsoft Kinect became a popular subject for researchers, who want to find out how this device might be applied in more advanced scenarios [4,15].

The second of the mentioned devices – inertial measurement unit (IMU) – can be easily found in almost every modern smartphone. From home user's point of view, the most noticeable functionality, implemented thanks to these devices, is a screen view rotation. Also applications that measure number of pedestrian's steps base on them [11,29]. Of course, these devices also have some flaws and limitations that need to be taken into consideration in order to achieve accurate and stable results.

Mentioned controllers data fusion methods were also studied as to increase tracking performance compensating relative devices imprecisions [2,5,13,18]. Nevertheless authors have concentrated mostly on different types of Kalman filter raw data fusion rather then devices inherent characteristics correction.

© Springer International Publishing AG 2016
L.J. Chmielewski et al. (Eds.): ICCVG 2016, LNCS 9972, pp. 316–328, 2016.
DOI: 10.1007/978-3-319-46418-3_28

Basing on self experiments as well as on existing publications, presented paper describes thorough characteristics of both devices and propose a new method compensating their major imperfections and limits. Suggested method focuses on individual devices as well as on their fusion, what allows to compensate incompleteness of information that both types devices have.

## 2  Kinect Characteristics

Microsoft Kinect version 1 is an RGB-D camera built from two CMOS cameras and integrated infrared (IR) projector. One of these CMOS is responsible for an RGB signal and the second one is calibrated to record IR beam's view. However, the most important part is the main chip created by PrimeSense company, which is responsible for the body motion tracking and the body gesture recognition. The simplified device schema is presented in Fig. 1.

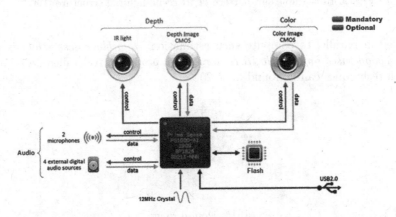

**Fig. 1.** Simplified Microsoft Kinect v.1controller build schema [12]

According to the official specification, an operation range of Kinect is between 0.8m and 4m in the field of view 57° horizontally (static) and 43° vertically. The specification doesn't include any information on the possible variety of measurements accuracy in this area. The range defined in the official specification is presented in Fig. 3. However, some users [26] and researchers [6] reported that different device series have a slightly different ranges where they operate, so above values should be treated as an average.

An important characteristic of Microsoft Kinect – object distance measurement – is directly related to the device design and used algorithm that bases on a structured light idea. Microsoft hasn't published any document describing how the algorithm actually works, but basing on original patent forms [8,24,25] and independent research, some rough description can be created [19], as well as an image of the used light pattern (1 out of 9 repeatable sub-patterns is presented in Fig. 2). Basing on the image of a structurally lighted scene, Kinect analyses the distortion of IR dots pattern to estimate objects' distance. Two techniques

**Fig. 2.** Repeatable sub-pattern of IR scene lighting structure [19]

are used in parallel to compute such estimation: *dots blurriness analysis* and *stereo-vision based on a single IR camera and a projector*. A detailed description of both techniques can be found in [7, 20].

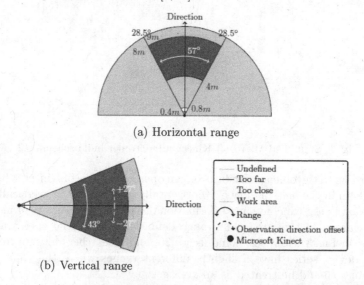

(a) Horizontal range

(b) Vertical range

**Fig. 3.** Microsoft Kinect v.1 work range

A human skeleton estimation is based on the previously estimated depth map and pattern recognition built on about 100 000 predefined samples. Pose classification process bases mostly on machine learning and random decision forest as well as some object detection algorithms i.e. Viola-Jones [22,23]. It is worth noticing that a signal recorded from an RGB camera is not used at all in the human skeleton estimation process.

One of the basic limitations of this device is the sun light sensitivity. Scene depth estimation relies on the IR light, whereas the sun light contains a full colours spectrum in both, visible and an invisible range. This causes a noise in the light pattern. The great example of the sun light impact on measurements can be found in [27]. That makes Kinect useless in outdoor scenarios and makes it difficult to use two or more Kinects simultaneously. However, despite Microsoft recommendation to not use multiple Kinect controllers in one room, scientists worked on and published methods on combining signals from several devices [1,14,21].

Other significant limitation is related to completeness of information gathered from the device. An inherent skeleton estimation algorithm retrieves positions of 20 joints and rotations of bones between these joints. However, every joint is reduced to a single point and bones rotations are estimated basing on these points, what results in the lack of information about rotation along the bone (roll).

Two other limitations: occlusions and variety of the depth measurements accuracy in the field of observation, are treated also as significant. The first one occurs when a part of user's body is covered by another object or is hidden behind any other body part (self-occlusion). When the occlusion happens, Kinect tries to estimate the location of the covered joint or stops tracking it, when it is not able to provide any rough estimation. The occlusion by an external object seems to be intuitive and doesn't require any additional explanation, but self-occlusion is connected with Kinect's sensitivity to user's rotation to the camera. The official specification mentions that Kinect is designed to work in a *face off pose*. However, this document doesn't define what *face off* means and what is the exact angle between the human and the device when the occlusion occurs. Self experiments allow to observe how measurements change when the user rotates in front of the camera. The angle $\alpha$ (Fig. 4) represents such a rotation and has been calculated with Eq. (1). It is also worth to mention that each joint can be in any of 3 tracking states:

- *Tracked* – set for fully visible, not noised joint with directly measured position.
- *Interfered* – joint which position can be estimated but not measured.
- *NotTracked* – joint which position cannot be measured nor estimated.

Occluded joints can be in *Interfered* or *NotTracked* state.

$$P_{Dev}.Z = P_{Dev_1}.Z - P_{Dev_2}.Z = 0$$
$$P_{Dev}.X = P_{Dev_1}.X - P_{Dev_2}.X = -1$$
$$P_{Sh}.Z = P_{Sh_L}.Z - P_{Sh_R}.Z$$
$$P_{Sh}.X = P_{Sh_L}.X - P_{Sh_R}.X$$
$$\alpha = \begin{cases} |atan(\frac{P_{Dev}.Z}{P_{Dev}.X}) - atan(\frac{P_{Sh}.Z}{P_{Sh}.X})| = atan(\frac{P_{Sh}.Z}{P_{Sh}.X}) & , P_{Sh}.X \neq 0 \\ |atan(\frac{P_{Dev}.Z}{P_{Dev}.X}) - \frac{\Pi}{2})| = \frac{\Pi}{2} & , P_{Sh}.X = 0 \end{cases}$$

$$(1)$$

where: $P_{Dev_1}.X, P_{Dev_1}.Z, P_{Dev_2}.X, P_{Dev_2}.Z$ – X and Z axes coordinates of Kinect camera. $P_{Sh_L}.X, P_{Sh_L}.Z$ – X and Z axes coordinates of user's left shoulder. $P_{Sh_R}.X, P_{Sh_R}.Z$ – X and Z axes coordinates of user's right shoulder.

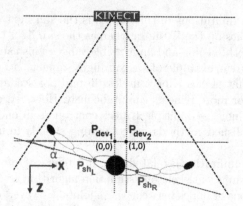

**Fig. 4.** Rotation angle $\alpha$ between user and Kinect

Charts form Figs. 5(a) and (b) show measured joints tracking states and elbow angle changes during rotation respectively. All the time, observed joint has been visible to the camera and its angle hasn't changed (rotation in "T-pose"). As we can see in Fig. 5(b), when angle is greater than 50° measurements turn to be unstable and unreliable.

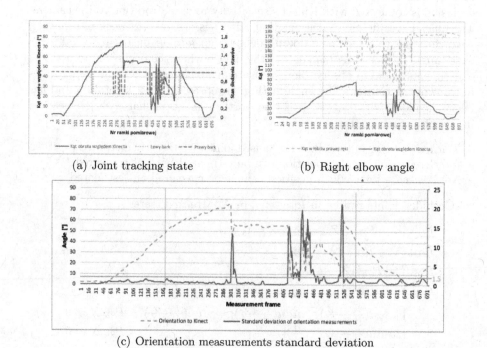

(a) Joint tracking state          (b) Right elbow angle

(c) Orientation measurements standard deviation

**Fig. 5.** Joints measurements reflecting user orientation changes in relation to the Kinect

Fluctuations in depth measurement accuracy have been observed in experiment with a professional Vicon Motion Capture system. During that experiment, the user had to move back in the distance from 0.8 m to 4 m from the camera and such distance has been measured by Kinect and Vicon simultaneously. The results show that in the close range Kinect slightly underestimates the distance and in the far range it overestimates it. The optimum is located at the distance of 2 m–2.3 m from the camera. Basing on measured values, model function has been estimated as the 3rd order polynomial ($y = a_0 + a_1x + a_2x^2 + a_3x^3$) calculated according to Eq. (2).

$$X = \begin{bmatrix} x_1^0 & x_1^1 & x_1^2 & x_1^3 \\ x_2^0 & x_2^1 & x_2^2 & x_2^3 \\ x_3^0 & x_3^1 & x_3^2 & x_3^3 \\ \dots \\ x_n^0 & x_n^1 & x_n^2 & x_n^3 \end{bmatrix}, A = \begin{bmatrix} a_0 \\ a_1 \\ a_2 \\ a_3 \end{bmatrix}, Y = \begin{bmatrix} y_0 \\ y_1 \\ y_2 \\ \dots \\ y_n \end{bmatrix} \tag{2}$$

$$X^T X A = X^T Y$$

where: $n$ – number of measured samples, $X$ – matrix of sample points arguments, $A$ – matrix of coefficients that need to be estimated, $Y$ – matrix of sample points values

Calculated matrix of coefficients has values as follow:

$$\begin{bmatrix} a_0 \\ a_1 \\ a_2 \\ a_3 \end{bmatrix} = \begin{bmatrix} -0.25 \\ 0.27 \\ -0.11 \\ 0.02 \end{bmatrix}$$

Estimated function that describes relation of distance measurement accuracy to the real user distance from Kinect is presented in Fig. 6.

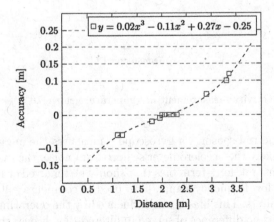

**Fig. 6.** Microsoft Kinect depth measurement accuracy by user distance

# 3    IMU Characteristics

IMU devices are in the professional usage for decades i.e. gyroscopes in rockets during II World War or in navigation systems in the aircrafts. Such devices became popular in home devices since they were implemented in MEMS architecture. In this article, all experiments were performed with the usage of IvenSense MPU-6050 module, which integrates accelerometer, gyroscope and thermometer on a single PCB. Both inertial sensors signals are affected by the external noise with different frequency characteristics and it needs to be filtered out to make these signals usable.

An accelerometer is a sensor responsible for a linear acceleration measurement in a form of the *g-force*, so the device at rest measures the force of $1g$ ($1g = 9.81 \frac{m}{s^2}$) in upwards direction. However, accelerometer measures every single temporary force that works on this device and this is treated as a high frequency noise. That means, the filter used to remove such incorrect data must be one of the low pass filters. Also the technology used to build such sensor – capacitive – results in the sensitivity to operating temperature changes. Such influence was the subject of some scientists' researches [9,10]. The same influence was also observed in the used device, during the experiment, when the device measured g-force in the temperature range $10°C - 50°C$. The results of these measurements are presented in Fig. 7. If the IMU device is placed on a human body, its temperature rises up to approx. $30°C$, so it requires some sort of the compensation. The temperature model formula can be estimated according to Eq. (2) as well.

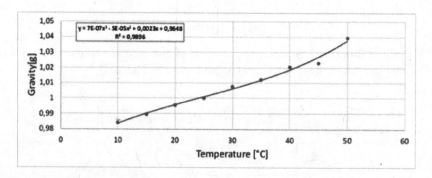

**Fig. 7.** Gravity measurement in temperature range $10°C - 50°C$

The second inertial sensor – a gyroscope – measures the angular velocity in *deg/s* units. Unlikely the accelerometer's short-term noise, the gyroscope suffers mostly from a constant, long-term bias that should be removed or limited. As this kind of noise is a low frequency signal, filter used to compensate it should be one of the high pass filters. This bias is also influenced by the operating temperature, however, there was no difference observed in filtered signals over the temperature range. It means that no additional compensation is required here.

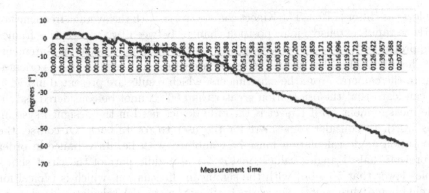

**Fig. 8.** Gyroscope drift in non moved device

In these types of devices we can also notice the incomplete information problem. The accelerometer, even though it measures forces along all 3 axes, allows us to calculate orientation around two of them only. The orientation (or the rotation) around the gravity vector is unmeasurable for such device. Theoretically, it is possible to calculate the orientation around all 3 axes with the gyroscope signal and its integration over the time. However, even the filtered signal contains some noise that grows rapidly due to the numerical integration and it quickly results in the significant drift that makes such measurements useless. Figure 8 shows how noise affects the motion drift. During measurements, device was laying on table without any move, however, due to the uncompensated noise, estimation shows it has nominally rotated about 60°.

# 4   Measurements Imperfections Compensation Method

## 4.1   Kinect

The compensation of Kinect measurements focuses on two aspects:

– reducing the distance estimation inaccuracy according to the known model
– filtering unreliable joints positions estimations

The first aspect can be improved by the correction of the depth value ("$z$" in Kinect's coordination space) by function $f(z)$ according to Eq. (3)

$$z' = f(z) = -0.02 * z^3 + 0.11 * z^2 - 0.27 * z + 0.25 \tag{3}$$

where: $z'$ – joint distance correction value.

This function is opposite to the function estimated from raw distance accuracy measurements, so adding it to the raw "$z$" value, reduces both: under- and overestimation.

The second problem – unreliable measurements filtration – can be reduced by the combination of few tools. First of all, joints positions should be filtered with the low pass filter (LPF). The Kinect camera works with the average frequency of 30 Hz so rapid, extensive joint position changes between two consecutive frames is improbable. If such phenomena appears, LPF will remove such measurement.

The other thing that should be taken into consideration is the user's orientation to the camera. From the experiments, which results are presented in Fig. 5, we can learn that the orientation greater than 50° cannot be considered as reliable measurement, so if Kinect is the only device used in the designed system, it is worth to consider some alert for the user to rotate back. Of course, the orientation angle calculation must be combined with i.e. its variance in order to prevent "false" angles values (in Fig. 5 the middle part of the chart shows values lower that 50°, but with the significant fluctuation, which is typical for unreliable measurements). For correct values the standard deviation is close to 0, as there are no rapid changes in measurements (Fig. 5(c)).

To summarize, decision if user's rotation to the Kinect is within reliable range takes into consideration following information:

– both shoulders have tracking state set to *Tracked*,
– orientation angle $\alpha$ is lower than 50°,
– standard deviation of last 5 measured orientation angles is lower than 1.5°.

## 4.2    Inertial Measurement Unit

The accelerometer and the gyroscope measurements are usually fused together in order to compensate the noise that affects both signals and to estimate the device orientation in the space. The most popular methods to achieve such fusion are Kalman filter [3,17] and lately, Madgwick filter [13]. The accuracy comparison of these two filters can be found in the literature i.e. [16]. Both of them can be described as a sort of complementary filters where two signals with low and high frequency noises are fused together with the proper noise reduction and some fusion factors. That allows to join together the same information from both sources with different level of importance. As the accelerometer signal needs to be filtered with LPF and its measurement is sensitive to the temperature, before it is fused with the gyroscope, the correction according to the temperature should be done. The regression analysis (Eq. (2)) allowed to estimate the formula of accelerometer signal correction, described with Eq. (4).

$$A' = \frac{A}{1 + \beta(T - T_0)} \tag{4}$$

where: $A'$ – corrected accelerometer measurement, $A$ – accelerometer measurement, $T$ – temperature measurement, $T_0$ – device reference operating temperature. For used device $T_0 = 25°C$, $\beta$ – correction factor. For used device $\beta = 0.0011$.

The results of such correction, influenced by different $\beta$ is presented in Fig. 9. Parameter $\beta$ has been estimated on sample measurements analysis and chosen based on average error between expected and actual values in each measurement point. Next, these signals can be used in the fusion filter.

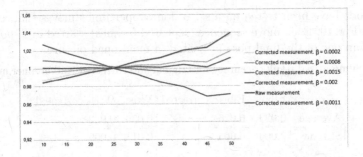

**Fig. 9.** Gravity measurement compensation due to the temperature and $\beta$ factor.

## 4.3   Information Incompleteness Correction

Compensation methods presented previously are able to improve the quality of data gathered from both types of devices, however, are not able to add the missing information about rotations (Kinect – roll – rotation along the bone; IMU – yaw – rotation around gravity vector). To achieve that, both signals: from Kinect and IMU must be fused together. Then, the combined data will include full set of information. In the literature there are presented several methods of Kinect and IMU data fusion [2, 13, 28] and each of them has different approach to such fusion and the different accuracy (Kalkbrener [13] declared standard deviation of the joint coordinates measurements of $\pm 2.20$ cm for *face off* trunk position). To verify influence of flaws described in this article, series of experiments has been performed with algorithm proposed by Kalkbrenner and implemented according to published description. Results returned by this implementation had slightly different accuracy than declared and they differed for both joints: $\pm 2.90$ cm for elbow and $\pm 3.60$ cm for wrist. Then, original method has been modified by adding IMU temperature and Kinect distance corrections as well as decreasing importance of Kinect measurements if user was considerably rotated to the camera.

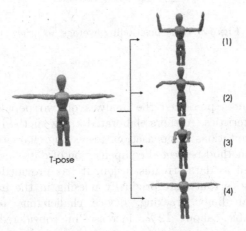

**Fig. 10.** Movement sequences performed during tests.

Methods have been tested on a set of four upper limbs moves that are presented in Fig. 10. Each move sequence (repeated 5 times) started in *T-pose* and ended up in one of the final pose presented in mentioned picture.

**Table 1.** Summarized results accuracy for original and corrected Kalkbrenner methods

|            | Elbow | Elbow corrected | Wrist | Wrist corrected |
|------------|-------|-----------------|-------|-----------------|
| Average    | 0.029 | 0.026           | 0.036 | 0.032           |
| Std. dev.  | 0.006 | 0.005           | 0.01  | 0.009           |

Average improvement of joints positioning accuracy has been noticed for about 12 %. Comparison of results of both methods has been presented in Table 1 and in Figs. 11 and 12.

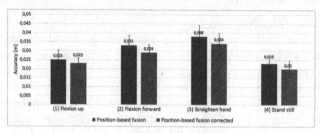

**Fig. 11.** Elbow positioning average accuracy

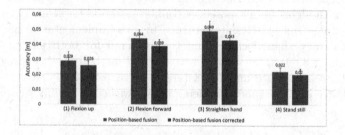

**Fig. 12.** Wrist positioning average accuracy

# 5 Summary

In this paper authors presented the analysis of two popular motion tracking devices characteristics. Authors elaborated a new method of measurements imprecision and limitations compensation, respecting characteristics of considered devices. The method respected compensation of data flaws for each device individually, as well as data streams fusion. It has provided set of estimated sensors characteristics that were originally missing in the individual devices. Aggregated, human limbs tracking, device challenging, experiments have revealed considerable, about 12 %, increase in considered joints tracking accuracy.

# References

1. Asteriadis, S., et al.: Estimating human motion from multiple Kinect sensors. In: Proceedings of 6th International Conference on Computer Vision/Computer Graphics Collaboration Techniques and Applications, MIRAGE 2013 (2013)
2. Bo, A.P., Lanari,et al.: Joint angle estimation in rehabilitation with inertial sensors and its integration with Kinect. In: Proceedings of the Annual International Conference of the IEEE Engineering in Medicine and Biology Society, EMBS/2011 (2011)
3. Caron, F., et al.: GPS/IMU data fusion using multisensor Kalman filtering: introduction of contextual aspects. Inf. Fusion **7**, 221–230 (2006)
4. Chang, Y.-J., et al.: A Kinect-based system for physical rehabilitation: a pilot study for young adults with motor disabilities. Res. Dev. Disabil. **32**(6), 2566–2570 (2011)
5. Destelle, F., et al.: Low-cost accurate skeleton tracking based on fusion of kinect and wearable inertial sensors. In: Proceedings of the 22nd European IEEE Signal Processing Conference (EUSIPCO), pp. 371–375 (2014)
6. DiFilippo, N.M., Jouaneh, M.K.: Characterization of different microsoft kinect sensor models. IEEE Sens. J. **15**(8), 4554–4564 (2015)
7. Fofi, D., Sliwa, T., Voisin, Y.: A comparative survey on invisible structured light. In: SPIE Electron. Imaging Machine Vision Applications in Industrial Inspection, XII, San José (2004)
8. Freedman, B., et al.: Depth mapping using projected patterns. Patent: 20100118123
9. Gebhardt, S., Scheinert, G., Uhlmann, F.H.: Temperature influence on capacitive sensor structures. In: Information Technology and Electrical Engineering - Devices and Systems, Materials and Technologies for the Future (2006)
10. Grigorie, M., de Raad, C., Krummenacher, F., Enz, C.: Analog temperature compensation for capacitive sensor interfaces (1996)
11. Jayalath, S., Murray, I.: A gyroscope based accurate pedometer algorithm. In: International Conference on Indoor Positioning and Indoor Navigation, p. 31, October 2013
12. iFixIt:Xbox 360 Kinect Teardown - iFixit. https://www.ifixit.com/Teardown/Xbox+360+Kinect+Teardown/4066. Accessed 12 Apr 2016
13. Kalkbrenner, C., et al.: Motion capturing with inertial measurement units and kinect - tracking of limb movement using optical and orientation information. In: Proceedings of the International Conference on Biomedical Electronics and Devices (2014)
14. Kitsikidis, A., et al.: Dance analysis using multiple kinect sensors (2011)
15. Lange, B., et al.: Interactive game-based rehabilitation using the Microsoft Kinect. In: 2012 IEEE Virtual Reality (VRW), pp. 171–172, March 2012
16. Madgwick, S.O.H.: An efficient orientation filter for inertial and inertial/magnetic sensor arrays (2010)
17. Mccarron, B.: Low-Cost IMU implementation via sensor fusion algorithms in the arduino environment (2013)
18. Feng, S., Murray-Smith, R.: Fusing kinect sensor and inertial sensors with multi-rate Kalman filter. In: IET Conference on Data Fusion Target Track. 2014 Algorithms Application (2014)
19. Reichinger, A.: Kinect pattern uncovered. https://azttm.wordpress.com/. Accessed 12 Apr 2016
20. Rzeszotarski, D., Strumiłło, P., et al.: System Obrazowania Stereoskopowego Sekwencji Scen Trójwymiarowych. Zesz. Nauk, Elektron (2006)

21. Schröder, Y., et al.: Multiple Kinect Studies Technical report (2011)
22. Shotton, J., et al.: Semantic texton forests for image categorization and segmentation. In: Proceedings of IEEE CVPR (2008)
23. Shotton, J., et al.: Real-time human pose recognition in parts from single depth images. In: Proceedings of IEEE CVPR (2011)
24. Shpunt, A., Zalevsky, Z.: Depth-varying light fields for three dimensional sensing. Patent: 20080106746
25. Shpunt, A.: Depth mapping using multi-beam illumination. Patent: 20100020078
26. Stackoverfow community: precision of the kinect depth camera. Accessed 12 Apr 2016
27. Suarez, J., Murphy, R.R.: Using the Kinect for search and rescue robotics. In: 2012 IEEE International Symposium on Safety, Security, and Rescue Robotics (SSRR) (2012)
28. Tian, Y., et al.: Upper limb motion tracking with the integration of IMU and Kinect. Neurocomputing **159**, 207–218 (2015)
29. Walklogger.     https://play.google.com/store/apps/details?id=com.walklogger.pedometer. Accessed 17 Apr 2016

# Face Photo-Sketch Transformation and Population Generation

Georgy Kukharev[1] and Andrei Oleinik[2(✉)]

[1] Saint Petersburg Electrotechnical University "LETI", St. Petersburg, Russia
[2] ITMO University, St. Petersburg, Russia
andrey_oleynik@niuitmo.ru

**Abstract.** The problem of the automatic recognition and processing of face photos and sketches is of significant importance for law enforcement applications. A photo-sketch transformation is a convenient way to reduce dissimilarities between a face sketch and a photo before employing one of the existing face recognition techniques. In this paper, we propose to generate a photo (sketch) population instead of a single image. This approach improves face recognition rate and reduces the effect of different appearance variations. The proposed method is based on the modified version of the Eigenface/Eigensketch approach. We carried out the experiments on the photo-sketch transformation and population generation. The obtained results confirm the capability of the proposed technique to transform sketches of various styles to photos and introduce an inter-population diversity that is sufficient to cover various face appearance deviations.

**Keywords:** Forensic sketch · Face recognition · Eigenface · Eigensketch · Face image population

## 1  Introduction

Today, the problem of the automatic comparison of face sketches and photos is of significant importance for law enforcement applications. Often, a face sketch is based on a subjective evidence obtained from a witness. Meanwhile, a photo of a suspect usually has a poor quality along with unpredictable pose and lighting variations. For these reasons, the correspondence between a face photo and a sketch is often ambiguous and depends on multiple uncontrollable factors. Thus, the majority of existing face recognition techniques cannot be directly applied for the photo-sketch recognition problem.

In order to reduce the undesired dissimilarity between sketches and photos, the photo-sketch transformation is performed. Depending on the particular case, one may prefer to convert a photo to a sketch or, alternatively, a sketch to a photo.

There are different kinds of sketches [1]: *Viewed Sketch* (drawn by an artist in the presence of the person or his/her photo), *Composite Sketch* (based on a testimony of an eyewitness and created by means of the primitives library), *Artist Sketch* (a digital picture modified by an artist) and *Composite Forensic Sketch* (a composite sketch created from a verbal portrait by a criminologist).

© Springer International Publishing AG 2016
L.J. Chmielewski et al. (Eds.): ICCVG 2016, LNCS 9972, pp. 329–340, 2016.
DOI: 10.1007/978-3-319-46418-3_29

Due to the diversity of sketch types, in many cases obtained results are valid only for a particular dataset or a drawing style. The ambiguity of the photo-sketch relationship typically reduces the synthesis quality and recognition rate. Thus, it is reasonable to generate a *population* of images instead of a single one [2,3].

In this paper, we propose a method for the photo-sketch population generation based on the modified version of the Eigensketch approach [4]. Random variations are introduced into the principal components of a generated photo/sketch, creating a population with semantically significant differences. Proposed solution allows both photo-to-sketch and sketch-to-photo transforms and does not directly use the training sample during the synthesis process. Moreover, we introduce a similar transformation approach based on two-dimensional Principal Component Analysis (2D PCA) [5].

We conduct the experiments on the *sketch-to-photo* transformation and photo population generation, since this operation is more challenging than the photo-to-sketch transformation and rarely considered in the literature. Of course, our solution may be used to perform the inverse operation as well.

Though various applications of the approach are possible, we assume it is the most suitable for the enhancement and modification of existing photo-sketch datasets as well as face hallucination. This will significantly increase their representativeness and improve the overall recognition rate.

## 2    Related Work

A straightforward way to perform a photo-sketch transformation is to use a set of facial components (e.g. mouths, noses and eyes) to synthesize a composite sketch [6]. Despite being simple, this technique is restricted to a limited set of possible sketches and allows solely photo-to-sketch transformation.

The 2D and 3D caricature synthesis technique based on Mean Value Coordinates [7] can be applied for the sketch synthesis problem as well. It provides a flexible way to transform different parameters of the face image, along with limited photo synthesis capabilities.

In [8], Embedded Hidden Markov Models (E-HMM) have been applied for the face information modeling. It is capable of capturing a nonlinear relationship between photos and sketches, but its potential is limited by the E-HMM structure.

A photo-sketch transformation method based on Markov Random Fields (MRF) concept [9,10] implies a division of face images into rectangular overlapping patches. These patches form a library that is employed to create new images, while MRF is used to maintain the coherence between different regions of the synthesized image. This method is capable of performing sketch-to-photo generation. However, it tends to disregard global features of a face causing artefacts and distortions.

One of the most perspective and versatile approaches is utilization of *subspace methods* such as *Principal Component Analysis* (PCA). With respect to the face recognition problem, this class of methods is often referred as *Eigenfaces* [11,12]. Later, the concept of *Eigensketches* have been introduced and subspace methods have been applied to perform the photo-sketch transformation [4,13,14]. Moreover, other powerful subspace methods like *Canonical Correlation Analysis* (CCA) and *Partial Least Squares* (PLS) have been utilized for processing and recognition of photo-sketch face images [15,16]. In contrast to the primitives library approach, subspace methods allow combination of different face parts into new ones. In addition, these techniques are capable of synthesizing both sketches and photos, providing extra flexibility. The weak points of subspace methods include their sensitiveness to shift and scale variations in processed images and the tendency to introduce blurring distortions into generated photos/sketches.

In this paper, we employ the modification of the approach [4]. According to that method, the sketch-to-photo transformation is performed as follows (the inverse operation is carried out in the similar way). The key idea is the *assumption of the similarity of photo and sketch eigenspaces*. Given a training set of face photos and corresponding sketches, following computations are carried out. On the training phase, eigenvalues and eigenvectors of the sketches' covariance and Gram matrices are evaluated. On the synthesis phase, a new sketch is represented as a linear combination of the sketches from the training set. Taking into account the aforementioned eigenspaces similarity assumption, the sketches in this linear combination are substituted with the corresponding photos. The summation of the weighted training photos finalizes the synthesis process.

## 3 Photo-Sketch Transformation and Population Generation

In this section we describe a method for the photo-sketch transformation and population generation. As a basic algorithm, we employ the modification of the technique presented in [4] that does not explicitly use the training set during the synthesis process. Further, we extend it to gain the population generation capability.

For the sake of brevity and clarity we further describe only the sketch-to-photo transformation algorithm. The inverse (photo-to-sketch) procedure is carried out in the similar way by swapping sketches and photos.

Table 1 presents principal notations used in this paper. Figure 1 summarizes the procedure of sketch-photo population generation.

First, the sketch and photo images from the training dataset are converted into vectors by concatenating their rows (or columns). These vectors are combined into the data matrices $\mathbf{S}$ and $\mathbf{P}$.

The transformation is performed on the *centered* data matrices $\bar{\mathbf{S}}$ and $\bar{\mathbf{P}}$, which are computed by subtracting the mean sketch $\mathbf{m_S}$ and the mean photo $\mathbf{m_P}$ from the each column of the corresponding data matrices $\mathbf{S}$ and $\mathbf{P}$.

The centered sketch data matrix $\bar{\mathbf{S}}$ can be represented as a product of the three matrices by means of *Singular Value Decomposition* (SVD):

$$\bar{\mathbf{S}} = \mathbf{U_S}\mathbf{\Lambda_S}^{\frac{1}{2}}\mathbf{V_S^\top}. \tag{1}$$

**Table 1.** Principal notations.

| Notation | Meaning |
|---|---|
| $K$ | number of photo-sketch pairs in the dataset |
| $M$ | number of images' rows |
| $N$ | number of images' columns |
| $L$ | the desired number of images in the generated population |
| $\mathbf{S}$ | $MN \times K$ sketch matrix |
| $\mathbf{P}$ | $MN \times K$ photo matrix |
| $\mathbf{m_S}$ | mean sketch |
| $\mathbf{m_P}$ | mean photo |
| $\mathbf{\bar{S}}$ | $MN \times K$ sketch matrix centered relative to $\mathbf{m_S}$ |
| $\mathbf{\bar{P}}$ | $MN \times K$ photo matrix centered relative to $\mathbf{m_P}$ |
| $\mathbf{U_S}$ | $MN \times K$ matrix of eigenvectors of the covariance matrix $\mathbf{\bar{S}\bar{S}}^\top$ |
| $\mathbf{\Lambda_S}$ | $K \times K$ diagonal matrix of eigenvalues of the Gram matrix $\mathbf{\bar{S}}^\top\mathbf{\bar{S}}$ |
| $\mathbf{V_S}$ | $K \times K$ matrix of eigenvectors of the Gram matrix $\mathbf{\bar{S}}^\top\mathbf{\bar{S}}$ |
| $\mathbf{T_{SP}}$ | $MN \times K$ sketch-to-photo transformation matrix |
| $\mathbf{S_{new}}$ | column vector with $MN$ elements, obtained by concatenating rows (or columns) of a new sketch image |
| $\mathbf{\bar{S}_{new}}$ | column vector with $MN$ elements, obtained by centering the matrix $\mathbf{S_{new}}$ relative to $\mathbf{m_S}$ |
| $\mathbf{J}$ | column vector with $K$ elements, denoting the projection of $\mathbf{\bar{S}_{new}}$ |
| $\xi_l$ | a random column vector with $K$ elements |
| $\mathbf{\tilde{H}}$ | $K \times L$ matrix, containing modified versions of $\mathbf{J}$ in its columns |
| $\mathbf{\bar{P}_{pop}}$ | $MN \times L$ photo population matrix centered relative to $\mathbf{m_P}$ |
| $\mathbf{P_{pop}}$ | $MN \times L$ photo population matrix |

In most of the cases $K < MN$ and thus the covariance matrix $\mathbf{\bar{S}\bar{S}}^\top$ is singular. Therefore, it is reasonable to compute $\mathbf{V_S}$ and $\mathbf{\Lambda_S}$ as eigenvectors and eigenvalues of the Gram matrix $\mathbf{\bar{S}}^\top\mathbf{\bar{S}}$, which is unlikely to be singular. The matrix $\mathbf{U_S}$ containing $K$ eigenvectors of the covariance matrix is expressed as

$$\mathbf{U_S} = \mathbf{\bar{S}}\left(\mathbf{V_S}\mathbf{\Lambda_S}^{-\frac{1}{2}}\right). \tag{2}$$

This procedure is essentially PCA performed on the sketch set.

Next, we adopt the assumption of the *similarity of the sketch and photo eigenspaces' structures*, which has been proposed in [4]. In [4], the authors obtain a representation of a sketch $\mathbf{\bar{S}_{new}}$ as a linear combination of the training sketches stored in $\mathbf{\bar{S}}$. Then, they replace $\mathbf{\bar{S}}$ with $\mathbf{\bar{P}}$, achieving a desired estimate of the photo $\mathbf{\bar{P}_{new}}$. In this paper, we do not explicitly use the training set at the syn-

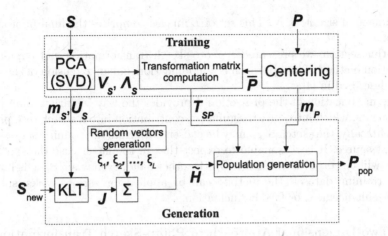

**Fig. 1.** Illustration of sketch-photo transformation and population generation process.

thesis stage, but employ a *sketch-to-photo transformation matrix*, defined as:

$$\mathbf{T_{SP}} \overset{\text{def}}{=} \bar{\mathbf{P}} \left( \mathbf{V_S \Lambda_S}^{-\frac{1}{2}} \right). \tag{3}$$

Similarly to $\mathbf{U_S}$, the matrix $\mathbf{T_{SP}}$ contains a set of $K$ vectors as its columns. These vectors can be considered as a "combined" sketch-photo basis. It can be used to approximately restore a photo from a vector in the sketch eigenspace.

*Remark.* In our version, we do not explicitly use the training set on the synthesis phase and compute the matrix $\mathbf{T_{SP}}$ instead. In the case of large $K$, it may be beneficial to reject the columns of $\mathbf{U_S}$ and $\mathbf{T_{SP}}$, corresponding to the small eigenvalues. This will reduce computational costs of the algorithm without any significant loss of the synthesis quality.

Since the matrices $\mathbf{U_S}$ and $\mathbf{T_{SP}}$ are computed, the population synthesis may be carried out as follows. For a new (centered) sketch $\bar{\mathbf{S}}_{\text{new}}$, a projection $\mathbf{J}$ on the eigenspace is computed by means of *Karhunen-Loève Transform* (KLT):

$$\mathbf{J} = \mathbf{U_S^\top \bar{S}_{\text{new}}}. \tag{4}$$

To generate a population instead of a single photo, we introduce random variations into $\mathbf{J}$ by generating $L$ random vectors $\xi_l$ and adding them to $\mathbf{J}$. As a result, we obtain a matrix of "noised" projections $\tilde{\mathbf{H}}$:

$$\tilde{\mathbf{H}} = [\mathbf{J} + \xi_1, \ \mathbf{J} + \xi_2, \ \dots, \ \mathbf{J} + \xi_L]. \tag{5}$$

The population is generated by means of multiplication by $\mathbf{T_{SP}}$:

$$\bar{\mathbf{P}}_{\text{pop}} = \mathbf{T_{SP}} \tilde{\mathbf{H}}. \tag{6}$$

The resulting photo population matrix $\mathbf{P}_{\text{pop}}$ is restored by adding the mean photo $\mathbf{m_P}$ to each column of $\bar{\mathbf{P}}_{\text{pop}}$. Further, each column of $\mathbf{P}_{\text{pop}}$ is converted to an image of size $M \times N$. This set of $L$ images comprises the final photo population.

In this section, we presented a photo-sketch transformation and population generation method. This approach is a modification and an extension of the technique described in [4].

The modification of the projection $\mathbf{J}$ provides the way to variate only those components, which introduce a significant contribution into a sketch or a photo.

Technically, the sketch $\mathbf{S}_{\text{new}}$ may be chosen both from the training set or some different source. It is reasonable to expect that in the latter case the synthesis quality will be considerably lower. On the other hand, even when $\mathbf{S}_{\text{new}}$ is limited to the training dataset, the method can be applied for various tasks, such as dataset enhancement or face hallucination.

## 3.1   Two-Dimensional Approach to Photo-Sketch Transformation

2D PCA/2D KLT method involves computation of two eigenbases (for the image rows and columns) and evaluation of two-dimensional Karhunen-Loève Transform [5]. This approach does not require conversion of images to vectors.

In this subsection, $\mathbf{p}_1, \ldots, \mathbf{p}_K$ and $\mathbf{s}_1, \ldots, \mathbf{s}_K$ denote two sets of *centered* $M \times N$ photos and sketches. We define row and column data matrices as follows:

- $\mathbf{P}_{\text{col}} = (\mathbf{p}_1 \cdots \mathbf{p}_K)$ of size $M \times NK$;
- $\mathbf{S}_{\text{col}} = (\mathbf{s}_1 \cdots \mathbf{s}_K)$ of size $M \times NK$;
- $\mathbf{P}_{\text{row}} = (\mathbf{p}_1^\top \cdots \mathbf{p}_K^\top)$ of size $N \times MK$;
- $\mathbf{S}_{\text{row}} = (\mathbf{s}_1^\top \cdots \mathbf{s}_K^\top)$ of size $N \times MK$.

2D PCA seeks the solutions of the eigenproblems for two covariance matrices: $\mathbf{S}_{\text{col}}\mathbf{S}_{\text{col}}^\top$ and $\mathbf{S}_{\text{row}}\mathbf{S}_{\text{row}}^\top$. Thus, we obtain the eigenvector matrices $\mathbf{U}_{\mathbf{S}_{\text{col}}}$ ($M \times M$) and $\mathbf{U}_{\mathbf{S}_{\text{row}}}$ ($N \times N$) along with the corresponding eigenvalue matrices $\mathbf{\Lambda}_{\mathbf{S}_{\text{col}}}$ and $\mathbf{\Lambda}_{\mathbf{S}_{\text{row}}}$. The eigenvector matrices $\mathbf{V}_{\mathbf{S}_{\text{col}}}$ ($NK \times M$) and $\mathbf{V}_{\mathbf{S}_{\text{row}}}$ ($MK \times N$) for the Gram matrices $\mathbf{S}_{\text{col}}^\top\mathbf{S}_{\text{col}}$ and $\mathbf{S}_{\text{row}}^\top\mathbf{S}_{\text{row}}$ are expressed as follows:

$$\mathbf{V}_{\mathbf{S}_{\text{col}}} = \mathbf{S}_{\text{col}}^\top \mathbf{U}_{\mathbf{S}_{\text{col}}} \mathbf{\Lambda}_{\mathbf{S}_{\text{col}}}^{-\frac{1}{2}}, \tag{7}$$

$$\mathbf{V}_{\mathbf{S}_{\text{row}}} = \mathbf{S}_{\text{row}}^\top \mathbf{U}_{\mathbf{S}_{\text{row}}} \mathbf{\Lambda}_{\mathbf{S}_{\text{row}}}^{-\frac{1}{2}}. \tag{8}$$

In the same way as is done in the one-dimensional case, we replace $\mathbf{S}_{\text{col}}$ with $\mathbf{P}_{\text{col}}$ and $\mathbf{S}_{\text{row}}$ with $\mathbf{P}_{\text{row}}$. As a result, we obtain two transformation matrices:

$$\mathbf{T}_{\mathbf{SP}_{\text{col}}} \overset{\text{def}}{=} \mathbf{P}_{\text{col}} \left( \mathbf{V}_{\mathbf{S}_{\text{col}}} \mathbf{\Lambda}_{\mathbf{S}_{\text{col}}}^{-\frac{1}{2}} \right) \overset{(7)}{=} \mathbf{P}_{\text{col}} \mathbf{S}_{\text{col}}^\top \mathbf{U}_{\mathbf{S}_{\text{col}}} \mathbf{\Lambda}_{\mathbf{S}_{\text{col}}}^{-1}, \tag{9}$$

$$\mathbf{T}_{\mathbf{SP}_{\text{row}}} \overset{\text{def}}{=} \mathbf{P}_{\text{row}} \left( \mathbf{V}_{\mathbf{S}_{\text{row}}} \mathbf{\Lambda}_{\mathbf{S}_{\text{row}}}^{-\frac{1}{2}} \right) \overset{(8)}{=} \mathbf{P}_{\text{row}} \mathbf{S}_{\text{row}}^\top \mathbf{U}_{\mathbf{S}_{\text{row}}} \mathbf{\Lambda}_{\mathbf{S}_{\text{row}}}^{-1}. \tag{10}$$

The operation of two-dimensional projection of a new sketch $\mathbf{s}_{\text{new}}$ is implemented as $\mathbf{J}_{rc} = \mathbf{U}_{\mathbf{S}_{\text{col}}}^\top \mathbf{s}_{\text{new}} \mathbf{U}_{\mathbf{S}_{\text{row}}}$. The photo reconstruction is performed as $\tilde{\mathbf{P}} = \mathbf{T}_{\mathbf{SP}_{\text{col}}} \mathbf{J}_{rc} \mathbf{T}_{\mathbf{SP}_{\text{row}}}^\top$.

Photo-to-sketch transformation matrices $\mathbf{T}_{\mathbf{PS}_{\text{col}}}$ and $\mathbf{T}_{\mathbf{PS}_{\text{row}}}$ can be obtained in a similar way. Furthermore, introduction of random noise into the projection $\mathbf{J}_{rc}$ leads to the two-dimensional photo-sketch population generation method.

## 4   Experimental Results

We performed the sketch-photo transformation and population generation experiments on CUHK Face Sketch Database (CUFS) and CUHK Face Sketch FERET Database (CUFSF) [9,17,18]. Moreover, we used a sample of face photos and contour sketches presented in [6]. Figure 2 shows example photo-sketch pairs from these datasets. Note that the images from the employed databases have the same alignment and scale, so we do not carry out any preprocessing in our experiments. In practice, when performing the sketch-to-photo (or photo-to-sketch) transformation, one should provide a sketch (or a photo) with the correct scale and alignment.

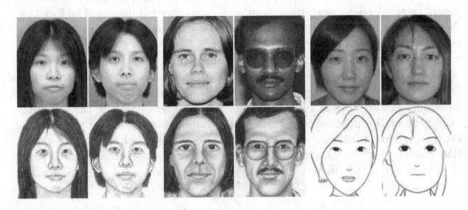

**Fig. 2.** Face photo-sketch pairs from CUFS dataset (columns 1–2), CUFSF dataset (columns 3–4) and the contour sketches sample (columns 5–6).

In the experiments, we transformed sketches to photos. The inverse operation can be conducted in a similar way and will yield analogous results.

In this paper, we present the results of the following experiments:

1. Sketch-to-photo synthesis;
2. Additional experiments on photo reconstruction from contour sketches [6] and low resolution sketches;
3. Generation of photo populations from sketches.

Due to the ambiguity of the photo-sketch relation (mentioned in Sect. 1) and the subjectivity of face image perception it is hard to propose an appropriate quality metric for generated photos. Thus, the evaluation of the photo generation quality is based on visual assessment of the synthesized images.

In the extreme case when no population is generated ($L = 1$, $\xi_1 \equiv 0$) our method and the algorithm of Tang and Wang [4] will yield similar results. But in contrast to the approach of Tang and Wang [4], we deal with the problem of *multiple* photo generation. Thus, the resulting populations should demonstrate two following properties at the same time. Firstly, all photos from the population should retain the individual features of the original sketch. Secondly, the generated photos should not be identical, i.e. the population should have a good variability. Further, we show that the proposed method generates populations which exhibit both of these properties.

## 4.1 Sketch-to-Photo Synthesis

*In the sketch-to-photo synthesis* experiment, we performed the computational procedure described in Sect. 3 without population generation ($L = 1$, $\xi_1 \equiv 0$). Generally, here we followed the framework described in [4] with the exception of the different computational procedure. Figure 3 presents the mean sketch and photo, eigenvalues $\Lambda_S$ and two examples of reconstructed photos. The fact that the eigenvalues decrease exponentially means that only a few principal components have a significant impact on the appearance of a face. Figure 4 shows examples of the photos synthesized from the training and testing sketches. The algorithm achieves a perfect reconstruction on the training set, while the transformation of the testing sketches causes the blurring effect and the loss of some individual features of the faces. The blurring may be caused by the imperfect alignment of the photo-sketch pairs and variability of the faces' shapes. The loss of individual features emerges due to the dataset limitations. We expect that large and representative photo-sketch databases may improve the synthesis quality given that images from those databases have good alignment and a similar scale.

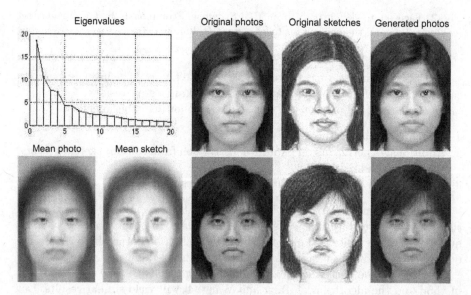

**Fig. 3.** Sketch-to-photo transformation performed on the training set.

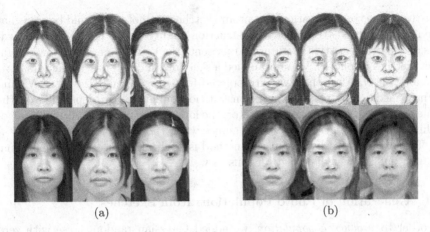

**Fig. 4.** Photo synthesis performed on the training sample (a) and the testing set (b). First row shows the original sketches, while the bottom row contains synthesised photos.

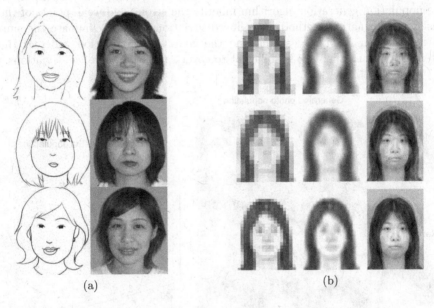

**Fig. 5.** Results of the experiments on the photo reconstruction from contour sketches (a) and from low resolution sketches (b). To process the low resolution sketches, interpolation was carried out prior to the photo synthesis (see (b), middle column). The scale factor was set to 7 %, 9 % and 13 % (from the top row to the bottom one).

## 4.2  Photo Reconstruction from Contour and Subsampled Sketches

We conducted the experiments on the reconstruction of photos from *contour drawings* (see [6] for the original images) and *low resolution sketches*. Figure 5 (a) illustrates the transformation of contour sketches to photos. It could be seen that the method achieves a perfect reconstruction quality on the training set regardless of the drawing style. Figure 5 (b) presents the transformation of low resolution sketches to photos. We subsampled a sketch with different scale factors (7 %, 9 % and 13 %). After that, we interpolated it to the original size ($M \times N$) and transformed to the photo. The reconstruction quality varies depending on the scale factor (the smaller the scale factor, the lower is the photo quality). The algorithm achieves the acceptable performance when the scale factor reaches 13 %.

This experiment shows that the method is applicable not only to the original images, but to their distorted versions as well.

## 4.3   Generation of Photo Populations from Sketches

In order to *produce a population*, we added Gaussian random noise with zero mean $\xi_l$ to a sketch projection **J**. Figure 6 presents a generated population and a 3D visualization of its first three principal components. Figure 7 shows examples of generated populations for the training and testing sets. As expected, the population generation algorithm inherits the strong and weak points of the basic transformation method. Introduced variations do not eliminate the similarity between the initial sketch and the generated population, whereas the inter-population difference is sufficient to cover various appearance deviations.

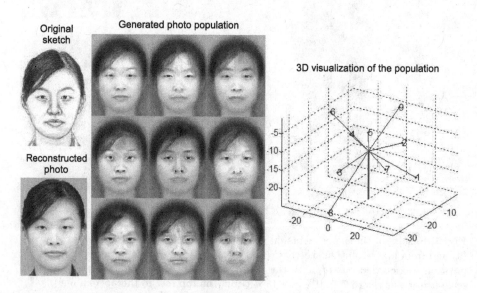

**Fig. 6.** Photo population generated from the sketch (on the left) and the 3D visualization of its projection on the first three principal components (on the right). Each photo of the generated population corresponds to a point on the plot. Note the considerable differences between the population photos and their projections.

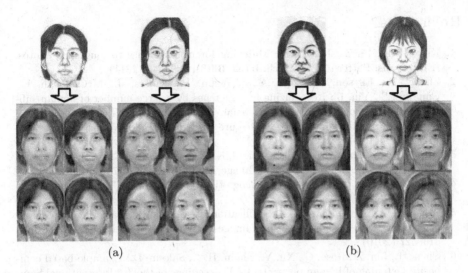

**Fig. 7.** Populations generated from the training (a) and testing sketches (b).

## 5   Discussion

In this paper, we presented an approach to the bidirectional photo-sketch transformation and population generation. We thoroughly considered the case of the sketch-to-photo transformation; the inverse operation is performed in a similar way. The construction of the sketch-photo transformation model involves the evaluation of the matrix $\mathbf{T_{SP}}$. On the generation stage, a new sketch is transformed into a single photo or a population of photos. The proposed solution can be based on one-dimensional (conventional) PCA as well as on 2D PCA.

In order to investigate different aspects of the one-dimensional variant of the proposed approach, we conducted the experiments on the three datasets. In all cases, adequate results were obtained. The proposed approach can be applied to the modification and enhancement of existing photo-sketch datasets as well as to superresolution problems.

Moreover, there are various potential applications of the presented approach. They include processing of heterogeneous face images (photos in the visible light spectrum, near infrared, thermal infrared and 3D face models) [19] and cross-modal multimedia retrieval. In addition to this, the application area of our approach is not limited to the transformation of face images. It can be employed for the processing of arbitrary image sets, in case the assumption of the eigenspaces structural similarity holds for those images. The research of the potential applications of the proposed approach is the subject of the further study.

**Acknowledgements.** This work was partially financially supported by the Government of the Russian Federation, Grant 074-U01. The authors express their sincere appreciation to Yuri Matveev, Head of SIS Department for his critical remarks and advice that significantly improved this paper.

# References

1. Klare, B.F., Li, Z., Jain, A.K.: Matching forensic sketches to mug shot photos. IEEE Trans. Pattern Anal. Mach. Intell. **33**(3), 639–646 (2011)
2. Zhang, Y., Ellyson, S., Zone, A., Gangam, P., Sullins, J., McCullough, C., Canavan, S., Yin, L.: Recognizing face sketches by a large number of human subjects: a perception-based study for facial distinctiveness. In: IEEE International Conference on Automatic Face & Gesture Recognition and Workshops, pp. 707–712. IEEE (2011)
3. Kukharev, G., Matveev, Y., Shchegoleva, N.: New solutions for face photo retrieval based on sketches. Pattern Recogn. Image Anal. **26**(1), 165–175 (2016)
4. Tang, X., Wang, X.: Face sketch recognition. IEEE Trans. Circuits Syst. Video Technol. **14**(1), 50–57 (2004)
5. Shchegoleva, N., Kukharev, G.: Application of two-dimensional principal component analysis for recognition of face images. Pattern Recogn. Image Anal. **20**(4), 513–527 (2010)
6. Chen, H., Liu, Z., Rose, C., Xu, Y., Shum, H.Y., Salesin, D.: Example-based composite sketching of human portraits. In: Proceedings of the 3rd International Symposium on Non-Photorealistic Animation and Rendering, pp. 95–153. ACM (2004)
7. Yu, H., Zhang, J.J.: Mean value coordinates-based caricature and expression synthesis. Sig. Image Video Process. **7**(5), 899–910 (2013)
8. Gao, X., Zhong, J., Li, J., Tian, C.: Face sketch synthesis algorithm based on E-HMM and selective ensemble. IEEE Trans. Circuits Syst. Video Technol. **18**(4), 487–496 (2008)
9. Wang, X., Tang, X.: Face photo-sketch synthesis and recognition. IEEE Trans. Pattern Anal. Mach. Intell. **31**(11), 1955–1967 (2009)
10. Zhang, W., Wang, X., Tang, X.: Lighting and pose robust face sketch synthesis. In: Daniilidis, K., Maragos, P., Paragios, N. (eds.) ECCV 2010. LNCS, vol. 6316, pp. 420–433. Springer, Heidelberg (2010). doi:10.1007/978-3-642-15567-3_31
11. Kirby, M., Sirovich, L.: Application of the Karhunen-Loeve procedure for the characterization of human faces. IEEE Trans. Pattern Anal. Mach. Intell. **12**(1), 103–108 (1990)
12. Turk, M., Pentland, A.: Eigenfaces for recognition. J. Cogn. Neurosci. **3**(1), 71–86 (1991)
13. Liu, Q., Tang, X., Jin, H., Lu, H., Ma, S.: A nonlinear approach for face sketch synthesis and recognition. In: IEEE Computer Society Conference on Computer Vision and Pattern Recognition (CVPR), vol. 1, pp. 1005–1010. IEEE (2005)
14. Li, Y.H., Savvides, M.: Faces from sketches: a subspace synthesis approach. Proc. SPIE **6202**, 62020K (2006)
15. Sharma, A., Jacobs, D.W.: Bypassing synthesis: PLS for face recognition with pose, low-resolution and sketch. In: IEEE Conference on Computer Vision and Pattern Recognition (CVPR), 2011, pp. 593–600. IEEE (2011)
16. Ouyang, S., Hospedales, T., Song, Y.-Z., Li, X.: Cross-modal face matching: beyond viewed sketches. In: Cremers, D., Reid, I., Saito, H., Yang, M.-H. (eds.) ACCV 2014. LNCS, vol. 9004, pp. 210–225. Springer, Heidelberg (2015). doi:10.1007/978-3-319-16808-1_15
17. CUFS dataset. http://mmlab.ie.cuhk.edu.hk/archive/facesketch.html
18. CUFSF dataset. http://mmlab.ie.cuhk.edu.hk/archive/cufsf/
19. Guo, G.: Heterogeneous face recognition: an emerging topic in biometrics. Intel Technol. J. **18**(4), 80–97 (2014)

# Similarity Measures for Face Images: An Experimental Study

Maciej Smiatacz[✉]

Faculty of Electronics, Telecommunications and Informatics,
Gdańsk University of Technology, Narutowicza 11/12, 80-233 Gdańsk, Poland
slowhand@eti.pg.gda.pl

**Abstract.** This work describes experiments aimed at finding a straight-forward but effective way of comparing face images. We discuss properties of the basic concepts, such as the Euclidean, cosine and correlation metrics, test the simplest version of elastic templates, and compare these solutions with distances based on texture descriptors (Local Ternary Patterns). The influence of selected image processing methods (e.g. bilateral filtering) on image comparison results is also considered. Additionally, the new metric, in which differences between LTP histograms are weighted with alignment coefficients, is proposed.

## 1 Introduction

Measuring image similarity is one of computer vision open issues. Ultimately, we would like to have algorithms performing this task as efficiently and accurately as humans do. In general the problem is extremely complex as it may be related to scene understanding, mechanisms of learning and perception, or even principles of artificial intelligence on the whole. In the specific context of face recognition, however, it seems to be much more straightforward, or even trivial, if we assume that images are frontal, taken under stable lighting conditions and properly cropped. Unfortunately, this intuition is confusing and may lead to false conclusions. For example, an appropriate similarity measure is necessary to evaluate the outcomes of illumination normalization methods. In this case, we want to know how closely the processed image of a badly lit face resembles the image of the same face taken under neutral lighting. In many publications (e.g. [1]) the simple Euclidean distance between the two images is used as a satisfactory measure of their similarity. If the nearest neighbor algorithm based on the Euclidean metric is able to classify the normalized image correctly, it means that the relighting method produces a good result. In fact such a test is not particularly useful. From the Euclidean point of view the image in Fig. 1a is more similar to the image shown in Fig. 1c than to the one in Fig. 1b. Consequently, application of the Euclidean metric might lead to the rejection of a good normalization method or to the acceptance of a bad one.

The Euclidean metric is still widely used as the image similarity measure, although the problems that it causes were noticed many years ago. The authors

© Springer International Publishing AG 2016
L.J. Chmielewski et al. (Eds.): ICCVG 2016, LNCS 9972, pp. 341–352, 2016.
DOI: 10.1007/978-3-319-46418-3_30

of [2] introduced the IMED (IMage Euclidean Distance), which is robust to small perturbations, and at the same time they showed that applying this metric is equivalent to smoothing the images being compared. In other words, they proved that blurring noiseless images can still increase the recognition rate. This suggests that other image processing methods may also be beneficial for calculating the similarity of images, although the mathematical background of the process may be difficult to discover. Therefore, we decided to verify this idea experimentally.

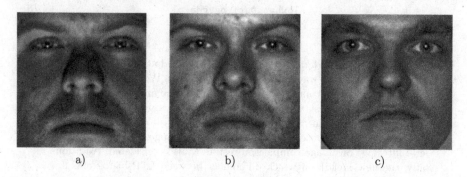

a)                    b)                    c)

**Fig. 1.** Euclidean distance between image (a) and (c) is smaller than between (a) and (b).

Several ways of measuring the distance between images were proposed in the literature [3–5]. Many of them, however, have serious disadvantages; for example, they do not obey the triangle inequality (two dissimilar images can be both similar to the third one). On the other hand, metric learning has gained considerable popularity in recent years [6,7]. According to this concept, the distance function is constructed by means of training, performed on large datasets. This approach proved to be helpful in solving problems such as face verification. Unfortunately, metrics of this type are neither available for general use nor can be easily created (several thousands of training samples are necessary). Moreover, they are trained to return low values when two images depict the same object, but it often does not mean that the images are similar (Fig. 2).

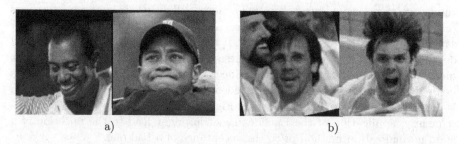

a)                              b)

**Fig. 2.** In the sense of the metric defined in [6] each pair (a) and (b) contains similar images – although they are completely different.

The goal of the research described in this paper was to find the image similarity measure that would be easy to implement (not requiring any large-scale training), and could properly assess the similarity of face *images* (not necessarily the faces themselves), without obvious mistakes such as the one illustrated in Fig. 1. We focused on different strategies involving raw images as well as their representations based on texture descriptors (namely Local Ternary Patterns [8]). Moreover, we wanted to check how the specific image processing techniques influence results of image comparison. The rest of this paper mostly describes the experimental work. New ideas regarding the face image distance are presented mainly in Sect. 5.

## 2  Experimental Setup

We compared different forms of image similarity measures with the help of a specially designed face recognition experiment. Each person was represented by only one training image and the simplest nearest neighbor algorithm was used as a classifier. The recognition error depended only on the metric, and served as a measure describing the quality of a given solution (the lower the better). It is important to point out that our work was not aimed at constructing a face recognition system. An efficient face recognition method must be able to identify every registered person in several substantially different images (for example the pose or illumination conditions may vary). We did not expect such robustness from the similarity measures that we tested. They were only supposed to handle relatively small variations, usually insignificant for human observers.

Out of the many data sets available [9], the CMU-PIE database [10] was chosen as the main source of face images. Training samples came from the *gallery* folder containing portraits of 68 persons. The testing set included frontal images captured under constant illumination but from three slightly different positions (1209 images taken by cameras no 07, 09 and 27 during the *expression* and *talking* sessions). In some experiments images from the Extended Yale B database (EYB) [11] were also used (38 persons in the gallery, testing set including

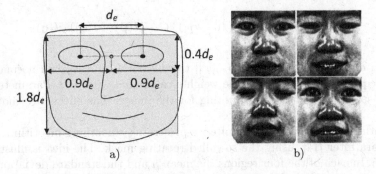

**Fig. 3.** (a) The cropping procedure, (b) sample testing images from one class.

429 frontal images with small illumination variations visible). Eye centers were automatically detected on every image, and the interocular distance $d_e$ was used to delineate the cropping region (Fig. 3a). Finally, the images were scaled to the size of $128 \times 128$ pixels (Fig. 3b).

Two editions of the Betaface service [12] were used to obtain the precise localization of eye centers (and 99 other landmark points) for each face. Although the newest version (from 2016) provided more accurate results that the one from 2014, the testing images from the CMU-PIE database were processed by both of them. As a result, two slightly different testing sets (CMU-14 and CMU-16) were created.

## 3   Image Processing Methods

One of the goals of the research was to check if certain image processing techniques could be helpful in defining the face image similarity measure. In particular we were interested in transformations that would filter out the noise together with small and unimportant features, and introduce the higher level of abstraction to the process of image comparison. Gaussian blur and median filtering are the simplest forms of such operations. Histogram equalization, on the other hand, is essential in highlighting the most important visual information, regardless of the distribution of the image intensity levels.

The typical Gaussian filter calculates the new value $I_n(\mathbf{p})$ of a pixel located at point $\mathbf{p} = (x, y)$ as a weighted sum of the pixels belonging to some neighborhood of $\mathbf{p}$ (denoted by $\Omega$). The weights are the values of a Gaussian function $G_{\sigma_s}$ centered at $\mathbf{p}$, so that the closer neighbors of $\mathbf{p}$ have higher impact on the value of $I_n(\mathbf{p})$. Since only the *distances* of neighboring pixels are taken into account, the Gaussian filter blurs the edges, which is unfavorable in most of the cases. As a solution to this problem the bilateral filter was proposed [13]. It preserves the edges by introducing another Gaussian term to the calculation of weights, this time treating the difference of *intensities* of the neighboring pixels as the argument of the Gaussian function $G_{\sigma_r}$. Now, the pixels whose intensities differ much from $I_n(\mathbf{p})$, i.e. the original intensity of $\mathbf{p}$, contribute less to the final result. Formally the bilateral filter is defined by:

$$I_n(\mathbf{p}) = \frac{1}{w_\mathbf{p}} \sum_{\mathbf{q} \in \Omega} G_{\sigma_s}\left(\|\mathbf{p} - \mathbf{q}\|\right) \cdot G_{\sigma_r}\left(I(\mathbf{p}) - I(\mathbf{q})\right) \cdot I(\mathbf{q}) \tag{1}$$

where $\mathbf{q}$ denotes a neighbor of $\mathbf{p}$, $\| \cdot \|$ the $L2$ norm, and $w_\mathbf{p}$ is a normalizing factor, equal to the sum of all the weights calculated within $\Omega$. Parameters $\sigma_s$ and $\sigma_r$ specify the amount of filtering for the image. The effects are shown in Fig. 4b.

Another interesting example of edge-preserving smoothing algorithm is the Kuwahara filter [14], using the so-called rotating mask. The idea is illustrated in Fig. 5. In each of the four regions the mean $\mu$ and the standard deviation $\sigma$ of pixel intensities is calculated, and the mean extracted from the region with the lowest level of $\sigma$ is treated as the new value $I_n(\mathbf{p})$. Figure 4c presents the results.

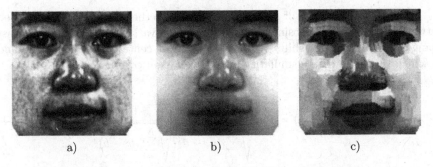

**Fig. 4.** Image processing methods: (a) the original image, (b) the image after bilateral filtering ($\sigma_s = \sigma_r = 30$) and, (c) after Kuwahara filtering ($5 \times 5$ mask).

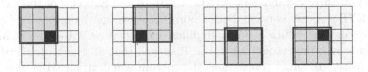

**Fig. 5.** The rotating mask of the Kuwahara filter.

## 4 Basic Measures

A digital grayscale image is just an $n \times m$ array of intensity values, which can be easily converted into a column vector containing $N = nm$ elements. The similarity of images represented by two vectors **a** and **b** can be measured with the help of the Euclidean distance:

$$d_E(\mathbf{a}, \mathbf{b}) = \sqrt{(\mathbf{a} - \mathbf{b}) \cdot (\mathbf{a} - \mathbf{b})} = \sqrt{(\mathbf{a} - \mathbf{b})^{\mathrm{T}}(\mathbf{a} - \mathbf{b})} \qquad (2)$$

where $(\cdot)$ denotes the dot product. Although this is a well-known and widely used method of comparing feature vectors in general, special care must be taken when the features are simply the raw pixel intensities. We have to remember that the Euclidean metric is not invariant to shifting and scaling, which means that even hardly noticeable changes of contrast or brightness may result in large distance values – much larger than the distances between substantially different images. The metric often provides counterintuitive results (Fig. 1) and is sensitive to small perturbations, insignificant for human observers [2].

Another simple method of distance calculation, often applied to vectors containing image data, is based on the cosine similarity:

$$d_{\cos}(\mathbf{a}, \mathbf{b}) = 1 - \frac{\mathbf{a} \cdot \mathbf{b}}{\|\mathbf{a}\| \, \|\mathbf{b}\|} = 1 - \frac{\sum\limits_{i=1}^{N} a_i b_i}{\sqrt{\sum\limits_{i=1}^{N} a_i^2} \sqrt{\sum\limits_{i=1}^{N} b_i^2}} \qquad (3)$$

Typically the elements of **a** and **b** are positive so the value of $d_{cos}$ is bounded between 0 and 1. The cosine distance is only invariant to scaling (contrast changes). Invariance to shifts requires the use of centered versions of **a** and **b**, which turns the cosine similarity into the Pearson correlation:

$$d_{corr}(\mathbf{a}, \mathbf{b}) = 1 - \frac{\sum\limits_{i=1}^{N} (a_i - \bar{a})(b_i - \bar{b})}{\sqrt{\sum\limits_{i=1}^{N} (a_i - \bar{a})^2}\sqrt{\sum\limits_{i=1}^{N} (b_i - \bar{b})^2}} \tag{4}$$

where $\bar{a}$ denotes the mean of vector **a** elements.

Table 1 presents results of the simple recognition experiment (as described in Sect. 2) on three databases: CMU-14, CMU-16 and Subset 2 of the Extended Yale B (EYB). As we can see, better normalization (i.e. more precise localization of eye centers), which is the main difference between CMU-14 and CMU-16, greatly improves the recognition rates. It means that all the basic metrics are highly sensitive to small translations. Histogram equalization (HE) also lowers the error rates and almost entirely eliminates differences between the performance of the three methods, since the invariance to brightness and contrast changes is no longer important. This is not exactly true (error rates increase) for the EYB database, in which the pose and expression of each face is precisely fixed but differences in images appear as a result of small illumination changes. We assume, however, that the illumination normalization should be performed before similarity measurements, so the EYB dataset will not be used in further experiments.

**Table 1.** Error rates provided by the basic metrics for different datasets

| Metric | CMU-14 | CMU-16 | EYB | CMU-14 | CMU-16 | EYB |
|---|---|---|---|---|---|---|
| | Histogram equalization OFF | | | Histogram equalization ON | | |
| $d_E$ (2) | **48.83** | **29.53** | 14.45 | 33.45 | **25.89** | 14.45 |
| $d_{cos}$ (3) | 55.34 | 37.55 | **8.86** | **33.27** | **25.89** | 14.45 |
| $d_{corr}$ (4) | 48.91 | 32.67 | 10.26 | 33.36 | 26.06 | **14.22** |

Having taken a look at the results obtained for CMU-16 database (especially when HE is off) one might come to the conclusion that Euclidean distance is actually the best choice. It is not. Better performance of the Euclidean metric only tells us something about the dataset characteristics – namely, it means that some of the faces can be classified correctly on the basis of brightness and contrast levels. Since we want to compare the contents of images, not their photometric parameters, only $d_{corr}$ metric (4) will be used in the subsequent tests.

The next task was to check how the selected image processing operations influence the results. Table 2 contains error rates obtained for CMU-14 dataset, but exactly the same tendencies were observed for CMU-16. GB($s$) denotes Gaussian blur with $s$ variance, MB($d$) – median blur in $d{\times}d$ window, BL($\sigma_r, \sigma_s$) –

bilateral filter (1), KW($d$) – the Kuwahara filter with $d \times d$ mask. Gaussian and median filtering was preceded by histogram equalization, but in the case of the Kuwahara and bilateral filters histogram equalization was performed as the second step.

**Table 2.** Influence of image filtering on the classification error ($d_{corr}$, CMU-14)

| Filter | Error | Filter | Error | Filter | Error | Filter | Error |
|--------|-------|--------|-------|--------|-------|--------|-------|
| GB(1) | 32.75 | MB(3) | 32.84 | BL(10,10) | 33.45 | KW(3) | 32.32 |
| GB(3) | 30.41 | MB(7) | 32.41 | BL(30,30) | 43.70 | KW(7) | 29.71 |
| GB(5) | 29.71 | MB(21) | **27.28** | BL(50,50) | 56.30 | KW(9) | 28.06 |

The results confirm the observation formulated in [2] – indeed, smoothing the images before comparison makes sense. Heavy median blur proved to be particularly effective, the Kuwahara method provided similar results at a higher computational cost, while the application of bilateral filter appeared to be counterproductive.

In another experiment landmark coordinates supplied by the Betaface service were used to create three regions of interest for each face, defining the eye, nose, and mouth templates. This way we employed some external knowledge about the nature of the object presented on images. As a consequence, similarity measures utilizing the templates were no longer universal, but targeted specifically at human faces. The simplest metric, $d_T$ expressed the distance as a sum of differences between regions of interest. The center of each testing template was aligned with the center of the equivalent template extracted from the gallery image, and then the regions covered by the testing template were compared using $d_{corr}$ measure. In second version of the metric, $d_{TW}$, each template was assigned a separate weight. In another two variants, $d_{TM}$ and $d_{TWM}$, the testing template was allowed to move along the spiral path filling the $a \times a$ box and starting from the center of the gallery template; the best (i.e. the lowest) score was treated as the distance value.

The weights of the templates were determined by means of the simple optimization process executed on CMU-14 and EYB datasets. For CMU-14 the best results were obtained with weights for eyes, nose and mouth equal to, respectively, $w_e = 0.61$, $w_n = 0.34$ and $w_m = 0.05$. For EYB the optimal values were 0.71, 0.20 and 0.09. In both cases eyes appeared to be most important, but the expression changes noticeable in CMU-14 images diminished their role, and increased the weight assigned to the relatively stable nose region. To avoid overfitting, the generalized values of 0.65, 0.25 and 0.1 were used throughout the experiment. Table 3 compares the performance of template-based metrics (a = 13 for $d_{TM}$ and $d_{TWM}$).

As we can see, the raw application of ROIs only worsens the results. However, by allowing the template to search for the best match within some limited zone we are able to compensate for the imprecise normalization, which is mainly the problem of CMU-14. With the addition of proper weighting the lowest error rates so far could be obtained. Interestingly, the median blur was no longer necessary.

**Table 3.** Performance of template-based metrics ($d_{corr}$ given for reference)

| Metric | CMU-14 | CMU-16 | CMU-14 | CMU-16 |
|--------|--------|--------|--------|--------|
|        | HE only | | HE + MB(21) | |
| $d_T$    | 53.78 | 45.33 | 42.83 | 37.39 |
| $d_{TW}$  | 39.88 | 32.59 | 33.36 | 28.29 |
| $d_{TM}$  | 29.12 | 28.29 | 31.45 | 27.30 |
| $d_{TWM}$ | **22.85** | **18.45** | 24.85 | 19.02 |
| $d_{corr}$ | 33.36 | 26.06 | 27.28 | 19.52 |

# 5 Measures Using Local Ternary Patterns

Local Binary Pattern (LBP) operator, proposed in [15], considers a small ($3 \times 3$ in the basic case) neighborhood of each pixel, and performs binarization in this area, using intensity $i_c$ of the central point $\mathbf{p}_c$ as the threshold value. The sequence of 0 and 1 values obtained in this way can be treated as a binary code describing the texture around $\mathbf{p}_c$. The idea of local texture descriptors inspired many authors who created their own solutions, but according to the recent comparison [16] in the case of face recognition the differences between them are negligible. Still, in our previous study [17], we showed that the modification of LBP introduced in [8], called Local Ternary Pattern (LTP), has certain advantages. Thus, we decided to verify its potential in measuring the similarity of images. The LTP operator generates a sequence S containing $N$ ternary values $(-1, 0, 1)$, which form the local texture descriptor ($N$ is the number of neighbors). The $n$-th element of S is defined as:

$$s_n(i_n, i_c, t) = \begin{cases} 1 & i_n \geq i_c + t \\ 0 & |i_n - i_c| < t \\ -1 & i_n \leq i_c - t \end{cases} \tag{5}$$

where $i_n$ is the intensity of the $n$-th neighbor, and $t$ denotes the parameter that introduces some level of tolerance to the binarization process. Following the results presented in [17], we use the circular neighborhood with radius $r = 1.5$ (interpolation is necessary), $N = 12$ and $t = 7$. Typically the image is described by a set of histograms of LTP codes. In our configuration the histograms are created for regions located around the nodes of the regular $11 \times 11$ grid. More precisely, each LTP code is converted into two LBP codes with the help of the following operations: (a) $-1 \rightarrow 0$, (b) $1 \rightarrow 0$, $-1 \rightarrow 1$. Consequently the LTP histogram is twice as big as the LBP version. Having computed two sets of histograms for two images $\mathbf{A}$ and $\mathbf{B}$, we can measure their similarity using the following formula:

$$d_H(\mathbf{A}, \mathbf{B}) = \sum_{i,j} w_i \frac{(a_{i,j} - b_{i,j})^2}{a_{i,j} + b_{i,j}} = \sum_i w_i d_H^{(i)}(\mathbf{A}, \mathbf{B}) \tag{6}$$

where $a_{i,j}$ denotes the value of the $j$-th bin in the $i$-th histogram describing image **A** and $w_i$ is the weight that indicates the importance of the $i$-th region (by default all weights are equal).

Table 4 shows the results of experiments involving LTP codes and several image processing methods (each filter was combined with histogram equalization), performed on CMU-16 dataset. LTP outperforms template-based method, delicate smoothing with Gaussian or median blur lowers the error rate slightly, bilateral filtering appears to be useless once again, but the Kuwahara filter with $9 \times 9$ window improves the results noticeably.

**Table 4.** Influence of image processing methods on the classification error ($d_H$, CMU-16)

| Filter | Error | Filter | Error | Filter | Error | Filter | Error |
|--------|-------|--------|-------|----------|-------|--------|-------|
| none | 17.54 | GB(5) | 15.30 | BL(10,10) | 13.15 | KW(3) | 13.23 |
| HE only | 13.23 | MB(5) | 11.33 | BL(30,30) | 14.97 | KW(7) | 9.34 |
| GB(1) | 11.33 | MB(21) | 15.72 | BL(50,50) | 18.69 | KW(9) | **9.02** |

Since the introduction of different weights for eye, nose and mouth regions proved to be advantageous in the case of template-based metrics, we applied the same concept to the regions for which LTP histograms were created. To this end the central point of each region was assigned the three coefficients $c_e^{(i)}$, $c_n^{(i)}$, $c_m^{(i)}$, derived from distances ($d_e^{(i)}$, $d_n^{(i)}$, $d_m^{(i)}$) to the nearest landmarks labeled, respectively, as eye, nose or mouth points by the Betaface service. For example:

$$c_e^{(i)} = 1 \Big/ \left(1 + d_e^{(i)}\right) \tag{7}$$

($c_n^{(i)}$ and $c_m^{(i)}$ are defined analogously) so that each coefficient is bounded to the 0..1 range. After additional normalization $c_e^{(i)} + c_n^{(i)} + c_m^{(i)} = 1$. The weight of the $i$-th LTP region can then be expressed as:

$$w_i = \left(w_e c_e^{(i)} + w_n c_n^{(i)} + w_m c_m^{(i)}\right) / W, \quad W = \sum_i \left(w_e c_e^{(i)} + w_n c_n^{(i)} + w_m c_m^{(i)}\right) \tag{8}$$

Because LTP histograms are created for the fixed set of rectangular regions, the relative positions of landmark points with respect to the nodes of the LTP grid change from image to image. Each node in image **A** can be characterized by the vector ($\mathbf{v_A}^{(i)}$) containing distances to all the landmark points. If the difference between two vectors $\mathbf{v_A}^{(i)}$ and $\mathbf{v_B}^{(i)}$ (which represent corresponding nodes from two images **A** and **B**) is high, the two histograms describe different face fragments. Assuming that better aligned regions should play more important role in image comparison, we can set the weight of $i$-th region to:

$$w_i = 1 \Big/ \left(1 + \sqrt{\sum_{k=1}^{K} z_k^{(i)} (v_{\mathbf{A}k}^{(i)} - v_{\mathbf{B}k}^{(i)})^2}\right) = 1 \Big/ \left(1 + d_{EW}(\mathbf{v}_\mathbf{A}^{(i)}, \mathbf{v}_\mathbf{B}^{(i)})\right) \tag{9}$$

where $K$ is the number of landmarks and $v_{\mathbf{A}k}^{(i)}$ denotes the distance between $i$-th node and $k$-th landmark in image $\mathbf{A}$ (the normalization factor is skipped for clarity). Since the landmarks which are positioned far from the node should not influence the value of $w_i$, another set of weights, denoted as $z_k^{(i)}$, must be introduced:

$$z_k^{(i)} = \left(1 - q_k^{(i)}/K\right)^2 \tag{10}$$

where $q_k^{(i)}$ is the position of $k$-th landmark in the sequence sorted by distances to $i$-th node. Well aligned nodes showing high similarity are particularly important for comparison. Therefore, if $d_{EW}(\mathbf{v}_{\mathbf{A}}^{(i)}, \mathbf{v}_{\mathbf{B}}^{(i)}) < t_1$ and $d_H^{(i)}(\mathbf{A}, \mathbf{B}) < t_2$ we increase the weight of $i$-th region by setting $z_k^{(i)} \leftarrow 3z_k^{(i)}$. Since maximum observed value of $d_{EW}(\mathbf{v}_{\mathbf{A}}^{(i)}, \mathbf{v}_{\mathbf{B}}^{(i)})$ was equal to 16.29, and the average value of $d_H^{(i)}(\mathbf{A}, \mathbf{B})$ equal to 0.94, we used $t_1 = 5$ and $t_2 = 0.9$.

Experiments showed that assigning different weights, defined by (7) and (8), to the eye, nose and mouth regions, slightly improved the performance of the LTP-based similarity metric only when the Kuwahara filtering was turned off. On the other hand, weighting LTP histogram distances with the level of the corresponding LTP regions alignment (9) provided good results, summarized in Table 5.

**Table 5.** Results of experiments involving LTP region weighting (CMU-16)

| Method | Error |
|---|---|
| LTP, histogram equalization only, different weights for eyes, nose and mouth | 12.90 |
| LTP, histogram equalization only, alignment weighting (9) | 10.92 |
| LTP, histogram equalization, Kuwahara $7 \times 7$, alignment weighting (9) | 8.44 |
| LTP, histogram equalization, Kuwahara $9 \times 9$, alignment weighting (9) | **8.27** |

# 6 Combined Metrics

The goal of the last series of experiments was to check if it is possible to obtain better results by combining different types of measures into one ultimate metric. Four methods forming four channels were considered: (1) $d_{corr}$ with HE and median blur using $21 \times 21$ window (the best holistic option), (2) $d_{TWM}$ with HE (the best template-based option), (3) $d_H$ with HE and the weighting (9) (the best description of the unchanged texture), (4) $d_H$ with HE, Kuwahara filtering using $9 \times 9$ window, and the weighting (9) (the best LTP-based solution). The results showed that the first two channels are not useful but slightly lower error rate (8.02 on CMU-16) can be achieved by combining options 3 and 4 (using 0.2 and 0.8 weights).

# 7   Conclusions

Practitioners looking for a simple but effective way of comparing face images may be interested in the following suggestions, formulated as a result of the experiments described in this paper.

- The use of the Euclidean or cosine metrics is misleading, only correlation (4) is invariant to contrast and brightness fluctuations (error rate of 32.67 on CMU-16).
- The simple histogram equalization lowers the error significantly (to 26.06), but results are much better (19.52) when the intense median blur is also applied.
- When faces are not precisely cropped, but the locations of eyes, nose and mouth can be easily determined, the use of weighted elastic templates is beneficial (error falls from 27.28 to 22.85 on CMU-14), otherwise the improvement (in comparison with the straightforward median blur) is much smaller (18.45 error on CMU-16). We suggest the following weights for the eye, nose, and mouth regions: 0.65, 0.25, 0.1.
- Local Ternary Patterns are worth implementing: the error immediately drops to 13.23 on CMU-16.
- The Kuwahara filter (using $9 \times 9$ window) is very useful when combined with LTP – it lowers the error rate to 9.02.
- When landmark positions are available, further improvements are possible through the application of the advanced weighting (9) of LTP histograms. It results in the lowest observed error rate, equal to 8.02 on CMU-16.

The gain provided by the Kuwahara filtering is worth noticing. Although no formal explanation of this phenomenon is currently available, application of this simple image processing method made the behavior of the LTP-based metric closer to the human perception.

# References

1. Lai, Z.-R., Dai, D.-Q., Ren, C.-X., Huang, K.-K.: Multilayer surface albedo for face recognition with reference images in bad lighting conditions. IEEE Trans. Image Process. **23**, 4709–4723 (2014)
2. Wang, L., Zhang, Y., Feng, J.: On the Euclidean distance of images. IEEE Trans. Pattern Anal. Mach. Intell **27**, 1334–1339 (2005)
3. Huttenlocher, D.P., Klanderman, G.A., Rucklidge, W.J.: Comparing images using the hausdorff distance. IEEE Trans. Pattern Anal. Mach. Intell. **15**, 850–863 (1993)
4. Simard, P., LeCun, Y., Denker, J.S.: Efficient pattern recognition using a new transformation distance. In: Hanson, S., Cowan, J., Giles, C. (eds.) Advances in Neural Information Processing Systems, pp. 50–58. Morgan Kaufman, San Mateo (1993)
5. Li, J., Lu, B.-L.: An adaptive image Euclidean distance. Pattern Recognit. **42**, 349–357 (2009)
6. Guillaumin, M., Verbeek, J., Schmid, C.: Is that you? metric learning approaches for face identication. In: ICCV 2009 - International Conference on Computer Vision, pp. 498–505. IEEE (2009)

7. Cao, X., Wipf, D., Wen, F., Duan, G., Sun, J.: A practical transfer learning algorithm for face verification. In: ICCV 2013 - International Conference on Computer Vision, pp. 3208–3215 (2013)
8. Tan, X., Triggs, B.: Enhanced local texture feature sets for face recognition under difficult lighting conditions. IEEE Trans. Image Process. **19**, 1635–1650 (2010)
9. Forczmański, P., Furman, M.: Comparative analysis of benchmark datasets for face recognition algorithms verification. In: Bolc, L., Tadeusiewicz, R., Chmielewski, L.J., Wojciechowski, K. (eds.) ICCVG 2012. LNCS, vol. 7594, pp. 354–362. Springer, Heidelberg (2012). doi:10.1007/978-3-642-33564-8_43
10. Sim, T., Baker, S., Bsat, M.: The CMU pose, illumination, and expression (PIE) database. In: Proceedings of the 5th International Conference on Automatic Face and Gesture Recognition (2002)
11. Georghiades, A.S., Belhumeur, P.N., Kriegman, D.J.: From few to many: illumination cone models for face recognition under variable lighting and pose. IEEE Trans. Pattern Anal. Mach. Intell. **23**, 643–660 (2001)
12. http://www.betafaceapi.com/
13. Tomasi, C., Manduchi, R.: Bilateral filtering for gray and color images. In: ICCV 1998 - International Conference on Computer Vision, pp. 839–846. IEEE (1998)
14. Kuwahara, M., Hachimura, K., Eiho, S., Kinoshita, M.: Processing of RI-Angiocardiographic images. In: Preston Jr, K., Onoe, M. (eds.) Digital Processing of Biomedical Images, pp. 187–202. Springer, New York (1976)
15. Ojala, T., Pietikainen, M., Harwood, D.: A comparative study of texture measures with classification based on featured distributions. Pattern Recognit. **29**, 51–59 (1996)
16. Bereta, M., Karczmarek, P., Pedrycz, W., Reformat, M.: Local descriptors in application to the aging problem in face recognition. Pattern Recognit. **46**, 2634–2646 (2013)
17. Smiatacz, M., Rumiński, J.: Local texture pattern selection for efficient face recognition and tracking. In: Burduk, R., Jackowski, K., Kurzyński, M., Woźniak, M., Żołnierek, A. (eds.) CORES 2015. Advances in Intelligent Systems and Computing, vol. 403, pp. 359–368, Springer (2016)

# Log-Gabor Transforms and Score Fusion to Overcome Variations in Appearance for Face Recognition

Mithat Çağri Yildiz[1]([✉]), Omid Sharifi[2], and Maryam Eskandari[2]

[1] Department of Electronic and Electrical Engineering,
Gaziantep University, Gaziantep, Turkey
m.cagri.yildiz@hotmail.com
[2] Department of Computer and Software Engineering,
Toros University, Mersin, Turkey
{omid.sharifi,maryam.eskandari}@toros.edu.tr

**Abstract.** In this paper a new hybrid scheme for overcoming variations in facial images based on the score fusion strategy is considered. The scheme takes into account Log-Gabor transform to extract facial features. The implemented scheme applies Backtracking Search Algorithm (BSA) as a novel feature selection method and Linear Discriminant Analysis (LDA) as a feature transformation method to reduce the number of features and computational cost. Then Weighted Sum Rule (WS) fusion technique is applied to fuse the produced scores for our face recognition system. The robustness of schemes is tested using FERET and ORL database. Experimental results show a significant improvement of proposed scheme over implemented methods in this study.

## 1 Introduction

Face recognition is considered as one of the most attractive areas in a variety of applications such as pattern recognition, computer vision, human-computer interaction, etc. [1–6]. In this respect, extracting the most significant facial features is still an interesting and challenging research area. Basically, two typical facial extraction techniques are employed in face recognition applications namely holistic and local feature based methods. The holistic approaches concentrate on features extraction from the whole face image of a subject by transforming the facial features. However, the performance of these kinds of techniques usually is affected due to variations in pose, illumination, facial expression and partial occlusion [7]. On the other hand, local-feature based techniques extract the partial facial features of local regions and they are considered to be more robust in uncontrolled conditions. One of the most significant local-feature based technique for facial recognition is Log-Gabor transforms [8]. The result of studying this method under uncontrolled conditions demonstrates its superior performance [9]. However, high dimensionality is considered as a problem of facial extraction using Log-Gabor transforms that subsequently affects the recognition performance [10]. Indeed, one of the most significant questions in this area is how to

© Springer International Publishing AG 2016
L.J. Chmielewski et al. (Eds.): ICCVG 2016, LNCS 9972, pp. 353–361, 2016.
DOI: 10.1007/978-3-319-46418-3_31

reduce the number of features for further processing. In order to solve this problem, typically two different strategies are used namely feature transformation and feature selection.

The focus of feature selection methods is on selecting an optimal subset of original feature sets according to a certain objective function. Various feature selection methods such as Particle Swarm Optimization (PSO), Genetic Algorithm (GA), and Sequential Forward Floating Selection (SFFS), have been applied for purpose of optimization [11–15]. On the other hand, feature transformation techniques reduce the features by transforming the feature vector into another vector space. Principal Component Analysis (PCA), Linear Discriminant Analysis (LDA), Kernel Principal Component Analysis (KPCA), and Independent Component Analysis (ICA) are typical ones of feature transformation techniques [16]. In this study, designing a facial recognition system to be robust against variations in appearance for face recognition and also be able to solve the high dimensionality problem is interested. We study the effect of feature transformation and feature selection techniques separately and together on recognition performance of facial systems under variations when Log-Gabor transforms is applied. We additionally propose a hybrid facial fusion system according to feature transformation and feature selection produced score to overcome the problem of high dimensionality and variations.

The contribution of this work is to use the advantages of both feature transformation and feature selection strategies on Log-Gabor transforms to enhance the recognition performance using score fusion. Especially, applying Backtracking Search Algorithm (BSA) [17] as a novel evolutionary algorithm to reduce the number of facial features leads to lower computational time and memory compared to other feature selection strategies. The implemented scheme is appropriate to be applied in face recognition systems including different variations in appearance such as pose, aging and illumination. Therefore, by a robust suggestion of extracting intelligent information from multiple levels of fusion the scheme maximizes the identification and verification performance of face recognition systems under variations.

The organization of paper is as follows. Section 2 summarizes face recognition using Log-Gabor transforms. Section 3 presents the facial feature selection, while the proposed recognition scheme is explained in Sect. 4. Databases and experimental results are explained in Sect. 5. Finally Sect. 6 draws some conclusions.

## 2   Face Recognition Using Log-Gabor Transforms

Face recognition is considered as a very interesting area of biometric systems in last two decades. The typical processing steps done on face images in this study can be presented as preprocessing, feature extraction and match scores generation. All the face images in preprocessing step are resized to 60 × 60, and subsequently histogram equalization (HE) and mean-variance normalization (MVN) [18] techniques are used on face images to reduce the illumination effect of resized images.

According to linear frequency scale, Log-Gabor transform extracts the facial features by using transfer function presented in Eq. 1 [8]:

$$G(\omega) = \exp\left\{\frac{-\log\left(\frac{\omega}{\omega_0}\right)^2}{2 \times \log\left(\frac{k}{\omega_0}\right)^2}\right\} \tag{1}$$

where $\omega_0$ is the filter center frequency, $\omega$ is the normalized radius from center and $k$ is the standard deviation of angular component. The computation of constant shape filter is done by representing the ratio $\left(\frac{k}{\omega_0}\right)^2$ to be constant for varying values of $\omega_0$. In this paper, four different scales and eight orientations for the Log-Gabor transform are considered according to different trial results. The generated Log-Gabor transformed image is later down sampled by six. In this way, the final size of Log-Gabor transformed image is reduced to $40 \times 80$. In order to produce the matching scores, Manhattan distance measurement is applied in this paper.

## 3   Facial Feature Selection

Log-Gabor transforms is considered as a robust local-feature based technique for facial recognition under uncontrolled conditions [9]. However, as mentioned earlier high dimensionality is considered as a problem of facial extraction using Log-Gabor transforms. Therefore, designing a robust scheme to solve high dimensionality problem and consequently improving system performance is motivated. To design a robust facial recognition system consideration of a successful and efficient feature selection and/or transformation method for removing the redundant and irrelevant facial data is needed. In this study, we attempt to apply both feature selection and feature transformation techniques on extracted facial features using Log-Gabor transforms in order to find the most optimized facial feature sets. In fact, we find the best facial feature selection strategy under variations.

We first introduce the Log-Gabor transform based BSA as an effective technique to select the optimized set of Log-Gabor features. BSA is a novel population-based iterative evolutionary algorithm that is successfully used in many numerical optimization benchmark problems [17]. BSA eliminates the effect of problems encountered in Evolutionary Algorithms (EA) such as excessive sensitivity to control parameters, premature convergence and slow computation. This feature selection strategy searches local and global optimum in an optimization problem according to a certain objective function. BSA memory uses previous generation experiences to generate trial population. Algorithm 1 demonstrates the general architecture of BSA algorithm.

Selection of Log-Gabor facial features is done according to a binary bit string (1' means the feature is selected and '0' not selected) of length $M$. The objective function in this study is considered as recognition performance. In this study, we also propose to change the original trial population T of BSA to be appropriate for binary number generation as in Eq. 2:

---

**Algorithm 1.** General Structure of Backtracking Search Algorithm [17].
    1. Initialization
  **Repeat**
    2. Selection-I
  **Generation of Trial-Population**
      3. Mutation
      4. Crossover
  **End**
    5. Selection-II
  **Until stopping conditions are met**

---

$$T = P \vee (map \wedge F) \wedge |(oldp - P)| \tag{2}$$

where $F$ controls the amplitude of search direction matrix $(oldp - P)$ and it is set experimentally, $\vee$ and $\wedge$ are logical $OR$ and $AND$ operators. Additionally, achieving maximum number of iteration, or obtaining the optimal fitness value or failing to update the last best solution after 400 evaluations is considered as the stopping condition. In this study, we set $F = 1$, $mix - rate = 1$, population and iteration size are both set to 60. On the other hand, feature transformation methods can be considered to reduce the dimensionality and redundancy effect of large-scale facial features. LDA as a feature transformation strategy alleviate dimensionality while preserving as much of the class discriminatory information as possible. So, in this study we also implement Log-Gabor transforms based LDA to investigate the effect of class discriminatory strategies on performance and dimensionality of facial images under variations. Generally, LDA attempts to discriminate the input data by projecting input data into a lower dimensional space. LDA aim is to find the best projection by discriminating the patterns as much as possible. Indeed, LDA maximizes the between-class scatter and at the same time minimizes the within-class scatter in the projective feature vector space. We therefore apply Log-Gabor transform based LDA on facial images to reduce dimensionality problem while preserving as much of the class discriminatory information as possible. The number of eigenvectors applied in LDA projection is constrained by $L - 1$, where $L$ is number of individuals.

## 4   Proposed Scheme

The proposed scheme fuses the produced match scores of Log-Gabor transforms with BSA and LDA match scores to improve the recognition performance of Log-Gabor transforms based facial systems under variations and high dimensionality problems. In score fusion techniques, each single system provides matching scores and then the matching scores are combined to improve matching performance of the system. In general, fusion of multiple matchers for biometric recognition improvement has achieved considerable attention [19, 20] due to reporting high recognition performance. Among different fusion strategies score fusion can be considered as the best due to its simplicity and good performance. In fact, the optimized facial feature sets obtained by BAS and LDA can be combined as shown in Fig. 1 to provide richer information for a better matching. Indeed, fusion of scores produced by Log-Gabor transforms as a robust algorithm against variations with optimized scores obtained by BSA and LDA as proposed scheme can improve the recognition performance.

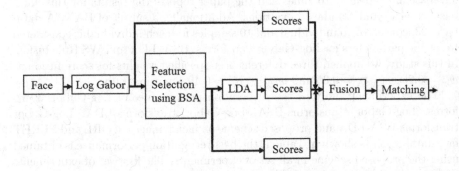

**Fig. 1.** Block diagram of proposed scheme

The extracted facial features using Log-Gabor transforms first are optimized by BSA and then LDA is used to discriminant the optimized features as much as possible. The scheme attempts to improve the recognition performance of the facial system by fusing the computed matching scores of Log-Gabor transforms, BSA and LDA. In this study, Weighted Sum Rule technique is applied to fuse scores of Log-Gabor transforms, BSA and LDA. We applied user-specific weight strategy to calculate the weighted sum of scores. Weighted Sum Rule (WS) of different score matchers can be calculated as in Eq. 3:

$$ws = w_1 \times s_1 + w_2 \times s_2 + \ldots + w_n \times s_n \qquad (3)$$

where $w_1, w_2, \ldots w_n$ are the assigned weights for different algorithms and $s_1, s_2, \ldots, s_n$ are the computed scores.

## 5  Databases and Experimental Results

The proposed facial recognition scheme is evaluated using ORL [21] and FERET [22] face databases. ORL face database considers different appearance based variations such as open/closed eyes, smiling/non-smiling and moderate pose and scale variations for the images and totally contains 40 individuals with 10 different frontal face images. All 40 subjects of ORL database are used to evaluate the scheme where randomly selected set of 5 images per individual are considered for training and the rest 5 for testing. We also consider the standard subsets of FERET database to perform the experiments. The gallery images are constructed using images in category Fa (1196 pictures) for four probe sets, Fb, Fc, Dup1 and

Dup2. Fb includes 1195 pictures having variations in expressions, Fc contains 194 pictures with variations in cameras and illumination conditions, 722 images of Dup1 are recorded at different times compared to Fa. Dup2 contains 234 images and it is a subset of Dup1, this dataset pictures are taken at least 18 months later after the gallery image was taken. Dup1 and Dup2 images can be used to study the effect of aging on recognition performance. The experiments for ORL face database are repeated 10 times and the paper reports the results for this database as mean and standard deviations. Additionally, a subset of BANCA database [23] consist of 40 individual and 10 samples for each individual is considered to set the parameters for Log-Gabor transforms, BSA, LDA and WS Rule fusion. In this study, we applied three different user-specified weights for score fusion as $w_{lg} = 0.25$, $w_{lgBSA} = 0.35$ and $w_{lgBSALDA} = 0.40$ experimentally.

The experiment analyzes the recognition performance of Log-Gabor transforms, Log-Gabor transforms-BSA, Log-Gabor transforms-LDA, Log-Gabor transforms-BSA-LDA and proposed scheme on facial images of ORL and FERET face databases. As shown in Table 1, the best recognition performance is obtained using the proposed scheme in all set of experiments. The first set of experiments evaluates the effect of Log-Gabor transforms with and without feature selection and feature transformation strategies along with the proposed scheme on ORL database. This database contains different kind of variations in the face images. Analyzing the results shows the effectiveness of feature transformation and selection methods on Log-Gabor transforms recognition performance. However, according to the experiments, for this database the recognition performance is better whenever BSA feature selection method is applied compared to the time that feature transformation method (LDA) is applied for feature reduction. We can also state that, the combination of feature selection and feature transformation methods leads to better recognition performance. Indeed, based on the experiments applying BSA feature selection to select the optimized set of facial features and then discriminating these optimized features by LDA causes a better performance compared to the time LDA is applied first and then BSA. However, the best recognition result is obtained using the proposed scheme including the scores of Log-Gabor transforms, BSA and LDA as 97.32 %.

In order to analyze the effect of different variations separately on face images, we repeated the experiments on standard subsets of FERET database as presented in Table 1. It can be observed that in all the scenarios the proposed scheme outperforms other methods. Precisely analyzing the table demonstrates the effect of score fusion on aging and illumination. On the other words, the recognition performance of proposed scheme and Log-Gabor + BSA + LDA for Fb subset of FERET database is 96.23 %. However, the proposed scheme for Fc, Dup1 and Dup2 subsets of FERET face database has achieved 1.03 %, 1.37 % and 2.08 % improvement over Log-Gabor + BSA + LDA that shows the robustness of proposed scheme against aging and illumination variations in facial images. Our investigation on effect of feature selection and feature transformation methods for Log-Gabor transforms shows in overall feature selection strategies work better in presence of different variations.

**Table 1.** Identification performance of different methods on ORL and FERET database.

| Method | ORL | FERET Fb | FERET Fc | FERET Dup1 | FERET Dup2 |
|---|---|---|---|---|---|
| Log-Gabor | 93.04 ± 2.06 | 90.29 | 71.13 | 65.24 | 63.58 |
| Log-Gabor + LDA | 94.83 ± 1.77 | 93.72 | 74.17 | 68.35 | 63.20 |
| Log-Gabor + BSA | 96.12 ± 2.11 | 95.06 | 77.74 | 69.12 | 65.16 |
| Log-Gabor + LDA + BSA | 95.94 ± 2.51 | 95.39 | 77.83 | 69.01 | 64.90 |
| Log-Gabor + BSA + LDA | 97.02 ± 1.46 | 96.23 | 80.41 | 71.92 | 66.00 |
| Proposed Scheme | **97.32 ± 2.21** | **96.23** | **81.44** | **73.29** | **68.08** |

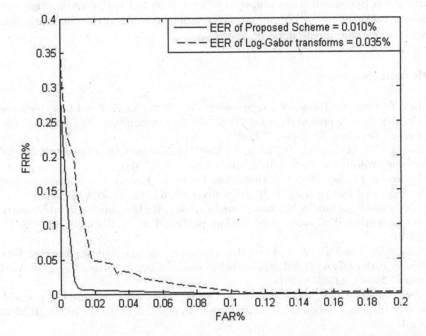

**Fig. 2.** ROC curves of proposed scheme and Log-Gabor transforms on ORL database

Figure 2 demonstrates the Receiver Operating Characteristic (ROC) analysis of the proposed method and Log-Gabor transforms. The figure compares the Equal Error Rate (EER) of proposed scheme and Log-Gabor transforms. As it is shown on the top of Fig. 2, the proposed scheme achieved better EER compared to Log-Gabor transforms that shows the superiority of the proposed scheme to overcome variations in appearance for face recognition. In addition, all the algorithms in this study are implemented on MATLAB 8.1. The computer is Intel(R) Core(TM) i5-5200U, 2.20 GHz CPU, 4 GB RAM and the system is Windows 10.

# 6   Conclusion

In this paper we investigate the effect of Log-Gabor transforms, BSA feature selection method and LDA feature transformation method on facial images under variations. On the other words, we studied the impact of feature transformation and feature selection techniques separately and together on recognition performance of facial systems under variations when Log-Gabor transforms is applied. We also proposed to fuse the produced scores of Log-Gabor transforms with the scores obtained using the same algorithm after feature selection and transformation. According to our experiment results the proposed scheme outperforms other implemented methods in this study. The experiment results demonstrated the effectiveness of proposed scheme for all variations in appearance studied in this work. Specifically, the proposed scheme achieved better recognition performance under aging and illumination variations compared to other variations based on the experiments done in this paper.

# References

1. Lei, Y., Guo, Y., Hayat, M., Bennamoun, M., Zhou, X.: A Two-Phase Weighted Collaborative Representation for 3D partial face recognition with single sample. Pattern Recognit. **52**, 218–237 (2016)
2. Zhanga, T., Li, X., Tao, D., Yang, J.: Multimodal biometrics using geometry preserving projections. Pattern Recognit. **41**, 805–813 (2008)
3. Juefei-Xu, F., Savvides, M.: Multi-class Fukunaga Koontz discriminant analysis for enhanced face recognition. Pattern Recognit. **52**, 186–205 (2016)
4. Al-Maadeed, S., Bourif, M., Bouridane, A., Jiang, R.: Low-quality facial biometric verification via dictionary-based random pooling. Pattern Recognit. **52**, 238–248 (2016)
5. Cao, N.T., Ton-That, A.H., Choi, H.I.: Facial expression recounting based on local binary pattern features and support vector machine. Int. J. Pattern Recognit. Artif. Intell. **28**(06), 1456012 (2014)
6. Fernández-Martínez, J.L., Ana, C.: Exploring the uncertainty space of ensemble classifiers in face recognition. Int. J. Pattern Recognit. Artif. Intell. **29**(03), 1556002 (2015)
7. Chen, S., Zhu, Y.: Subpattern-based principle component analysis. Pattern Recognit. **3**, 1081–1083 (2004)
8. Zhitao, X., Chengming, G., Ming, Y., Qiang, L.: Research on log gabor wavelet and its application in image edge detection. In: Proceedings of 6th International Conference on Signal Processing (ICSP-2002), USA, pp. 592–95 (2002)
9. Kavita, R.S., Mukesh, A.Z., Mukesh, M.R.: 3Face identification under uncontrolled environment with LGFSV face representation technique. Cent. Eur. J. Comput. Sci. **3**(3), 129–148 (2013)
10. Murugan, D., Arumugam, S., Rajalakshmi, K., Manish, T.: Performance evaluation of face recognition using Gabor filter, Log Gabor filter, and discrete wavelet transform. Int. J. Comput. Sci. Technol. (IJCSIT) **2**(1), 234 (2010)
11. Eskandari, M., Toygar, Ö.: Fusion of face and iris biometrics using local and global feature extraction methods. Sig. Image Video Process. **8**(6), 995–1006 (2014). Springer-Verlag, London

12. Eskandari, M., Toygar, Ö., Demirel, H.: A new approach for Face-Iris multimodal biometric recognition using score fusion. Int. J. Pattern Recognit. Artif. Intell. **27**(3), 1356004 (2013)

13. Gökberk, B., Irfanoğlu, M.O., Akarun, L., Alpaydın, E.: Learning the best subset of local features for face recognition. Pattern Recognit. **40**, 1520–1532 (2007)

14. Eskandari, M., Toygar, Ö., Demirel, H.: Feature extractor selection for face-iris multimodal recognition. Sig. Image Video Process. **8**(6), 1189–1198 (2014). Springer-Verlag London

15. Eskandari, M., Toygar, Ö.: Selection of Optimized features and weights on Face-Iris fusion using distance images. Comput. Vis. Image Underst. **137**, 63–75 (2015)

16. Zhang, D., Jing, X., Yang, J.: Biometric Image Discrimination (BID) Technologies. IGP/IRM Press edition, USA (2006)

17. Civicioglu, P.: Backtracking Search Optimization Algorithm for numerical optimization problems. Appl. Math. Comput. **219**, 8121–8144 (2013)

18. Pujol, P., Macho, D., Nadeu, C.: On real-time mean-and- variance normalization of speech recognition features. In: IEEE International Conference on Acoustics, Speech and Signal Processing (ICASSP 2006), Toulouse, France, pp. 773–776 (2006)

19. Nandakumar, K., Chen, Y., Dass, S.C., Jain, A.K.: Likelihood ratio-based biometric score fusion. IEEE Trans. Pattern Anal. Mach. Intell. **30**(2), 342–347 (2008)

20. Ross, A., Nandakumar, K., Jain, A.K.: Handbook of Multibiometrics. Springer, New York (2006). (Springer-Verlag Edition)

21. AT & T Laboratories Cambridge, The ORL Database of Faces (2000). http://www.camorl.co.uk

22. Philips, P.J., Wechsler, H., Huang, J., Rauss, P.: The FERET database and evaluation procedure for face recognition algorithms. Image Vis. Comput. **16**(5), 295–306 (1998)

23. Bailly-Balliére, E., et al.: The BANCA database and evaluation protocol. In: Kittler, J., Nixon, M.S. (eds.) AVBPA 2003. LNCS, vol. 2688, pp. 625–638. Springer, Heidelberg (2003). doi:10.1007/3-540-44887-X_74

# Medical Image Analysis

# Optimization of Numerical Calculations of Geometric Features of a Curve Describing Preprocessed X-Ray Images of Bones as a Starting Point for Syntactic Analysis of Finger Bone Contours

Marzena Bielecka[✉] and Adam Piórkowski

Chair of Geoinformatics and Applied Computer Science, Faculty of Geology,
Geophysics and Environmental Protection, AGH University of Science
and Technology, Mickiewicza 30, 30-059 Kraków, Poland
{bielecka,pioro}@agh.edu.pl

**Abstract.** Analysis of bone contours in X-ray images is crucial for the detection of pathological changes such as erosions and osteophytes. The analysis is done by using shape languages. In this approach the contour received from the preprocessing procedure is segmented into fragments according to geometrical properties of the contour. The properties are characterized by monotonicity and convexity of the contour. Two aforementioned features are deduced by using the first and second derivatives that are calculated numerically. On the one hand the used numerical procedure can smooth the analyzed contour. On the other hand, however, the more smoothed the contour is, the more chance that the small pathological changes remain undetected. Finding the optimal numerical procedure for X-ray hand images is the aim of this paper. (This paper was supported by the AGH - University of Science and Technology, Faculty of Geology, Geophysics and Environmental Protection as a part of the statutory project).

**Keywords:** Palm radiographs · Image preprocessing · Shape languages · Primitives · Numerical calculations of geometric features

## 1 Introduction

X-ray examination remains the basic method used as the basis for arthritis and musculoskeletal disorders diagnosis. In the case of hand images, changes in the border of finger joint surfaces observed on hand radiographs are crucial to medical diagnosis and support important pieces of information for estimation of a disease development and therapy efficiency. However, they are difficult to detect precisely by a human expert, due to the quantity of joints. Therefore, it is crucial to work out automatic analysis of radiographs by using computer algorithms [3,9,23]. This paper is focused on this topic and is a continuation of studies described in [1,2,4–6].

© Springer International Publishing AG 2016
L.J. Chmielewski et al. (Eds.): ICCVG 2016, LNCS 9972, pp. 365–376, 2016.
DOI: 10.1007/978-3-319-46418-3_32

Analysis of bone contours in X-ray images is crucial for the detection of pathological changes such as erosions and osteophytes. The analysis is done by using shape languages. In this approach the contour received from the preprocessing procedure is segmented into fragments according to geometrical properties of the contour. The properties are characterized by monotonicity and convexity of the contour. Two aforementioned features are deduced by using the first and second derivatives that are calculated numerically. On the one hand the used numerical procedure can smooth the analyzed contour. On the other hand, however, the more smoothed the contour is, the more chance that the small pathological changes remain undetected. Finding the optimal numerical procedure for X-ray hand images is the aim of this paper.

This paper is organized in the following way. In the next section motivations for the studies are referred. Then, the applied preprocessing procedure is described. In Sect. 4 the analysis of effectiveness of numerical procedures depending on the length of the minimal step of calculations is done.

## 2    Motivations

Bone contour analysis allows us to detect bone erosions and osteophytes which is important in medical diagnostics of inflammations and degenerations in joints. The automatization of X-ray images analysis is demanded because of the great number of radiograph examinations that are done every day [18,19]. Furthermore, it is important to detect changes at the early stages of the disease and tracing of the disease development. In the both aforementioned cases, very small changes should be detected. Radiographs have its own specificity. The problems concern preprocessing of this type of images are among them. Effective preprocessing of X-ray images is difficult and methods worked out for other types of images turn to be ineffective for X-ray images. Syntactic methods are applied to bone contours analysis but they are sensitive to distortions. Therefore, obtaining smooth contour as a result of preprocessing procedure is crucial for effective analysis by using syntactic methods. On the other hand, however, the smoothing procedure should not smooth small lesions. This means, that the smoothing process should be two-staged. The preliminary step should be done during preprocessing. The second step should be conjugate with the analyzing procedure. The balance between smoothness and preservation of the small pathological changes is crucial for effective analysis.

## 3    Preprocessing

Preprocessing is an important initial stage of the image analysis. There are a lot of image processing methods that can be applied to extract the desired components of the image. The fact that the quality of preprocessing is strongly dependent on various properties of the processed image is one of the crucial problems. For instance, hand radiographs have various resolutions which influence the preprocessing quality. Another problem is the luminance dynamic in the image, which is dependent on the radiograph acquisition parameters on the equipment and on the patient's hand anatomical features. The optimal preprocessing of the hand phalanges images should provide a precise contour of the bone, irrespective to the input image quality. Finding such a universal algorithm is probably impossible. Therefore, researches often create a dedicated solutions for the analysis of certain types of images. In [22] the Sobel gradient was used to obtain a separation of lines of fingers phalanxes. The preprocessing consisted in background removal based on dynamic thresholding. The $3 \times 3$ structural mask was used to remove all small noisy elements. In the further research the authors presented a new approach based on independent background removal for each highest peak which reflects the soft and bony structures, in relation to the average intensity of the background level as a solution for image nonuniformity [21]. The issue of identification of the borders of the upper and lower surfaces of phalanxes is also presented in [7,8,25]. The authors constructed an algorithm, which computes the path running through the borders of both surfaces.

## 3.1   SDA Algorithm to Extract Bone Contour

The Statistical Dominance Algorithm was developed for preprocessing of a group of images with various dynamic and noise level [17]. It describes in a statistical way whether the point belongs to an object or not. The main idea of SDA is to calculate all points in the selected neighborhood, that dominate over the central point. That pixels, which have a bigger value, belong to the object. Additional parameter is a threshold, that allows us to select only points which are definitely dominating, and therefore they belong to the object.

The algorithm can be defined by the formula:

$$
p\prime(x,y) = \sum_{i=-N, j=-N}^{i=N, j=N} \begin{cases} p'(x,y) := p'(x,y) + 1, & p(x+i, y+j) \geq p(x,y) + t, \\ & i^2 + j^2 \leq R^2 \\ p'(x,y) := p'(x,y), & \text{otherwise} \end{cases}
$$

$$(1)$$

where:

- $p(x,y)$ - the value of pixel $(x,y)$ in input image,
- $p'(x,y)$ - the value of pixel $(x,y)$ in output image,
- $R$ - radius of neighborhood,
- $N$ - size of neighborhood mask, $N = \lceil R \rceil$
- $t$ - *threshold* - the optional difference to be checked.

The main advantage of the algorithm is small sensitivity to the pixel values variance, because it accounts only the relation between pixels. This often allows us to omit a local thresholding. Similar approach exploiting statistical information about image content is used for skin and bone contour localization in USG images [15].

## 3.2    The Stages of Preprocessing

At the initial stage of preprocessing an optional smoothing is performed. It is needed in the case of significant level of noise in a radiograph. The main step is to use the SDA algorithm with adjusted parameters (radius - dependent of the image resolution, threshold - 10 % of image dynamic range) - see Fig. 1. Next, the output image is binarised (threshold of 1). The fourth stage contains a contour extraction using the following square mask - see Table 1, [24]:

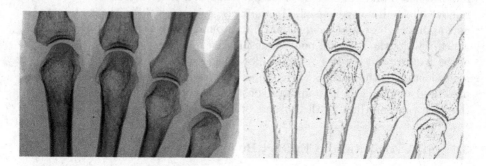

**Fig. 1.** The example of fingers radiograph and the output image of SDA (R = 25, t = 100).

**Table 1.** A mask for contour extraction

| 1 | 1 | 1 |
|---|---|---|
| 1 | 1 | 1 |
| 1 | 1 | 1 |

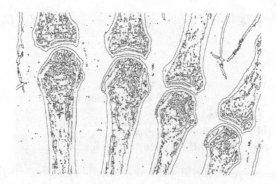

**Fig. 2.** The result of binarisation of the output of SDA and contour extraction.

The result of binarisation is shown in Fig. 2. The output segmentation can be additionally smoothed by using thinning with a set of masks presented in [16].

In the end, the removal of small objects is performed to keep only a contour of phalanxes.

# 4    Numerical Procedure Analysis

The next stage of the analysis of a received contour is its description by so-called primitives. The contour is analyzed as a curve on the Euclidean plane. It is divided into fragments which are segments with constant values of four components $[c', c'', c^x, c^y]$ which constitute a vector $\mathbf{c}$. The first component $c'$ encodes the properties of the tangent line. They can be vertical, horizontal, increasing or decreasing. The second component encodes whether the contour fragment is concave, convex, flat vertical or flat horizontal. The components $c^x$ and $c^y$ encode increase of the $x$ coordinate and the $y$ coordinate, respectively. As a result the analyzed contour, let it be denoted as $k$, can be described by a string of primitives i.e. the maximal fragments for which the vector $\mathbf{c} = [c', c'', c^x, c^y]$ is constant. Let us denote the possible vectors $\mathbf{c}$ by using bi-index as $p_{ij}, i, j \in \{1, 2, 3, 4\}$. Each of these vectors corresponds to one of the quadrants of the Cartesian plane - the index $i$. Then, the contour $k$ can be characterized by its descriptor as a string of primitives: $des(k) = p_{i_1 j_1} p_{i_2 j_2} ... p_{i_n j_n}$. Next, by using a transducer a key of the contour $k$ is received that represents it in the subsequent stages of the recognition process. The proposed primitives were defined in [1]. It should be noticed that the transducer is widely used both in engineering and medical applications [13, 14, 20]. The output of the transducer is denoted by $key(k) = a_0 b_0 w_0 \cdot a_1 b_1 w_1 \cdots a_{n+1} b_{n+1} w_{n+1}$ where every pair $a_i b_j$ determines transition between $i$-sinquad to $j$-sinquad [1] and $w_i \in \{0, 1\}$. If $w_i = 0$ then the analyzed fragment of a contour will be concave. If $w_i = 1$ then the analyzed fragment of a contour will be convex [13]. Such approach is sufficient to detect changes in a bone contour i.e. erosions and osteophytes.

As the primitives are calculated in a numerical way it also means that an analyzed contour is additionally smoothing. However the result of such smoothing can be unsatisfactory. It can cause that small lesions in the bone contour can be neglected. Therefore it is needed to set such a step of computations that small changes in the contour (as erosions and osteophytes) could be noticed. The experiment was carried out by using the data set of 600 joint surfaces acquired from the University Hospital in Kraków, Poland. Only the upper joint surface of the second joint of every finger was considered. It can also be done for the first joint but then other type of patterns have to be considered. The set contains 6 examples of osteophtes and 15 examples of erosions. For every received contours the calculations were conducted for a step $s$ equals 3 points, 5 points and 7 points. Thus every contour was described by three descriptors. If a given contour $k_1$ does not have any lesions - see Fig. 3 then its descriptor after using a transducer is represented by a key:

$$key(k_1) = 341.411.140.411.121,$$

The accepted value of $s$ obviously does not have any meaning. In every case the received key is the same and represents the class of healthy contours - see Table 2.

**Table 2.** Keys of a healthy contour for different values of s

| s - number of points | received keys |
| --- | --- |
| 3 | 341.411.140.411.121 |
| 5 | 341.411.140.411.121 |
| 7 | 341.411.140.411.121 |

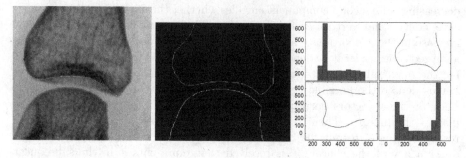

**Fig. 3.** The examples of a healthy joint with an outline made by an expert (first from the left) and with outline received by using the statistical dominance algorithm (middle and right).

In the case of erosions and osteophytes the keys are different. If a given contour $k_2$ has left osteopyte Figs. 4 and 5 then its key is following:

$$\text{key}(k_2) = 341.430.341.411.140.411.121,$$

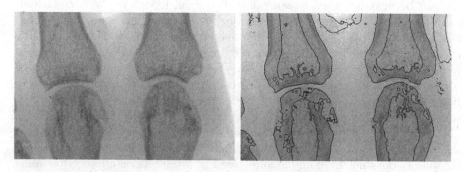

**Fig. 4.** The examples of joints with osteophytes (left) and theirs outlines made by using the statistical dominance algorithm (right).

The accepted value of $s$ can influence the received key. In the analyzed examples for every accepted values of $s$ osteophytes were recognized - see Table 3. The received key represents the $LE$ class i.e. the class of contours with left osteophyte (Table 3).

**Table 3.** Keys of a contour with left osteophyte for different values of s

| s - number of points | received keys |
|---|---|
| 3 | 341.430.341.411.140.411.121 |
| 5 | 341.430.341.411.140.411.121 |
| 7 | 341.430.341.411.140.411.121 |

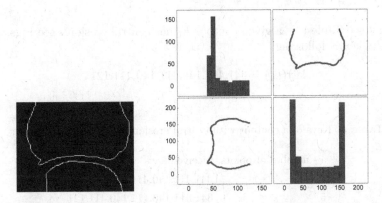

**Fig. 5.** The contour of a joint with left osteophyte made by using the statistical dominance algorithm.

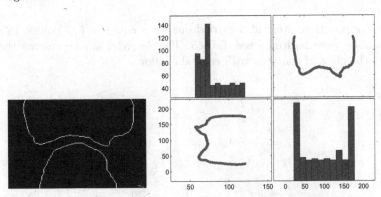

**Fig. 6.** The contour of a joint with right osteophyte made by using the statistical dominance algorithm.

If a given contour $k_3$ has right osteophyte - see Figs. 4 and 6 then its key is following:

$$\text{key}(k_3) = 341.411.140.411.121.210.121,$$

The accepted value of s can influence the received key. In the analyzed examples for s equals 3 points and 5 points right osteophyte was recognized. However, for s equals 7 points the smoothing of contour made the right osteophyte invisible and as a result the received key is exactly the same as for a healthy

**Table 4.** Keys of a contour with right osteophyte for different values of s

| s - number of points | received keys |
| --- | --- |
| 3 | 341.411.140.411.121.210.121 |
| 5 | 341.411.140.411.121.210.121 |
| 7 | 341.411.140.411.121 |

contour - see Table 4. If a given contour $k_4$ has central erosion - see Figs. 7 and 8 then its key is following:

$$\text{key}(k_4) = 341.411.140.411.140.411.121,$$

**Table 5.** Keys of a contour with central erosion for different values of s

| s - number of points | received keys |
| --- | --- |
| 3 | 341.411.140.411.140.411.121 |
| 5 | 341.411.140.411.140.411.121 |
| 7 | 341.411.140.411.140.411.121 |

The computations were also carried out for $s$ equals $3, 5, 7$ points. In every case erosions were noticed - see Table 5. The received key represents the $CE$ class i.e. the class of contours with central erosion.

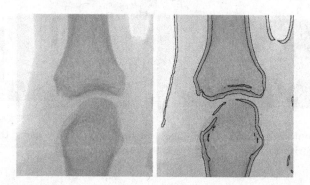

**Fig. 7.** The example of a joint with central erosion (left) and its outline made by using the statistical dominance algorithm (right).

If a given contour $k_5$ has left erosion - see Fig. 9 and Fig. 10 then its key is following:

$$\text{key}(k_5) = 341.430.341.411.140.411.121,$$

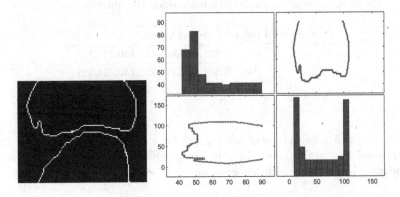

**Fig. 8.** The contour of a joint with central erosion made by using the statistical dominance algorithm.

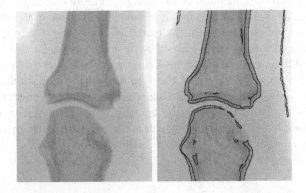

**Fig. 9.** The example of a joint with left erosion (left) and its outline made by using the statistical dominance algorithm (right).

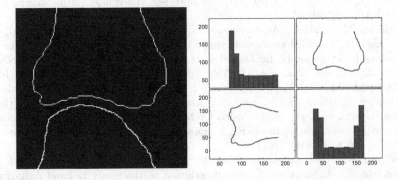

**Fig. 10.** The contour of a joint with left erosion made by using the statistical dominance algorithm.

**Table 6.** Keys of a contour with left erosion for different values of s

| s - number of points | received keys |
| --- | --- |
| 3 | 341.430.341.411.140.411.121 |
| 5 | 341.430.341.411.140.411.121 |
| 7 | 341.430.341.411.140.411.121 |

The computations were also carried out for $s$ equals $3, 5, 7$ points. In every case erosions were noticed - see Table 6. The received key represents the $LE$ class i.e. the class of contours with left erosion.

## 5  Concluding Remarks

The SDA algorithm used as a preprocessing procedure turned to be effective for obtaining bone contours in hand X-ray images. The obtained contours numerical procedure, for which three, five and seven points were the minimal step of calculations, has been tested. In the examined cases the smallest lesions were smoothed and, as a consequence, cannot be detected except for seven points procedures. Such differences in effectiveness can be utilized in the detection of early pathological changes. The length of the step for which the pathological change is smoothed is a good measure for its size and, as a consequence, development of the disease. The keys that describe healthy bones, bones with erosion and bones with osteophyte are different, which is the starting point for the syntactic analysis of the contour in the context of medical diagnosis.

## References

1. Bielecka, M., Korkosz, M.: Generalized shape language application to detection of a specific type of bone erosion in X-ray images. In: Rutkowski, L., Korytkowski, M., Scherer, R., Tadeusiewicz, R., Zadeh, L.A., Zurada, J.M. (eds.) ICAISC 2016. LNCS (LNAI), vol. 9692, pp. 531–540. Springer, Heidelberg (2016). doi:10.1007/978-3-319-39378-0_45
2. Bielecka, M., Bielecki, A., Korkosz, M., Skomorowski, M., Wojciechowski, W., Zieliński, B.: Modified jakubowski shape transducer for detecting osteophytes and erosions in finger joints. In: Dobnikar, A., Lotrič, U., Šter, B. (eds.) ICANNGA 2011. LNCS, vol. 6594, pp. 147–155. Springer, Heidelberg (2011). doi:10.1007/978-3-642-20267-4_16
3. Benerjee, S., Bhunia, S., Schaefer, G.: Osteophyte detection for hand osteoarthritis identification in X-ray images using CNNs. In: Proceedings of the Annual International Conference of the IEEE Engineering in Medicine and Biology Society, EMBS, vol. 6196–6199 (2011)
4. Bielecka, M., Bielecki, A., Korkosz, M., Skomorowski, M., Wojciechowski, W., Zieliński, B.: Application of shape description methodology to hand radiographs interpretation. In: Bolc, L., Tadeusiewicz, R., Chmielewski, L.J., Wojciechowski, K. (eds.) ICCVG 2010. LNCS, vol. 6374, pp. 11–18. Springer, Heidelberg (2010). doi:10.1007/978-3-642-15910-7_2

5. Bielecka, M., Piórkowski, A.: Adaptive preprocessing of X-ray hand images. In: Piętka, E., Kawa, J., Wieclawek, W. (eds.) Information Technologies in Biomedicine, Volume 3. AISC, vol. 283, pp. 61–70. Springer, Heidelberg (2014). doi:10. 1007/978-3-319-06593-9_6

6. Bielecka, M., Skomorowski, M., Zieliński, B.: A fuzzy shape descriptor and inference by fuzzy relaxation with application to description of bones contours at hand radiographs. In: Kolehmainen, M., Toivanen, P., Beliczynski, B. (eds.) ICANNGA 2009. LNCS, vol. 5495, pp. 469–478. Springer, Heidelberg (2009). doi:10.1007/ 978-3-642-04921-7_48

7. Bielecki, A., Korkosz, M., Wojciechowski, W., Zieliński, B.: Identifying the borders of the upper and lower metacarpophalangeal joint surfaces on hand radiographs. In: Rutkowski, L., Scherer, R., Tadeusiewicz, R., Zadeh, L.A., Zurada, J.M. (eds.) ICAISC 2010. LNCS (LNAI), vol. 6113, pp. 589–596. Springer, Heidelberg (2010). doi:10.1007/978-3-642-13208-7_73

8. Bielecki, A., Korkosz, M., Zieliński, B.: Hand radiographs preprocessing, image representation in the finger regions and joint space width measurements for image interpretation. Pattern Recogn. 41, 3786–3798 (2008)

9. Bottcher, J., Pfeil, A., Rosholm, A., Petrovitch, A., Seidl, B.E., Malich, A., Schäfer, M.L., Kramer, A., Mentzel, H.J., Lehmann, G., Hein, G., Kaiser, W.A.: Digital X-ray radiogrammetry combined with semiautomated analysis of joint space widths as a new diagnostic approach in rheumatoid arthritis: a cross-sectional and longitudal study. Arthritis Rheum. 52, 3850–3859 (2006)

10. Choi, S., Lee, G.J., Hong, S.J., Park, K.H., Urtnasan, T., Park, H.K.: Development of a joint space width measurement method based on radiographic hand images. Comput. Biol. Med. 41, 987–998 (2011)

11. Davis, L., Theobald, B.-J., Toms, A., Bagnall, A.: On the extraction and classification of hand outlines. In: Yin, H., Wang, W., Rayward-Smith, V. (eds.) IDEAL 2011. LNCS, vol. 6936, pp. 92–99. Springer, Heidelberg (2011). doi:10. 1007/978-3-642-23878-9_12

12. Davis, L., Theobald, B.J., Lines, J., Toms, A., Bagnall, A.: On the segmentation and classification of hand radiographs. Int. J. Neural Syst. 22, 1250020–1250036 (2012)

13. Jakubowski, R.: Extraction of shape features for syntactic recognition of mechanical parts. IEEE Trans. Syst. Man Cybern. 15, 642–651 (1985)

14. Jakubowski, R.: A structural representation of shape and its features. Inf. Sci. 39, 129–151 (1986)

15. Nurzynska, K., Smolka, B.: Automatic finger joint synovitis localization in ultrasound images. In: Proceedings of the SPIE, vol. 9897, pp: 98970N–98970N-11 (2016). doi:10.1117/12.2227638

16. Piórkowski, A., Gronkowska–Serafin, J.: Towards precise segmentation of corneal endothelial cells. In: Ortuño, F., Rojas, I. (eds.) IWBBIO 2015. LNCS, vol. 9043, pp. 240–249. Springer, Heidelberg (2015). doi:10.1007/978-3-319-16483-0_25

17. Piórkowski, A.: A statistical dominance algorithm for edge detection and segmentation of medical images. In: Piętka, E., Badura, P., Kawa, J., Wieclawek, W. (eds.) Information Technologies in Medicine. AISC, vol. 471, pp. 3–14. Springer, Heidelberg (2016). doi:10.1007/978-3-319-39796-2_1

18. Ogiela, M., Tadeusiewicz, R.: Picture languages in automatic radiological palm interpretation. Int. J. Appl. Math. Comput. Sci. 15, 305–312 (2005)

19. Ogiela, M.R., Tadeusiewicz, R., Ogiela, L.: Image languages in intelligent radiological palm diagnostics. Pattern Recogn. 39, 2157–2165 (2006)

20. Ogiela, M.R., Tadeusiewicz, R.: Syntactic pattern recognition for X-ray diagnosis of pancreatic cancer-algorithms for analyzing the morphologic shape of pancreatic ducts for early diagnosis of changes in the pancreas. IEEE Eng. Med. Biol. Mag. **19**, 94–105 (2000)

21. Pietka, E., Gertych, A., Pospiech-Kurkowska, S., Cao, F., Huang, H., Gilzanz, V., et al.: Computer-assisted bone age assessment: graphical user interface for image processing and comparison. J. Digit. Imaging **17**(3), 175–188 (2004)

22. Pietka, E., Gertych, A., Pospiech, S., Cao, F., Huang, H., Gilsanz, V.: Computer-assisted bone age assessment: Image preprocessing and epiphyseal/metaphyseal ROI extraction. IEEE Trans. Med. Imaging **20**(8), 715–729 (2001)

23. Sharp, J., Gardner, J.: Bennett E: Computer-based methods for measuring joint space and estimating erosion volume in the finger and wrist joints of patients with rheumatoid arthritis. Arthritis Rheum. **43**, 1378–1386 (2000)

24. Tadeusiewicz, R., Korohoda, P.: Computer analysis and image processing. Progress of Telecommunication Foundation Publishing House, Cracow (1997)

25. Zieliński, B., Skomorowski, M., Wojciechowski, W., Korkosz, M., Sprężak, K.: Computer aided erosions and osteophytes detection based on hand radiographs. Pattern Recogn. **48**, 2304–2317 (2015)

# Construction of a 3D Geometric Model of a Presynaptic Bouton for Use in Modeling of Neurotransmitter Flow

Andrzej Bielecki[1], Maciej Gierdziewicz[1(✉)], Piotr Kalita[2], and Kamil Szostek[3]

[1] Chair of Applied Computer Science, Faculty of Electrical Engineering,
Automation, Computer Science and Biomedical Engineering, AGH University
of Science and Technology, Al. Mickiewicza 30, 30-059 Kraków, Poland
{bielecki,gierdzma}@agh.edu.pl
[2] Chair of Optimization and Control Theory, Faculty of Mathematics and Computer
Science, Jagiellonian University, Łojasiewicza 6, 30-348 Kraków, Poland
kalita@ii.uj.edu.pl
[3] Chair of Geoinformatics and Applied Computer Science, Faculty of Geology,
Geophysics and Environmental Protection, AGH University of Science
and Technology, Al. Mickiewicza 30, 30-059 Kraków, Poland
kamil.szostek@agh.edu.pl

**Abstract.** This paper refers strongly to mathematical modeling of diffusive process in a presynaptic bouton. Creation of a robust three-dimensional model of the bouton geometry is the topic of the paper. Such a model is necessary for partial differential equations that describe the aforementioned flows. The proposed geometric model is based on ultra-thin sections obtained by using electron microscopy. The data structure which describes the surface of the whole bouton as well as the surfaces of some internal organelles is created as the result of the modeling procedure.

**Keywords:** Presynaptic bouton · Partial differential equations model · Three-dimensional bouton geometry · Finite elements method

## 1 Introduction

Signal conductivity in a synapse is one of the crucial topics in neurophysiological studies. These investigations have both strong experimental and theoretical aspects. Numerous measurements and observations concerning processes that take place in the presynaptic bouton, the synaptic cleft and the postsynaptic membrane are performed [8–10,17,21]. Theoretical models that not only complement them but also allow us to describe and understand deeply the dynamics of conductive phenomena are worked out as well [6,7]. Mathematical models, based on differential equations, among them on partial ones, are one of the main ways of modeling of the aforementioned phenomena. Partial differential equations need a good geometric model of the structure, in which the processes that are described by the model, occur [2–7].

© Springer International Publishing AG 2016
L.J. Chmielewski et al. (Eds.): ICCVG 2016, LNCS 9972, pp. 377–386, 2016.
DOI: 10.1007/978-3-319-46418-3_33

In this paper we refer to the partial differential model of neurotransmitter flow in a presynaptic bouton. The creation of a robust three-dimensional model of the bouton geometry is the topic of this paper. It should be stressed that the described considerations are a continuation of the studies presented in [2,3,5].

## 2    Motivation

Partial differential equations are used for modeling the dynamics of neurotransmitter flows because this type of model can reflect both temporal and spatial aspects of the described phenomenon. The spatial aspect, however, needs an accurate model of the geometry of the physical structures that are the scene for the modeled dynamic processes. In the considered case this means that it is necessary to create a data structure that describes the geometry of the presynaptic bouton, including internal organelles. Taking into consideration the specificity of the finite elements method (FEM) which is used for numerical solution of the obtained differential nonlinear equations with a given boundary condition, the surfaces of both the bouton and internal organelles should be approximated by using triangles or quadrangles. They are the basis for generation of a tetrahedral mesh to the vertices of which the numerical calculations refer. Creating both the aforementioned data structure and the mesh is not a trivial task. Therefore, frequently, very simplified geometric models are used for numerical calculations - for instance in [3] numerical simulations were performed in two dimensions. The more accurately the geometric aspects are described, the better the whole model reflects all aspects of the considered phenomena and, as a consequence, the more the model is useful. Therefore, creating a robust model of the geometric aspects of the biological structures in which the neurotransmitter flows take place is crucial for founding the adequate mathematical description.

## 3    The Model of Neurotransmitter Dynamics

The model of a presynaptic bouton is needed to estimate the neurotransmitter density. Both the theoretical foundations of the model and its application in a simplified two-dimensional case have been already presented [2-5]. In the methodology applied to reach that goal in the cited papers it has been assumed that neurotransmitter density changes are governed by a partial differential equation with two terms: a "diffusive" term and a "synthesis" term, accomplished by the initial condition (the initial distribution of the neurotransmitter) and the boundary condition (the lack of flow of the neurotransmitter outside the bouton except periodical time intervals of stimulation in a specific release zone of the bouton membrane). This paper describes the next step in modeling i.e. the 3D model of a presynaptic bouton, required for calculating the spatial distribution of the density of the neurotransmitter within the bouton and the changes of that density in time. The model is based on the description of average bouton modeling [23] where the author presents the approximated model of the bouton from a rat brain. The model was built on the basis of multiple images from electron microscopy (EM). Ultrathin sections obtained from EM were used to reconstruct the physical properties of a synaptosome: its size, shape and organelle composition as well. The author prepared and reconstructed more than 60 different boutons. Despite the noticeable diversity of physical characteristics of the boutons, the average model was created and described. Also, the amount of synaptic vesicles was approximated as a linear function of a bouton size. What is more, both in the above cited paper and in the work [24], the absolute protein composition of a presynaptic terminal has been quantified.

To simulate vesicles propagation, the FEM method requires a tetrahedral (or hexahedral) 3D model of the synaptosome. To reach that goal, the methods similar to those presented before, for example in [11,20,22], can be applied. The significant feature of the 3D modeling is, that first a surface mesh on the boundary of the modeled domain must be generated. This mesh is next used as an input data for volume mesh generation algorithms. In [22] the author describes both the whole-heart modeling obtained with similar techniques and its possibilities in various heart simulations. After the surface mesh is generated, a tetrahedral model required for FEM calculations can be constructed semi-automatically with, for example, TetGen(R) software [14,15,18].

## 4   The Bouton 3D Model

Based on the work in [23], the 3D model of the typical (average) bouton was prepared. The computer program used in that stage of the project was 3D designing software 3D Studio Max 2014 from Autodesk [1], since it has a wide spectrum of possibilities to create and manipulate various kinds of 3D objects. With that program, the approximated model was created from a default geoshperical object, i.e., the approximation of the sphere by using planar triangles. The radius of the geosphere was $0.77\,\mu m$ and the volume was $1.93\,\mu m^3$. This objects are constructed by using triangles that are as close to the equilateral triangle as possible. First, the standard *Perlin noise* modifier was applied to make the surface pleated. Its strength was set to $0.07\,\mu m$ in all directions and scaled to 220. Then, the object was converted into editable mesh and adjusted manually to reflect main bouton surface features. The model was manually shaped by carefully moving surface vertices to achieve target volume of $1.1\,\mu m^3$. Afterwards, some of the triangles were detached to open the bouton, what corresponds to an axon exit. The detached triangles, flattened to construct a cap, were intended to be used to close the mesh since it is required for the tetrahedral mesh generation. This cap was further modified to include the mitochondrion body model opening. Then, final shape adjustments were performed using *Scale* tool to reflect the physical properties like volume and surface, presented in Table 1. The selected approach is considered to be sufficient, as the boutons vary significantly in size and shape (cf. Fig. 3.7A in [23]). The process of constructing the mesh is illustrated in Fig. 1.

The mitochondrion was constructed in a slightly different manner.

First, a simple box object with only a small number of triangles was constructed. It was then modified by hand and a *MeshSmooth* modifier, which

**Table 1.** Physical parameters of the bouton ([23] p. 55.)

| Parameter | Value |
|---|---|
| Volume | $1.1 \pm 0.1\,\mu m^3$ |
| Surface | $4.4 \pm 0.3\,\mu m^2$ |
| Number of vesicles | $383.7 \pm 37.9$ |
| Volume occupied by vesicles | $0.015 \pm 0.001\,\mu m^3$ |
| Number of active zones per synapse | $0.71 \pm 0.09$ |
| Average size of active zone | $0.21 \pm 0.04\,\mu m^2$ |
| Number of mitochondria per synapse | $0.65 \pm 0.08$ |
| Average size of mitochondria | $0.18 \pm 0.04\,\mu m^3$ |

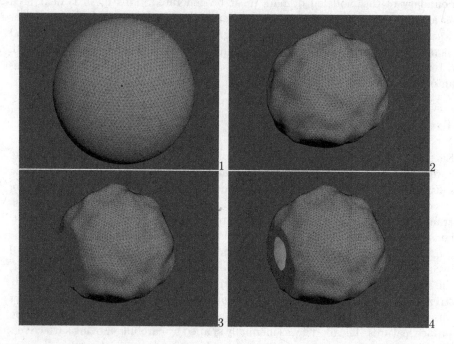

**Fig. 1.** The steps of the modeling the bouton surface mesh. First the sphere (1), then a *Noise* modifier applied (2), the axon exit flattening (3) and the result with the closing cap (4).

increases number of triangles and creates smooth mesh using NURMS (non-uniform rational mesh smooth) subdivision algorithm, was applied. This technique, known as box modeling, is one of the oldest methods used in computer graphics [13,16]. Figure 2 shows the mitochondrion in relation to the bouton surface.

The bottom part of the bouton was marked as the active zone for further simulations.

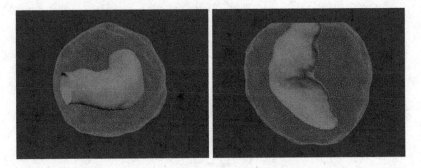

**Fig. 2.** The model of mitochondrion in the bouton: the perspective and top view

This zone, as described in, e.g., [4], is the area of releasing neurotransmitter molecules into the synaptic cleft, and was presented in Fig. 3.

**Fig. 3.** The area marked and detached as a neurotransmitter release zone, required for the further simulation

The size of the bouton varies, therefore the model was created with volume of about $1.0\,\mu m^3$ and the area about $4.65\,\mu m^2$. The bouton is built of 14 467 triangles with average area of $3.60 \times 10^{-6}\,\mu m^2$ and median $3.89 \times 10^{-6}\,\mu m^2$. The histogram of their areas is presented in Fig. 4.

The mitochondrion is built of 3 840 triangles, with average area of $512 \times 10^{-6}\,\mu m^2$ and median $382 \times 10^{-6}\,\mu m^2$. The histogram in Fig. 5 shows the distribution of triangle areas.

The two histograms differ because of the different techniques used to create the meshes.

Besides the bouton surface, vesicles were created. Each synaptic vesicle was constructed using default sphere object with 960 triangles each. The number and distribution of the vesicles were approximated according to Table 1 and equals 380, which gives us the cumulative volume of all vesicles $0.015\,\mu m^3$.

The quality of the generated triangular mesh can be measured by calculating the ratio of the longest side to the radius of the inscribed circle [12]. The

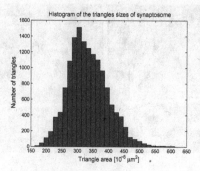

**Fig. 4.** The histogram of triangles sizes of bouton mesh

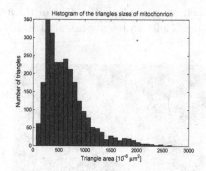

**Fig. 5.** The histogram of triangles sizes of mitochondrion mesh

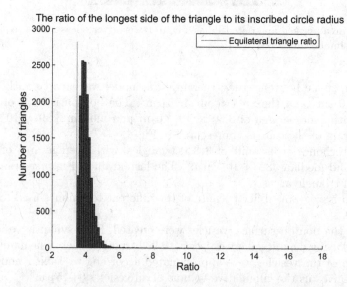

**Fig. 6.** Histogram of triangles quality for generated surface mesh

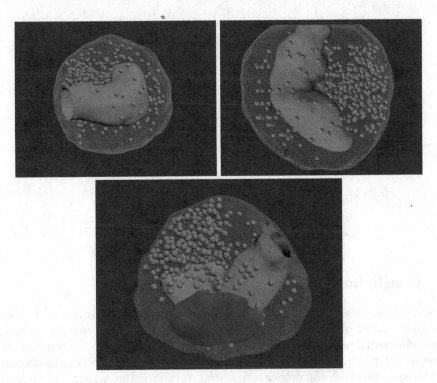

**Fig. 7.** The results of bouton modeling

smaller this parameter is, the closer is the triangle to the equilateral one and, simultaneously, the numerical properties of the mesh are better. Calculated data for the generated mesh is presented in Fig. 6 and Table 2.

Additionally, a script was written and used to distribute all synaptic vesicles inside the bouton. The script randomly positions the vesicles and verifies that the objects do not intersect with each other. The vesicles are presented in Fig. 7.

The results of modeling, presented in Fig. 7 and Table 3, were exported using Wavefront .obj file format [19], which is a format created for use with Wavefront's Advanced Visualizer (Table 2). This text file contains information about vertices, edges and triangles and can be easily imported into other software.

**Table 2.** Measure of generated mesh quality versus the corresponding ideal value for equilateral triangle.

| | Mean value | Median value | Equilateral triangle |
|---|---|---|---|
| $\frac{\text{Longest side}}{\text{Inscribed circle radius}}$ | 4.03 | 3.96 | 3.46 |

**Table 3.** Physical parameters of the modeled boutons

| Parameter | Value |
|---|---|
| Synaptosom volume | $1.0\,\mu m^3$ |
| Synaptosom dimensions | $1.30 \times 1.18 \times 1.12\,\mu m^3$ |
| Synaptosom surface area | $4.65\,\mu m^2$ |
| Vesicle volume | $38.17 \times 10^{-6}\,\mu m^3$ |
| Vesicle diameter | $0.0197\,\mu m$ |
| Number of vesicles | 380 |
| Cumulative vesicle volume | $0.0145\,\mu m^3$ |
| Mitochondrion volume | $0.147\,\mu m^3$ |
| Mitochondrion surface area | $1.79\,\mu m^2$ |
| Active Zone area | $0.273\,\mu m^2$ |

# 5    Concluding Remarks

It should be stressed that this paper summarizes one of the stages of a more complex project of modeling the dynamics of processes in the synaptic bouton with differential equations. Once the surface structure of the bouton and its internal components have been modeled, the next stage will be filling the domain of the equations with the proper tetrahedral mesh structure which is to be used to investigate processes and phenomena in the synapse. Therefore the quality of the surface mesh is absolutely essential. Too small number of vertices would introduce numerical errors; on the other hand, too large number would result in the dramatic increase of computational costs. The presented solution is a compromise between accuracy of geometric representation (and, consequently, the degree of reflecting the reality) and the efficiency of planned calculations, and is suitable for implementing in future the algorithm of numerical integration to model neurotransmitter flow in the presynaptic bouton.

**Acknowledgement.** The work of Piotr Kalita has been supported by the National Science Center of Poland under the Maestro Advanced Project No. DEC-2012/06/A/ST1/00262.

# References

1. AutoDesk 3DS max software. http://www.autodesk.pl/products/3ds-max/
2. Bielecki, A., Kalita, P.: Model of neurotransmitter fast transport in axon terminal of presynaptic neuron. J. Math. Biol. **56**, 559–576 (2008)
3. Bielecki, A., Kalita, P., Lewandowski, M., Siwek, B.: Numerical simulation for a neurotransmitter transport model in the axon terminal of a presynaptic neuron. Biol. Cybern. **102**, 489–502 (2010)
4. Bielecki, A., Kalita, P., Lewandowski, M., Skomorowski, M.: Compartment model of neuropeptide synaptic transport with impulse control. Biol. Cybern. **99**, 443–458 (2008)

5. Bielecki, A., Kalita, P.: Dynamical properties of the reaction-diffusion type model of fast synaptic transport. J. Math. Anal. Appl. **393**, 329–340 (2012)
6. Bobrowski, A.: Boundary conditions in evolutionary equations in biology. In: Banasiak, J., Mokhtar-Kharroubi, M. (eds.) Evolutionary Equations with Applications in Natural Sciences. LNM, vol. 2126, pp. 47–92. Springer, Heidelberg (2015). doi:10.1007/978-3-319-11322-7_2
7. Bobrowski, A., Morawska, K.: From a PDE model to an ODE model of dynamics of synaptic depression. Discreté Continuous Dyn. Syst. Ser. B **17**, 2313–2327 (2012)
8. Bui, L., Glavinovic, M.: Synaptic activity slows vesicular replenishment at excitatory synapses of rat hippocampus. Cogn. Neurodyn. **7**, 105–120 (2013)
9. Bui, L., Glavinovic, M.: Is replenishment of the readily releasable pool associated with vesicular movement? Cogn. Neurodyn. **8**, 99–110 (2014)
10. Bui, L., Glavinovic, M.: Temperature dependence of vesicular dynamics at excitatory synapses of rat hippocampus. Cogn. Neurodyn. **8**, 277–286 (2014)
11. Burger, B., Bettinghausen, S., Hesser, R., Hesser, J.: Real-time GPU-based ultrasound simulation using deformable mesh models. IEEE Trans. Med. Imaging **32**(3), 609–618 (2013)
12. Ciarlet, P.G.: The Finite Element Method for Elliptic Problems (Classics in Applied Mathematics). 2nd edn. Society for Industrial and Applied Mathematics (SIAM) (2002)
13. Derakhshani, D., Munn, R.L.: Introducing 3ds Max 9: 3D for Beginners. pp. 164–177 (2007). ISBN 9781118058541
14. Hang, S.: TetGen: a quality tetrahedral mesh generator and 3D delaunay triangulator, version 1.4 user manual. WIAS - Weierstrass Institute for Applied Analysis and Stochastics (WIAS) (2006)
15. Hang, S.: TetGen, a Delaunay-based quality tetrahedral mesh generator. ACM Trans. Math. Softw. **41**(2), (2015). Article 11
16. Hughes, J.F., van Dam, A., McGuire, M., Sklar, D.F., Foley, J.D., Feiner, S.K., Akeley, K.: Computer Graphics: Principles and Practice, 3rd edn. Addison-Wesley Professional, Boston (2013)
17. Knodel, M.M., Geiger, R., Ge, L., Bucher, D., Grillo, A., Wittum, G., Schuster, C., Queisser, G.: Synaptic bouton properties are tuned to best fit the prevailing firing pattern. Front. Comput. Neurosci. **8**, Article 101 (2014)
18. Miller, G., Talmor, D., Teng, S.H., Walkington, N., Wang, H.: Control volume meshes using sphere packing: generation, refinement and coarsening. In: Proceedings of the Fifth International Meshing Roundtable, pp. 47–61 (1996)
19. Murray, J.D., Van Ryper, W.: Encyclopedia of Graphics File Formats, 2nd edn. O'Reilly Media, USA (1996)
20. Oñate, E., Rojek, J., Taylor, R., Zienkiewicz, O.: Finite calculus formulation for incompressible solids using linear triangles and tetrahedra. Int. J. Numer. Methods Eng. **59**, 1473–1500 (2004)
21. Saleewong, T., Srikiatkhachorn, A., Maneepark, M., Chonwerayuth, A., Bongsebandhu-Ghubhakdi, S.: Quantyfying altered long-term potential in the CA1 hippocampus. J. Integr. Neurosci. **11**, 243–264 (2012)
22. Trayanova, N.A.: Whole-heart modeling: applications to cardiac electrophysiology and electromechanics. Circ. Res. **108**(1), 113–128 (2011)
23. Wilhelm, B.G.: Stoichiometric biology of the synapse. Dissertation in partial fulfillment of the requirements for the degree "Doctor of Natural Sciences (Dr. rer. nat)" in the Neuroscience Program at the Georg August University Göttingen, Faculty of Biology, Göttingen, Germany (2013)

24. Wilhelm, B.G., Mandad, S., Truckenbrodt, S., Kröhnert, K., Schäfer, C., Rammner, B., Seong, J.K., Gala, A.C., Krauss, M., Haucke, V., Urlaub, H., Rizzoli, S.O.: Composition of isolated synaptic boutons reveals the amounts of vesicle trafficking proteins. Science **344**, 1023–1028 (2014)

# Application of the Point Distance Histogram to the Automatic Identification of People by Means of Digital Dental Radiographic Images

Dariusz Frejlichowski(✉)

Faculty of Computer Science and Information Technology, West Pomeranian
University of Technology, Żołnierska 52, 71-210 Szczecin, Poland
dfrejlichowski@wi.zut.edu.pl

**Abstract.** In this paper, an approach for the identification of people
based on digital orthopantomogram images is proposed and experimentally investigated. This approach is composed of four main stages. In the
first stage, the image quality is enhanced using the Laplacian pyramid.
In the second stage, the image is segmented into individual sub-images,
each containing a single tooth. To do this, the line that separates the
upper and lower jaw is obtained using integral projections, and then
information about the intensity and location of particular types of tooth
is applied. The extraction of the shapes of the teeth is the third stage.
This stage also later involves each particular shape being represented
using the Point Distance Histogram algorithm to obtain its description.
Finally, the resultant descriptions are matched with the objects stored
in a template base for a person and, using these, biometric identification
is performed.

## 1 Introduction

Automatic identification of people using dental information is evidently less popular than identification from other biometric modalities, such as facial, fingerprint, iris or voice information. However, dental records are commonly used
for forensic human identification [1]. They are, for example, used more commonly than other types of biometric records when establishing the identity of
an individual, which is to be later used in judicial proceedings alongside DNA
and fingerprint information. This is because a person's teeth and bite are both
robust to decomposition and highly discriminant [2]. As a result, there is continuously growing usage of this type of biometric data. An example that illustrates
this is the existence of the Dental Task Force (DTF), a special service created
by the Federal Bureau of Investigation (FBI) for improving the use of digital
dental information in legal issues [3]. The group has, for example, created an
Automated Dental Identification System (ADIS), the main goal of which is to
retrieve from large image databases any dental images that have features similar to a provided input image [4]. A typical ADIS implementation executes in
four main stages: (1) image pre-processing; (2) image segmentation; (3) feature

© Springer International Publishing AG 2016
L.J. Chmielewski et al. (Eds.): ICCVG 2016, LNCS 9972, pp. 387–394, 2016.
DOI: 10.1007/978-3-319-46418-3_34

extraction; (4) feature recognition [5]. The first stage may for example use a wavelet-transform [6,7] or a Laplacian pyramid [8,9], resulting in the decomposition of the image into layers that each contain a subset of the information derived from the original image information. For the second stage, the layers are processed independently so as to improve or degrade particular image characteristics. During the segmentation process, either integral projections [10,11] or active contour models [8] are applied. The third stage, involving the extraction of particular features, mainly the shapes of the teeth, is then executed by, for example, either the active shapes model [12], line scanning [10] or watersheds [13] methods. The first two of these methods are designed specifically for intraoral images. Hence, their application to pantomograms sometimes fails as a result of frequent occlusions. Under such circumstances the latter method works better. For the final stage, any shape description and recognition approach can be applied.

In this paper, a complete approach for the identification of people based on the recognition of teeth that are visible on an orthopantomogram image is proposed. Some algorithms that have been designed for the aforementioned stages are firstly described. Then the experiments on real data — i.e. pantomograms that have been used with courtesy of Pomeranian University of Medicine in Szczecin, Poland — are described and discussed.

## 2    Image Preprocessing, Segmentation and Extraction of Tooth Shapes

The image enhancement process applied in the approach starts with the Laplacian decomposition [14]. The images given by particular layers of the Laplacian pyramid contain lower frequencies. Thanks to this one can obtain and emphasize various aspects of the dental data. For example, the trabecular structures of the mandible and maxilla are better visible after modifying the first layer, the contours of teeth and bones are sharpened using consecutive layers, operating on the last layer modifies the brightness.

The previously performed experiments gave the conclusion that the most effective approach for the dental image enhancement can be based on the following three steps — the averaging of the antepenultimate and penultimate layers, unsharp filter on the second layer, and the contrast enhancement [9].

Figure 1 provides an exemplary result of the preprocessed image. Most important is the visible emphasis of the roots and the teeth, which is especially desirable for the appropriate results during the consecutive steps of the whole approach.

The second stage of the approach is the segmentation of an image. Firstly, the integral projections are applied in order to separate the upper and lower jaws. The horizontal projection around the central point of the image with the smallest value is taken as the starting point of the separation line. This is a modification comparing to the original approach described in [10]. The rest of the process is similar.

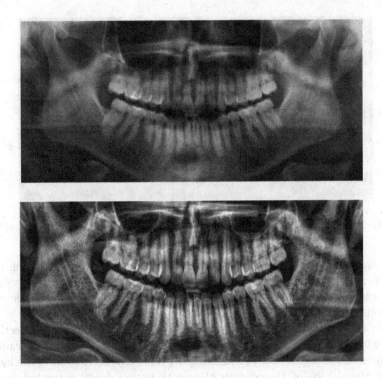

**Fig. 1.** An original and enhanced orthopantomogram obtained using a combination of the three described methods.

This curve is later used for the estimation of the position of the neck of every tooth. Then the points on each spline corresponding to a gap between the necks of two adjacent teeth are selected. Also, the value-inverted original image is multiplied with its local range filtered version. The search of the appropriate spike value that indicates the gap between the necks of teeth is based on the Bayesian probability.

The described method is efficient enough to find the reliable separation lines. However, sometimes the vertical line can be insufficient for the distinction between two occluding teeth. In those cases, additionally a point between them is localised using the greedy method described in [11]. The last step is the removal of the areas lying below the teeth roots.

The exemplary result of the segmentation stage is given in Fig. 2.

During the extraction of teeth shapes firstly an image is morphologically opened in order to reduce the noise and to create larger areas of similar intensity range. It is later entropy filtered and segmented by means of the watersheds approach. For each obtained segment a few attributes are derived, i.e. the centroid, the normalised mean intensity, and the normalised vertical distance from the centroid to the curve separating the jaws. Later, the Euclidean distance between each of the obtained centroids is calculated and the 50 segments that

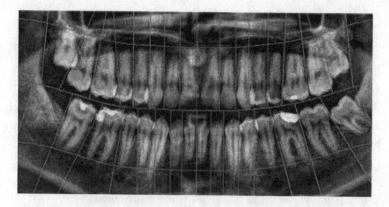

**Fig. 2.** A result of the segmentation stage obtained using the described approach.

are the lowest distance from each obtained segment are selected. Using these, the average intensity and the distinction values are derived. In order to select which segments belong to a tooth, a fitness function is applied [13]. The values this function takes depend on the type of the tooth analysed.

After all fitness functions have been derived for all segments, the selection of those that belong to a tooth starts using the pre-assumed function parameters [13]. The selected regions are morphologically dilated so as to remove the borders between them. Finally, the contour of a tooth is traced and extracted for later recognition.

An example of the results obtained using the described approach is presented in Fig. 3.

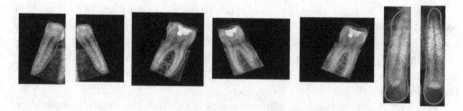

**Fig. 3.** Examples of the segmented teeth images.

## 3    Representation of Tooth Contours Using the Point Distance Histogram

Each tooth contour, that had been extracted using the discussed approach, was represented using the Point Distance Histogram — an algorithm for shape description [17]. The method starts with the calculation of the centroid $O$ of the planar shape:

$$O = (O_p, O_q) = (\frac{1}{s} \sum_{i=1}^{s} p_i, \frac{1}{s} \sum_{i=1}^{s} q_i), \qquad (1)$$

where:

$s$ — is the number of points in a contour of a planar shape,

$p_i$, $q_i$ — Cartesian coordinates of the $i$-th point of the projected shape.

The obtained polar coordinates are put into two vectors $\Theta^i$ for angles (in degrees) and $P^i$ for radii:

$$\rho_i = \sqrt{(p_i - O_p)^2 + (q_i - O_q)^2}, \qquad \theta_i = atan\left(\frac{q_i - O_q}{p_i - p_x}\right). \qquad (2)$$

The resultant values in $\theta_i$ are converted into nearest integers:

$$\theta_i = \begin{cases} \lfloor \theta_i \rfloor, & if\ \theta_i - \lfloor \theta_i \rfloor < 0.5 \\ \lceil \theta_i \rceil, & if\ \theta_i - \lfloor \theta_i \rfloor \geq 0.5 \end{cases}. \qquad (3)$$

The next step is the rearrangement of the elements in $\Theta^i$ and $P^i$ according to the increasing values in $\Theta^i$. This way we achieve the vectors $\Theta^j$, $P^j$. For equal elements in $\Theta^j$ only the one with the highest corresponding value $P^j$ is selected. That gives a vector with at most 360 elements, one for each integer angle. For further work only the vector of radii is taken — $P^k$, where $k = 1, 2, ..., m$ and $m$ is the number of elements in $P^k$ ($m \leq 360$). Now, the normalization of elements in vector $P^k$ is performed:

$$G = \max_k \{\rho_k\}, \qquad \rho_k = \frac{\rho_k}{G}, \qquad (4)$$

The elements in $P^k$ are assigned to $r$ bins in histogram ($\rho_k$ to $l_k$):

$$l_k = \begin{cases} r, & if\ \rho_k = 1 \\ \lfloor r\rho_k \rfloor, & if\ \rho_k \neq 1 \end{cases}. \qquad (5)$$

The obtained histograms representing two objects — one for a template and one for a test object — can be matched together by means of any dissimilarity measure. In the experiments the Euclidean distance was applied. The template object representing a base class with the smallest dissimilarity measure according to the test object was indicating the recognized class.

## 4    Discussion of Experimental Conditions and Results

The algorithms described in the paper were experimentally tested using 60 digital pantomograms, selected in a very specific way. They belonged to 30 individuals, and for each person exactly two images were taken at separate points in time. One image was treated as a template pattern, while the second one was used for recognition purposes.

Each image was firstly enhanced and segmented, and then each tooth shape was extracted and represented using the Point Distance Histogram algorithm. Obviously, the descriptions were matched.

The information about the location of each tooth was preserved. It was required, because the matching of obtained objects was limited to particular types of teeth. Hence all incisors extracted from the test pantomograms were matched with incisors from the template images, test canines were compared with template canines, premolars with template premolars, and finally, molars with template molars. This assumption was important, since the shapes of different types of tooth vary.

The best matching results (i.e. identifications of the correct people) were obtained for molars. However, since for certain people this particular type of tooth was not always present, other types were also considered. More precisely, the strategy was to perform the identification process separately for each of four quarters of an image (i.e. four sub–images). For each sub–image, a comparison was performed that started from the back of the jaw and continued towards the image's centre. Only when a tooth was present at a particular position in both the test and template sub–images would matching using the Euclidean distance be performed. This indicated a possible match of a person for a single tooth. For an analysed pantomogram, the voting was then finally performed. The template class with the largest number of indications was selected as the recognised person.

The testing procedure described above gave the following results — 18 of the 30 test objects were identified properly. That gives the efficiency (recognition rate) of 60 %. This result seems far from ideal, however various aspects can be taken into account in future works. Above all, several other shape description algorithms could be investigated. It is possible that another approach will be more successful. Despite the good results obtained from the enhancement and segmentation, other image processing techniques could also be analysed. Finally, the method of making a final decision about the identified person could be improved.

## 5   Conclusions

In this paper, a complete approach towards the identification of persons based on orthopantomograms was described. It started with the image enhancement process. Later an image was segmented so as to divide it into sub-areas covering individual teeth. Then, each tooth was extracted separately using the outer contour of its shape. Finally, particular tooth shapes were described using the Point Distance Histogram algorithm and matched with objects stored in the database that were represented by the same shape descriptor. The number of matching results for particular teeth was calculated and the template image corresponding to a person was indicated as the identified one if it obtained the highest number of matches.

Using the method described in the paper, a test on 60 pantomograms acquired from 30 people was performed. The dataset was divided equally: half of the images were selected as templates assigned to particular persons, while the other half was used as test data. Obviously, this means that during the experiment two images obtained at separate points in time were used for each person. The obtained identification efficiency was equal to 60 %. Although the result is not yet sufficient for practical purposes, one must keep in mind the particularly difficult character of dental orthopantomogram images.

Moreover, further work on the problem needs to be carried out. Above all, other shape representation methods should be applied and experimentally evaluated. Some of these could possibly give better recognition rates. Although the earlier stages of the approach work well, the analysis of other image processing methods is still possible, since they could produce even better results.

**Acknowledgements.** The author of this paper wishes to thank gratefully MSc R. Wanat for his significant help in developing and exploring the described approach.

# References

1. Bowers, M.C.: Forensic Dental Evidence. Elsevier, Boston (2004)
2. Lee, S., et al.: The diversity of dental patterns in Orthopantomography and its significance in human identification. J. Forensic Sci. **49**(4), 784–786 (2004)
3. Nassar, D., Ammar, H.H.: A prototype automated dental identification system (ADIS). In: Proceedings of the 2003 Annual National Conference on Digital Government Research, pp. 1–4 (2003)
4. Abdel-Mottaleb, M., et al.: Challenges of developing an automated dental identification system. In: IEEE Mid-west Symposium for Circuits and Systems, Cairo, Egypt, pp. 411–414 (2003)
5. Fahmy, G., et al.: Towards an automated dental identification system (ADIS). In: Zhang, D., Jain, A.K. (eds.) ICBA 2004. LNCS, vol. 3072, pp. 789–796. Springer, Heidelberg (2004). doi:10.1007/978-3-540-25948-0_107
6. Lu, J., Healy Jr., D.M.: Contrast enhancement of medical images using multiscale edge representation. In: Proceedings of SPIE: Wavelet applications, Orlando, 5–8 April 1994
7. Dippel, S., Stahl, M., Wiemker, R., Blaffert, T.: Multiscale contrast ehnahncement for radiographies: laplacian pyramid versus fast wavelet transform. IEEE Trans. Med. Imaging **21**(4), 343–353 (2002)
8. Zhou, J., Abdel-Mottaleb, M.: A content-based system for human identification based on bitewing dental X-ray images. Pattern Recogn. **38**(11), 2132–2142 (2005)
9. Frejlichowski, D., Wanat, R.: Application of the laplacian pyramid decomposition to the enhancement of digital dental radiographic images for the automatic person identification. In: Campilho, A., Kamel, M. (eds.) ICIAR 2010. LNCS, vol. 6112, pp. 151–160. Springer, Heidelberg (2010). doi:10.1007/978-3-642-13775-4_16
10. Jain, A.K., Chen, H.: Matching of dental X-ray images for human identification. Pattern Recogn. **37**(7), 1519–1532 (2004)
11. Frejlichowski, D., Wanat, R.: Automatic segmentation of digital orthopantomograms for forensic human identification. In: Maino, G., Foresti, G.L. (eds.) ICIAP 2011. LNCS, vol. 6979, pp. 294–302. Springer, Heidelberg (2011). doi:10.1007/978-3-642-24088-1_31
12. Chen, H., Jain, A.: Automatic forensic dental identification. In: Jain, A.K., Flynn, P., Ross, A.A. (eds.) Handbook of Biometrics, pp. 231–251. Springer, USA (2008)

13. Frejlichowski, D., Wanat, R.: Extraction of teeth shapes from orthopantomograms for forensic human identification. In: Real, P., Diaz-Pernil, D., Molina-Abril, H., Berciano, A., Kropatsch, W. (eds.) CAIP 2011. LNCS, vol. 6855, pp. 65–72. Springer, Heidelberg (2011). doi:10.1007/978-3-642-23678-5_6

14. Burt, P.J., Adelson, E.H.: The laplacian pyramid as a compact image code. IEEE Trans. Commun. **31**(4), 532–540 (1983)

15. Vuylsteke, P., Schoeters, E.: Image processing in computed radiography. In: Proceedings of International Symposium on Computerized Tomography for Industrial Applications and Image Processing in Radiology, Berlin, Germany, 15–17 March 1999

16. Stahl, M., Aach, T., Buzug, T.M., Dippel, S., Neitzel, U.: Noise-resistant weak-structure enhancement for digital radiography. SPIE **1999**(3661), 1406–1417 (1999)

17. Frejlichowski, D.: The point distance histogram for analysis of erythrocyte shapes. Pol. J. Environ. Stud. **16**(5B), 261–264 (2007)

# Airway Segmentation, Skeletonization, and Tree Matching to Improve Registration of 3D CT Images with Large Opacities in the Lungs

Duván Alberto Gómez Betancur[1], Anna Fabijańska[2],
Leonardo Flórez-Valencia[3], Alfredo Morales Pinzón[1,4],
Eduardo Enrique Dávila Serrano[4], Jean-Christophe Richard[4],
Maciej Orkisz[4(✉)], and Marcela Hernández Hoyos[1]

[1] Systems and Computing Engineering Department, School of Engineering,
Universidad de Los Andes, Bogotá, Colombia
{da.gomez16,alf-mora,marc-her}@uniandes.edu.co
[2] Institute of Applied Computer Science, Łódź University of Technology,
18/22 Stefanowskiego Street, 90-924 Łódź, Poland
anna.fabijanska@p.lodz.pl
[3] Facultad de Ingeniería, Pontificia Universidad Javeriana, Bogotá, Colombia
florez-l@javeriana.edu.co
[4] Univ Lyon, INSA-Lyon, Université Lyon 1, UJM-Saint Etienne, CNRS, Inserm,
CREATIS UMR 5220, U1206, 69621 Lyon, France
{davila,jean-christophe.richard,maciej.orkisz}@creatis.insa-lyon.fr

**Abstract.** In this work, we address the registration of pulmonary images, representing the same subject, with large opaque regions within the lungs, and with possibly large displacements. We propose a hybrid method combining alignment based on gray levels and landmarks within the same cost function. The landmarks are nodes of the airway tree obtained by specially developed segmentation and skeletonization algorithms. The former uses the random walker approach, whereas the latter exploits the minimum spanning tree constructed by the Dijkstra's algorithm, in order to detect end-points and bifurcations. Airway trees from different images are matched by a modified best-first-search algorithm with a specially designed distance function. The proposed method was evaluated on computed-tomography images of subjects with acute respiratory distress syndrome, acquired at significantly different mechanical ventilation conditions. It achieved better results than registration based only on gray levels, but also better than hybrid registration using a standard airway-segmentation method.

# 1 Introduction

## 1.1 Context

Pulmonary image analysis receives an increasing attention justified by various clinical applications. In particular, thoracic computed tomography (CT) images

© Springer International Publishing AG 2016
L.J. Chmielewski et al. (Eds.): ICCVG 2016, LNCS 9972, pp. 395–407, 2016.
DOI: 10.1007/978-3-319-46418-3_35

are analyzed for the purpose of diagnosis, treatment planning, and follow-up of such diseases as lung cancer and chronic obstructive pulmonary disease (COPD). Analysis comprises lung, vessel, and airway segmentation and registration, the latter being particularly useful to align and compare images acquired at different time-points and/or with different ventilation conditions, in cases requiring mechanical ventilation, such as acute respiratory distress syndrome (ARDS).

Generally, CT images of the lung present good contrasts. Nevertheless, their registration is challenging due to a violation of two assumptions usually made in this field: image-intensity is not preserved owing to density variations induced by volume changes, and continuous/smooth transformations cannot be used to represent the *sliding motion* of the lungs against the thoracic wall. Despite these difficulties, recent methods achieve good accuracy [15], with alignment errors of the order of one millimeter [16]. It should be noted however, that in the most frequently addressed diseases – lung cancer and COPD – the methods were devised for and evaluated on images with relatively small displacements: in the former, several images representing different phases of the respiratory cycle (with small movements from one phase to another) are typically available; in the latter, images are acquired at different sessions, but the respiratory phase is approximately the same, *e.g.*, end-inspiration. Additionally, in these diseases, the contrasts remain similar to those in healthy lungs, and opaque regions within lungs – such as nodules – (if any) are focal, *i.e.*, relatively small and localized. Registration of pulmonary images with large opaque regions, typically encountered in ARDS, is much more difficult, as demonstrated by the LOLA11 challenge[1], where all participating algorithms obtained poor results in images with large opacities.

In this work, we address the registration of pulmonary images, from the same subject, with large opaque regions within the lungs, and with possibly large displacements, such as between opposite respiratory phases or – even larger – induced by significantly different settings of mechanical ventilation (Fig. 1). Towards this objective, we propose a method combining alignment based on image gray-levels, and landmark matching, where the landmarks are bifurcations and leaves of the airway tree. The latter requires appropriate airway segmentation and skeletonization, as well as symbolic description by oriented graphs (trees).

## 1.2   Related Work

*Airway Segmentation.* Numerous algorithms have been proposed to segment lower airways from CT scans. Most of them are 3D region-growing approaches using various rules to stop or control the leakage into the lung parenchyma [11, 17, 19]. Nevertheless airway segmentation is still an open problem, where a tradeoff is sought between the number/length of detected branches and the amount of leakages. Additionally, most of the reported approaches consider subjects with normal contrasts (without large opaque regions), where the airways appear as tubes with dark lumen and bright walls, on a dark background. In the case of subjects with large opacities, considered in this study, this pattern is locally invalid. The proposed method aimed at coping with these specific contrast variations.

---

[1] http://www.lola11.com/ - let us note that the focus of the challenge was lung segmentation, but many participating methods were based on atlas registration.

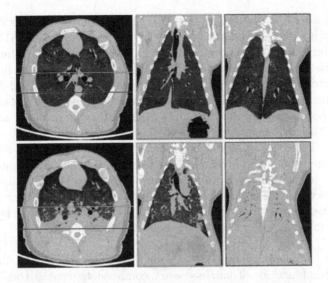

**Fig. 1.** CT images of a subject (pig) with ARDS, at significantly different mechanical ventilation pressures: high (top) and low (bottom). The axial slices (left) and the coronal slices (middle and right) with color frames corresponding to lines in coronal slices, show the contrast loss at low pressure, and a large displacement of the diaphragm.

*Skeletonization and Tree Construction.* The skeleton of a tree-like structure with tubular branches is a union of the centerlines of all its branches. It can be constructed from a minimum spanning tree, if an appropriate cost function is used, such that the cost is lowest on the tube centerlines. To construct its symbolic description (oriented graph), detection of bifurcations and end-points is needed. Skeletonization has been thoroughly studied since many years and has classically been based on morphological erosion with precautions taken to prune spurious branches and avoid shortening the actual branches (see [18] for a recent survey of skeletonization methods). Though mathematical morphology can also be used to detect bifurcations and end-points, a popular solution implemented in the AnalyseSkeleton plugin[2] of ImageJ is based on the Depth-First Search graph-analysis algorithm. A recent approach [21] has used graph theory at both steps: the Dijkstra's algorithm [3] was first applied to the segmented image to construct the minimum spanning tree, then this tree was recursively analyzed to extract the skeleton and infer its symbolic description. Our method follows a similar approach, but fully takes advantage of the minimum spanning tree constructed by the Dijkstra's algorithm, so as to detect the end-points, and to build the symbolic description during backtracking from these points across the tree. A preliminary, slower version of the algorithm was presented in [6].

*Tree Matching.* When dealing with anatomical trees, various geometrical and topological distortions must be considered, so the problem cannot be directly

---

[2] http://fiji.sc/AnalyzeSkeleton.

solved by seeking a graph isomorphism [8]. The number of methods devised for airway trees is relatively limited – see [5,17] for a review – *e.g.*, [13,20] built an association graph and performed the maximum-clique search to find the best match. Topological changes were handled either implicitly, or by explicitly defining valid distortions [8]. Different algorithms used such geometrical features as branch diameters or angles, distances between nodes, branches, or entire paths, etc. Let us note however, that distances usually increase in distal airway generations, so their use requires special precautions. According to [5], algorithms for anatomical-tree matching can be classified into inter- and intra-subject categories. In the former, reported results were good, but matching was generally used for the purpose of atlas-based labeling, limited to thirty landmarks [20]. In the latter, where more than hundred nodes have to be matched, results were moderate. We propose a method for intra-subject airway-tree matching, which successfully matches a significantly increased number of nodes.

*Registration.* Numerous methods developed to align 3D medical images can be seen as combinations of four necessary components: spatial transformation model, dissimilarity function, attributes on which this function is applied, and optimization strategy used to find the transformation parameters leading to minimal dissimilarity. Pulmonary-image registration [15] requires non-rigid transformations with continuity constraint restricted by a mask accounting for the *sliding motion*. Often, an additional component is a multi-scale strategy devised to avoid local minima, particularly in the case of large displacements. Nevertheless, methods using only attributes based on gray levels are still likely to be trapped by local minima. Attributes based on anatomical landmarks are expected to be more robust, but – when used alone – provide too sparse information. Therefore, hybrid methods combining gray-levels and landmarks have been proposed [1,15]. Blood vessels in CT images have the same gray-levels as non-aerated lung, so vascular landmarks used in [1] partly disappear in ARDS images, whereas airways remain visible (see dark "holes" in Fig. 1). In [22], registration of airway landmarks was used to initialize the subsequent gray-level registration. The results were more accurate than with gray-levels alone, but only healthy volunteers were used for evaluation. In ARDS subjects, opacities change in shape, extent, and density, so the gray-level registration still may diverge despite an initialization close to the good solution. We propose to restrict the solution by combining gray-levels and airway-tree landmarks in a single dissimilarity measure.

## 2    Methods

Figure 2 summarizes the proposed registration method. Its key point is a combination of image gray-level information with airway-tree-node matches, assuming that these matches are accurate (small number of false positives), numerous (large number of true positives), and available all throughout the lung, including within the opacities. These assumptions imposed constraints on the development of the components that will be detailed in the subsequent subsections.

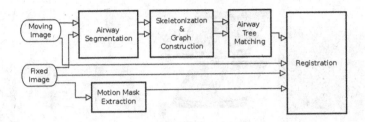

**Fig. 2.** Flowchart of the proposed method.

## 2.1 Airway Segmentation

The aim is to obtain a binary representation, $\mathcal{A}(\mathbf{x}) : \Omega \subset \mathbb{R}^3 \rightarrow \{0,1\}$, of each airway tree, with as many branches as possible and without leakages. The proposed solution, adapted from [4], relies on the *random walker* (RW) algorithm [9]. RW represents the image by an undirected graph $G = (V, E)$, where vertices $v \in V$ correspond to pixels, and edges $e \in E \subseteq V \times V$ are weighted: each edge $e_{ij} = (v_i, v_j)$ is assigned a weight (cost) $w_{ij}$ describing the similarity of the vertices $v_i$ and $v_j$. The $V$ set contains a subset $V_L = V_L^1 \cup V_L^0$ of seeds, *i.e.*, vertices labeled as *object* ($V_L^1$) or *background* ($V_L^0$), and a subset $V_U$ of unlabeled ones, $V_L \cup V_U = V$. The algorithm simulates random walkers released from each unlabeled vertex $v \in V_U$, and preferring edges with lower costs. A vertex $v \in V_U$ is assigned the label 1, if the probability that its random walker will first reach an *object* vertex is greater than the probability that it will first reach a *background* vertex, and 0 otherwise. Our airway-tree segmentation uses the random walker's ability of obeying discontinuous boundaries to avoid leakages into the lungs.

Prior to RW-based segmentation, coarse airway extraction is done using the seeded-region-growing method proposed by Mori *et al.* [14]: the growth starts from a seed-point $\mathbf{x}_0 \in \Omega$, and uses an initially low (here $-950\,\mathrm{HU}$) intensity threshold increased by steps of 10 HU until leakage – defined as a sudden increase (10 %) in the number of extracted voxels – is detected. The last result before leakage, $\mathcal{A}_0$, constitutes the initial subset $V_L^1$ of *object* labels. The values of the percentage and of all parameters were determined empirically on training data.

When applied in 3D, RW algorithm tends to miss smaller airways. Therefore, the random walker is applied slice-by-slice using 2D 4-connectivity, and the segmentation result, $V^{1,n}$, from slice $I^n$ guides and constrains the growth in slice $I^{n+1}$. This step also uses a "tubularness" measure [7], $\mathcal{F}$, calculated on the negative of the input CT image. *Object* seeds, $V_L^{1,n+1}$, in slice $I^{n+1}$ are pixels $v$ corresponding to locations such that $\mathcal{F}(v) > \tau$, with a low value of the threshold $\tau$ (equal to 5 % of the maximal tubularness value), and restricted by $v \in V^{1,n} \cup \mathcal{A}_0$ (green in Fig. 3a). *Background* seeds, $V_L^{0,n+1}$, in $I^{n+1}$ are pixels having $\mathcal{F}(v)$ below $\tau$ (red in Fig. 3a). The 2D RW-segmentation results, $V^{1,n}$, update the final 3D result $\mathcal{A}$. This procedure grows the tree "down" from the first to the last slice. Then, it is repeated backwards, and is alternated in both

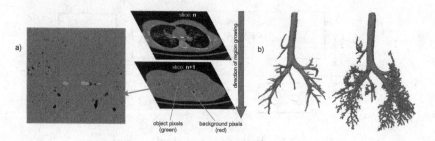

**Fig. 3.** Airway tree segmentation: (a) seed selection; (b) sample results (blue - initial coarsely segmented airways, $\mathcal{A}_0$; red - final segmentation result, $\mathcal{A}$). (Color figure online)

directions, as long as new airways are added. Figure 3b displays an example of initial (blue) and final (red) segmentation result.

## 2.2   Skeletonization and Graph Construction

Using the segmented airways, $\mathcal{A}$, and the user-defined point, $\mathbf{x}_0$, from the previous stage, this stage simultaneously extracts the skeleton, $\mathcal{S}$, and its symbolic description, $\mathcal{T}$, based on the detection of end-points and bifurcations. It was devised to avoid small spurious branches that might result from irregularities of the segmented airways. The algorithm is composed of four main steps: $(a)$ compute a medialness map, $D(\mathbf{x})$, $(b)$ build a minimum spanning tree, $\Gamma_{\mathbf{x}_0}$, $(c)$ extract end-points, $\mathcal{E} \equiv \{\mathbf{e}_i \in \Gamma_{\mathbf{x}_0}\}$, and bifurcations, $\mathcal{Y} \equiv \{\mathbf{y}_j \in \Gamma_{\mathbf{x}_0}\}$, $(d)$ construct an oriented graph, actually a *rooted tree*, $\mathcal{T}(V, E, r)$.

The medialness function, $D(\mathbf{x}) : \Omega \rightarrow \mathbb{R}$, calculated in step $(a)$, is the Maurer's exact signed Euclidean distance map [12], selected because of its low computational cost. As mentioned in Sect. 1.2, we chose Dijkstra's algorithm [3] to compute the minimum spanning trees in step $(b)$. To encourage fast propagation along airway centerlines, a function $c(u, v) : \Omega \times \Omega \rightarrow \mathbb{R}^+$, which expresses the *positive* cost of traveling from vertex $u$ to vertex $v$, was defined:

$$c(u, v) = \begin{cases} \infty & ; D(v) < 0, \\ \dfrac{1}{D^2(v) + 1} & ; D(v) \geq 0. \end{cases} \tag{1}$$

Step $(c)$ builds on the fact that Dijkstra's algorithm finds all minimum-cost paths going from $\mathbf{x}_0$ to any other point in $\mathcal{A}$, and these paths are stored in the minimum spanning tree $\Gamma_{\mathbf{x}_0}$. The point $v \in \Gamma_{\mathbf{x}_0}$ that simultaneously has the greatest cost $C(v)$ accumulated along the minimal path, and a small value of the distance $D(v)$, is likely to be located at the tip of the longest branch in the tree. This point, denoted $\mathbf{e}_{max}$, is selected by seeking the maximum of an "endness" function defined as $\epsilon(v) = C(v)/D^2(v)$, and is added to $\mathcal{E}$ set. The skeleton, $\mathcal{S}$, of the corresponding branch is extracted by backtracking the minimal path from $\mathbf{e}_{max}$ to $\mathbf{x}_0$; all the points that belong to $\mathcal{S}$, and the points of

$\mathcal{A}$ – within a distance $\rho(v)$ – around them, are marked as visited. In this way, the next maximum-endness point, not visited yet, should belong to the next longest branch. With an appropriately selected value of $\rho(v) > D(v)$ (we set $\rho = 1.5D$), irregularities of $\mathcal{A}$ surface can be marked as visited, and will never be selected as end-points, so small spurious branches in the skeleton can be avoided. When backtracking a new branch, along the minimal path from $\mathbf{e}_i$ towards $\mathbf{x}_0$, the process is likely to reach a point belonging to an already extracted part of the skeleton, $\mathcal{S}$. Such a point is considered as a bifurcation, $\mathbf{y}_j$, and is added to $\mathcal{Y}$ set. The procedure is repeated until all tree points in $\mathcal{A}$ are marked, thus completing the construction of $\mathcal{S}$, $\mathcal{E}$, and $\mathcal{Y}$ sets. Step $(d)$ uses these results to build a *rooted tree*, $\mathcal{T}(V, E, r)$, where the root is $r = \mathbf{x}_0$, the node set is $V = \mathcal{E} \cup \mathcal{Y}$ (with $\mathcal{E}$ corresponding to the terminal nodes), and each node, $v \in V$, stores the list of points in $\mathcal{S}$ corresponding to the edge, $e \in E$, connecting $v$ to its parent.

## 2.3   Tree Matching

The tree matching (Algorithm 1) recursively pairs sub-trees of two rooted trees, $\mathcal{T}_1(V_1, E_1, r_1)$ and $\mathcal{T}_2(V_2, E_2, r_2)$, as long as non-marked nodes remain in the search space (line 2). The algorithm is based on three characteristics enabling it to manage geometrical and topological differences between the matched trees. The first one is the *successive translation/matching*: after two nodes, $v \in \mathcal{T}_1$ and $w \in \mathcal{T}_2$, were matched at a given recursion level, the sub-trees, $\mathcal{T}_1^u, \mathcal{T}_2^w$, respectively rooted in $v$ and $w$, are translated (line 1) in order to superimpose their roots, before seeking the next best match (line 7). This allows the algorithm to cope with increasing spatial gaps between corresponding branches – as observed in distal airway regions in images acquired at different ventilation conditions – and thus to successfully use the second characteristic, called *father/family distance* (line 3). The latter is the sum of path-to-path distances between all branches composing the compared sub-trees, *i.e.*, between father branches and between their children. This distance allows the algorithm to improve the discrimination in complex topological and geometrical configurations. The third characteristic is a strategy called *Q-Best-First search* that seeks the best match in a space limited to the descendent nodes until the $Q^{\text{th}}$ generation. Expanding the search space by taking $Q > 1$ augments the ability of the algorithm to overcome topological differences between trees, but increases the execution time. As *Q-Best-First search* may lead to multiple matches for the same node, topological consistency is verified (line 4) before marking the pair of matched nodes (line 5), and adding it to the set of confirmed matches, $\mathcal{M} = \{(u, w) \in V_1 \times V_2\}$ (line 6). Moreover, the search is actually carried out simultaneously in both trees, $\mathcal{T}_1, \mathcal{T}_2$, so an identifier, $idT$, is used to specify if a given match was found by seeking in $\mathcal{T}_2$ a sub-tree best fitting a model taken from $\mathcal{T}_1$ or vice-versa, and to mark the appropriate node in case of a topologically inconsistent match (line 9).

**Algorithm 1.** MatchTrees

---

**input:** $T_1(V_1, E_1, r_1)$, $T_2(V_2, E_2, r_2)$, $Q$, $\mathcal{M}$

1  $TranslateTreesToSuperimposeRootNodes(T_1, T_2)$;
2  **while** $GetNumberOfNonMarkedNodesInSearchSpace(T_1, T_2, Q) > 0$ **do**
3       $[u \in V_1, w \in V_2, idT] \leftarrow GetBestFatherFamilyMatch(T_1, T_2, Q)$;
4       **if** $TopologicalConsistency(T_1, T_2, u, w, \mathcal{M})$ **then**
5           $MarkNode(u)$;   $MarkNode(w)$;
6           $\mathcal{M}.add(u, w)$;
7           $MatchTrees(T_1^u, T_2^w, Q, \mathcal{M})$;
8       **else**
9           $MarkInconsistentNode(u, w, idT)$;

---

## 2.4  Hybrid Registration

We propose a registration method devised to align a pair of 3D CT images representing lungs that undergo large deformations and contain wide opacities changing in size and density. To take into account the sliding motion, the method uses motion masks, $\mathcal{K}$: the usual continuity and smoothness constraints on the transformation, $\mathbb{T}_\mu$, are relaxed in the direction tangential to the surface of the motion mask [2]. Therefore, the surface of a motion mask must fit the interior of the ribcage, but it must extend below the lungs, to avoid artificial discontinuities near the diaphragm. Hence, motion masks are extracted in three steps. First, the thoracic cage is segmented. Then, limits in the intercostal spaces, and between the ribs and the sternum, are defined. Third, the abdominal region is delineated.

Our main contribution to the registration is the design of a cost function allowing a simultaneous optimization with respect to two different image-based criteria: landmark correspondences and gray-level similarities. Let $\mathcal{I}_F$ and $\mathcal{I}_M$ stand for the fixed and moving images, respectively, while $T_F$ and $T_M$ account for the corresponding trees. The landmarks are the previously matched node pairs $(v_F, v_M) \in \mathcal{M}$. We redefine the registration cost function $\mathcal{C}$, as

$$\mathcal{C}(\mathcal{I}_F, \mathcal{I}_M, \mathcal{K}, \mathcal{M}, \mathbb{T}) = \Big( \underbrace{(1 - \beta)\, \mathcal{D}_g(\mathcal{I}_F, \mathcal{I}_M, \mathbb{T})}_{\text{gray-level}} + \underbrace{\beta\, \mathcal{D}_l(\mathcal{M}, \mathbb{T})}_{\text{landmark}} \Big) + \underbrace{\alpha\, \mathcal{R}(\mathcal{K}, \mathbb{T})}_{\substack{\text{regularizing} \\ \text{term}}}, \quad (2)$$

$$\underbrace{\phantom{\Big( (1 - \beta)\, \mathcal{D}_g(\mathcal{I}_F, \mathcal{I}_M, \mathbb{T}) + \beta\, \mathcal{D}_l(\mathcal{M}, \mathbb{T}) \Big)}}_{\text{new data-attachment term}}$$

where $\mathcal{D}_g$ is the sum of gray-level dissimilarities, $\mathcal{D}_l$ is the sum of Euclidean distances between landmark locations, $\mathcal{R}$ controls the regularity of the transformation $\mathbb{T}$, separately within and beyond the motion mask $\mathcal{K}$ (see [2] for details), $\beta$ represents a weight used to balance the two distance terms, and $\alpha$ is used to set a trade-off between regularity constraint and data-attachment terms.

The registration algorithm was implemented in `elastix` framework [10] using the following settings: stochastic optimizer, B-Spline interpolator, and multi-resolution approach with three-level pyramid registrations. Furthermore, $\mathbb{T}$ used multiple B-Spline transformations, as in [2], $\mathcal{D}_g$ used the normalized mutual information, because it is robust to intensity changes, $\mathcal{D}_l$ used the Euclidean distance, and the weights were empirically set to $\alpha = 1, \beta = 0.01$.

## 2.5  Evaluation

*Data.* The method was assessed on 3D CT images from a study of an animal model (pig) with ARDS induced, where 20 image pairs (end-inspiration/end-expiration), acquired at various volume/pressure settings, were available for each pig. Two pigs were chosen and, for each of them, 3 image pairs were selected, corresponding to extreme and intermediate positive-end-expiratory-pressure (PEEP) values (20, 10 and $2\,\mathrm{cm\,H_2O}$) – to ensure large displacements and density changes – with constant tidal volume $V_t = 5\,\mathrm{ml/kg}$. Thus 12 images with various ventilation conditions were used, containing from 418 (pig B) to 469 (pig A) $512 \times 512$-voxel slices with voxel size $0.58 \times 0.58 \times 0.7\,\mathrm{mm^3}$.

*Criteria.* Registration was performed intra-subject, *i.e.*, separately for pigs A and B, and both intra- and inter-pressure, *i.e.*, between inspiration and expiration at fixed PEEP values, and in inspiration between different PEEP values (high-medium, medium-low, and high-low). Results were assessed qualitatively and quantitatively. Visualization of the moving image superimposed onto the fixed one was used to qualitatively assess the alignment of lung boundaries and anatomical landmarks perceptible despite the opacities. Quantitative assessment of this alignment used two measures. The alignment of lung surface was evaluated indirectly: the lungs were first segmented by an expert, then the transformation, $\mathbb{T}$, resulting from the registration was applied to the lung mask from the moving image, and the Dice similarity score, between this deformed mask and the lungs segmented in the fixed image, was calculated. The second measure quantified the residual Euclidean distance, after transformation, between anatomical landmarks identified by an expert in moving and fixed images. The latter were available only for one experiment (single pig, two pressures, five landmark pairs) in the most difficult (postero-caudal) region, where even expert's annotations are not very reliable, so the result must be interpreted with precautions.

Additionally, the tree-matching algorithm was evaluated separately by two observers visually checking and counting correct, incorrect, and missing matches. The skeletonization algorithm was also tested on five synthetic trees, to assess its reproducibility: the starting point, $\mathbf{x}_0$, was varied within a radius of five pixels, and the locations of the identified bifurcations were compared.

## 3  Results

In synthetic trees, the skeletonization algorithm achieved 100 % reproducibility *i.e.*, the locations of the detected bifurcations were always the same, regardless the starting point. In the segmentation of real airways, no leakage was detected by visual inspection. The tree-matching algorithm found 94.3 % of correct matches, 7.4 % of matches were incorrect, and 5.7 % of matches were missed.

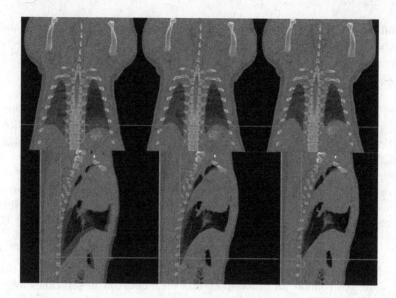

**Fig. 4.** Moving and fixed images superimposed: before registration (left), after registration using only gray levels (middle), and after hybrid registration (right). Red haircrosses specify the locations of the respective coronal and sagittal slices. Green crosses point out the location of one selected landmark in both images. Color highlights the regions, where gray levels differ between the images due to lack of alignment and/or to density changes in diseased zones. Sagittal slices (bottom) show successful alignment in most regions, except the posterior part of the diaphragm. Coronal slices (top) show the posterior region, where the lack of contrast hampered the registration, but the hybrid method performed better than the gray-level-based one. (Color figure online)

Figure 4 shows how the initial large displacement (left) between medium and high pressures, 10 and 20 cm $H_2O$, was compensated by a gray-level-based registration (middle) and the proposed hybrid registration (right). Green crosses represent the locations of one selected landmark: the upper cross represents the landmark in the medium-pressure image, whereas the lower one represents the same landmark in the high-pressure image before registration (left) and after the two different registration methods. Both registration methods successfully aligned well-contrasted regions, but the hybrid one performed better in the postero-caudal region, where a large opacity was present at low pressure.

Indirect evaluation of the lung-surface alignment, by means of Dice similarity scores, provided the following results: the hybrid registration achieved a score of 0.91, on average (0.88 and 0.93, for pigs A and B, respectively), whereas the average score obtained by the gray-level-based registration was of 0.83 (0.81 and 0.85, respectively). Residual distances between user-selected landmarks (available only in pig A) were of 14.6 mm, on average (range 4.9 − 29.5 mm), whereas the average distance obtained by the gray-level-based registration was of 23.5 mm (range 20.4 − 26.3 mm). These residual distances are to be compared with the distances before registration: average 25.3 mm, range 21.9 − 29.7 mm.

# 4   Discussion and Conclusions

In this work, we proposed a hybrid registration method devised for pulmonary CT images of the same subject with pathological infiltrations in the lung tissue, acquired at strongly differing ventilation conditions. The method was therefore expected to cope with large displacements and dramatic changes in contrast. The method combines, in a single cost function, airway-tree correspondences and gray-level similarities. To this purpose, new airway segmentation, skeletonization, symbolic description, and matching methods were developed. Evaluated on image pairs presenting such characteristics, the whole work-flow performed overall better than registration based on gray-levels alone.

The airway segmentation method successfully coped with contrast variations. It may represent a good trade-off between the number of detected branches and the risk of adding spurious branches, although qualitative assessment reported in this article needs to be confirmed by a quantitative evaluation against an independent standard. In future work, a faster implementation will be sought.

Skeletonization and symbolic description are performed simultaneously by an algorithm that fully exploits the minimum-spanning-tree constructed by the Dijkstra's algorithm. The algorithm has proved well-suited to the application tackled: it is fast and has provided reliable trees that were successfully matched. In particular, the strategy used to define the end-points has automatically discarded small irregularities of the segmented surface, thus avoiding the generation of small spurious branches and considerably reducing the need for pruning.

The tree-matching method showed good sensitivity, higher than the values reported in the literature, which guarantees that most of the detected airway-tree branches were effectively used for the purpose of hybrid registration. Nevertheless, it can still be improved to eliminate false-positive matches that may potentially lead to local errors in the transformation.

In the hybrid registration, gray-level correspondences aligned well-contrasted structures, landmark matches successfully attracted the tissues in regions lacking contrast, but residual misalignment remained where neither contrasts nor landmarks were present. This problem will be investigated in future work.

In conclusion, the proposed hybrid registration method outperformed gray-level-based registration of pulmonary structures in images with large displacements and severe contrast loss observed in subjects with ARDS. It may therefore be helpful in quantifying the lung-parenchyma aeration and in choosing patient-specific settings of the ventilator. Further investigation is necessary to improve the alignment in the absence of both contrast and airway landmarks. Future work will also tackle assessing the sensitivity of the method to the parameter settings and evaluating its accuracy on more datasets, including humans, and using an independent standard.

**Acknowledgments.** The authors thank Colciencias for doctoral scholarships granted to D. Gómez Betancur and A. Morales Pinzón, and also for its support through the French-Colombian ECOS-NORD program C15M04 grant. This work was also supported by the French-Polish PHC Polonium 34852WG grant.

# References

1. Cao, K., Ding, K., et al.: Improving intensity-based lung CT registration accuracy utilizing vascular information. Int. J. Biomed. Imaging **2012**, 17 (2012). doi:10. 1155/2012/285136. Article ID 285136
2. Delmon, V., Rit, S., et al.: Registration of sliding objects using direction dependent B-splines decomposition. Phys. Med. Biol. **8**(5), 1303–1314 (2013)
3. Dijkstra, E.W.: A note on two problems in connexion with graphs. Numer. Math. **1**, 269–271 (1959)
4. Fabijanska, A.: Segmentation of pulmonary vascular tree from 3D CT thorax scans. Biocybern. Biomed. Eng. **35**(2), 106–119 (2015)
5. Feragen, A., Petersen, J., Owen, M., Lo, P., Hohwü Thomsen, L., et al.: Geodesic atlas-based labeling of anatomical trees: Application and evaluation on airways extracted from CT. IEEE Trans. Med. Imaging **34**, 1212–1226 (2015)
6. Flórez-Valencia, L., Morales Pinzón, A., et al.: Simultaneous skeletonization and graph description of airway trees in 3D CT images. In: Proceedings of the 25th GRETSI (2015)
7. Frangi, A.F., Niessen, W.J., et al.: Model-based quantitation of 3-D magnetic resonance angiographic images. IEEE Trans. Med. Imaging **18**(10), 946–956 (1999)
8. Graham, M.W., Higgins, W.E.: Optimal graph-theoretic approach to 3D anatomical tree matching. In: Proceedings of the 3rd ISBI, pp. 109–112 (2006)
9. Grady, L.: Random walks for image segmentation. IEEE Trans. Pattern Anal. Mach. Intell. **28**(11), 1768–1783 (2006)
10. Klein, S., Staring, M., Murphy, K., Viergever, M.A., Pluim, J.P.W.: elastix: a toolbox for intensity based medical image registration. IEEE Trans. Med. Imaging **29**, 196–205 (2010)
11. Lo, P., van Ginneken, B., Reinhardt, J.M., Tarunashree, Y., et al.: Extraction of airways from CT (EXACT 2009). IEEE Trans. Med. Imaging. **31**, 2093–2107 (2012)
12. Maurer, C.R., Qi, R., Raghavan, V.: A linear time algorithm for computing exact Euclidean distance transforms of binary images in arbitrary dimensions. IEEE Trans. Pattern Anal. Mach. Intell. **25**(2), 265–270 (2003)
13. Metzen, J.H., Kröger, T., Schenk, A., et al.: Matching of anatomical tree structures for registration of medical images. Image Vis. Comput. **27**, 923–933 (2009)
14. Mori, K., Hasegawa, J., Toriwaki, J., Anno, H., Katada, K.: Recognition of bronchus in three-dimensional X-ray CT images with applications to virtualized bronchoscopy system. In: Proceedings of the 13th International Conference on Pattern Recognition, vol. 3, pp. 528–532 (1996)
15. Murphy, K., van Ginneken, B., Reinhardt, J.M., Kabus, S., Ding, K., Deng, X., et al.: Evaluation of registration methods on thoracic CT the EMPIRE10 challenge. IEEE Trans. Med. Imaging **30**(11), 1901–1920 (2011)
16. Polzin, T., Rühaak, J., Werner, R., Strehlow, J., Heldmann, S., et al.: Combining automatic landmark detection and variational methods for Lung CT registration. In: Proceedings of the MICCAI 5th International Workshop on Pulmonary Image Analysis, pp. 85–96 (2013)
17. Pu, J., Gu, S., Liu, S., Zhu, S., Wilson, D., et al.: CT based computerized identification and analysis of human airways: a review. Med. Phys. **39**, 2603–2616 (2012)
18. Saha, P.K., Borgefors, G., Sanniti di Baja, G.: A survey on skeletonization algorithms and their applications. Pattern Recogn. Lett. **76**, 3–12 (2016)

19. van Rikxoort, E.M., van Ginneken, B.: Automated segmentation of pulmonary structures in thoracic computed tomography scans: a review. Phys. Med. Biol. **58**, 187–220 (2013)
20. Tschirren, J., Mclennan, G., Palagyi, K., et al.: Matching and anatomical labeling of human airway tree. IEEE Trans. Med. Imaging **24**, 1540–1547 (2005)
21. Verscheure, L., Peyrodie, L., Dewalle, A.S., Reyns, N., Betrouni, N., et al.: Three-dimensional skeletonization and symbolic description in vascular imaging: preliminary results. Int. J. Comput. Assist. Radiol. Surg. **8**(2), 233–246 (2013)
22. Yin, Y., Hoffman, E.A., Ding, K., Reinhardt, J.M., Lin, C.-L.: A cubic B-spline-based hybrid registration of lung CT images for a dynamic airway geometric model with large deformation. Phys. Med. Biol. **56**, 203–218 (2011)

# Regions of Interest in a Fundus Image Selection Technique Using the Discriminative Analysis Methods

Nataly Ilyasova[1,2]([✉]), Rustam Paringer[1,2], and Alexander Kupriyanov[1,2]

[1] Samara National Research University, Samara, Russia
ilyasova@smr.ru
[2] Image Processing Systems Institute - Branch of the Federal
Scientific Research Centre, "Crystallography and Photonics" of Russian
Academy of Sciences, Samara, Russia

**Abstract.** A technique of formation of the effective features for the identification of regions of interest (ROI) in fundus images during laser coagulation is proposed. The technique is based on the texture analysis of selected image patterns. The analysis of informative value of obtained feature space and the selection of the most effective features is performed using the data discriminative analysis. The best values of image fragmentation dimensions for the image segmentation and the feature sets providing the precise identification required for regions of interest are determined herein.

**Keywords:** Fundus images · Image processing · Diagnostic features · Laser coagulation · Texture analysis

## 1 Introduction

The main reason for the irreversible blindness among employable population in developed countries is diabetic retinopathy (DR). At diabetic retinopathy all parts of the eye's retina are damaged, however, in particular, changes in central parts in the form of the diabetic macula edema may cause the quickest and the most irreversible visual decrement [1] (Fig. 1). Treatment of the diabetic macula edema is rather a complicated process including both conservative and surgical laser methods. Laser coagulation of the eye's retina is "the golden standard" for medical treatment, the effectiveness of which was proved by a large-scale

This work was partially supported by the Ministry of education and science of the Russian Federation in the framework of the implementation of the Program of increasing the competitiveness of SSAU among the world's leading scientific and educational centers for 2013–2020 years; by the Russian Foundation for Basic Research grants (#14-07-97040, # 15-29-03823, # 15-29-07077, #16-57-48006); by the ONIT RAS program # 6 "Bioinformatics, modern information technologies and mathematical methods in medicine" 2016.

© Springer International Publishing AG 2016
L.J. Chmielewski et al. (Eds.): ICCVG 2016, LNCS 9972, pp. 408–417, 2016.
DOI: 10.1007/978-3-319-46418-3_36

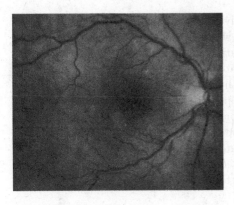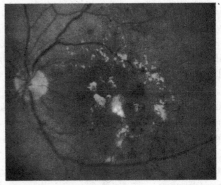

**Fig. 1.** The example of a fundus diagnostic image without pathology (left) and with pathology detected (right)

study (ETDRS 1987) [2]. During laser treatment a series of metered microscopic thermal wounds – laser coagulates – are applied in the edema zone on the eye's retina. Coagulates are overlayed either one by one or in series located in the form of a specified regular-shaped figure – a pattern, or with a preliminarily planned coagulate location with subsequent overlapping the obtained plan onto a retina image in online mode [3]. The optimum location of coagulates is most preferable, that means that they are to be located in the edema zone at maximum equal distances between each other, and their intrusion onto vessels are avoided. Preliminarily planned coagulates are overlayed by an automatic beam positioning control system that allows to give medical treatment with high accuracy (Fig. 2) [4,5].

The main disadvantage of this approach is that there is no optimum location of coagulates in conditions of high diversity of edema forms and retinal vascular patterns therein. First, this is due to a limited choice of patterns forms which often correspond neither to the edema form nor to a status of vessels. If the

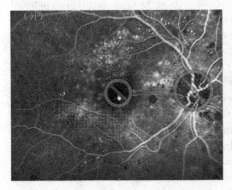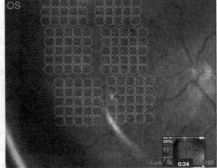

**Fig. 2.** Examples of patterns NAVILAS [4,5]

arrangement is conducted manually only by coagulate, their optimal position will be experience based and more time will be required for planning [6].

Thus, the development of the information technology, including methods and algorithms for optimal automatic coagulate filling in the defined edema zone with different arrangements of blood vessels therein, is currently a critical task.

To computerize a laser coagulation procedure it is necessary to make the image segmentation for particular regions of interest which are characterized by the presence of four classes of objects, i.e. exudates, blood vessels, intact sectors and the macula. The macular edema region is to be defined by aggregated exudation zones. During laser therapy it is recommended by doctors to avoid the zone of blood vessels, and it is strongly forbidden to overlay coagulates on the macula zone.

The authors [7–9] propose a review on the current segmentation algorithms used for medical images. Algorithms are classified according to their principal methodologies, namely the ones based on thresholds, the ones based on clustering techniques, the ones based on deformable models. To solve our problem we offer an algorithm that is based on clustering techniques using textural features. Textural features showed good results in recognizing biomedical images and their further diagnosis [10,11]. To evaluate informativeness of textural features based on a classification efficiency criterion and in order to form new features required to improve a segmentation quality a method of discriminative analysis of sample data is used [12]. The method is universal enough to be applied to improve the informativeness of any combination of features.

## 2    The Discriminative Analysis to Form the Informative Feature Space

There are a few approaches used for increasing the informativeness of the features: correlation analysis, regression analysis, factor analysis, cluster analysis, discriminant analysis. From the point of view of classification efficiency the most promising method is the discriminant analysis, the interpretation of intergroup differences, to be exact. This kind of analysis is a section of multidimensional statistical analysis which makes it possible to investigate the differences between two or more classes of objects by a few variables simultaneously [12]. The possibility to discriminate the classes by using a particular set of features is evaluated, and a set of features providing the best classification efficiency is found. So the addition of a discriminant-analysis-based algorithm for generation of effective features will allow us to distinguish between normal and pathological cases more efficiently.

The basic idea of the discriminant analysis is that the smaller the departure of feature space points from the intra-class centroid and the greater the inter-centroid distance are, the more effective the classification is [12].

If two or more classes available (in our case there are 4 classes including exudates, blood vessels, intact sectors and the macula), the objective of feature selection is to select those features which are the most efficient in accordance with the class separability [12–14]. In the discriminative analysis the class separability criteria are formed using scatter matrixes inside classes and scatter matrixes between classes [14].

Let there be a sample of $n$ elements divided in $g$ classes and holding $p$ features. The scatter matrix inside classes demonstrates a variety of objects with respect to mean vectors of classes: $\mathbf{W} = \sum_{k=1}^{g}(\mathbf{X}_k - \bar{\mathbf{x}}_k)(\mathbf{X}_k - \bar{\mathbf{x}}_k)^T$, where $k$-th class data will correspond to the mean vector $\bar{\mathbf{x}}_k = [\bar{x}_{1k}\bar{x}_{21k}...\bar{x}_{pk}]$. Elements of the scatter matrix between classes $\mathbf{B}$ is counted by the formula:

$$b_{ij} = \sum_{k=1}^{g} n_k(\bar{x}_{ik} - \bar{x}_i)(\bar{x}_{jk} - \bar{x}_j), i,j = \overline{1,p}, \tag{1}$$

where $\bar{x}_i = (1/n)\sum_{k=1}^{g} n_k\bar{x}_{ik}$, is a mean feature value of $i$-th feature in all classes, $n_k$ is a number of objects in $k$-th class, $\bar{x}_{ik} = 1/n_k \sum_{m=1}^{n_k} \bar{x}_{ikm}$ is the mean feature value in class $k$, and $x_{ikm}$ is a value of $i$-th feature for $m$-th object in $k$-th class. Elements of the scatter matrix inside classes is counted by the formula:

$$w_{ij} = \sum_{k=1}^{g} \sum_{m=1}^{n_k} (x_{ikm} - \bar{x}_{ik})(x_{jkm} - \bar{x}_{jk}), i,j = \overline{1,p} \tag{2}$$

The matrices $\mathbf{W}$ and $\mathbf{B}$ contain all basic information about interrelationships inside and between classes. In order to obtain the class separability criterion some number is to be associated to these matrixes. This number should be increased with the increase of scattering between classes or with the decrease of scattering inside classes. For this purpose the following criterion is more frequently used [12]: $J = tr(\mathbf{T}^{-1}\mathbf{B})$, where $\mathbf{T} = \mathbf{B} + \mathbf{W}$. The greater the value of the criterion – the more separability of classes.

Let $\mathbf{x} = [x_1, x_2...x_p]^T$ is the initial vector of features. Let us consider the algorithm of generation of new $m$ features: $\mathbf{y} = [y_1, y_2...y_m]^T$.

1. Let us define eigenvectors $\mathbf{v}_i$, $i = \overline{1,m}$ for matrix $\mathbf{T}^{-1}\mathbf{B}, m \leq p$ [12].
2. Let us determine the vectors of normalized coefficients $\boldsymbol{\beta}_i = [\beta_0, \beta_1...\beta_p]$, $i = \overline{1,m}$, where elements $\boldsymbol{\beta}_i$ are computed as

$$\beta_0 = -\sum_{i=1}^{p} \beta_i\bar{x}_i, \beta_i = v_i\sqrt{n-g}, i = \overline{1,p}. \tag{3}$$

3. Let us calculate the vector elements of new features by formula:

$$y_i = \beta_0 + \beta_1 x_1 + ...\beta_p x_p, i = \overline{1,m}. \tag{4}$$

The number of new features cannot exceed the number of original ones. Note that we can use the standardized coefficients [14]

$$c_i = \beta_i + \sqrt{w_{ii}/n-g}, i = \overline{1,p} \tag{5}$$

to evaluate the contribution of each original feature into each new feature.

If the magnitude of the coefficient (5) for a variable is small, we can omit this variable and reduce the number of variables [12,14].

## 3  The Technique of Defining Regions of Interest Based on the Texture Analysis of Biomedical Images

The segmentation is to be performed by making a decision on the membership of fragmented zones to one of the four given classes of object images. The fragmentation was carried out by dividing the image into several square-shaped blocks, which were classified using a technique of selection of effective recognition features (Fig. 3).

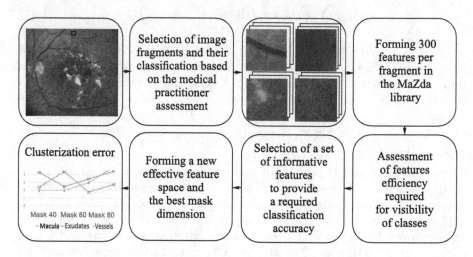

**Fig. 3.** The technique of formation of the effective features for the identification of regions of interest in fundus images

At the initial stage, the technique is used to select proper-sized fragments and to preliminarily classify them, thus involving medical practitioners to provide the recognition system training. The analysis of the fragments showed that they may differ well enough by their textural characteristics. We used the known MaZda library which allows us to calculate up to 300 different texture features [15,16]. Different texture features such as correlation, homogeneity, short run emphasis, long run emphasis, run percentage and many more were extracted from the digital fundus images. Texture features derived from 6 different statistical image descriptors can be computed by MaZda. The features are derived respectively from image histogram, image gradient, run-length matrix, co-occurrence matrix, autoregressive model, wavelet transform, each calculated for up to 16 predefined ROIs.

With such a large number of features, it is very difficult to predict, which ones will be most useful for texture classification. Also, the large number of features requires very large number of data samples to provide reliable discriminant analysis results, from the statistical point of view. The required large number of samples are not normally available. Finally, almost 300 features are difficult to manage (for presentation, displaying, analysis). For these reasons, there is a need for feature reduction, to provide a compact parameter set useful for texture discrimination and classification.

The effectiveness of the obtained feature set was evaluated based on the discriminative analysis [14,17,18]. The purpose of the research is to select, from this enormous amount of features, a subset of the most informative ones for our class of biomedical images, which provide a minimum clusterization error. It is necessary herewith to define the best dimension of a mask, by means of which the system will process the image and make the automatic selection of regions of interest during the laser coagulation procedure.

As follows from the discriminative analysis, the best features were identified for each sample of objects based on a separability criterion. In order to evaluate the separability quality, we calculated the clusterization error for each feature set and various fragmentation window sizes. Feature sets were formed through selecting the best ones, based on values of individual separability criteria. We used a K-means clusterization method, and the Euclidean and Mahalanobis distance was used as a similarity measure [12]. The required minimum size of a fragmentation window and the similarity measure were selected according to the criterion of the minimum clusterization error.

## 4   Experimental Results

The experiments were carried out on samples formed while analyzing 70000 fragments, which contained different image classes. The experiments were aimed at selecting the best feature set and the fragmentation window to identify regions of interest with a prescribed accuracy. Specific characteristics of the analyzed diagnostic image thereby impose restrictions on the size of the fragmentation window. The smallest window size ensures the highest segmentation quality obtained during laser coagulation. Therefore, while analyzing relationships obtained during the experiments, we select the smallest value of the fragmentation window, at which there is a quantum leap in values of the clusterization error and the separability criterion. Figure 4 shows the interrelationship of values of the group separability criterion and the fragmentation size at various amounts of selected features characterized by the maximum individual separability criterion.

The experiments show that the largest group separability criterion is possessed by sets of 14–20 features when the minimum fragmentation window size is 47 pixels. The second quantum leap in the separability criterion arises at the level of 64 pixels. The specified sets are thereby characterized with their close interrelationships. If we consider the interrelationship of the clusterization error and fragmentation sizes for three lowest-dimensional feature sets, i.e. 14–16 (Fig. 5), it can be observed that the least error with the fragmentation window 47 pixels in size is possessed by the set of 16 features.

From Fig. 6, which illustrates the interrelationship of maximum, average and minimum clusterization errors depending on the type of features (the subset of original features MaZda with the maximum separability criterion and newly

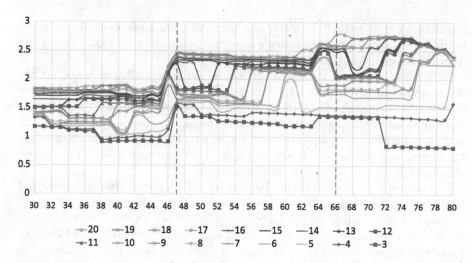

**Fig. 4.** The interrelationship of values of the group separability criterion and the fragmentation size at various amounts of selected features with the maximum individual separability criterion

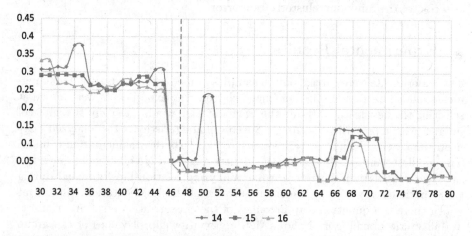

**Fig. 5.** The interrelationship of the clusterization error and the fragmentation window size when using the Mahalanobis similarity measure and the sets of 14, 15 and 16 features with the maximum separability criterion

formed features based on the discriminative analysis) and the type of similarity measures, and from Fig. 7 it may be concluded that the best clusterization result may be provided by the Mahalanobis distance and the set of newly formed features obtained from 16 original features.

It is thereby recommended to use the fragmentation window 47 pixels in size. This shall provide at least 95 % of identification certainty of regions of interest.

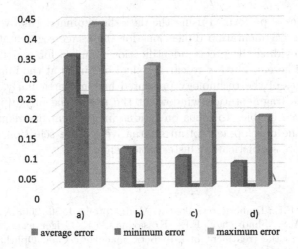

**Fig. 6.** Illustration of various types of the clusterization error depending on the types of features and various similarity measures: (a) Euclidean distance and original features; (b) Mahalanobis distance and original features (c) Euclidean distance and set of newly formed features; (d) Mahalanobis distance and set of newly formed features

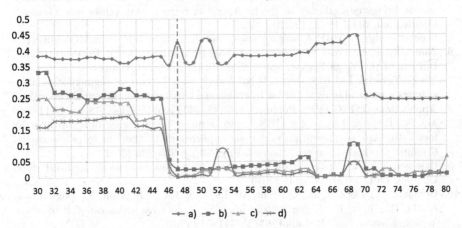

**Fig. 7.** The interrelationship of the clusterization error and the fragmentation window size at various similarity measures when using 16 features with the maximum separability criterion: (a) Euclidean distance and original features; (b) Mahalanobis distance and original features (c) Euclidean distance and set of newly formed features; (d) Mahalanobis distance and set of newly formed features

## 5   Conclusion

A technique of formation of the effective features for the identification of regions of interest in fundus images during laser coagulation is proposed. The technique is based on the texture analysis of selected image patterns. The analysis of informative value of obtained feature space and the selection of the most effective features is performed using the data discriminative analysis. The best values of image fragmentation dimensions for the image segmentation and the feature sets providing the precise identification required for regions of interest are determined herein. Further researches shall be aimed at the improvement of individual stages of the technology presented herein, particularly, shape modifications of the fragmentation window, at the use of the image preprocessing procedure, which enables to focus on fundus image elements required for the analysis, and the development of an alternative feature selection method and the use of a more sophisticated clusterization algorithm.

# References

1. Shadrichev, F.E.: Diabetic retinopathy. Mod. Optom. **4**, 36 (2008) (in Russian)
2. Astakhov, Y.S., Shadrichev, F.E., Krasavina, M.I., Grigoryeva, N.N.: Modern approaches to the treatment of a diabetic macular edema. Ophthalmol. Sheets **4**, 59–69 (2009) (in Russian)
3. Kernt, M., Cheuteu, R., Liegl, R.G., et al.: Navigated focal retinal laser therapy using the NAVILAS system for diabetic macula edema. Ophthalmology **109**, 692–700 (2012)
4. Chhablani, J., Kozak, I., Barteselli, G., El-Emam, S.: A novel navigated laser system brings new efficacy to the treatment of retinovascular disorders. Oman J. Ophthalmol. **6**(1), 18–22 (2013)
5. Navilas navigated PRP 4. https://www.youtube.com/watch?v=mtMOYdIuyvI
6. Zamytsky, E.A.: Laser treatment of a diabetic macular edema. In: Postgraduate Bulletin of the Volga Region, vol. 1–2, p. 79. (2015) (in Russian)
7. Ma Z., Tavares, J.M.R.S., Jorge, R.N.: A review on the current segmentation algorithms for medical images. In: 1st International Conference on Imaging Theory and Applications (IMAGAPP), Portugal, pp. 135–140 (2009). ISBN: 978-989-8111-68-5
8. Ma, Z., Tavares, J.M., Jorge, R.N., Mascarenhas, T.: A review of algorithms for medical image. segmentation and their applications to the female pelvic cavity. Comput. Methods Biomech. Biomed. Eng. **13**(2), 235–246 (2010)
9. Ilyasova, N.Y.: Methods for digital analysis of human vascular system. Lit. Rev. Comput. Opt. **37**(4), 517–541 (2013)
10. HeiShun, Y., Tischler, B., Qureshi, M.M., Soto, J.A., Anderson, S., Daginawala, N., Li, B., Buch, K.: Using texture analyses of contrast enhanced CT to assess hepatic fibrosis. Eur. J. Radiol. **85**(3), 511–517 (2016)
11. Acharya, U.R., Ng, E.Y., Tan, J.H., Sree, S.V., Ng, K.H.: An integrated index for the identification of diabetic retinopathy stages using texture parameters. J. Med. Syst. **36**(3), 2011–2020 (2012)
12. Fukunaga, K.: Introduction to Statistical Pattern Recognition. Academic Press, New York and London (1972)
13. Ilyasova, N., Kupriyanov, A.V., Paringer, R.A.: Formation of features for improving the quality of medical diagnosis based on discriminant analysis method. Comput. Opt. **38**(4), 751–756 (2014) (in Russian)
14. Kim, J.-A., Myuller, C., Klekka, W.R.: Factor, discriminant and cluster analysis. In: "Financy I Statistica" Publisher, Moscow, p. 215 (1989) (in Russian)
15. Strzelecki, M., Strzelecki, M., Szczypinski, P., Materka, A., Klepaczko, A.: A software tool for automatic classification and segmentation of 2D/3D medical images. Nucl. Instr. Methods Phys. Res. Sect. A: Accelerators, Spectrometers, Detectors Associated Equipment **702**, 137–140 (2013)

16. Szczypiski, P.M., Strzelecki, M., Materka, A., Klepaczko, A.: MaZda–a software package for image texture analysis. Comput. Methods Programs Biomed. **94**(1), 66–76 (2009)
17. Ilyasova, N., Kupriyanov, A.V., Paringer, R.A.: The discriminative analysis application to refine the diagnostic features of blood vessels images. Opt. Memory Neural Netw. (Inf. Opt.) **24**(4), 309–313 (2015)
18. Ilyasova, N., Paringer, R.A.: Research effectiveness of features for the vascular pathologies diagnosis. Scientific Journal of "Proceedings of the Samara Scientific Center of the Russian Academy of Sciences", Samara Scientific Center of the Russian Academy of Sciences, vol. 17, no. 2(5), pp. 1015–1020 (2015) (in Russian)

# Blue Whitish Veil, Atypical Vascular Pattern and Regression Structures Detection in Skin Lesions Images

Karol Kropidlowski[1]([⊠]), Marcin Kociolek[1], Michal Strzelecki[1], and Dariusz Czubinski[2]

[1] Institute of Electronics, Łódź University of Technology,
Wolczanska 211/215, 90-924 Łódź, Poland
{karol.kropidlowski,marcin.kociolek,michal.strzelecki}@p.lodz.pl
[2] DerMed Training Center, Piotrkowska 48, 90-265 Łódź, Poland
dariusz@czubinski.pl

**Abstract.** There is no suitable standard for the detection of blue whitish veil atypical vascular pattern and regression structures applied to skin lesion images. This information however is important in assessment of melanoma in skin dermatoscopic images. Thus there is a need for development of image analysis techniques that satisfy at least subjective criteria required by dermatologists. In this paper the application of color based image features for detection of blue whitish veil and atypical vas-cular pattern is presented. Preliminary test results are promising; for analyzed melanoma images the accuracy of developed methods provides 78 % correctly detected blue whitish veils, 84 % correctly detected atypical vascular pattern, and 86,5 % correctly detected regression structures. This paper is a contribution to the computer aided diagnostic system implementing the ELM 7-point check-list aimed at melanoma detection.

**Keywords:** Malignant melanoma · Image processing · Blue whitish veil · Typical and atypical vascular pattern · 7-point checklist · Regression structures · Color based classification

## 1 Introduction

The malignant melanoma [1] is a skin cancer that grows fast and easily metastasizes thus being extremely lethal if not early diagnosed. Annually over 77 thousand people die from malignant melanoma worldwide [2]. If early diagnosed, a cure rate can reach 90 %. So there is a need for accurate diagnosis methods.

A clinical evaluation of the melanoma usually relays on: the five-point Clark [1] scale and the four-point Breslow [1] scale. Such evaluation is invasive because it utilizes a histological material. The thin needle biopsy is not applicable because in case of melanoma it can produce the metastasis. Thus the only way to get histological material is wide extraction which removes whole nevus. Such procedure is impractical because most of the nevi is harmless so its removal is not necessary.

© Springer International Publishing AG 2016
L.J. Chmielewski et al. (Eds.): ICCVG 2016, LNCS 9972, pp. 418–428, 2016.
DOI: 10.1007/978-3-319-46418-3_37

For an initial diagnosis of a melanocytic nevi, a trained dermatologist performs a visual inspection usually supported by the epiluminescence microscopy (also called dermoscopy) [3]. Such inspection relies on one of three available diagnosis models [4]: the pattern analysis, the ABCD-rule or the ELM 7-point checklist.

Application of image processing and analysis algorithms in dermatology has a long tradition [5] and demonstrated its usefulness in extracting of diagnostically important quantitative information. Such methods can also support melanoma diagnosis performed by dermatologists or even general physicians, ensuring objective and user independent results. The idea of creating a computer-based system for melanoma detection is not new. Several research groups are working on such systems development. Good review of image analysis based detection methods can be found in [6]. Jaworek-Koriakowska and Tadeusiewicz [7] described the implementation of border irregularity from ABCD rule. The same rule was applied by Grzymala-Busse in [8] in the data mining system. Also, Smaoui presented the implementation of the ABCD rule in [9]. Betta and his team published series of papers [3,4,10,11] describing implementation of the ELM 7-point checklist. However, accuracy of presented systems for discovering melanoma is not yet satisfactory. There is still a need for improving existing and developing new methods in order to increase credibility and robustness of image processing framework aimed at diagnosis support of melanoma lesions.

This paper describes recent research which is part of the struggle to develop an image analysis based tool for the recognition of the malignant melanoma utilizing the ELM 7-point checklist. This is a continuation of previous studies where the skin nevi semiautomatic segmentation tool was presented [12] and preliminary works on discovering two criterions from the ELM 7-point checklist: irregular streaks and the atypical pigmentation [13] was showed. In this work another three of seven criteria from the ELM 7-point checklist are covered, namely the blue whitish veil, the atypical vascular pattern and regression structures.

The structure of the paper is as follows: the second section contains description of analyzed images; the third section presents developed image analysis algorithms while the fourth one presents some tests results and discussion of the proposed methods. The last section sums up the paper.

## 2   Materials

193 digital images of skin nevi acquired by means of the digital camera (Nikon D90) equipped with the dermatoscope (Heine Delta 20) were analyzed. The resolution of these images was 2848 x 4288 pixels. The rectangular field of the view covers an area of 10 by 15 mm. Original images were stored using Nikon Electronic Format (RGB 12bits per pixel). Three of seven criteria from the ELM 7-point checklist were investigated. Those are the presence of the atypical vascular pattern, the blue whitish veil and regression structures (Fig. 1).

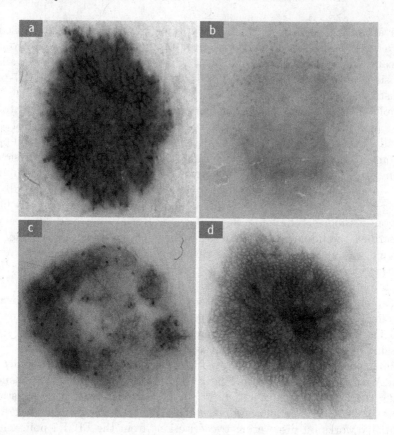

**Fig. 1.** Fragments of images containing blue whitish veil (a), irregular vascular pattern (b), regression (c) and nevus without three discussed structures (d).

Analyzed images were divided into six subsets which were identified by the trained dermatologist:

(a) 32 images with the atypical vascular pattern,
(b) 161 without the atypical vascular pattern,
(c) 84 images with the blue whitish veil,
(d) 109 images without the blue whitish veil,
(e) 32 images with regression structures,
(f) 161 images without regression structures.

## 3   Methods

All acquired images were affected by the non-uniform illumination introduced by the dermatoscope. The illumination model described in [12] was used to correct brightness nonuniformity over the entire image.

Alike the blue whitish veil (Fig. 1a) and the atypical vascular pattern (Fig. 1b) visually differ in color from the other nevi structures. The blue whitish veil color is something between white and light blue while atypical vascular patterns are red. Other structures have different shades of brown or are close to black. Therefore, separate color channels and its combinations from various color spaces (RGB, HSV, YCbCr) were tested. It was found that for the blue whitish veil and the atypical vascular patterns differences of Red-Green channels (Fig. 2B) and Green-Blue channels (Fig. 2c) from RGB space are most discriminative.

Figure 3. shows histograms calculated for regions with and without blue whitish veil for channels Green-Blue and Red-Green.

In Fig. 4, histograms calculated for regions with and without atypical vascular pattern for channels Red-Green and Green-Blue are presented.

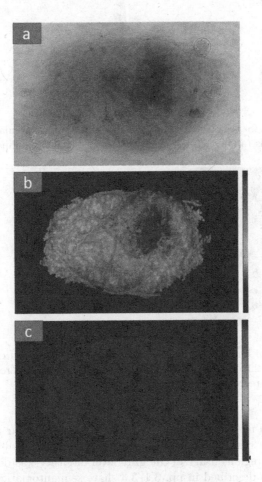

**Fig. 2.** Example image with atypical vascular pattern: original image (a) Red-Green channels (b) Green-Blue channels (c). (Color figure online)

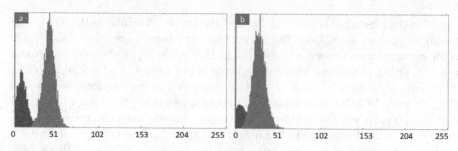

**Fig. 3.** Histograms for region with (red) and without blue whitish veil (green) Red-Green channels (a) Green-Blue channels (b). (Color figure online)

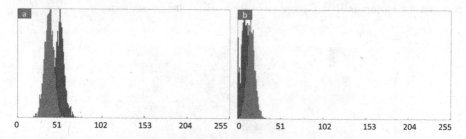

**Fig. 4.** Histograms for region with (red) and without atypical vascular pattern (green) Red-Green channels (a Green-Blue) channels (b). (Color figure online)

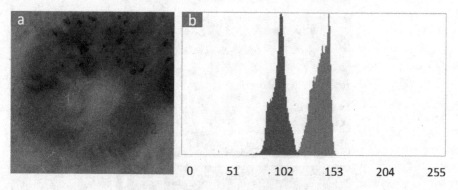

**Fig. 5.** A gray level image with marked regression region 1.(green circle) and region without regression 2.(red circle) (a), histograms for the regression region (green) and the region without regression (red) (b). (Color figure online)

The regression regions (Fig. 1c) have an appearance similar to the skin outside nevus. Those regions are significantly brighter from nevus regions, so for discovery of such regions usage of the gray level intensity was decided. (Fig. 5a)

All algorithms described in pp. 3.1–3.3 share semiautomatic image segmentation method presented in [12] which leads to extraction of the nevus region.

## 3.1   Recognition of the Blue Whitish Veil

In order to discover presence of the blue whitish veil the algorithm consisting of the following steps is applied:

(1) The segmentation of the investigated image in order to extract the nevus region.
(2) Difference images for R-G and G-B channels are calculated.
(3) Binary mask $M(x,y)$ is built to identify image pixels satisfying the following condition:

$$M(x, y) = \begin{cases} 1 & \text{if } I_{R-G}(x,y) < T_{R-G} \text{ and } I_{G-B}(x,y) < T_{G-B} \\ 0 & \text{otherwise} \end{cases}$$

Where:
$I_{R-G}(x,y)$ pixel intensity in R-G channel,
$I_{G-B}(x,y)$ pixel intensity in G-B channel,
$T_{R-G}$ threshold for the R-G channel,
$T_{G-B}$ threshold for the G-B channel,

(4) The morphological closing is applied into $M(x,y)$
(5) The morphological erosion is applied into $M(x,y)$
(6) Counting of nonzero pixels belonging to $M(x,y)$, $S = \sum M(x,y)$
(7) If $S > T_s$ (size threshold) the blue whitish veil is detected.

In above mentioned algorithm the segmentation is applied to input image after illumination equalization, common for all algorithms. According to performed tests, differential images R-G an G-B carry most discriminative information for discovering of the blue whitish veil. Empirically chosen thresholds were on the levels: $T_{R-G} < 5$ and $T_{G-B} < 9$. The morphological closing (circular structuring element with diameter of 50 pixels) fills small holes in detected regions. Additional morphological erosion (circular structuring element with diameter of 40 pixels) removes small groups of misclassified pixels. The final decision is taken based on empirically selected $T_s$ which was 5000 in this study.

## 3.2   Recognition of Atypical Vascular Pattern

The algorithm for discovering the atypical vascular pattern consists of following steps:

(1) R-G and G-B channel difference images are calculated.
(2) Binary mask $M(x,y)$ is built to identify image pixels satisfying the following condition:

$$M(x, y) = \begin{cases} 1 & \text{if } I_{R-G}(x,y) > T_{R-G} \text{ and } I_{G-B}(x,y) < T_{G-B} \\ 0 & \text{otherwise} \end{cases}$$

(3) Morphological opening is applied into $M(x,y)$
(4) Labeling separate objects in $M(x,y)$ to obtain labeled image $L(x,y)$
(5) Remove regions with area over area threshold
(6) Counting of nonzero pixels belonging to $L(x,y)$, $S = \sum \begin{cases} 1 & \text{if } L(x,y) > 0 \\ 0 & \text{otherwise} \end{cases}$
(7) If $S > T_s$ (size threshold) the atypical vascular pattern is detected.

This algorithm is similar to the one described in Sect. 3.1. The difference lays in different threshold values and the post processing. For the atypical vascular pattern the following thresholds were used: $T_{R-G} > 51$ and $T_{G-B} < 26$. The post processing starts from morphological opening. This time we are looking for small elements so this step causes separation of small areas. The labeling and removing of large objects exclude those which area does not satisfy definition of atypical vascular patterns (is bigger than 300 pixels). The final decision is taken based on empirically selected threshold $T_s$ applied to sum of remaining objects which was 600 in this study.

## 3.3   Recognition of Regression Regions

In order to discover the presence of the regression the following algorithm is applied:

(1) Average filtering of grey level image,
(2) Semiautomatic segmentation to detect the lesion, resulting in binary image $R(x,y)$;
(3) Conversion from original RGB to grey level image;
(4) Application of Otsu thresholding on nevus region (brighter region is used for further analysis), resulting in binary mask $M(x,y)$.
(5) Morphological erosion applied to the $R(x,y)$, resulting in $Re(x,y)$;
(6) Estimation of $H(x,y)=Re(x,y)$ and $M(x,y)$;
(7) Counting of nonzero pixels belonging to $H(x,y)$, $S = \sum H(x,y)$
(8) If $S > T_s$ (size threshold) the regression is detected.

Average filtering smooths the nevus region thus small structures like a pigmentation network will be removed. The conversion to the gray scale follows our discovery that the brightness is most discriminative factor between the regression and other nevus regions. The external boundary of the nevus is brighter than internal thus the Otsu thresholding will pick it together with the regression. In order to remove this region from further analysis an erosion of external boundary is performed with a relatively large structuring element. Its size is proportional to the size of the entire nevus. The final decision is taken based on empirically selected $T_s$ which was 5000 in this study.

## 4   Results and Discussion

Application of algorithm described in Sect. 3 allows for the detection of the blue whitish veil, the atypical vascular pattern and regression structures. Figure 6 shows examples of properly detected structures.

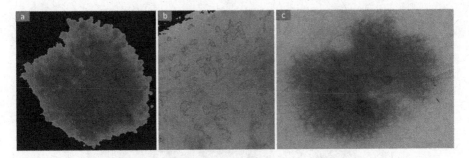

**Fig. 6.** Examples of properly discovered structures blue whitish veil (a), atypical vascular pattern (b) and regression structures (c).

**Table 1.** Classification results on test images.

| Criterion | True positives | True negatives | False positives | False negatives | Total error | Sensitivity | Specificity |
|-----------|----------------|----------------|-----------------|-----------------|-------------|-------------|-------------|
| Blue whitish veil | 80 (41.5%) | 71 (36.8%) | 38 (19.7%) | 4 (2.1%) | 42 (22%) | 95.3% | 65.2% |
| Atypical vascular pattern | 28 (14.5%) | 134 (69.4%) | 27 (14%) | 4 (2.1%) | 31 (16%) | 87.5% | 83.2% |
| Regression structures | 29 (15%) | 137 (71%) | 23 (11.9%) | 3 (1.6%) | 26 (13.5%) | 90.6% | 85.6% |

The combined quantitative analysis results are shown in the Table 1.

As it can be easily seen from Table 1, false negative cases are at relatively low level. On the other hand, the number of false positives is still large. This is due the fact that algorithms parameters were tuned in a pro-safe way ensuring minimal number false negatives. The highest classification error was observed when detecting blue whitish veil. This is related with relatively high number of false positives (see specificity in Table 1). The most accurate detection was obtained for regression. Obtained results were compared with those published in work of Di Leo et al. [4] (Table 2).

Presented results represent better sensitivity for detection of blue whitish veil and regression structures and negligibly smaller for atypical vascular pattern.

**Table 2.** Comparison of sensitivity and specificity for our approach and those presented in [4].

| | Blue whitish veil | | Atypical vascular pattern | | Regression structures | |
|---|---|---|---|---|---|---|
| | Our approach | Competetive approach | Our approach | Competetive approach | Our approach | Competetive approach |
| Sensitivity | 95.1% | 90% | 87.5% | 88% | 90.6% | 80% |
| Specificity | 65.1% | 93% | 83.2% | 82% | 85.6% | 83% |

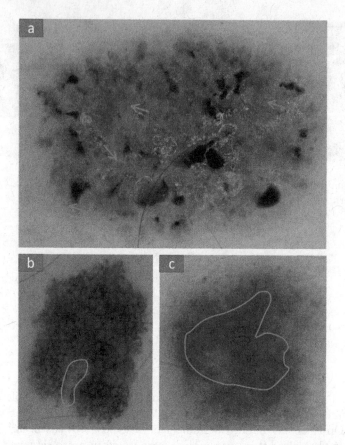

**Fig. 7.** Examples of false negatives discoveries (manually marked), the atypical vascular pattern(a), regression (b), blue whitish veil (c).

Proposed method has significantly lower specificity for recognition of blue whitish veil and slightly better for atypical vascular pattern and regression structures. Figure 7 shows examples of false negatives.

The atypical vascular pattern from Fig. 7a is covered by the strong blue whitish veil which was properly identified. Regression on Fig. 7b is in the early stage of development so its appearance in gray level scale is rather more similar to the rest of the nevus than to the healthy skin around. The blue whitish veil from Fig. 7c is quite gentle and it was just missed by the algorithm.

Further tuning of algorithms parameters is still possible and desired. Parameters (intensity and size thresholds) used in this study were selected on small tuning set (around 40 images). Thus larger data set should be considered to tune the parameters in order to improve algorithms robustness.

# 5  Summary

In this paper implementation of three criteria from seven points checklist for malign melanoma diagnosis were presented. Those are presence of the blue whitish veil, the atypical vascular pattern and the regression structures. Application of proposed detection algorithms gives promising results. Quantitatively, they are slightly better when compared to competitive approach presented in [4]. This work is part of larger project aimed at implementation and clinical verification of the 7-point checklist for automatic detection of melanoma lesions. Future works will focus on further testing and improving of already created algorithms as well as at development of image analysis methods that implement remaining criteria.

# References

1. Jablonska, S., Chorzelski, T.: Choroby Skory, 5th edn. PZWL, Warszawa (2001)
2. LeDuc, T.: World Life Expectancy. www.worldlifeexpectancy.com
3. Betta, G., Di Leo, G., Fabbrocini, G., Paolillo, A., Sommella, P.: Dermoscopic image-analysis system: estimation of atypical pigment network and atypical vascular pattern. In: IEEE International Workshop on Medical Measurement and Applications, MeMeA 2006, vol. 2006, pp. 63–67, April 2006
4. Di Leo, G., Paolillo, A., Sommella, P., Fabbrocini, G., Rescigno, O.: A software tool for the diagnosis of melanomas. In: IEEE International Instrumentation and Measurement Technology Conference (I2MTC) (2010)
5. Janowski, P., Strzelecki, M., Brzezinska-Blaszczyk, E., Zalewska, A.: Computer analysis of normal and basal cell carcinoma mast cells. Med. Sci. Monitor $7(2)$, 260–265 (2001)
6. Sathiya, S.B., Kumar, S.S., Prabin, M.: A survey on recent computer-aided diagnosis of Melanoma. In: 2014 International Conference on Control, Instrumentation, Communication and Computational Technologies, pp. 1387–1392 (2014)
7. Jaworek-Korjakowska, J., Tadeusiewicz, R.: Determination of border irregularity in dermoscopic color images of pigmented skin lesions. In: 2014 36th Annual International Conference of the IEEE Engineering in Medicine and Biology Society (EMBC), pp. 6459–6462 (2014)
8. Grzymala-Busse, P., Grzymala-Busse, J. W., Hippe, Z.S.: Melanoma prediction using data mining system LERS. In: 25th Annual International Computer Software and Applications Conference, COMPSAC 2001, pp. 615–620 (2001)
9. Smaoui, N.: A developed system for melanoma diagnosis. Int. J. Comput. Vis. Signal Process. $3(1)$, 10–17 (2013)
10. Betta, G., Di Leo, G., Fabbrocini, G., Paolillo, A., Scalvenzi, M.: Automated application of the; 7-point checklist; diagnosis method for skin lesions: estimation of chromatic and shape parameters. In: 2005 IEEE Instrumentationand Measurement Technology Conference Proceedings, vol. 3, pp. 17–19, May 2005
11. Di Leo, G., Paolillo, A., Sommella, P., Fabbrocini, G.: Automatic diagnosis of melanoma: a software system based on the 7-point check-list. In: Proceedings of Annual Hawaii International Conference on System Science, pp. 1–10 (2010)

12. Kropidłowski, K., Kociołek, M., Strzelecki, M., Czubiński, D.: Model based approach for melanoma segmentation. In: Chmielewski, L.J., Kozera, R., Shin, B.-S., Wojciechowski, K. (eds.) ICCVG 2014. LNCS, vol. 8671, pp. 347–355. Springer, Heidelberg (2014). doi:10.1007/978-3-319-11331-9_42
13. Kropidlowski, K., Kociolek, M., Strzelecki, M., Czubinski, D.: Nevus atypical pigment network distinction and irregular streaks detection in skin lesions images. In: Signal Processing: Algorithms, Architectures, Arrangements, and Applications (SPA), Poznan, pp. 66–70 (2015)

# Applying Artificial Neural Network for the Classification of Breast Cancer Using Infrared Thermographic Images

Vanessa Lessa$^{(\boxtimes)}$ and Mauricio Marengoni

Presbiterian University Mackenzie, São Paulo 01302-907, Brazil
vslessa@terra.com.br, mauricio.marengoni@mackenzie.br

**Abstract.** The second type of cancer that kills more women in the world is breast cancer. If the prognosis is done at an early stage of the disease, women can have a better chance of cure. However, the access to medical exams in poor countries is usually precarious. This work describes the study of a computer-assisted diagnostic system using thermal imaging. The images are generated by a thermographic camera that has a lower cost than the equipment used in conventional exams. We propose a system that classifies the thermographic breasts images in "normal" and "abnormal". We have analyzed 8 statistical characteristics: mean, variance, standard deviation (SD), skewness, kurtosis, entropy, range and median. The classification used an Artificial Neural Network (ANN) and got a result of 87 % in sensitivity, 83 % in specificity and 85 % in accuracy.

**Keywords:** Image processing · Thermography · Breast cancer · Artificial neural network

## 1 Introduction

Breast cancer is the second most common type of cancer in the world and the most common among women, corresponding to 25.2 % of new cases every year [1]. When breast cancer is detected at an early stage, the chance of cure is 85 %, but when it is detected at an advanced stage, the percentage drastically drops to 10 % [2].

A tumor may be identified through a series of tests such as mammography, ultrasound, tomosynthesis (3D mammography), magnetic resonance imaging and computed tomography. These tests can be painful, invasive, expose the patient to ionizing radiation or can require the use of contrast [3].

Cancerous cells were normal cells that suffered some kind of deformation. They have suffered an imbalance in the metabolic activity that makes the cell consumes a large amount of glucose and releases large amounts of lactate, causing regional vasodilation in the early stages of the disease and an increase in the formation of new blood vessels [4]. The increase of blood flow in the area causes a growth in the body temperature in the cancer area when compared to normal

© Springer International Publishing AG 2016
L.J. Chmielewski et al. (Eds.): ICCVG 2016, LNCS 9972, pp. 429–438, 2016.
DOI: 10.1007/978-3-319-46418-3_38

tissue temperature. The increase in temperature helps to detect cancerous tissue with infrared cameras, because they capture thermal information.

Recently, several studies have been using thermographic images to help on the diagnosis of breast cancer. Thermographic images is a non-invasive, painless method and does not need radiation or the use of contrast to generate images. Thus, it is completely safe for children and pregnant women. Our main contribution in this paper is to develop a system for the diagnosis of breast abnormalities using statistical characteristics and an artificial neural network.

## 2    Bibliography Review

Many authors are conducting experiments with breast thermographic images. The results shown the effectiveness of different statistical parameters and different classifiers in early detection and classification of breast cancer. The results are presented in Table 1, where the sample used in each experiment and in parenthesis the number of healthy patients and the number of patients with some abnormality. The authors presented some statistical measures to evaluate the performance of the experiment. Sensitivity is the ability of a diagnosis to identify the true positives in the individuals that are actually sick. Specificity is the ability of a diagnosis to identify the true negatives in individuals that are actually healthy. Accuracy is the ratio of successes, the total of true positive and true negative within the sample.

Koay et al. [11] used images of 19 patients, among which 14 patients were healthy and 5 of them had some breast abnormality. The extracted features were: average temperature, standard deviation, median, maximum, minimum, skewness, kurtosis, entropy, area and amount of heat. After the features extraction they have used the statistical software SPSS (Statistical Package for Social Sciences) to determine the correlation between the features. According to the authors, five characteristics are highly correlated: average temperature, standard deviation, skewness, kurtosis and amount of heat. They used an artificial neural network (ANN) with a single hidden layer, reporting only 10 % of false negatives. According to the authors, the failure of the experiment was due to the small number of images.

Tang et al. [12] analysed thermograms of a hundred and seventeen patients, among which forty-seven had malignant tumors and seventy patients had benign tumors. The authors suggested an analysis of a characteristic named by them "Local Temperature Increase" (LTI), which is an abnormality in the vascular patterns on the thermogram, with presence of very high temperatures. The proposed method of classification considers that the possible presence of a cancer is proportional to the maximum amplitude of the skin temperature in the suspicious region.

Arora et al. [13] analyzed ninety-two patients, among which fifty-eight cases had malignant tumors and thirty-four had benign tumors. They used a proprietary system (Sentinel Breast Scan) with unknown characteristics and classification with ANN model.

Wishart et al. [14] did not report extracted features. For the classification, they have used four tests: screening test, clinical examination, ANN and an artificial intelligence based method developed by the authors, called "No Touch Breast Scan" (NTBS). The results obtained using the NTBS had 48 % of sensitivity and 70 % of specificity.

Umadevi et al. [15] developed a software called "Infrared Thermography Based Image Construction" (ITBIC) for the interpretation of breast thermograms. The system captures three images of each patient (front, left and right side) and generates a simplified image. The simplified image is analyzed from logical decisions based on hot skin areas that have been extracted.

Acharya et al. [16] presented a study in which they used 50 breast thermograms, 50 % of them were normal and 50 % had breast cancer. The authors used sixteen characteristics based on texture: homogeneity, energy, entropy, the four first moments calculated by the matrix of co-occurrence, the second angular moment, contrast, median, emphasis in long primitives, uniformity in the level of grey scale and percentage of primitives. After comparison, only four characteristics were considered significant for classification: first moment, third moment, percentage of primitives and uniformity of the level of grey scale. The classifier used was a "Support Vector Machine" (SVM).

Bonini [3] used statistical measures as features: histogram, Higuchi fractal dimension and three methods of geostatistics: Geary coefficient, Moran index and Ripley's K function. The classification of these characteristics was performed by a "Support Vector Machine" (SVM).

**Table 1.** Comparison of results

|  | Sample | Sensitivity | Specificity | Acuracy |
|---|---|---|---|---|
| Koay et al. [11] | 19 (14/5) | 60 % | 100 % | 89.5 % |
| Tang et al. [12] | 117 (70/47) | 93.6 % | 44.3 % | - |
| Arora et al. [13] | 94 (34/60) | 97 % | 44 % | - |
| Wishart et al. [14] | 106 (41/65) | 48 % | 70 % | - |
| Umadevi et al. [15] | 50 (44/6) | 66.7 % | 97.7 % | - |
| Acharya et al. [16] | 50 (25/25) | 85.7 % | 90.5 % | 88.1 % |
| Borchartt [3] | 51 (14/37) | 91.9 % | 78.6 % | 88.2 % |

## 3    Database

The thermographic images used for this paper came from DMR (Database for Mastology Research) [5]. To feed the database, a FLIR SC-620 camera, with a 640 × 480 pixels resolution was used. Currently, the DMR database has breast images in grey scale of normal patients and patients with some anomaly. We randomly selected 47 patients and 94 breasts images for our experiment: 48 of them had normal breasts and 46 had some anomaly.

# 4    Analysis of Breast Thermograms

As mentioned above, due to the temperature difference one can detect cancerous tissue. Patients with normal tissue have a symmetry in the breasts temperature. A small difference in the thermal pattern may denote an anomaly. However, tumors in both breasts at the same time are uncommon. Thus, a small difference in the breasts temperature may indicate an abnormal tissue.

In this paper, the method used for analysis of thermograms consists of an evaluation of quantitative temperature parameters for each patient. For the analysis of asymmetric thermograms the following steps were integrated:

1. Pre-processing
2. Segmentation
3. Feature extraction for asymmetry analysis
4. Classification

## 4.1    Pre-processing of Breast Thermograms

The extraction of the region of interest in thermal imaging is challenging because there is no clear limit among the regions. In the pre-processing method, we extracted all the unnecessary areas were extracted before processing the image [9]. The background has to be removed manually and the image must be at grey scale to be pre-processed.

## 4.2    Segmentation of Breast Thermograms

The segmentation of the region of interest (ROI) plays a very important role. We need to separate the areas of the right breast and the left breast properly, because the feature extraction and classification depend on this process. The Fig. 1 (Left) shows the original image acquired from DMR. To segment the region of interest, we need to create a mask Fig. 1 (Right), that is why we apply in the original image the Canny edge detector [6] using a threshold for the lower dish of each breast. With the help of the mask presented in Fig. 1 (Right) it is possible to

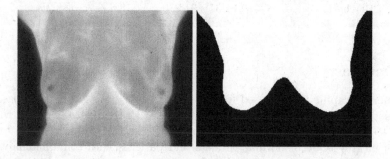

**Fig. 1.** Segmentation: (left) original image; (right) mask

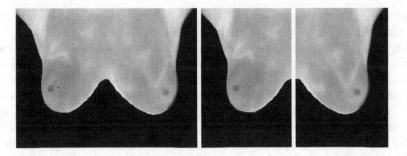

**Fig. 2.** Segmentation: (left) mamas segmented; regions of interest: (center) left breast (LB); (right) right breast (RB)

segment the original breast image as shown in Figure 2 (Left) and then separate the regions of interest, locating the center of the breasts, as shown in Fig. 2 (Center,Right) right breast and the left breast.

### 4.3    Feature Extraction for Asymmetry Analysis

Texture characteristics are most efficient for breast analysis thermograms [7]. Statistics measures allows extracting information from the breasts temperature to understand the relationship between the temperature values of healthy breasts and the ones with some pathology.

To analyze the pixels intensity distribution in each thermogram a histogram was used, where X indicates the temperature or the intensity (radiant heat), and Y represents the number of pixels for each intensity value. Figure 3 presents the histogram of the right and left breasts of two volunteers. We can observe that the breast with some anomaly have a higher pixel concentration where the temperature is higher (values near to 255). In other words, the lighter the

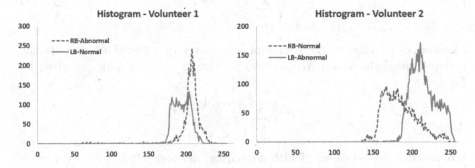

**Fig. 3.** Histogram of the left and right breast: (left) Volunteer 1 - Right breast abnormal and left breast normal; (right) Volunteer 2 - Right breast normal and left breast abnormal

image the higher the temperature. Thus, we conclude that the histogram is an important feature of asymmetry analysis in thermograms.

The first order statistical measures do not consider neighboring pixels and can be calculated directly from the image's histogram. The statistical measures of second order consider a pair of pixels at a random distance, orientation and position. Considering the difference presented in the histograms presented in Fig. 3, we have considered the first order statistical measurements: mean, variance, standard deviation (SD), skewness, kurtosis, entropy, range and median. If $P(i)$ is the probability of $i$ happening, where $i$ represents each grey level in the image $f(x, y)$ and G is the total number of grey levels:

**Mean:** Indicates the data concentration of a distribution. The mean can show the global temperature of the region of interest, as shown in Eq. 1.

$$\mu = \sum_{i=0}^{G-1} i * P(i) \tag{1}$$

**Variance:** Represents the deviation value of the image's grey levels related to the mean grey level. The Variance is computed using Eq. 2.

$$\sigma^2 = \sum_{i=0}^{G-1} (i - \mu)^2 * P(i) \tag{2}$$

**Standard Deviation:** Shows the dispersion of data around the mean. A low standard deviation indicates that the values are very close to the mean, while a high standard deviation indicates a wide dispersion of values towards the mean. The standard deviation presents a bigger or a smaller homogeneity or heterogeneity in the image, and it is computed using Eq. 3.

$$\sigma = \sqrt{\sum_{i=0}^{G-1} (i - \mu)^2 * P(i)} \tag{3}$$

**Skewness:** It refers to the degree of asymmetry of a distribution of specific feature around the mean. We can have positive or negative values, as given by Eq. 4.

$$\gamma_1 = \mu^{-3}[\sum_{i=0}^{G-1} (i - \mu)^3 * P(i)] \tag{4}$$

**Kurtosis:** It is also called "fourth normalized moment". It measures the levelling of a distribution with relation to a normal distribution, according to Eq. 5.

$$\gamma_2 = \mu^{-4}[\sum_{i=0}^{G-1} (i - \mu)^4 * P(i)] \tag{5}$$

**Entropy:** It measures the information contained in the segmented images and the amount of disorder in the system. The more symmetric the temperature distribution, the smaller the entropy. Individuals that have widely differing entropy in the images of the breasts (left and right) have a larger asymmetry and an increased probability of abnormality. The entropy is computed using Eq. 6.

$$H = \sum_{i=0}^{G-1} P(i) * log_2[P(i)] \tag{6}$$

**Range:** It indicates the temperature variation $(\Delta t)$ inside the region of interest. The value is calculated from the difference between the highest and lowest temperature $(t)$ in the region of interest. It is computed according to Eq. 7.

$$\Delta t = max_{0 \leq i \leq G-1} t_i - min_{0 \leq i \leq G-1} t_i \tag{7}$$

**Median:** It is the numerical value that divides the probability distribution in equal parts. The greater the difference between the median of the breasts of a patient, the greater the likelihood of a breast having an abnormality. Likewise, the smaller the difference, the greater the likelihood of no anomalies.

**Table 2.** Measure of asymmetry in left and right breast

| Statistical features | Volunteer 1 | | Volunteer 2 | |
|---|---|---|---|---|
| | Left breast normal | Right breast abnormal | Left breast abnormal | Right breast normal |
| Mean | 167.507 | 176.067 | 173.854 | 110.225 |
| Variance | 738.495 | 1050.057 | 1597.971 | 3563.663 |
| SD | 27.1752 | 32.4045 | 39.9746 | 59.6964 |
| Skewness | 1.2152 | 0.5795 | 1.3427 | 1.4518 |
| Kurtosis | 1.824 | 2.324 | 1.956 | 2.255 |
| Entropy | 4.8910 | 4.7182 | 5.0893 | 4.2360 |
| Range | 148 | 187 | 110 | 113 |
| Median | 194 | 205 | 215 | 184 |

Table 2 shows the statistical measures of right and left breasts of two volunteers. The features used can assist in the diagnosis of abnormalities in the breast, only with the analysis of differences. Because the probability distributions of the histograms are concentrated at higher temperatures, i.e., in the clearer pixels, the features "Mean and Median" showed higher values in the abnormal breast compared to the normal breast. The "Skewness" feature showed a lower degree of asymmetry for the abnormal breast. The other features were not conclusive for the selected volunteers.

# 5   Classification of Breast Thermograms

In order to classify the thermal breast images into "normal" or abnormal", we used an artificial neural network (ANN), which is widely used in pattern recognition problems. Artificial neural networks are computer models inspired by the central nervous system of an animal, particularly the brain. Neurons are arranged in layers and interconnected by connections known as synaptic weights, which represent the network knowledge. They are able to perform machine learning, as well as pattern recognition [10], with one layer of input neurons, one layer of output neurons and one or more intermediate layers [8].

We compare two ANN classification models. The first ANN used a single intermediate layer - this model is capable of solving a linearly separable problem, that is, a problem that can be separated by tracing a straight line on a hyperplane (Fig. 4 left), since the algorithm is able to adjust only one weight layer. The second ANN solves problems of non-linear classification using an algorithm to adjust more than one layer (Fig. 4 right) [17].

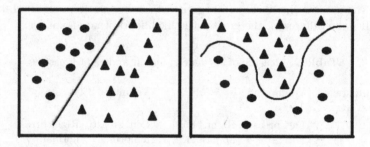

**Fig. 4.** Classification: (left) linear; (right) non-linear

After segmentation and feature extraction, we randomly selected 25 images with some anomaly and 25 normal images for ANN training. For the experiments, we used the 8 statistical features extracted from each image to the ANN training network and the backpropagation algorithm, which calculates the gradient of the sum according to a quadratic error function related to weights. It is an optimization method capable of finding the weight coefficients and thresholds for the neural network given a training set [10].

For linear classification, the training was considered satisfactory when it achieved the error rate equal to 0.205. The next step was to submit all the features of the 94 images for classification (47 of right breast and 47 of left breast). The displayed output is the data model in the interpretation network. For non-linear classification, the training was considered satisfactory when it achieved the error rate equal to 0.016. The ANN used has an input layer with 8 neurons, that are related to the features extracted from the image. The output layer has two neurons enabling the classification and 1 hidden layer with 5

**Table 3.** Matrix of confusion

|  |  | Linear | | Non-linear | |
|---|---|---|---|---|---|
|  |  | Normal | Abnormal | Normal | Abnormal |
| Real | Normal | 33 | 15 | 40 | 8 |
|  | Abnormal | 20 | 26 | 6 | 40 |

neurons. The number of neurons was calculated based on the arithmetic mean of the input and output size of the network.

To analyze the ANNs performance, we calculated some statistical measures using the information present in the confusion matrix presented in Table 3. The non-linear model showed the best result reaching 87 % of sensitivity, 83 % of specificity and 85 % of accuracy. The linear classification had a lower result, showing 57 % of sensitivity, 69 % of specificity and 63 % of accuracy. The results presented by both ANNs concluded that a non-linear ANN best solves the problem.

## 6   Conclusion

The main objective of identifying breast cancer is to reduce the mortality rate caused by the disease. The earlier the prognosis the better the chances of cure. The thermographic image is a non-invasive, painless process, and does not need radiation or contrast to generate the image. It is therefore completely safe for children and pregnant women and the cost of equipment is low.

The experiments showed that we could have good results in cancer identification using thermographic images and classifying them with non-linear neural network.

This paper presents the first phase of analysis and experiments conducted for the development of a diagnostic computer-assisted system. The results indicate a possibility of further exploration for diagnosis using thermographic images. As future work, we will use other features and other classifiers in order to improve results.

## References

1. Ferlay, J., Soerjomataram, M., Ervik, M., Dikshit, R., Eser, S., Mathers, C., Rebelo, M., Parkin, D., Forman, D., Bray, F.: Cancer Incidence and Mortality Worldwide: IARC Cancer Base n 11 (2012). http://globocan.iarc.fr
2. Ng, E., Sudharsan, N.: Numerical computation as a tool to aid thermographic interpretation. J. Med. Eng. Technol. **25**, 53–60 (2001)
3. Borchartt, T.: Thermographic Image Analysis for the Change of Classification in Breast. Univerisadade Federal Fluminense, Brasil (2013)
4. Thomsen, L., Miles, D.: Happerfield: nitrie oxide synthase activity in human breast. Br. J. Cancer **72**, 41 (1995)

5. Silva, L.F., Saade, D.C.M., Sequeiros, G.O., Silva, A.C., Paiva, A.C., Bravo, R.S., Conci, A.: A new database for breast research with infrared image. J. Med. Imaging Health Inf. **4**(1), 92–100 (2014)
6. Canny, J.: A computational approach to edge detectiion. IEEE Trans. Pattern Anal. Mach. Intell. **6**, 679–698 (1995)
7. Nurhayati, O., Susanto, A., Sri Widodo, T., Tjokronagoro, M.: Principal component analysis combined with first order statistical method for breast thermal images classification. Int. J. Comput. Sci. Technol. (JCST) **2**(2), 12–18 (2011)
8. Freeman, J.A., Skapura, D.M.: Neural Networks: Algorithms, Applications, and Programming Techniques. Addison-Wesley, New York (1992)
9. Zhou, Q., Li, Z., Aggarwal, J.K.: Boundary extraction in thermal images by edge map. In: Proceedings of the ACM Symposium on Applied Computing, pp. 254–258 (2004)
10. Haykin, S.: Neural networks: principles and practice. Trad. Paulo Martins Engel, Porto Alegre, Bookman, 2nd edn., p. 893 (2008)
11. Koay, J., Herry, C., Frize, M.: Analysis of breast thermography with an artificial neural network. In: Conference of Proceedings IEEE Engineering in Medicine and Biology Society, vol. 2, p. 1159 (2004)
12. Tang, X., Ding, H., Yuan, Y., Wang, Q.: Morphological measurement of localized temperature increase amplitudes in breast infrared thermograms and its clinical application. In: Biomedical Signal Processing and Control, vol. 3(4), p. 312, October 2008
13. Arora, N., Martins, D., Ruggerio, D., Tousimis, E., Swistel, A., Osborne, M., Simmons, R.: Effectiveness of a noninvasive digital infrared thermal imaging system in the detection of breast cancer. Am. J. Surg. **196**, 523–526 (2008)
14. Wishart, G.C., Campisi, M., Boswell, M., Chapman, D., Shackleton, V., Iddles, S., Hallett, A., Britton, P.D.: The accuracy of digital infrared imaging for breast cancer detection in women undergoing breast biopsy. Euro. J. Surg. Oncol. (EJSO) **36**, 535–540 (2010)
15. Umadevi, V., Raghavan, S.V., Jaipurkar, S.: Interpreter for breast thermogram characterization. In: Conference on Biomedical Engineering and Sciences (IECBES), Kuala Lumpur, p. 150 (2010)
16. Acharya, U.R., Ng, E.Y.K., Tan, J.H., Sree, S.V.: Thermography based breast cancer detection using texture features and support vector machine. J. Med. Syst. **36**, 1503–1510 (2012)
17. Bishop, C.: Neural Networks for Pattern Recognition. Oxford University Press, Oxford (1995)

# Fully-Automatic Method for Assessment of Flow-Mediated Dilation

Bartosz Zieliński[1]([✉]), Agata Dróżdż[2], and Marzena Frołow[2]

[1] Institute of Computer Science and Computer Mathematics,
Faculty of Mathematics and Computer Science,
Jagiellonian University, ul. Łojasiewicza 6, 30-348 Kraków, Poland
bartosz.zielinski@uj.edu.pl
[2] Jagiellonian Centre for Experimental Therapeutics (JCET), Jagiellonian
University, ul. Bobrzyńskiego 14, 30-348 Kraków, Poland
{agata.drozdz,marzena.frolow}@jcet.eu

**Abstract.** The most popular method for assessment the endothelial
function, called flow-mediated dilation, is based on monitoring how the
brachial artery diameter changes in hyperemia state. All of the existing methods that assess FMD are exceedingly time consuming, as they
require supervising analysis of the whole video. The presented method
fully-automatically analyzes the videos and returns the FMD value using
region of interest (ROI) defined by the operator. The main contributions
of this paper are: minimizing inter and intra-observer variability; elim-
inating supervision from the analysis; applying more informative techniques than edge detectors; providing dataset which can be used by other
researchers to test their fully-automatic methods.

**Keywords:** Ultrasound videos · Flow-mediated dilation · Computer-
aided diagnosis · Machine learning · Computer vision · Line descriptor

## 1 Introduction

Endothelial cells that form a thin layer inside the blood vessels play a key role in various processes in human body. Their dysfunction leads to various
pathologies [10] and has been observed from patients with inflammatory and
infectious diseases [7]. There exist clinical evidences on the diagnostic, prog-
nostic, and therapeutic significance of the endothelial function, and hence a
number of methods have been introduced for its assessment. The most popular one, called flow-mediated dilation (FMD; [3]), is based on monitoring how
the brachial artery diameter changes in hyperemia state. FMD is computed as
$(maxHyper - base)/base$, where $maxHyper$ and $base$ correspond to the maximal
artery diameter in the hyperemia state and the artery diameter under normal
conditions, respectively. FMD is usually different in case of the endothelial cells
with and without dysfunction [2].

Both $base$ and $maxHyper$ values are usually obtained by analyzing ultrasound videos. Value of $base$ can be determined easily, as the artery diameter changes insignificantly under normal conditions; therefore, even a short 5 s

© Springer International Publishing AG 2016
L.J. Chmielewski et al. (Eds.): ICCVG 2016, LNCS 9972, pp. 439–450, 2016.
DOI: 10.1007/978-3-319-46418-3_39

long video, containing around 100 frames, is sufficient. However, the time when *maxHyper* occurs varies depending on the patient; therefore, at least 120 s long video, containing around 6000 frames, has to be analyzed. For this reason, all of the existing methods that assess FMD are exceedingly time consuming, as they require supervising analysis of the whole video (see Sect. 2 for details).

The presented method fully-automatically analyzes the ultrasound video and returns the FMD value using region of interest (ROI) defined by the operator. Each frame of the video is analyzed separately in order to produce line segments which are candidates for upper and lower artery walls. The lines are described and classified as located or not located on the artery walls. Classifier was trained on 40 ultrasound videos and testing on remaining 30 videos. The experiment was repeated ten times for different training and test sets.

The main contributions of this paper are:

- to present a fully-automatic method for assessment of FMD which minimize inter and intra-observer variability,
- to eliminate supervision from analysis of large number of ultrasound videos in post-processing mode,
- to apply computer vision and machine learning techniques which are more informative than currently used edge detectors,
- to provide dataset which can be used by other researchers to test their fully-automatic methods (the ultrasound videos are available together with the ground truth artery walls).

## 2    Problem Statement

FMD is based on monitoring how the brachial artery diameter changes in the hyperemia state. For this purpose, after some time of baseline conditions, occlusion of flow to the forearm is provoked and maintained for 5 min by a cuff inflated to suprasystolic pressure around the upper forearm. The reactive hyperemia is introduced by sudden cuff deflation, resulting in rapid brachial artery dilation that reaches its maximum approximately 1 min after cuff deflation. The whole process is recorded as 2D ultrasound video (see Fig. 1a–f) which can be analyzed in real-time or in post-processing mode. The artery should be recorded continuously from 30 s before to 2 min after cuff deflation. [4, 16].

Most of the existing methods determine how the artery diameter changes in time by tracking the artery walls in successive frames, computing distance between them and then use such distances to determine FMD.

Liang et al. [12] use dynamic programming with cost function of multiple image features, such as echo intensity, intensity gradient, and boundary formation (all of them represented as fuzzy expressions).

Woodman et al. [17] use IMAQ automatic binary thresholding to convert ROI (which contains inner part of the vessel) into black and white mode. Each column of black and white ROI is then analyzed to determine the longest sequence of black pixels. Once all columns are processed, they are sorted into numerical

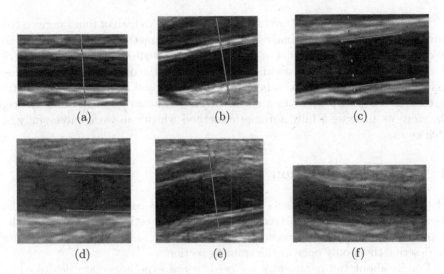

**Fig. 1.** Easy (a, b and c) and difficult to analyze (d, e and f) ROIs and the ground truth artery walls.

order, and the median column length of binary zeros is taken to be the diameter of the artery.

Sidhu et al. [14] developed artificial neural network wall detection method that automatically detects and tracks the anterior and posterior walls within a user-defined ROI. The vessel diameter is determined by averaging a large number of local vessel diameters.

According to Hiltawsky et al. [11], the vessel wall is known to be a continuous and smooth boundary, which can be described using an active contour model (snake). Therefore, they represented a contour by a number of points and minimized the sum of internal and external energies in order to find the optimal contour. Similar approach was presented in [18].

In [5], the averaged profile plot is produced along a direction orthogonal to the longitudinal arterial axis to determine the maximal derivative values of the profile at the blood-wall interfaces.

Gemignani et al. [9] use edge detector called "mass center of the gray-level variability", where border points are corrected by iteratively computing the mass center of the gray level variability inside the circular domain. As a result, the border points are moved closer to the discontinuity (edge).

At the beginning, Bartoli et al. [1] use contrast enhancement by histogram stretching and sharpening via a negative Laplacian filter of size $3 \times 3$. Then, two cubic splines are independently fitted to the artery walls and progressively propagated along the video sequence.

The comparison of two most popular FMD software, FMD Studio [9] and Brachial Analyzer [15] is presented in [6].

Although many methods are used to determine FMD, all of them were tested using so-called supervising analysis. In case of some methods, such analysis can be conducted in real-time, what allows a continuous feedback about the quality of the acquired ultrasound images and reduces the number of examinations lost due to low-quality videos. On the other hand the supervised analysis is problematic in case of the post-processing analysis of large number of ultrasound videos, therefore we propose a fully-automatic method which can work successfully in such cases.

# 3   Method Description

The method description consists of two parts. In first part we describe how the classifier is trained, while the second part refers to testing phase. Some of the steps are similar for both phases, like lines extraction and description, therefore we describe them only once in the training section.

Details about the parameters we used in the experiment are described in Sect. 4.

## 3.1   Training Phase

For each video from training set we randomly choose frames for training the classifier. Each ROI from the chosen frames is processed with the Laplacian filter in order to extract the edges (see Fig. 2a). Then, the standard Hough transform is computed, and the peaks are identified. In result, a set of line segments (candidates for upper and lower artery walls) is obtained (see Fig. 2b).

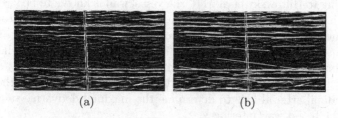

(a)                                     (b)

**Fig. 2.** A ROI from Fig. 1 processed with the Laplacian filter (a), and the candidates for upper and lower artery walls (yellow line segments in b). (Color figure online)

In the next step, the line segments are divided into two groups: positive and negative candidates (separately for upper and lower artery walls). A line segment is considered as positive candidate if the mean distance between the line and the ground truth artery wall is small. However, the line segments which does not overlap the ground truth artery walls (in accordance with the horizontal coordinates) are rejected from further analysis (see Fig. 3a–b). Naturally, there is much more negative candidates (the group of positive candidates contains approximately 10 % of the line segments).

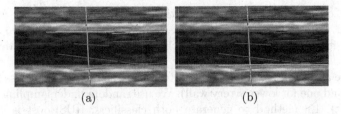

(a)                                         (b)

**Fig. 3.** A ROI from Fig. 1 with positive (yellow color) and negative (red color) candidates for upper (a) and lower (b) artery walls. Green line segments represent the ground truth artery walls. (Color figure online)

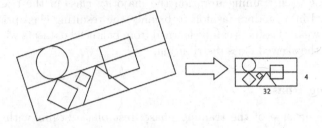

**Fig. 4.** Transforming neighborhood of line segment into the fixed size matrix using rotation and scaling.

The line descriptor we use takes the neighborhood of the line segment and transforms it (using rotation and scaling) into the fixed size matrix in a way presented in Fig. 4. The matrix is reshaped to vector with successive rows of the

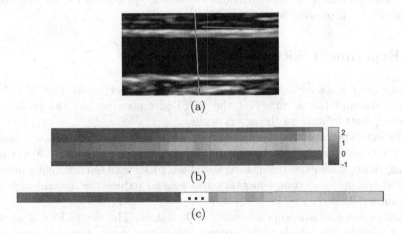

(a)

(b)

(c)

**Fig. 5.** The example of line (a) together with its transformed neighborhood with standardized values (b) and description vector (c). In this example, we take 5 pixels above and 5 pixels below the line as the neighborhood, and then transform it to the matrix of size $32 \times 4$, therefore description vector length is 128.

matrix. In order to make such description vector more robust, its values are normalized using standardization. The example of line is presented in Fig. 5 together with its transformed neighborhood and plot of resulting description vector.

Positive and negative description vectors are used to train two classifiers (one for upper and one for lower artery wall). We use random undersampling boosting (RUSBoost) [13] method to generate both classifiers. RUSBoost is similar to AdaBoost [8] which is an ensemble method that combines the weighted decisions of weak classifiers to obtain a final decision for a given input sample. RUSBoost extends this concept by a data sampling strategy that enforces similar class priors. During each training iteration the majority class in the training set is undersampled in a random fashion to balance the resulting class priors. In this manner, the weak classifiers can be learned from balanced datasets without being biased from the skewed class distribution.

## 3.2   Testing Phase

Similarly like in case of the training phase, test phase begins with generating set of line segments (candidates for upper and lower artery walls) together with description vectors.

In the next step, description vectors are analyzed by both classifiers. Two lines with the highest scores (one for each classifier) are denoted as upper and lower artery walls. The distance between those two lines is considered as artery diameter.

As the result of analyzing all frames, we determine vector $auto$ which describes how the artery diameter changes in time. Both $auto$ and ground truth ($gt$) vector for one of the test ultrasound videos are plotted in Fig. 6. To stabilize the result, we process $gt$ and $auto$ with median filter.

## 4   Experiment Setup

In our experiments we investigate the robustness and expressiveness of the line descriptors, and the accuracy of the RUSBoost classifier for the problem of detecting lines located on the artery walls.

For our experiments, we employ a dataset of 70 ultrasound videos together with the ground truth lines. We use 40 videos in training phase and 30 videos in testing phase. Each experiment is repeated ten times with ten different randomly selected training and complementary test sets to reduce the dependency from the training data.

Each video contains approximately 3000 frames. The size of ROI is approximately $300 \times 200$. pixels. The ground truth lines have been obtained with supervised analysis described in [18]. The examples of artery ROI with ground truth artery walls are presented in Fig. 1a–f. Dataset is publicly available (see Appendix).

Details about the parameters we used in method from Sect. 3:

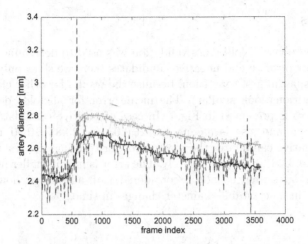

**Fig. 6.** This plot presents how the artery diameter changes in time. It was obtained for one of the test ultrasound videos. Dashed green and black lines represent ground truth (*gt*) and automatic results (*auto*), respectively. Solid green and black lines represents *gt* and *auto* processed with median filter, respectively. The systematic error is caused by the fact that positive candidates for artery walls are localized slightly below or above the ground truth artery walls (see Fig. 3a-b), where the edge values are maximal. This error can slightly influence the FMD value. (Color figure online)

- we randomly choose 100 frames from each training video to learn the classifier (the indices of randomly chosen frames are available online for reproducibility; see Appendix),
- in Hough transform we use 25 peaks, threshold equals 0.3 of the maximal value in Hough space, and minimum length of line segment equals 0.2 of the ROI's width,
- we consider a line segment as positive candidate if the mean distance between the line and the ground truth artery wall is smaller than 0.1 mm (around 3 pixels),
- we reject the line segments which does not overlap 0.5 of the ground truth artery walls (in accordance with the horizontal coordinates),
- as the neighborhood of the line segment for simple line descriptor we take 5 pixels above and 5 pixels below the line,
- the size of description matrix is $32 \times 4$, therefore description vector length is 128,
- in RUSBoost classifier we use 500 trees with minimum leaf size equals 5, and 0.1 learning rate,
- we use only 100 trees from RUSBoost in testing phase.

The value of FMD (*autoFMD*) is approximated by $(max(auto) - min(auto))/min(auto)$. Such approximation is made only for the experiment and in the real examination $min(auto)$ should be replace by *base*, as described in Sect. 1.

## 5   Results

In the training phase, 5-fold cross validation was used to determine the classification error for positive and negative candidates (here we show only the results for lower classifier in first repetition, because the results for other classifiers and in other repetitions look similar). The mean error for all folds depending on number of trees is presented in Fig. 7. In case of positive candidates the mean error for training and test data equal $0.09 \pm 0.03$ and $23.83 \pm 0.90$, respectively. In case of negative candidates the mean error for training and test data equals $0.01 \pm 0.01$ and $3.26 \pm 0.20$, respectively. The error is much smaller in case of the negative candidates what usually is considered as disadvantage, however in this case it results in much stable diameter changes in time.

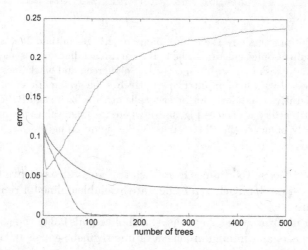

**Fig. 7.** The mean error for all folds depending on number of trees for positive (green lines) and negative (red lines) candidates. Dashed lines represent error for training data, while solid lines represent error for test data. (Color figure online)

The relation of automatically generated FMD ($autoFMD$) to ground truth FMD ($gtFMD$) for overall test samples (all test samples from all ten repetitions) is presented in Fig. 8. As can be observed, most of the results lie on the perfect correlation line (green line in Fig. 8). The rareness of large $abs(gtFMD - autoFMD)$ values is additionally visible in Fig. 9 where only outliers are larger than 5 %. There are 38 outliers out of 300 overall test samples (12.67 %).

Moreover, most of the outliers can be detected automatically, taking into consideration that according to Bots et al. [2], the absolute value of FMD should be less than 20 %. Therefore, 33 out of 38 outliers in overall test samples (86.84 %) can be automatically rejected from the analysis, as their $autoFMD$ were greater than 20 % (see Fig. 8).

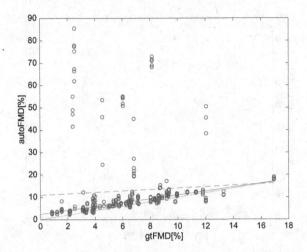

**Fig. 8.** The relation of automatically generated FMD to ground truth FMD. Green line represents perfect correlation, red dashed line represents regression for all results, and red solid line represents correlation for all results except those automatically rejected. The correlation without rejected results equals 0.82 ($autoFMD'$ corresponds to all results except those automatically rejected). (Color figure online)

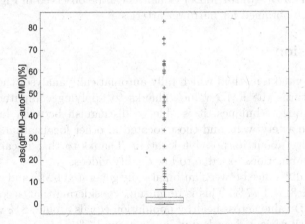

**Fig. 9.** Difference between automatically generated FMD and ground truth FMD. The mean value without automatically rejected results equals $1.81 \pm 1.77\%$. The differences are considered as outliers if they are greater than $q_3 + w(q_3 - q_1)$ or less than $q_1 - w(q_3 - q_1)$, where $q1$ and $q3$ are the $25^{th}$ and $75^{th}$ percentiles of the sample data, respectively.

When ignoring the rejected results, the mean value of $abs(gtFMD' - autoFMD')$ equals $1.81 \pm 1.77\%$ ($autoFMD'$ corresponds to all results except those automatically rejected).

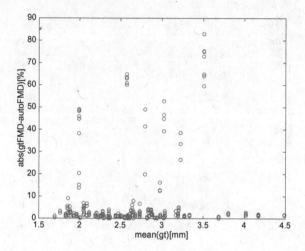

**Fig. 10.** The relation of difference between automatically generated FMD and ground truth FMD to mean ground truth diameter.

Additional analysis was performed to investigate if mean diameter influences on the $abs(gtFMD' - autoFMD')$ value. As can be observed in Fig. 10, most of the outliers are obtained for narrower arteries.

## 6   Discussion

We have presented a method which fully-automatically analyses the ultrasound video and returns the FMD value. Thanks to applying computer vision and machine learning techniques, it is able to distinguish between line segments located on the artery walls and those located in other localization without any prior knowledge about its possible location. Thanks to that it can reduce the number of examinations lost due to low quality videos.

The mean difference between automatically generated FMD and ground truth FMD equals $1.81 \pm 1.77\%$. This is promising, considering that according to [2], the mean FMD value across healthy population equals around $8\%$ while in case of patients with various disorders it equals around $3\%$.

According to our knowledge there is no other dataset with that kind of data available online, therefore sharing it with other researchers can contribute to the formation of other fully-automatic methods.

Although the method was created to work in post-processing mode, some additional effort should be made to speed it up. For this purpose, we attend to use faster line detectors and descriptors (also those based on the pyramids) and AdaBoost with linear SVM classifier as a week learner. This should speed up the testing phase which is crucial for clinical applications (naturally, class priors should be taken into consideration when learning linear SVM).

The systematic error between ground truth and automatic artery diameter (see Fig. 6) has to be eliminated, as it can influence the FMD value. Moreover, the dataset was generated using only one method of supervised analysis and therefore may contain errors. Therefore, we encourage other researches to run their supervised methods on our dataset and to send us their results (unfortunately most of the methods are not publicly available, therefore we were not able to do it ourselves). This hopefully result in more accurate dataset, which could be used by all researchers.

**Acknowledgement.** Dataset used in this paper was acquired from Jagiellonian Centre for Experimental Therapeutics (JCET) at Jagiellonian University in Kraków, Poland. The ultrasound videos were obtained during the study supported by European Union from the resources of the European Regional Development Fund under the Innovative Economy Programme (grant coordinated by JCET-UJ, No POIG. 01.01.02-00-069/09). We gratefully acknowledge the support from Prof. Stefan Chłopicki that were instrumental to carry out this study.

## Appendix: Code and dataset

The code of application and dataset used in experiment are publicly available under the following link: www.ii.uj.edu.pl/~zielinsb.

## References

1. Bartoli, G., Menegaz, G., Lisi, M., Di Stolfo, G., Dragoni, S., Gori, T.: Model-based analysis of flow-mediated dilation and intima-media thickness. J. Biomed. Imaging **2008**, 16–16 (2008)
2. Bots, M.L., Westerink, J., Rabelink, T.J., de Koning, E.J.: Assessment of FMD of the brachial artery: effects of technical aspects of the FMD measurement on the FMD response. Eur. Heart J. **26**(4), 363–368 (2005)
3. Celermajer, D.S., Sorensen, K., Gooch, V., Sullivan, I., Lloyd, J., Deanfield, J., Spiegelhalter, D., et al.: Non-invasive detection of endothelial dysfunction in children and adults at risk of atherosclerosis. Lancet **340**(8828), 1111–1115 (1992)
4. Corretti, M.C., Anderson, T.J., Benjamin, E.J., Celermajer, D., Charbonneau, F., Creager, M.A., Deanfield, J., Drexler, H., Gerhard-Herman, M., Herrington, D., et al.: Guidelines for the ultrasound assessment of endothelial-dependent flow-mediated vasodilation of the brachial artery: a report of the international brachial artery reactivity task force. J. Am. Coll. Cardiol. **39**(2), 257–265 (2002)
5. Craiem, D., Chironi, G., Gariepy, J., Miranda-Lacet, J., Levenson, J., Simon, A.: New monitoring software for larger clinical application of brachial artery flow-mediated vasodilatation measurements. J. Hypertens. **25**(1), 133–140 (2007)
6. Faita, F., Masi, S., Loukogeorgakis, S., Gemignani, V., Okorie, M., Bianchini, E., Charakida, M., Demi, M., Ghiadoni, L., Deanfield, J.E.: Comparison of two automatic methods for the assessment of brachial artery flow-mediated dilation. J. Hypertens. **29**(1), 85–90 (2011)
7. Flammer, A.J., Anderson, T., Celermajer, D.S., Creager, M.A., Deanfield, J., Ganz, P., Hamburg, N.M., Lüscher, T.F., Shechter, M., Taddei, S., et al.: The assessment of endothelial function from research into clinical practice. Circulation **126**(6), 753–767 (2012)

8. Freund, Y., Schapire, R.E.: A decision-theoretic generalization of on-line learning and an application to boosting. J. Comput. Syst. Sci. **55**(1), 119–139 (1997)
9. Gemignani, V., Faita, F., Ghiadoni, L., Poggianti, E., Demi, M.: A system for real-time measurement of the brachial artery diameter in b-mode ultrasound images. IEEE Trans. Med. Imaging **26**(3), 393–404 (2007)
10. Gryglewski, R.J.: Pharmacology of vascular endothelium. FEBS J. **272**(12), 2956–2967 (2005)
11. Hiltawsky, K., Wiegratz, A., Enderle, M., Ermert, H.: Real-time detection of vessel diameters with ultrasound. echtzeiterkennung von gefäßdurchmessern mit ultraschall. Biomedizinische Technik/Biomedical. Engineering **48**(5), 141–146 (2003)
12. Liang, Q., Wendelhag, I., Wikstrand, J., Gustavsson, T.: A multiscale dynamic programming procedure for boundary detection in ultrasonic artery images. IEEE Trans. Medi. Imaging **19**(2), 127–142 (2000)
13. Seiffert, C., Khoshgoftaar, T.M., Van Hulse, J., Napolitano, A.: Rusboost: A hybrid approach to alleviating class imbalance. IEEE Trans. Syst. Man Cybern. Part A Syst. Hum. **40**(1), 185–197 (2010)
14. Sidhu, J., Newey, V., Nassiri, D., Kaski, J.: A rapid and reproducible on line automated technique to determine endothelial function. Heart **88**(3), 289–292 (2002)
15. Sonka, M., Liang, W., Lauer, R.M.: Automated analysis of brachial ultrasound image sequences: early detection of cardiovascular disease via surrogates of endothelial function. IEEE Trans. Med. Imaging **21**(10), 1271–1279 (2002)
16. Thijssen, D.H., Black, M.A., Pyke, K.E., Padilla, J., Atkinson, G., Harris, R.A., Parker, B., Widlansky, M.E., Tschakovsky, M.E., Green, D.J.: Assessment of flow-mediated dilation in humans: a methodological and physiological guideline. Am. J. Physiol. Heart Circulatory Physiol. **300**(1), H2–H12 (2011)
17. Woodman, R., Playford, D., Watts, G., Cheetham, C., Reed, C., Taylor, R., Puddey, I., Beilin, L., Burke, V., Mori, T., et al.: Improved analysis of brachial artery ultrasound using a novel edge-detection software system. J. Appl. Physiol. **91**(2), 929–937 (2001)
18. Zielinski, B., Roman, A., Drozdz, A., Kowalewska, A., Frolow, M.: A new approach to automatic continuous artery diameter measurement. In: 2014 Federated Conference on Computer Science and Information Systems (FedCSIS), pp. 247–251. IEEE (2014)

# Motion Analysis, Tracking and Surveillance

# Orthogonal Gradient-Based Binary Image Representation for Vehicle Detection

Zbigniew Czapla[✉]

Faculty of Transport, Silesian University of Technology,
ul. Krasinskiego 8, 40-019 Katowice, Poland
zbigniew.czapla@polsl.pl

**Abstract.** The paper presents a novel method of image conversion into binary representation. This method of image conversion is based on small orthogonal image gradients. The input image sequence consist of consecutive frames taken from the video stream obtained from the camera placed over a road. Images from the input image sequence are processed separately into binary image representation. Layout of logical values of binary image representation is in accordance with edges of objects comprised in the source image. Vehicle detection is performed by the analysis of changes of the detection field state. The state of the detection field is determined on the basis of appropriate sums of logical values calculated within the detection field. The proposed method of image conversion into binary representation is efficient and attractive computationally. Gradient-based binary image representation is intended for application in road traffic systems. Experimental results are provided.

## 1 Introduction

Image data can be utilized in road traffic systems for traffic monitoring and measurement of traffic parameters. Road traffic systems using cameras are often more attractive comparing to systems of other kind. In addition to vehicle detection, systems using cameras can perform various other functions e.g., vehicle classification, counting of vehicles in individual classes, determination of lane occupancy or vehicle tracking.

Road traffic systems using image data are usually complex and multistage. In these systems various methods of vehicle detection are applied. The popular method of vehicle detection consist in calculation of the difference between current image and the current background, binarization of the result with the use of a threshold value and background updating [1,2]. The background can be determine by adaptive modelling as mixture of Gausians [3]. In [4] vehicles are detected by detecting corners as regions in which brightness changes in more than one direction. In [5] vehicles are detected by analysis of intensity differences which occur along defined slits. In [6] vehicle detection is carried out by generating images on the basis of virtual detection lines, application of Canny edge detector and morphological operations.

© Springer International Publishing AG 2016
L.J. Chmielewski et al. (Eds.): ICCVG 2016, LNCS 9972, pp. 453–461, 2016.
DOI: 10.1007/978-3-319-46418-3_40

In static images vehicles can be detect with the use of edge detection. The popular edge detection methods are gradient methods using convolution of digital functions [7] and methods using Gaussian filters [8]. There are also known other edge detection methods based on e.g., maximizing objective function [9] or fuzzy classifiers [10]. In static images vehicle detection can be also performed by application of thresholding techniques on the basis of e.g., histogram shape, clustering, entropy or object attributes [11].

The proposed image representation is among binary image representations created on the basis of small gradients [12]. Image conversion into orthogonal gradient-based binary representation considers only gradients in perpendicular directions and it utilizes smoothing operations. The proposed orthogonal gradient-based binary image representation is intended for application in road traffic systems.

## 2    Small Orthogonal Gradients

A digital image is described by the two-dimensional discrete function $f(m, n)$, which assigns an integer intensity value to each pair of integer coordinates $(m, n)$. The gradient $G(m, n)$ of the function $f(m, n)$ is a vector and it can be expressed as composition of the row gradient $G_R(m, n)$ and the column gradient $G_C(m, n)$

$$G(m, n) = [G_R(m, n), G_C(m, n)]. \tag{1}$$

The gradient magnitude is given by

$$|G(m, n)| = \left[ G_R(m, n)^2 + G_C(m, n)^2 \right]^{\frac{1}{2}}. \tag{2}$$

The small orthogonal gradients are defined in horizontal (rows) and vertical (columns) neighbours. The small row gradient is given by the equation

$$G_R(m, n) = f(m, n) - f(m - 1, n) \tag{3}$$

and the small column gradient by the equation

$$G_C(m, n) = f(m, n) - f(m, n - 1). \tag{4}$$

Small orthogonal row and column gradients can be determined by calculation of running differences of pixels along image rows and columns respectively.

## 3    Conversion into Gradient-Based Binary Representation

The source greyscale image of intensity resolution $k$ bits per pixel and size of $M \times N$ (columns x rows) pixels is described by the function $f(m, n)$. Pixel values of the source image $f(m, n)$ are placed into source image matrix $\mathbf{A}$

$$\mathbf{A} = [a_{n,m}] : \quad n = 0, \dots, N - 1, \quad m = 0, \dots, M - 1. \tag{5}$$

Elements of source image matrix $\mathbf{A}$ are read by rows consecutively except border elements $(1 \leq n \leq N - 2,\ 1 \leq m \leq M - 2)$ and for each read element small orthogonal gradient magnitudes are determined. The small row gradient magnitude is determined by the equation

$$|G_R(m, n)| = |a_{n,m} - a_{n,m-1}| \qquad (6)$$

and the small column gradient magnitude by the equation

$$|G_C(m, n)| = |a_{n,m} - a_{n-1,m}|. \qquad (7)$$

The maximum value of magnitudes of the orthogonal gradients is calculated according to the equation

$$|G_{\max}(m, n)| = \begin{cases} |G_R(m, n)| & \text{for} \quad |G_C(m, n)| \leq |G_R(m, n)|, \\ |G_C(m, n)| & \text{for} \quad |G_C(m, n)| > |G_R(m, n)|. \end{cases} \qquad (8)$$

Logical values are written into target binary matrix $\mathbf{B}$

$$\mathbf{B} = [b_{n,m}]: \quad n = 0, \ldots, N - 1, \quad m = 0, \ldots, M - 1 \qquad (9)$$

on the basis to the maximum values of small gradient magnitudes and the preset threshold value denoted by $T$ as follows:

$$b_{n,m} = \begin{cases} 0 & \text{for} \quad |G_{\max}(m, n)| \leq T, \\ 1 & \text{for} \quad |G_{\max}(m, n)| > T. \end{cases} \qquad (10)$$

Elements of matrix $\mathbf{B}$, which satisfy $b_{n,m} = 1$ are called the edge points. Layout of the edge points corresponds to edges of objects contained in the source image. Elements of matrix $\mathbf{B}$ form target orthogonal gradient-based binary image representation.

## 4    Smoothing Operations

The quality of the target binary image contained in matrix $\mathbf{B}$ can be improved by application of smoothing operations. For each element of matrix $\mathbf{B}$ except border elements $(1 \leq n \leq N - 2,\ 1 \leq m \leq M - 2)$, the new value $b_{n,m}$ is calculated using the smoothing logical operations for initial values $b_{n,m} = 0$ and $b_{n,m} = 1$ respectively.

For the initial value $b_{n,m} = 1$ the isolated edge points are removing in the orthogonal neighbourhood

$$b_{n,m} = b_{n-1,m} + b_{n+1,m} + b_{n,m-1} + b_{n,m+1} \qquad (11)$$

and in the diagonal neighbourhood

$$b_{n,m} = b_{n-1,m-1} + b_{n+1,m+1} + b_{n+1,m-1} + b_{n-1,m+1}. \qquad (12)$$

For the initial value $b_{n,m} = 0$ the edge points are supplemented in the orthogonal neighbourhood

$$b_{n,m} = (b_{n,m-1} \cdot b_{n,m+1}) + (b_{n-1,m} \cdot b_{n+1,m}) \tag{13}$$

and in the diagonal neighbourhood

$$b_{n,m} = (b_{n-1,m-1} \cdot b_{n+1,m+1}) + (b_{n+1,m-1} \cdot b_{n-1,m+1}). \tag{14}$$

Smoothing operations improve the quality of the target binary images and should be carried out. However, if the quality of the target images is satisfying, smoothing operations can be omitted.

## 5    Test Input Image Sequence

The input image sequence consists of consecutive frames taken from the video stream obtained from the camera placed over a road. The video stream is of 30 frames per second. Each image of the input image sequence is a grayscale image of 8 bits intensity resolution and of size $256 \times 256$ pixels. Images in the input image sequence are labelled by the ordinal number denoted by $i$. The selected images of the input image sequence are shown in Fig. 1.

(a)                              (b)                              (c)

**Fig. 1.** Selected images from the input image sequence (a) $i = 9$ (b) $i = 23$ (c) $i = 37$

All images of the input image sequence are converted into orthogonal gradient-based binary image representation with the threshold value set $T = 8$. The selected images from the input image sequence after conversion into orthogonal gradient-based binary representation are shown in Fig. 2. In images the edge points are marked by black dots.

Smoothing operations are carried out after image conversion into orthogonal gradient-based binary representation for all images of the input image sequence. The selected images from the input image sequence after smoothing operations are shown in Fig. 3. In images the edge points are marked by black dots.

Layout of the edge points in orthogonal gradient-based image binary representation corresponds to edges of objects contained in the source image. After smoothing operations layout of the edge points better corresponds to edges of objects in images than before smoothing operations.

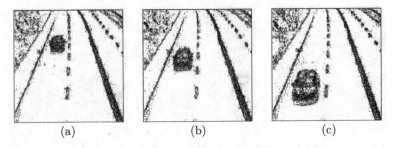

**Fig. 2.** Selected images from the input image sequence after conversion into orthogonal gradient-based binary representation (a) $i = 9$ (b) $i = 23$ (c) $i = 37$

**Fig. 3.** Selected images from the input image sequence after smoothing operations (a) $i = 9$ (b) $i = 23$ (c) $i = 37$

## 6    Detection of vehicles

Detection of vehicles is carried out with the use of the input image sequence. Each image of the input image sequence is converted into orthogonal gradient-based binary image representation. For each processed image smoothing operations are performed after conversion.

For each image of the input image sequence the same detection field is defined and the sums of the edge points within the detection field are calculated [12]. The detection field is rectangular described by 4 vertices. Position of individual vertices is determined by the following vertex coordinates: the left, upper vertex by $(m_L, n_U)$, the right, upper vertex by $(m_R, n_U)$, the left, bottom vertex by $(m_L, n_B)$ and the right, bottom vertex by $(m_R, n_B)$. Selected images of the input image sequence, with the marked detection field, are shown in Fig. 4.

Conversion and smoothing operations are performed for each image of the input image sequence. Selected images of the input image sequence after conversion and smoothing operations, with the marked detection field, are shown in Fig. 5. The black dots in images denote the edge points.

For the current image $i$ from the input image sequence, after conversion into binary representation and smoothing operations, the arithmetic sum of the edge points inside of the detection field is calculated using the equation

$$S_i = \sum_{n=n_U}^{n_B} \sum_{m=m_L}^{m_R} b_{n,m} : b_{n,m} = 1 \tag{15}$$

**Fig. 4.** Selected images of the input image sequence with the marked detection field (a) $i = 9$ (b) $i = 23$ (c) $i = 37$

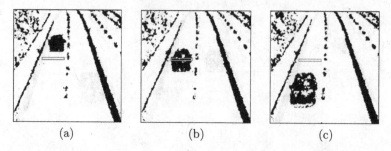

**Fig. 5.** Selected images of the input image sequence after conversion and smoothing operations, with the marked detection field (a) $i = 9$ (b) $i = 23$ (c) $i = 37$

As a vehicle is driving through the detection field the sum of the edge points inside of the detection field is changing for consecutive images. The sums of the edge points within the detection field for selected images of the input image sequence are shown in Fig. 6.

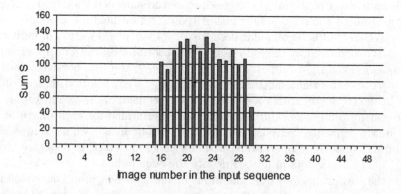

**Fig. 6.** Sums of the edge points within the detection field for images of the input image sequence

A vehicle driving through the detection field causes changes of its state. The state of the detection field is determined on the basis of the average sum of the edge points within the detection field. The average sum of the edge points within the detection field, for the current image $i$ and $P$ previous images, is expressed in the form

$$R_i = \frac{1}{P+1} \sum_{j=i-P}^{i} S_j \qquad (16)$$

The state of the detection field changes from "detection field free" to "detection field occupied" if the condition $R_i > R_O$ is satisfied, where $R_O$ is the threshold value for the change to the state "detection field occupied". The state of the detection field changes from "detection field occupied" to "detection field free" if the condition $R_i < R_F$ is satisfied, where $R_F$ denotes the threshold value for the change to the state "detection field free".

## 7    Estimation of Efficiency

Estimation of efficiency of the vehicle detection method utilizing image conversion into orthogonal gradient-based binary representation is performed with the use of traffic images obtained from the cameras placed in test measuring stations. Source images, images after conversion into binary representation and images after smoothing operations are shown in Figs. 7, 8 and 9 respectively. All image conversions into binary representation were performed with the threshold value set $T = 8$.

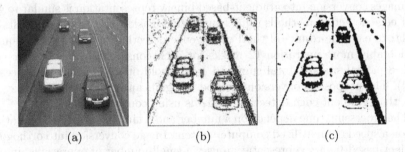

(a)                          (b)                          (c)

**Fig. 7.** Processing result for an image from measuring station 1 (a) source image (b) image after conversion (c) image after smoothing operations

For all images, taken from various measuring stations, the obtained results are similar. The quality of images after conversion into binary representation and smoothing operations, meant as number of edge points corresponding to objects contained in an image, is sufficient to correct detection of vehicles. Conversion into orthogonal gradient-based binary image representation allows to detect vehicles of various classes. In typical weather conditions, image conversion into binary representation can be carried out with the same threshold value.

(a)                              (b)                              (c)

**Fig. 8.** Processing result for an image from measuring station 2 (a) source image (b) image after conversion (c) image after smoothing operations

(a)                              (b)                              (c)

**Fig. 9.** Processing result for an image from measuring station 3 (a) source image (b) image after conversion (c) image after smoothing operations

Images conversion into gradient-based binary representation is similar to gradient edge detection methods using convolution masks. The obtained results are similar to e.g., the results of the Prewitt edge detection method which requires considerably more operation (2 masks for each considered direction, for each mask 8 partial sums, 1 total sum and 1 threshold operation for one processed pixel). The proposed conversion method is significantly simpler and more efficient than gradient edge detection methods using convolution masks.

The processing time depends on a number and a kind of performed operations and on a speed of an utilized computer system. Image conversion into orthogonal gradient-based binary representation uses a small number of operations, integer and logical mainly, which makes this method very fast. In typical weather conditions and without disruption, achieved efficiency of vehicle detection can be near to hundred per cent.

## 8   Conclusions

Image conversion into orthogonal gradient-based representation transform an image in the bitmap format into an image in the binary form. Position of the edge points in proposed binary image representation corresponds well to edges of objects contained in a source image. Detection of vehicles driving through the detection field is carried out by analyses of changes of the detection field state. The detection field state is determined by simple calculations of the sums of the edge points inside of the detection field. The proposed method of image conversion into binary representation is simpler and faster then majority of the well-known edge detection methods, in particular the gradient methods using discrete convolution, and it can be applied instead of them for image processing. Vehicle detection utilizing image conversion into orthogonal gradient-based binary representation requires a small number of operations which makes this method efficient and attractive computationally. Orthogonal gradient-based binary image representation is suitable for vehicle detection and this representation can be apply in road traffic systems.

# References

1. Gupte, S., Masoud, O., Martin, R.F.K., Papanikolopoulos, N.P.: Detection and classification of vehicles. IEEE Trans. Intell. Trans. Syst. **3**(1), 37–47 (2002)
2. Hsieh, J., Yu, S.H., Chen, Y.S., Hu, W.F.: An automatic traffic surveillance system for vehicle tracking and classification. IEEE Trans. Intell. Trans. Syst. **7**(2), 175–187 (2006)
3. Stauffer C., Grimson, W.E.L.: Adaptive background mixture model for real-time tracking. In: Proceedings IEEE Computer Society Conference on Computer Vision and Pattern Recognition, vol. 2, pp. 246-252 (1999)
4. Coifman, B., Beymer, D., McLauchlan, P., Malik, J.: A real-time vision system for vehicle tracking and traffic surveillance. Trans. Res. Part C **6**, 271–288 (1998)
5. Kamijo, S., Matsushita, Y., Ikeuchi, K., Sakauchi, M.: Traffic monitoring and accident detection at intersections. IEEE Trans. Intell. Trans. Syst. **1**(2), 108–118 (2000)
6. Mithun, N.C., Rashid, N.U., Rahman, S.M.M.: Detection and classification of vehicles from video using multiple time-spatial images. IEEE Trans. Intell. Trans. Syst. **13**(3), 1215–1225 (2012)
7. Muthukrishnan, R., Radha, M.: Edge detection techniques for image segmentation. Int. J. Comput. Sci. Inf. Technol. (IJCSIT) **3**(6), 259–267 (2011)
8. Basu, M.: Gaussian-based edge detection methods-a survey. IEEE Trans. Syst. Man Cybern. Part C: Appl. Rev. **32**(3), 252–260 (2002)
9. Kang, C.-C., Wang, W.-J.: A novel edge detection method based on the maximizing objective function. Pattern Recogn. **40**, 609–618 (2007)
10. Liang, L.R., Looney, C.G.: Competitive fuzzy edge detection. Appl. Soft Comput. **3**(2), 123–137 (2003)
11. Sezgin, M., Sankur, B.: Survey over image thresholding techniques and quantitative performance evaluation. J. Electr. Imaging **13**(1), 146–168 (2004)
12. Czapla, Z.: Point image representation for efficient detection of vehicles. In: Burduk, R., Jackowski, K., Kurzyński, M., Woźniak, M., Żołnierek, A. (eds.) Proceedings of the 9th International Conference on Computer Recognition Systems CORES 2015. AISC, vol. 403, pp. 691–700. Springer, Heidelberg (2016). doi:10.1007/978-3-319-26227-7_65

# Multi-view Data Aggregation for Behaviour Analysis in Video Surveillance Systems

Paweł Forczmański[✉] and Adam Nowosielski

Faculty of Computer Science and Information Technology, West Pomeranian University of Technology, Żołnierska Str. 49, 71–210 Szczecin, Poland
{pforczmanski,anowosielski}@wi.zut.edu.pl

**Abstract.** Detecting restricted or security critical behaviour on roads is crucial for safety protection and fluent traffic flow. In the paper we propose an algorithm for the analysis of movement trajectory of vehicles using vision-based techniques. It works on video sequences captured by road cameras in multi-view mode. We integrate methods of background modelling, object tracking and homographic projection. Individual views are projected into a single, planar surface of road surface and then the detected movement path is compared with a template associated with an illegal movement. The effectiveness of the proposed solution is confirmed by experimental studies.

**Keywords:** Visual surveillance · Tracking · Multi-view integration · Movement path comparison

## 1 Introduction

There are four major causes of the road congestion in the contemporary road traffic [1,2]: (i) poor planning of transport routes, (ii) existence of bottlenecks, (iii) lack of the adaptation of existing infrastructure to the current traffic load, (iv) accidents.

The last of these reasons is mostly associated with the lack of awareness of drivers and their tendency to omit some inconvenient traffic regulations. Similarly as in the case of speed control systems, which force the driving at a safe speed, solutions for automatic critical behaviour detection should enforce the appropriate driving thus reducing the number of potential accidents. Such problem of the analysis and identification of vehicles motion patterns is referred in the literature as Vehicle Behaviour Analysis [3].

Illegal movements of vehicles can be detected using vision-based techniques applied to video sequences captured by road cameras. The main advantage of using computer vision techniques is their non-intrusive application not requiring the installation of the sensors directly onto or into the road surface [2]. Such system is also capable of the immediate (real-time) automatic response and alerting in case of the occurrence of an unfortunate accident.

© Springer International Publishing AG 2016
L.J. Chmielewski et al. (Eds.): ICCVG 2016, LNCS 9972, pp. 462–473, 2016.
DOI: 10.1007/978-3-319-46418-3_41

The image-based techniques have already been utilized for variety of tasks in Intelligent Transportation Systems (ITS) providing complete traffic flow information for the situations related to [3]: traffic management [4], public transportation, information service, surveillance, security and logistics management. The tasks successfully implemented with vision-based techniques include [2]: reading vehicle registration plates (ALPR - Automatic License Plate Recognition), vehicle counting, congestion calculation, traffic jam detection, lane occupancy readings, road accident detection, traffic light control, comprehensive statistics calculation, etc. Computer vision techniques are also increasingly willing utilized by driver assistant systems (ADAS - Advanced Driver Assistance Systems). Many vehicles are equipped with on board cameras which form the basis for systems such as [5,6]: TSR - Traffic Sign Recognition, CAV - Collision Avoidance (by pedestrians or surrounding vehicles detection and tracking), LDW - Lane Departure Warning (adaptive cruise control), and driver fatigue detection.

The main drawback of vision-based solutions is susceptibility to poor visibility conditions and occlusions [7]. Researchers, however, actively respond to the challenge and propose solutions that deal with those difficulties (e.g. occluded traffic signs recognition [8], behaviour analysis in multi-view environment [10]). In the paper we focus on the extension of our previous work on the automatic analysis of vehicle behaviour (presented in [2]) with the emphasis on poor visibility conditions and occlusions. The main contribution of the paper is a novel approach to the vehicle trajectory analysis on data aggregated from multiple views.

## 1.1  Approaches to Behaviour Analysis

Vehicle behaviour analysis in the surveillance context is mostly limited to the detection of restricted or security critical events on roads [2,9,11]. The task can be solved successfully with the analysis of moving vehicle trajectory [2,9, 11]. Figure 1 presents an exemplary intersection with a compulsory right turn (adopted from proprietary Google Maps and Google Street View services). In the situation presented, the driver is obliged to follow the path approximately outlined by a green dashed line. Red trajectories denote possible but illegal and dangerous movements. As presented in the example two categories of trajectories are possible: the correct (legal) and the forbidden (illegal). Such distinction can be applied to all traffic situations. The trajectories, in terms of their geometry, may take a variety of shapes and may consist of different number of points. The key factor is the comparison with the template. Such template trajectory might be the appropriate or the forbidden one. In the first case, a discrepancy will reveal restricted behaviour. In the second case, the same discovery is possible through the similarity to a forbidden trajectory. In fact, it is specific to a road system that determines whether it is better to take as a template legal or illegal trajectory.

In video-based approaches the trajectory of moving vehicle is obtained through the vehicle detection and the successive tracking algorithm. The activity

**Fig. 1.** Compulsory right turn example and possible vehicle movements (red - illegal, green - appropriate) (Color figure online)

perception and the detection of abnormal events are detected by high level vision algorithms [9]. The following abnormal events detection can be distinguished [2]:

- illegal left and right turns,
- illegal U-turn,
- illegal lane change and violation of traffic line,
- overtaking in prohibited places,
- wrong-way driving,
- illegal retrograde,
- illegal parking.

## 1.2   Related Works

Most algorithms for behaviour analysis proposed in the literature consider the single view. Presented solutions can be divided into supervised and unsupervised methods [9]. In the first case, the manual intervention for specifying patterns of behaviour is required. In an unsupervised mode the algorithm learns abnormal activity from the sample data. The process is automatic and the outcome might be sometimes unexpected. Generally, the process requires a reasonable amount of data and is time consuming.

The trajectory-based solution for the illegal behaviour detection can be adopted to most locations. The greatest difficulty is the susceptibility to poor visibility conditions and occlusions. The use of one camera view is burdened with considerable risk when camera field of view is obscured with large or close object. Problems with vehicle detection and segmentation using the single view may adversely affect the location of a vehicle. Due to errors the vehicle may temporarily disappear and the calculated position may not always be determined reliably. Multi-view observation is resistant to such cases. When a tracked vehicle is occluded in one view and the tracking procedure is interrupted, the other views can be used to merge the information and link the interrupted parts of the trajectory.

The most similar solution to the one proposed in this paper is presented in [10]. Multiple camera views are used in [10] to remove occlusion and to extract abnormal vehicles behaviour more accurately. The vehicles trajectory analysis is based on support vector machine (SVM). The system is constructed using the distributed architecture. The analysis is performed using individual views only. Later the results are aggregated and supplemented using other views. This approach is different from the one presented here, which firstly integrates the information from all views, then calculates the trajectory.

The trajectory analysis alone does not allow to discover some specific dangerous movements like: sharp brake, sharp turn or sharp turn brake. To detect these dangerous behaviours the velocity information is necessary. An exemplary solution allowing the detection of the above-mentioned events using the rate of velocity variation and the rate of direction variation has been proposed in [12].

## 2   Method Description

In this paper we present a visual surveillance system aimed at vehicle detection and tracking. Like any typical visual surveillance system aimed at gathering information about certain phenomena in order to execute or suggest certain actions, especially in case of situations dangerous to human life, health or property, proposed system's purpose is to alarm about probable hazardous road situations. Visual surveillance in this case is often realized using a closed-circuit television system (CCTV) that consists of static camera (or cameras) aimed at one fixed point in space. In order to simplify the problem, we assume that the focal length of each camera lens is constant as well (hence Pan-Tilt-Zoom cameras are excluded from out investigations). The solution proposed in this paper integrates the information about the movement of vehicles observed by more than one camera. During the development we assumed that vehicles are tracked only in the area covered by a specified number of cameras and we consider only those vehicles that are observed by assumed number of cameras. The proposed solution consists of the following modules (Fig. 2):

- background modeling - independently detects foreground areas in each view;
- object detection - determines silhouettes of moving objects and selects vehicles in each view;
- integrator - integrates information coming from all views (homographic projection);
- object detector - detects vehicles in projected (aggregated) view;
- tracker - estimates detected vehicles trajectories.

Since most of scenes observed by CCTV cameras are not static, the process of background separation has to take into consideration many different environmental conditions, such as variable lighting [13], atmospheric phenomena and changes caused by different actions. Hence, background modeling is a crucial task since its efficiency determines the capabilities of the whole system. Until now, many methods of background modeling have been proposed. They are based

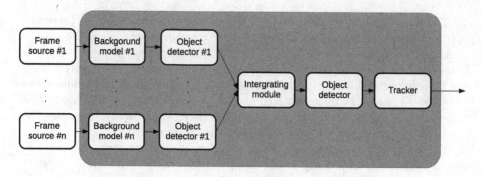

**Fig. 2.** Scheme of processing in a multi-view environment

on different assumptions and principles, however all of them can be divided into two main categories: pixel-based and block-based approaches. The former class of methods analyses each individual pixel in the image, while the latter considers an image decomposed into segments (often overlapping). For each pixel or segment certain features are calculated and used later at the classification stage (into pixels or segments belonging to background and foreground). In many typical approaches, each detected object (or blob) is also tracked. The authors often assume that the movement is constant and the direction does not change in a considerable way within certain number of frames [14,15], which further simplifies the algorithm. The last stage of processing may involve object recognition or classification. The selection of a method used at this stage depends mainly on the object type and its invariant features. For example, in a system presented in [16] each detected object is described by mean area it occupies – a similar approach is also applied in this work.

## 2.1   Background Modeling

In our solution, the background model employs a pixel-based approach similar to the one proposed in [13]. Here, every pixel is modeled by a set of five mixtures of Gaussians in R, G and B channels. According to the research, such number of Gaussians increases the robustness of the model in the comparison to the one presented in [17]. Similar approach, successfully employed for human motion tracking has been already presented in [18].

In our case, the first 200 frames from video stream are used for learning the parameters of the background model. The further frames are processed in a stepwise manner, and the parameters of the model are updated.

During the processing loop, every pixel from the current frame is checked against the existing Gaussians in the corresponding position in the model. If there is no match the least probable Gaussian is replaced by the new one using current pixel value as a mean value. Then, the weights of all Gaussians are updated according to the following rule: weights of distributions that do not correspond with the new pixel value are decreased, while the weights of

**Fig. 3.** Two camera views and their foreground masks obtained by background modeling

distributions that suite it are increased. Parameters of unmatched distributions remain unchanged. The parameters of the distribution which matches the new observation are updated according to the following formulas:

$$\mu_t = (1 - \rho)\mu_{t-1} + \rho X_t, \tag{1}$$

$$\sigma_t^2 = (1 - \rho)\sigma_{t-1}^2 + \rho(X_t - \mu_t)^T(X_t - \mu_t), \tag{2}$$

$$\rho = \alpha\eta(X_t|\mu_k, \sigma_k), \tag{3}$$

where $X_t$ is a new pixel value, $\eta$ is a Gaussian probability density function, $\alpha$ is a learning rate, $\mu$ and $\sigma$ are distribution parameters, and $\rho \in \langle 0, 1 \rangle$.

After that, each weight of each distribution is updated as follows:

$$\omega_t = \begin{cases} (1 - \alpha)\omega_{t-1} + \alpha & \text{if a pixel fits the distribution} \\ (1 - \alpha)\omega_{t-1} & \text{otherwise.} \end{cases} \tag{4}$$

Background subtraction operation results in a binary image mask of possible foreground pixels which are grouped using connected components (see Fig. 3). Unfortunately, this approach does not suppress shadows and certain reflections from being considered as moving objects, thus it can cause certain serious problems, namely false detections of non-existent objects. In the proposed system we use a shadow detection and elimination method based on [19]. It assumes that casted shadow lowers the luminance of the point while chrominance is unchanged. This observation is valid for HSV color space, used in our solution.

## 2.2   Homographic Transformation

The proposed solution of integrating information from multiple cameras uses a simplified method of projection, originally described in [20]. As it was already mentioned, projective transformation allows for mapping of one plane to another. In our algorithm, we use it to find ground position of vehicles seen in different camera views. Projecting transformation is expressed by the equation:

$$
\begin{bmatrix} x_1 \\ y_1 \\ 1 \end{bmatrix} = \begin{bmatrix} h_{11} & h_{12} & h_{13} \\ h_{21} & h_{22} & h_{23} \\ h_{31} & h_{32} & h_{33} \end{bmatrix} \begin{bmatrix} x_2 \\ y_2 \\ 1 \end{bmatrix}, \tag{5}
$$

where $x_1$ and $y_1$ are the coordinates of a single point on the input plane, $x_2$ and $y_2$ are the coordinates on the output plane, $H$ is a transformation matrix.

**Fig. 4.** Two camera views (with calibration rectangle marked) and their projections onto a planar surface

In order to calculate $H$ by means of least squares method we need to collect four pairs of so called calibration points. Such an approach is a compromise between computational complexity and the quality of the resulting transformation. More precise results can be obtained by means of non-linear mapping, described i.e. in [20]. Exemplary calibration points, forming rectangles in two camera views are presented in Fig. 4.

## 2.3   Data Integration

The individual projections of foreground masks are taken as an input for data integration module. We assume that each foreground mask resembles a shadow of a moving object cast onto the ground plane. If we integrate (superimpose) all individual projections we obtain a complex image, where the common part represents the object viewed by each camera. All false detections, like shadows or reflections are often visible in single view only, hence they are not taken into consideration by this method.

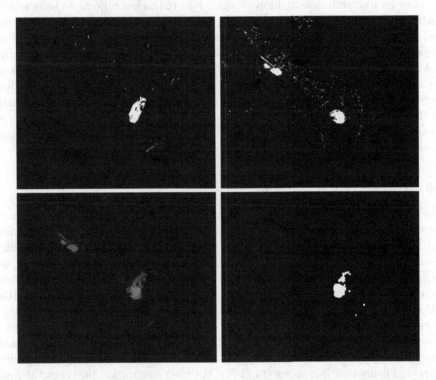

**Fig. 5.** Foreground masks for camera 1 and 2 (upper row), their superposition (lower left) and output, projected, foreground mask (lower, right)

The blobs detected at this stage are described by their geometrical properties, among others by their centroids, which represent their ground position. An exemplary mapping for the data from PETS benchmark is presented in Fig. 5. As it can be seen, a car that is closer to the viewer is observed in two camera-views, hence its integrated blob is depicted in the final foreground mask. The other, further car, is visible in the second camera view only, hence it is not taken for the further processing. In the presence of multiple views, different strategies of joining individual views can be applied. Taking into consideration the environmental conditions and purpose, voting (majority) strategy (e.g. two-out-of-three) may be used.

## 2.4    Trajectory Calculation

In the next step we calculate the trajectories of foreground objects using a simplified Object Tracker. Objects, detected in integrated projection, are tracked from frame to frame in a stepwise manner. For each tracked object (labelled using unique number) we store an information about its bounding box and its position in current frame. We use historical data (previous frames) to decide about the object label. Besides such numerical data, the database contains, for each object, its binary mask (in each frame) and cropped video frame.

In order to match detected foreground blobs to tracked objects an association matrix similar to the one proposed in [21] is used. For all pairs of foreground blobs and tracked objects we measure Euclidean distance from last stored position of object to the center of the foreground blob. If a foreground blob intersects with last remembered bounding box of the tracked object we measure distance from the center of a bounding box to the center of the blob. After distance calculation between all pairs blob-object, object list is updated using blobs which are closest to them. In case when a blob has no matched object, a new tracked object is created. On the other hand when the object has not been associated to any foreground blob for several frames, it is removed.

## 2.5    Trajectory Comparison

The behaviour analysis based on the comparisons with the reference trajectory is frequently performed using the Hausdorff distance or its modifications (e.g. [2,9,22,23]). The main advantage is the resistance of this measure to the different number of point coordinates of compared trajectories. This measure in the form of Modified Hausdorff Distance (MHD) proposed by [24] is also used in this paper. The MHD, in fact, combines (takes the maximum) two directional MHDs which are sometimes referred to as FHD (forward) or RHD (reverse). Characteristics of these measures are presented in graphical form in Fig. 6. There are two trajectories presented in these figures. The template trajectory has an upward direction (top right of Fig. 6). The analysed vehicle trajectory is a real trajectory extracted using multiple views (top left). For the presentation purposes the first few coordinates corresponding to the retrograde have been removed. The MHD measure presented in the middle of Fig. 6 has at the beginning high value which correspond to the RHD. The FHD value is comparatively small (in the first phase of the movement) since all tested trajectory points finds their equivalents in the template trajectory. Due to the similarity of the movement to template trajectory all the values are decreased.

The MHD, unfortunately, is unable to differentiate the direction of the movement. It considers only the mutual relationships of trajectory points which are treated as a set. To discriminate the trajectory direction we further analyse the X and Y projections of all coordinate points. The bottom parts of Fig. 6 presents projections of trajectory points onto X and Y axes. As it can be seen, both projections coincide. Hence we can decide about movement direction.

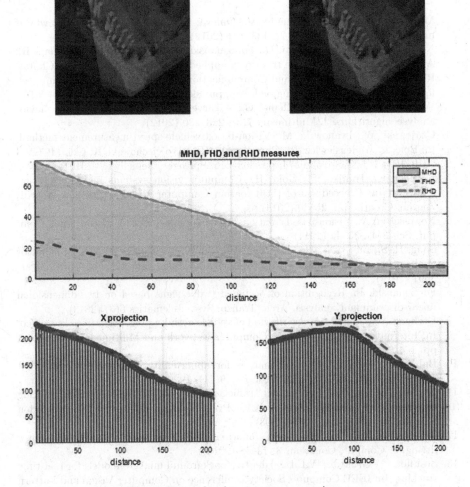

**Fig. 6.** Example of trajectory comparison

# 3   Conclusions

In this paper we proposed a method for the detection of restricted or security critical behaviour on roads by vehicle trajectory analysis. Our proposal contains two novel elements. The first one is a combined, multi-view background modeling approach that integrates foreground masks in order to more precisely calculate the trajectory of moving vehicles. The second element is an improvement of the original Modified Hausdorff Distance-based method by incorporating the X and Y projections in the final trajectory matching algorithm. Such solution solves the problem of the movement direction, specific trajectory configuration (found in e.g. roundabout case) and possible occlusions. Accompanied with ALPR technology the system can be a good deterrent from dangerous and illegal driving behaviour contributing for safety protection and fluent traffic flow.

# References

1. Munuzuri, J., Cortés, P., Guadix, J., Onieva, L.: City logistics in Spain: why it might never work. Cities **29**(2), 133–141 (2012)
2. Nowosielski, A., Frejlichowski, D., Forczmański, P., Gościewska, K., Hofman, R.: Automatic analysis of vehicle trajectory applied to visual surveillance. In: Choraś, R.S. (ed.) Image Processing and Communications Challenges 7. Advances in Intelligent Systems and Computing, vol. 389, pp. 89–96. Springer, Switzerland (2016)
3. Wu, J., Cui, Z., Chen, J., Zhang, G.: A survey on video-based vehicle behavior analysis algorithms. J. Multimedia **7**(3), 223–230 (2012)
4. Czajewski, W., Iwanowski, M.: Vision-based vehicle speed measurement method. In: Bolc, L., Tadeusiewicz, R., Chmielewski, L.J., Wojciechowski, K. (eds.) ICCVG 2010, Part I. LNCS, vol. 6374, pp. 308–315. Springer, Heidelberg (2010)
5. Kovacic, K., Ivanjko, E., Gold, H.: Computer vision systems in road vehicles: a review. In: Proceedings of the Croatian Computer Vision Workshop, Year 1, Zagreb, Croatia, pp. 25–30 (2013)
6. Nowosielski, A.: Vision-based solutions for driver assistance. J. Theor. Appl. Comput. Sci. **8**(4), 35–44 (2014)
7. Song, H.-S., Lu, S.-N., Ma, X., Yang, Y., Liu, X.-Q., Zhang, P.: Vehicle behavior analysis using target motion trajectories. IEEE Trans. Veh. Technol. **63**(8), 3580–3591 (2014)
8. Forczmański, P.: Recognition of occluded traffic signs based on two-dimensional linear discriminant analysis. Arch. Transp. Syst. Telematics 6(3) (2013)
9. Desheng, W., Jia, W.: A new method of vehicle activity perception from live video. In: International Symposium on Computer Network and Multimedia Technology, pp. 1–4 (2009)
10. Babaei, P.: Vehicles behavior analysis for abnormality detection by multi-view monitoring. Int. Res. J. Appl. Basic Sci. **9**(11), 1929–1936 (2015)
11. Hu, W., Xiao, X., Xie, D., Tan, T.: Traffic accident prediction using vehicle tracking and trajectory analysis. In: 2003 IEEE Proceedings of Intelligent Transportation Systems, vol. 1, pp. 220–225 (2003)
12. Jiang, E., Wang, X.: Analysis of abnormal vehicle behavior based on trajectory fitting. J. Comput. Commun. **3**, 13–18 (2015)
13. Stauffer, C., Grimson, W.E.L.: Adaptive background mixture models for real-time tracking. In: IEEE Computer Society Conference on Computer Vision and Pattern Recognition (CVPR), pp. 246–252 (1999)
14. Comaniciu, D., Ramesh, V., Meer, P.: Kernel-based object tracking. IEEE Trans. Pattern Anal. Mach. Intell. **25**(5), 564–577 (2003)
15. Okarma, K., Mazurek, P.: Application of shape analysis techniques for the classification of vehicles. In: Mikulski, J. (ed.) TST 2010. CCIS, vol. 104, pp. 218–225. Springer, Heidelberg (2010)
16. Li, L., Ma, R., Huang, W., Leman, K.: Evaluation of an IVS system for abandoned object detection on PETS 2006 datasets. In: Ninth IEEE International Workshop on Performance Evaluation of Tracking and Surveillance (PETS), pp. 91–98 (2006)
17. Tian, Y., Feris, R.S., Hampapur, A.: Real-time detection of abandoned and removed objects in complex environments. In: IEEE International Workshop on Visual Surveillance (in conjunction with ECCV 2008), Marseille, France (2008)
18. Forczmański, P., Seweryn, M.: Surveillance video stream analysis using adaptive background model and object recognition. In: Bolc, L., Tadeusiewicz, R., Chmielewski, L.J., Wojciechowski, K. (eds.) ICCVG 2010, Part I. LNCS, vol. 6374, pp. 114–121. Springer, Heidelberg (2010)

19. Cucchiara, R., Grana, C., Piccardi, M., Prati, A., Sirotti, S.: Improving shadow suppression in moving object detection with HSV color information. In: IEEE Intelligent Transportation Systems, pp. 334–339 (2001)
20. Auvinet, E., Grossmann, E., Rougier, C., Dahmane, M., Meunier, J.: Left-luggage detection using homographies and simple heuristics. In: Proceedings of 9th IEEE International Workshop on Performance Evaluation in Tracking and Surveillance (PETS 2006), pp. 51–58 (2006)
21. Lv, F., Song, X., Wu, B., Singh, V.K., Necatia, R.: Left-luggage detection using bayesian inference. In: Ninth IEEE International Workshop on Performance Evaluation of Tracking and Surveillance (PETS 2006), pp. 83–90 (2006)
22. Wang, X., Tieu, K., Grimson, W.E.L.: Learning semantic scene models by trajectory analysis. In: Leonardis, A., Bischof, H., Pinz, A. (eds.) ECCV 2006. LNCS, vol. 3953, pp. 110–123. Springer, Heidelberg (2006)
23. Yang, Y., Cui, Z., Wu, J., Zhang, G., Xian, X.: Trajectory analysis using spectral clustering and sequence pattern mining. J. Comput. Inf. Syst. 8(6), 2637–2645 (2012)
24. Dubuisson, M.P., Jain, A.K.: A Modified Hausdorff distance for object matching. In: Proceedings of the 12th IAPR International Conference on Pattern Recognition ICPR94, pp. 566–568 (1994)

# Moving Object Detection Using SIFT Matching on Three Frames for Advanced Driver Assistance Systems

Jeongmok Ha[1]($\boxtimes$), WooYeol Jun[2], and Hong Jeong[1]

[1] POSTECH, Pohang, South Korea
{jmokha,hjeong}@postech.ac.kr
[2] VADAS Co., Ltd., Pohang, South Korea
wyjun@vadas.co.kr

**Abstract.** Detecting moving objects in a dynamic scene is a difficult task in computer vision. We propose a moving object detection algorithm for advanced driver assistance systems that uses only images from a monocular camera. To distinguish moving objects from standing objects when the camera is moving, we used an epipolar line constraint and an optical flow constraint. When evaluated using the KITTI scene flow 2015 dataset, the proposed algorithm detected moving objects in the image successfully even when the monocular camera was moving. The runtime of the proposed algorithm is $< 1\,\mathrm{s}$, so it is feasible for practical uses.

## 1 Introduction

*Moving object detection* (MOD) is a technique to identify objects that change positions in successive images [13,30]. MOD has become a key technique for *advanced driver assistance systems* (ADAS) and intelligent vehicles [7,28]. By detecting moving objects in an image, a system can warn drivers about dangerous situations; this is one of the most important tasks to protect drivers and pedestrians from being struck by vehicles, so algorithms that find obstacles that are approaching an ego-vehicle are crucial.

Most previous MOD techniques to warn drivers of obstacles have been based on object detection [25], which finds objects in images and shows the positions of the detected objects [2]. By using object detection in ADAS and intelligent vehicles, candidate obstacles (e.g., pedestrians, vehicles, trees, curbs, and buildings) can be found using a camera mounted on a vehicle. Especially, pedestrians and vehicles are the most significant objects to avoid while driving, because they are moving. Therefore, pedestrian detection [6,7] and vehicle detection [28] have been the main research topics.

The limitation of methods based on object detection is that they find all objects regardless of whether they are moving. Object detection algorithms only use local features such as gradient, edges, and corners to locate an object in an image; they do not consider whether the object is moving [1,8,21].

© Springer International Publishing AG 2016
L.J. Chmielewski et al. (Eds.): ICCVG 2016, LNCS 9972, pp. 474–485, 2016.
DOI: 10.1007/978-3-319-46418-3_42

From a driver's point of view, stationary objects are not interesting. Standing pedestrians and stationary vehicles are lumped together with immovable objects such as buildings, trees, traffic signs, and traffic lights, so identifying stationary objects and warning the driver about them is not a useful task.

In contrast, the goal of MOD is to detect only *moving objects* in the image [12, 14,17]. MOD does not find motionless pedestrians and vehicles because they are not relevant to drivers. The most dangerous situation while driving is that an object approaches the vehicle, so algorithms that find the object's trajectory are important.

The most difficult problem for a MOD algorithm is to detect moving objects when the camera is also moving (i.e., a *dynamic scene*). Research to detect moving objects in a scene in which the camera is not moving (i.e., a *static scene*) have achieved quite accurate results [16,27], but in a dynamic scene the positions of the pixels changes, so local temporal information is not useful. For this reason, recently MOD algorithms use the optical flow technique to obtain motion information by comparing consecutive frames [14].

However, dense optical flow algorithms need huge computation time to get reliable motion information [4,10], so they are not suitable for use in ADAS and intelligent vehicles. Some algorithms based on background subtraction, segmentation, and a tracking scheme have been developed, but they often give inferior results in road environments [5,15,18,24,26]. A recent development is scene flow, which is a hybrid of stereo matching and optical flow, but which requires a stereo camera [17,19,22]. An MOD algorithm that uses data from a laser scanner has been proposed [23]. Algorithms that use scene flow and laser scanner can be used only when the camera or scanner is on the car, which are unusual cases.

To overcome these problems, we propose an MOD algorithm that uses epipolar geometry constraints to detect moving objects in a dynamic scene [11]. To reduce computational time significantly, an epipolar line constraint between two consecutive frames is used. In image coordinates, the positions of all pixels change if the camera moves, but in world coordinates, object's position is independent of the movement of the camera, so standing objects are stationary even the camera is moving. This means that the pixels of standing objects (i.e., *background pixels*) remain on the epipolar line regardless of camera movement; pixels of moving objects (i.e., *foreground pixels*) do not remain on this line. We exploited this property to detect moving objects in dynamic scenes.

However, the epipolar line constraint cannot detect an object that is moving along the epipolar line. Therefore, to supplement the epipolar line constraint, we also used the optical flow constraint, which is based on the fact that two consecutive optical flows of the background pixel are the same if camera frame rate is sufficiently high. By comparing two consecutive optical flows of a pixel, foreground pixels can be identified if two consecutive flows are different. To avoid the immense computational time of existing algorithms, the proposed algorithm computes optical flows only for keypoints in the image that are estimated using scale invariant feature transform (SIFT) [21] (Fig. 1).

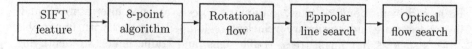

**Fig. 1.** A block diagram of proposed algorithm

The main contributions of this study are

- An algorithm for MOD that works in dynamic scenes but requires only data from a monocular camera.
- A method that uses epipolar line constraint and optical flow constraint.
- Short computation time.

## 2 Problem Statement

Goal of this study is to obtain the positions of moving objects in a dynamic road scene. When a camera is mounted on the vehicle and the vehicle is moving, the camera is also moving, so the problem is to distinguish foreground pixels (moving objects) from background pixels (stationary objects) when all pixels are moving.

Assuming that current frame is $n \in [0, \cdots, N-1]$, we denote (1) a point in world coordinates at $n$ as $\mathbf{P}_n = (X, Y, Z)$, (2) a pixel in image coordinates at $n$ as $\mathbf{p}_n = (y, x)$, and (3) the image plane in frame $n$ as $P_n$. If the camera is not moving, one point of the background in world coordinates is always projected onto the same pixel in image coordinates ($\mathbf{p}_n = \mathbf{p}_{n-1}$). However, when the camera is moving, one point of the background in world coordinates is projected onto the pixels in image coordinates ($\mathbf{p}_n \neq \mathbf{p}_{n-1}$). This is the most important characteristics of MOD in a dynamic scene.

To solve this problem, the epipolar constraint is used to distinguish foreground pixels $\mathbf{p}_n^1$ from background pixels $\mathbf{p}_n^0$. We denote the epipole in $P_n$ as $\mathbf{e}_n$, and the epipolar line as $\mathbf{l}_n$. The epipolar constraint means that when background is static, one pixel $\mathbf{p}_n$ on $P_n$ is always projected to one pixel $\mathbf{p}_{n-1}$ on the epipolar line $\mathbf{l}_{n-1}$ in image plane $P_{n-1}$, and vice versa. Regardless of movement of the camera, all pixels in $P_n$ must be projected on the epipolar line in $P_{n-1}$ when the background is static.

However, objects that are moving in world coordinates violate the epipolar line constraint: i.e., foreground pixel $\mathbf{p}_n$ in $P_n$ is not projected to epipolar line $\mathbf{l}_{n-1}$ in $P_{n-1}$ and vice versa. Based on this fact, foreground pixel can be distinguished from background pixels in image coordinates. However, if an object is moving along the epipolar line, its foreground pixels in $P_n$ are projected onto epipolar line in $P_{n-1}$. To identify the moving object in this case, three consecutive frames are used; the method is based on the fact that the distances that the objects between $\mathbf{p}_n$ and $\mathbf{p}_{n-1}$ and between $\mathbf{p}_n$ and $\mathbf{p}_{n+1}$ will be almost the same when the image frame rate is sufficiently high.

# 3   Epipole Alignment

To use two epipolar geometry constraints in consecutive frames, all epipoles of consecutive frames must be aligned to each other [29]. Here, alignment means that the epipoles of three consecutive frames become the same. Epipole alignment should be performed before the two constraints are used.

Assuming that all objects are static and that only the camera mounted on the vehicle is moving, only ego-motion of the vehicle affects variation of the pixels, so ego-motion is the basic source of information that can be used to estimate the epipole and epipolar lines in dynamic scene. Because ego-motion in world coordinates is projected to epipolar flow in image coordinates, epipolar flow must be estimated using consecutive frames to align epipoles and epipolar lines.

Epipolar flow $\mathbf{u}(\mathbf{p}) = (u_y(\mathbf{p}), u_x(\mathbf{p}))$ of pixel $\mathbf{p}$ consists of rotational flow $\mathbf{u}^r(\mathbf{p})$ and translation flow $\mathbf{u}^t(\mathbf{p}, d(\mathbf{p}))$:

$$\mathbf{u}(\mathbf{p}) = \mathbf{u}^r(\mathbf{p}) + \mathbf{u}^t(\mathbf{p}, d(\mathbf{p})), \tag{1}$$

where $d(\mathbf{p})$ is the distance from the camera to the pixel. Rotational flow is related to the rotational component in epipolar flow, and translational flow is related to the distance component in epipolar flow. When rotational flow is compensated for, translational flow with respect to distance value is projected along the epipolar line. Therefore, to align epipoles of frame $n-1$, $n$, and $n+1$, rotational flow must be estimated and compensated for.

To obtain rotational flow, we used SIFT [21] features in two consecutive frames to identify discriminative pixels in the image, which are then used to estimate rotational flow. We use SIFT because it achieves stable keypoint results and can use only discriminative background pixels for the estimation. If foreground pixels affect estimation of rotational flow, epipoles and epipolar lines are incorrectly estimated. Assuming that the number of background pixels significantly outnumber the foreground pixels, *random sample consensus* (RANSAC) [3] is used to remove foreground pixels from estimating rotational flow.

Assuming that rotational flow is small, $\mathbf{u}^r(\mathbf{p})$ can be represented as a function of five elements $\mathbf{a} = (a_1, a_2, a_3, a_4, a_5)^\top$ [20]

$$\mathbf{u}^r(\mathbf{p}) = \begin{pmatrix} a_1 - a_3\bar{y} + a_4\bar{x}^2 + a_5\bar{x}\bar{y} \\ a_2 + a_3\bar{x} + a_4\bar{x}\bar{y} + a_5\bar{y}^2 \end{pmatrix}, \tag{2}$$

where $\bar{y} = y - y_c$ and $\bar{x} = x - x_c$, and $x_c$ and $y_c$ are principle points of $x$-axis and $y$-axis, respectively. All elements are related to focal length and principle points. By using keypoints in the image, $\mathbf{a}$ is computed using the 8-point algorithm [9].

After obtaining rotational flow between $n$ and $n-1$, and between $n$ and $n+1$, pixels in $P_{n-1}$ and $P_{n+1}$ are compensated according to $P_n$. The epipoles and epipolar lines of three image planes are the same after compensation: $\mathbf{e}'_{n-1} = \mathbf{e}_n = \mathbf{e}'_{n+1}$ and $\mathbf{l}'_{n-1} = \mathbf{l}_n = \mathbf{l}'_{n+1}$, where $\mathbf{e}'_n$ and $\mathbf{l}'_n$ represents compensated epipole and epipolar line at frame $n$, respectively. Then the two epipolar geometry constraints can be applied to distinguish foreground pixels from background pixels.

# 4  Moving Object Detection Using Epipolar Constraints

In the following, we assume that all epipoles of three consecutive frames have been aligned. In an aligned image, all background pixels that are not moving in world coordinates are positioned on an epipolar line, and foreground pixels that are moving in world coordinates are usually not positioned on this line; if they are, optical flow constraint is also used.

## 4.1  Epipolar Line Search

The first condition to separate foreground pixel from background pixels is to determine whether the pixel is positioned on the epipolar line. We denote a compensated pixel in a frame as $n-1$ and $n+1$ as $\mathbf{p}'_{n-1}$ and $\mathbf{p}'_{n+1}$. For the background pixels, the compensated pixels $\mathbf{p}'_{n-1}$ and $\mathbf{p}'_{n+1}$ must lay on the epipolar line $\mathbf{l}_n(\mathbf{p}_n)$. For the foreground pixels, the compensated pixels $\mathbf{p}'_{n-1}$ and $\mathbf{p}'_{n+1}$ usually do not lay on $\mathbf{l}_n(\mathbf{p}_n)$. These relations are represented as

$$\mathbf{l}_n(\mathbf{p}_n^0)^\top \mathbf{p}'^0_{n-1} = 0, \tag{3}$$

$$\mathbf{l}_n(\mathbf{p}_n^0)^\top \mathbf{p}'^0_{n+1} = 0, \tag{4}$$

$$\mathbf{l}_n(\mathbf{p}_n^1)^\top \mathbf{p}'^1_{n-1} \neq 0, \tag{5}$$

$$\mathbf{l}_n(\mathbf{p}_n^1)^\top \mathbf{p}'^1_{n+1} \neq 0. \tag{6}$$

Using these relations, we filter out foreground pixels. Using epipolar line at frame $n$ and compensated pixel at frame $n-1$ and $n+1$, background pixels can be distinguished from foreground pixels

$$L(\mathbf{p}) = \begin{cases} 0, & \|\mathbf{l}_n(\mathbf{p}_n)^\top \mathbf{p}_{n-1}\| \leq \lambda_1 \cap \|\mathbf{l}_n(\mathbf{p}_n)^\top \mathbf{p}_{n+1}\| \leq \lambda_1 \\ 1, & \text{otherwise,} \end{cases} \tag{7}$$

where $L(\mathbf{p})$ is estimated label of pixel $\mathbf{p}$ and $\lambda_1$ is threshold value that is applied to decide whether the pixel lays on the epipolar line. The label '0' indecates that $\mathbf{p}$ is a background pixel and '1' indicates that it is a foreground pixel.

## 4.2  Optical Flow Search

Epipolar line search successfully identified moving objects, unless they were approaching the ego-vehicle along this line. In this case, foreground pixel is moving along the epipolar line. To identify moving objects in this situation, optical flow between frames $n-1$ and $n$, and between frames $n$ and $n+1$ are compared. These optical flows are different if the object is moving, and the same if it is not. These characteristics are used to identify foreground pixels.

The position of a stationary object in world coordinate is static so $\mathbf{P}_{n-1} = \mathbf{P}_n = \mathbf{P}_{n+1}$. As shown in Fig. 2, in world coordinates, we denote $\mathbf{O}_n$ as the position of the camera during frame $n$, $\mathbf{V}$ as an orthogonal point between $\mathbf{P}$ and the vanishing line, $D$ as distance between $\mathbf{V}$ and $\mathbf{P}$, $Z_n$ as distance between $\mathbf{V}$

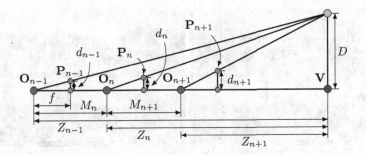

**Fig. 2.** World coordinates model of a stationary object.

and $O_n$, and $M_n$ as distance between $O_n$ and $O_{n-1}$. In the image coordinates, we denote $f$ as focal length and $d_n$ as the distance between the epipole $e_n$ and pixel $p_n$.

Based on trigonometry, the proportion between frame $n-1$, $n$, and $n+1$ is represented by $f$, $d_n$, $D$, and $Z_n$

$$D : Z_{n-1} = d_{n-1} : f, \tag{8}$$

$$D : Z_n = d_n : f, \tag{9}$$

$$D : Z_{n+1} = d_{n+1} : f. \tag{10}$$

By replacing $Z_{n-1} = Z_n + M_n$ and $Z_{n+1} = Z_n - M_{n+1}$, Eqs. (8) and (10) become $D : Z_n + M_n = d_{n-1} : f$ and $D : Z_n - M_{n+1} = d_{n+1} : f$, respectively.

Organizing proportional expressions with respect to $M_n$ yields the relationships

$$\frac{M_{n+1}}{M_n} = \frac{d_{n-1}(d_{n+1} - d_n)}{d_{n+1}(d_n - d_{n-1})}. \tag{11}$$

If frame rate is sufficiently high that the speed of ego-vehicle does not change between consecutive frames, then $M_n = M_{n+1}$. Therefore, for the background pixels, Eq. (11) must equal '1'.

To use Eq. (11), we used a conditional function to classify foreground and background pixels:

$$L(\mathbf{p}) = \begin{cases} 0, & |d_{n-1}(d_{n+1} - d_n) - d_{n+1}(d_n - d_{n-1})| \leq \lambda_2 \\ 1, & \text{otherwise}, \end{cases} \tag{12}$$

where $\lambda_2$ is a threshold value for the optical flow constraint. To apply both epipolar geometry constraints, both Eqs. (7) and (12) must be used.

## 5   Experimental Results

To show the accuracy and runtime of proposed algorithm, we compare it to the TriTrack method [17], which uses sparse scene flow segmentation for object

**Fig. 3.** Moving object detection results of proposed algorithm (left column) and Tri-Track [17] (right column) in consecutive frames when vehicle is moving.

tracking. We compared only TriTrack because no public dataset is available that contains monocular images with dynamic scenes to evaluate MOD algorithms and no code is available to compare.

We used KITTI scene flow dataset 2015 multi-view extension version that provides 200 scenes of different road scenarios, each with 20 consecutive frames. Because this dataset is not intended from use in evaluating MOD algorithms, it contains no ground truth data, so we evaluated the algorithms by counting the number of detected objects manually. Not all images have moving objects, and we eliminated out some scenarios that include moving objects. Image sizes were approximately 1340×375, and we used $\lambda_1 = 20$ and $\lambda_2 = 100$ for all tested images. Our experimental settings consisted of an Intel i7-3770 3.4 Ghz CPU, 8 GB memory, Microsoft Windows 8.1 (64-bit), Microsoft Visual Studio 2013 C++, and OpenCV 3.0.

Based on the movement of the ego-vehicle, two common scenarios were considered: (1) moving ego-vehicle (dynamic scene); and (2) stationary ego-vehicle.

**Fig. 4.** Moving object detection results of proposed algorithm (left column) and Tri-Track [17] (right column) in various scenes when vehicle is moving.

Usually, when the ego-vehicle is moving on a road, other vehicles approach it. When the ego-vehicle is stopped, other vehicles cross the video horizontally.

**Dynamic Scene.** When the ego-vehicle was moving, the proposed algorithm successfully found the approaching vehicle (Figs. 3 and 4, left column). In this case, the approaching car was moving along the epipolar line, so foreground pixels were not easily distinguished from background if only the epipolar line constraint is used. So, two epipolar geometry constraints were used to detected moving cars. Some result images show incorrectly-detected points. This error occurs because of mismatches from the SIFT feature.

MOD results obtained using TriTrack (Figs. 3 and 4, right column) sometimes do not detect approaching vehicles, but the method can detect cars that cross in front of the ego-vehicle. If the goal is to prevent car accidents, then warning of the approach of objects that are on a collision course is more important than warning about objects will miss (or that have missed) the ego-vehicle. The failure of Tritrack to detect moving objects when the camera is moving, even when a stereo camera provides depth information, emphasize the difficulty of MOD in dynamic scene. Consequently, the proposed algorithm's successful use of data from only one camera to detect an approaching object even when camera mounted on a moving vehicle is a remarkable accomplishment.

**Static Scene.** When the ego-vehicle was stopped and other vehicles were moving horizontally, the proposed algorithm always detected moving cars in the image (Figs. 5 and 6), whereas TriTrack sometimes failed to detect them, but generally, both algorithms identified moving objects when the camera was stationary. This result proves that MOD is much easier in a static scene than in a dynamic scene.

**Fig. 5.** Moving object detection results of proposed algorithm (left column) and Tri-Track [17] (right column) in consecutive frames when vehicle is stopped.

**Quantitative Evaluation.** Evaluation of MOD algorithms in dynamic scenes is a difficult task because dynamic MOD has not ground truth, and because no evaluation metric exists. Therefore, we used an evaluation metric is commonly used in industry: from the first to last frames in which moving object appears, we noted whether the algorithm detected the object correctly at least once. This metric usually used when evaluation of an algorithm is difficult.

We counted the number of relevant moving objects in all image frames. Among the 129 objects in the dataset, the proposed algorithm detected 83, and TriTrack detected 89. The proposed algorithm sometimes cannot detect moving objects when the ego-vehicle is turning quickly; in this case, keypoint matching is difficult, so estimating the fundamental matrix is also difficult. In general cases, the proposed algorithm detects moving objects successfully.

**Fig. 6.** Moving object detection results of proposed algorithm (left column) and Tri-Track [17] (right column) in various scenes when vehicle is stopped.

**Runtime Evaluation.** To show the effectiveness of our proposed algorithm, we compared its runtime to that of TriTrack. For the tested images, the proposed algorithm took ~0.98 s to get detection results, whereas TriTrack required ~1.34 s; i.e., the proposed algorithm is about 1.35 times faster than TriTrack. The speedup occurs because our proposed algorithm is based on sparse features and uses a monocular camera.

The proposed algorithm only takes time to compute SIFT, rotational flow, epipolar line constraint, and optical flow constraint. Among them, computing SIFT feature takes ~0.94 s which is almost 95 % of all runtime. When the ego-vehicle is moving forward or stopped, the algorithm need not calculate SIFT feature, epipole, or epipolar line, so the computation time of the proposed algorithm could be reduced severely by using rotational information from the ego-vehicle's steering system.

## 6   Conclusion

In this study, we proposed an MOD algorithm for dynamic scene. In general, finding the position of a moving object when camera is moving is a very difficult task because all pixels in the image are moving. To overcome this difficulty, we proposed an algorithm based on epipolar line search and optical flow search. Epipolar line search is based on the property that background pixels of three consecutive frames are always on the epipolar lines, otherwise it is a foreground pixel. Optical flow search is based on the property that two optical flows over three consecutive frames are the same when frame rate is sufficiently fast. By using these two constraints, foreground pixels can be distinguished from background pixels. We evaluated our proposed algorithm using KITTI scene flow dataset. Our proposed algorithm detected moving objects sufficiently in and images that were obtained in dynamic scenes even though it uses only a monocular camera. The proposed algorithm is sufficiently fast to have practical uses.

**Acknowledgement.** This work was supported by the Human Resource Training Program for Regional Innovation and Creativity through the Ministry of Education and National Research Foundation of Korea.

# References

1. Dalal, N., Triggs, B.: Histograms of oriented gradients for human detection. In: IEEE Computer Society Conference on Computer Vision and Pattern Recognition, 2005, CVPR 2005, vol. 1, pp. 886–893. IEEE (2005)
2. Felzenszwalb, P.F., Girshick, R.B., McAllester, D., Ramanan, D.: Object detection with discriminatively trained part-based models. IEEE Trans. Pattern Anal. Mach. Intell. **32**(9), 1627–1645 (2010)
3. Fischler, M.A., Bolles, R.C.: Random sample consensus: a paradigm for model fitting with applications to image analysis and automated cartography. Commun. ACM **24**(6), 381–395 (1981)
4. Fortun, D., Bouthemy, P., Kervrann, C.: Optical flow modeling and computation: a survey. Comput. Vis. Image Underst. **134**, 1–21 (2015)
5. Fu, H., Xu, D., Zhang, B., Lin, S.: Object-based multiple foreground video co-segmentation. In: 2014 IEEE Conference on Computer Vision and Pattern Recognition (CVPR), pp. 3166–3173. IEEE (2014)
6. Gavrila, D.M.: Pedestrian detection from a moving vehicle. In: Vernon, D. (ed.) ECCV 2000. LNCS, vol. 1843, pp. 37–49. Springer, Heidelberg (2000). doi:10.1007/3-540-45053-X_3
7. Geronimo, D., Lopez, A.M., Sappa, A.D., Graf, T.: Survey of pedestrian detection for advanced driver assistance systems. IEEE Trans. Pattern Anal. Mach. Intell. **7**, 1239–1258 (2009)
8. Harris, C., Stephens, M.: A combined corner and edge detector. In: Alvey Vision Conference, vol. 15, p. 50. Citeseer (1988)
9. Hartley, R.I.: In defense of the eight-point algorithm. IEEE Trans. Pattern Anal. Mach. Intell. **19**(6), 580–593 (1997)
10. Horn, B.K., Schunck, B.G.: Determining optical flow. In: 1981 Technical Symposium East, pp. 319–331. International Society for Optics and Photonics (1981)
11. Jun, W.: MOD for collision warning using monocular camera in dynamic scene. Master's thesis, Pohang University of Science and Technology (2016)
12. Jun, W., Ha, J., Jeong, H.: Moving object detection using energy model and particle filter for dynamic scene. In: Bräunl, T., McCane, B., Rivera, M., Yu, X. (eds.) PSIVT 2015. LNCS, vol. 9431, pp. 111–122. Springer, Heidelberg (2016). doi:10.1007/978-3-319-29451-3_10
13. Klappstein, J., Stein, F., Franke, U.: Monocular motion detection using spatial constraints in a unified manner. In: 2006 IEEE Intelligent Vehicles Symposium, pp. 261–267. IEEE (2006)
14. Klappstein, J., Vaudrey, T., Rabe, C., Wedel, A., Klette, R.: Moving object segmentation using optical flow and depth information. In: Wada, T., Huang, F., Lin, S. (eds.) PSIVT 2009. LNCS, vol. 5414, pp. 611–623. Springer, Heidelberg (2009). doi:10.1007/978-3-540-92957-4_53

15. Kwak, S., Lim, T., Nam, W., Han, B., Han, J.H.: Generalized background subtraction based on hybrid inference by belief propagation and bayesian filtering. In: 2011 IEEE International Conference on Computer Vision (ICCV), pp. 2174–2181. IEEE (2011)

16. Lee, D.S.: Effective Gaussian mixture learning for video background subtraction. IEEE Trans. Pattern Anal. Mach. Intell. **27**(5), 827–832 (2005)

17. Lenz, P., Ziegler, J., Geiger, A., Roser, M.: Sparse scene flow segmentation for moving object detection in urban environments. In: 2011 IEEE Intelligent Vehicles Symposium (IV), pp. 926–932. IEEE (2011)

18. Lim, J., Han, B.: Generalized background subtraction using superpixels with label integrated motion estimation. In: Fleet, D., Pajdla, T., Schiele, B., Tuytelaars, T. (eds.) ECCV 2014, Part V. LNCS, vol. 8693, pp. 173–187. Springer, Heidelberg (2014)

19. Lindström, M., Eklundh, J.O.: Detecting and tracking moving objects from a mobile platform using a laser range scanner. In: Proceedings of 2001 IEEE/RSJ International Conference on Intelligent Robots and Systems, 2001, vol. 3, pp. 1364–1369. IEEE (2001)

20. Longuet-Higgins, H.C., Prazdny, K.: The interpretation of a moving retinal image. Proc. R. Soc. Lond. B: Biol. Sci. **208**(1173), 385–397 (1980)

21. Lowe, D.G.: Distinctive image features from scale-invariant keypoints. Int. J. Comput. Vision **60**(2), 91–110 (2004)

22. Menze, M., Geiger, A.: Object scene flow for autonomous vehicles. In: Proceedings of the IEEE Conference on Computer Vision and Pattern Recognition, pp. 3061–3070 (2015)

23. Mertz, C., Navarro-Serment, L.E., MacLachlan, R., Rybski, P., Steinfeld, A., Suppe, A., Urmson, C., Vandapel, N., Hebert, M., Thorpe, C., et al.: Moving object detection with laser scanners. J. Field Rob. **30**(1), 17–43 (2013)

24. Mumtaz, A., Zhang, W., Chan, A.B.: Joint motion segmentation and background estimation in dynamic scenes. In: 2014 IEEE Conference on Computer Vision and Pattern Recognition (CVPR), pp. 368–375. IEEE (2014)

25. Shashua, A., Gdalyahu, Y., Hayun, G.: Pedestrian detection for driving assistance systems: single-frame classification and system level performance. In: 2004 IEEE Intelligent Vehicles Symposium, pp. 1–6. IEEE (2004)

26. Shimada, A., Nagahara, H., Taniguchi, R.I.: Background modeling based on bidirectional analysis. In: 2013 IEEE Conference on Computer Vision and Pattern Recognition (CVPR), pp. 1979–1986. IEEE (2013)

27. Stauffer, C., Grimson, W.E.L.: Learning patterns of activity using real-time tracking. IEEE Trans. Pattern Anal. Mach. Intell. **22**(8), 747–757 (2000)

28. Sun, Z., Bebis, G., Miller, R.: On-road vehicle detection: a review. IEEE Trans. Pattern Anal. Mach. Intell. **28**(5), 694–711 (2006)

29. Yamaguchi, K., Kato, T., Ninomiya, Y.: Vehicle ego-motion estimation and moving object detection using a monocular camera. In: 18th International Conference on Pattern Recognition, 2006, ICPR 2006, vol. 4, pp. 610–613. IEEE (2006)

30. Zhou, X., Yang, C., Yu, W.: Moving object detection by detecting contiguous outliers in the low-rank representation. IEEE Trans. Pattern Anal. Mach. Intell. **35**(3), 597–610 (2013)

# FPGA Implementation of the Flux Tensor Moving Object Detection Method

Piotr Janus, Kamil Piszczek, and Tomasz Kryjak$^{(\boxtimes)}$

Faculty of Electrical Engineering, Automatics, Computer Science and Biomedical Engineering, AGH University of Science and Technology, Kraków, Poland
{kertoip,aldarel}@student.agh.edu.pl, tomasz.kryjak@agh.edu.pl

**Abstract.** In this paper a hardware implementation in a field programmable gate array (FPGA) device of moving object segmentation using the flux tensor (FT) method is presented. The used algorithm and its parallelized version are described in details. The designed module has been verified on the VC 707 development board with Virtex 7 FPGA device for the following video stream parameters: 720 × 576 @ 50 fps (25 MHz pixel clock), 1280 × 720 @ 50 fps (74.25 MHz pixel clock) and 1920 × 1080 @ 50 fps (148.5 MHz pixel clock). Additionally, the computing performance and power consumption have been estimated. The proposed module outperforms the previous FT implementations both in terms of real-time processing capabilities for high-definition stream, as well as energy efficiency.

## 1 Introduction

Moving object detection is one of the most important elements of an advanced automated video surveillance system. It can be used to segment people, vehicles or animals. However, it should be noted, that this approach may be insufficient is some cases. Good examples are stopped objects e.g. pedestrians waiting at a bus stop or an abandoned bag. On the other hand, not all moving elements present in the scene are important, especially flowing water (a river, a fountain), flapping flags, etc. This brief analysis delineates the complexity of the so-called foreground object segmentation. This issue is beyond the scope of this article – an extensive discussion can be found in the book [3]. Moving object segmentation is usually an integral part of foreground object segmentation algorithms. It is used as a cue, which allows to improve the obtained results. Therefore, designing and implementing this kind of algorithms is fully justified.

In recent years a significant cost reduction of vision sensors and cameras could be observed. This also includes high resolution devices – 720p, 1080p or 2160p[1]. In addition, the number of surveillance cameras in public spaces increases. This implies two important problems: who will analyse the video streams and where this task should be conducted. Traditional methods involving "manual"

---

[1] 720p denotes that the vertical resolution of the image equals 720 lines and progressive scanning is used (not interlacing). Usually 720p means a 1280 × 720 resolution.

© Springer International Publishing AG 2016
L.J. Chmielewski et al. (Eds.): ICCVG 2016, LNCS 9972, pp. 486–497, 2016.
DOI: 10.1007/978-3-319-46418-3_43

analysis by trained operators are very poorly scalable and generate significant costs. Humans are not able to effectively concentrate for a long period of time on this task. Especially because during 99.99 % of the time nothing important happens – only typical behaviours can be observed. Also the number of different video streams, that a person can analyse at the same time is limited. Both factors contribute to the necessity of frequent staff rotation and this increases the cost of the whole system. Due to the mentioned above reasons, a very dynamic development of automated surveillance video analysis algorithms and systems can be observed. However, the aim is not to replace the human operator, but to support his work by identifying situation that pose potential threats. This includes: violation of forbidden zone detection (e.g. track crossing at a railway station), abandoned luggage detection, incorrect motion direction or violent behaviour detection.

The used high resolution cameras are a source of an increasing video stream. For example, a typical colour (RGB), 24 bit per pixel video in so-called full high definition resolution (FullHD) i.e. $1920 \times 1080$ @ 50 fps (frames per second) means over 2.3 GB of uncompressed data per second. This data must be processed, analysed and also archived (usually in a compressed form). This can be done centrally (in the surveillance centre) or in a distributed manner. In the second case, the so-called smart camera approach is used – image processing, analysis and recognition are performed immediately after image acquisition (close to the sensor) [2]. This allows to obtain a significant reduction in the required communication bandwidth. In typical conditions only analysis result in form of meta-data are transmitted.

When designing a smart camera a very important decision is the selection of a proper computing platform. It should have the following characteristics: real-time video stream processing support (the ability to process all data from the image sensor without pixel or frame dropping), flexibility (easy algorithm upgrade, especially important in novel solutions) and energy efficiency (low power consumption). Among the possible solutions worth mentioning are: general purpose processors (GPP), application specific integrated circuits (ASIC), field programmable gate arrays (FPGA) and heterogeneous system on chip (e.g. Zynq SoC – the integration of an ARM processor and reprogrammable logic in one housing). Each of these computing platforms has its advantages and disadvantages, whose comprehensive discussion is beyond the scope of this paper. In the proposed system a FPGA device was used. According to authors opinion, it meets all the presented above requirements. It is also a proven platform for implementing many different vision systems – from simple operations like pre-processing and filtration [8], to advanced pedestrian detection systems with multi-scale image analysis. A comprehensive presentation of various FPGA image processing applications can be found in the book [1].

In this paper a hardware implementation in FPGA of the flux tensor moving object detection method is presented. The main contributions of this paper are twofold:

– to the authors best knowledge, this is the first reported FPGA implementation of this algorithm,

– several modifications in the data processing path were proposed, which allowed to optimize FPGA resource usage.

The rest of this paper is organized as follows. In Sect. 2 the flux tensor method and in Sect. 3 the proposed hardware architecture are described. Implementation and evaluation results are presented in Sect. 4. The paper ends with a short summary and further research direction discussion.

## 2   The Flux Tensor Algorithm

As stated in the introduction, moving object detection is an important issue in many vision systems. In practise several method are used. The simplest one is consecutive frame differencing (CFD). It can be performed for colour (RGB, YCbCr) or greyscale images. This method is easy to implement and very computationally efficient, but very prone to all kinds of noise.

Another often used solution is optical flow i.e. the computation of a vector filed which describes the motion of each pixel between two successive frames. In this case the moving object mask is obtained by thresholding the magnitude of particular vectors. The two basic algorithms are Lucas-Kanade and Horn-Schunck. More information on this issue can be found in the review paper [7].

The flux tensor (FT) algorithm was first proposed in the papers [4,5] in 2007. It is based on the previously described structure tensor method for 3D greyscale images [11]. The authors of FT emphasize that in comparison to standard optical flow computation, their method provides more spatial coherent results with less noise. Moreover, they claim that its basic advantage is the ability to reliably detect motion in difficult scenarios: the presence of illumination changes, variable camera focus, shadow occurrence, small movement (water, leaves) and sensor noise. It should also be noted that FT does not involve the computationally complex eigenvalues decomposition.

In the mentioned works, the flux tensor method has been used in a people detection and tracking system. The approach involved visible and infra-red image fusion. This solution consisted of four modules: FT calculation for infra-red image, FT segmentation results improvement (filling holes and correcting object boundaries) using level set based geodesic active contour, multiple object tracking using correspondence graphs and trajectory analysis and improvement using a clustering approach.

This method was also used for segmentation of biological objects [6,13], as well as an exemplary algorithm in a surveillance video analysis framework [15]. Furthermore, it is a key component of an advanced foreground object segmentation algorithm – Flux-Tensor with Split Gaussian models (FTSG) [16].

However, the FT algorithm is rather computationally complex. This is a consequence of the spatio-temporal filtrations and weighted integration operations in the 3D volume. In the work [14] the method was accelerated on a multi-core Cell Broadband Engine processor (available in Play Station 3). Using an appropriate architecture and techniques like: vectorization, loop unrolling, short vector fused multiply add operations and double-buffering optimizations allowed to obtain 12 to 40 times speed-up in comparison to a GPP reference implementation for 1920 × 1080 image resolution. Furthermore, a 50 times improvement in energy efficiency was reported.

## 2.1 Mathematical Formulation of the Flux Tensor

The flux tensor is composed of temporal variations in the optical field within the local 3D spatio-temporal volume. The method is based on horizontal and vertical edge detection and calculating temporal derivatives to determine moving elements in the scene. In the considered version of the algorithm greyscale input images are used. Let $I(x, y, t)$ denote the brightness of the pixel at position $x, y$ in the frame with time index $t$. To simplify the equations let $v = (x, y, t)$. If $\Omega$ is a pixel neighbourhood, then the flux tensor is given by the following matrix:

$$J_F(i) = \begin{pmatrix} \int_\Omega \left(\frac{\partial^2 I(v)}{\partial x \partial t}\right)^2 dv & \int_\Omega \frac{\partial^2 I(v)}{\partial x \partial t} \frac{\partial^2 I(v)}{\partial y \partial t} dv & \int_\Omega \frac{\partial^2 I(v)}{\partial x \partial t} \frac{\partial^2 I(v)}{\partial^2 t} dv \\ \int_\Omega \frac{\partial^2 I(v)}{\partial y \partial t} \frac{\partial^2 I(v)}{\partial x \partial t} dv & \int_\Omega \left(\frac{\partial^2 I(v)}{\partial y \partial t}\right)^2 dv & \int_\Omega \frac{\partial^2 I(v)}{\partial y \partial t} \frac{\partial^2 I(v)}{\partial^2 t} dv \\ \int_\Omega \frac{\partial^2 I(v)}{\partial^2 t} \frac{\partial^2 I(v)}{\partial x \partial t} dv & \int_\Omega \frac{\partial^2 I(v)}{\partial^2 t} \frac{\partial^2 I(v)}{\partial y \partial t} dv & \int_\Omega \left(\frac{\partial^2 I(v)}{\partial^2 t}\right)^2 dv \end{pmatrix} \tag{1}$$

The matrix trace is used in moving object segmentation:

$$trace(J_F) = \int_\Omega \left\| \frac{\partial}{\partial t} \nabla I(v) \right\|^2 dv \tag{2}$$

It is computed for each pixel. If it's value is greater than a predefined threshold $T$ the pixel is considered as a moving one. Let:

$$I_{xt} = \frac{\partial^2 I(x, y, t)}{\partial x \partial t}, \quad I_{yt} = \frac{\partial^2 I(x, y, t)}{\partial y \partial t}, \quad I_{tt} = \frac{\partial^2 I(x, y, t)}{\partial^2 t} \tag{3}$$

Then Eq. (2) can be rewritten as:

$$trace(J_F) = \int_\Omega \left( I_{xt}^2(v) + I_{yt}^2(v) + I_{tt}^2(v) \right) dv \tag{4}$$

The components $I_{xt}$ and $I_{yt}$ correspond to detected moving edges and the component $I_{tt}$ corresponds to brightness changes in time.

## 2.2 Numerical Computations

The determination of components $I_{xt}$, $I_{yt}$ and $I_{tt}$ necessary to compute the matrix trace can be implemented using convolution operations. A straightforward solution involves 3D kernels and is computationally inefficient. Therefore, in practise, a decomposition into three separate 1D kernels is used. This allows to reduce to computational complexity from $O(n^3)$ to $O(n)$. Additionally, in order to improve the numerical stability and reduce noise, the authors of the algorithm proposed to use some additional smoothing filters. They are applied to the third component, which is not required in the current second derivative calculation [14]. For example, in case of $I_{xt}$ the derivative filters in the $x$ and $t$ dimension are used and smoothing is applied for the $y$ dimension. The required integral operator is also implemented as three 1D averaging filters. A scheme of the required calculations is presented in Fig. 1.

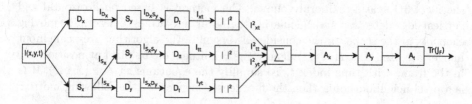

**Fig. 1.** Scheme of the operations required to obtain the matrix trace $J_F$ – source [14]

Where: $D_x$ and $D_y$ – spatial derivative filters for $x$ and $y$ dimensions, $S_x$ and $S_y$ – spatial smoothing filters, $D_t$ and $D_{tt}$ – the first and second temporal derivatives, $A_x, A_y, A_t$ – averaging filters.

It should be noted that the scheme presents a computation flow with certain optimizations for a sequential architecture. For example, the sum operation is carried out before averaging to save memory resources. Summing up, to determine the trace for a single pixel eight 1D filtrations are required in the spatio-temporal derivative stage and three 1D convolutions in the averaging stage.

## 2.3 Software Model

In the first step the flux tensor algorithm was implemented in C++ with the use of an open-source image processing library OpenCV [12]. Also parameters of individual filters were determined. In case of the smoothing operation a one-dimensional Gaussian filter with $\sigma = 3$ was used. For derivative computation the following masks were used ($n$ – filter size, also used as a pre-fix): $n = 3$ – $[-\frac{1}{2}, 0, \frac{1}{2}]$, $n = 5$ – $[\frac{1}{12}, -\frac{2}{3}, 0, \frac{2}{3}, -\frac{1}{12}]$, $n = 7$ – $[-\frac{1}{60}, \frac{3}{20}, -\frac{3}{4}, 0, \frac{3}{4}, -\frac{3}{20}, \frac{1}{60}]$.

For simplification it can be assumed that spatial filters have the same size i.e.: $nSx = nSy = nSs$, $nDx = nDy = nDs$ and $nAx = nAy = nAt$. Furthermore, the first and second temporal derivative have the same size $nDt = nDtt$. Also, derivative and smoothing filter sizes are equal ($nDs = nSs$). Finally, according to the above presented assumptions, the algorithm has 5 parameters: $T$ – moving object detection threshold, $nDs, nAs$ – spatial filters sizes and $nDt, nAt$ – temporal filter sizes (i.e. number of frames). The following parameters were used in this study: $T = 25, nDs = nDt = nAs = nAt = 5$. Consequently, three FIFO (First In First Out) buffers of size $nDt - 1$ and one of size $nAt - 1$ are required for the computing architecture presented in Fig. 1 – in total 16 frames have to be buffered.

# 3  Hardware Implementation of the Flux Tensor Algorithm

The flux tensor moving object segmentation method is computationally and memory complex, especially when compared to simple consecutive frame differencing. On the other hand, the obtained moving object mask have quite high quality. Additionally, the algorithm can be described as data driven and straightforward to parallelize. Therefore, it's implementation in a FPGA device is fully justified.

## 3.1  The Proposed Implementation

The main aim of the presented work was the design of an energy efficient flux tensor hardware module able to perform real-time video processing for the following video resolutions $720 \times 576$, $1280 \times 720$ and $1920 \times 1080$ pixels (the video source was a HDMI camera). It was decided to implement and test it on a FPGA based video processing system. The used computing platform supports all levels of parallelism from fine to coarse grained, pipeline data processing and is quite energy efficient. It should be noted that in the HDMI image transmission standard (as well as in other serial ones) in each pixel clock cycle one pixel is provided (usually 24 bits in RGB – 8 bits per pixel). Therefore, the pixels are received by the processing system line by line, frame by frame. If there is no buffering implemented, it is impossible to access image data in a random fashion (unlike in a PC based system). The above stated conditions have a significant impact on the hardware module design.

A preliminary analysis of the algorithm depicted in Fig. 1 revealed two main implementation challenges. Firstly, buffering of 16 image frames was required. The currently available FPGA devices do not have sufficient memory resources to even buffer a single HD frame[2] and therefore, external RAM memory had to be used.

Secondly, due to the way pixels are transmitted from the camera, the implementation of computations directly according to the diagram presented in Fig. 1 would be ineffective. If the operations for the $x$ dimensions were performed first, then three modules for vertical context generation would be required ($y$ dimension). In a pipelined vision system, this module requires so-called long delay lines (also referred to as circular buffers, FIFOs). To obtain a $n$ pixel context $n - 1$ image lines have to be buffered. In FPGA delay lines are usually implemented using internal block memory resources (BRAM). A more comprehensive description of this issue is provided in the work [9], where the hardware implementation of the peer group filtering algorithm is presented. Obtaining the context for the $x$ dimension is much easier and requires only a small number of register resources. Therefore, swapping the operation order, i.e. first executing $S_y$ and $D_y$, allowed

---

[2] Even if the available memory resources are greater than the required 47 Mb, combining many distributed across the FPGA device block RAM modules is very problematic and inefficient.

to use only one vertical context generation module and save a lot of hardware resources. The modified computing architecture is depicted in Fig. 2. The considered modules are highlighted.

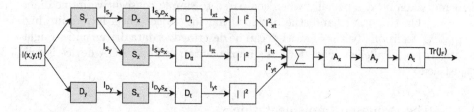

**Fig. 2.** Scheme of the flux tensor computation used in the hardware implementation

As mentioned above, the computation of temporal derivatives and averages $(D_t, D_{tt}, A_t)$ involves the buffering of previous frames – $I_{S_y D_x}$, $I_{S_y S_x}$, $I_{D_y S_x}$ and $I_{sum}$. The buffer size depends on the used mask size. For the considered default parameters (all sizes equal 5), for a single pixel $(5 - 1) \cdot 4 \cdot 8$ bits $= 128$ bits have to be stored and for the maximal considered mask size 7–192 bits. These values do not exceed the capabilities of modern FPGA devices with access to fast DDR3 or DDR4 memory, even for high definition video stream (1920 × 1080). Nevertheless, to ensure an appropriate transfer to and from the external memory a carefully designed controller has to be used [10].

## 3.2    Overview of the Proposed System

A high-level scheme of the implemented embedded vision system is presented in Figure 3. All modules were described in the Verilog hardware description language. The Vivado 2015.4 integrated development environment from Xilinx was used.

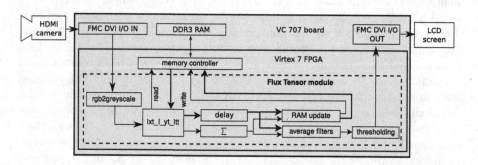

**Fig. 3.** High-level scheme of the embedded vision system with flux tensor based moving object detection

The source of the video stream was a Sony HDR-CX280 camera with HDMI output. It supports the following video parameters: $720 \times 576$ @ 50 fps, $1280 \times 720$ @ 50 fps and $1920 \times 1080$ @ 50 fps. The moving object detection results were displayed on a typical LCD monitor with HDMI input. The VC 707 development board from Xilinx was used as the main computing platform. It is equipped with a Virtex 7 FPGA device (XC7VX485T-2FFG1761). The system used also external DDR3 RAM and a HDMI input/output module (Avnet FMC DVI I/O).

In the first step, the input stream was converted from RGB colour space to greyscale (module `rgb2greyscale`). The applied transformation was compatible with the OpenCV library.

In the next module, the $I_{xt}, I_{yt}, I_{tt}$ values were computed (a detailed description in Subsect. 3.3). Calculating the temporal derivatives required access to external RAM via a memory controller (module `memory controller`). Then the results were squared and summed – module $\Sigma$. In parallel, the data read from RAM was delayed (module `delay`).

The results obtained in previous operations were then passed to two modules:

- `RAM update` – the data which should be stored in external RAM was updated. This involved a FIFO operation i.e. the removal of the oldest sample, shifting the remaining data and adding a new sample.
- `average filters` – realization of averaging filters $(A_x, A_y, A_t)$ – detailed description in Subsect. 3.4.

The last step of the algorithm involved thresholding (module `thersholding`).

During implementation, one of the goals was the reduction of hardware resource usage by limiting the length of used delay lines. This was especially important for data stored in external RAM memory (word width of 128 bits). Firstly, the data was read exactly when it was needed (i.e. after computing the $y$ context). Secondly, the $I_{sum}$ instead of the $I_{sum}$ after spatial averaging ($A_x$ and $A_y$) value was stored in RAM . On one hand, this solution required the realisation of $A_x$ and $A_y$ filtration for all pixel in the temporal context (i.e. 5 for the considered parameters). If only long delay lines (BRAM) are considered, then $4 \cdot 5 \cdot 8 \cdot XX = 160 \cdot XX$ bits need to be buffered ($XX$ – horizontal image resolution). However, the alternative, i.e. a direct implementation of the data flow presented in Figure 2 requires the buffering of $4 \cdot 128 \cdot XX = 512 \cdot XX$ bits plus additional $8 \cdot 4 \cdot XX$ bits.

It is worth noting that the applied solution has other advantages. For example, if the FT module is used as a part of a larger vision system and other modules also require access to data in external RAM, then a short RAM word path results in an even greater resource saving (assuming the path for the other module is shorter) and easier co-operation with the rest of the system.

### 3.3   Trace Computation Module

A detailed scheme of the module `I_xt_I_ty_I_tt` is presented in Fig. 4. In the first step, the vertical context was determined – `y_context`. The delay line approach, described in details in work [9], was used. When the full context was valid i.e. 5 pixels were available, a RAM read signal was generated (**read**). The RAM word had the following form: $[I_{S_y D_x(t-1)}, ..., I_{S_y D_x(t-nDt+1)}, I_{D_y S_x(t-1)}, ..., I_{D_y S_x(t-nDt+1)}, I_{S_y S_x(t-1)}, ..., I_{S_y S_x(t-nDt+1)}, I_{sum(t-1)}, ..., I_{sum(t-nAt+1)}]$.

In the second step, in parallel the derivative filter $D_y$ and smoothing filter $S_y$ were realized. Then the $S_x$ (two times) and $D_x$ operations were executed. In the third stage, temporal derivatives $D_t$ and $D_{tt}$ were computed. The data from external RAM was delayed in modules $DEL\_D_y S_x$, $DEL\_S_y D_x$ and $DEL\_S_y S_x$. Additionally, data required later during spatial averaging was also delayed – $DEL\_I_{sum}$. The output of module consists of $I_{xt}, I_{yt}, I_{yt}$ values and data word from RAM (with $R\_$ prefix).

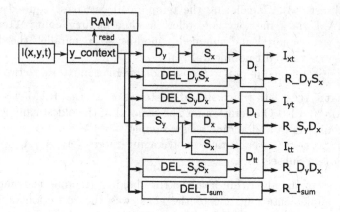

**Fig. 4.** Matrix trace calculation module (I_xt_I_ty_I_tt)

## 3.4  Spatial Averaging

Scheme of the **average_filters** module is depicted in Fig. 5. The inputs are $I_{sum}$ and $nAt - 1$ $I_{sum}$ values from previous frames (prefix $R\_$). In the first step the data was separated into $nAt$ values. Then, the $A_x$ and $A_y$ operations were performed. In the next stage, the results were combined into a temporal context and the $A_t$ operation was executed. As result the matrix trace $Tr(J_F)$ was obtained.

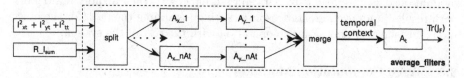

**Fig. 5.** Scheme of the spatial averaging module $A_x, A_y, A_t$

# 4   Evaluation of the Implemented FT Module

In the first step, the designed FT module was tested using the simulator available in the Vivado software. Particular submodules described in Verilog were compared with the software model in C++. Then the FT block was integrated into a vision system on the VC 707 development board.

The system was positively tested for the following video stream parameters: 720 × 576 @ 50 fps (25 MHz pixel clock), 1280 × 720 @ 50 fps (74.25 MHz pixel clock) and 1920 × 1080 @ 50 fps (148.5 MHz pixel clock). The Vivado Power Report tool estimated the power usage for the design at 3.468 W (on-chip, with 200 MHz clock). Furthermore, real power consumption measurements using a wattmeter were conducted. Four designs were considered: board in reset state (Idle), simple video capture and display (VS), consecutive frame differencing (CFD) and flux tensor (FT). The results are summed up in Table 1.

**Table 1.** Power usage analysis

| Resolution | Pixel clock | Idle | VS | CFD | FT |
|---|---|---|---|---|---|
| 720 × 576 @ 50 Hz | 27 MHz | 16 W | 16.8 W | 20.7 W | 20.7 W |
| 1280 × 720 @ 50 Hz | 74.25 MHz | 16 W | 17.4 W | 21.1 W | 21.5 W |
| 1920 × 1080 @ 50 Hz | 148.5 MHz | 16 W | 18.3 W | 22.2 W | 23.6 W |

Four issues should be emphasized. First, power usage is strictly frequency dependent. Second, the external RAM operations rise the power usage by about 4W (CFD or FT minus VS). Third, the difference between CFD and FT also heavily depends on the image resolution. Finally, the Power Report tool is quite accurate but is does not include RAM operations.

Computing the flux tensor for a single pixel involves 104 operations (addition, subtraction, multiplications etc.). This results in the following GOPS (Giga Operations Per Second) values: 2.1 GOPS, 4,8 GOPS 10,8 GOPS for the three considered resolutions. Respectively the GOPS/W coefficient equals: 0.1 GOPS/W, 0.2 GOPS/W and 0.5 GOPS/W. The proposed module does not require large logic resources (Table 2). The quite high BRAM usage results mainly from the used external RAM controller, which involves large FIFOs.

The proposed hardware module allows real time video stream processing for all considered resolutions at 50 frames per second. Our software reference application in C++ running on a i7-3630QM @ 2.40 GHz processor obtained the following frame per second rate: 720 × 576 –12 fps, 1280 × 720 – 6 fps, 1920 × 1080 – 3 fps.

Comparing the above results to the presented in paper [14] two issues should be emphasized. First, for the same filter configuration and 1920 × 1080 image resolution, the proposed PS-3 Cell/B.E. processor implementation achieved about 30 fps and our FPGA based 50 fps. Second, the Cell processor system uses about

**Table 2.** FPGA resource usage of the flux tensor module and whole vision system

| Resources | Usage | Avaliable | % used |
|-----------|-------|-----------|--------|
| FF | 951–10298 | 607200 | 0.16–1.7 |
| LUT | 890–10905 | 303600 | 0.29–3.59 |
| DSP 48 | 28–28 | 2800 | 1–1 |
| BRAM | 36–101.5 | 1030 | 3.5–9.85 |

135 W, whereas ours only 24 W (with an overhead introduced by elements on the board which are not used but powered on – the idle board requires 16 W).

A visual comparison of the flux tensor and consecutive frame differencing method is presented in Fig. 6a–c. Additionally, in Fig. 6d the used test setup and demo of the working system is shown.

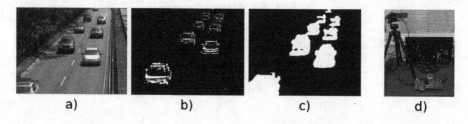

**Fig. 6.** Segmentation examples and working system: (a) input image, (b) consecutive frame differencing, (c) flux tensor, (d) working system

## 5   Summary

In this article the hardware implementation of the flux tensor moving object segmentation algorithm was described. The designed module enables real-time image processing for the following video streams: $720 \times 576$ @ 50 fps, $1280 \times 720$ @ 50 fps and $1920 \times 1080$ @ 50 fps. It was verified on the VC 707 development board with Virtex 7 FPGA device. The proposed solution is also energy efficient. The whole system uses only about 24 W for a $1920 \times 1080$ video stream. It outperforms our software model, as well as the parllelized solution presented in [14]. The FT module is a part of the flux tensor with split Gaussian models foreground object segmentation method [16]. Therefore, in the near future we will concentrate on a FPGA implementation of this algorithm. Moreover, FT can be used in other vision system, as an alternative to very simple consecutive frame differencing and quite complex optical flow computations.

**Acknowledgements.** The work presented in this paper was supported by AGH University of Science and Technology project number 15.11.120.879.

# References

1. Bailey, D.G.: Design for Embedded Image Processing on FPGAs. Wiley, Singapore (2011)
2. Belbachir, A.N.: Smart Cameras. Springer, USA (2010)
3. Bouwmans, T., Porikli, F., Hferlin, B., Vacavant, A.: Background Modeling and Foreground Detection for Video Surveillance. Chapman and Hall/CRC, Boca Raton (2014)
4. Bunyak, F., Palaniappan, K., Nath, S.K., Seetharaman, G.: Geodesic active contour based fusion of visible and infrared video for persistent object tracking. In: IEEE Workshop on Applications of Computer Vision (2007)
5. Bunyak, F., Palaniappan, K., Nath, S.K.: Flux tensor constrained geodesic active contours with sensor fusion for persistent object tracking. J. Multimedia 2(4), 20–33 (2007)
6. Ersoy, I., Palaniappan, K.: Multi-feature contour evolution for automatic live cell segmentation in time lapse imagery. In: 30th Annual International Conference of the IEEE Engineering in Medicine and Biology Society, pp. 371–374 (2008)
7. Fortun, D., Bouthemy, P., Kervrann, C.: Optical flow modeling and computation: a survey. Comput. Vis. Image Underst. 134, 1–21 (2015)
8. Gorgon, M., Tadeusiewicz, R.: Hardware-based image processing library for virtex FPGA. In: Proceedings of SPIE 4212 - Reconfigurable Technology: FPGAs for Computing and Applications II, pp. 1–10 (2000)
9. Kryjak, T., Gorgon, M.: Pipeline implementation of peer group filtering in FPGA. Comput. Inf. 31(4), 727–741 (2012)
10. Kryjak, T., Komorkiewicz, M., Gorgon, M.: Real-time background generation and foreground object segmentation for high-definition colour video stream in FPGA device. J. Real-Time Image Process. 9(1), 61–77 (2014)
11. Nath, S.K., Palaniappan, K.: Adaptive robust structure tensors for orientation estimation and image segmentation. In: Bebis, G., Boyle, R., Koracin, D., Parvin, B. (eds.) ISVC 2005. LNCS, vol. 3804, pp. 445–453. Springer, Heidelberg (2005)
12. OpenCV. http://opencv.org/. Accessed 17 April 2016
13. Palaniappan, K., Ersoy, I., Nath, S.K.: Moving object segmentation using the flux tensor for biological video microscopy. In: Ip, H.H.-S., Au, O.C., Leung, H., Sun, M.-T., Ma, W.-Y., Hu, S.-M. (eds.) PCM 2007. LNCS, vol. 4810, pp. 483–493. Springer, Heidelberg (2007)
14. Palaniappan, K., Ersoy, I., Seetharaman, G., Davis, S.R., Kumar, P., Rao, R.M., Linderman, R.: Parallel flux tensor analysis for efficient moving object detection. In: Proceedings of the 14th International Conference on Information Fusion (FUSION), pp. 1–8 (2011)
15. Thissell, W.R., Czajkowski, R., Schrenk, F., Selway, T., Ries, A.J., Patel, S., McDermott, P.L., Moten, R., Rudnicki, R., Seetharaman, G., Ersoy, I., Palaniappan, K.: A scalable architecture for operational FMV exploitation. In: 2015 IEEE International Conference on Computer Vision Workshop (ICCVW), pp. 1062–1070 (2015)
16. Wang, R., Bunyak, F., Seetharaman, G., Palaniappan, K.: Static and moving object detection using flux tensor with split gaussian models. In: 2014 IEEE Conference on Computer Vision and Pattern Recognition Workshops, Columbus, OH, pp. 420–424 (2014)

# Visual Target Tracking Using a Low-Cost Methodology Based on Visual Words

Andrzej Śluzek[✉], Aamna Alali, Amna Alzaabi, and Alia Aljasmi

Khalifa University, Abu Dhabi, UAE
andrzej.sluzek@kustar.ac.ae

**Abstract.** The paper discusses methodology and presents preliminary results of a low-cost method for visual tracking (in an exemplary setup consisting of a mobile agent, e.g. a drone, with an on-board that follows a mobile ground object randomly changing its location). In general, a well-known concept of keypoint-based image representation and matching has been applied. However, the proposed techniques have been simplified so that the future system can be prospectively installed on board of low-cost drones (or other similarly inexpensive agents). The main modifications include: (1) target localization based on statistical approximations, (2) simplified vocabulary building (and quantization of descriptors into visual words), and (3) a prospective use of dedicated hardware.

## 1 Introduction

Visual detection and (subsequently) tracking predefined objects in unstructured environments remains a difficult task with a large variety of proposed algorithms and techniques, e.g. [6,21]. In particular, it is stated in [21] that: *recently, automatic object detection has become quite successful to the degree that tracking of a single object may be achieved by performing detection in every frame.* The presented solution is based on this observation. We propose to use a typical *content-based visual information retrieval* (CBVIR) approach, where global and semi-local image similarities (i.e. similarities between either whole images of there fragments) are analyzed using the concept of keypoint matching.

Keypoint-based algorithms are a well-established tool in the retrieval of similar visual contents. However, for various retrieval objectives diversified requirements and limitations are imposed on the underlying keypoint-based methods. For example, CBVIR in large datasets and keypoint-based visual search/tracking are problems with rather opposite requirements, which can be summarized in three major differences.

1. In CBVIR, individually submitted query images are compared to huge collections of images, e.g. [7,22], while in visual detection & tracking tasks very small datasets (sometimes containing just a single image of the object of interest) are matched against continuously submitted queries (video-frames captured by a camera to a mobile agent).

© Springer International Publishing AG 2016
L.J. Chmielewski et al. (Eds.): ICCVG 2016, LNCS 9972, pp. 498–508, 2016.
DOI: 10.1007/978-3-319-46418-3_44

2. In visual tracking, image pre-processing (i.e. keypoint detection and description, quantization into visual words, etc.) are the bottleneck operations, with the computational costs exceeding complexity of the actual image matching and retrieval. Additionally, the available hardware/software resources might be limited (e.g. on-board controllers only) so that both steps should be performed at minimum costs. In typical CBVIR tasks, the costs of image pre-processing are considered negligible compared to the costs of matching and retrieval operations.
3. In CBVIR, query images are usually unrelated so that no redundancy between the subsequent queries can be assumed/exploited. In visual tracking, subsequent queries (video-frames) are highly correlated so that *recall* characteristics of individual frame processing can be compromised and more targeted matching (i.e. over selected image fragments only) can be attempted after the tracked object has been detected and localized.

Nevertheless, in typical keypoint-based applications the same basic functional components are used (e.g. [25]), i.e. (a) keypoint detection and description, (b) descriptor quantization into words from a visual vocabulary, (c) image matching by exploiting individual keypoint correspondences or distributions of visual words in both images, and (d) supplementary operations performed to verify validity of preliminarily established matches between keypoints and/or images.

In this paper, we discuss and preliminarily evaluate a keypoint-based scheme for target detection and tracking, in which we exploit the above-mentioned properties of visual search. In particular, we propose a low-cost method for building the visual vocabulary and, subsequently, similarly inexpensive quantization of keypoint descriptors into visual words. Additionally, the usage of hardware accelerators is discussed (based on solutions developed both in our group and externally). Finally, a simplified target localization method is proposed, which shares some principles with RANSAC, [5], but has lower computational costs. In this method, individual keypoint correspondences are not verified geometrically. Instead, the average coordinates within a cloud of keypoints matching the target keypoints are considered the target location.

As mentioned above, standard CBVIR mechanisms are used as the low-level tools of the proposed solution, i.e. we apply affine-invariants keypoint-detectors (either MSER, [10], or Harris-affine, [12]) combined with popular descriptors (SIFT, [9], and SURF, [1], are our choices). Descriptors are quantized into a relatively large vocabulary of $64K$ words. Details of the image pre-processing operations are described in Sect. 2.

If the following Sects. 3 and 4, details of the tracking algorithm and an overview of the feasibility-study implementation are, correspondingly, discussed. Section 5 concludes the paper.

## 2   Image Pre-processing

Generally, in any typical image matching task (either for retrieval, detection or tracking applications) keypoint detection and description are the fundamental tools. We decided to use affine-invariant detectors, because they better represent perspective distortion which unavoidably exist in tracking tasks in 3D world. Preliminarily, we use Harris-affine (*harraf*) detector, [12], but the ultimate choice is MSER detector, [10], which has only marginally lower performances (see [13]) but is also more suitable for hardware implementation. He have verified that even for simple targets represented by binary images, detected keypoints are numerous enough to ensure sufficient numbers of correspondences in detection and tracking tasks (see examples in Figs. 1 and 2).

A recently developed ASICS chip (based in the patent [18]) for MSER detection has the area of less than $2mm^2$, with only $7mW$ power, and it can process

**Fig. 1.** An exemplary logo image and *harraf* keypoints detected in it.

**Fig. 2.** An exemplary video-frame (containing the logo from Fig. 1) captured from a drone, and *harraf* keypoints detected in it.

frames faster than the frame rates of typical UAV-mounted cameras. It is also important that the output of this chip, i.e. elliptic approximations of MSER regions, can be directly used in the next processing stage, i.e. for keypoint description.

Two options have been selected for numerical keypoint representation. Both of them are well-proven and popular descriptors, namely SIFT (see [9]) and SURF (see [1]). SURF has been selected for the prospective future implementation because of its significantly lower computational complexity (and, therefore, can be more easily converted into a dedicated hardware, e.g. [2,4], which would be our ultimate objective).

Regardless the selected keypoint descriptor, the descriptor vectors are quantized into visual words. Published results (e.g. [14,22]) indicate that the recommended sizes of visual vocabularies for large-database visual search are in the range of millions, especially if *precision* is more important than *recall*. In our application, however, the image diversity is constrained, so that a smaller vocabulary size is proposed. Both SIFT and SURF descriptors are quantized into $64k$ words. I has been verified experimentally that such a number well compromises *recall* (which is needed to robustly detect targets) and *precision* (which determines confidence of detection and localization).

Since in small databases computational costs of the typical descriptor quantization into words (i.e. *near neighbor* or *approximate nearest neighbor*)are comparable to the costs of direct descriptor mathing (see Point (3) in Sect. 1)) a simpler quantization method has been adopted, which is a further simplification of [20].

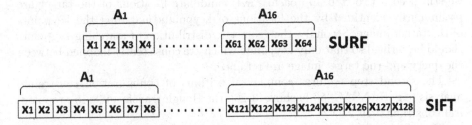

**Fig. 3.** Visualization of the descriptor vector partition into fields used for vocabulary building and word assignments.

Each SIFT or SURF vector is partitioned into 16 fields of, correspondingly, 8 or 4 elements $\{A_1, ..., A_{16}\}$, as shown in Fig. 3. The aggregated sums for the field are calculated as:

$$\text{SIFT } A_k = \sum_{i=1}^{8} x_{8 \times (k-1)+i}, \text{for } k = 1, ..., 16 \tag{1}$$

$$\text{SURF } A_k = \sum_{i=1}^{4} x_{4 \times (k-1)+i}, \text{for } k = 1, ..., 16 \tag{2}$$

The values of $A_k$ are averaged off-line over a huge number (over 500 million) of keypoints extracted from numerous images to be subsequently used for vocabulary building and word assignment.

Let $Avrg_k$ be those average values, and $AC_k$ be the aggregated sums calculated for the current keypoint descriptor according to Eqs. 1 and 2. Then the visual word $N$ assigned to this keypoint is given by

$$N = \sum_{k=1}^{16} p_k \times 2^k, \tag{3}$$

where $p_k = 1$ if $AC_k \geq Avrg_k$ and 0 otherwise.

Then, the descriptor quantization into words requires just a small number of additions and comparisons, which can be done instantaneously. In the next section algorithms, two keypoints are considered a match if they are assigned the same visual word.

## 3   Target Detection and Tracking

A keypoint-based target detection is actually a special case of *sub-image retrieval*. Generally, the objective of sub-image retrieval is to identify images which contain fragments visual similar to unspecified fragments of the query image (while the other fragments of both images can be completely different). In target detection, the objective is simplified because the database image(s) contain only the target.

Nevertheless, the major difficulties of sub-image retrieval remain, because we still need a two-step approach. First, candidate locations of the target are preliminarily identified by the locations of keypoints matching the keypoints of the target image. Secondly, the geometric distribution of matching keypoints should be verified so that only keypoints which are consistently mapped between the query and the target image are retained.

The second step requires complex algorithms of configuration constraints analysis (e.g. RANSAC [5], hashing [3,26], the Hough transform [8,15], topological constraints [19,23].

Therefore, we propose an extremely simplified algorithm where ALL keypoints of the current frame which match the target image are taken into account (without any geometric verification) to approximately localize the target, i.e. the estimated coordinates $[xt, yt]$ of the central part of the target are:

$$[xt, yt] = \frac{\sum_{j=1}^{M} [x_j, y_j]}{M}, \tag{4}$$

where $[x_j, y_j]$ are coordinates of the current frame keypoints matching the target image keypoints ($M$ indicates the total number of those keypoints).

Then, the error of the target localization by Eq. 4 can be statistically approximated as

$$[\Delta xt, \Delta yt] \approx \frac{m}{M-m} \left([Xc, Yc] - [\widetilde{xt}, \widetilde{yt}]\right), \tag{5}$$

where $m$ is the number of *false positive* keypoint matches, $[Xc, Yc]$ indicates the image center, and $[\widetilde{xt}, \widetilde{yt}]$ is the hypothetical localization obtained by excluding the *false positive* matches.

Thus, the error depends primarily on the background content (which affects the number of keypoint *false-positively* matching the target keypoints) so that performances (localization accuracy) of the applied methods can be assessed qualitative only as follows:

In case of frames which do not contain the target, the results of Eq. 4 are obviously random, so that we assume (based on experimental verification) the equation is applied only for frames with $M$ equal at least to 40 % of the total number of keypoints in the reference image of the target (e.g. Fig. 1) called *target keypoints*. Otherwise, no target detection is considered in the current frame at all.

Since, as highlighted in the next section, the objective is to keep the target as close as possible to the image center, the $([Xc, Yc] - [\widetilde{xt}, \widetilde{yt}])$ component of the error equation Eq. 5 is expected to be gradually reduced. The numbers of *false positive* keypoint matches $m$ are, however, less predictable (depending, obviously, on the background content). In typical cases they are outnumbered by *true positives*, but there might be frames with a majority a keypoint matches are *false-positives*. In the most pessimistic scenario (when the total number of matches exceeds 40 % of the total number of template keypoints, but none of them is a *true-positive*) the error reaches infinity, which is a mathematical representation of localizing a non-existing target. In the conducted experiments, however, no such case was found, and in typical frames containing the target the value of $m$ is sufficiently small to keep the localization error within tolerable limits.

The following Figs. 4, 5 and 6 and an exemplary video attached to the submission illustrate the above conclusions.

**Fig. 4.** Localization of a non-existing target. The total number of matching keypoints is only 10 % of the number of keypoints in the reference target image (Fig. 1).

## 4    Feasibility-Study Implementation

The proposed concept has been preliminarily implemented using a platform consisting of a drone with a mounted camera (images shown in this paper have been

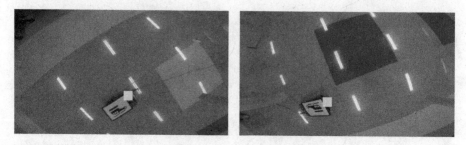

**Fig. 5.** Examples of less accurate localization. The target is smaller (i.e. relative fewer correct keypoint matches can be found) and/or it is further away from the image center.

**Fig. 6.** Examples of more accurate localization. The target is larger (i.e. more correct keypoint matches can be found) and/or it is closer to the image center.

mostly captured by this camera) and a small ground vehicles with a nearly-planar logo attached to its top. The task for the drone is to follow the ground vehicle so that the logo can be kept in the middle of the camera-captured video frames. Thus, the setup partially corresponds to the tasks specified for the Mohamed Bin Zayed International Robotics Challenge to be held in Abu Dhabi in 2017. Exemplary views of the indoor environment (visually challenging because of the illumination and reflection issues) are given in Fig. 7.

The camera-capture images are not processed on-board. Instead, they are transmitted to a ground station (a laptop) which performs all the calculations. Even though all the calculations are performed in Matlab (which can be hardly considered a software platform suitable for real-time applications) the rate of a few frames per second has been achieved. It depends on the complexity of

**Fig. 7.** Exemplary photos from the conducted experiments.

background (i.e. on the number of detected keypoints) and varies between 2 and 5 frames/second. In the ultimate system, the predicted performance (based on performances of the developed hardware and C++ implementation of the required operations) will be at least 15 frames/second.

Additionally, a PID controller has been designed which can be used to control the drone so that the system attempts to keep the target in the center of the video-frames. Details of the controller are not discussed in this paper. Nevertheless, in the presented solution (where only the approximate location of the target within the image is determined, but not the target's size) the controller can only track the target in 2D coordinates, i.e. lowering the drone to approach the target (or to land on it) is currently not possible.

As a future improvement, we plan to use the Kalman filter to estimate and track the target location smoothly, e.g. [16,17]. Currently, unusual changes of the background (or temporarily increased level of noise) can generate a noisy trajectory of the target positions and, correspondingly, jerky motions of the tracking drone.

The video attached to the paper shows the detection/tracking results (computed offline) superimposed on a video actually captured by a drone.

## 5    Concluding Remarks

The paper presents a simple (compared to typical *state-of-the-art* solutions) method of visual detection and tracking of an individual target (represented by a good-quality template image). The method performs target detection in every frame so that initialization or re-initialization of the tracked object is not needed. The detection process is based on CBVIR principles, namely on keypoint detection and matching.

Compared to typical CBVIR approaches, the following algorithmic simplifications have been introduced:

- Visual vocabulary building is base on simple aggregation of statistical properties of keypoint descriptors, so that the costs of descriptor quantization become negligibly small.
- In target detection/tracking, only the number of matching keypoints (and their coordinates) are taken into account. Thus, no geometric verification (which is a bottleneck of sub-image retrieval) is not used at all.

As an additional improvement, the usage of hardware accelerators for the low-level operations is anticipated and explained (although details of those hardware components are not discussed - they are developed by another team within our institution).

It has been verified that, under reasonable assumptions, such a method is a feasible solution. Nevertheless, several limitations still exist:

- Without the Kalman filter (which is planned for the next phase of the project) the estimated trajectory of the target is jerky (which might adversely affect the drone control algorithm).
- In case of background contents too similar to the target, the localization accuracy can be very poor and even tracking a non-existing target might be attempted.

Altogether, we consider the presented results an important step towards development of very-low-cost drones to be prospectively used in a number of tracking-related applications, e.g. delivery services to mobile, non-cooperative clients. Thus, the presented project is a part of the institutional preparations to the Mohamed Bin Zayed International Robotics Challenge (MBZIRC) to be held in 2017 [11]. The project was also presented at Think Science Fair 2016 [24].

# References

1. Bay, H., Ess, A., Tuytelaars, T., Gool, L.: Speeded-up robust features (SURF). Comput. Vis. Image Underst. **110**(3), 346–359 (2008)
2. Cai, S., Liu, L., Yin, S., Zhou, R., Zhang, W., Wei, S.: Optimization of speeded-up robust feature algorithm for hardware implementation. Sci. China Inf. Sci. **57**(4), 1–15 (2014)
3. Chum, O., Perdoch, M., Matas, J.: Geometric min-hashing: Finding a (thick) needle in a haystack. In: Proceedings of the IEEE Conference CVPR 2009, pp. 17–24 (2009)
4. Cornelis, N., Gool, L.V.: Fast scale invariant feature detection and matching on programmable graphics hardware. In: Proceedings of the IEEE Computer Vision and Pattern Recognition Workshops, CVPRW 2008, pp. 1–8. Anchorage (Alaska) (2008)

5. Fischler, M., Bolles, R.: Random sample consensus: a paradigm for model fitting with applications to image analysis and automated cartography. In: Proceedings of the 4th European Conference on Computer Vision (ECCV 1996), pp. 683–695. Cambridge (UK) (1996)

6. Hu, W., Tan, T., Wang, L., Maybank, S.: A survey on visual surveillance of object motion and behaviors. IEEE Trans. SMC Part C Appl. Rev. **34**(3), 334–352 (2004)

7. Jegou, H., Douze, M., Schmid, C.: Improving bag-of-features for large scale image search. Int. J. Comput. Vis. **87**(3), 316–336 (2010)

8. Lowe, D.G.: Object recognition from local scale-invariant features. In: Proceedings of the 7th IEEE International Conference on Computer Vision, vol. 2, pp. 1150–1157 (1999)

9. Lowe, D.G.: Distinctive image features from scale-invariant keypoints. Int. J. Comput. Vis. **60**(2), 91–110 (2004)

10. Matas, J., Chum, O., Urban, M., Pajdla, T.: Robust wide baseline stereo from maximally stable extremal regions. Image Vis. Comput. **22**, 761–767 (2004)

11. MBZIRC: http://www.mbzirc.com/. Accessed 20 Apr 2016

12. Mikolajczyk, K., Schmid, C.: Scale and affine invariant interest point detectors. Int. J. Comput. Vis. **60**, 63–86 (2004)

13. Mikolajczyk, K., Tuytelaars, T., Schmid, C., Zisserman, A., Matas, J., Schaffalitzky, F., Kadir, T., Gool, L.V.: A comparison of affine region detectors. Int. J. Comput. Vis. **65**, 43–72 (2005)

14. Nistér, D., Stewénius, H.: Scalable recognition with a vocabulary tree. In: Proceedings of the IEEE Conference on CVPR 2006, vol. 2, pp. 2161–2168 (2006)

15. Paradowski, M., Śluzek, A.: Local keypoints and global affine geometry: triangles and ellipses for image fragment matching. In: Kwaśnicka, H., Jain, L.C. (eds.) Innovations in Intelligent Image Analysis. SCI, vol. 339, pp. 195–224. Springer, Heidelberg (2011)

16. Pinho, R., Tavares, J.: Tracking features in image sequences with kalman filtering, global optimization, mahalanobis distance and a management model. Comput. Model. Eng. Sci. **46**(1), 51–75 (2009)

17. Pinho, R., Tavares, J., Correia, M.: A movement tracking management model with kalman filtering, global optimization techniques and mahalanobis distance. Lect. Ser. Comput. Comput. Sci. **4A**, 463–466 (2005)

18. Salahat, E., Saleh, H., Sluzek, A., Al-Qutayri, M., Mohammad, B., Elnaggar, M.: Architecture and method for real-time parallel detection and extraction of maximally stable extremal regions (msers). U.S. Patent 9311555, April 2016

19. Schmid, C., Mohr, R.: Object recognition using local characterization and semilocal constraints. Technical report, INRIA (1996)

20. Śluzek, A.: Visual detection of objects by mobile agents using cbvir techniques of low complexity. In: Proceedings of the FedCSIS 2015 (Annals of Computer Science and Information Systems), vol. 5, pp. 241–246 (1996)

21. Smeulders, A., Chu, D., Cucchiara, R., Calderara, S., Dehghan, A., Shah, M.: Visual tracking: An experimental survey. IEEE Trans. PAMI **36**(7), 1442–1468 (2014)

22. Stewénius, H., Gunderson, S., Pilet, J.: Size matters: Exhaustive geometric verification for image retrieval. In: Proceedings of the ECCV 2012, vol. II, pp. 674–687. Florence (2012)

23. Tell, D., Carlsson, S.: Combining appearance and topology for wide baseline matching. In: Heyden, A., Sparr, G., Nielsen, M., Johansen, P. (eds.) ECCV 2002, Part I. LNCS, vol. 2350, pp. 68–81. Springer, Heidelberg (2002)

24. Think-Science-Fair: http://www.thinkscience.ae/en/join/. Accessed 10 May 2016
25. Vedaldi, A., Zisserman, A.: http://www.robots.ox.ac.uk/vgg/practicals/instance-recognition/index.html. Accessed 20 Apr 2016
26. Wolfson, H., Rigoutsos, I.: Geometric hashing: An overview. IEEE Comp. Sci. Eng. **4**(4), 10–21 (1997)

# Reference Data Set for Accuracy Evaluation of Orientation Estimation Algorithms for Inertial Motion Capture Systems

Agnieszka Szczęsna[1(✉)], Przemysław Skurowski[1], Przemysław Pruszowski[1], Damian Pęszor[1], Marcin Paszkuta[1], and Konrad Wojciechowski[2]

[1] Institute of Informatics, The Silesian University of Technology, Gliwice, Poland
{Agnieszka.Szczesna,Przemyslaw.Skurowski,
Przemyslaw.Pruszowski,Damian.Peszor,Marcin.Paszkuta}@polsl.pl
[2] The Polish-Japanese Academy of Information Technology, Warsaw, Poland
Konrad.Wojciechowski@polsl.pl

**Abstract.** In this paper, we describe the freely available repository, RepoIMU, proposed for the needs of orientation estimation algorithm evaluation for inertial motion capture systems. Such algorithms fuse data from IMU sensors - accelerometer, magnetometer and gyroscope. Although such systems gain in popularity, the evaluation of methods used in their development is still not well covered in literature. In presented repository, unlike many others, signals from IMU sensors combined into easily interpretable kinematic chain are synchronized, and not only cropped to, reference orientation obtained from accurate optical motion capture system.

## 1 Introduction

Inertial Motion Capture (IMC) systems rely on orientation estimated on the basis of inertial measurement units (IMU). The orientations of the sensors are estimated by fusing a measurements of a gyroscope ($\omega$), an accelerometer ($a$), a magnetometer ($m$) and reference values such as Earth's gravity vector ($g$) and magnetic field vector ($mg$). The main idea is to combine high frequency angular rate information in a complementary manner with accelerometer and magnetometer data through the use of a sensor fusion algorithms such as complementary [1] or Kalman filters [2–7]. Example of application of such IMC system can be found in costume for out-door acquisition of human motion [8,9]. **RepoIMU**[1] repository is proposed for the needs of algorithm testing on the basis of the output of IMU sensors ($a$, $\omega$, $m$). Quaternion coded data from optical motion capture system (Vicon Nexus) are used as a reference. Although data are from two different systems, they were synchronized and properly cropped for the sake of user's convenience.

Features that differentiate **RepoIMU** from other databases include:

---

[1] http://zgwisk.aei.polsl.pl/index.php/en/research/projects/61-repoimu.

© Springer International Publishing AG 2016
L.J. Chmielewski et al. (Eds.): ICCVG 2016, LNCS 9972, pp. 509–520, 2016.
DOI: 10.1007/978-3-319-46418-3_45

- signals from IMU sensors (accelerometer, magnetometer, gyroscope) synchronized with reference orientation quaternion from optical motion capture system;
- data from two kinematic sets: wand (T-stick) and 3-segment pendulum;
- a full range of orientation angles' changes;
- recording with different acceleration values.

The need to create an IMC-oriented motion repository stems from the fact that numerous approaches for the sensor fusion and filtering were proposed whereas there is no common and comprehensive reference data set available. Such a data set would allow the researchers for the objective quality evaluation of their results and to compare those to results obtained through the use of other methods with no need for their reimplementation.

## 2    Inertial Motion Capture Repositories-Review

A similar repository was not found. Available data sets are created for navigation [10], autonomous driving [11] and activity recognition purposes [12–14], but there is a lack of data strictly appropriate for the purpose of evaluation of the orientation calculating algorithms. Most of them do not contain all the sensor signals; for example, in activity recognition datasets, we were able to find only acceleration output values, while gyroscope and magnetometer data was not present. Another problem, is lack of synchronization between sensors' signals and accurate reference orientation.

After careful review, we can point the following interesting proposals, however none of them meets all of our objectives.

1. *Reference Data Sets for Multisensor Pedestrian Navigation.*
   This reference data is intended for the analysis and verification of algorithms based on foot mounted inertial sensors (Xsens MTx-28A53G25) [10]. The data set provides measurements (accelerometer, magnetometer and gyroscope) from shoe mounted inertial sensor array, as well as synchronous data from the optical tracking system (Vicon Bonita 8 IR cameras) providing ground truth for location and orientation. The data was synchronized manually by finding the offset between optical and inertial system. The data is from experiments that rely on walking (mainly only from right shoe). While the reference system used is both well proven and accurate, the orientation do not vary over the whole angle range and thus might not be enough to test developed algorithm. It is also worth to note, that while manual synchronization might be enough for cropping, it certainly does not cover for stability of sampling frequency, which in practice can vary over time.
2. *Opportunity Activity Recognition Challenge Dataset.*
   The benchmarking Opportunity dataset contains rich sensor data of subjects performing activities at home. [13]. The sensors include, among others, 12 accelerometers and 7 inertial measurement units worn on the body. The dataset is labelled and comprises of activities ranging from simple motion

primitives and gestures to composite activities. From our point of view, data from IMU sensors is most important, this consists of output from accelerometer, magnetometer, gyroscope and also the orientation quaternion. In dataset, there is however no orientation reference data from different source than inertial system itself. While it can be used to train a system for activity recognition, it does not provide ground truth that could be used to validate tested algorithms and therefore is missing on a key element that our repository provides. Smaller but similar to Opportunity dataset for physical activity recognition is PAMAP2 [14]. Dataset is performed by subjects wearing 3 inertial measurement units.

3. *Multimodal Kinect-IMU Dataset.*
   The entire dataset is comprised of three smaller sets of data. First, the HCI set, contains a subject performing gestures of drawing geometrical symbols with his right hand. In the second set, named Fitness, subject performs six fitness exercises. The third and last set, named Background, contains primitive movements (translation, rotation) that can be useful in order to detect more complex activities. The acquisition setup used to create dataset is comprised of five Xsens inertial measurement units (one on each lower arm, one on each upper arm and one on back), five additional prototype sensors placed at various body parts and data obtained from Kinect sensor. The Kinect sensor provides 3D coordinates of 15 body joints, which is based on fitting a human skeleton to depth map obtained using structural lighting method. As such, the data is constrained by performance of Kinect system. While it can certainly be used in order to achieve a proper results, for example, developing a gesture recognition system, the coordinates obtained through Kinect are hardly stable and do not represent actual center of rotations in joints. Neither original depth map nor video data is included in the database, however the provided measurements are said to be resampled offline for the sake of synchronization. The exact method of synchronization is not presented.
   This dataset has been originally collected to investigate the possibility of translating activity recognition systems to another set of sensors [15]. The dataset may be also used for gesture spotting and continuous activity recognition. While the dataset is certainly worth using in development of Kinect-based solutions, the data is not appropriate for the testing of algorithms based on the output of IMU sensors, since Kinect data can hardly be used as ground truth, especially when the Kinect sensor used was since replaced with by it's developer with second edition, which improves the resolution.

## 3   RepoIMU Repository Organization

### 3.1   Data Collection Protocol

The **RepoIMU** repository contains data from two kinematic sets: wand and 3-segment pendulum. The repository contains a total of 95 recordings. The reference vectors for possible estimation filters are Earth gravity vector $g = [0, 0, -9.81]^T$ and magnetic north vector $mg = [\cos(\varphi^L) - \sin(\varphi^L)]^T$, where $\varphi^L$

is the geographical latitude angle. For the geographical position of the laboratory (geographic coordinates: 50.35363, 18.9148285), where measurements were done, we have $\varphi^L = 66^o = 1.1519$ rad.

**Wand.** Experiments were carried out using a wand (T-stick) made of plastic to which the Xsens sensor (type MTi-G-28 A53 G35) and Vicon markers were attached in accordance with the diagram in Fig. 1, where sensors X axis was approximately matched along the longer arm, Y axis along the shorter one and Z axis was perpendicular to the both arms.

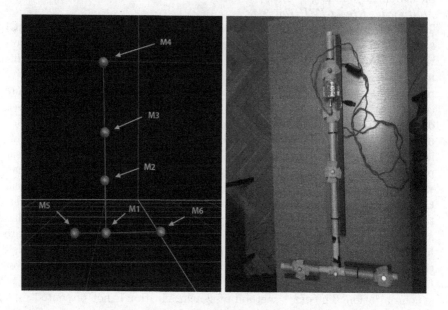

**Fig. 1.** Schema and photo of the T-stick.

Each experiment was recorded using Vicon system Nexus with a frequency of 100 Hz.

**Pendulum.** The pendulum was built with three segments connected by movable joints. An IMU sensor built at the *Silesian University of Technology, Department of Automatic Control and Robotics* [16] was fixed to each segment. These IMU sensors have been marked as IMU1, IMU2 and IMU3 (Fig. 2). Markers were also attached to the pendulum, each marked as R1, R2, W1, W2, W3, W4, W5 and W6.

The recorded movement is characterized by high values of acceleration amplitudes of about 20 $m/s^2$. The scenarios relied on forcing motion (Low or High swing) to a certain segment (upper 1st, middle 2nd or lowest 3rd segment) of the pendulum. Each experiment was recorded using Vicon system Nexus with a frequency of 100 Hz.

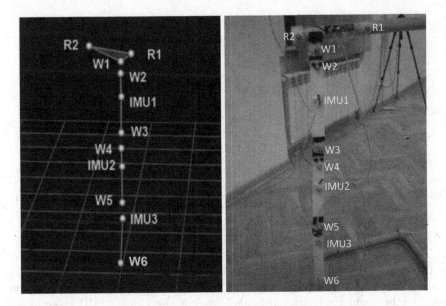

**Fig. 2.** Schema and photo of the pendulum.

## 3.2 Data Synchronization

Providing the orientation data from inertial devices along with the reference ones obtained with the optical system requires matching the tested one to the reference in the time domain. The need for synchronization is twofold - to identify corresponding time intervals (to match begin and end) and to compensate for the intermediate clock inconsistencies which are caused by technological limitations within motion capture system.

Alignment of two time series of the same sampling frequency is a well known and closely related to problem which is solved in various ways - naive shift estimation with the cross correlation, dynamic time warping (DTW), shotgun analysis (used in DNA sequence analysis) and others. Synchronization of orientation sequence to the IMU sensor values is a quite specific problem; the time of the matched sequence has to be fitted to reference one only, contrary to the common DTW based methods [17,18], which can be considered as a kind of denoising filter that might affect the final evaluation of results. Furthermore, the data are multivariates of slightly different, but related types, prone to noise with no common coordinate system which might be rotated to each other. The begin and end matching problem can be solved using dedicated hardware triggering device e.g. Xsens Awinda Station or Xsens Sync Station, although it is not available for the other vendors/technologies or a custom built IMC system. They also do not provide solution for the intermediate clock discrepancies where the time can be distorted in various ways (linear and nonlinear) - changes can even occur just temporarily resulting in such artefacts as shifts due to data transmission loss or lags, compression or expansion due to clock skew.

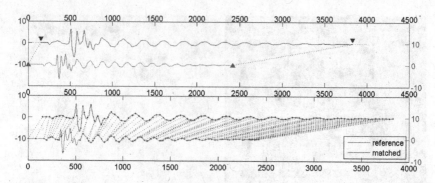

**Fig. 3.** Vicon data (matched) synchronization to IMU data (referenced) based on first PCA component (Pendulum, Test05, Trial 1, Segment 2).

To address problems presented above, we adopted the solution [19] based on two step alignment of blocks for the first component of principal component analysis defined for the quaternions (PCA-TSA). The key difference is that we matched the angular velocities instead of orientations – for the IMU we employed gyroscope values whereas for reference Vicon orientations we obtained it as a numerical first derivative of orientations. Since the angular velocities are not in circular domain – they add linearly, we could employ conventional linear PCA.

The synchronization pipeline can be summarized in a few key points:

1. First, ordinary PCA on angular velocities is employed, in order to aggregate as much of overall motion in a single dimension as possible, thanks to this all next steps are completely agnostic to the coordinates rotation.
2. Then, as first alignment, we match begins and ends using block matching and we trim protruding parts outside of the common time range.
3. Next, secondary alignment, spans a pool of nodal points in reference sequence and matches corresponding points using surrounding block matching with a sum of absolute difference.
4. Using known reference time for known nodal points, we interpolate time between the nodal points for the matched sequence.
5. Finding matched time series is done by interpolating matched sequence values using 1D linear interpolation - using phase of complex numbers as a representation for the orientation angles (Fig. 3).
6. The rotation between coordinate systems is identified as an average angular difference between the two sequences.

## 3.3   Data Structure

The repository is organized into separate files containing comma separated values (CSV). First row contains the headers, so the files are quite self explanatory. Acquired measures contain sensor values: timestamps in milliseconds (1 column); reference orientation quaternion (4 columns); accelerometer $[\frac{m}{s^2}]$ (3 columns);

gyroscope $[\frac{rad}{s}]$ (3 columns); magnetometer $[\mu T]$ (3 columns). If in the record there is more than one segment and sensor they are stored in separate files of the same structure, having common main name part and suffix with segment number. Remarks on the assumed notation:

- timestamp is relative in milliseconds from the beginning,
- the orientation quaternion first parameter is a rotation scalar (real part), the remainder is vector part of quaternion (imaginary part),
- accelerometer and magnetometer triplets of sensor measures are in XYZ order,
- gyroscope measurements are in XYZ convention as well (contrary to the most common *yaw-pitch-roll* which is ZYX order).

## 3.4    The Data

The wand data set comprises 2–3 trials of the following tests (Table 1):

1. Static test with empty reference orientation to get noise level in sensor;
2. Slow rotation about sensor X axis (longer arm);
3. Slow rotation about sensor Y axis (shorter arm);
4. Slow rotation about sensor Z axis (perpendicular to arms);
5. Fast rotation about sensor X axis (longer arm);
6. Fast rotation about sensor Y axis (shorter arm);
7. Fast rotation about sensor Z axis (perpendicular to arms);
8. Push (translation) along X sensor axis;
9. Push (translation) along Y sensor axis;
10. Push (translation) along Z sensor axis;
11. Free slow rotation about all three axes.

**Table 1.** Wand test set.

| Name | Trials | Sampling [Hz] | Duration [sec.] |
|------|--------|---------------|-----------------|
| Test01 | 1 | 100 | 181.53 |
| Test02 | 2 | 100 | 89.92, 89.99 |
| Test03 | 3 | 100 | 89.62, 88.52, 88.17 |
| Test04 | 3 | 100 | 88.42, 89.54, 89.99 |
| Test05 | 3 | 100 | 88.11, 89.99, 89.29 |
| Test06 | 2 | 100 | 87.31, 89.99 |
| Test07 | 3 | 100 | 89.99, 89.99, 89.99 |
| Test08 | 3 | 100 | 89.99, 89.99, 89.99 |
| Test09 | 3 | 100 | 89.99, 89.28, 89.99 |
| Test10 | 3 | 100 | 88.78, 87.91, 89.99 |
| Test11 | 3 | 100 | 89.94, 89.69, 89.66 |

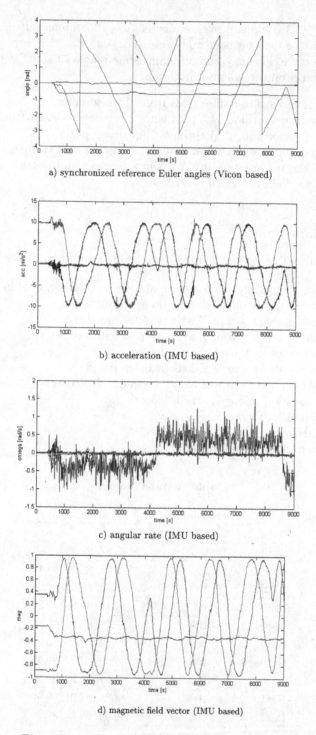

a) synchronized reference Euler angles (Vicon based)

b) acceleration (IMU based)

c) angular rate (IMU based)

d) magnetic field vector (IMU based)

**Fig. 4.** Repository data for T-stick - Test02, Trial2.

Repository data for Test02, slow rotation about sensor X axis are presented in Fig. 4.

The pendulum data set (Table 2) comprises of two long swinging sequences with repeated extortions on the first segment (Test02a and Test02b) and a set of sequences containing short swinging with initial extortion on different pendulum segments, two initial swings, with small and large inclination, are used:

1. Static test;
2. Long, multiple (9–10) iterations of damped pendulum swinging, extortions to the 1st segment;
3. Extorsion to the 3rd segment (end of kinematic chain) - large amplitude;
4. Extorsion to the 3rd segment (end of kinematic chain) - small amplitude;
5. Extorsion to the 2nd segment (middle of kinematic chain) - large amplitude;
6. Extorsion to the 2nd segment (middle of kinematic chain) - small amplitude;
7. Extorsion to the 1st segment (beginning of kinematic chain) - large amplitude;
8. Extorsion to the 1st segment (beginning of kinematic chain) - small amplitude.

**Table 2.** Pendulum test set.

| Name | Trials | Sampling [Hz] | Duration [sec.] |
| --- | --- | --- | --- |
| Test01a | 1 | 90 | 179.15 |
| Test01b | 1 | 166 | 79.237 |
| Test02a | 1 | 90 | 174.11 |
| Test02b | 1 | 90 | 216.71 |
| Test03 | 3 | 166 | 25.719, 27.117, 25.725 |
| Test04 | 3 | 166 | 18.579, 18.355, 22.331 |
| Test05 | 3 | 166 | 26.058, 27.639, 27.806 |
| Test06 | 3 | 166 | 19.647, 20.159, 21.951 |
| Test07 | 3 | 166 | 22.754, 25.252, 24.685 |
| Test08 | 3 | 166 | 21.668, 22.262, 22.683 |

## 3.5   Note on Potential Pitfall

The authors would like to precaution users not to be confused with rotated coordinate systems. The IMU sensor coordinate system and global coordinate system conform each-other just vaguely as the sensors were attached manually with no rigours control of the angle between axes of IMU and object – it is a common case for the body mounted sensors. When using IMU sensor measurements provided with this paper to compute orientations and comparing them to the orientations provided, it is necessary to cancel the rotation between coordinate systems. Matching IMU to global is preferred. One can achieve it using the quaternion representation, as it was proposed in [19] to find a systematic rotation between coordinate systems. First, we need to compute momentary differences of IMU $(Q_i)$ and reference $(Q_i^{ref})$ orientation quaternions as:

$$\Delta Q_i = Q_i \cdot \text{conj}(Q_i^{ref}),$$

then we need to compute mean difference $(\bar{\Delta Q})$ with QUTEM [20] procedure. Next, we need to rotate orientations from IMU coordinates to the reference with:

$$Q_i^{rot} = \text{conj}(\bar{\Delta Q}) \cdot Q_i.$$

## 4   Summary

The **RepoIMU** is an IMC oriented motion repository for testing orientation estimation algorithms for single segment and also for kinematic chain with use of kinematic constrains. Algorithms can be evaluated on the basis of reference orientation from accurate optical motion capture system.

The repository is an ongoing effort of a group of researchers involved in inertial motion acquisition. The described set of recordings will be subject to change - as new representative recordings are prepared, they will be included into the repository. The progress will be reported in future papers – one of examples is a recording of the same motion with IMU sensors from various vendors. Also, the motions of human skeleton kinematic chain, like leg or arm, are planned to be recorded in the near future. Partial data from the repository were already used in the following publications [6, 7, 19].

**Acknowledgement.** This work was supported by statute project (BK/263/RAU-2/2015) and Young Scientist Project (BKM/515/RAU-2/2015, task, Motion data acquisition for the purpose of interactive graphic applications) of the Silesian University of Technology, Institute of Informatics. This work was also partly conducted using the infrastructure supported by the POIG.02.03.01-24-099/13 grant: GCONiI - Upper-Silesian Center for Scientific Computation.

Data was recorded in *Human Motion Laboratory* (http://bytom.pja.edu.pl.) of Polish-Japanese Academy of Information Technology in Bytom, Poland

## References

1. Mahony, R., Hamel, T., Pflimlin, J.M.: Nonlinear complementary filters on the special orthogonal group. IEEE Trans. Autom. Control **53**(5), 1203–1218 (2008)
2. Yun, X., Bachmann, E.R.: Design, implementation, and experimental results of a quaternion-based kalman filter for human body motion tracking. IEEE Trans. Robot. **22**(6), 1216–1227 (2006)
3. Yun, X., Aparicio, C., Bachmann, E.R., McGhee, R.B.: Implementation and experimental results of a quaternion-based kalman filter for human body motion tracking. In: Proceedings of the 2005 IEEE International Conference on Robotics and Automation, ICRA, 18–22 April 2005, Barcelona, Spain, pp. 317–322 (2005)

4. Sabatini, A.M.: Quaternion-based extended kalman filter for determining orientation by inertial and magnetic sensing. IEEE Trans. Biomed. Eng. **53**(7), 1346–1356 (2006)

5. Sabatini, A.M.: Estimating three-dimensional orientation of human body parts by inertial/magnetic sensing. Sensors **11**(2), 1489–1525 (2011)

6. Słupik, J., Szczęsna, A., Polański, A.: Novel lightweight quaternion filter for determining orientation based on indications of gyroscope, magnetometer and accelerometer. In: Chmielewski, L.J., Kozera, R., Shin, B.-S., Wojciechowski, K. (eds.) ICCVG 2014. LNCS, vol. 8671, pp. 586–593. Springer, Heidelberg (2014)

7. Szczęsna, A., Pruszowski, P., Słupik, J., Pęszor, D., Polański, A.: Evaluation of improvement in orientation estimation through the use of the linear acceleration estimation in the body model. In: Gruca, A., Brachman, A., Kozielski, S., Czachórski, T. (eds.) Man–Machine Interactions 4. AISC, vol. 391, pp. 377–387. Springer, Heidelberg (2016). doi:10.1007/978-3-319-23437-3_32

8. Kulbacki, M., Koteras, R., Szczęsna, A., Daniec, K., Bieda, R., Słupik, J., Segen, J., Nawrat, A., Polański, A., Wojciechowski, K.: Scalable, wearable, unobtrusive sensor network for multimodal human monitoring with distributed control. In: Lacković, I. (ed.) 6th European Conference of the International Federation for Medical and Biological Engineering. IFMBE Proceedings, vol. 45, pp. 914–917. Springer, Heidelberg (2015)

9. Roetenberg, D., Luinge, H., Slycke, P.: Xsens MVN: full 6D of human motion tracking using miniature inertial sensors. Technical Report, Xsens Motion Technologies BV (2009)

10. Angermann, M., Robertson, P., Kemptner, T., Khide, M.: A high precision reference data set for pedestrian navigation using foot-mounted inertial sensors. In: 2010 International Conference on Indoor Positioning and Indoor Navigation (IPIN), pp. 1–6. IEEE (2010)

11. Geiger, A., Lenz, P., Stiller, C., Urtasun, R.: Vision meets robotics: The KITTI dataset. Int. J. Robot. Res. (IJRR) **32**(11), 1231–1237 (2013)

12. Zhang, M., Sawchuk, A.A.: USC-had: a daily activity dataset for ubiquitous activity recognition using wearable sensors. In: Proceedings of the 2012 ACM Conference on Ubiquitous Computing, pp. 1036–1043. ACM (2012)

13. Chavarriaga, R., Sagha, H., Calatroni, A., Digumarti, S.T., Tröster, G.: Millán, J.d.R., Roggen, D.: The opportunity challenge: A benchmark database for on-body sensor-based activity recognition. Pattern Recogn. Lett. **34**(15), 2033–2042 (2013)

14. Reiss, A., Stricker, D.: Creating and benchmarking a new dataset for physical activity monitoring. In: Proceedings of the 5th International Conference on PErvasive Technologies Related to Assistive Environments. ACM (2012). Article No. 40

15. Banos, O., Calatroni, A., Damas, M., Pomares, H., Rojas, I., Sagha, H., Millan, D.R., Tröster, G., Chavarriaga, R., Roggen, D., et al.: Kinect= IMU? learning mimo signal mappings to automatically translate activity recognition systems across sensor modalities. In: 2012 16th International Symposium on Wearable Computers (ISWC), pp. 92–99. IEEE (2012)

16. Jędrasiak, K., Daniec, K., Nawrat, A.: The low cost micro inertial measurement unit. In: 2013 8th IEEE Conference on Industrial Electronics and Applications (ICIEA), pp. 403–408. IEEE (2013)

17. Zhou, F., Torre, F.: Canonical time warping for alignment of human behavior. In: Advances in Neural Information Processing Systems, pp. 2286–2294 (2009)

18. Sessa, S., Zecca, M., Lin, Z., Bartolomeo, L., Ishii, H., Takanishi, A.: A methodology for the performance evaluation of inertial measurement units. J. Intell. Robot. Syst. **71**(2), 143–157 (2013)
19. Skurowski, P., Pruszowski, P., Pęszor, D.: Synchronization of motion sequences from different sources. In: AIP Conference Proceedings (ICNAAM 2015), vol. 1738, p. 180013 (2016)
20. Johnson, M.P.: Exploiting Quaternions to Support Expressive Interactive Character Motion. Ph.D. Thesis, MIT (2003)

# Security and Protection

# Selection of Relevant Filter Responses
# for Extraction of Latent Images
# from Protected Documents

Victor Fedoseev[1,2(✉)] and Elena Mishkina[1]

[1] Samara National Research University, Samara, Russia
vicanfed@gmail.com, truelentyay@gmail.com
[2] Image Processing Systems Institute, Russian Academy of Sciences, Samara, Russia

**Abstract.** In this paper we propose a method for automatic selection of relevant filter responses which are used for extraction of latent images from printed documents containing means of protection. In other words, it constitutes a part of the latent image extraction technique developed earlier, which is based on convolving an analyzing document image with an adaptively constructed Gabor filter bank. Previously selection a set of relevant filter responses was performed manually. Therefore the motivation of this paper is to design an automatic procedure for this stage. The proposed procedure consists in joint classification of both magnitude and phase parts of filter responses using specific feature sets. The results of experimental investigations showing high precision of the method are given.

## 1 Introduction

Latent, or hidden images is a popular means for protection of printed media such as documents, banknotes, financial securities etc. [6]. All of them usually contain a fine high-quality dot or line grid which variations in period or width represent different tones of color. Latent images are formed by area-specific variations of some parameters of the grid (frequency, direction, shift) which are chosen to be invisible by the human eye. Moreover, such elements are usually difficult for alteration. The problem of automatic extraction of latent images from printed documents is extremely important for authenticity checking, as well as for detection of secure communication within printed materials.

Recently in papers [7,8] we proposed a technique for latent image detection and extraction, which is based on convolving an analyzing image (which is a fragment of high-resolution document scanning result) with an adaptively constructed Gabor filter bank [5] and subsequent post-processing stages. These stages include selection and grouping of relevant responses, and multicomponent clustering, which uses the selected responses as feature fields.

The filter response selection stage is necessary because the constructed filter bank usually consists of filters which reference frequencies match all valuable textures detected in a particular image. At the same time, not all of the textures

© Springer International Publishing AG 2016
L.J. Chmielewski et al. (Eds.): ICCVG 2016, LNCS 9972, pp. 523–531, 2016.
DOI: 10.1007/978-3-319-46418-3_46

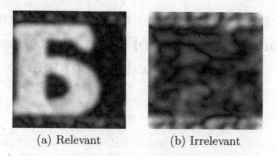

(a) Relevant                    (b) Irrelevant

**Fig. 1.** Two examples of magnitude responses

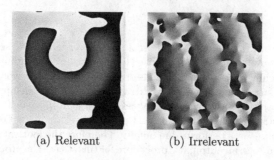

(a) Relevant                    (b) Irrelevant

**Fig. 2.** Two examples of phase responses

change their parameters in a considered part of the document. As our experiments shown, after the first filtering stage 10–20 responses are usually created, but only 1–2 of them, at the most − 4, are relevant (see Figs. 1 and 2 for examples of responses of different significance).

In the mentioned works [7,8] filter response selection was performed manually. In this paper we suggest an automatic procedure based on joint classification of both magnitude and phase parts of filter responses using specific feature sets. The article organized as follows. First of all in Sect. 1 we revise the filtering stage and discuss the properties of relevant and irrelevant responses. Next section presents the proposed method. After that different feature sets for image classification are considered. The final sections contain experimental results, discussion and conclusion.

## 2  Principles of Relevant Response Selection

As known [5], Gabor filter impulse response is a complex function:

$$h_{\omega_1^0,\omega_2^0}(n_1,n_2) = A\,exp\left(-\frac{n_1^2+n_2^2}{2\sigma^2}\right)\,exp\left[i\left(\omega_1^0 n_1 + \omega_2^0 n_2\right)\right], \qquad (1)$$

where $A \approx 1/\left(2\pi\sigma^2\right)$ is a factor, $\sigma$ is a scale parameter of the Gaussian weighting function of the filter, and $\omega_1^0, \omega_2^0$ are the reference frequencies. Therefore it is convenient to consider filtering results

$$g_{\omega_1^0,\omega_2^0}(n_1,n_2) = h_{\omega_1^0,\omega_2^0}(n_1,n_2) * * f(n_1,n_2), \tag{2}$$

as a pair of two components: a magnitude and a phase (in 2 $f(n_1,n_2)$ is a source image):

$$A_{\omega_1^0,\omega_2^0}(n_1,n_2) = \left| g_{\omega_1^0,\omega_2^0}(n_1,n_2) \right|, \tag{3}$$

$$\varphi_{\omega_1^0,\omega_2^0}(n_1,n_2) = Arg\left[ g_{\omega_1^0,\omega_2^0}(n_1,n_2) \right] - \omega_1^0 n_1 - \omega_2^0 n_2, \tag{4}$$

$$\left| \varphi_{\omega_1^0,\omega_2^0}(n_1,n_2) \right| \leq \pi.$$

Relevant magnitude components should have high values in those parts of image filled with a texture which reference frequency is close to the frequencies $\omega_1^0, \omega_2^0$ of the considered filter, and low values in all other parts of the image. In other words, they can be easily segmented into two clusters.

Consequently, we can perform such a clusterization to get some useful features for classification of filter responses. These features include means, standard deviations, pixel numbers for each cluster and so on. Then a particular magnitude image ought to be classified as irrelevant in the following cases:

- when its maximal value is quite low (it means that the analyzing frequency is week in the image);
- when cluster means are considerably similar and its deviations are high (it indicates homogeneity of the frequency component over the image);
- if number of pixels in one of two cluster is extremely low, etc.

It should be noticed that in last two cases a phase response corresponding to the analyzed magnitude response could be relevant, whereas it is impossible in the first case. The hard pieces of evidence against informativity of a given phase response are:

- high density of unclosed lines of phase discontinuity caused by its periodicity modulo $2\pi$ (points to the absence of any texture which frequency is close the filter frequency);
- considerable amount of nearly parallel lines of phase discontinuity (indicates a period mismatch between image texture and Gabor filter).

On the contrary, low density of phase discontinuity lines and their closeness reflect an accurate tuning of the Gabor filter to one of main harmonics the of the texture spectrum. It indicates that the filter response could be relevant. But final decision should be taken after a phase unwrapping stage which is converting a matrix of principal phase values $\varphi_{\omega_1^0,\omega_2^0}(n_1,n_2)$ to a matrix of absolute phase values $\Phi_{\omega_1^0,\omega_2^0}(n_1,n_2)$. It is obvious that absolute phase could help to understand better the nature of the analyzing signal so far as it is not limited by $\pm\pi$. To date, a lot of phase unwrapping methods are developed [1,3], which are mostly used for interferometry tasks.

For further analysis of the unwrapped phase $\Phi_{\omega_1^0,\omega_2^0}(n_1,n_2)$, the considered stages of clusterization, feature calculation and classification can also be carried out by a similar manner.

## 3    Method Description

Fig. 3 shows a flowchart of a method for one filter response significance check.

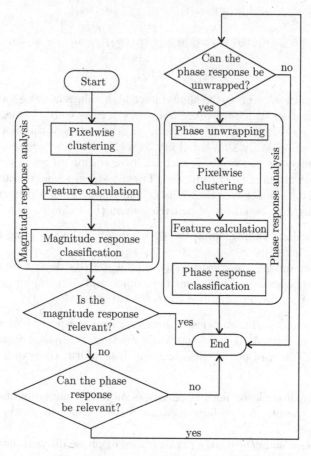

**Fig. 3.** A flowchart of the developed method

The method begins with analyzing a magnitude image, including the discussed stages of two-class clustering, feature calculation and classification. At this point, the response may be assigned to one of three possible classes: relevant, completely irrelevant, and irrelevant by magnitude while possible phase significance. First two cases lead to end of the processing, while the third one initiates analysis of a phase image.

At the beginning of work with the phase image it is tested whether or not it can be unwrapped. If no, the processing stops. Otherwise, phase is unwrapped, and then similar stages of two-class clustering, feature calculation and classification are applied to it. Herein there are two possible classes: relevant or not.

At the output, the procedure answers the question of the response significance (yes/no) and returns the relevant part of the complex response.

## 4    Features Used for Classification

As a clustering algorithm we decided to choose Expectation-Maximization (EM) algorithm for gaussian mixtures [2] due to two reasons. Firstly, a pixel value distribution for relevant responses usually looks like a mixture of two Gaussian distributions (see Fig. 4). Secondly, EM algorithm makes it possible to estimate parameters of each distribution.

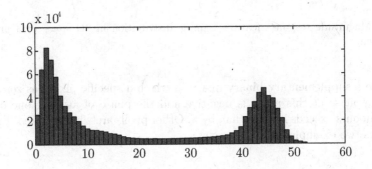

**Fig. 4.** The histogram of the image in Fig. 1a

Let us label the found clusters as 0 and 1. Then $K_0$ and $K_1$ are pixel numbers in each cluster, $m_0^{EM}$ and $m_1^{EM}$ are means, estimated by EM algorithm for mixture components (at that $m_0^{EM} \leq m_1^{EM}$), $\sigma_0^{EM}$ and $\sigma_1^{EM}$ are standard deviations estimated by the same manner. To these features we have added $\hat{m}_0$, $\hat{m}_1$, $\hat{\sigma}_0$ and $\hat{\sigma}_1$ which are sampling estimations of mean and deviation within cluster pixels, and also the lowest $v_{min}$ and highest $v_{max}$ magnitude values.

Besides that some derived features have been included into the entire feature vector: $\max\left(\sigma_0^{EM}, \sigma_1^{EM}\right)$, $\max\left(\hat{\sigma}_0, \hat{\sigma}_1\right)$, $\max\left(K_0, K_1\right)$ and $K_1/K_0$. The resulting vector is denoted as **f**.

For preliminary analysis of class separability using the chosen features, we calculated principal components (PCs) [4] by a specific labeled dataset containing the **f** values for several hundreds of test images and then projected the dataset onto a 3-dimensional space of first three PCs. A colored point cloud in Fig. 5 shows the result of this transformation. It is evident that three classes are separable in the given space.

The stage of phase response analysis is preceded by testing the possibility of its unwrapping. For that, we used a simple algorithm checking the presence of unclosed phase discontinuity lines which do not reach image boundaries. This algorithm consists of the following steps:

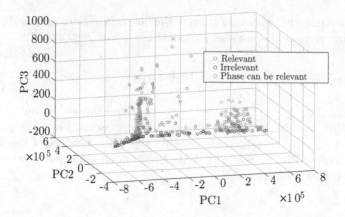

**Fig. 5.** Magnitude response features sample distribution in 3D space of 3 principal components

1. Make a supplementary binary image in which a specific pixel has zero value if the phase at this point is negative and the phase of at least one of its 4 neighbours exceeds it more than by $\pi$. Other pixels are white-colored. Figure 6 shows two examples of such images.

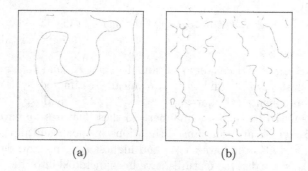

       (a)                       (b)

**Fig. 6.** Phase discontinuity lines for images in Fig. 2

**Fig. 7.** Unwrapped phase image from Fig. 2a

2. Find black pixels (not lying on the image border) which do not have two black nonadjacent neighbours (in 8-neighborhood). Such pixels are the ends of unclosed phase discontinuity lines.

If at least one such a pixel was detected, the phase response was accepted as irrelevant. Otherwise for further analysis the Constantini's phase unwrapping method [1] was employed (see Fig. 7).

To classify phase responses the same feature vector could be used, but obviously many of its components are unnecessary. That is why another, short vector of only two features was also tested in the experiments:

$$\mathbf{g} = \left(v_{\max} - v_{\min}, m_1^{EM} - m_0^{EM}\right). \tag{5}$$

## 5  Experimental Results

In the experiments there was used a support vector machines classifier (SVM) in linear and nonlinear (with radial basis kernel) forms [4]. For quality assessment we utilized $k$-fold cross-validation procedure with $K = 10$ with F-measure estimation. As noted above, $\mathbf{f}$ was tested for classification of magnitude responses,

**Table 1.** Numbers of images in the experimental set (class labels are: A - relevant, B - irrelevant, C - phase can be relevant)

| Image type | Magnitude responses | | | | Phase responses | | |
|---|---|---|---|---|---|---|---|
| | Classes | | | Sum | Classes | | Sum |
| | A | B | C | | A | B | |
| Scanned | 154 | 230 | 112 | 496 | 26 | 37 | 63 |
| Synthesized | 144 | 166 | 109 | 419 | 45 | 58 | 103 |

**Fig. 8.** Examples of magnitude images from training set. Three lines contain relevant responses, irrelevant responses and responses which phase part can be relevant consequently. In each line first four examples were obtained using scanned images, whereas last four using synthesized ones

**Fig. 9.** Examples of phase images from training set. Two lines contain relevant and irrelevant phase responses consequently. In both lines first four examples were obtained using scanned images, whereas last four using synthesized ones

and both vectors **f** and **g** were used for phase responses. In addition to the entire vector **f**, we also tested a vector made of its principal components, with automatic selection of its number by quality evaluation (for that, PCs were added to the tested vector one by one while F-measure was growing).

Training and test data for the experiments were collected in two ways: by scanning actual documents having security elements, and by artificial synthesis of images with latent insertions. The necessity of the second method is explained by the lack of a sufficient number of actual data for learning.

To avoid overfitting on irrelevant in real conditions data the set of phase responses was formed with taking into account the principal scheme of the processing procedure (Fig. 3). This means that we added into the set only those phase images which can be unwrapped and which corresponding magnitude responses are assigned to the third class.

Totally we have collected 915 amplitude response images and 166 phase response images (both having size of $1024 \times 1024$ pixels) for training and evaluating the classifiers. Table 1 shows particular amounts of the used filtered scanned and synthesized images for each class. Figures 8 and 9 show some of these images.

As a result, the better results have been achieved with the use of non-linear classifiers. The performance of magnitude response classifier has shown $F = 0.8410$. Its typical confusion matrix is presented in Table 2.

**Table 2.** Typical magnitude response classification confusion matrix

|        |   | Predicted |    |     |
|--------|---|-----------|----|-----|
|        |   | 1         | 2  | 3   |
| Actual | 1 | 71        | 1  | 18  |
|        | 2 | 0         | 57 | 10  |
|        | 3 | 5         | 12 | 102 |

**Table 3.** Typical phase response classification confusion matrix

Predicted

|  |  | 1 | 2 |
|---|---|---|---|
| Actual | 1 | 20 | 2 |
|  | 2 | 5 | 24 |

At phase classification, the vector g has shown itself the best, reaching $F = 0.9354$, while a classifier by the first PC made by the vector f has achieved only $F = 0.9037$. A typical confusion matrix for the best model is presented in Table 3.

# 6  Conclusion

In the paper a relevant Gabor filter response selection method have been proposed which can be used for detection of latent images in printed documents. The method analyzes both magnitude and phase components of filter responses and performs their sequential classification. The experiments have shown high accuracy of the used classifiers which indicates that the method can be integrated to existing document verification systems to speed up their processing (by excluding manual response image selection) without significant quality loss.

**Acknowledgements.** This work was supported by RFBR (project No. 15-07-05576) and the Russian Ministry of Education and Science by President's grant MK-4506.2015.9, state contract 2014/198 (code 2298) and Project 5-100.

# References

1. Costantini, M.: A novel phase unwrapping method based on network programming. IEEE Trans. Geosci. Remote Sens. **36**(3), 813–821 (1998)
2. Dempster, A.P., Laird, N.M., Rubin, D.B.: Maximum likelihood from incomplete data via the EM algorithm. J. R. Stat. Soc. Ser. B (Methodol.) **39**(1), 1–38 (1977)
3. Ghiglia, D.C., Pritt, M.D.: Two-Dimensional Phase Unwrapping: Theory, Algorithms, and Software, vol. 4. Wiley, New York (1998)
4. James, G., Witten, D., Hastie, T., Tibshirani, R.: An Introduction To Statistical Learning, vol. 112. Springer, New York (2013)
5. Movellan, J.R.: Tutorial on gabor filters. Open Source Document (2002)
6. van Renesse, R.L.: Hidden and scrambled images: a review. Proc. SPIE **4677**, 333–348 (2002)
7. Sergeyev, V., Fedoseev, V.: Extraction of latent images from printed media. In: Proceedings of SPIE, vol. 9875, pp. 98750X–98750X-5 (2015). http://dx.doi.org/10.1117/12.2228405
8. Sergeyev, V., Fedoseev, V.: A method for extracting watermarks from textured printed documents. Comput. Opt. **38**(4), 825–832 (2014)

# Comparing Images for Document Plagiarism Detection

Marcin Iwanowski[1]([⊠]), Arkadiusz Cacko[1], and Grzegorz Sarwas[2]

[1] Institute of Control and Industrial Electronics, Warsaw University of Technology,
ul. Koszykowa 75, 00-662 Warszawa, Poland
{marcin.iwanowski,arkadiusz.cacko}@ee.pw.edu.pl
[2] Lingaro Sp. z o.o., ul. PułAwska 99a, 02-595 Warszawa, Poland
grzegorz.sarwas@lingaro.com

**Abstract.** The paper presents results of research oriented towards an application of image processing methods into document comparisons in view of their application into plagiarism-detection systems. Among all image processing methods, the feature-point ones, thanks to their invariance to various image transforms, are best suited for computing image similarity. In the paper various combination of feature point detectors and descriptors are investigated as potential tool for finding similar images in document. The methods are tested on the database consisting of scientific papers containing 5 well known image processing test images. Also, an idea is presented in the paper how the algorithms computing the image similarity may extend the functionality of plagiarism detection systems.

## 1 Introduction

The paper is focused on the image processing methods applied to document plagiarism detection. It presents results of research oriented towards an application of image processing methods into detection of similar pictures in various documents. Also, an idea is discussed in the paper how the image similarity computing algorithms may extend the functionality of plagiarism detection systems.

An important property of contemporary documents is their multimodality. The pure-text documents are very rare nowadays, usually text is supported by pictures in printed materials and also by movies in digital ones. The document plagiarism detection methods are however focusing on text, rejecting other media during the similarity analysis. Due to multimedia properties of documents, such a rejection may negatively affect the effectiveness of the plagiarism detection methods. At first images themselves may be copyrighted and their reuse might be illegal. But even if they are used properly and legally, their presence in two documents being compared may indicate that the text content of one document is based on the content of another one. This may be useful if the main thoughts and ideas presented in one document are copied from another one, but formulated using other words, phrases or in different language.

© Springer International Publishing AG 2016
L.J. Chmielewski et al. (Eds.): ICCVG 2016, LNCS 9972, pp. 532–543, 2016.
DOI: 10.1007/978-3-319-46418-3_47

The comparison of two documents based on similarity of included pictures requires extraction of images from the documents and their consecutive matching. As soon as all images from the document has been processed, one can compute the similarity metric indicating the number of similar images from the document under study that are present in reference documents. Based on such metric one may find the most similar documents in the reference database (if there are any).

Among all image processing methods, the feature-point ones, thanks to their invariance to various image transforms, are best suited for computing image similarity. For a given image, they result in a set of descriptor vectors is produced, that contains numerical description of an image. In the paper various combination of feature point detectors and descriptors are investigated in view of their application to finding similar images in document. The methods are tested on the database consisting of scientific papers containing 5 well known image processing test images.

The paper is organized as follows. Section 2 an application of feature-point methods to finding similar images in documents is presented. In Sect. 3, the experiments are described. Section 4 is focused on the discussion on the application of image comparison into plagiarism-detection. Finally, Sect. 5 concludes the paper.

## 2   Finding Similar Images in Documents

When a human is comparing images, their *content* is usually taken into account. It implies that a recognition process must be performed in order to first understand the image content so that it may be compared with the content of an another image. Hopefully, in case of the search for the images that served as pictures illustrating a document, the content understanding process, due to its complexity, does not have to be performed. This is due to the fact that, in this particular case, not the content of the image is crucial, but the image itself. For example when looking at two documents about an Eiffel Tower one can expect that both are illustrated by pictures presenting the tower. However, as soon as two different (in terms of a point of view, position of a photograph etc.) pictures have been used, one can exclude a plagiarism. But if both documents are presenting the tower in a way that it looks exactly in the same way at both figures, we might suspect (although we cannot be sure) that a picture used in one document was copied from the other one.

To perform such content-based image comaprisons, various methods are in common use (see e.g. [5]). However, the feature-point methods are particularily well-suited to this purpose. It became very popular within the image processing community over the last 15 years. They allow to extract valuable features of the visual scene represented by descriptors of feature points pointing at meaningful places of the visual scene. The most important feature of feature points is their invariance to various image transformations. Most of the feature point methods are performed by means of two-step process consisting of feature point detector followed by extractor of the descriptor. In the current study several feature point detectors has been applied in combination with some descriptor extractors. In particular, the following detectors have been studied: Harris [6], SIFT [10], SURF [2], FAST [15], BRISK [9] and MSER [12,13]. In order to describe the surrounding of feature points extracted by means of above detectors, the following descriptors has been used: SURF [2], HoG [3], BRISK [9] and FREAK [1]. In addition, the simplest approach to describe the neighborhood of the feature point was used. It is based on simple storing the values of pixels within given, square neighborhood of the feature point. Such an approach will be referred to as *block* method.

To validate the applicability of the feature-point-based image comparison for picture plagiarism detecting we propose a framework based on the database of the scientific papers containing some pictures. In the computer vision scientific domain almost all papers include some pictures of processed images. Moreover, in this scientific domain, the authors very often use standard test images, widely recognized by the members of scientific community in the computer vision area. Reading the scientific papers in this domain one can often find those images, in most of cases both original and distorted by various image manipulations. Thanks to all above facts, papers on computer vision are characterized by relatively high (and higher than in other domains) level of image repeatability. From the legal point of view it is not a plagiarism (standard test images can be freely used by scientists in their research and consequently may be published in scientific papers), but from technical one the situation is exactly the same as if it would be a plagiarism. Due to that fact, based on it an good framework for testing the plagiarism image-based detection methods may be created.

**Fig. 1.** Five test (reference) images: B – 'baboon', C – 'cameraman', L – 'Lena', P – 'peppers', G – 'girl'.

In order to validate the image comparison methods, at first the *document database* has been prepared. It consist of 20 scientific papers, each of which contains at least one of the five computer vision test images: 'baboon', 'cameraman', 'Lena', 'peppers', 'girl', shown in Fig. 1. The *main image database* has been created by extracting from all those papers, the total number of 162 images. Among them are images that consist of single pictures (properly extracted) and also images that are mixtures of *multiple* figures (improperly extracted, not separated). In this paper we focus solely on the image comparison. In fact when investigating picture-driven comparison of documents, there is another important task that must be done – extraction of pictures from documents. Due however to space limitation this process of automatic image extraction from papers is out of scope of this paper. Moreover this task may be validated separately and independently from the image comparison.

Images published in the chosen papers were often altered by various image transforms. We made our tests considering the image manipulation that may be found in real documents. The images may suffer from change of contrast, lightness, resolution etc. They also may be modified by rotation by 90 deg., or sometimes by small angles (what could be caused by inaccurate placement of the document in the scanner). The latter modification was not observed in our database, but according to separate tests that has been done, such a image swinging of image do not influence much the feature point matching. Another image modification the was considered was the compression artefacts. But in the case of document picture plagiarism such an issue happens extremely rare. This is due to the fact that pictures in documents must be of possibly high quality and free from distortions, so pictures with high-compression rates are not used – the readability of the document with such pictures would dramatically go down.

Considering possible image manipulations, next two categories has been be introduced – *clear* images that are were not modified comparing to the original test image and *modified*. Both multiple and modified categories of images was intentionally kept in the database in order to obtain wide spectrum of possible situations that could happen in the real document analysis. The total number of images in particular categories is presented[1] in Table 1. In order to further validate the quality of detection, the images from papers was manually marked, as one of the reference images or none of them. Consequently, the ground-truth data became easily available for further experiments.

**Table 1.** Number of images of various categories in the main database

| Category | B | C | L | P | G | Other |
|----------|----|----|----|----|----|-------|
| Clear | 4 | 3 | 10 | 5 | 1 | |
| Modified | 6 | 6 | 32 | 2 | 0 | |
| Multiple | 8 | 0 | 32 | 5 | 0 | |
| **Total** | 18 | 9 | 74 | 12 | 1 | 62 |

Apart from the main image database, a separate, small, *reference image database* consisting of 'pure' versions of 5 test images has also been created (images from this database are shown in Fig. 1). Both image databases (main and reference) were used to test the feature point methods in view of their applicability to detects similar images in the database. Two group of experiments was performed. The first one was based on both databases. In this test the presence of images from the reference database in the main database was investigated. In such a way the presence of reference images in all papers was tested. The second group of tests were using exclusively the main database. In this case each paper were tested towards the remainder papers in the database in a figure-to-figure

---

[1] The total number of images in the last row of the Table 1 does not sum up to 162 (total number of images) because some multiple images consist of several test ones.

manner. In other words, all figures extracted from this paper were compared with all figures from other papers.

At first the comparison of the images is performed. In order to compare images, the feature point methods are applied. The point detection and description were separated in order to be able to validate various combinations of detectors and descriptors. The total number of combinations of 6 detectors and 5 descriptors was equal to 30. In order to find the similarity between two images, at first, feature points from each of them were extracted and their descriptors were computed. Next, for each point descriptor of the first image, the closest point descriptor in the second one is searched for. The distance is computed based on sum of absolute differences (SAD, Manhattan distance) metric. If the distance to this closest descriptor is lower than the given threshold $T$, point of the first image is matched with the point of the second one. If the distance is above the threshold, points remains unmatched. The same operation is performed for all point descriptors located in the second image, matching them with point descriptors of the first one. Finally point descriptors are considered as ultimately matched if and only if they are matched in both directions. The number of ultimately matched points is a similarity metric of two images.

The number of point belonging to the set of matched pixels may suggest image similarity (the higher number of such points, the more similar the images could be) but it does not imply it. It does not consider the relative position of points, just their surrounding characterized by point descriptors. Since possible modification of images in various documents may refer to geometric image transforms, like rescaling, rotation, etc., one should investigate whether there exist a geometric transform that converts one set of points into another one. This investigation is performed using the MSAC algorithm [16] which is a generalization of RANSAC algorithm [4]. In these algorithms at the beginning, from the original set of matched points $M$, the subset of corresponding points $M'$ is randomly selected. A size $M'$ depends on type of transformation which can be used between test images. Next, for each matched points, the symmetric transfer error for a planar transformation is calculated. This error is defined as sum of the squared distances between a point achieved after both side transformation. Then, if the error is smaller for the some threshold we define this pair as inlier. In RANSAC the score of this transformation is described by the number of inlier pairs. This kind of estimator is not the best, because we do not know anything about quality of inline pairs for the high value of threshold, therefore we use MSAC (M-estimator SAmple and Consensus), where outlier pairs have also fixed penalty value, but know how inliers are fitted. This algorithm is executed given number of times taking into consideration different $M'$ to select the transformation producing the smallest value of score function. As a result of this algorithm, from a set of matched points, a subset $M_g$ is extracted, that consists of pixels that – in addition to the first matching, based on descriptors – are geometrically matched (inlier). In order to validate the quality of image matching, the cardinality of the latter set of matched points $M_g$ are considered. The following condition is checked to validate if both images are similar or not (binary decision): $|M_g| > \lambda$, where $\lambda$ stands for the minimal number of geometrically matched points that implies the similarity of images (first condition).

Based on the above measures and assumptions, two groups of experiments were performed. During the first group tests all figures extracted as images from all papers are compared with 5 reference images (as shown in Fig. 1) using all combinations of detectors/descriptors. Thank to the fact that ground-truth was available (information on real similarity extracted manually during the database preparation process), the typical factors has been evaluated in an one-to-one manner (i.e. each image from reference database to each image from main one) as the number of images belonging to one of the below categories: *true-positives (TP)* are images from documents properly classified as belonging to their actual categories (e.g. 'peppers' from a document recognized as reference 'peppers' image), *true-negatives (TN)* are images properly classified as not belonging to another category than their actual (e.g. 'peppers' recognized as not belonging to reference 'babooon' class), *false-positives (FP)* are images improperly classified as belonging to given category (e.g. 'peppers' recognized as 'baboon'), *false-negatives (FN)* are images improperly classified as not belonging to their actual category (e.e. 'peppers' recognized as not belonging to the reference 'peppers' class).

Based on the above factors, three known coefficients has been finally computed in order to validate the image similarity computation method: precision $p$, recall $r$, and accuracy $a$ defined as, respectively:

$$p = \frac{TP}{TP+FP}, \; r = \frac{TP}{TP+FN}, \; a = \frac{TP+TN}{TP+TN+FP+FN} \tag{1}$$

Evaluation of detection and description methods has been performed using the above factors computed based on entire databases test for each combination detector-descriptor.

The second group of test was performed based on the same principles and assumptions, but this time the reference set of 5 test images was not used. Instead, figures from each document was compared with images from all other documents. The appropriate factors were thus evaluated for presence the reference image from document A in the document B.

## 3    Experiments

First series of tests was performed using the reference and main databases. The aim of this series was to the check the ability of finding reference images in documents. The task was to simulate the anti-plagiarism operation where the reference documents' images are given (and stored in the reference database). The images from the reference database was in this test confronted with pictures included in document (stored in the main database). The similarity of each image from the main image database and each of 5 images from the reference image database was computed. Based on these similarity measures, each picture was classified as belonging or not to reference classes. Owing to the fact that the ground-truth information was available, the classification results could have been validated. It was done by means of mentioned before measures of quality – precision, recall and accuracy. The results are presented in Table 2 – case 1. Several combinations of detector and descriptor produced valuable results, which may be estimated based on three factors. Those factors was calculated for each of 30 detector-descriptor pairs. Based on the values of three factors, each combination descriptor/detector was validated. Each of three factors reflects different aspect of the results.

The first measure – precision refers to (computed for the whole database) ratio of detected actually plagiarized images (detected plagiarized that are indeed plagiarized) to all detected as plagiarized. The lower (closer to 0) value of this ratio is the higher is the number of false charges of plagiarism. Since such accusations are quite a delicate matter, this factor should be as high as possible (close , or – in the best case – equal to 1). The recall measure is defined as the ration of detected actually plagiarized images to all plagiarized. This rate refers to the efficiency of the detector – the lower this rate is, the lower percentage of detected plagiarized images is. Low value of this factor results in low sensibility of the detector. The value of the last factor – accuracy is the rate of correct outputs of the classifier to the total number of compared images. The higher accuracy is, the better is the detector, and the number of mistakes – lower.

Based on above interpretation one can indicate as the best detector the SURF method. This detector may not be necessarily combined with SURF descriptor. Also BRISK and FREAK binary descriptors produced almost equally good

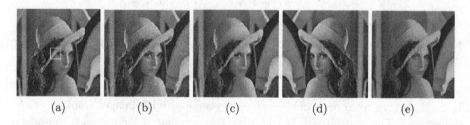

**Fig. 2.** Correctly identified Lena pictures: (a) with added frame, (b) with noise, (c) subsampled, (d) mirrored, (e) modified

**Fig. 3.** Example of errors: (a) poor quality, (b) mixture, (c) cropping

results. But the best results have been obtained with the proprietary SURF descriptor. This observation is important in view of the practical implementation of detectors and descriptors since these descriptors performs usually faster that SURF. Other combinations of detector-descriptors suffers from low either precision or recall factor which have huge influence on performance quality.

The second group of tests was based solely on the main database. Every paper was compared with each other by computing similarity between pictures included in those papers. The task was to determine whether an image of one paper is plagiarised version of another. To compute results of all detector-descriptor pairs and all articles images (in total number of 162) the number of about 0.5 million comparisons of images must have been computed. Similarly to the previous group of tests, for every such combination, precision, recall and accuracy metrics, was computed. The results are presented in Table 2 – case 2. Results are not as good as in first test because images in science articles often aren't in original versions. Therefore it's more difficult to compare i.e. two distorted Lenas. Again SURF detector with FRISK and SURF descriptors have the best results.

Different matching threshold for both tests $T$ values and vector distance metrics SAD and SSD were investigated (results of this experiments will not be presented in this paper). Finally, experiments have shown that the best results were achieved for sum of absolute difference (SAD) with $T = 15$ (result for this combination of parameters are presented in Table 2). Another conclusion was that major parameter affecting the quality of the classifier is a $\lambda$. Best results was for $\lambda = 5$ (which was presented in both tables). Higher values of $\lambda$ does not improve the results.

Apart from the analysis of the results at the highest level, considering above described factors, it has also been performed at lower level – similarity of particular images. Experiments carried-out confirmed the known advantages of feature-point methods. Owing to the fact that considered documents – papers on image processing methods – were on one hand repeatable (the same test image in various papers) but on the other test images were modified by various image processing methods, one can validate the robustness of those methods to such modifications. Feature-point methods are invariant to them. Examples of images proving such invariance are shown in Fig. 2. The figure presents various versions of the Lena image that were created by adding a small frame (a), introducing some noise (b), subsampling providing some blocks of pixels (c), mirroring (d) and strong non-linear filtering (e). All those variant of the original image (shown in Fig. 1) were properly classified as the Lena image using a majority of combinations of detector/descriptor (including the best one – SURF).

On the other hand some of images were improperly classified. Examples of such images are shown in Fig. 3. There were three major reasons of improper classification of images, that refer to consecutive pictures presented in Fig. 3: destruction of an image (considerably lower quality), mixture of the proper image with other ones, and cropping too small part of the original image. The source of the first and third reasons are detector and descriptor algorithms. The second one is related to the process of extraction of images from the document. The presence of images consisting of a mixture of multiple images decreases the effectiveness of the image plagiarism detection methods.

**Table 2.** Test results for $T = 15$, $\lambda = 5$, SAD – case 1: presence of images from the reference database in the main database , case 2 – only images from the main database, case 3 – presence of images from the reference database in the main database without mixtures of images. The names of methods has been abbreviated to their first two letters

| Det. | Desc. | Case 1 | | | Case 2 | | | Case 3 | | |
|------|-------|------|------|------|------|------|------|------|------|------|
| | | $p$ | $r$ | $a$ | $p$ | $r$ | $a$ | $p$ | $r$ | $a$ |
| Fa | Bl | 0.97 | 0.33 | 0.91 | 0.97 | 0.33 | 0.87 | 0,96 | 0,42 | 0,94 |
| | Br | 1 | 0.13 | 0.89 | 0.99 | 0.15 | 0.84 | 1 | 0,13 | 0,91 |
| | Fr | 1 | 0.23 | 0.9 | 0.99 | 0.25 | 0.85 | 1 | 0,25 | 0,92 |
| | Ho | 0.8 | 0.31 | 0.9 | 0.93 | 0.33 | 0.86 | 0,78 | 0,39 | 0,92 |
| | Su | 0.86 | 0.29 | 0.9 | 0.94 | 0.33 | 0.87 | 0,82 | 0,36 | 0,92 |
| Ms | Bl | 0.22 | 0.43 | 0.72 | 0.36 | 0.35 | 0.75 | 0,2 | 0,55 | 0,72 |
| | Br | 1 | 0.2 | 0.89 | 0.98 | 0.22 | 0.85 | 1 | 0,23 | 0,92 |
| | Fr | 0.76 | 0.62 | 0.92 | 0.84 | 0.43 | 0.87 | 0,75 | 0,8 | 0,95 |
| | Ho | 0.26 | 0.45 | 0.76 | 0.39 | 0.42 | 0.76 | 0,24 | 0,52 | 0,78 |
| | Su | 0.44 | 0.74 | 0.84 | 0.54 | 0.68 | 0.83 | 0,42 | 0,92 | 0,86 |
| Su | Bl | 0.97 | 0.3 | 0.91 | 0.99 | 0.31 | 0.86 | 0,96 | 0,36 | 0,93 |
| | Br | 1 | 0.71 | 0.96 | 0.99 | 0.48 | 0.9 | 1 | 0,88 | 0,99 |
| | Fr | 1 | 0.73 | 0.96 | 0.99 | 0.61 | 0.92 | 1 | 0,91 | 0,99 |
| | Ho | 1 | 0.39 | 0.92 | 0.99 | 0.38 | 0.88 | 1 | 0,5 | 0,95 |
| | Su | 1 | 0.76 | 0.97 | 0.99 | 0.65 | 0.93 | 1 | 0,91 | 0,99 |
| Br | Bl | 1 | 0.2 | 0.89 | 0.97 | 0.1 | 0.83 | 1 | 0,25 | 0,92 |
| | Br | 1 | 0.07 | 0.88 | 0.9 | 0.02 | 0.81 | 1 | 0,09 | 0,9 |
| | Fr | 1 | 0.11 | 0.88 | 0.95 | 0.03 | 0.81 | 1 | 0,16 | 0,91 |
| | Ho | 1 | 0.22 | 0.9 | 0.97 | 0.13 | 0.83 | 1 | 0,28 | 0,92 |
| | Su | 1 | 0.26 | 0.9 | 0.97 | 0.14 | 0.83 | 1 | 0,34 | 0,93 |
| Ha | Bl | 0.95 | 0.39 | 0.92 | 0.98 | 0.34 | 0.87 | 0,94 | 0,52 | 0,95 |
| | Br | 1 | 0.16 | 0.89 | 0.99 | 0.18 | 0.84 | 1 | 0,2 | 0,92 |
| | Fr | 1 | 0.4 | 0.92 | 0.99 | 0.29 | 0.86 | 1 | 0,55 | 0,95 |
| | Ho | 1 | 0.38 | 0.92 | 0.98 | 0.33 | 0.87 | 1 | 0,5 | 0,95 |
| | Su | 1 | 0.31 | 0.91 | 0.97 | 0.32 | 0.87 | 1 | 0,44 | 0,94 |
| Si | Bl | 0.95 | 0.2 | 0.89 | 0.99 | 0.26 | 0.86 | 0,94 | 0,25 | 0,92 |
| | Br | 1 | 0.21 | 0.9 | 0.99 | 0.25 | 0.85 | 1 | 0,23 | 0,92 |
| | Fr | 1 | 0.2 | 0.89 | 0.99 | 0.28 | 0.86 | 1 | 0,22 | 0,92 |
| | Ho | 1 | 0.27 | 0.9 | 0.99 | 0.3 | 0.86 | 1 | 0,34 | 0,93 |
| | Su | 1 | 0.25 | 0.9 | 0.99 | 0.36 | 0.87 | 1 | 0,33 | 0,9 |

In order to confirm the above statement yet another experiment was conducted. It was done in according to the same rules as the first test (reference vs. main databases), but, this time, the mixtures of images was removed from the database. Results are presented in Table 2 – case 3. When comparing the number with those presented in Table 2 – case 1, is became clear how important is the process of extraction images from the documents. All measures: precision, recall and accuracy for almost all combinations of detector and descriptor are closer to the ideal value of 1.

In order to perform the comparative tests, the MATLAB computing environment was used[2]. Tests was performed using different combinations of detector and descriptor methods. Every feature point detector and descriptor method was executed with parameters fine-tuned to reflect the diersity of the set of images from the databases.

## 4   Application to Plagiarism Detection

The research carried-out proved that similar images may be successfully identified in documents. As the second group of tests have shown, a document may be investigated in view of a presence of images published in this document in other documents present in a database. This property allows us to formulate the idea of a system that supports classic text-based plagiarism [7,8,11,14] and extends it by adding image plagiarism detection functionality.

The structure of image-based plagiarism detection system could consist of two main activity blocks responsible for extending of the source documents database and for comparing documents. The first activity is divided into the following phases (new source document makes the input):

1. Extract all figures from the document and store them separately as images
2. Process extracted images one-by-one by extracting from each the set of feature points
3. Store sets of feature points along with link to appropriate image and document in the database.

Such step should be performed for each document added to the source database. The second activity, document comparison, consist in turn of the following steps:

1. Extract all figures from the document and store them separately as images
2. Process extracted images one-by-one by extracting from each the set of feature points
3. Compare each set of feature points (from every image from the document) with all sets of feature point in the databases
4. Based on image comparisons compute the similarity metrics between the document under study and all the document in the source database
5. Send to the output all the document all the source documents for which the value of a metric is higher than a given threshold.

The document similarity metrics is based on the similarities of images included in two compared documents. For example, it may equal to the number of similar images, or, alternatively, to the percentage of such images in the total number of images included in the document.

---

[2] The implementation of all but one detectors and descriptors was based on the appropriate procedures included in *MATLAB Computer Vision Systems Toolbox*. Only the code for the SIFT method was taken from the *VLfeat* external MATLAB toolbox.

# 5   Conclusions and Future Work

The paper was focused on the comparison of images and its possible application to plagiarism-detection systems. The methods based on feature-points detection was investigated. Some of the most popular among them was tested and compared in order to validate the possibility of their application to comparison of images from documents. To perform necessary tests, images that served as pictures in scientific papers related to image processing was chosen and included in the main test database. This database along with the second, reference one was used to test combinations of most popular feature point detectors and descriptors. Finally, based on the test results, the SURF detector [2] appeared as the most effective one.

The above results of tests proved that the feature-point image comparison methods may be successfully applied to detect similar images in various documents. Based on this conclusion the proposal for image-based document plagiarism detection module was discussed. Such a module may improve the results of text-based document comparison methods, the arguments supporting this statement was also pointed out in the paper.

The possible directions of the future research may be focused on considering the specificity of various types of figures in documents. The experiments in this work was focused on classic test images, produced from real photographs, which does not reflect the spectrum of possible types of figures that could be found in documents. Other kinds of possible figure types are: charts, drawings, and other artificially generated graphical content. In order to compare such figures feature-point methods could not be sufficient, or even appropriate. To solve such cases other image processing approaches might be useful.

The obtained results that are promising in view of the application of image similarity computations into document plagiarism detection. Also, above mentioned area of further research are prospective. Undertaking this research may lead to creation of an effective, fully-functional image-similarity-based module supporting the main text-based system for document plagiarism detection.

**Acknowledgments.** This work was partially supported by the European Union within the European Regional Development Fund. The authors would like also to thank prof. Marek Kowalski for support and fruitful discussions on the plagiarism detection topic.

# References

1. Alahi, A., Ortiz, R., Vandergheynst, P.: FREAK: fast retina keypoint. In: 2012 IEEE Conference on Computer Vision and Pattern Recognition (CVPR), pp. 510–517 (2012)
2. Bay, H., Ess, A., Tuytelaars, T., Van Gool, L.: Speeded-up robust features (SURF). Comput. Vis. Image Underst. **110**(3), 346–359 (2008). Similarity Matching in Computer Vision and Multimedia

3. Dalal, N., Triggs, B.: Histograms of oriented gradients for human detection. In: IEEE Computer Society Conference on Computer Vision and Pattern Recognition, CVPR 2005, vol. 1, pp. 886–893 (2005)

4. Fischler, M.A., Bolles, R.C.: Random sample consensus: a paradigm for model fitting with applications to image analysis and automated cartography. Commun. ACM 24(6), 381–395 (1981)

5. Forczmanski, P., Frejlichowski, D.: Strategies of shape and color fusions for content based image retrieval. In: Kurzynski, M., Puchala, E., Wozniak, M., Zolnierek, A. (eds.) Computer Recognition Systems 2. Advances in Intelligent and Soft Computing, vol. 45, pp. 3–10. Springer, Heidelberg (2007)

6. Harris, C., Stephens, M.: A combined corner and edge detector. In: Proceedings of Fourth Alvey Vision Conference, pp. 147–151 (1988)

7. Irving, R.W.: Plagiarism and collusion detection using the Smith-Waterman algorithm, University of Glasgow, p. 9 (2004)

8. Kang, N.O., Gelbukh, A., Han, S.Y.: PPChecker: plagiarism pattern checker in document copy detection. In: Sojka, P., Kopeček, I., Pala, K. (eds.) TSD 2006. LNCS (LNAI), vol. 4188, pp. 661–667. Springer, Heidelberg (2006). doi:10.1007/11846406_83

9. Leutenegger, S., Chli, M., Siegwart, R.: BRISK: binary robust invariant scalable keypoints. In: 2011 IEEE International Conference on Computer Vision (ICCV), pp. 2548–2555 (2011)

10. Lowe, D.: Object recognition from local scale-invariant features. In: The Proceedings of the Seventh IEEE International Conference on Computer Vision, vol. 2, pp. 1150–1157 (1999)

11. Lyon, C., Barrett, R., Malcolm, J.: A theoretical basis to the automated detection of copying between texts, and its practical implementation in the ferret plagiarism and collusion detector. Prevention, Practice and Policies, Plagiarism (2004)

12. Matas, J., Chum, O., Urban, M., Pajdla, T.: Robust wide baseline stereo from maximally stable extremal regions. In: Proceedings of British Machine Vision Conference (2002)

13. Nistér, D., Stewénius, H.: Linear time maximally stable extremal regions. In: Forsyth, D., Torr, P., Zisserman, A. (eds.) ECCV 2008. LNCS, vol. 5303, pp. 183–196. Springer, Heidelberg (2008). doi:10.1007/978-3-540-88688-4_14

14. Parker, A., et al.: Computer algorithms for plagiarism detection. IEEE Trans. Educ. 32(2), 94–99 (1989)

15. Rosten, E., Drummond, T.: Fusing points and lines for high performance tracking. In: IEEE International Conference on Computer Vision, vol. 2, pp. 1508–1511 (2005)

16. Torr, P., Zisserman, A.: MLESAC: a new robust estimator with application to estimating image geometry. Comput. Vis. Image Underst. 78(1), 138–156 (2000)

# Remote Sensing Data Copy-Move Forgery Protection Algorithm

Andrey Kuznetsov[✉]

Samara National Research University, Samara, Russia
kuznetsoff.andrey@gmail.com

**Abstract.** Copy-move attack is one of the most popular digital image forgery attacks. The main problem is that existing studies do not provide high detection accuracy with low computational complexity. High complexity of existing feature based solutions makes impossible to use them for large remote sensing snapshots analysis. In this paper there is proposed a copy-move detection algorithm based on perceptual hash value calculation. Hash values are evaluated using the result of binary gradient contours computation. The proposed solution showed high detection accuracy and low computational complexity for copy-move detection in remote sensing data.

## 1 Introduction

Nowadays digital images play an important role in information retrieval. Digital photos are used as evidence for events, satellite images show territory state, etc. Remote sensing data is a special type of digital images. In a radical departure from ordinary images, satellite snapshots have larger size ($5000 \times 5000$ pixels and more). This fact does not allow to use ordinary image processing methods. New versions of existing methods are developed to be able to process large amount of data. One of the most popular digital image processing task is image security. Speaking about remote sensing data, they should be secured well from image data hiding and altering.

The most frequently used forgery method is copy and paste the local area of the same image. These attacks are called copy-move, and copied image regions are called duplicates. Copy-move procedure consists of three main steps: copying some image fragment from one place of an image, transforming it and pasting to the place of the same image that needs to be hidden by some reason. There is a number of works [1–3], where copy-move detection algorithms are proposed: the common step of these methods is development of features that are invariant to various changes of duplicates (contrast, compression, noise, geometry, etc.) and are calculated in an overlapping window mode to reduce computational complexity. These methods can be easily used for ordinary digital images, but not for remote sensing data. In [4,5] another approach to copy-move detection is proposed – it is based on perceptual hash values calculation in a sliding window mode. The main disadvantage of this solution is that it can not be used to

© Springer International Publishing AG 2016
L.J. Chmielewski et al. (Eds.): ICCVG 2016, LNCS 9972, pp. 544–552, 2016.
DOI: 10.1007/978-3-319-46418-3_48

detect transformed duplicates. At the same time it has very low computational complexity and average satellite image (10000 × 10000) analysis time equals to 12 s [5]. The analysis time changes linearly with image size increase because hash values are calculated recursively. In this paper it is proposed a combination of feature based solution with hash values calculation. The developed algorithm allows to detect transformed duplicates in remote sensing data very fast. The main problem is a narrow range of transformation parameters, so investigations in this field will be continued.

This paper consists of five main sections. Section 2 contains a brief outline of binary gradient contours (BGC). They are calculated on the basis of initial image pixels and form a code map of it. BGC code map generation is a preprocessing step of the proposed algorithm. Section 3 is devoted to the description of preceptual hash function used in the algorithm. Section 4 is devoted to the proposed copy-move detection algorithm. Section 5 presents results of conducted experiments and comparison of our approach with existing solutions [1,6]. In Sect. 6 conclusion and recommendations for using of the developed algorithm are presented.

## 2  Binary Gradient Contours

BGC were proposed by Fernndez et al. [7]. BGC belong to the class of descriptors based on pairwise comparison of pixel values selected in a clockwise order from a neighborhood using some pre-defined route. Obviously the number of different BGC construction methods depends on the number of different routes that can be created for a given neighborhood. Three ways of BGC calculation proposed in [7] will be denoted later as $BGC_1$, $BGC_2$ and $BGC_3$.

Let $f$ be an analyzed image. Its pixels are defined as $f_i = f(x_i, y_i)$, where $x_i, y_i$ are pixel coordinates. The first two methods use one route for the 3 × 3 neighborhood of the central pixel $(x_c, y_c)$ to generate the code. The first method is described by the following sequence {0,1,2,3,4,5,6,7,0}, where '0' denotes to the index of the upper left pixel in the neighborhood. In this case the BGC code is calculated as follows:

$$BGC_1(x_c, y_c) = \sum_{i=0}^{7} I(f_i - f_{(i+1) \bmod 8} \geq 0) \cdot 2^i. \qquad (1)$$

The second method is based on the route of the form {0,3,6,1,4,7,2,5,0}. In this case the BGC code is calculated as follows:

$$BGC_2(x_c, y_c) = \sum_{i=0}^{7} I(f_{3i \bmod 8} - f_{3(i+1) \bmod 8} \geq 0) \cdot 2^i. \qquad (2)$$

Both methods degenerate $2^8 - 1$ different code values.

The third method of BGC code calculation is different from the previous ones. It is based on two different routes usage {1,3,7,5,1} and {0,2,4,6,0}. Every route usage leads to $2^4 - 1$ different codes and the whole BGC code is calculated as follows:

$$BGC_3(x_c, y_c) = (2^4 - 1) \cdot \sum_{i=0}^{3} I(f_{2i} - f_{2(i+1) \bmod 8} \geq 0) \cdot 2^i$$

$$+ \sum_{i=0}^{3} I(f_{2i+1} - f_{(2i+3) \bmod 8} \geq 0) \cdot 2^i - 2^4. \tag{3}$$

## 3  Perceptual Hash Calculation

There are exist two types of hash functions: cryptographic and perceptual. Hash functions of the first type rely on the effect of a small change in input value creating a large change in output value. Perceptual hash values are close if input values are similar. In this work the perceptual hash function based on Rabin-Karp rolling hash is used.

In the proposed solution hash values are calculated in a sliding window with size $a \times b$. A hash value for an image fragment at position $(m, n)$ of the sliding window will be calculated as a 2D generalization of the Rabin-Karp rolling hash [5]:

$$H(m, n, f) \equiv f(m, n) \cdot 2^{q(ab-1)} + f(m, n+1) \cdot 2^{q(ab-2)} + \ldots$$

$$\ldots + f(m, n+b-1) \cdot 2^{q(ab-b)} + \ldots + f(m+a-1, n) \cdot 2^{q(b-1)} \tag{4}$$

$$+ f(m+a-1, n+1) \cdot 2^{q(ab-1)} + \ldots + f(m+a-1, n+b-1) \cdot 2^0,$$

where $q$ defines the number of bits used to store a pixel value.

Storing such hash values in RAM of an ordinary workstation is difficult because of the following problems:

– no standard numeric types for operating with large numbers;
– it is unavailable to allocate memory to store hash table of required size (hash table usage will be described in Sect. 4).

Further solution is used to consider restrictions mentioned above. According to Chinese remainder theorem R modular representations of (4) can be defined in the following way:

$$H_r(m, n, f) \equiv H(m, n, f) \bmod b_r, \tag{5}$$

where $b_r$ are coprime numbers. Moreover a system of R functions (5) guarantees one-to-one correspondence of an analyzed image fragment to a hash value. This fact allows to use any of remainders (5) as a hash value. Further $b_r$ value will be taken in order to accept the following limitation: $b_r \gg 2^q - 1$.

Let us define a standard form of the function $H_r(m, n, f)$:

$$H_r(m, n, f) \equiv \left( \left( f(m,n) \bmod b_r \cdot 2^{q(ab-1)} \bmod b_r \right) \bmod b_r \right.$$
$$+ \left( f(m, n+1) \bmod b_r \cdot 2^{q(ab-2)} \bmod b_r \right) \bmod b_r + \ldots \tag{6}$$
$$\left. \ldots + f(m+a-1, n+b-1) \bmod b_r \right) \bmod b_r.$$

Let us further consider the following simplifications:

- $f(m,n) \bmod b_r = f(m,n)$, because $f(m,n) \in [0, 2^q - 1]$;
- $p_r^i = 2^{qi} \bmod b_r, i \in [1, ab-1]$ can be calculated once before image analysis;
- $\bmod b_r$ for every summand can be discarded.

Considering these simplifications, Eq. (6) is changed to the following form:

$$H_r(m, n, f) \equiv \left( f(m,n) p_r^{ab-1} + \ldots + f(m+a-1, n+b-1) \right) \bmod b_r. \tag{7}$$

Recursive calculation of hash value (4) is used in order to reduce computational complexity and to provide invariance to the analyzed image size. The following equations are used for rows and columns recursive hash calculation correspondingly:

$$H(m, n+1, f) = 2^q H(m, n, f) - 2^{qab} f(m, n)$$
$$+ \sum_{i=1}^{a-1} 2^{qb(a-i)} \left( f(m+i-1, n+b-1) - f(m+i, n) \right)$$
$$+ f(m+a-1, n+b-1),$$
$$H(m+1, n, f) = 2^{qb} \left( H(m, n, f) - \sum_{i=0}^{b-1} 2^{q(ab-i-1)} f(m, n+i) \right) \tag{8}$$
$$+ \sum_{i=1}^{b-1} 2^{q(b-i)} f(m+a, n+i).$$

It should be mentioned that multiplication by powers of 2 are computed effectively using shift operations. This simplification leads to the hash value calculation time reduce.

## 4 Copy-Move Detection Algorithm

Most of the copy-move detection algorithms [1–3] developed nowadays follow a typical structure:

- features calculation in an overlapping windows;
- nearest neighbor search step to detect close features;
- postprocesing filtering step to reduce false detection.

Such algorithms have a major problem - nearest neighbor search step has high computational complexity with features set size increase. This is why sliding window mode can not be used on the first step.

To solve the problem of computational complexity here it is proposed a copy-move detection algorithm based on perceptual hash value calculation. The list of parameters to be fixed includes the sliding window size $a \times b$ and the prime number $b_r$. When this step is done, the algorithm below will provide you with the result image:

- calculate BGC codes using (1), (2) or (3) in a sliding window $3 \times 3$ and put them in the code map;
- compute the hash values (8) in the sliding window $a \times b$ using pixels of the code map;
- place hash values in a hash table to calculate their absolute frequencies;
- if the absolute frequency of a particular hash value is greater than 1, then this hash value corresponds to an image fragment of a potential duplicate;
- potential duplicates are marked in an output image generated by the algorithm.

One of the main advantages of the proposed algorithm is low computational complexity and false negative error. This statement is proved according to the following assumptions:

- the analysis is made using sliding window approach;
- hash values are calculated for every sliding window position;
- hash values are calculated using fast computed BGC codes;
- hash calculation algorithm is recursive.

As it was already mentioned, the main problem of the proposed solution is a narrow range of transformation parameters, so investigations in this field will be continued.

## 5   Experiments

To carry out research there was used a standard PC (Intel Core i5-3470 3.2 GHz, 8 GB RAM). 10 halftone satellite images (Geoeye, SPOT-4) with size $5000 \times 5000$ were selected to create forgeries using a self-developed automatic copy-move generation procedure. Using the developed procedure, there were generated 1200 forgeries: 120 images for each of the 10 initial images (60 images for each transform type), which were further analyzed using the detection algorithm (Sect. 4). This procedure allows to control the size of duplicates and the values of transform parameters. The forgeries were generated using the following transform types:

- contrast enhancement;
- additive Gaussian and impulse noise.

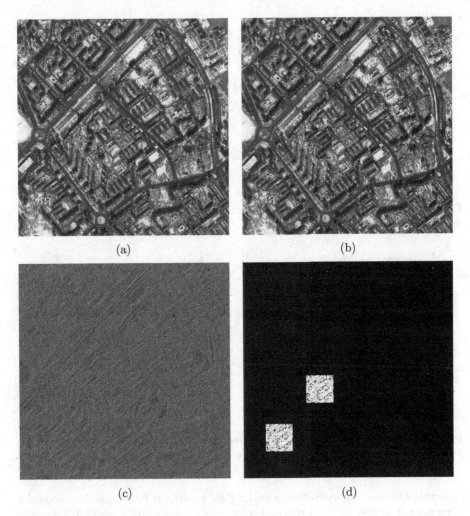

**Fig. 1.** Initial image (a), forgery (b), BGC code map (c) and copy-move detection result (d).

In Fig. 1 there is presented an initial Geoeye image (a), its altered version (b), generated BGC code map (c) and copy-move detection result (d) (contrast enhancement and 'salt & pepper' noise were used to transform a duplicate). It can be seen that the number of false errors is very low, whereas the copy-move block is detected precisely.

The proposed hash based solution shows higher or equal Precision and Recall values in comparison with SIFT and DCT feature based approach in contrast enhancement and additive noise detection. The dataset of 120 images with size $512 \times 512$ was used to compare two types of algorithms: feature based and hash based. Figure 2 shows accuracy of duplicates detection (transformed with linear

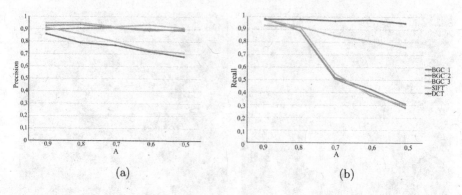

(a)                                              (b)

**Fig. 2.** Precision (a) and Recall (b) values comparison when detecting copy-move transformed with contrast enhancement.

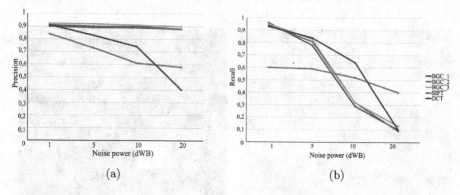

(a)                                              (b)

**Fig. 3.** Precision (a) and Recall (b) values comparison when detecting copy-move transformed with additive noise.

contrast enhancement operation $y = Ax + B$, where $x$ is initial pixel value and $y$ is an output value) by the proposed solution and using SIFT and DCT feature based methods. Figure 3 shows copy-move detection accuracy comparison when additive noise is applied to duplicates.

The proposed solution leads to higher Recall values for small values of transformations' parameters. This means that with increase in distortion, the number of missed copy-move regions increases more for the proposed solution. At the same time, Precision values are higher for all the range of distortions' parameters. This result shows that the number of false detected copy-move regions is significantly lower for the hash based solution.

At the same time, the developed solution has much lower computational complexity than SIFT and DCT feature based approaches. SIFT and DCT features calculation for every sliding window position leads to high computational complexity because these features can not be calculated recursive and the process of their values calculation is more costly than perceptual hash values calculation.

**Table 1.** Detection time (ms) comparison for the proposed algorithm, SIFT and DCT feature based approaches

| Time, ms | Perceptual hash | SIFT | DCT |
|---|---|---|---|
| 500 × 500 | 311 | 6210 | 15870 |
| 1000 × 1000 | 870 | 21587 | 25544 |
| 2500 × 2500 | 2812 | 43124 | 118456 |
| 5000 × 5000 | 5688 | 709678 | 1070120 |

Three solutions were used for the work time comparison. There were used halftone images with 4 different sizes (500 × 500, 1000 × 1000, 2500 × 2500 and 5000 × 5000) and calculated analysis time in ms for the two feature based solutions and the proposed hash based algorithm. Obtained results are shown in Table 1. It can be seen that the proposed solution has lower computational complexity than feature based approach. Moreover, the proposed algorithm is capable of sliding window use (size of a window used was 11 × 11 pixels), whereas feature based approaches are applied only with intersected windows mode (during experiments the size of a window used was 16 × 16 pixels, the shift of a window was equal to 8).

## 6   Results and Conclusion

In this paper it is proposed a fast copy-move detection algorithm based on the usage of BGC codes and perceptual hash values calculation. The developed solution showed high accuracy for detection of altered duplicates using several types of transformations: contrast enhancement and additive noise. At the same time, the developed method has low computational complexity in comparison with popular existing copy-move detection algorithms. Although, Rabin-Karp perceptual hash usage does not allow to detect duplicates distorted with a wide range of transform parameters, experiments showed that the proposed algorithm is suitable for large remote sensing data analysis. Further research will be carried out in perceptual hash functions analysis: DCT based, Marr-Hildreth operator based, Radial Variance based and Block Mean based. It is assumed that this investigation will help to reduce the number of missed duplicates and, as a result, will lead to Recall value increase for a wide range of distortion parameters. However, the proposed method can be applied in remote sensing data analysis systems as well as in digital image analysis software to prevent the usage of forgeries.

**Acknowledgements.** This work was financially supported by the Russian Scientific Foundation (RSF), grant no. 14-31-00014 "Establishment of a Laboratory of Advanced Technology for Earth Remote Sensing".

# References

1. Christlein, V., Riess, C., Jordan, J., Angelopoulou, E.: An evaluation of popular copy-move forgery detection approaches. IEEE Trans. Inf. Forensics Secur. **7**(6), 1841–1854 (2012)
2. Amerini, I., Ballan, L., Caldelli, R., Del Bimbo, A., Serra, G.: A SIFT-based forensic method for copy move attack detection and transformation recovery. IEEE Trans. Inf. Forensics Secur. **6**(3), 1099–1110 (2011)
3. Bayram, S., Sencar, H., Memon, H.: An efficient and robust method for detecting copy-move forgery. IEEE Int. Conf. Acoust. Speech Signal Process. **2009**, 1053–1056 (2009)
4. Glumov, N., Kuznetsov, A., Myasnikov, V.: Algorithms for detection of plain copy-move regions in digital images. Pattern Recogn. Image Anal. **25**(3), 423–429 (2015)
5. Vladimirovich, K.A., Valerievich, M.V.: A fast plain copy-move detection algorithm based on structural pattern and 2D rabin-karp rolling hash. In: Campilho, A., Kamel, M. (eds.) ICIAR 2014. LNCS, vol. 8814, pp. 461–468. Springer, Heidelberg (2014). doi:10.1007/978-3-319-11758-4_50
6. Davarzani, R., Yaghmaie, K., Mozaffari, S., Tapak, M.: Copy-move forgery detection using multi-resolution local binary patterns. Forensic Sci. Int. **231**(1–3), 61–72 (2013)
7. Fernndez, A., lvarez, M.X., Bianconi, F.: Image classification with binary gradient contours. Opt. Lasers Eng. **49**(910), 1177–1184 (2011)

# Applications

# Time Series Prediction for Electric Power Industry with the Help of Syntactic Pattern Recognition

Mariusz Flasiński[✉], Janusz Jurek, and Tomasz Peszek

Information Technology Systems Department, Jagiellonian University
in Cracow, ul. prof. St. Łojasiewicza 4, 30-348 Kraków, Poland
{Mariusz.Flasinski,janusz.jurek}@uj.edu.pl
http://www.ksi.uj.edu.pl/en/index.html

**Abstract.** Load prediction is one of the most important problems in electric power industry. The prediction is usually made with the help of standard time series analysis models. The novel syntactic pattern recognition-based model for the load prediction is defined in the paper. The Syntactic Pattern Recognition-based Electrical Load Prediction (SPRELP) System is described and the results concerning the reduction of the forecasting error with the comparison with other methods are presented.

## 1 Introduction

There are two general paradigms in pattern analysis. The decision-theoretic paradigm consists in representing patterns as *vectors of (numerical) features* and ascribing them to pre-defined classes in feature space. The syntactic/structural paradigm consists in representing patterns as *structures*, e.g., *string* (linear) *structural patterns*, which are constructed of elementary structural elements, called *primitives* [7]. The symbolic representations of these structures are treated as *words* of some *formal language* and they are recognized/classified with the help of *formal automata*.

Electrical load forecasting is one of the most important application areas of IT prediction systems [3,14]. A lot of deterministic and probabilistic parameterized *numerical-based* models have been developed since now, e.g. [1,2,9,10,12,15]. Electrical load patterns are typical time series patterns. Such patterns (e.g., ECG, EEG, stock chart patterns) have been analyzed with the syntactic pattern recognition methods [7].

In the paper we present results of the research into constructing the formal model of the Syntactic Pattern Recognition-based Electrical Load Prediction, SPRELP, System, which has been developed with TAURON Energy Holding[1],

---

[1] TAURON Energy Holding is one of the biggest electricity/heat generation and distribution companies in the Central-East Europe. The holding supplies over 45 TWh of electricity to over 5.3 million customers per year.

© Springer International Publishing AG 2016
L.J. Chmielewski et al. (Eds.): ICCVG 2016, LNCS 9972, pp. 555–563, 2016.
DOI: 10.1007/978-3-319-46418-3_49

the one of biggest such business organizations in Poland. The model has been constructed within the hybrid Artificial Intelligence paradigm based on artificial neural networks used at the first phase of electrical load pattern processing, and fuzzy syntactic/structural pattern recognition applied for the final analysis of the pattern for the purpose of electrical load forecasting.

The model of representation and processing of electrical load patterns treated as noisy structures is introduced in the next section. Syntactic pattern recognition-based method using the fuzzy transducer as a tool for the electrical load prediction is defined in Sect. 3. In the fourth section Syntactic Pattern Recognition-based Electrical Load Prediction (SPRELP) System implemented on the basis of the model defined is described and experimental results are presented and compared with the results published in the literature. The final section contains the concluding remarks.

## 2    Representation and Processing of Electrical Load Pattern as Noisy Structure

The main drawback of syntactic pattern recognition results from the fact that if one handles with distorted/noisy data, which often takes place in practical applications, then during converting such data into symbolic representation such noisiness is, somehow, enhanced. In our model the generation of the electrical load forecast is made on the basis of the vector of input data, which define conditions influencing the forecast e.g. forecasted temperature and forecasted insolation. Since such forecasted numerical data are noisy, they are transformed by Forecast Preprocessor, consisting of probabilistic neural networks [13], into the forecast fuzzy symbolic representation (cf. Fig. 1). This representation, which defines structural features of the input signal, is analysed in the next, syntactic pattern recognition-based phase. Let $\Sigma = \{a_1, ..., a_n\}$ be a set of symbols, which represent structural primitives. A *fuzzy symbolic representation of a structural primitive* is defined as a vector $((a_{i_1}, p_{i_1}), ..., (a_{i_s}, p_{i_s})), i_1, ..., i_s \in \{1, ..., n\}$, where $a_{i_1}, ..., a_{i_s} \in \Sigma$ are different symbols, $p_{i_1}, ..., p_{i_s}$ are probabilistic measures corresponding to each symbol such that: $p_{i_k} > 0, k = 1, ..., s$ ; $p_{i_1} + ... + p_{i_s} \leq 1$ ; $p_{i_1} \geq ... \geq p_{i_s}$. The string of fuzzy primitives over $\Sigma$ is denoted by $FP_\Sigma$.

In the forecast fuzzy symbolic representation noisiness is expressed with respect to each structural primitive separately. However, we want to make the electric load prediction on the basis of the string of these primitives, i.e. on the basis of the structural/syntactic pattern consisting of these primitives defined in time-series. Thus, for the string of fuzzy primitives in time-series the set of possible structural/syntactic patterns with corresponding probabilities is recognized by automata/transducers of the special type in the second phase (cf. Fig. 1). This set is called *the symbolic (variant) identification*, denoted $SI_\Sigma$, and contains pairs $(w_i, p_i)$, where $w_i \in \Sigma^*$ ($\Sigma^*$ is the Kleene star on $\Sigma$) is one of the high-probability-recognized words describing the fuzzy pattern, and $p_i$ is the probability of the recognition of the fuzzy pattern as the word $w_i$. The symbolic identifications of

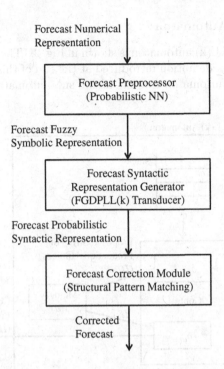

**Fig. 1.** The scheme of the hybrid model for the electric load forecasting

fuzzy patterns create the forecast probabilistic syntactic representation and are used for the forecast correction in the last phase (cf. Fig. 1).

The forecast correction is performed in the straightforward way. The database of Forecast Correction Module contains structural patterns for historical data used in past for the load forecasting. The correction is made as the weighted (probabilities $p_i$ of the symbolic variant identification are used as weights) sum of corrections being differences between the words represented historical structural patterns and words $w_i$ of the symbolic variant identification generated in the previous phase.

## 3    Fuzzy Transducer as a Tool for Electrical Load prediction

The essence of the method consists in the generation of the adequate symbolic variant identification of the noisy pattern on the basis of the string of fuzzy primitives. It is performed by the fuzzy transducer, abbrev. FGDPLL(k). The transducer uses the pool of deterministic automata, called GDPLL(k) automata [6,8]. These automata have the sufficient discriminative power to recognize context-like structural patterns representing time-series, which are generated by GDPLL(k) grammars [6,8]. We introduce them in the following subsection.

## 3.1  GDPLL(k) Automaton

The scheme of GDPLL(k) automaton is shown in Fig. 2. (The symbols in brackets are used in the formal definition introduced at the end of this subsection.) As we can see, in fact, the automaton consists of two sub-automata: LLA(k) and OIA.

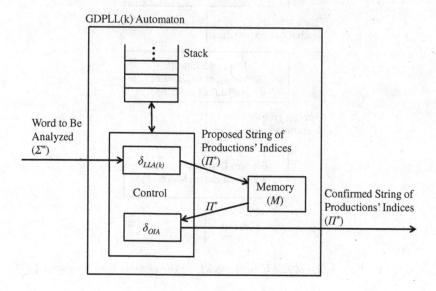

**Fig. 2.** The scheme of GDPLL(k) automation

The LLA(k) automaton is a kind of the pushdown automaton. It differs from the LL(k) automaton [11] known from the compiler design theory in analyzing much broader class of formal languages, i.e. the class of the so-called quasi-sensitive languages. (The standard LL(k) automaton is "too weak" to analyze such patterns like those representing real-world signals.) However, it can choose more than one production/reduction at a given derivational step. It means that LLA(k) is the non-deterministic automaton, which, of course, would mean the non-polynomial time complexity.

In order to obtain the polynomial, O(n), complexity LLA(k) cooperates at each reduction step with Operation Interpreter Automaton - OIA, which chooses the proper production out of the possible ones on the basis of the well-known formalism of the predicate of applicability.

Now, we can defined GDPLL(k) automaton in a formal way.

**Definition 1.** A *GDPLL(k)* *automaton* is a seven-tuple

$$A = (\Sigma, \Gamma, \Pi, M, \delta_{LLA(k)}, \delta_{OIA}, Z_0), \text{ where:}$$

$\Sigma$ is a finite set of input symbols,
$\Gamma$ is a finite set of stack symbols,

$\Pi$ is a set of productions' indices of the corresponding GDPLL(k) grammar,
$M$ is an automaton memory,
$\delta_{LLA(k)} : \Gamma \times \Sigma^* \longrightarrow \Pi^* \times \Gamma^*$ is the transition function choosing the set of possible productions,
$\delta_{OIA} : \Pi \times M \longrightarrow \{True, False\} \times M$ is the transition function determining the production that fulfills the conditions stored in the memory $M$,
$Z_0 \in \Gamma$ is the initial symbol of the stack.

## 3.2  FGDPLL(k) Transducer

As we have mentioned in Sect. 2, FGDPLL(k) transducer obtains the string of noisy primitives, i.e. the forecast fuzzy symbolic representation $FP_{Sigma}$, and it generates the symbolic variant identification $SI_\Sigma = \{(w_i, p_i), i = 1, ..., m\}$. In fact, it sends $FP_\Sigma$ to the pool of GDPLL(k) automata and each automaton generates the string of indices of productions belonging to GDPLL(k) grammar, as it is shown in Fig. 3. Each string of productions' indices corresponds to the generation of one $w_i$. At the same time the control of the transducer computes the proper probabilities pi using the auxiliary memory for this purpose.

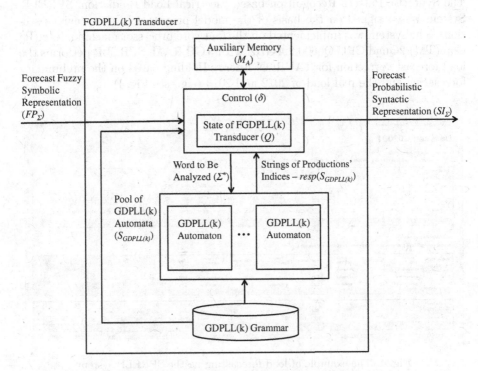

**Fig. 3.** The scheme of FGDPLL(k) transducer

At the end of this section let us define FGDPLL(k) transducer formally.

**Definition 2.** An *FGDPLL(k) transducer* is a seven-tuple

$$T = (Q, \Sigma, M_A, \delta, q_0, F, S_{GDPLL(k)}), \text{ where:}$$

$Q$ is a finite set of states,
$\Sigma$ is a finite set of input symbols,
$M_A$ is an auxiliary memory,
$\delta : Q \times FP_\Sigma \times M_A \times resp(S_{GDPLL(k)}) \longrightarrow Q \times M_A \times SI_\Sigma$ is the transition function, in which $FP_\Sigma$ is the string of fuzzy primitives, $resp(S_{GDPLL(k)}) \in \{prod : prod \in \Pi^*, \Pi$ is set of productions' indices of the corresponding GDPLL(k) grammar$\}$ is the response of the pool of GDPLL(k) automata, $SI_\Sigma$ is the symbolic identification,
$q_0 \in Q$ is the initial state,
$F \subseteq Q$ is a set of final states,
$S_{GDPLL(k)} = \{A_{GDPLL(k)} : A_{GDPLL(k)}$ is a GDPLL(k) automaton$\}$ is a pool of GDPLL(k) automata.

## 4   SPRELP System - Application and Results

The Syntactic Pattern Recognition-based Electrical Load Prediction, SPRELP, System was designed on the basis of the model presented in the previous sections. The system was implemented on the four core processor machine, Intel(R) Core(TM) 2Quad CPU Q6600 2.4 GHz, with 3 GB RAM. SPRELP performs the load forecast correction for TAURON Energy Holding based on the preliminary forecasting and the real load of 2012 and 2013 (e.g., see Fig. 4).

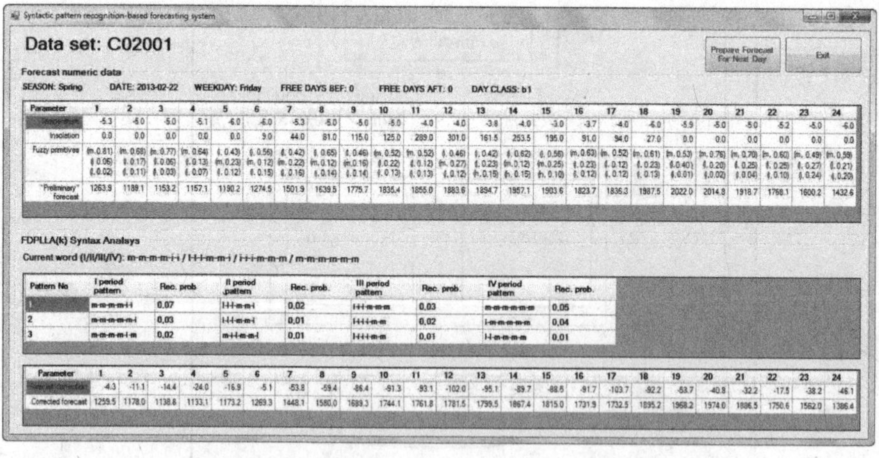

**Fig. 4.** The example of load forecasting by the SPRELP system

The minimization of the mean absolute percentage error, MAPE, is the main objective of the SPRELP learning process. The learning process concerns both

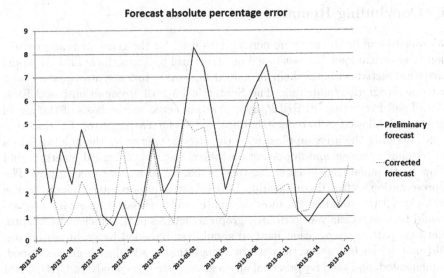

**Fig. 5.** The example of the comparison of MAPE for preliminary forecasting vs. forecasting corrected by SPRELP system for historical data of 2013.

the stochastic neural network at the forecast pre-processing stage and the construction of the GDPLL(k) grammar defining the control table for the pool of GDPLL(k) parsers, which are the basis for processing at the forecast syntactic representation generation. The tuning of the SPRELP is performed via the improvement of MAPE for historical data (e.g., see Fig. 5).

The SPRELP system has allowed us to reduce the forecasting error, with respect to the method used previously by TAURON Energy Holding, by 5.2 %. The mean absolute percentage error, MAPE, obtained after the correction equals to 2.9 %. Thus, the accuracy of the short-term load forecasting, STLF, in case of the SPRELP is similar to the accuracy of other STLF methods known from the literature (cf. Table 1).

**Table 1.** The comparison of the accuracy of the STLF methods

| Methodology | Reference | MAPE(%) |
| --- | --- | --- |
| Neural Network (NN) | Adepoju et al. 2007 [2] | 2.45 |
| Neural Network (NN) | Taylor & McSharry 2008 [15] | 2.25 |
| Neural Network (NN) | Satish et al. 2004 [12] | 4.00 |
| Fuzzy Logic | Popławski 2008 [10] | 3.55 |
| Fuzzy Logic | Manoj & Shah 2014 [9] | 2.26 |
| ARIMA | Abdel-Aal & Al-Garni 1997 [1] | 3.80 |
| Syntactic pattern recognition/NN | our method | 2.90 |

# 5  Concluding Remarks

In order to handle the noisy numerical data used for the generation and correction of electrical load forecast based on structural patterns the hybrid AI model was constructed with the help of neural networks, fuzzy syntactic/structural pattern recognition/matching. The Syntactic Pattern Recognition-based Electrical Load Prediction, SPRELP, System constructed on the basis of the model introduced, allowed us to reduce significantly the forecasting error. On the other hand, dividing the area supplied with the electric energy by the holding into a set of many subareas and important customers (e.g., big chemical plants) would allow us to make load forecast for these subareas in a more precise way. The representation of this decomposition into subareas/important recipients by the graph structure would be the most adequate model. However, in such a case we should be able to analyse attributed graph structures in the efficient way. Thus, syntactic pattern recognition method should be extended by graph automata. Fortunately, such a syntactic pattern recognition model has been developed, implemented, and used for practical applications, like scene analysis, CAD/CAM integration [4,5,7]. The use of this model for the purpose of the electrical load prediction will the subject of the further research.

# References

1. Abdel-Aal, R.E., Al-Garni, A.Z.: Forecasting monthly electric energy consumption in eastern Saudi Arabia using univariate time-series analysis. Energy **22**, 1059–1069 (1997)
2. Adepoju, G.A., Ogunjuyigbe, S.O.A., Alawode, K.O.: Application of neural network to load forecasting in Nigerian electrical power system. Pac. J. Sci. Technol. **8**, 68–72 (2007)
3. Alfares, K.H., Nazeeruddin, M.: Electric load forecasting: literature survey and classification of methods. Int. J. Syst. Sci. **33**, 23–34 (2002)
4. Flasiński, M.: On the parsing of deterministic graph languages for syntactic pattern recognition. Pattern Recogn. **26**, 1–16 (1993)
5. Flasiński, M.: Use of graph grammars for the description of mechanical parts. Comput. Aided Des. **27**, 403–433 (1995)
6. Flasiński, M., Jurek, J.: Dynamically programmed automata for quasi context sensitive languages as a tool for inference support in pattern recognition-based real- time control expert systems. Pattern Recogn. **32**, 671–690 (1999)
7. Flasiński, M.: Syntactic pattern recognition: paradigm issues and open problems. In: Chen, C.H. (ed.) Handbook of Pattern Recognition and Computer Vision, 5th edn, pp. 3–25. World Scientific, New Jersey (2016)
8. Jurek, J.: Recent developments of the syntactic pattern recognition model based on quasi-context sensitive languages. Pattern Recogn. Lett. **26**, 1011–1018 (2005)
9. Manoj, P.P., Shah, A.P.: Fuzzy logic methodology for short term load forecasting. Int. J. Res. Eng. Technol. **3**, 322–328 (2014)
10. Popławski, T.: The short-term fuzzy load prediction model. Acta Electrotechnica et Informatica **8**, 39–43 (2008)
11. Rosenkrantz, D.J., Stearns, R.E.: Properites of deterministic top-down grammars. Inf. Control **17**, 226–256 (1970)

12. Satish, B., Swarup, K.S., Srinivas, S., Hanumantha Rao, A.: Effect of temperature on short term load forecasting using an integrated ANN. Electr. Power Syst. Res. **72**, 95–101 (2004)
13. Specht, D.F.: Probabilistic neural networks. Neural Netw. **3**, 109–118 (1990)
14. Tadeusiewicz, R.: Introduction to intelligent systems. In: Wilamowski, B.M., Irvin, J.D. (eds.) The Industrial Electronics Handbook Intelligent Systems, pp. 1-1–1-12. CRC Press, Boca Raton (2011). Chap. 1
15. Taylor, J.W., McSharry, P.E.: Short-term load forecasting methods: an evaluation based on European data. IEEE Trans. Power Syst. **22**, 2213–2219 (2008)

# Simultaneous Mixed Vertical and Horizontal Handwritten Japanese Character Line Detection

Tomotaka Kimura[1]([✉]), Chinthaka Premachandra[2], and Hiroharu Kawanaka[3]

[1] Department of Electrical Engineering, Tokyo University of Science,
6-3-1 Niijuku, Katsushika-ku, Tokyo 125-8585, Japan
kimura@ee.kagu.tus.ac.jp
[2] Department of Electronic Engineering, Shibaura Institute of Technology,
3-7-5, Toyosu, Koto-ku, Tokyo 135-8548, Japan
chintaka@shibaura-it.ac.jp
[3] Graduate School of Engineering, Mie University,
1577 Kurimamachiya-cho, Tsu, Mie 514-8507, Japan

**Abstract.** Teachers consume considerable time and their energy in process of marking examination sheets. To reduce this burden on teachers, we have been developing an automatic marking system. To mark examination sheets automatically, handwritten character lines are extracted, and then the characters on those lines are recognized. In this paper, we discuss how character lines are extracted from Japanese handwritten examination sheets without ruled lines. Japanese characters can be written vertically and horizontally, so examination sheets written in Japanese are consisted of mixed vertical and horizontal (MVH) character lines. Conventional character line extraction methods cannot deal with MVH lines, because they have been developed to consider only horizontal character lines. This paper focuses on the simultaneous detection of MVH character lines. The result of experiments using appropriate examination sheet images shows that our method can detect MVH character lines effectively.

## 1 Introduction

In academic institutions, various paper-based examinations are conducted to evaluate the academic performance of students. In general, academic institutes in Japan provide two types of answer sheets: *marking sheets* and *writing sheets*. The former is a special mark sheet, and can thus be marked automatically by automated marking systems. These marking sheets are used in most university entrance examinations in Japan. In such examinations, students place a mark next to their chosen answer on the sheet, and the sheet is then automatically evaluated by a computer. In contrast, writing sheets require handwritten answers. Although the latest character recognition software can recognize most printed characters with high accuracy, the accuracy with handwritten characters is not especially high. In particular, characters written in Japanese are very complicated, and some characters are very similar in shape, making them difficult to distinguish.

© Springer International Publishing AG 2016
L.J. Chmielewski et al. (Eds.): ICCVG 2016, LNCS 9972, pp. 564–572, 2016.
DOI: 10.1007/978-3-319-46418-3_50

We have been developing an automatic marking system for Japanese handwritten examination sheets. An automatic marking system that can accurately process these handwritten examination sheets is a desirable applications, because teachers expend considerable time and their energy for marking handwritten examination sheets. The creation of an automatic marking system for such complicated handwritten examination sheets will reduce the burden on teachers in academic institutes.

To recognize the characters within handwritten documents such as examination sheets, character line extraction is often used. Figure 1 illustrates a typical example of a Japanese handwritten examination sheet. Japanese characters can be written vertically and horizontally, so the sheet consists of mixed vertical and horizontal (MVH) character lines. In Fig. 1, the lower left section is written horizontally, whereas the other parts are written vertically. Therefore, to extract character lines from the image, horizontal and vertical character lines must be detected.

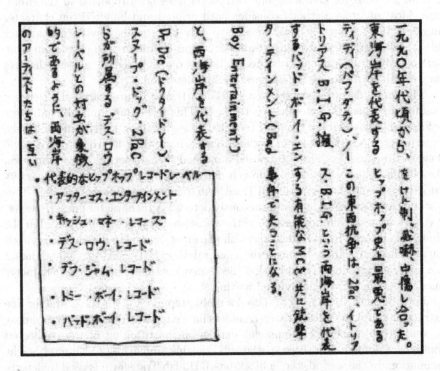

**Fig. 1.** An example of a Japanese handwritten sheet, where the lower left of the image is written horizontally and other parts are written vertically.

This paper focuses on the problems encountered by MVH handwritten character line extraction. Several character line extraction methods have been considered in the literature [1–9]. These methods are generally time-consuming and deal with only horizontal character lines. Hence, they cannot simultaneously extract MVH handwritten lines. Previously, we have considered the horizontal handwritten character line extraction problem of reducing the computation time [6]. In this paper, we tackle the MVH handwritten character line extraction problem. Our method for MVH character lines results in a high extraction rate. In addition, our method reduces the computation time compared with existing horizontal character line extraction methods.

The reminder of this paper is organized as follows. Section 2 introduces and discusses previous approaches to handwritten character line extraction. Section 3 describes the details of our method for the simultaneous extraction of MVH character lines. Section 4 presents and discusses the experimental results obtained in this study. Finally, Sect. 5 concludes the paper.

## 2   Related Studies on Character Line Detection

Several methods for character line extraction have been reported in the literature. Most of these methods consider both printed and handwritten character line detection, though some studies have only targeted handwritten character lines. Moreover, these existing studies focus on character line extraction from horizontally written documents. To the best of our knowledge, no study has yet targeted the problem of MVH character line detection.

The methods proposed by Adachi et al. [1] and Tsuruoka et al. [7] use a thinning approach to detect character lines. This technique thins all characters before using their gravity points to detect the character lines. Unfortunately, experiments suggest that these methods require more than 40 s to process a single image. Hirabayashi et al. [3] proposed a method that detects character lines via the Hough Transform. Their approach detects the gravity points of characters are detected, and then uses Hough Transform to identify the character lines. This method can also be used to simultaneously detect MVH character lines. However, it is very time-consuming because of the voting-based processing involved in the Hough Transform. In addition, this method cannot be used to detect handwritten curved character lines, because the classical Hough Transform cannot detect randomly curved lines. Examination sheets may contain lots of curved character lines, depending on the individual writing style.

Louloudisa et al. [5] have proposed a multi-step method for the character line extraction problem. The first step conducts image binarization and enhancement is conducted, connected component extraction, partitioning of the connected component domain into three spatial sub-domains, and average character height estimation. In the second step, a block-based Hough Transform is used to detects potential text lines. A third step then corrects possible splitting, detects text lines that the previous step did not reveal, and separates vertically connected characters and assigns them to text lines. This method is also very time-consuming, because connected component detection and the Hough Transform are computationally expensive.

Chaudhuri et al. [2] proposed a method that detects character lines by following the gap between two lines. This method is interesting, though it is less accurate when the gap between two lines is very small. In addition, it is difficult to employ this method for MVH character line detection problem since the gaps between and vertical and horizontal character lines become confused.

Yin and Liu [8,9] proposed a character line detection method based on minimum spanning tree (MST) clustering with new distance measures. First, the connected components of the document image are grouped into a tree by the MST clustering with a new distance measure. The edges of the tree are then dynamically cut to form text lines using a new objective function to determine the number of clusters. However, this method also requires time-consuming connected component analysis, which is especially problematic when processing large document images.

Khayya et al. [4] developed a handwritten text line detection method by applying an adaptive mask to morphological dilation. This method first identifies the characteristics of the document and its connected components to set the parameters and thresholds of the algorithm. The final smearing of the document is then determined by the dynamic mask. A recursive function plays an important role in the method as it breaks up blobs according to the attraction and repulsion of the text within those blobs. This is another interesting concept, though the connected component analysis process requires very time-consuming.

More recently, Premachandra et al. [6] proposed a method that reduces the character line detection time by analyzing block-based histograms, which is a relatively simple process. Experiments on a number of examination sheets demonstrated that the detection time of their method is lower than that of the method in [9].

## 3   Proposed MVH Line Detection Method

The proposed method draws multiple vertical and horizontal lines, such as depicted in Fig. 2(a), and then examines histograms of black pixels in both directions. To distinguish between vertical and horizontal writing, the proposed method uses the difference between the deviations of each histogram. When creating a histogram in the vertical direction for an document written horizontally, the line spacing between each sentence causes a number of peaks to appear (see Fig. 2(b)). In contrast, when creating a histogram in the horizontal direction, a series of connected peaks appear because the characters have been written continually (see Fig. 2(c)). These observations indicate that the histogram formed horizontally more closely represents a uniform distribution than the histogram formed vertically. Therefore, the calculation of the Kullback–Leibler distance between the uniform distribution and the histogram for the horizontal orientation is less than that between the uniform distribution and the histogram for the vertical orientation. Using this observation, we can determine whether the document is written horizontally or vertically.

The procedure of the proposed method is detailed as follows, where we assume that figures in examination sheets can be removed using the technique described in [6].

(a) An example image written horizontally with multiple vertical and horizontal lines.

(b) Histogram in the vertical direction.

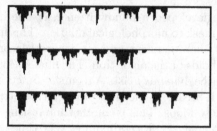

(c) Histogram in the horizontal direction.

**Fig. 2.** Concept of the proposed method.

**Step 1:** A $N \times M$ pixel image is divided into small regions. By setting each small region to have width $w$, we draw $\lfloor N/w \rfloor$ straight lines in the horizontal direction and $\lfloor M/w \rfloor$ straight lines in the vertical direction. Therefore, the image is divided into $\lceil N/w \rceil \times \lceil M/w \rceil$ regions. Further, $A_{n,m}$ represents the $n$th region in the horizontal direction and the $m$th region in the vertical direction.

**Step 2:** The number of black pixels is counted for each region $A_{n,m}$, and the total number of black pixels is denoted as $S_{n,m}$.

**Step 3:** For each region $A_{n,m}$, we set $v_{n,m}(i)$ for $i \in \{0, 1, \ldots, w-1\}$, as follows:

$$v_{n,m}(i) = \sum_{j=0}^{w-1} \frac{f(nw+i, mw+j)}{S_{n,m}},$$

where $f(k,l)$ is a function such that when the pixel at $(k,l)$ is black, $f(k,l) = 1$; otherwise, $f(k,l) = 0$.

For each region $A_{n,m}$, we also set $h_{n,m}(j)$ for $j \in \{0, 1, \ldots, w-1\}$ as follows:

$$h_{n,m}(j) = \sum_{i=0}^{w-1} \frac{f(nw+i, mw+j)}{S_{n,m}}.$$

**Step 4:** We set $u(i) = 1/w$ for $i \in \{0, 1, \ldots w - 1\}$. For each region $A_{n,m}$, we calculate the Kullback-Leibler distance for $u(i)$ and $v_{n,m}(i)$, and denote its value as $V_{n,m}$.

$$V_{n,m} = \sum_{i=0}^{w-1} v_{n,m}(i) \log \frac{v_{n,m}(i)}{u(i)}.$$

We also calculate the Kullback-Leibler distance for $u(i)$ and $h_{n,m}(i)$, and denote its value as $H_{n,m}$.

$$H_{n,m} = \sum_{i=0}^{w-1} h_{n,m}(i) \log \frac{h_{n,m}(i)}{u(i)}.$$

**Step 5:** $V_{n,m}$ is compared with $H_{n,m}$. For $V_{n,m} < H_{n,m}$, region $A_{n,m}$ is considered to contain vertical writing. For $V_{n,m} > H_{n,m}$, region $A_{n,m}$ is considered to contain horizontal writing. For $V_{n,m} = H_{n,m}$, we cannot distinguish whether the region $A_{n,m}$ contains vertical or horizontal writing. In the following, we refer to regions for $V_{n,m} < H_{n,m}$ and $V_{n,m} > H_{n,m}$ as *vertical-writing regions* and *horizontal-writing regions*, respectively. Figure 3(b) shows the estimation result of Fig. 1, where black and gray regions indicate horizontal-writing and vertical-writing regions, respectively.

**Step 6:** The peak of each region is determined and all peaks are plotted on the borders of regions, as illustrated in Fig. 3(c). For vertical-writing and horizontal-writing regions, peaks are plotted on the horizontal and vertical borders, respectively.

**Step 7:** We extract straight horizontal or vertical lines with a technique similar to that described in [6]. If there are more than two consecutive regions with horizontal writing, we draw a straight horizontal line between these regions. More specifically, we draw a straight line from the first peak to the last peak in the consecutive regions (see Fig. 3(d)). If there are more than two consecutive regions with vertical writing, we draw a straight vertical line between these regions.

## 4 Experiments

### 4.1 Experimental Environment

All experiments were conducted using a computer with the following configuration:

OS: Mac OS 10.10,    CPU: Core i5 3.5 GHz
RAM: 8.00 GB,    Programming language: C++

The images used in the experiments had the following specifications:

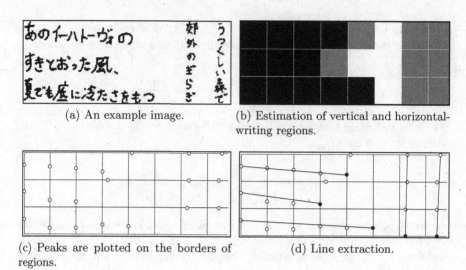

(a) An example image.

(b) Estimation of vertical and horizontal-writing regions.

(c) Peaks are plotted on the borders of regions.

(d) Line extraction.

**Fig. 3.** An example of applying the proposed method.

Handwritten examination sheets: 30
Image Size: 1646 × 2079
Number of character lines: 660

Experiments were conducted to verify the performance of the proposed character line extraction method and its required processing time. Further, we compared the performance of our method with that of a HT (Hough Transform)-based method.

## 4.2   Experimental Results

Figure 4 shows the character line extraction results obtained using our method. All lines in Fig. 4(a) are extracted correctly, whereas in Fig. 4(b) the third horizontal line from the bottom cannot be extracted because the line spans multiple blocks. This result indicates that the setting of the block-width $w$ is important to extract lines with the proposed method. We leave the appropriate setting of the block-width $w$ for future works.

Table 1 shows the character line extraction rate of the proposed method and the HT-based method. The average processing time of our method is 3.2 s. The results indicate that our proposed method gives better character line extraction and reduced processing time compared with the existing method.

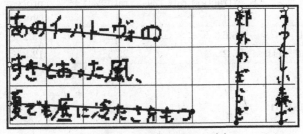

(a) Extraction from Fig. 3(a)

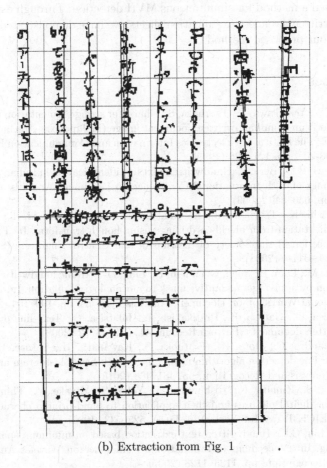

(b) Extraction from Fig. 1

**Fig. 4.** Character line extraction results.

**Table 1.** Comparison of extracted character lines.

| Method | Character line extraction rate [%] | False positive rate [%] | Average processing time [s] |
|---|---|---|---|
| Proposal | 95.6 | 1.2 | 3.2 |
| HT-based method | 95.2 | 23.5 | 12.8 |

## 5   Conclusion

In this paper, we have considered the MVH character line extraction problems and described a method for simultaneous MVH detection. Through experiments with handwritten Japanese examination sheets, we have demonstrated the effectiveness of our proposed method.

## References

1. Adachi, Y., Yoshikawa, T., Tsuruoka, S.: Character string segmentation using thinning algorithm from handwritten document image (in Japanese), Technical report of IEICE (The Institute of Electronics Information and Communication Engineers), PRMU98-208, pp. 121–126 (1999)
2. Chaudhuri, B.B., Bera, S.: Handwritten text line identification in Indian scripts. In: Proceedings of 10th International Conference on Document Analysis and Recognition, pp. 636–640 (2009)
3. Hirabayashi, K., Tsuruoka, S., Kawanaka, H., Takase, H., Ozaki, T.: Character line segmentation from blackboard image using hough transform. In: Proceedings of Mie Section of the Society of Instrument and Control Engineers (SICE-Mie), pp. B11-1–B11-4 (2008)
4. Khayyat, M., Lam, L., Suen, C.Y., Yin, F., Liu, C.L.: Arabic handwritten text line extraction by applying an adaptive mask to morphological dilation. In: 10th IAPR International Workshop on Document Analysis Systems, pp. 100–104 (2012)
5. Louloudisa, G., Gatosb, B., Pratikakisb, I., Halatsisa, C.: Text line detection in handwritten documents. Pattern Recogn. **41**, 3758–3772 (2008)
6. Premachandra, C., Goto, K., Tsuruoka, S., Kawanaka, H., Takase, H.: Speedy character line detection algorithm using image block-based histogram analysis. In: Image Analysis and Recognition, pp. 481–488 (2015)
7. Tsuruoka, S., Kimura, F., Yoshimura, M., Yokoi, S., Miyake, Y.: Thinning algorithms for digital pictures and their application to hand-printed character recognition. IEICE Trans. Inf. Syst. **J66–D(5)**, 525–532 (1983)
8. Yin, F., Liu, C.L.: Handwritten text extraction based on minimum spanning tree clustering. In: Proceedings of International Conference on Wavelet Analysis and Pattern Recognition, pp. 1123–1128 (2007)
9. Yin, F., Liu, C.L.: A variational bayes method for handwritten text line segmentation. In: Proceedings of 10th International Conference on Document Analysis and Recognition, pp. 436–440 (2009)

# Determination of Road Traffic Flow Based on 3D Daubechies Wavelet Transform of an Image Sequence

Marcin Jacek Kłos[(✉)]

Faculty of Transport, Silesian University of Technology,
ul.Krasinskiego 8, Katowice, Poland
marcin.j.klos@polsl.pl

**Abstract.** Daubechies wavelet transform is proposed to represent the contents of the image sequence. In order to account for temporal changes of the contents a 3D transform is used. 3D DWT, Daubechies based, is chosen for calculations to determine the coefficients. A method of mapping road traffic flow is developed. The method uses a linear function of the wavelet coefficients for describing the changes in detection fields, which is in turn is converted to traffic flow. The parameters of the linear function are determined by minimizing the MSE of fitting this function to corresponding traffic flow values. The method is validated using a set of video sequences.

## 1 Introduction

Reliable non-intrusive road traffic measuring devices are crucial for providing data for processing in intelligent transportation systems. ITS contribute significantly to the efficiency of transportation systems in urban areas. The transportation system determines to a large extent the quality of life in cities. Traffic flow and density are the basic parameters, which describe vehicle movement on roads. Determination of these parameters is essential for the traffic lights control systems. Methods used for collecting data, describing the traffic situation occurring at the intersections, currently fall into two main categories: video based and sensor based where sensors recognize traffic participants by detecting e.g. wireless transmissions, magnetic signatures of vehicles. The sensors may be linked together to function in a network. Wireless sensor network (WSN) proliferate in this data collection field. Authors in [1] present an analysis of traffic collected using different topologies of wireless sensor networks. Results of the analysis confirm the effectiveness of this method to determine traffic parameters. Paper [2] presents a method of using WSN to determine traffic parameters: density and traffic flow. Obtained values are used to determine the length of the green light in a traffic light cycle.

Video based methods comprise a wide range of processing approaches for determining traffic parameters. This paper presents the results of elaborating a method, that processes the video sequence content without extracting individual

© Springer International Publishing AG 2016
L.J. Chmielewski et al. (Eds.): ICCVG 2016, LNCS 9972, pp. 573–580, 2016.
DOI: 10.1007/978-3-319-46418-3_51

vehicles. The traffic flow is determined on the basis of the transform of the video stream from the camera.

This paper is organized as follows: Sect. 2 provides a literature background positioning the proposed transform approach for determining traffic parameters. Section 3 presents the characteristics of DWT based on Daubechies wavelets which is the basis of the traffic parameters mapping. This is followed by Sect. 4, which describes the methodology of using DWT and the design of the processing method. The results of evaluating road traffic parameters are described in Sect. 5. Section 6 of the paper contains conclusions and propositions for future work.

## 2    Literature Review

Image processing methods are used for extracting the parameters of moving objects in the video sequences. These are related to the basic traffic parameters: congestion, mean speed, density and traffic flow. The movement parameters are evaluated using transforms: discrete wavelet transform, fast Fourier transform or with tracking methods [3].

Author in paper [4] compares the use of discrete wavelet transform and fast Fourier transform for evaluating the level of congestion. Characteristics of the transformations are discussed. The author stresses the limitation of fast Fourier transformation for detecting traffic congestion. An algorithm is proposed for processing a set of pixels - a line on a strech of a traffic lane, using DWT to evaluate the congestion of this traffic lane. One-dimensional wavelet transformation is used, the obtained DWT coefficients are coverted to congestion values.

The author in paper [5] discuses methods for estimating the level of traffic congestion. Fast Fourier transform and discrete wavelet transform characteristic are again analysed. The analysis proves that the wavelet transform gives a higher accuracy of estimating traffic, because it has the feature of localization of events in time and space. Principal component analysis (PCA) is used for reducing the number of discrete wavelet transform coefficients, which represent the traffic parameters.

Authors in [6] present the application of two-dimensional discrete Haars transform for determining vehicle speeds. The described method is based on the analysis of the content of successive video frames.

Three-dimensional transform complements the representation with data on changes of the video stream content in time [7]. This property is desirable in obtaining road parameters from a video sequence. Author in [8] describes the method of using three-dimensional wavelet transform with Haars wavelets. Traffic flow and density are evaluated, based on the rate of the change of the sum of coefficients in a defined detection field in the observation plane.

Author in [9, 10] introduces a method of mapping the traffic parameters using transform coefficients. The traffic parameters are mapped using a polynomial. The coefficients of the polynomial are estimated using MSE and real traffic data.

An important criterion for choosing a transformation for representing the stream contents is its computational complexity. This characteristic determines the cability to process large datasets in real time (eg. video streams with a resolution of 4K). Fast Fourier transform requires order of $O(nlog2(n))$ operations whereas fast wavelet transform requires $O(n)$ operations [11]. DWT is a preferable transformation for representing stream content.

Daubechies wavelets are noted for use in various application fields. Author in [12] present the design and implementation of a three-dimensional Daubechies transformation for medical image compression. Author ascertain that Daubechies wavelets have excellent performance in image compression applications. Paper [13] presents a colour image steganography technique, based on Daubechies DWT. The author compares the results of two dimensional transformations: Haar and Daubechies. Test shows the superior characteristics of Daubechies DWT.

Daubechies wavelets are used to filter objects with different textures features. The number of vanishing moments of the transformation limits the wavelets ability to represent polynomial behaviour of a signal. This in a way reflects the smoothness of represented features of the image content [14]. A properly selected wavelet enables an efficient representation of smooth-edged objects such as vehicles. These properties reveal their merit in image compression applications [15].

The Daubechies wavelet transformation is defined in the similar way as the Haar transformation. It is based on computing running averages and differences using scalar products [16]. The difference between them is the way the scaling signals are defined [14].

## 3    Daubechies Coefficients

Three dimensional Daubechies (4, 4) transformation is chosen for the investigation of the representation of traffic flow based on the content of a video stream. The third dimension is used to represent the change of the content of the video stream in time. This characteristic allows to represent object movement parameters, which are the basic elements of traffic.

The lifting scheme is chosen for calculating the transform coefficients. This approach significantly reduces the complexity of calculations which is desirable because a hardware implementation is planned in the future [17]. Equation 1 presents formulas of prediction $d_{1,i}$ and update $s_{1,i}$ of Daubechies (4, 4) discrete wavelet transformation.

$$d_{1,i} = s_{0,2+1} - [9(s_{0,2i} + s_{0,2+2i})/16 - (s_{0,2i-2} + s_{0,2+4i})/16 + 1/2]$$
$$s_{1,i} = s_{0,2i} + [9(d_{1i-1} + d_{1i})/32 - (d_{1i-2} + d_{1i+1})/32 + 1/2] \tag{1}$$

The set of eight consecutive frames are used for the calculation of 3D DWT. This defines the resolution and dynamics of vehicles movement which is described by the coefficients.

Multi-resolution sub-band coefficients comprise three elements. For example $C1 - sds$, the first position (s) maps information related to changes of pixel values in time, the following (d) gives horizontal changes and the last position (s) maps vertical changes of image pixel values (Table 1).

**Table 1.** Daubechies coefficients

| Coefficients | Multi-resolution sub-band coefficients | Description |
|---|---|---|
| C0 | sss | Averagining in time |
| C1 | sds | Averagining in time |
| C2 | ssd | Averagining in time |
| C3 | sdd | Averagining in time |
| C4 | ddd | Detail in time |
| C5 | dsd | Detail in time |
| C6 | dss | Detail in time |
| C7 | dds | Detail in time |

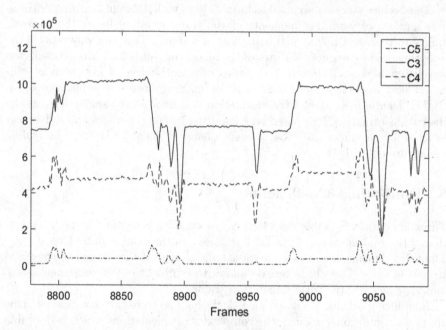

**Fig. 1.** Graph of the sum of the coefficients of the defined detection field - C3, C4, C5.

Figure 1 shows the graph of the sum of the coefficients of the defined detection field (Fig. 2). The analysis of the obtained coefficients sums is used for evaluating the occupation of the detection field and counting of vehicles for determination of traffic flow.

## 4   Implementation

The aim of the analysis is to elaborate an algorithm to derive traffic flow values from wavelet representation of video streams.

**Fig. 2.** The defined detection field on analysed film frame.

Figure 2 shows an example from the dataset of video sequences obtained from measuring stations, which work in real time. The video sequences are registered with the use of video stream registering equipment directly from road cameras. The road cameras are mounted on horizontal gantries at the intersections.

The developed solution uses a linear function of Daubechies wavelet coefficients for approximating the content of a defined detection field, where the objects appear (pass through). The problem of calculating the function parameters and determination of the detection thresholds is tackled. A large number of factors affect the contents of the detection field, especially highly changeable ambient light conditions, so it is necessary to devise a method to account for them. Instead of determining individual detections traffic flow is recognized as an overall measure of the detection field occupation. The function parameters are determined by finding the optimal fit of the graph of the traffic flow and the graph of content description using Daubechies wavelet coefficients.

Equation 2 expresses the occupancy of the detection field defined on an image of a video sequence.

$$Y = w_1 \frac{(C1 + C2)}{(C7 + C5)} + w_2 \frac{(C0 + C3)}{(C6 + C4)} > P \tag{2}$$

Y - detection function, w1, w2 - linear function scales; C0, C1, C2, C3, C4, C5, C6, C7 - wavelet coefficients, P - threshold value.

Figure 1 shows the differences between coefficients. Equation 2 include normalization of the coefficients. Averaging coefficients are placed in the numerator and the detail coefficients are placed in the denominator.

The threshold value is estimated using MSE and real traffic values. Detection function is validated using a set of different threshold values.

## 5   Results

A method of mapping road traffic flow is developed. The method uses a linear function of the wavelet coefficients for describing the changes in detection fields, which is in turn is converted to traffic flow. Traffic flow is calculated every 5 min using 15 min vehicle counts (Fig. 3).

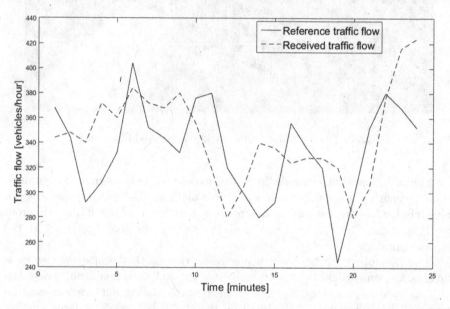

**Fig. 3.** Graph presenting the comparison of the reference traffic flow and traffic flow obtained using the elaborated detection function.

Figure 3 shows the comparison of reference traffic flow and traffic flow obtained using the elaborated detection function. Mean square error between reference and calculated traffic flow amounts to 11,7 %. Test results prove that the designed method can be applied to determine traffic flow values for control systems.

## 6   Conclusion

Three dimensional wavelet transformation with Daubechies wavelets gives a representation of an image sequence, which is useful for evaluating traffic flow. The proposed method uses a linear function of the wavelet coefficients for describing the occupation of detection fields, which generates vehicle counts. The counts linked with the counting periods define traffic flow values. The method is validated using a dataset of video sequences. The elaborated method allows to determine traffic flow with an accuracy adequate for local traffic controllers. Future work will include calculating traffic density and using different wavelets.

# References

1. McEachen, l.C., Beng Wang, W.: Characterization of traffic in wireless sensor networks. In: 15th IEEE International Conference on Networks, pp. 437–442 (2007)
2. Zhou, B., Cao, J., Zeng, X., Wu, H.: Adaptive traffic light control in wireless sensor network-based intelligent transportation system. In: Proceedings of the IEEE 72nd VTC-Fall, pp. 1–5 (2010)
3. Moeslund, T.: Image acquisition. In: Introduction to Video and Image Processing Building Real System and Application. Springer Publisher, London (2012)
4. Klosowski, M.: Hardware accelerated implementation of wavelet transform for machine vision in road traffic monitoring system. In: 1st International Conference on Information Technology, IT 2008, pp. 1–4 (2008)
5. Zhu, W., Barth, M.: Vehicle trajectory-based road type and congestion recognition using wavelet analysis. In: Proceedings of the IEEE ITSC 2006 Intelligent Transportation Systems Conference Toronto, Canada, September 17–20 (2006)
6. Kong, J., Xin, H., Lu, Y., Li, B., Li, Y.-W.: Vehicle tracking and traffic parameter extraction based on discrete wavelet transform. In: Sattar, A., Kang, B.-H. (eds.) AI 2006. LNCS (LNAI), vol. 4304, pp. 482–490. Springer, Heidelberg (2006)
7. Wu, Y., Shen, J., Dai, M.: Traffic object detections and it's action analysis. Pattern Recogn. Lett. **26**, 1963–1984 (2005)
8. Pamula, W.: Determination of road traffic parameters based on 3D wavelet representation of an image sequence. In: Bolc, L., Tadeusiewicz, R., Chmielewski, L.J., Wojciechowski, K. (eds.) ICCVG 2012. LNCS, vol. 7594, pp. 541–548. Springer, Heidelberg (2012)
9. Kłos, M.J.: Determination of road traffic flow based on 3D wavelet transform of an image sequence. In: Burduk, R., Jackowski, K., Kurzyński, M., Woźniak, M., Żołnierek, A. (eds.) Proceedings of the 9th International Conference on Computer Recognition Systems CORES 2015. AISC, vol. 403, pp. 501–507. Springer, Heidelberg (2016). doi:10.1007/978-3-319-26227-7_47
10. Kłos, M.: Metoda określania natężenia ruchu drogowego z wykorzystaniem falkowej reprezentacji strumienia wideo z kamery obserwacyjnej. Logistyka **3**, 2211–2218 (2015)
11. Fessler, J.A., Sutton, B.P.: Nonuniform fast fourier transforms using min-max interpolation. IEEE Trans. Sig. Process. **51**(2), 560–574 (2003)
12. Ahmad, A., Ja'afar, N.H., Amira, A.: FPGA-based implementation of 3-D daubechies for medical image compression. In: IEEE EMBS Conference on Biomedical Engineering and Sciences (IECBES). IEEE (2012)
13. Shrestha, A., Timalsina, A.: Color image steganography technique using daubechies discrete wavelet transform. In: 2015 9th International Conference on Software, Knowledge, Information Management and Applications (SKIMA). IEEE (2015)

14. Wahid, K.: Low complexity implementation of daubechies wavelets for medical imaging applications. In: INTECH Open, pp. 122–134 (2011)
15. Daubechies, I.: Ten lectures on wavelets. In: SIAM (1992)
16. Walker, J.S.: A Primer on Wavelets and Scientific Applications (1999)
17. Daubechies, I., Sweldens, W.: Factoring wavelet transforms into lifting steps. J. Fourier Anal. Appl. 4(1998), 247–269 (1998)

# Robust Knot Segmentation by Knot Pith Tracking in 3D Tangential Images

Adrien Krähenbühl[1]([✉]), Jean-Romain Roussel[4], Bertrand Kerautret[1]([✉]),
Isabelle Debled-Rennesson[1], Frédéric Mothe[2,3], and Fleur Longuetaud[2,3]

[1] LORIA, UMR CNRS 7503, Université de Lorraine,
54506 Vandœuvre-les-nancy, France
{adrien.krahenbuhl,bertrand.kerautret,isabelle.debled-rennesson}@loria.fr
[2] INRA, UMR1092 LERFoB, 54280 Champenoux, France
[3] AgroParisTech, UMR1092 LERFoB, 54000 Nancy, France
{mothe,fleur.longuetaud}@nancy.inra.fr
[4] CRMR, Départ. des sciences du bois et de la foret, Laval, Québec, Canada
jean-romain.roussel.1@ulaval.ca

**Abstract.** This paper proposes a fast, accurate and automatic method
to segment wood knots from images obtained by X-Ray Computed
Tomography scanner. The wood knot segmentation is a classical problem
where the most popular segmentation techniques produce unsatisfactory
results. In a previous work, a method was developed to detect knot areas
and an approach was proposed to segment the knots. However this last
step is not entirely satisfactory in the presence of sapwood. This paper
presents a novel approach for knot segmentation, based on the original idea considering slices tangential to the growth rings. They allow to
track the knot from the log pith to the bark. Knots are then segmented
by detecting discrete ellipses in each slice. A complete implementation is
proposed on the TKDetection software available online.

## 1 Introduction

Outside the classical medical applications, Computer Tomography (CT) is also
used to study wooded structures from tree logs. Forest sciences researchers and
sawmills are the main clients of such analysis. The firsts are looking for accurate
knot measurements while the aim at the sawmills is to localize knots with real
time constraints in order to perform sawing optimization.

In presence of wet areas, the knot segmentation remains a well known challenge. As shown in Fig. 1(a), recent segmentation algorithms like the Power
Watershed [8] fails to precisely segment the knots even with a manual setting of
background/foreground thresholds (see also [12] for other experiments). Different authors have explored some original strategies to limit the influence of wet
areas: the use of knot models by Andreu and Rinnhofer [3], the deformable models of Aguilera *et al.* [2] or the exploitation of neural networks by Nordmark [14].
Even if these approaches permit to obtain satisfactory results, the segmentation
results inside such areas were not specifically measured by authors.

© Springer International Publishing AG 2016
L.J. Chmielewski et al. (Eds.): ICCVG 2016, LNCS 9972, pp. 581–593, 2016.
DOI: 10.1007/978-3-319-46418-3_52

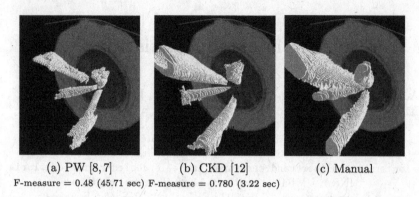

(a) PW [8, 7]              (b) CKD [12]              (c) Manual
F-measure = 0.48 (45.71 sec)  F-measure = 0.780 (3.22 sec)

**Fig. 1.** 3D reconstructions of segmented knots. Image (a) shows the limitations of classical image segmentation algorithm to segment such a wet wood image in comparison to previous method (b) and manual segmentation (c).

In a previous work was proposed a first solution to address the problem of knot segmentation in wet areas [12]. The idea was first to detect knot areas [13] and then to exploit the geometric information of curvature computed from discrete contours [9]. As shown in Fig. 1(b), this method named CKD (Curvature-based Knot Detection) is robust to wet sapwood areas and gives better results than the other general approaches. The classical statistics of *precision, recall* and *F-measure* obtained from the manual segmentation (c) support these improvements. However the segmentation quality can still be improved. In particular, the resulting shapes present different artifacts in some specific 2D slices ((b) vs. (c) in Fig. 1). Such artifacts do not have a significant influence for the *F-measure* values but can be preponderant for the knot curvature estimation.

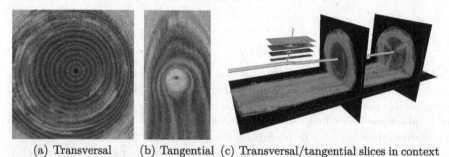

(a) Transversal    (b) Tangential  (c) Transversal/tangential slices in context

**Fig. 2.** Illustration of the pith extraction process for the log (in light blue) and knot (light red). Image (a) (respectively (b)) shows one of the source image exploited to obtain such a pith extraction for the log (respectively the knot). (Color figure online)

In the context of CKD, the slice-by-slice strategy taken in the main log axis does not allow to add new simple geometric constraints to improve the segmentation process. 2D slices in a direction tangential to the annual growth rings (see

Fig. 2(b)) seems more suitable to exploit and include prior shape informations in the segmentation algorithm. In particular, as stated in the work [15], such a strategy permits to track the pith of knots as illustrated on tangential image (b) of Fig. 2, and to automatically estimate the characteristics of the knot shape.

The contribution of this paper is to propose a fully automatic segmentation process TKD (Tangential-based Knot Detection) to extract the set of 3D voxels belonging to the knots. The first step relies on the knot areas detection [13] which overview is given in the next section. An extraction of tangential images is then presented in Sect. 4 before describing the knot pith tracking in Sect. 5. The segmentation process is finally achieved by the analysis of elliptic shapes in 2D images.

## 2   Knot Areas Detection with Z-Motion

The method proposed in [13] isolates each knot of a log on a knot area. Briefly, this method is based on the z-motion notion. It assumes that knots are the tree defects with the biggest movements visible when the scanned slices are scrolled. The first step identifies the groups of slices containing knot whorls. A second step, applied on each group of slices, isolates the knots of a whorl by analyzing the z-motion by angular sector centered on the pith.

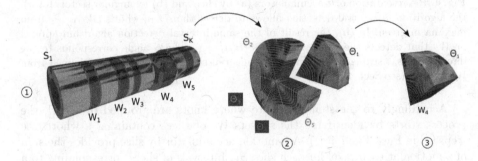

**Fig. 3.** Process of the knot area detection. From a log taken a set of slices $S_k$, the step ① identifies the whorls of knots $W$, subsets of slices. Then, during the second step ②, each knot of each whorl is isolated in an interval of angular sectors. Finally, each knot is contrained inside a knot area (③), sub-domain of the initial log.

### 2.1   Z-Motion

The z-motion, introduced in [13], considers a log as an image sequence taken along the z-axis. During the scrolling of this sequence, the knots seem to move between the pith and the bark of the stem. The z-motion can be seen as a measurement of this motion computed as a discrete derivative. More formally, a set $(S_k)_{1 \leq k \leq K}$ of log slices is considered (see Fig. 3), $S_k \in \mathbb{Z}^3$. The z-motion slice $Z_k$ for $2 \leq k \leq K$ is computed as: $Z_k = |S_k - S_{k-1}|$.

## 2.2   Knot Areas

A knot area is a log area containing only one knot. A knot area is cropped in two similar steps based on the z-motion analysis. These two steps (see Fig. 3) use a z-motion accumulator [12] in order to detect areas with a high value of z-motion.

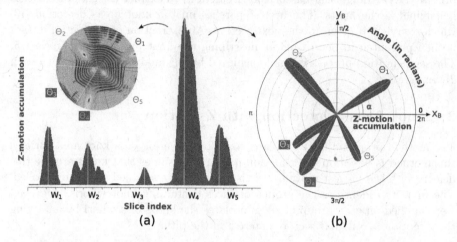

**Fig. 4.** Representation of z-accumulators (a) by slice and (b) by angular sector. In (a), the algorithm of interval detection allows to detect the set of whorls $(W_i)_{1 \leq i \leq 5}$ from maxima in green. In (b), the result of the same interval detection algorithm applied on $W_2$ that detects the angular intervals $(\Theta_j)_{1 \leq j \leq 5}$. The $\alpha$ angle corresponds to the direction of $s_\alpha$, segment directing the tangential slices of the knot area defined from $W_1$ and $\Theta_1$ (see Sect. 4.1).

Accordingly to the stem structure where knots are grouped by whorl, the process starts by identifying the subsets $W_i$ of slices containing a whorl (see steps ① in Figs. 3 and 4(a)). A z-motion accumulator by slice provides the sum of z-motion at each pixel for each slice $S_k$. Intervals of slices corresponding to a whorl are localized by a dedicated algorithm of interval detection based on the maximum localization on the z-accumulation representation (see details in [12]). The second step is applied on each identified whorl (② on Fig. 3). It requires to know the pith position on each slice of the whorl. The whorl is split in angular sectors centered on the pith position. A z-motion accumulator by angular sector provides the sum of z-motion at each pixel of this angular sector on all the whorl slices. The intervals $\Theta_j$ of angular sectors containing a knot are localized by the same algorithm of interval detection as in the first step (see Fig. 4(b)). Finally, each of the resulting knot area, similar to the shape ③ in Fig. 3, contains one knot. The knot areas will be used as starting elements for the new tangential segmentation method presented in the next section. More details about the knot area detection could be found in [12,13].

Note that this knot area detection can also be obtained by using the recent method allowing to extract individual knot [10].

## 3    Tangential Segmentation Overview

The proposed segmentation method, TKD (Tangential-based Knot Detection) is built on a unique assumption: the knot cross-sections are circular on planes directed orthogonally to the local knot pith trajectory (see Fig. 2). It considers each knot as a series $(T_l)_{1 \leq l \leq L}$ of slices "tangential" to the annual growth rings. In this context, knots appear as ellipses on each slice $T_l$ (see Fig. 5). Elliptical appearance of a knot on a slice $T_l$ derives from two aspects: the voxel aspect ratio on a tangential slice and the vertical inclination of the knot inside the log. These two aspects are combined to compute the knot elliptical coefficient $\tau$ of each tangential slice. A profile of elliptical cumulated intensities allows then to identify the major radius of the best ellipse fitting the knot contour. However, ellipse computing is usually intricate on tangential slices close to the stem pith and to the bark. An extrapolation followed by the LOWESS algorithm [5] avoid outlier ellipses.

Tested on few samples of knots in [15], the next sections propose several improvements. They allow to generalize the process to various tree species and to automate it for complete logs.

## 4    Tangential Slices

This is the first step of the segmentation of one knot area. It consists in generating the set $(T_l)$ of slices tangential to the annual growth rings (see Fig. 5).

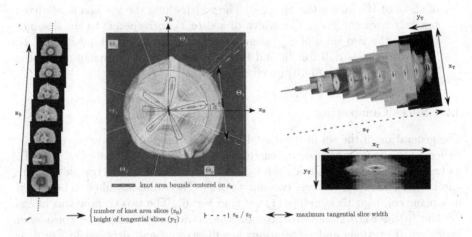

knot area bounds centered on $s_\alpha$

number of knot area slices ($z_B$)
height of tangential slices ($y_T$)    $\vdash$ - - -$\dashv$ $s_\alpha$ / $z_T$    maximum tangential slice width

**Fig. 5.** Process to generate tangential slices. On the left a slice set detected as containing a knot whorl. In the middle, a log slice with a diagram representing the z-motion accumulator by transparency. For the $\Theta_1$ angular sector interval, the $s_\alpha$ segment is drawn as red dashed from the pith to the bark. $s_\alpha$ is oriented in the direction of the maximum of the z-motion accumulation (in green). Initial knot area bounds (white lines) are reoriented to have $s_\alpha$ as bisectrix. All tangential slices on the right are generated throughout $s_\alpha$ with an increasing width from 0 to the orange segment width. (Color figure online)

## 4.1    Position and Dimensions

The $(T_l)$ set of tangential slices of the knot area must be (1) directed, (2) positioned and (3) bounded in the $(O_B, x_B, y_B, z_B)$ space of the log (see Fig. 5).

(1) *Directions.* The $T_l$ slices are directed orthogonally to a main segment denoted $s_\alpha$. This segment is orthogonal to the $z_B$ axis, in the $(x_B, y_B)$ plan. In this plan, $s_\alpha$ is oriented by an $\alpha$ angle determined from the direction of the maximum of z-motion for $\Theta_j$ (see $\Theta_1$ in Figs. 4(b) and 5). Orientation of the knot area bisectrix, median angle of $\Theta_j$, is not used because the knot is not necessarily angularly centered in the knot area but always in the direction of the maximum of z-motion of $\Theta_j$. Contrariwise, the knot area magnitude is retained to consider an angular interval of same magnitude, with $s_\alpha$ as bisectrix (in white dashes and lines in Fig. 5).

(2) *Position.* The $s_\alpha$ segment starts at the stem pith level and finishes at the bark limit (in red dots in Fig. 5). The start point for $s_\alpha$ is fixed as the position of the stem pith on the log slice corresponding to the middle of the $W_i$ whorl. To determine the bark position, end point of the knot pith, the first value lower than $-900$[1] is searched from the start point in the $s_\alpha$ direction. This step could be simplified by using the stem radii computed during the knot area localization step. The $s_\alpha$ length is used to determine the number of tangential slices.

(3) *Bounds.* The dimensions of the tangential slices are differently fixed horizontally and vertically. The height along the $y_T$ axis is simply the number of slices of $W_i$ (along the $z_B$ axis). The width along the $x_T$ axis is not fixed but increases along $s_\alpha$. The width of a slice $T_l$ corresponds to the distance between the two sides of $\Theta_j$ taken orthogonally to $s_\alpha$ at the position of $T_l$. This distance is null for $T_0$ and increases linearly to be maximum at the bark (orange line in Fig. 5) on the $T_L$ slice.

## 4.2    Slices Generating

The generating of the set of tangential slices $(T_l)$ is performed slice by slice. For a slice $T_l$, the process consists in searching for each pixel coordinate $(x_t, y_t)$ of $T_l$, its $(x_b, y_b, z_b)$ coordinates inside the log. Three rotations and two translations are applied to each $(x_t, y_t)$ integer coordinate of $T_l$. The rotations allow to be placed in a plane collinear to $s_\alpha$ (steps ① to ④ in Fig. 6). The two translations (steps ⑤ and ⑥ in Fig. 6) allow to position the coordinates inside the considered knot area. Rotations and translations are illustrated and detailed in Fig. 6. If the position is searched as integer coordinates $(s_t, y_t)$, rotations and translations provide decimal coordinates $(x_b, y_b, z_b)$. A trilinear interpolation allows then to improve quality of tangential images and consequently the next segmentation steps.

---

[1] $-900$ (in Hounsfield Unit) corresponds to a wood density of $100 \text{kg/m}^3$.

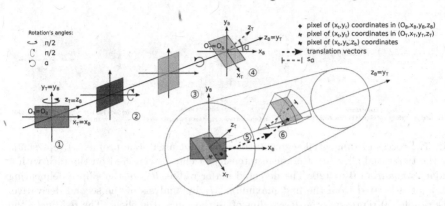

**Fig. 6.** Matching process between the coordinates of a tangential slice $T_l$ and the log coordinates. Rotations ① to ④ positioned the coordinates in a plane collinear to $s_\alpha$. Translations ⑤ and ⑥ move the coordinates at their exact position in the stem coordinate system: ⑤ links $O_B$ to the pith position in the middle slice of $W_i$ and ⑥ links the pith position in the middle slice of $W_i$ to the intersection of $T_l$ with $s_\alpha$.

## 5  Knot Pith Tracking

The knot pith tracking is the first and the most critical step of the tangential segmentation of knots. A good localization of the pith ensures a best precision for ellipse detection. The pith is tracked with help of the Boukadida et al. algorithm [4]. This algorithm is based on a Sobel edge detection, where edges correspond here to the border of the knot cross-section, and the Hough accumulation principle. This detection algorithm, designed to retrieve log pith using circular shape of growth rings appears to be robust with ellipticity but several steps of this algorithm must be optimized in the context of the knot pith, where some problems appear with the original algorithm version:

*Tangential Slice Shape.* The increasing width of the tangential slices must be considered for all steps of the algorithm. Due to the angular interval of the knot area, the increasing width ensures to only deal with one knot. It also implies that the narrowest slices do not contain enough informations to be segmented.

*Extrapolation Step.* The last step is an extrapolation of first and last slices. In the original algorithm dedicated to the stem pith, invalid slices at the start and at the end do not contain a tree part and can be ignored. On the tangential slices, first slices necessarily contain the knot start but its apparent diameter is low. It is complicated to precisely localize the pith position on these narrow slices. Similarly, when the knot reaches the bark, the last slices contain the knot ending inside an increasingly small part of wood due to the tree circularity. Moreover, the additional presence of sapwood at this position makes it hard to differentiate the knot contour points from the noise. For these two reasons, the knot pith position is extrapolated by using the local slope of the first and last valid slices to determine the knot pith direction.

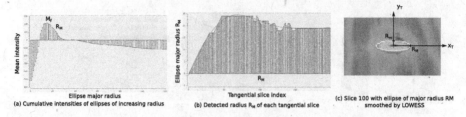

Ellipse major radius
(a) Cumulative intensities of ellipses of increasing radius

Tangential slice index
(b) Detected radius $R_M$ of each tangential slice

(c) Slice 100 with ellipse of major radius RM smoothed by LOWESS

**Fig. 7.** Process of tangential segmentation in a knot area. The profile (a) represents, for the tangential slice (c), the mean intensity of ellipses centered on the pith with a major radius from 0 to 120. The detected major radius $R_M$ of the ellipse delineating the knot is located from the first maximum $M_f$ by analysis of the second derivative. The profile (b) represents the $R_M$ radius of all the tangential slices. The red line is the ellipse radius $R_M$ found on the profile (a). The blue curve represents the final ellipse major radius obtained by LOWESS regression. On the (c) tangential slice is drawn in red the pith position. The white ellipse is parameterized with the smoothed radius. (Color figure online)

## 6    Elliptical Segmentation

The elliptical segmentation is independently applied to each knot area. The elliptical segmentation step requires to have generated the set of tangential slices $(T_l)_{1 \leq l \leq L}$ of the knot area (see Sect. 4) and to know the knot pith position on each tangential slice $T_l$ (see Sect. 5).

The process consists in finding, for each slice $T_l$, the parameters of the ellipse delineating the knot, centered on the knot pith. This assumes that apparent knot sections would be circular shaped on slices directed orthogonally to the knot pith trajectory. The elliptical segmentation is performed in three steps:

A. Elliptical coefficient computing
B. Ellipse major radius detection
C. Local regression of the ellipse radius series.

Note that steps (A) and (B) is local to each slice $T_l$ while step (C) concern the global ellipse set $(T_l)_{1 \leq l \leq L}$.

### 6.1    Elliptical Coefficient Computing

On each tangential slice $T_l$, the elliptical coefficient $\tau$ of the apparent knot section is the $R_m/R_M$ ratio where $R_m$ is the ellipse minor radius, in the $y_T$ axis direction, and $R_M$ is the ellipse major radius, in the $x_T$ axis direction (see Fig. 7(c)). Two factors impact the $\tau$ value: (1) the pixel aspect ratio of the slice and (2) the local vertical inclination of the pith.

(1) The pixel aspect ratio $w{:}h$ of a tangential slice is common to all the $T_l$ slices. It is directly deduced from the voxel aspect ratio of the log. The two first rotations (① to ③ in Fig. 6) of the tangential slice generating implies that

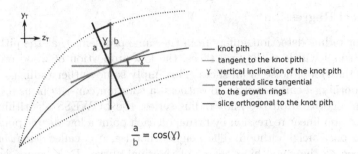

**Fig. 8.** Details of the factor of the elliptical coefficient due to the use of slices tangent to the growth rings. Ellipses would be circles on slices orthogonal to the local knot pith direction.

$w$ is equal to the initial inter-slice spacing (rotations lead to match $y_T$ with $z_B$ as illustrated in Fig. 6). The $\alpha$ angle of the last rotation (③ to ④ in Fig. 6) and the pixel aspect ratio of transversal slices allow to determine the $h$ coefficient.

(2) The vertical inclination of the knot pith computed locally to a tangential slice generates the second term of $\tau$, factor inversely proportional to the cosine of the vertical inclination (see Fig. 8). Here, the vertical direction refers to the $z_B$ axis, and therefore the $y_T$ axis (see Fig. 5). Indeed,the more the knot is vertically inclined, the more $R_m$ decreases. The vertical inclination of the pith is computed from the discrete local derivative of the vertical knot position.

The final elliptical coefficient $\tau$ is computed as:

$$\tau = \frac{R_m}{R_M} = \frac{w}{h} \times \frac{1}{cos(\gamma)}$$

## 6.2 Major Radius Detection

This second step assumes to know the knot pith position and the computed elliptical coefficient $\tau$ of the apparent knot section on $T_l$. It aims to find the best ellipse delineating the apparent knot section among the set of ellipses centered on the pith, with an integer major radius. From each ellipse $E$ of this set, the mean of intensity values of pixels composing $E$ is computed. Pixels composing $E$ are determined with help of the midpoint algorithm, extension of the Bresenham's circle algorithm to the elliptical case [16]. The profile in Fig. 7(a) represents the series of elliptical means of the ellipse set.

This profile shows a characteristic shape allowing to select the $R_M$ major radius of the best ellipse. Specifically, the first maximum $M_f$ is identified. If $M_f$ is found after the half of the profile, the first profile value is considered. Then we iteratively analyze the slope after $M_f$ to determine the position where the second derivate becomes positive. This position corresponds to the $R_M$ radius of the ellipse delineating the apparent knot section at best.

The minor radius $R_m$ is directly deduced by the formula $R_m = \tau \times R_M$.

## 6.3  Local Regression

The major radius detection suffers from the same problems that the pith detection: the small width of the first slices, the low proportion of wood on in last ones and the global noise in all slices. This imply some outlier radii.

A smoothing being sensitive to outliers, a solution consists in using a local regression algorithm on the knot radius series: the LOWESS algorithm [5]. It performs a non linear regression by fitting on each point a low-degree polynomial computed on a neighborhood. The neighborhood size is called *bandwidth* and can be seen as the smoothing degree of the final curve. To be more resistant, the LOWESS algorithm apply two times by interposing an outlier interpolation based on an inter-quartile statistic computed on the residue between initial data and the first LOWESS curve. The final major radius $R_M$ (see Fig. 7(b)) is given by the LOWESS curve after the second pass.

## 7  Discussions and Comparisons

The knot segmentation based on the tangential approach is advantageous for two main reasons: the knot pith tracking efficient inside the wet sapwood and the low computing time. The knot pith tracking is presently the best way to determine the knot trajectory on wet areas. In [12], the knot position inside the sapwood was extrapolated from estimation of the knot curvature at the heartwood/sapwood limit. In this paper, the knot center is exactly detected from the log pith until the bark. The elliptical constraint led to an accurate detection process of the knot volume contour. Second reason, the computing time is close to 1 s for a whorl, without any parallelization. This is particularly important for sawmills to include the knot segmentation step on the wood sawing analysis process.

The complete TKD method proposed in this paper is implemented in the software TKDetection [11] freely available online. It allows to test and validate TKD with other log samples. The Fig. 9 compares the reconstructions of volumes detected by TKD to the Power Watershed (implemented in [7]) and CKD algorithms. Artifacts visible on these two other methods disappear with the TKD. The classical measurements of precision, recall and *F-measure* were computed and compared for each method. The results presented in Table 1 show that the proposed method has the best *F-measure* scores for each species and the first or second rank for the precision or recall scores. Moreover by mean for all species, TKD is almost 5× faster in comparison to CKD. We also apply segmentation quality measure by using the curvature of the shape computed by a recent multigrid convergent curvature estimator based on integral invariants [6]. This estimator available through the DGtal library [1] is adapted to the digital objects and needs only the setting of one parameter associated to the radius of the ball used in the estimation (set to 10 in these experiments). To estimate the segmentation quality with curvature, we first associate each surface element (surfel) $s_s$ of the segmented shape to the nearest surfel $s_r$ of the reference shape. Then, the curvature comparison is obtained from the mean squared errors of curvature $\kappa$ given in the two surfels:

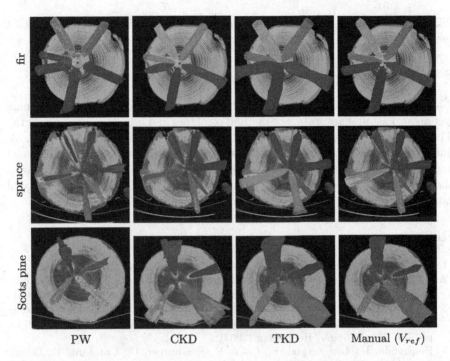

**Fig. 9.** Comparisons of segmentation algorithms: the Power Watershed (PW) [8], CKD [12], the tangential approach TKD and a manual segmentation.

**Table 1.** Segmentation comparisons of our algorithm with the PW and CKD algorithms. For each criterion, the best ranks are highlighted with these ranges: first , second values. Computing times are given in seconds.

| Species | Spruce | | | | Fir | | | | Scots pine | | | |
|---|---|---|---|---|---|---|---|---|---|---|---|---|
| Method | time | precision | recall | F-mes | time | precision | recall | F-mes | time | precision | recall | F-mes |
| PW | 47.7 | 0.835 | 0.297 | 0.438 | 38.21 | 0.820 | 0.858 | 0.839 | 45.71 | 0.894 | 0.328 | 0.480 |
| CKD | 5.88 | 0.856 | 0.633 | 0.728 | 5.35 | 0.921 | 0.787 | 0.849 | 3.22 | 0.752 | 0.811 | 0.780 |
| TKD | 1.21 | 0.766 | 0.774 | 0.770 | 1.98 | 0.856 | 0.844 | 0.850 | 0.86 | 0.762 | 0.852 | 0.805 |

| Species | Spruce | | Fir | | Scots pine | |
|---|---|---|---|---|---|---|
| Method | $MSE(\kappa)$ | $MaxE(\kappa)$ | $MSE(\kappa)$ | $MaxE(\kappa)$ | $MSE(\kappa)$ | $MaxE(\kappa)$ |
| PW | 0.0126 | 0.1187 | 0.0015 | 0.0445 | 0.0051 | 0.0816 |
| CKD | 0.0044 | 0.0872 | 0.0022 | 0.0264 | 0.0041 | 0.1706 |
| TKD | 0.0036 | 0.0833 | 0.0014 | 0.0373 | 0.0025 | 0.0374 |

$MSE(\kappa) = (\kappa(s_s) - \kappa(s_r))^2$. Associated to this measure, we also compute the maximal squared error $MaxE(\kappa)$. As for the previous measure, the results of the proposed method TKD outperform the previous approach CKD with almost the best results (see second part of Table 1). Note that the overlapped orange knot of spruce specie (manual segmentation of Fig. 9) is not segmented by TKD since the knot detection method detects a single angular sector containing in fact two different knots. Such limitation could be improved by using an individual knot detection [10].

## 8   Conclusion

This paper proposes an automatic knot segmentation process on logs containing wet areas. Fast and accurate, the method combines and improves ideas of [12, 15]. The method is fully implemented in the TKDetection software [11] available online. First experiments show very good results with regard to the biologist and sawmills expectations. Knots segmented with TKD are the most similar to the knots manually segmented. Experiments will be applied to a wider range of samples with a more detailed analysis of the obtained volumes of knots.

## References

1. DGtal: digital geometry tools and algorithms library. http://dgtal.org
2. Aguilera, C., Sanchez, R., Baradit, E.: Detection of knots using X-ray tomographies and deformable contours with simulated annealing. Wood Res. **53**, 57–66 (2008)
3. Andreu, J.-P., Rinnhofer, A.: Modeling knot geometry in norway spruce from industrial CT images. In: Bigun, J., Gustavsson, T. (eds.) SCIA 2003. LNCS, vol. 2749, pp. 786–791. Springer, Heidelberg (2003)
4. Boukadida, H., Longuetaud, F., Colin, F., Freyburger, C., Constant, T., Leban, J.M., Mothe, F.: Pithextract: a robust algorithm for pith detection in computer tomography images of wood - application to 125 logs from 17 tree species. Comput. Electr. Agric. **85**, 90–98 (2012)
5. Cleveland, W.S.: Robust locally weighted regression and smoothing scatterplots. JASA **74**, 829–836 (1979)
6. Coeurjolly, D., Lachaud, J.-O., Levallois, J.: Integral based curvature estimators in digital geometry. In: Gonzalez-Diaz, R., Jimenez, M.-J., Medrano, B. (eds.) DGCI 2013. LNCS, vol. 7749, pp. 215–227. Springer, Heidelberg (2013). doi:10. 1007/978-3-642-37067-0_19
7. Couprie, C., Grady, L., Najman, L., Talbot, H.: The power watershed algorithm c/c++ code. http://sourceforge.net/projects/powerwatershed/
8. Couprie, C., Grady, L., Najman, L., Talbot, H.: Power watersheds: a unifying graph-based optimization framework. IEEE PAMI **33**(7), 1384–1399 (2010)
9. Kerautret, B., Lachaud, J.O.: Curvature estimation along noisy digital contours by approximate global optimization. PR **42**(10), 2265–2278 (2009)
10. Krähenbühl, A., Kerautret, B., Feschet, F.: Knot Detection from Accumulation Map by Polar Scan. In: Barneva, P.R., et al. (eds.) IWCIA 2015. LNCS, vol. 9448, pp. 352–362. Springer, Heidelberg (2015). doi:10.1007/978-3-319-26145-4_26
11. Krähenbühl, A.: TKDetection (2012). https://github.com/akrah/TKDetection/
12. Krähenbühl, A., Kerautret, B., Debled-Rennesson, I.: Knot segmentation in noisy 3D images of wood. In: Gonzalez-Diaz, R., Jimenez, M.-J., Medrano, B. (eds.) DGCI 2013. LNCS, vol. 7749, pp. 383–394. Springer, Heidelberg (2013)
13. Krähenbühl, A., Kerautret, B., Debled-Rennesson, I., Longuetaud, F., Mothe, F.: Knot detection in X-Ray CT images of wood. In: Bebis, G., Boyle, R., Parvin, B., Koracin, D., Fowlkes, C., Wang, S., Choi, M.-H., Mantler, S., Schulze, J., Acevedo, D., Mueller, K., Papka, M. (eds.) ISVC 2012, Part II. LNCS, vol. 7432, pp. 209–218. Springer, Heidelberg (2012)

14. Nordmark, U.: Value recovery and production control in the forestry-wood chain using simulation technique. Ph.D. thesis, Luleå University of Technology (2005)

15. Roussel, J.R., Mothe, F., Krähenbühl, A., Kerautret, B., Debled-Rennesson, I., Longuetaud, F.: Automatic knot segmentation in CT images of wet softwood logs using a tangential approach. Comput. Electr. Agric. **104**, 46–56 (2014)

16. Van Aken, J.: An efficient ellipse-drawing algorithm. IEEE Comput. Graph. Appl. **4**, 24–35 (1984)

# Artificial Neural Network Based Sinhala Character Recognition

H. Waruna H. Premachandra[1]([⊠]), Chinthaka Premachandra[2],
Tomotaka Kimura[3], and Hiroharu Kawanaka[4]

[1] ICT Center, Wayamba University of Srilanka, Makadura, Sri Lanka
warunaprema@yahoo.com
[2] Department of Electronic Engineering, Shibaura Institute of Technology,
3-7-5 Toyosu Koto-ku, Tokyo 135-8548, Japan
chintaka@shibaura-it.ac.jp
[3] Tokyo University of Science, 6-3-1 Niijuku Katsushika-ku, Tokyo 125-8585, Japan
kimura@ee.kagu.tus.ac.jp
[4] Graduate School of Engineering, Mie University,
1577 Kurimamachiya-cho, Tsu City, Mie 514-8507, Japan
kawanaka@elec.mie-u.ac.jp

**Abstract.** Sinhala is the main language spoken by the majority of the
population of Sri Lanka. There is a clear need for an optical character
recognition (OCR) system for the Sinhala language. However, the language contains very similar characters, which makes it very difficult to
distinguish them except on feature analysis. The character recognition
rates of previous systems proposed for Sinhala character recognition are
low, and so further improvement is needed. Consequently, in this paper,
we propose a new Sinhala character recognition method that uses character geometry features and artificial neural network (ANN). The results
of experiments conducted using various documentary images of the Sinhala language indicate that the proposed method has better character
recognition performance than conventional methods.

**Keywords:** Character recognition · Sinhala script · Character geometry
features · Artificial neural networks

## 1  Introduction

Optical character recognition (OCR) technology is used to convert information
available in printed or handwritten documents to machine-editable electronic
forms. In this paper, we discuss the development of an optical character reader
for the Sinhala language, which is one of the major languages in Sri Lanka.
Sophisticated OCR solutions are available for many languages in the world,
such as English, Japanese, French, German, and Chinese. In the case of the
Sinhala language, several studies have proposed various methods for recognizing
Sinhala characters. However, the few currently available Sinhala OCR systems
are not effective, since they are personal dependent, i.e., they are successful only

© Springer International Publishing AG 2016
L.J. Chmielewski et al. (Eds.): ICCVG 2016, LNCS 9972, pp. 594–603, 2016.
DOI: 10.1007/978-3-319-46418-3_53

for a limited predefined set of characters and their character recognition rate is low. Furthermore, the proposed methods are focused on recognizing only a very limited number of characters.

## 1.1  Characteristics of the Sinhala Language

Sinhala scripts evolved from ancient Brahmi scripts. They comprise approximately 18 vowels and 41 consonants. Some of those vowels and consonants are illustrated in Fig. 1. In addition, a variety of 17 modifier symbols is also included in the Sinhala language, as illustrated in Fig. 2. A modified character is created by combining a consonant and a modifier symbol (see Fig. 3). Many modified characters are available, some of which are very similar in shape because some of the modifier symbols have virtually similar shapes. Human beings can distinguish each character correctly. However, it is very difficult for a computer to recognize them separately following the current OCR technologies. In this paper, we focus on this interesting and rather complex recognition problem.

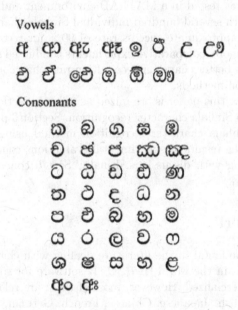

**Fig. 1.** Vowels and consonants of the Sinhala language

**Fig. 2.** Some modifier symbols

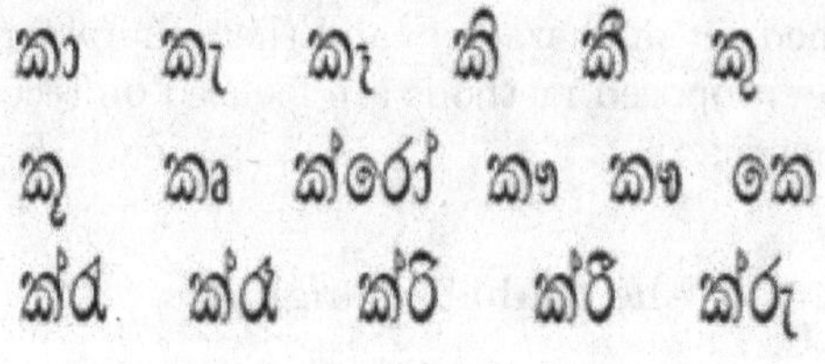

කා   කැ   කෑ   කි   කී   කු
කූ   කෘ   ක්රෝ   කෲ   කෟ   කේ
ක්ඍ   ක්ඎ   ක්ඍ   ක්ඏ   ක්ඐ

**Fig. 3.** Some modified characters

The studies in the literature have not considered recognition of the above modified characters, although experiments have been conducted using the images of some consonants and vowels. In this paper, our target is recognition of modified characters as well as consonants and vowels. Recognition of the modified characters is comparatively harder than that of consonants and vowels because several modified characters have virtually similar shapes. In order to overcome this complex problem, we develop a new Sinhala character recognition method using character geometric features (CGF) and artificial neural networks (ANN). The proposed method was tested in a MATLAB environment and evaluated using a testing database with several hundred individual Sinhala character images. The results indicate an approximate success rate of 90 % for recognition of Sinhala characters. Furthermore, comparative experiments conducted show that the proposed method has a better character recognition rate than conventional Sinhala character recognition methods.

The remainder of this paper is organized as follows. Section 2 describes previous approaches to Sinhala character recognition. Section 3 presents the details of the proposed Sinhala character recognition method using CGF and ANN. Section 4 presents the results of experimental evaluations conducted of the proposed method, along with discussions. Finally, Sect. 5 concludes and outlines plans for future work.

## 2   Related Work

Many studies can be found in the literature dealing with character recognition of various languages in the world [1–7]. OCR software for some languages has already been commercialized. However, most of them are related to major languages such as English, Japanese, Chinese, French, German, and Spanish. The overall shape of characters in a language has its own features. For example, English characters are very simple and most of them are different in shape. Further, they are written using very few linear or curved strokes. In the case of the Chinese language, a Chinese character is written using many strokes, including both linear and curved strokes, and some of them have virtually the same shape. Considering those conditions, it is difficult to apply English or Chinese character recognition methods without having a means of modification to achieve effective character recognition of the other language. In the case of the Sinhala language, most of the characters are written using round strokes. Furthermore, several characters have almost similar shapes because of the combinations of modifier symbols and consonants, as shown in the Fig. 3.

Consequently, Sinhala character recognition is a complex problem on which several studies have been conducted within the last several years [8–12]. Most of these studies have proposed the use of soft computing and statistical approaches such as Fuzzy logic and Hidden Markov Models.

Hewavitharana et al. [8] proposed an offline Sinhala character recognition method that conducts Sinhala character recognition using hidden Markov models (HMMs). Their experimental environment consisted of the most commonly used 25 characters, and modified Sinhala characters were not considered. Experimental results showed that their method has an accuracy rate of 64.3 %.

Premarathna et al. [11] proposed a linear symmetry (LS)-based approach in which characters are initially recognized through a multi-level filtering process using the LS feature. The recognized characters are then segmented to identify the associated modifier symbols. In this case, the results of experiments conducted using various fonts showed a success rate of 84 %.

Kodituwakku et al. [12] proposed another soft computing-based Sinhala character recognition method in which a character is segmented into meaningful segments through fuzzy characteristics. That approach responds well to smoothly written characters and characters that do not tend to conflict with other characters such as modified characters.

In this paper, we propose a Sinhala character recognition method that performs better than the above conventional methods. Whereas limited types of Sinhala characters were used in the experiments conducted in the above studies, we tested using the 55 types of printed characters and different fonts, as well as a bit of handwritten characters by different people in our experiments. The details of the proposed method are given below.

## 3  Proposed Method for Sinhala Character Recognition

The new proposal includes three main processing steps: preprocessing, recognition, and post-processing, as illustrated in Fig. 4.

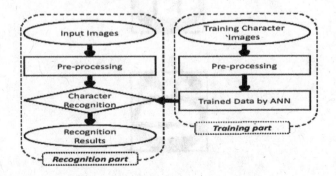

**Fig. 4.** Main processing steps in the proposed method

The proposed method extracts a set of geometry-based features from the characters. These features are based on the basic line types that form the character skeleton. The system then gives a feature vector as its output. The feature vector, which is generated from a training set, is used to train the pattern recognition engine of an ANN. The main steps related to the proposal are described below.

## 3.1    Universe of Discourse and Zoning

During the preprocessing stage, scanned images are prepared for the recognition process. Cleaning and de-skewing of the images are initially conducted. Then, the images are scaled and binarized [13].

Universe of discourse (UOD) [14] is defined as the shortest matrix that covers the entire character skeleton, illustrated in the Fig. 5. The UOD is used to extract the character image region. Therefore, every character image should be independent of its image size.

**Fig. 5.** Example of UOD

Following extraction of the character image region, it is divided into a number of windows of similar size vertically and then horizontally, as illustrated in Fig. 6.

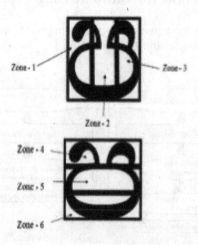

**Fig. 6.** Vertical and horizontal zoning

## 3.2  Distinguishing Line Segments

After conducting the above zoning process in each and every zone, the following four types of line particles are presented:

(a) Horizontal line
(b) Vertical line
(c) Right diagonal line
(d) Left diagonal line

A direction vector is then extracted from every line segment and used to determine each line type. As stated above, feature extraction is applied to each individual zone rather than the entire image, which gives more information about the character skeleton.

## 3.3  Feature Extraction

Following determination of the line type segment, a feature vector [15] is formed based on this information. Consequently, every zone is associated with a corresponding feature vector. This results in every zone having a feature vector nine components in length. The contents of each zone feature vector are as follows:

(1) Number of horizontal lines.
(2) Number of vertical lines.
(3) Number of right diagonal lines.
(4) Number of left diagonal lines.
(5) Normalized length of all horizontal lines.
(6) Normalized length of all vertical lines.
(7) Normalized length of all right diagonal lines.
(8) Normalized length of all left diagonal lines.
(9) Normalized area of the skeleton.

The feature vectors for the characters in the training set are obtained as explained above. This feature vector is then fed into an ANN; specifically, a feed-forward error back-propagation neural network. The ANN and the overall system was implemented using MATLAB version 7.8.8.0.347 (R2009a), and the output of the ANN tested using another set of testing images.

## 3.4  Character Recognition Through ANN

Geometry-based line features were extracted from the character training images in a character image database, fed into the ANN, and trained accordingly. Subsequently, by using the testing images in the character image database, character recognition was conducted. This process is illustrated in Fig. 4.

The neural network toolkit in MATLAB version 7.8.8.0.347(R2009a) was used to implement the neural network for the initial training and testing purposes. In this paper, we evaluate the effectiveness of proposed pre-processing and features extraction methods, so that we use a simple neural network. The neural network was implemented with 26 neurons in the hidden layer, tansig as the transfer function for the hidden layers, and traingd as the back-propagation network training function. The number of epochs was set to 800,000 and the MSE was 3e-5. All training functions and values were obtained experimentally. We determined this setup to be the optimum for the neural network after running the system more than one hundred times and changing the parameters experimentally. The neural network implementation is defined in Eq. (1) below:

$$net = newff(minmax(actualTrainingSet); [261]);,$$
$$\{\text{'tansig purelin'}\}, \text{'traingd'}); \hspace{3cm} (1)$$
$$net.trainParam.lr = 0.05;$$
$$net.trainParam.goal = 3e - 5;$$
$$net.trainParam.epochs = 800000;$$

As it returns only one output character as per one input character, we have a one neuron in the output layer and 'purelin' would be one of an appropriate transfer function for the output layer, as it is more a Regression than a Classification in the ANN.

## 4   Character Recognition Evaluation

### 4.1   Testing Environment

The preliminary evaluation was conducted in the system itself following the training of the image database. Recognition of 44 different characters in the Sinhala language was conducted. The training database consisted of 968 character images, with each Sinhala character comprising 22 different printed and handwritten versions.

In our implementation, we utilized a computer with the following configuration: Intel(R) Core(TM) i7-2600 CPU@3.40 GHz, 4.00 GB RAM.

### 4.2   Results

We conducted evaluations for the consonants, vowels, and modified characters separately. To do this, we use a database that consists of 1000 character images, and we evaluate the success rate of the proposed method. Formally, the success rate of each character $c$ is defined as follows:

$$\text{success rate} = \frac{\# \text{ of successes in recognition}}{\text{total } \# \text{ of character } c}.$$

We also tested the success rate of one of the best methods found in the literature [11].

Table 1 shows the success rate for some consonants and vowels while Table 2 shows the success rate for some modified characters. Table 3 shows the average success rate for all the characters used in the experiments.

**Table 1.** Character recognition results for consonants and vowels

| Consonants and vowels (Pronunciation) | Success rate by proposed method (%) | Success rate by conventional method (%) |
|---|---|---|
| අ (a) | 96 | 83 |
| ඔ (o) | 91 | 85 |
| ව (wa) | 87 | 82 |
| න (na) | 89 | 81 |
| ත (tha) | 90 | 81 |
| ක (ka) | 91 | 84 |
| ප (pa) | 93 | 86 |

**Table 2.** Character recognition results for modified characters

| Modified characters (Pronunciation) | Success rate by proposed method (%) | Success rate by conventional method (%) |
|---|---|---|
| ආ (aa) | 93 | 84 |
| කා (kaa) | 89 | 81 |
| ති (thi) | 91 | 85 |
| නු (nu) | 90 | 82 |
| ප් (p) | 92 | 82 |
| බැ (bae) | 91 | 85 |
| මෙ (me) | 88 | 81 |

**Table 3.** Overall character recognition evaluation

| Type of Characters | Average success rate by proposed method(%) | Average success rate by conventional method(%) |
|---|---|---|
| 44 | 90 | 84 |

### 4.3   Discussions

The overall results of the recognition experiments indicate that our proposed method has a better performance than that of one of the best methods in the literature [11].

As stated in the introduction, Sinhala character recognition is a complex problem because some characters have similar shapes. Our proposed method achieved a better success rate for consonants and vowels than for the modified characters. The modified characters were generated by combining consonant and modifier symbols. In some cases, a consonant was combined with multiple modifier symbols to generate multiple modified characters, as illustrated in Fig. 7. In the figure, the left part of the three characters is a single consonant and it is combined with the three different modifier symbols to generate the three different modified characters. As Fig. 7 illustrates, the three modifier symbols have almost the same shape. Consequently, false detection occurred very easily in the case of modified character recognition.

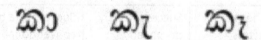

**Fig. 7.** Example of three similar modified characters

In the case of the consonants and vowels, a few characters also had similar shapes. However, the number of such characters was small compared to that for the modified characters. Furthermore, the similarity was weak. Consequently, the proposed method had a better recognition rate for consonants and vowels than with the modified characters.

In future work, we plan to further improve the character recognition rate by considering curve features in the feature extraction stage.

## 5   Conclusion

This research was conducted with the aim of devising a multi-faceted character recognition method for Sinhala characters. A new Sinhala character recognition method was developed using CGFs and ANNs. The results of experiments conducted using MATLAB and a database comprising hundreds of individual Sinhala character images indicate that the proposed method has a 90 % success rate in recognizing Sinhala characters.

We plan to further improve the proposed method by considering character curve features in the feature extraction stage. Moreover, we will tackle to com- pare performances of other state-of-the-art methods.

# References

1. Mahasukhon, P., Mousavinezhad, H., Song, J.Y.: Hand-printed english character recognition based on fuzzy theory. In: IEEE International Conference on Elec- tro/Information Technology (EIT), pp. 1–4 (2012)
2. Yuan, A., Bai, G., Jiao, L., Liu, Y.: Offline handwritten English character recogni- tion based on convolutional neural network. In: 10th IAPR International Workshop on Document Analysis Systems (DAS), pp. 125–129 (2012)
3. Pal, U., Kimura, F., Roy, K., Pal, T.: Recognition of english multi-oriented charac- ters. In: 18th International Conference on Pattern Recognition (ICPR), pp. 873– 876 (2006)
4. Sobu, Y., Goto, H., Aso, H.: Binary tree-based precision-keeping clustering for very fast Japanese character recognition. In: 25th International Conference of Image and Vision Computing New Zealand (IVCNZ), pp. 1–6 (2010)
5. Gao, Y., Jin, L., Yang, W.: An empirical comparative study of online handwrit- ing chinese character recognition: simplified vs. traditional. In: 12th International Conference on Document Analysis and Recognition (ICDAR), pp. 862–866 (2013)
6. Huang, L., Liu, C.: Handwritten Chinese character recognition method based on non-parametric dimensionality reduction. In: International Conference on Com- puter Design and Applications (ICCDA), pp. V1-217–V1-220 (2010)
7. Tran, D.C., Franco, P., Ogier, J.: Accented handwritten character recognition using SVM - application to French. In: International Conference on Frontiers in Hand- writing Recognition (ICFHR), pp. 65–71 (2010)
8. Hewavitharana, S., Fernando, H.C., Kodikara, N.D.: Off-line sinhala handwrit- ing recognition using hidden markov models. In: Indian Conference on Computer Vision, Graphics & Image Processing (ICVGIP), pp. 266–269 (2002)
9. Karunanayaka, M.L.M., Marasinghe, C.A., Kodikara, N.D.: Thresholding, noise reduction and skew correction of sinhala handwritten words. In: MVA IAPR Con- ference on Machine Vision Applications (2005)
10. Fernando, H.C., Kodikara, N.D.: A database of handwritten text recognition research in sinhala language. In: Seventh International Conference on Document Analysis and Recognition, pp. 1262–1264 (2003)
11. Premaratne, H.L., Bigun, J.: Recognition of printed sinhala characters using linear symmetry. In: The 5th Asian Conference on Computer Vision (2002)
12. Kodituwakku, S.R., Nilanthi, P.S.: Investigating a fuzzy approach for handwritten sinhala character recognition. Int. J. Eng. Sci. Technol. 2(11), 6031–6034 (2010)
13. Otsu, N.: A threshold selection method from gray-level histograms. IEEE Trans. Syst. Man Cybern. 9(1), 62–66 (1979)
14. Sagillo, J.M.: Domains of sciences, universe of discourse, and omega arguments. Hist. Philos. Logic 20, 267–280 (1999)
15. Gaurav, D.D., Ramesh, R.: A feature extraction technique based on character geometry for character recognition (2012). arXiv preprint arXiv:1202.3884

# Evolving Node Transfer Functions in Artificial Neural Networks for Handwritten Digits Recognition

Dmytro Vodianyk$^{(\boxtimes)}$ and Przemysław Rokita

Institute of Computer Science, Warsaw University of Technology,
Nowowiejska 15/19, 00-665 Warsaw, Poland
vodianyk@gmail.com, pro@ii.pw.edu.pl

**Abstract.** Feed-forward Artificial Neural Networks are popular choices among scientists and engineers for modeling complex real-world problems. One of the latest research areas in this field is evolving Artificial Neural Networks: NeuroEvolution. In this paper we investigate the effect of evolving a node transfer function and its parameters along with the evolution of connection weights in Evolutionary Artificial Neural Networks for the problem of handwritten digits recognition. The results are promising when compared with the traditional approach of homogeneous Artificial Neural Network with predefined transfer function.

## 1 Introduction

Evolutionary Artificial Neural Network (EANN) is a special class of ANNs in which evolution is another fundamental form of adaptation in addition to learning [1]. One of the important features of EANNs is their adaptability – ability to adapt to different environments and dynamic properties of these environments. Evolution and learning of EANNs make their adaptation to dynamic environments much more effective.

A significant advantage of EANNs is its ability to evolve the topology of ANNs along with connection weights. Topology evolving methods include: GNARL [2], NEAT [3], CGPANN [4]. Interestingly, EANNs can be used to optimize a Node Transfer Function (NTF) of each neuron within heterogeneous ANNs. However, this opportunity has been overlooked in recent research. Many ANN related publications indicated more research was required on optimization of NTF: "Selection and/or optimization of transfer functions performed by artificial neurons have been so far little explored ways to improve performance of neural networks in complex problems" [5], "The current emphasis in neural network research is on learning algorithms and architectures, neglecting the importance of transfer functions" [6].

The purpose of this research is to determine an impact of evolving the node transfer functions and its parameters along with the connection weights by resolving a multi-objective optimization problem. The paper concludes that the choice of node transfer functions and its parameters for each neuron in an ANN is as important as the choice of connection weights for each link between nodes.

© Springer International Publishing AG 2016
L.J. Chmielewski et al. (Eds.): ICCVG 2016, LNCS 9972, pp. 604–613, 2016.
DOI: 10.1007/978-3-319-46418-3_54

## 2    Evolution of Connection Weights in an Artificial Neural Network

Feed forward ANNs normally consist of three types of layers: input layer, hidden and output layer. A weighted sum of the neuron inputs specifies the activation function argument. For the best performance, this function is usually chosen to be nonlinear.

Backpropagation (BP) algorithm for training ANNs is well studied and has its own advantages and disadvantages. BP has drawbacks due to its use of gradient decent – often it gets trapped in a local minimum of the error function and it is incapable of finding a global minimum [7]. One way to overcome gradient-descent-based training algorithm's shortcomings is to use evolutionary algorithms (EA) – formulating a training process of an artificial neural network via evolution of its connection weights.

The evolutionary approach to weights training in ANNs consists of two major phases. The first phase is to decide the representation of connection weights: in form of binary strings or not. In the experiments performed in this paper connection weights represented as real-number matrices. The second one is the evolutionary process simulated by an EA, in which search operators, such as crossover and mutation, have to be defined in conjunction with the representation scheme. Different representation and search operators can lead to quite different training performance. A typical cycle of the evolution of connection weights is shown on Table 1.

**Table 1.** Evolution of ANN.

| |
|---|
| 1. Decode each individual (genotype) in the current generation into a set of connection weights and construct a corresponding ANN with connection weights. |
| 2. Evaluate effectiveness of each ANN by computing its total mean square error between actual and target outputs. The fitness of an individual is determined by the error. The higher the error, the lower the fitness. |
| 3. Select parents for reproduction based on their fitness. |
| 4. Apply search operators, such as crossover and / or mutation, to parents to generate offspring, which form the next generation. |

Most EAs are rather inefficient in fine-tuned local search problems, but are suitable for a global search. This is especially true for genetic algorithms (GA). The efficiency of evolutionary training can be drastically improved by introducing a local search step into the evolution – combining EA with a local search procedure. The local search algorithm could be a backpropagation algorithm. It was shown that a hybrid GA/BP approach is more efficient than ether the GA or BP algorithm used alone [8]. In the experiments in this paper BP algorithm was not combined with GA.

# 3    Evolution of the Node Transfer Function

The transfer function has been shown to be an important part of ANN's architecture and has significant impact on its performance [9]. The transfer function is often assumed to be the same for all the nodes in an ANN, at least for all the nodes in one layer. Usually a transfer function is predefined and chosen by human experts.

Evidently, the next step in improving the evolutionary approach in ANNs is to find the best-performing node transfer functions by applying evolutionary algorithms. It improves performance of an Evolutionary Artificial Neural Network and allows the evolutionary process to find a better solution without artificially placed limits for NTFs set by a client.

There are two main methods to evolve NTFs. In first method the NTF of each neuron is selected from a predetermined list of functions. Training approaches which use this method include General Neural Networks (GNN) [10], which randomly adds and removes logistic or Gaussian NTFs using an evolutionary method. GNN is also a hybrid approach, which makes use of backpropagation during training. Other NE methods, which select a specific NTF for each neuron, include Parallel Distributed Genetic Programming (PDGP) [11] and Cartesian Genetic Programming of Artificial Neural Networks (CGPANN) [4,12]. Both of these methods use genes to encode a NTF for each neuron. These genes are then subject to mutation during the training process.

The second way in which NE can optimize NTFs is to use functions, which are described by a number of parameters [6]. The training methods then optimize these parameters for each individual neuron. A simple version of this technique has been used by CGPANN [13], where the parameters of Gaussian functions were optimized for each neuron. The parameters associated with each neuron were encoded in the chromosome by the addition of an extra gene for each neuron.

The impact of evolving NTFs in ANNs was show in [14] and it was indicated that a further research is required to investigate an evolution of more complex NTFs described by multiple parameters and placing fewer restraints on the values each parameter can take. It also was stated that the further research could involve a combination of a heterogeneous ANN where each neuron also had parameters to be optimized. This paper concentrates on the mentioned two suggestions from [14] and shows that evolving complex NTFs with multiple parameters in each neuron improves the effectiveness of an ANN in a significant way.

# 4    Benchmarks

In this paper three different benchmarks were employed. The two of chosen benchmarks are classification problems and one is handwritten digits recognition. These benchmarks are chosen to show how evolving a node transfer functions along with its parameters affects different type of problems in machine learning.

### 4.1   Full Adder

The full adder benchmark is the task of implementing a full adder circuit using an ANN. The ANN has three inputs (two input bits and a carry in bit) and two outputs (one for the sum bit and the other for the carry out).

Input values and corresponding outputs shown in Table 2, where

$X_1$ - first input bit;

$X_2$ - second input bit;

$X_3$ - carry in bit;

$Y_1$ - sum bit of the first and second input bits including an effect of the carry in bit;

$Y_2$ - carry out bit.

**Table 2.** Full Adder.

| $X_1$ | $X_2$ | $X_3$ | $Y_1$ | $Y_2$ |
|---|---|---|---|---|
| 0 | 0 | 0 | 0 | 0 |
| 0 | 0 | 1 | 1 | 0 |
| 0 | 1 | 0 | 1 | 0 |
| 0 | 1 | 1 | 0 | 1 |
| 1 | 0 | 0 | 1 | 0 |
| 1 | 0 | 1 | 0 | 1 |
| 1 | 1 | 0 | 0 | 1 |
| 1 | 1 | 1 | 1 | 1 |

### 4.2   Monks Problem 1

The Monks Problems [15] are a set of three classification benchmarks intended for comparing different learning algorithms. The classification tasks are based on the appearance of robots, which are described by six attributes, each with a range of values, see Table 3 for more details. Only the first classification task is used here, where a robot belongs to a class if head_shape == body_shape OR jacket_color == red. 124 combinations were used for a training set and 432 combinations for the testing data, which includes the training set in it.

**Table 3.** Monks Problem.

| Description | Attributes |
|---|---|
| head_shape | round, square, octagon |
| body_shape | round, square, octagon |
| is_smiling | yes, no |
| holding | sword, balloon, flag |
| jacket_color | red, yellow, green, blue |
| has_tie | yes, no |

### 4.3   Handwritten Digits Recognition

For this benchmark problem MNIST [16] data set was used, which contains tens of thousands of scanned images of handwritten digits, together with their correct classifications. MNIST's name comes from the fact that it is a modified subset of two data sets collected by NIST, the United States' National Institute of Standards and Technology. Figure 1 shows a few images from the data set.

The MNIST data for this experiment comes in two parts: the first part contains 1,000 handwritten digits to be used as a training data and the second part of the data set is 2,000 images to be used as a testing data. These images are 28 by 28 pixels in size.

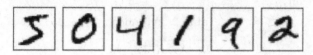

**Fig. 1.** Handwritten digit examples.

## 5   Experiment Set up

### 5.1   Architecture of the Artificial Neural Network

In the experiment, a predefined architecture of an artificial neural network was used. Therefore, the architecture is constant and is not being changed during the evolution process.

The feed-forward artificial neural network in this experiment has different numbers of inputs, hidden and output neurons for each benchmark problem. Figure 2 demonstrates the structure of the artificial neural network, where

$x_1, x_2, \ldots, x_n$ - input nodes;
$f_1, f_2, \ldots, f_h$ - node transfer functions of the hidden layer;
$g_1, g_2, \ldots, g_o$ - node transfer functions of the output layer;
$y_1, y_2, \ldots, y_m$ - output nodes, the result of the network.

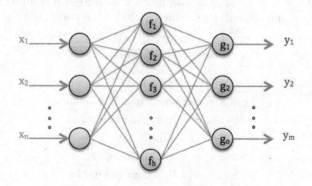

**Fig. 2.** The structure of the ANN.

Table 4 describes a shape of the networks used for each benchmarks. For example, a neural network with 3 input nodes, 6 hidden and 2 output nodes was used for the Full Adder benchmark.

Table 4. ANN shape for benchmarks.

| Benchmark problem | ANN shape |
|---|---|
| Full adder | 3, 6, 2 |
| Monks Problem 1 | 6, 12, 1 |
| Digits recognition | 784, 60, 10 |

## 5.2 Node Transfer Functions

The list of transfer functions was used to evolve the network. Table 5 shows which functions were used.

Table 5. List of node transfer functions.

| Function name | Equation |
|---|---|
| Step | $g(x) = \begin{cases} 1, & \text{if } x \geq 0 \\ 0, & \text{if } x < 0 \end{cases}$ |
| Unipolar Sigmoid | $g(x) = \dfrac{1}{1 + e^{-\frac{x-\mu}{\sigma}}}$ |
| Gaussian | $g(x) = e^{-\frac{(x-\mu)^2}{2\sigma^2}}$ |
| Sigmoid Prime | $g(x) = \dfrac{e^{-\frac{x-\mu}{\sigma}}}{(1 + e^{-\frac{x-\mu}{\sigma}})^2}$ |
| Hyperbolic Sigmoid | $g(x) = \dfrac{e^{\frac{x-\mu}{\sigma}} - e^{-\frac{x-\mu}{\sigma}}}{e^{\frac{x-\mu}{\sigma}} + e^{-\frac{x-\mu}{\sigma}}}$ |
| Bipolar Sigmoid | $g(x) = \dfrac{1 - e^{-\frac{x-\mu}{\sigma}}}{e^{\frac{x-\mu}{\sigma}} + e^{-\frac{x-\mu}{\sigma}}}$ |

The default values of $\mu$ and $\sigma$ for Unipolar Sigmoid, Sigmoid Prime, Hyperbolic and Bipolar functions are: $\mu = 0.0$, $\sigma = 1.0$. The default values of $\mu$ and $\sigma$ for Gaussian function are: $\mu = 4.5$, $\sigma = 4.5$.

## 5.3 Representation of the Evolutionary Artificial Neural Network

Since we are going to evolve an ANN, we should decide how it should be represented and which search operators should be used for the evolutionary process.

A chromosome should contain:

1. Connection weights as real numbers.
2. A list of transfer functions for hidden layer and output layer of the ANN.
3. Parameters for evolving transfer functions.

**Fig. 3.** A chromosome.

Figure 3 represents a chromosome of the EANN in the experiment, where $w_1, w_2, \ldots, w_n$ are connection weights between input-hidden and hidden-output nodes; $f_1, f_2, \ldots, f_h$, are node transfer functions of nodes in the hidden layer; $g_1, g_2, \ldots, g_o$ are node transfer functions of nodes in the output layer; $\mu$ and $\sigma$ are parameters of transfer functions.

## 5.4   Search Operators

After initial experiments it was decided to use a mutation search operator only for connection weights and node transfer functions.

Probability of the mutation in connection weights is 50 % for both hidden and output layers. Mutation operator creates a random index for each layer and changes a connection weight in it by assigning a random value between −15 and 15.

5 % mutation probability was chosen for evolving a node transfer function in the hidden layer and the output layer. The operator creates a random index for each layer and replaces a function located at that position with a random transfer function from the predefined list.

For evolving parameters in node transfer functions, the mutation operator changes values of $\mu$ and $\sigma$ parameters of Sigmoid, Sigmoid Prime, Hyperbolic and Bipolar functions between 1.0 and 5.0. For Gaussian function parameters vary between −5.0 and 5.0.

## 6   Results

For each benchmark problem 30 experiments were performed. 10 experiments for evolving connection weights only, 10 experiments for evolving connection weights along with node transfer functions and 10 experiments for evolving connection weights along with node transfer functions and its parameters simultaneously.

One experiment contains 32 evolutions of the artificial neural network. Each evolution contains 1,000 iterations. 100 iterations were used for Digits Recognition benchmark in order to reduce the time of the evolution.

**Table 6.** Results for Full Adder.

| N | 1 | 2 | 3 | 4 | 5 | 6 | 7 | 8 | 9 | 10 |
|---|---|---|---|---|---|---|---|---|---|----|
| $C_1$ | 0.02261 | 0.00045 | 0.01134 | 0.00803 | 0.02979 | 0.03303 | 0.03042 | 0.03197 | 0.00846 | 0.03473 |
| $C_2$ | 0.0 | 0.0 | 0.0 | 0.0 | 0.0 | 0.0 | 0.0 | 0.0 | 0.0 | 0.0 |
| $C_3$ | 0.0 | 0.0 | 0.0 | 0.0 | 0.0 | 0.0 | 0.0 | 0.0 | 0.0 | 0.0 |

**Table 7.** Results for Monks Problem.

| N | 1 | 2 | 3 | 4 | 5 | 6 | 7 | 8 | 9 | 10 |
|---|---|---|---|---|---|---|---|---|---|----|
| $C_1$ | 1.57206 | 4.05454 | 1.28225 | 4.81331 | 1.10062 | 2.86869 | 0.49146 | 4.02176 | 2.39384 | 10.378 |
| $C_2$ | 1.5 | 3.0 | 4.5 | 0.0 | 0.5 | 1.0 | 0.5 | 2.0 | 3.0 | 4.0 |
| $C_3$ | 1.074 | 0.5 | 1.0 | 0.5 | 4.0 | 4.5 | 2.5 | 0.0 | 2.0 | 1.0 |

**Table 8.** Results for Digits Recognition.

| N | 1 | 2 | 3 | 4 | 5 | 6 | 7 | 8 | 9 | 10 |
|---|---|---|---|---|---|---|---|---|---|----|
| $C_1$ | 922.17 | 931.45 | 934.14 | 943.58 | 925.00 | 926.70 | 926.66 | 941.74 | 913.05 | 943.72 |
| $C_2$ | 936.89 | 945.08 | 926.69 | 936.99 | 952.32 | 910.02 | 937.64 | 930.37 | 945.55 | 941.80 |
| $C_3$ | 883.32 | 895.30 | 883.35 | 885.37 | 880.44 | 899.17 | 895.06 | 878.96 | 901.96 | 910.56 |

The result of each experiment is a number, which represents the minimum cost associated with running a network on a testing data set after each evolution. The cost function is defined by means of the following formula:

$$C = \frac{1}{2} \sum_{i=0}^{n} (y_i - t_i)^2,$$

where:

$C$ - the total cost, which is the square of sum of differences between expected and actual results for all samples from the testing data divided by two;

$y_i$ - the expected result of neural network for $i_{th}$ sample from the testing set;

$t_i$ - the actual result of neural network for $i_{th}$ sample from the testing set;

$n$ - number of samples in the testing set.

Tables 6, 7 and 8 show results for each benchmark problem, where:

$N$ - experiment number;

$C_1$ - the minimum cost for the test data from evolving connection weights only;

$C_2$ - the minimum cost for the test data from simultaneously evolving connection weights and node transfer functions;

$C_3$ - the minimum cost for the test data from simultaneously evolving connection weights, node transfer functions and its parameters.

Table 9 shows an average cost associated with each evolutionary method.

**Table 9.** Average cost for each evolutionary method and benchmark problem.

| Cost/Benchmark | Full Adder | Monks Problem 1 | Digits Recognition |
|---|---|---|---|
| $\langle C_1 \rangle$ | 0.021083 | 2.995499 | 930.827271 |
| $\langle C_2 \rangle$ | 0 | 2 | 936.340773 |
| $\langle C_3 \rangle$ | 0 | 1.707375 | 891.354621 |

# 7   Conclusions

In this paper experiments were performed for different benchmark problems on an EANN by evolving connection weight only; connection weights with node transfer functions; and connection weights with node transfer functions and parameters.

The results demonstrate performance of an ANN can be increased by evolving both node transfer functions and parameters for each node. Performance gains are on par with methods where connection weights and transfer functions are evolved for the Full Adder benchmark problem. The performance boost of **5 %** to **15 %** is seen when evolving node transfer functions along with parameters for the Monks Problem 1 and Handwritten Digits Recognition benchmarks. The biggest improvement in recognizing unseen data using the proposed method was for Handwritten Digits Recognition.

Thus suggests the method of evolving node transfer functions and its parameters along with connection weights in an evolutionary artificial neural network should be considered to improve performance results. Evolving node transfer functions along with its parameters should be included in major research and toolbox software.

Further research is required to include an evolution of architecture in an artificial neural network; connections weights and node transfer functions along its parameters.

# References

1. Kent, A., Williams, J.G. (eds.): Evolutionary Artificial Neural Networks. Encyclopedia of Computer Science and Technology, vol. 33, pp. 137–170. Marcel Dekker, New York (1995)
2. Angeline, P.J., Saunders, G.M., Pollack, J.B.: An evolutionary algorithm that constructs recurrent neural networks. Neural Networks, pp. 54–65 (1994)
3. Stanley, K.O., Miikkulainen, R.: Evolving neural networks through augmenting topologies. Evol. Comput. **10**, 99–127 (2002)
4. Mahsal, K.M., Masood, A.A., Khan, M., Miller, J.F.: Fast learning neural networks using Cartesian genetic programming. Neurocomputing (2013)
5. Duch, W., Jankowski, N.: Transfer functions: hidden possibilities for better neural networks. In: ESANN, pp. 81–94 (2001)
6. Duch, W., Jankowski, N.: Survey of neural transfer functions. Neural Comput. Surv. **2**, 163–212 (1999)

7. Chauvin, Y., Rumelhart, D.E. (eds.): Backpropagation: Theory, Architectures, and Applications. Erlbaum, Hillsdale (1995)
8. Belew, R.K., McInerney, J., Schraudolph, N.N.: Evolving networks: using genetic algorithm with connectionist learning. University of California, San Diego, Technical report CS90-174 (1991)
9. Mani, G.: Learning by gradient descent in function space. In: Proceedings of the IEEE Internation Conference on System, Man, and Cybernetics, Los Angeles, CA, pp. 242–247 (1990)
10. Liu, Y., Yao, X.: Evolutionary design of artificial neural networks with different nodes. In: Proceedings of IEEE International Conference on Evolutionary Computation, pp. 670–675 (1996)
11. Poli, R.: Parallel distributed genetic programming. In: New Ideas in Optimization, Advanced Topics in Computer Science, pp. 403–431 (1999)
12. James, A.T., Miller, J.F.: Cartesian genetic programming encoded artificial neural networks: a comparison using three benchmarks. In: Proceedings of the Conference on Genetic and Evolutionary Computation (GECCO 2013), pp. 1005–1012 (2013)
13. Manning, T., Walsh, P.: Improving the performance of CGPANN for breast cancer diagnosis using crossover and radial basis functions. In: Vanneschi, L., Bush, W.S., Giacobini, M. (eds.) EvoBIO 2013. LNCS, vol. 7833, pp. 165–176. Springer, Heidelberg (2013)
14. James, A.T., Miller, J.F.: NeuroEvolution: The Importance of Transfer Function Evolution (2013)
15. Thrun, S.B., Bala, J., Bloedorn, E., Bratko, I., Cestnik, B., Cheng, J., De Jong, K., Dzeroski, S., Fahlman, S.E., Fisher, D., et al.: The monk's problems a performance comparison of different learning algorithms. Technical report, Carnegie Mellon University (1991)
16. The MNIST database of handwritten digits. http://yann.lecun.com/exdb/mnist/

# Mathematical Analysis, Estimation and Approximation

# Finding Line Segments in the Ulam Square with the Hough Transform

Leszek J. Chmielewski[✉] and Arkadiusz Orłowski

Faculty of Applied Informatics and Mathematics (WZIM),
Warsaw University of Life Sciences (SGGW),
ul. Nowoursynowska 159, 02-775 Warsaw, Poland
{leszek_chmielewski,arkadiusz_orlowski}@sggw.pl
http://www.wzim.sggw.pl

**Abstract.** The regularities present in the Ulam spiral provided an incentive for interesting observations in the number theory. Therefore, we have made the Ulam square an object of analysis from the image processing perspective. A version of the Hough transform designed specially for detecting sequences of pixels forming segments of straight lines with the slope defined by an irreducible fraction was used to find line segments in the Ulam spiral. Angles which described the slopes of the segments had tangents $p/q$ expressed by integers $p$ from 0 to 10 and $q$ from $-10$ to 10 (0 excluded). Due to storage limitations the squares with the side of length up to 5001 points which correspond to the largest prime 25 009 991 were analyzed at present. In such a square the longest segment has 16 primes and its tangent is 3 (3 up and 1 to the right). Segments of length 14 and 15 were absent. The number of shorter segments varied strongly, from one for a 13-point segment to tens of thousands for shorter ones.

**Keywords:** Ulam spiral · Line segments · Long · Contiguous · Hough transform · Image processing

## 1   Introduction and Motivation

The question of finding an efficient formula for generating prime number is still a challenge. The well known Euler formula $p = n^2 - n + 41$ generates primes for $n = 1, 2, \ldots, 40$ which form a continuous sequence, and for numerous other values of $n$ (cf. [1], last lines of the paper). When we look at the images of the Ulam spiral [2] with the primes generated by the Euler formula, one of the phenomena which strikes us is that some of the points which represent the primes compose themselves into regular sequences, like for example those for $n = 20, 21, \ldots, 40$. This is shown in Fig. 1.

In the following the prime and the point corresponding to this prime in the Ulam square will be treated as equivalent. The points in the square will also be called pixels, due to that the square will be treated as an image. The sequences of points located so that the ratio of increments of the two coordinates between

© Springer International Publishing AG 2016
L.J. Chmielewski et al. (Eds.): ICCVG 2016, LNCS 9972, pp. 617–626, 2016.
DOI: 10.1007/978-3-319-46418-3_55

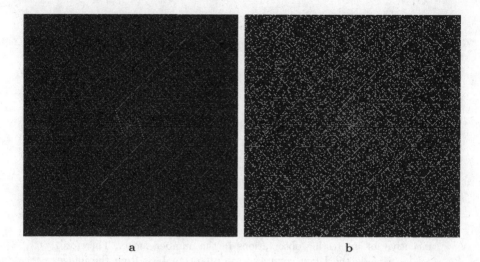

a                 b

**Fig. 1.** (a) Central part of the Ulam square ($301 \times 301$ points) with the points generated by the Euler formula. Yellow points ( ): primes generated by $n = 20, 21, \ldots, 40$; red, green and magenta points (■ ■): remaining primes generated by the formula; grey points (■): remaining primes (grey level $63/255$); white point ( ): number 1, black (■): other non-primes. The left yellow line segment contains 11 points, the right one has 10 points. There is no other 11-point segment in this image but there is another 10-point one – marked with green (■), and two 9-point ones – marked with magenta (■). Shorter segments are not separately marked. (b) The same part of the Ulam square as in (a), with just primes marked with white ( ), for comparison. (Color figure online)

consecutive points is constant, for example, $1:1$ or $3:1$, like in the lines marked with green or yellow in Fig. 1, will be called segments, in the same sense as the segments of a straight line. A sequence will be called a segment when its subsequent pixels are the nearest possible at a given ratio of increments. So, in the case of the ratio $1:1$ they will be immediate neighbors (with the Euclidean distance between their centers $\sqrt{2}$), while in the case of the ratio $1:3$ they will not, and their centers will be at an Euclidean distance of $\sqrt{10}$. In the latter case, the segment will be considered terminated if the next pixel is farther than this distance.

It is apparent that the primes generated by the Euler formula do form line segments. It can be said, informally, that the longer the segment generated by the formula, the better candidate for the prime-generator the formula is. Therefore, considering the Ulam square from the image processing perspective, we shall be interested in looking for long segments. We expect that finding long segments in the Ulam square will be helpful in exploring some aspects of the number theory.

As it can be seen in Fig. 1b, long segments can not be easily found with the unassisted human eye. The longest segment belonging to the results of the Euler formula is the left yellow segment which has 11 points. The right yellow segment has 10 points. A number of questions can be asked: are these segments the only segments 11 and 10 points long in the Ulam square? Are there longer segments in this image, an if so, how long, how many and in which locations?

The partial answers to some of these questions have been shown in Fig. 1a. In the Ulam square of the considered size, within the numbers generated by the Euler formula there are no more 11-point segments. There is one more 10-point segment besides the yellow one. Further, there are two 9-point segments, and so on. We shall see further in this paper that in this image there are more 10-point, 9-point, and shorter segments, but there is no other 11-point segment besides that generated by the Euler formula. We shall also see what is the longest segment in the square of $301 \times 301$ points. It will appear that there is no longer segment than that one in the Ulam square of the size up to $5001 \times 5001$ points.

A good method for finding lines and line segments in an image is the Hough transform (HT). After a broad review on HT [3] was published in 1993, there seemed to be a long break, intermitted only by the appearance of unpublished review reports, like for example [4]. This break was terminated by two recent review papers [5,6]. The first one is of interest for us because it reports on the papers in which differences between the Hough transforms for accurate and approximate objects were discussed. The comparison between the *digital* and *analog* Hough transforms was studied by Kiryati, Lindenbaum and Bruckstein [7]. They discuss the relation between the digital HT according to Cyganski, Noel and Orr [8,9], called there the Analytic Hough Transform, and the conventional HTs, which were analog in nature. Cyganski et al. analyzed digital arcs satisfying the chord property as well as those not satisfying the contiguity condition. They paid much attention to the question of representing all the possible digital straight lines being a digitization of a mathematical straight line segment.

In the Ulam square the points are not a representation of any real-world, analog lines. Neither they are the digital representations of any continuous digital lines passing the image. Therefore, the problem of their detection fits neither to the *analog*, nor to the *digital* version of the Hough transform in the sense defined in [7,8]. In this paper we shall use the version of the HT proposed by us previously in [10] and designed specially for the problem of our interest.

## 2   Method

The method was described in sufficient detail in [10]. Here we shall very briefly recall its main elements.

Let us locate the origin of the coordinate system $Opq$ in the central point of the Ulam square corresponding to the number 1. As written before, a line segment in the Ulam square is a sequence of pixels for which the increments $\Delta p, \Delta q$ of the coordinates $p, q$ between the subsequent pixels fulfil the condition $\Delta p / \Delta q = n_1 / n_2$, where $n_1, n_2$ are small integers and $n_1 / n_2$ is an irreducible fraction. This fraction represents the slope of the line. The slope will be represented as an element of an array $D_{ij}$, with $i = n_1$ and $j = n_2$, called the *direction array*. It is assumed $i \geq 0$ for uniqueness. To relate $(i, j)$ with the directions in the Ulam squares shown in the following, it should be said that $i$ is pointing up and $j$ is pointing to the right. Therefore, for example, the yellow segments in Fig. 1a have the direction $i : j = 3 : (-1)$ and the green one $1 : 1$. The dimensions of $D$ are $[0, N] \times [-N, N]$. Therefore, a restricted number of angles can be represented, which is in conformity with the nature of the problem. Those elements of $D$ which correspond to reducible and impossible fractions are not used. In each *used* element, the evidence for the existence of lines having the corresponding slope is accumulated.

The elemental subset of pixels in the Ulam square which defines a line is a pair. Each pair of prime numbers is a voting set. If the slope corresponds to an element of $D$, the pair is stored in $D_{ij}$, where $i/j$ is the reduced fraction $\Delta p/\Delta q$; otherwise it is neglected. In each element of $D$ the votes can be stored in a vector or a list; in the current implementation the vectors were used to avoid keeping large numbers of pointers in memory. For each vote the line offset (defined as the intercept with the axis $Op$ for horizontal lines and with $Oq$ for the remaining ones) is stored. To make it possible to analyze the results of accumulation, the locations of voting points are also stored and the pairs and their primes are counted.

After the accumulation process is finished the accumulator can be analyzed with respect to such evidence like the existence of lines with large numbers of primes, the contiguous strings of points representing long segments in the square, the directional structure of the Ulam spiral, etc.

In general, the voting sets should be formed by considering each possible pair of primes. In the case of the search for contiguous strings of pixels this time-consuming procedure can be replaced by taking into account only such pairs for which the differences of coordinates correspond to the used elements of the direction array $D$.

In the implementation used for the results presented in this paper the number $N$ which defines the dimensions of the direction array was assumed $N = 10$. It seemed reasonable not to consider pairs of pixels mutually farther than 10 as neighbors in the Ulam square.

At this stage we have used an implementation of the software which, due to the memory limit, restricted the size of the square to slightly more than $5001 \times 5001$ pixels. Therefore, the results for squares with side length up to 5001 will be presented. The number of primes in such a square is $1\,566\,540$ and the largest prime is $25\,009\,991$. The analysis of such a square with a typical PC took not more than several minutes. For smaller $N$, larger squares could be investigated, but the results were not increasingly interesting. Some of them will also be presented in the next Section. The memory limit can easily be overcome and in the future research we plan to analyze larger squares and larger prime numbers.

## 3    Results

### 3.1    Square of Size 301 × 301 Points

Segments shorter than 4 points do not indicate any stable tendency and are not interesting. Segments shorter than 6 points are very numerous and they will not be shown in this paper (see also Sect. 3.4). Segments of lengths from 6 to 16 points long will be presented here. We shall visualize them in the square $301 \times 301$ points due to that its size is small enough for presentation in the format of the paper. We briefly mention larger squares in the end of this Section.

We have already stated that the longest segment in the square of the considered size present in the set of primes generated by the Euler formula is 11 points long and there are no more segments of this length in this square. Now, we shall go on to segments 10 and 9 points long due to that they were already mentioned in relation with the Euler formula. There are four segments of length 10 and five segments of length 9. Their locations and slopes are shown in Fig. 2. Their relation to the primes generated by the Euler formula is outlined in the caption of this Figure. Shorter segments of the lengths 6, 7 and 8 points, can be seen in Fig. 3a, b and c.

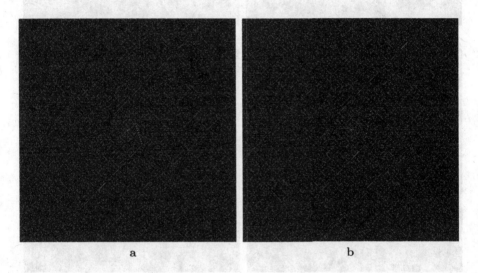

a                                        b

**Fig. 2.** (a) Segments 10 points long in the square of Fig. 1b. There are four such segments; two of them, marked with yellow ( ) and green (▒) belong to the set of points generated by the Euler formula, marked in Fig. 1a with the same colors, while the remaining two, marked blue (■) and magenta (■) do not belong to this set. (b) Segments 9 points long in the square of Fig. 1b. There are five such segments; two of them, marked magenta (■) belong to the set of points generated by the Euler formula, marked in Fig. 1a with the same colors, while the remaining three, marked red (■), blue (■) and cyan (▒) do not belong to this set. The colors: white ( ), grey (■) and black (■) have the same meaning as in Fig. 1a. (Color figure online)

The longest segment has 16 points and has the slope $i : j = 3 : 1$ (Fig. 3d). It consists of the primes:

$75\,227(-13, -137)$, $74\,131(-10, -136)$, $73\,043(-7, -135)$, $71\,963(-4, -134)$, $70\,891(-1, -133)$, $69\,827(2, -132)$, $68\,771(5, -131)$, $67\,723(8, -130)$, $66\,683(11, -129)$, $65\,651(14, -128)$, $64\,627(17, -127)$, $63\,611(20, -126)$, $62\,603(23, -125)$, $61\,603(26, -124)$, $60\,611(29, -123)$, $59\,627(32, -122)$

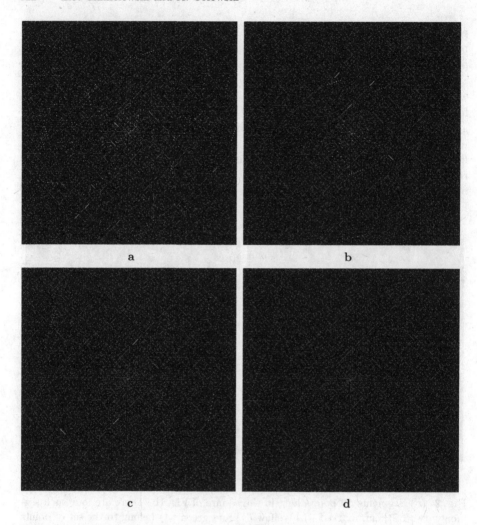

**Fig. 3.** Segments in the square of Fig. 1b: (**a**) 6 points long; (**b**) 7 points; (**c**) 8 points; (**d**) 16 points long – the longest segment in this square.

where $a(b,c)$ denote: $a$ – prime number, $(b,c)$ – its coordinates in the Ulam square. It can be seen that the points are not far from the center of the square. It is interesting to note that there are no segments of lengths from 12 to 15 points in the considered square.

## 3.2    Distribution of Lengths of the Segments

For the direction table of dimensions $[0, 10] \times [-10, 10]$ as specified before, the squares of dimensions up to $5001 \times 5001$ were analyzed. In the graph in Fig. 4

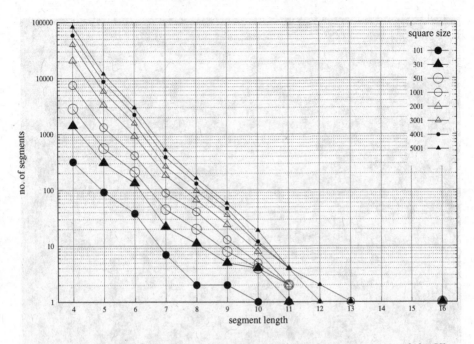

**Fig. 4.** Number of segments versus length of the segment for various sizes of the Ulam square. If the number of lines is zero the data point is absent.

it is shown what was the distribution of the numbers of segments versus their lengths, for the squares of different sizes.

It can be noticed that the numbers of short segments grow together with the size of the square, while the numbers of the longest segments change slightly or remain constant. As it can be expected, the longest segments are rare.

To show at least some of the results for longer segments and larger squares we have chosen the square of 1001 × 1001 points and the 9-point segments shown in Fig. 5.

More images and results are available online (see Sect. 3.4).

### 3.3   Larger Ulam Squares and Reduced Direction Table

To see whether a longer segment than 16 points can be found in larger squares, and to stay within the memory limit we have with the currently used software, some calculations were carried out with the limited set of directions. As it was written before, the dimensions of the direction table $D$ are $[0, N] \times [-N, N]$ and up till now the value of $N$ was 10. With $N$ limited to 5 the arrays up to 9001 × 9001 points, and with $N$ limited to 3 the arrays up to 10 001 × 10 001 points were analyzed. Some new segments of length 11 and 12 points were found. No new segment of length 13 points and no segments of length 14 and 15 points were found. No other segment of length 16 was found besides that already seen in 301 × 301 square. No segment longer than 16 points was found. The square

**Fig. 5.** Segments 9 points long in a 1001 × 1001 points Ulam square. For better visibility the white and color points were replaced with squares 3 × 3 pixels centered at respective points.

of 31 623 × 31 623 in which the largest prime would be over $10^9$ could not be analyzed even for $N$ limited to 1. Detailed results are available online (see next Section).

### 3.4  Online Resource

The results are in a large part in the form of images which are too large to be presented in a page of a paper. Also the volume of numerical data is too large to show them in tables. Therefore we have established a web page [11] in which the results of this one and our other papers on the prime numbers will be available.

## 4  Summary and Prospects

The Ulam square was analyzed form the image processing perspective. The straight line segments were looked for, in hope that this can be helpful in exploring the peculiarities of the number theory.

In the squares with the side of length up to 5001 points which correspond to the largest prime 25 009 991 the longest segment has 16 primes and its slope is 3:1 (3 up and 1 to the right). There were no segments of length 14 and 15. The number of shorter segments varied strongly, from one for 13-point segment to tens of thousands for shorter ones. Angles which described the slopes of the segments had tangents $p/q$ expressed by integers $p \in [0 : 10]$ and $q \in [-10, 10] \setminus \{0\}$. A version of the Hough transform designed specially for detecting such segments in the Ulam spiral was used. Detailed results can be seen in the web page [11].

In the future we shall develop the software with significantly weaker restrictions on memory, capable of analyzing a larger part of the Ulam square, and consequently, larger primes. Squares centered at other numbers than 1 will be possible to analyze.

In the data presented here it is not possible to observe to what extent the number of segments is going down together with the distance form the center of the square; however, such a phenomenon should be expected due to that the density of primes themselves is going down in this way. It would be interesting to see what is the relation of this decline to the decline in the density of primes according to the prime counting function.

## References

1. Euler, L.: Extrait d'un lettre de M. Euler le Pere à M. Bernoulli concernant le mémoire imprimé parmi œux de 1771. Nouveaux Mémoires de l'Académie Royale des Sciences et Belles-Lettres (1772), pp. 35–36. http://eulerarchive.maa.org/pages/E461.html
2. Stein, M.L., Ulam, S.M., Wells, M.B.: A visual display of some properties of the distribution of primes. Am. Math. Mon. **71**(5), 516–520 (1964). doi:10.2307/2312588
3. Leavers, V.F.: Which Hough transform? CVGIP Image Underst. **58**, 250–264 (1993). doi:10.1006/ciun.1993.1041
4. Antolovic, D.: Review of the Hough transform method, with an implementation of the fast Hough variant for line detection. Indiana University, Department of Computer Science (2008)
5. Mukhopadhyay, P., Chaudhuri, B.B.: A survey of Hough transform. Pattern Recogn. **48**(3), 993–1010 (2015). doi:10.1016/j.patcog.2014.08.027
6. Hassanein, A.S., Mohammad, S., Sameer, M., Ragab, M.E.: A survey on Hough trans-form, theory, techniques and applications. CoRR abs/1502.02160 arXiv:1502.02160 (2015)
7. Kiryati, N., Lindenbaum, M., Bruckstein, A.M.: Digital or analog Hough transform? Pattern Recogn. Lett. **12**(5), 291–297 (1991). doi:10.1016/0167-8655(91)90412-F
8. Cyganski, D., Noel, W.F., Orr, J.A.: Analytic Hough transform. In: Proceedings of SPIE: Sensing and Reconstruction of Three-Dimensional Objects and Scenes, vol. 1260, pp. 148–159 (1990). doi:10.1117/12.20013

9. Liu, Y., Cyganski, D., Vaz, R.F.: Efficient implementation of the analytic Hough transform for exact linear feature extraction. In: Proceedings of SPIE, Intelligent Robots and Computer Vision X: Algorithms and Techniques, vol. 1607, pp. 298–309 (1992). doi:10.1117/12.57109

10. Chmielewski, L.J., Orłowski, A.: Hough transform for lines with slope defined by a pair of co-primes. Mach. Graph. Vis. **22**(1/4), 17–25 (2013)

11. Chmielewski, L.J., Orłowski, A.: Prime numbers in the Ulam square (2016). http://www.lchmiel.pl/primes. Accessed 14 July 2016

# Analysis of 4D Hypercomplex Generalizations of Julia Sets

Andrzej Katunin[✉]

Institute of Fundamentals of Machinery Design, Silesian University of Technology,
18A Konarskiego Street, 44-100 Gliwice, Poland
andrzej.katunin@polsl.pl

**Abstract.** All possible 4D hypercomplex vector spaces were considered in the light of an ability of construction of Julia fractals in them. Both arithmetic fundamentals of the considered algebras as well as implementation procedures of such hypercomplex numbers are given. In the paper, the presented study summarizes well-known 4D hypecomplex fractals, like bicomplex and quaternionic ones, introduces a group of new hypercomplex fractals, like biquaternionic, and shows why other 4D hypercomplex vector spaces cannot produce the non-trivial Julia sets. All of the considered cases were enriched by several graphical representations of hypercomplex Julia sets with their graphical analysis.

## 1 Introduction

Mandelbrot and Julia ($\mathcal{M}$-$\mathcal{J}$) sets attracted a lot of attention when B. Mandelbrot popularized his multifractal set in a complex plane $\mathbb{C}$ which was further named after him. Numerous researchers and enthusiasts started studying properties of these fractal sets as well as a huge number of modifications of classical $\mathcal{M}$-$\mathcal{J}$ sets given by the following recursive equation:

$$z \to z^2 + c, \tag{1}$$

for $z, c \in \mathbb{C}$.

In spite of deep studies focused on $\mathcal{M}$-$\mathcal{J}$ sets on a $\mathbb{C}$-plane which have been continued until now, the generalized versions of $\mathcal{M}$-$\mathcal{J}$ sets with respect to a dimension of a vector space in which a given fractal set is constructed have become the subject of interest of many researchers and computer graphics enthusiasts, since Holbrook [4] introduced $\mathcal{M}$-$\mathcal{J}$ sets defined in quaternions $\mathbb{H}$ which is a 4-dimensional (4D) generalization of classical $\mathcal{M}$-$\mathcal{J}$ sets defined on a $\mathbb{C}$-plane. Two years later, Norton presented a 3D cross-sections of quaternionic Mandelbrot and Julia sets in [11]. Further studies of Norton [12] resulted in several variations of quaternionic $\mathcal{M}$-$\mathcal{J}$ sets. Wang and Sun [16] proposed a generalization of (1) with respect to a degree of polynomial $p$ for which (1) takes the form:

$$z \to z^p + c, \tag{2}$$

for $z, c \in \mathbb{H}$, $p \in \mathbb{N}$.

© Springer International Publishing AG 2016
L.J. Chmielewski et al. (Eds.): ICCVG 2016, LNCS 9972, pp. 627–635, 2016.
DOI: 10.1007/978-3-319-46418-3_56

Another type of 4D hypercomplex generalization of $\mathcal{M}$-$\mathcal{J}$ sets defined on a $\mathbb{C}$-plane was proposed by Rochon in [13], which was based on a tensor product of complex algebras $\mathbb{C} \otimes \mathbb{C}$ (or equivalently $\mathbb{C}_2$) known as bicomplex algebra. Several generalizations, including the one of type (2), were proposed by Zireh [17], and Wang and Song [15].

The last type of 4D hypercomplex generalization of $\mathcal{M}$-$\mathcal{J}$ sets described in the literature is a generalization to complexified quaternionic vector space, which is represented by a tensor product of algebras of complex numbers and quaternions $\mathbb{C} \otimes \mathbb{H}$. For the first time this type of hypercomplex fractal sets was described by Gintz [2], where he discussed a construction of biquaternionic $\mathcal{M}$-$\mathcal{J}$ sets and showed several 3D cross-sections of such sets. Later, Bogush [1] studied the properties of these structures. The mathematical description of these biquaternionic $\mathcal{M}$-$\mathcal{J}$ sets was provided in [7].

The mentioned generalizations of classical $\mathcal{M}$-$\mathcal{J}$ sets have their unique properties resulting from the properties of hypercomplex vector spaces, especially by the arithmetic operations on the hypercomplex numbers describing these sets. However, besides the three mentioned 4D hypercomplex generalizations of classical $\mathcal{M}$-$\mathcal{J}$ sets many others can be constructed, like those constructed in terms of split quaternions $\mathbb{H}'$, semiquaternions $\mathbb{H}^0$, split semiquaternions $\mathbb{H}'^0$, and $\frac{1}{4}$-quaternions $\mathbb{H}^{00}$ (see [14] for details). The aim of this study is to analyze the complete list of 4D hypercomplex algebras which can be considered for construction of the generalized versions of $\mathcal{M}$-$\mathcal{J}$ sets on the $\mathbb{C}$-plane, and perform an analysis concerning in which hypercomplex vector spaces the resulting generalizations are non-trivial and what influences on a resulting shape. The secondary goal is a graphical analysis of all the obtained 4D generalizations, and to distinguish the characteristic properties for each considered type of these generalizations.

## 2    4D Hypercomplex Algebras

In order to construct 4D hypercomplex generalizations of $\mathcal{M}$-$\mathcal{J}$ sets the corresponding hypercomplex vector spaces should be defined first. In this section all possible 4D hypercomplex algebras and fundamentals of calculus of hypercomplex numbers defined by these algebras are presented. Since during construction of $\mathcal{M}$-$\mathcal{J}$ sets only addition and multiplication operations are performed (see e.g. (2)), these operations are considered in this description.

The oldest and the simplest generalization of complex numbers is the algebra of quaternions $\mathbb{H}$ with a basis $1, i, j, k$, where $i, j, k$ are imaginary units, thus $i^2 = j^2 = k^2 = -1$. Quaternions do not fulfill the condition of commutativity:

$$q_1 q_2 = q_2 q_1, \tag{3}$$

where $q_1, q_2 \in \mathbb{H}$, which is an important difference when performing multiplication, e.g. if we consider the expression $q_1 q_2 = q_3$, by replacing multiplied quaternions we obtain: $q_2 q_1 = -q_3$. However, they fulfill the conditions of associativity and alternativity:

$$(q_1 q_2) q_3 = q_1 (q_2 q_3), \tag{4}$$

$$(q_2 q_1) q_1 = q_2 (q_1 q_1). \tag{5}$$

The addition of quaternions is performed element-wise, i.e. considering the symbolic form of a quaternion as $\mathbb{H} := \{q = a_1 + a_2 i + a_3 j + a_4 k \mid a_n \in \mathbb{R}\}$ we obtain:

$$(a_1, a_2, a_3, a_4) + (b_1, b_2, b_3, b_4) = (a_1 + b_1, a_2 + b_2, a_3 + b_3, a_4 + b_4), \tag{6}$$

while the multiplication is performed following the multiplication table presented in Table 1.

**Table 1.** Multiplication table for quaternions.

| $\times$ | 1 | $i$ | $j$ | $k$ |
|---|---|---|---|---|
| 1 | 1 | $i$ | $j$ | $k$ |
| $i$ | $i$ | $-1$ | $k$ | $-j$ |
| $j$ | $j$ | $-k$ | $-1$ | $i$ |
| $k$ | $k$ | $j$ | $-i$ | $-1$ |

The algebra of quaternions has numerous derivative algebras which differ from $\mathbb{H}$ with respect to bases. One can consider the algebra of split quaternions $\mathbb{H}'$ (also called the algebra of coquaternions) with a basis $1, i, j_1, j_2$, where $i^2 = -1$, $j_1^2 = j_2^2 = 1$. The multiplication of split quaternions is performed following Table 2.

**Table 2.** Multiplication table for split quaternions.

| $\times$ | 1 | $i$ | $j_1$ | $j_2$ |
|---|---|---|---|---|
| 1 | 1 | $i$ | $j_1$ | $j_2$ |
| $i$ | $i$ | $-1$ | $j_2$ | $-j_1$ |
| $j_1$ | $j_1$ | $-j_2$ | 1 | $-i$ |
| $j_2$ | $j_2$ | $j_1$ | $i$ | 1 |

The next derivative algebra of $\mathbb{H}$ is the algebra of semiquaternions $\mathbb{H}^0$ with a basis $1, i, \epsilon_1, \epsilon_2$, where $i^2 = -1$, $\epsilon_1^2 = \epsilon_2^2 = 0$, $i\epsilon_1 = -\epsilon_1 i = \epsilon_2$, $\epsilon_2 i = -i\epsilon_2 = \epsilon_1$, $\epsilon_1 \epsilon_2 = \epsilon_2 \epsilon_1 = 0$. Another derivative of $\mathbb{H}$-algebra is the algebra of split semiquaternions $\mathbb{H}'^0$ with a basis $1, j, \epsilon_1, \epsilon_2$, where $j^2 = 1$ and $\epsilon_1^2 = \epsilon_2^2 = 0$. The $\mathbb{H}'^0$-algebra has the same multiplication properties as the previous one. The last derivative algebra is the algebra of $\frac{1}{4}$-quaternions $\mathbb{H}^{00}$ with a basis $1, \epsilon_1, \epsilon_2, \epsilon_3$, where $\epsilon_1^2 = \epsilon_2^2 = \epsilon_3^2 = 0$, and $\epsilon_1 \epsilon_2 = -\epsilon_2 \epsilon_1 = \epsilon_3$, $\epsilon_1 \epsilon_3 = \epsilon_3 \epsilon_1 = \epsilon_2 \epsilon_3 = \epsilon_3 \epsilon_2 = 0$. All of the above-mentioned derivatives of $\mathbb{H}$-algebra are the associative algebras (they fulfill the conditions (4) and (5) only), and contain zero divisors, nilpotents and non-trivial idempotents.

Now let us consider a group of tensor product algebras. The next considered algebra is the algebra of bicomplex numbers $\mathbb{C}_2$ (known also as the algebra of tessarines) with a basis $1, i_1, i_2, j$, where $i_1^2 = i_2^2 = -1$, $j^2 = 1$, $i_1 i_2 = i_2 i_1 = j$.

In contrast to $\mathbb{H}$-algebra, $\mathbb{C}_2$ algebra is commutative, thus fulfills the conditions (3)–(5). Due to existence of non-trivial idempotents for $\mathbb{C}_2$, the addition and multiplication operations are performed element-wise. The multiplication is ruled by the multiplication table presented in Table 3.

**Table 3.** Multiplication table for bicomplex numbers.

| × | 1 | $i_1$ | $i_2$ | $j$ |
|---|---|---|---|---|
| 1 | 1 | $i_1$ | $i_2$ | $j$ |
| $i_1$ | $i_1$ | $-1$ | $j$ | $-i_2$ |
| $i_2$ | $i_2$ | $j$ | 1 | $i_1$ |
| $j$ | $j$ | $-i_2$ | $i_1$ | $-1$ |

Another generalization of $\mathbb{C}$-algebra is the algebra of biquaternions $\mathbb{C}\otimes\mathbb{H}$ with a basis $1, i, j, k$, where $i, j, k$ are imaginary units. The symbolic form of a biquaternion $\tilde{q}$ can be presented as follows: $\mathbb{C}\otimes\mathbb{H} := \{\tilde{q} = a_1 + a_2 i + a_3 j + a_4 k \mid a_n \in \mathbb{C}\}$. Biquaternions, similarly as quaternions, are not commutative, but are associative and alternative. The addition is performed element-wise, while the multiplication is ruled by Table 4.

**Table 4.** Multiplication table for biquaternions.

| × | 1 | i | $j$ | k |
|---|---|---|---|---|
| 1 | 1 | $i$ | $j$ | $k$ |
| i | $i$ | $-1$ | $-k$ | $-j$ |
| j | $j$ | $-k$ | 1 | $i$ |
| k | $k$ | $-j$ | $i$ | 1 |

## 3   Generalized Julia Sets in 4D Hypercomplex Spaces

Having defined all possible 4D hypercomplex algebras, one can perform an analysis of the resulting sets generated following the recursive polynomial (2). Since all of these geometrical structures are 4-dimensional, their 3D cross-sections are considered in further studies. The 3D cross-sections are obtained by setting the last coordinate to 0, i.e. each hypercomplex number is represented in the form $(a_1, a_2, a_3, 0)$. Such an approach was assumed by Hart et al. in [3] and many further studies.

In order to make possible the comparison and graphical analysis of generated Julia sets, it is essential to select the most known representations of Julia sets, namely the Dendrite $(0, 1, 0, 0)$, San Marco fractal $(-0.75, 0, 0, 0)$, and Siegel Disk $(-0.390541, 0.586788, 0, 0)$ as well as several other structures $(-1, -0.1, 0, 0)$, $(0.15, 0.4, 0.1, 0)$ and $(-0.6, -0.5, 0.22, 0.4)$. The values in brackets denote the coefficients of the elements of $c$ in (1). The rendering of these sets was performed in the ChaosPro freeware fractal generator, where the additional libraries for above-mentioned hypercomplex algebras were implemented (except the algebras of bicomplex numbers and quaternions). Preliminary analysis shows that only bicomplex, quaternionic and biquaternionic generalizations of $\mathcal{J}$ sets on a $\mathbb{C}$-plane are non-trivial, and have fractal properties for the most values of $c$. The mentioned examples for these cases are presented in Figs. 1, 2 and 3. The colors denote the distance from the origin of the 4D hypercomplex space.

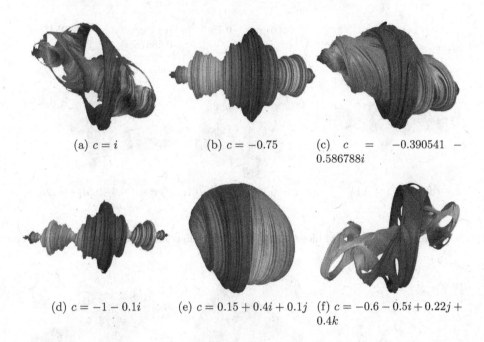

(a) $c = i$    (b) $c = -0.75$    (c) $c = -0.390541 - 0.586788i$

(d) $c = -1 - 0.1i$    (e) $c = 0.15 + 0.4i + 0.1j$    (f) $c = -0.6 - 0.5i + 0.22j + 0.4k$

**Fig. 1.** Examples of quaternionic $\mathcal{J}$-sets for various initial points $z_0 = c$.

It can be observed that quaternionic $\mathcal{J}$ sets reveal rotational symmetry around the axis of reals, while the bicomplex $\mathcal{J}$ sets are quadrilaterally symmetric, i.e. they are close to square shapes when performing cross-section normal to one of $\mathbb{C}$-planes. Moreover, when $c \in \mathbb{C}$ for the mentioned generalizations of $\mathcal{J}$ sets, they are trivial with respect to their analogues on a $\mathbb{C}$-plane (see e.g. Figs. 1(a)–(d) and 2(a)–(d)). This means that their 3D cross-sections are just the revolutions of their complex analogues (see Fig. 4 for instance). Analyzing the biquaternionic $\mathcal{J}$ sets presented in Fig. 3 one can observe that they are not trivial with respect to their analogues on a $\mathbb{C}$-plane even in $c \in \mathbb{C}$ (it is clearly visible in Fig. 3(b)–(d)), which is resulted by a complexification of a quaternion. Gintz [2] confirmed in his studies that "the [biquaternionic] fractal seemed to literally expand in all directions at once". However, if we visualize the same cross-sections for the cases presented in Fig. 3(a),(b) as for their quaternionic and bicomplex analogues shown in Fig. 4, we obtain the same shape in the plane of cross-section which proves the connection between complex and biquaternionic

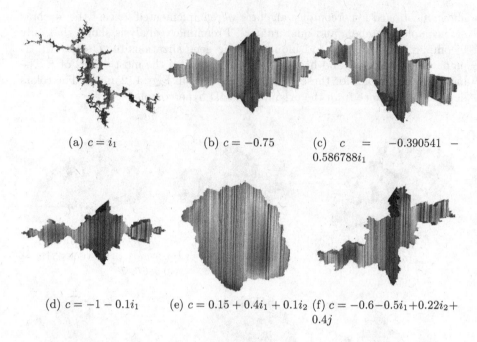

(a) $c = i_1$

(b) $c = -0.75$

(c) $c = -0.390541 - 0.586788i_1$

(d) $c = -1 - 0.1i_1$

(e) $c = 0.15 + 0.4i_1 + 0.1i_2$

(f) $c = -0.6 - 0.5i_1 + 0.22i_2 + 0.4j$

**Fig. 2.** Examples of bicomplex $\mathcal{J}$-sets for various initial points $z_0 = c$.

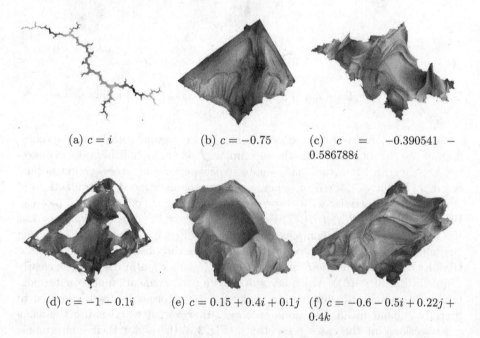

(a) $c = i$

(b) $c = -0.75$

(c) $c = -0.390541 - 0.586788i$

(d) $c = -1 - 0.1i$

(e) $c = 0.15 + 0.4i + 0.1j$

(f) $c = -0.6 - 0.5i + 0.22j + 0.4k$

**Fig. 3.** Examples of biquaternionic $\mathcal{J}$-sets for various initial points $z_0 = c$.

$\mathcal{J}$ sets. Taking into consideration the recursive equation generalized with respect to an order of a polynomial $p$, the quaternionic and bicomplex $\mathcal{J}$ sets tend to regular shapes [8,9], while in the case of biquaternionic $\mathcal{J}$ sets they remain of the fractal type (see [7] for details).

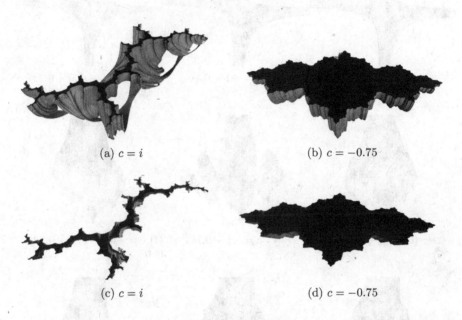

(a) $c = i$                    (b) $c = -0.75$

(c) $c = i$                    (d) $c = -0.75$

**Fig. 4.** Trivial cases of quaternionic $\mathcal{J}$-sets (a),(b), and bicomplex $\mathcal{J}$-sets (c),(d).

Now, let us consider the rest of hypercomplex spaces described in Sect. 2 and $\mathcal{J}$ sets constructed in them. The examples of 3D cross-sections of the generated $\mathcal{J}$ sets in these hypercomplex vector spaces are presented in Fig. 5. The rules of construction of these sets within particular hypercomplex vector spaces were described in [5,6,10]. In each case of the considered $\mathcal{J}$ sets constructed in $\mathbb{H}^0$, $\mathbb{H}'$, $\mathbb{H}'^0$ and $\mathbb{H}^{00}$ vector spaces are not limited, i.e. the generated $\mathcal{J}$ sets tend to infinity which causes that the critical points are not located in zero or even do not exist. In turn, this causes that the latter $\mathcal{J}$ sets are the degenerated ones and have no fractal properties as their analogues defined in $\mathbb{H}$, $\mathbb{C}_2$ and $\mathbb{C} \otimes \mathbb{H}$ vector spaces. Moreover, the degenerated $\mathcal{J}$ sets generalized with respect to a degree of polynomial also do not reveal any fractal properties.

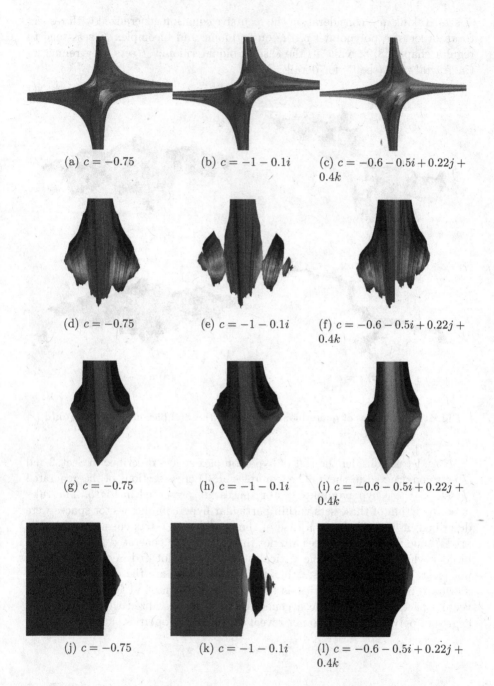

(a) $c = -0.75$

(b) $c = -1 - 0.1i$

(c) $c = -0.6 - 0.5i + 0.22j + 0.4k$

(d) $c = -0.75$

(e) $c = -1 - 0.1i$

(f) $c = -0.6 - 0.5i + 0.22j + 0.4k$

(g) $c = -0.75$

(h) $c = -1 - 0.1i$

(i) $c = -0.6 - 0.5i + 0.22j + 0.4k$

(j) $c = -0.75$

(k) $c = -1 - 0.1i$

(l) $c = -0.6 - 0.5i + 0.22j + 0.4k$

**Fig. 5.** Examples of split quaternionic (a)–(c), semiquaternionic (d)–(f), split semiquaternionic (g)–(i), and $\frac{1}{4}$-quaternionic (j)–(l) $\mathcal{J}$ sets for selected initial points $z_0 = c$.

# 4    Conclusions

In the presented study, all possible 4D hypercomplex generalizations of $\mathcal{J}$ sets are introduced and analyzed. After the mathematical preliminaries of 4D hypercomplex algebras and arithmetic operations within these algebras the selected $\mathcal{J}$ sets were visualized and analyzed. It was shown that only three of all possible 4D hypercomplex vector spaces are suitable for construction of non-trivial and non-degenerated $\mathcal{J}$ sets with the fractal properties, namely the quaternionic, bicomplex and biquaternionic ones. The other vector spaces generate the degenerated $\mathcal{J}$ sets which cannot be considered as fractals.

**Acknowledgements.** The publication is financed from the statutory funds of the Faculty of Mechanical Engineering of the Silesian University of Technology in 2016.

# References

1. Bogush, A.A., Gazizov, A.Z., Kurochkin, Y.A., Stosui, V.T.: Symmetry properties of quaternionic and biquaterionic analogs of Julia sets. Ukrainian J. Phys. **48**(4), 295–299 (2003)
2. Gintz, T.W.: Artist's statement CQUATS - a non-distributive quad algebra for 3D renderings of Mandelbrot and Julia sets. Comput. Graph. **26**(2), 367–370 (2002)
3. Hart, J.C., Sandin, D.J., Kauffman, L.H.: Ray tracing deterministic 3-D fractals. Comput. Graph. **23**(3), 289–296 (1989)
4. Holbrook, J.A.R.: Quaternionic Fatou-Julia sets. Ann. Sci. Math Que. **11**, 79–94 (1987)
5. Jafari, M.: Split semi-quaternions algebra in semi-euclidean 4-space. Cumhur. Sci. J. **36**(1), 70–77 (2015)
6. Jafari, M., Yayli, T.: Generalized quaternions and their algebraic properties. Sér. A1. Math. Stat. **64**(1), 15–27 (2015). Communications de la Faculté des Sciences de l'Université d'Ankara
7. Katunin, A.: The generalized biquaternionic M-J sets. Fractals, submitted (2016)
8. Katunin, A.: On the convergence of multicomplex M-J sets to the Steinmetz hypersolids. J. Appl. Math. Comput. Mech. **15**(3) (in press, 2016)
9. Katunin, A., Fedio, K.: On a visualization of the convergence of the boundary of generalized Mandelbrot set to $(n-1)$-sphere. J. Appl. Math. Comput. Mech. **14**(1), 63–69 (2015)
10. Mortazaasl, H., Jafari, M.: A study on semi-quaternions algebra in semi-euclidean 4-space. Math. Sci. Appl. E-notes **1**(2), 20–27 (2013)
11. Norton, A.V.: Generation and display of geometric fractals in 3-D. Comput. Graph. **16**(3), 61–67 (1982)
12. Norton, A.V.: Julia sets in the quaternions. Comput. Graph. **13**(2), 267–278 (1989)
13. Rochon, D.: A generalized Mandelbrot set for bicomplex numbers. Fractals **8**(4), 355–368 (2000)
14. Rosenfeld, B.: Geometry of Lie Groups, Mathematics and Its Applications, vol. 393. Springer, Dordrecht (1997)
15. Wang, X.Y., Song, W.J.: The generalized M-J sets for bicomplex numbers. Nonlinear Dyn. **72**(1), 17–26 (2013)
16. Wang, X.Y., Sun, Y.Y.: The general quaternionic M-J sets on the mapping $z \leftarrow z^\alpha + c$ ($\alpha \in \mathbf{N}$). Comput. Math. Appl. **53**(11), 1718–1732 (2007)
17. Zireh, A.: A generalized Mandelbrot set of polynomials of type $e_d$ for bicomplex numbers. Georgian Math. J. **15**(1), 189–194 (2008)

# 2D-Leap-Frog and Removal of Outliers in Noisy Photometric Stereo with Non-distant Illuminations

Ryszard Kozera[1,3](✉), Felicja Okulicka-Długewska[2], and Lyle Noakes[4]

[1] Faculty of Applied Informatics and Mathematics, Warsaw University of Life Sciences-SGGW, Nowoursynowska street 159, 02-776 Warsaw, Poland
`ryszard.kozera@gmail.com`
[2] Faculty of Mathematics and Information Science, Warsaw University of Technology, Koszykowa street 75, 00-662 Warsaw, Poland
`f.okulicka@mini.pw.edu.pl`
[3] School of Computer Science and Software Engineering, The University of Western Australia, 35 Stirling Highway, Crawley, Perth, WA 6009, Australia
[4] School of Mathematics and Statistics, The University of Western Australia, 35 Stirling Highway, Crawley, Perth, WA 6009, Australia
`lyle.noakes@uwa.edu.au`

**Abstract.** This paper discusses the reconstruction of a Lambertian surface $S_L$ in three-image noisy photometric stereo under the assumption that light-sources are not necessarily positioned at infinity. The corresponding multi-variable non-linear optimization task either incorporating or not an image boundary continuity enforcement (to remove outliers) is introduced. In addition, a feasible numerical scheme called 2D Leap-Frog is used to recover $S_L$ from three noisy images. The entire setting is tested for non-distant and distant illuminations. The comparison tests are conducted for different surfaces.

**Keywords:** Noisy photometric stereo · Non-distant illumination · Lambertian surface · 2D-Leap-Frog · Optimization

## 1 Introduction

A single image *shape-from-shading problem* is modelled by the so-called *image irradiance equation* (see [1]):

$$R(n_1(x,y,z), n_2(x,y,z), n_3(x,y,z)) = E(x,y), \tag{1}$$

considered over an image $\Omega \subset \mathbb{R}^2$. Here the function $E : \Omega \to [0,1]$ represents the intensity of the light reflected from the surface $S$ illuminated from the direction $p$. Commonly one assumes that $S = graph(u)$ with $u : \Omega \to \mathbb{R}$ defining a $C^k$ function ($k = 1, 2$). The mapping $R$ called *a reflectance map* depends on the material covering $S$. The vector fields $n(x,y,z) = (n_1(x,y,z), n_2(x,y,z), n_3(x,y,z))$

© Springer International Publishing AG 2016
L.J. Chmielewski et al. (Eds.): ICCVG 2016, LNCS 9972, pp. 636–648, 2016.
DOI: 10.1007/978-3-319-46418-3_57

defines a unit normal to $S$ at a point $s = (x, y, z) \in S$. The latter is proportional to $n(x, y) = (u_x(x, y), u_y(x, y), -1)$. For some materials the reflectance map $R$ can be determined (or closely approximated) by using laws of optics [1,2]. In particular, for the so-called *Lambertian surface* (denoted here as $S_L$), $R$ is proportional to $\cos \alpha(s)$, where $\alpha$ forms an angle between vectors $n(s)$ and $p$. Consequently, for any Lambertian surface $S_L$ the image irradiance equation (1) reads as (see [1]):

$$\frac{p_1 u_x(x, y) + p_2 u_y(x, y) - p_3}{\sqrt{p_1^2 + p_2^2 + p_3^2} \sqrt{u_x^2(x, y) + u_y^2(x, y) + 1}} = E_p(x, y), \qquad (2)$$

over some domain $\Omega_p$. Note that an arbitrary vertical shift of $u$ (and thus of $S_L$) in (2) is permitted as the shape of $S_L$ still remains unchanged. As demonstrated in [1,3–11], the Eq. (2) commonly yields an *ill-posed problem*. In order to disambiguate (2) various extra conditions can be imposed – see e.g. [1,10–15]. One of them (called *photometric stereo technique*) relies on consecutive illuminations of $S_L$ from multiple linearly independent directions i.e. by distant light-sources (see e.g. [1,12–15]).

*Two light-source photometric stereo* yields a generic uniqueness in the reconstruction process (see [13–15]). On the other hand, *three light-source photometric stereo* determines a unique Lambertian surface $S_L = graph(u)$ (modulo its vertical shift $C$) – see [1,12,13]. By (2), the reconstruction process is modelled here with the following system of three non-linear partial differential equations of the first order in two independent variables $(x, y)$:

$$\frac{\langle n | p \rangle}{||n|| \cdot ||p||} = E_p(x, y), \quad \frac{\langle n | q \rangle}{||n|| \cdot ||q||} = E_q(x, y), \quad \frac{\langle n | r \rangle}{||n|| \cdot ||r||} = E_r(x, y), \qquad (3)$$

defined over $\Omega = \Omega_p \cap \Omega_q \cap \Omega_r$. As shown in [1,12,13], the latter yields a unique vector field $v(x, y) = (v_1(x, y), v_2(x, y))$ (here $v_1 = u_x$ and $v_2 = u_y$) determined exclusively in terms of $E_p$, $E_q$, $E_r$, $p$, $q$ and $r$ which solves (3). Both symbols $\langle \cdot | \cdot \rangle$ and $|| \cdot ||$ appearing in (3) represent the Euclidean dot product and the corresponding norm in $\mathbb{R}^3$. In the next step *the integrability condition* $\int_{\gamma_c} u_x dx + u_y dy = 0$ (see [16]) must hold along each closed curve $\gamma_c \in C^1(\Omega)$ over simply-connected $\Omega$. Upon satisfaction of integrability constraint, the function $u$ (and thus $S_L$) is recovered according to (see e.g. [16–18]):

$$u(x, y) = u(x_0, y_0) + \int_\gamma v_1 dx + v_2 dy, \qquad (4)$$

which yields $u \in C^1(\Omega)$ (with a free constant $C = u(x_0, y_0)$ – see [17]). Here $\gamma \in C^1(\Omega)$ is an arbitrary curve joining any $(x, y) \in \Omega$ with a fixed $(x_0, y_0) \in \Omega$. Recall that the integrability condition for $u \in C^2(\Omega)$ over simply-connected $\Omega$ reads as (see e.g. [16–18]):

$$v_{1y} = v_{2x}. \qquad (5)$$

If the non-distant light-source is positioned at the point $\bar{p} = (\bar{p}_1, \bar{p}_2, \bar{p}_3)$ the incoming non-parallel beam direction varies at each $s \in S_L$ according to the simple formula $\tilde{p} = (\bar{p}_1 - x, \bar{p}_2 - y, \bar{p}_3 - u(x, y))$. Consequently, the image irradiance equation (2) for Lambertian surface $S_L$ illuminated by the light-source situated at $\bar{p}$ reformulates into (over $\Omega_{\bar{p}}$):

$$\frac{(\bar{p}_1 - x)u_x(x,y) + (\bar{p}_2 - y)u_y(x,y) - (\bar{p}_3 - u(x,y))}{\sqrt{(\bar{p}_1 - x)^2 + (\bar{p}_2 - y)^2 + (\bar{p}_3 - u(x,y))^2}\sqrt{u_x^2(x,y) + u_y^2(x,y) + 1}} = E_{\bar{p}}(x,y).$$
(6)

Taking into account (6), the system (3) for three light sources positioned at $\bar{p}$, $\bar{q}$ and $\bar{r}$ transforms into:

$$\frac{\langle n|\tilde{p}\rangle}{||n|| \cdot ||\tilde{p}||} = E_{\bar{p}}(x,y), \quad \frac{\langle n|\tilde{q}\rangle}{||n|| \cdot ||\tilde{q}||} = E_{\bar{q}}(x,y), \quad \frac{\langle n|\tilde{r}\rangle}{||n|| \cdot ||\tilde{r}||} = E_{\bar{r}}(x,y), \quad (7)$$

over $\Omega = \Omega_{\bar{p}} \cap \Omega_{\bar{q}} \cap \Omega_{\bar{r}}$. Here $\tilde{q}$ and $\tilde{r}$ are defined similarly to $\tilde{p}$ introduced above.

The real camera images $\hat{E}_p$, $\hat{E}_q$ and $\hat{E}_r$ (or $\hat{E}_{\bar{p}}$, $\hat{E}_{\bar{q}}$ and $\hat{E}_{\bar{r}}$) are digitized representations of $E_p$, $E_q$ and $E_r$ (or of $E_{\bar{p}}$, $E_{\bar{q}}$ and $E_{\bar{r}}$) calculated over each pixels instead of evaluating respective image intensities at each point $(x,y) \in \Omega$. An extra image contaminating component stems from the camera noise commonly assumed as Gaussian with mean $\mu = 0$ and standard deviation $\sigma \in [0.01, 0.10]$.

To deal with noisy photometric stereo various methods are originally introduced (coined here *linear rectification methods*) – see e.g. [17–20,22,23]. The main problem with such methods stems from the fact that the Gaussian noise is assumed as added to the computed vector field instead of input images. The gain is to rectify the computed non-integrable vector field upon solving merely the corresponding linear optimization. The next delicate aspect is to integrate (see (4)) a rectified vector field to $u$ and thus to $S_L$ – see [17–20,22,23]. Thus a need arises for non-linear optimization schemes (dealing with the genuine source of noise added to images) supplemented with the feasible computational methods for recovering $S_L$ from noisy photometric stereo images.

A *non-linear* digitized version of (2) is introduced in [24,25]. More specifically, for a given noisy image $\hat{E}_p$ (as for $\hat{E}_q$ and $\hat{E}_r$) with $N \times N$ pixel resolution, a central-difference derivative approximation transforms (2) into *a non-linear discrete minimization problem* in $\hat{u} \in \mathbb{R}^{N^2-4}$:

$$\mathcal{E}_p(\hat{u}) = \sum_{i,j=2}^{i,j=N-1} \left( \frac{p_1 \frac{\hat{u}_{i+1,j} - \hat{u}_{i-1,j}}{2\Delta x} + p_2 \frac{\hat{u}_{i,j+1} - \hat{u}_{i,j-1}}{2\Delta y} - p_3}{||p|| \sqrt{\left(\frac{\hat{u}_{i+1,j} - \hat{u}_{i-1,j}}{2\Delta x}\right)^2 + \left(\frac{\hat{u}_{i,j+1} - \hat{u}_{i,j-1}}{2\Delta y}\right)^2 + 1}} - \hat{E}_p(i,j) \right)^2,$$
(8)

where $\hat{E}_p(i,j)$ (and $\hat{u}_{i,j}$) represents the value of $\hat{E}_p$ (or of $\hat{u}$) at $(i,j)$-pixel. From now on, for simplicity we assume $\Delta x = \Delta y = \Delta$ and $\Omega = [0,1] \times [0,1]$. The boundary pixels $\in \partial\Omega$ are left out in (8) since central-difference derivative approximation is not applicable here. Four corner values of $\hat{u}_{1,1}$, $\hat{u}_{1,N}$, $\hat{u}_{N,1}$, $\hat{u}_{N,N}$ are also omitted due to the non-diagonal character of central-difference derivative approximation. In a similar fashion to (8) both $\mathcal{E}_q(\hat{u})$ and $\mathcal{E}_p(\hat{u})$ can be incorporated into *a total performance index*:

$$\mathcal{E}(\hat{u}) = \mathcal{E}_p(\hat{u}) + \mathcal{E}_q(\hat{u}) + \mathcal{E}_r(\hat{u}),$$
(9)

to be minimized with $\hat{u}_{opt} \in \mathbb{R}^{N^2-4}$. As shown in [24] problem (9) has non-isolated critical points. In addition, due to $N$ being large (reflecting a real image resolution) some optimization schemes like Newton's Method are confronted with multiple inversions of big size matrices $D^2\mathscr{E} \in M_{(N^2-4)\times(N^2-4)}(\mathbb{R})$. A Leap-Frog like scheme is applied in [24] (see also [26]) to handle this aspect while minimizing (9). However, the experiments demonstrate (see e.g. [24]) that most of the reconstructed surfaces are contaminated with the outliers commonly positioned along the boundary of $\Omega$. In order to cope with the latter (and to enforce computed critical points as isolated) a modified scheme to (9) is proposed in [27]. More specifically, for $\delta_{i,j} = (\hat{u}_{i+1,j} - \hat{u}_{i,j})^2$ and $\rho_{i,j} = (\hat{u}_{i,j+1} - \hat{u}_{i,j})^2$ the forward-difference continuity constraint over the left-boundary pixels reads as $\mathscr{E}_L(\hat{u}) = \sum_{j=2}^{N-1} \delta_{1,j} + \sum_{i=2}^{N-2} \rho_{i,1}$. In a similar fashion a continuity enforcement for $\mathscr{E}_T$, $\mathscr{E}_R$ and $\mathscr{E}_B$ is defined over top-, right- and bottom- boundaries of $\Omega$, respectively. Upon incorporating the above into (9) *a modified performance index function* reads as:

$$\mathscr{E}_M(\hat{u}) = \mathscr{E}(\hat{u}) + \mathscr{E}_L(\hat{u}) + \mathscr{E}_T(\hat{u}) + \mathscr{E}_R(\hat{u}) + \mathscr{E}_B(\hat{u}), \tag{10}$$

to be minimized with $\hat{u}_{opt} \in \mathbb{R}^{N^2-4}$. Thus the reconstruction of $S_L$ (illuminated by three distant light-sources) from noisy images reduces into a non-linear optimization – for the experimental results see [27]. Recall that the continuity enforcement in (9) (and hence in (10)) is only applied along boundary pixels. Indeed numerical differentiability (and thus continuity) is implicitly ascertained in (9) (and in (10)) over all internal pixels of $\Omega$.

This paper addresses the following issues:

1. Adaptation of (9) and (10) to the case of non-distant light-sources positioned at the points $\bar{p}$, $\bar{q}$ and $\bar{r}$ – see Sect. 2. The modified scheme (12) or (13) either does not or does rectify the potential outliers occurring in the reconstructed surface.
2. A non-linear 2D-Leap-Frog to examine the robustness of the above optimization schemes (i.e. to (9) and (10) or to (12) and (13)) is applied to both distant and non-distant illuminations. The experimental results are reported in Sect. 3.

## 2    Non-distant Light-Sources and 2D-Leap-Frog

Modelling a surface reconstruction based on three non-distant light-sources illuminations (positioned at $\bar{p}$, $\bar{q}$ and $\bar{r}$) can be now adapted from (10). Indeed, assume input data given by three noisy images $\hat{E}_{\bar{p}}$, $\hat{E}_{\bar{q}}$ and $\hat{E}_{\bar{r}}$ defined over an image $\Omega = \Omega_{\bar{p}} \cap \Omega_{\bar{q}} \cap \Omega_{\bar{r}}$. Similarly to (8), *a non-linear* digitized version of (6) leads into *a non-linear discrete minimization problem* in $\hat{u} \in \mathbb{R}^{N^2-4}$:

$$\mathscr{E}_{\bar{p}}(\hat{u}) = \sum_{i,j=2}^{i,j=N-1} \left( \frac{\tilde{p}_{i,j_1}\frac{\hat{u}_{i+1,j}-\hat{u}_{i-1,j}}{2\Delta x} + \tilde{p}_{i,j_2}\frac{\hat{u}_{i,j+1}-\hat{u}_{i,j-1}}{2\Delta y} - \tilde{p}_{i,j_3}}{\|\tilde{p}_{i,j}\|\sqrt{\left(\frac{\hat{u}_{i+1,j}-\hat{u}_{i-1,j}}{2\Delta x}\right)^2 + \left(\frac{\hat{u}_{i,j+1}-\hat{u}_{i,j-1}}{2\Delta y}\right)^2 + 1}} - \hat{E}_{\bar{p}}(i,j) \right)^2 ,$$

$$\tag{11}$$

where $(x_i, y_j)$ stands for the coordinates of the center of $(i,j)$-pixel, the vector $\tilde{p}_{i,j} = (\tilde{p}_{i,j_1}, \tilde{p}_{i,j_2}, \tilde{p}_{i,j_3}) = (\bar{p}_1 - x_i, \bar{p}_2 - y_j, \bar{p}_3 - \hat{u}_{i,j})$, $\hat{u}_{i,j} = \hat{u}(x_i, y_j)$ and $\hat{E}_{\bar{p}}(i,j) = \hat{E}_{\bar{p}}(x_i, y_j)$. Again for simplicity we assume here that $\Delta x = \Delta y = \Delta$ and $\Omega = [0,1] \times [0,1]$. Furthermore, as in (9) *a total performance index* reads as:

$$\bar{\mathscr{E}}(\hat{u}) = \mathscr{E}_{\bar{p}}(\hat{u}) + \mathscr{E}_{\bar{q}}(\hat{u}) + \mathscr{E}_{\bar{r}}(\hat{u}), \tag{12}$$

to be, as previously minimized with $\hat{u}_{opt} \in \mathbb{R}^{N^2-4}$. Finally, adding the continuity enforcement (as in (13)) yields *a modified performance index function*:

$$\bar{\mathscr{E}}_M(\hat{u}) = \bar{\mathscr{E}}(\hat{u}) + \mathscr{E}_L(\hat{u}) + \mathscr{E}_T(\hat{u}) + \mathscr{E}_R(\hat{u}) + \mathscr{E}_B(\hat{u}) \tag{13}$$

for three-image noisy photometric stereo with non-distant light-sources.

Finding numerically critical points for either (12) or (13) (or alternatively for either (9) or (10)) in case of high-resolution real images (i.e. with $N$ large) is confronted with heavy computational burden. To alleviate this problem a 2D-Leap-Frog can be deployed (see [21,24,25,27]). In this setting one covers the image $\Omega$ with overlapped sub-domains $\Omega_{s,t}$ (called snapshots) and optimize the respective performance index only over variables geometrically belonging to the selected snapshot $\Omega_{s,t}$. This diminishes the number of free variables while optimizing snapshot variables only. The computed local sub-optimal values over $\Omega_{s,t}$ replace the respective values of $\hat{u} \in \mathbb{R}^{N^2-4}$ representing values of $u$ over $\Omega$-pixels. The usual snapshot overlap involves either horizontal or vertical half-snapshot translations. The stopping condition for 2D-Leap-Frog often relies on imposing an a priori bound on a number of permitted iterations. Most 2D-Leap-Frog tests indicate that the corresponding performance index is substantially decreased only within the first 5–10 initial iterations. The subsequent iterations decrease marginally the energy in question while still consuming considerable execution time. The entire procedure can be run either sequentially (see e.g. [21]) or in parallel (see [27,28]). More specific information about 2D-Leap-Frog construction and its performance can be found in [21,24,25,27].

The *initial guess* for 2D-Leap-Frog for both distant and non-distant light sources can e.g. be taken as a substantial distortion of the ideal solution to (3) or (7) (assumed temporarily to be a priori given). This permits to test the appropriateness of (12) or (13) (or alternatively of either (9) or (10)) in modelling noisy photometric stereo and enables to verify the robustness of 2D-Leap-Frog as a feasible numerical scheme for minimizing optimization tasks in question. However, the weakness in choosing such initial guess stems from unavailability of the ideal solution to (3) (or to (7)).

The latter can be overcome for distant light-source illuminations with the aid of linear rectification methods – see Sect. 1. Indeed, as proved in [1,13] for noiseless three-image photometric stereo, the following integrable (for genuine Lambertian images) vector field $(u_x, u_y) = (f_1(p,q,r,E_p,E_q,E_r), f_2(p,q,r,E_p,E_q,E_r))$ determined by:

$$u_x = \frac{(q_2r_3-q_3r_2)E_p\|p\|+(p_3r_2-p_2r_3)E_q\|q\|+(p_2q_3-p_3q_2)E_r\|r\|}{(q_2r_1-q_1r_2)E_p\|p\|+(p_1r_2-p_2r_1)E_q\|q\|+(p_2q_1-p_1q_2)E_r\|r\|},$$

$$u_y = \frac{(q_3r_1-q_1r_3)E_p\|p\|+(p_1r_3-p_3r_1)E_q\|q\|+(p_3q_1-p_2q_3)E_r\|r\|}{(q_2r_1-q_1r_2)E_p\|p\|+(p_1r_2-p_2r_1)E_q\|q\|+(p_2q_1-p_1q_2)E_r\|r\|} \tag{14}$$

uniquely satisfies (3). Upon substituting noisy images $\hat{E}_p$, $\hat{E}_q$ and $\hat{E}_r$ into (14) one arrives at non-integrable vector field $(v_1, v_2) = (f_1(p, q, r, \hat{E}_p, \hat{E}_q, \hat{E}_r),$ $f_2(p, q, r, \hat{E}_p, \hat{E}_q, \hat{E}_r))$. As mentioned in Sect. 1, $(v_1, v_2)$ is rectifiable to the closest integrable vector field $(v_1^{opt}, v_2^{opt})$ by using various linear optimization schemes based on discretizing continuous integrability condition (5) – see e.g. [17–20, 22, 23, 29, 30]. Subsequently, an integrable vector field $(v_1^{opt}, v_2^{opt})$ via numerical analogue of integration formula (4) yields a requested initial guess.

In case of non-distant three light-sources, the formulas (14) applied to (7) yield $(u_x, u_y) = (f_1(\tilde{p}, \tilde{q}, \tilde{r}, E_{\tilde{p}}, E_{\tilde{q}}, E_{\tilde{r}}), f_2(\tilde{p}, \tilde{q}, \tilde{r}, E_{\tilde{p}}, E_{\tilde{q}}, E_{\tilde{r}}))$. Since $\tilde{p}_3 =$ $\bar{p}_3 - u(x, y)$, $\tilde{q}_3 = \bar{q}_3 - u(x, y)$ and $\tilde{r}_3 = \bar{r}_3 - u(x, y)$ depend on $u$ a previous linear integrability set-up to rectify the non-integrable field $(\bar{v}_1, \bar{v}_2) =$ $(f_1(\tilde{p}, \tilde{q}, \tilde{r}, \hat{E}_{\tilde{p}}, \hat{E}_{\tilde{q}}, \hat{E}_{\tilde{r}}), f_2(\tilde{p}, \tilde{q}, \tilde{r}, \hat{E}_{\tilde{p}}, \hat{E}_{\tilde{q}}, \hat{E}_{\tilde{r}}))$ is not anymore applicable. The remedy is to solve (7) for $(u_x, u_y)$ exclusively in terms of $\bar{p}$, $\bar{q}$, $\bar{r}$ and $E_{\bar{p}}$, $E_{\bar{q}}$ and $E_{\bar{r}}$ which remains an open problem. For the experiments in Sect. 3, an arbitrary condition $u = constant$ is used in $f_1$ and $f_2$.

The next section discusses the experimental results for noisy three-image photometric stereo with distant and non-distant illuminations.

## 3    Numerical Experiments

In this paper images only with $16 \times 16$ pixel resolutions are tested. Similar discussion for $32 \times 32$ and $64 \times 64$ resolutions is here omitted due to the page limitation. In addition, synthetic Lambertian input images $E_p$, $E_q$ and $E_r$ (or $E_{\bar{p}}$, $E_{\bar{q}}$ and $E_{\bar{r}}$) are exclusively generated. The latter is achieved by substituting the exact gradient $\nabla u = (u_x, u_y)$ (for which $S_L = graph(u)$) into (3) (or into (7)). Next the Gaussian noise is added to the ideal images $E_p$, $E_q$ and $E_r$ (or to $E_{\bar{p}}$, $E_{\bar{q}}$ and $E_{\bar{r}}$) to simulate the respective noisy images $\hat{E}_p$, $\hat{E}_q$ and $\hat{E}_r$ ($\hat{E}_{\bar{p}}$, $\hat{E}_{\bar{q}}$ and $\hat{E}_{\bar{r}}$). For simplicity we also assume $\Omega = [0, 1] \times [0, 1]$. The case of $(x, y) \in \Omega$ when $\cos \alpha(s) < 0$ (marking all shadowed sections of $S_L$ – see (2)) is here permitted to simplify the implementation of modified non-linear 2D-Leap-Frog. Thus we implicitly extend image irradiance equations (3) and (7) to all invisible part of $S_L$. Newton's Method is used for local snapshot 2D-Leap-Frog optimizations (a default option in *Mathematica FindMinimum* function). The initial guess for distant (non-distant) light-sources is computed with the conjugate gradient scheme [30] (with $u = 0$) applied to the linear setting of noisy photometric stereo – see [21, 30]. The experiments refer to both optimization schemes (12) or (9) (i.e. outlier insensitive) and to (13) or (10) (i.e. outlier sensitive).

*Example 1.* Let the Lambertian surface $S_{L_1} = graph(u_1)$ be defined by:

$$u_1(x, y) = \frac{3}{4} + \frac{1}{3}\left(1 - \tanh\left(25(\frac{1}{4}(x + y - 2)^2 + \frac{1}{4}(x - y)^2 - \frac{1}{3}))\right)\right),$$

over $\Omega = [0, 1] \times [0, 1]$. Three light-source directions are selected here as $p = (0, 0, -1)$, $q = (-\sin\frac{\pi}{12}, 0, -\cos\frac{\pi}{12})$ and $r = (\frac{1}{2}\sin\frac{\pi}{24}, \frac{\sqrt{3}}{2}\sin\frac{\pi}{24}, -\cos\frac{\pi}{24})$.

**Fig. 1.** Noiseless digitized images $E_p$, $E_q$ and $E_r$ for $S_{L_1}$.

**Fig. 2.** Noisy digitized images $\hat{E}_p$, $\hat{E}_q$ and $\hat{E}_r$ for $S_{L_1}$.

**Fig. 3.** Noiseless digitized images $E_{\bar{p}}$, $E_{\bar{q}}$ and $E_{\bar{r}}$ for $S_{L_1}$.

**Fig. 4.** Noisy digitized images $\hat{E}_{\bar{p}}$, $\hat{E}_{\bar{q}}$ and $\hat{E}_{\bar{r}}$ for $S_{L_1}$.

The digitized noiseless images $E_p$, $E_q$ and $E_r$ of $S_{L_1}$ are shown in Fig. 1 and the contaminated $\hat{E}_p$, $\hat{E}_q$ and $\hat{E}_r$ with Gaussian noise $\mathcal{N}(0.0, 0.05)$ are illustrated in Fig. 2. The non-distant light-sources are positioned here at $\bar{p} = (0, 0, 10)$, $\bar{q} = (0, -3, 10)$ and $\bar{r} = (3, 0, 10)$. The respective digitized noiseless images $E_{\bar{p}}$, $E_{\bar{q}}$ and $E_{\bar{r}}$ of $S_{L_1}$ are presented in Fig. 3 together with $\hat{E}_{\bar{p}}$, $\hat{E}_{\bar{q}}$ and $\hat{E}_{\bar{r}}$ contaminated by Gaussian noise $\mathcal{N}(0.0, 0.05)$ shown in Fig. 4. Furthermore, Fig. 5

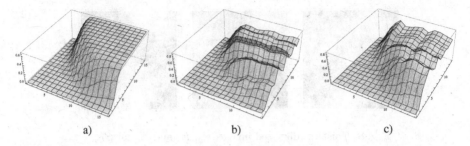

**Fig. 5.** (a) Ideal $S_{L_1}$, initial guess (b) $S_{L_{1a}}$ for $\hat{E}_p$, $\hat{E}_q$ and $\hat{E}_r$ (c) $\bar{S}_{L_{1a}}$ for $\hat{E}_{\bar{p}}$, $\hat{E}_{\bar{q}}$ and $\hat{E}_{\bar{r}}$.

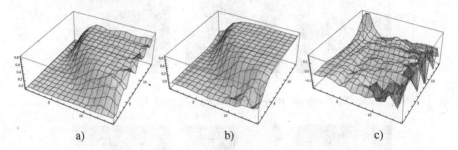

**Fig. 6.** $S_{L_1}$ reconstructed by 2D-Leap-Frog (after 6-th iterations) from $\hat{E}_p$, $\hat{E}_q$, $\hat{E}_r$: (a) $\hat{S}_{L_{1a}}^{o}$ for (9), (b) $\hat{S}_{L_{1a}}^{not(o)}$ for (10), (c) the difference between $\hat{S}_{L_{1a}}^{not(o)}$ and $\hat{S}_{L_{1a}}^{o}$.

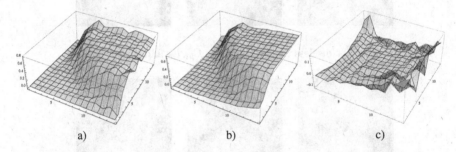

**Fig. 7.** $S_{L_1}$ reconstructed by 2D-Leap-Frog (after 6-th iterations) from $\hat{E}_{\bar{p}}$, $\hat{E}_{\bar{q}}$, $\hat{E}_{\bar{r}}$: (a) $\hat{S}_{L_{1a}}^{o}$ for (12), (b) $\hat{S}_{L_{1a}}^{not(o)}$ for (13), (c) the difference between $\hat{S}_{L_{1a}}^{not(o)}$ and $\hat{S}_{L_{1a}}^{o}$.

illustrates the ideal surface $S_{L_1}$ and the initial guesses $S_{L_{1a}}$ (or $\bar{S}_{L_{1a}}$) to optimize either (9) or (10) (or either (12) or (13)) from noisy images $\hat{E}_p$, $\hat{E}_q$, $\hat{E}_r$ (or $\hat{E}_{\bar{p}}$, $\hat{E}_{\bar{q}}$, $\hat{E}_{\bar{r}}$). The respective reconstructed surfaces without (i.e. $\hat{S}_{L_{1a}}^{o}$) and with (i.e. $\hat{S}_{L_{1a}}^{not(o)}$) outlier removal corrections obtained by 2D-Leap-Frog (after 6-th iterations) are shown in Fig. 6 (for distant illuminations) and in Fig. 7 (for non-distant illuminations). $\square$

**Fig. 8.** Noiseless digitized images $E_p$, $E_q$ and $E_r$ for $S_{L_2}$.

**Fig. 9.** Noisy digitized images $\hat{E}_p$, $\hat{E}_q$ and $\hat{E}_r$ for $S_{L_2}$.

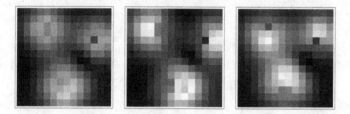

**Fig. 10.** Noiseless digitized images $E_{\bar{p}}$, $E_{\bar{q}}$ and $E_{\bar{r}}$ for $S_{L_2}$.

**Fig. 11.** Noisy digitized images $\hat{E}_{\bar{p}}$, $\hat{E}_{\bar{q}}$ and $\hat{E}_{\bar{r}}$ for $S_{L_2}$.

*Example 2.* Define a Lambertian surface $S_{L_2} = graph(u_2)$ according to:

$$u_2(x,y) = \frac{1}{16}\big(20f((x,y), w_1) - 15f((x,y), w_2) + 12f((x,y), w_3)\big),$$

with $w_1 = (\frac{3}{4}, \frac{1}{2})$, $w_2 = (\frac{1}{4}, \frac{1}{3})$, $w_3 = (\frac{1}{3}, \frac{4}{5})$ and $f(\tilde{v}_1, \tilde{v}_2) = e^{-100||\tilde{v}_1 - \tilde{v}_2||^2}$ for $\tilde{v}_1, \tilde{v}_2 \in \mathbb{R}^2$, over $\Omega = [0, 1] \times [0, 1]$. Three light-source directions are assumed to be $p = (0, 0, -1)$, $q = (0, \frac{1}{3}, -\frac{1}{\sqrt{2}})$ and $r = (\frac{1}{\sqrt{7}}, 0, -\frac{1}{\sqrt{2}})$. The respective noiseless

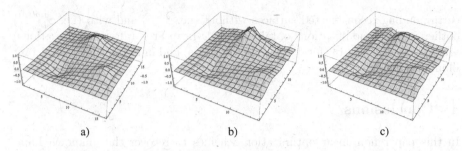

**Fig. 12.** (a) Ideal $S_{L_2}$, initial guess (b) $S_{L_{2a}}$ for $\hat{E}_p$, $\hat{E}_q$ and $\hat{E}_r$ (c) $\bar{S}_{L_{2a}}$ for $\hat{E}_{\bar{p}}$, $\hat{E}_{\bar{q}}$ and $\hat{E}_{\bar{r}}$.

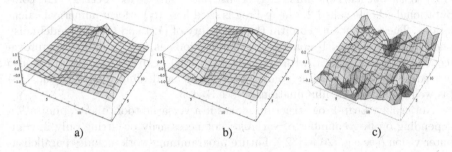

**Fig. 13.** $S_{L_2}$ reconstructed by 2D-Leap-Frog (after 6-th iterations) from $\hat{E}_p$, $\hat{E}_q$, $\hat{E}_r$: (a) $\hat{S}_{L_{2a}}^o$ for (9), (b) $\hat{S}_{L_{2a}}^{not(o)}$ for (10), (c) the difference between $\hat{S}_{L_{2a}}^{not(o)}$ and $\hat{S}_{L_{2a}}^o$.

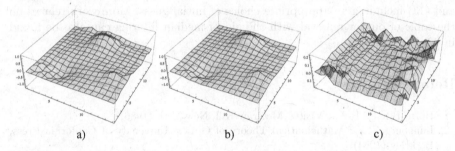

**Fig. 14.** $S_{L_2}$ reconstructed by 2D-Leap-Frog (after 6-th iterations) from $\hat{E}_{\bar{p}}$, $\hat{E}_{\bar{q}}$, $\hat{E}_{\bar{r}}$: (a) $\hat{S}_{L_{2a}}^o$ for (12), (b) $\hat{S}_{L_{2a}}^{not(o)}$ for (13), (c) the difference between $\hat{S}_{L_{2a}}^{not(o)}$ and $\hat{S}_{L_{2a}}^o$.

digitized images $E_p$, $E_q$ and $E_r$ of $S_{L_2}$ are shown in Fig. 8 and the contaminated $\hat{E}_p$, $\hat{E}_q$ and $\hat{E}_r$ with Gaussian noise $\mathcal{N}(0.0, 0.05)$ are presented in Fig. 9. The non-distant light-sources are situated here as previously at $\bar{p} = (0, 0, 10)$, $\bar{q} = (0, -3, 10)$ and $\bar{r} = (3, 0, 10)$. The respective noiseless digitized images $E_{\bar{p}}$, $E_{\bar{q}}$ and $E_{\bar{r}}$ of $S_{L_2}$ are shown in Fig. 10 together with $\hat{E}_{\bar{p}}$, $\hat{E}_{\bar{q}}$ and $\hat{E}_{\bar{r}}$ contaminated by Gaussian noise $\mathcal{N}(0.0, 0.05)$ illustrated in Fig. 11. Next Fig. 12 shows the ideal surface $S_{L_2}$ and the initial guesses $S_{L_{2a}}$ (or $\bar{S}_{L_{2a}}$) to optimize either (9) or (10) (or either (12) or (13)) from noisy images $\hat{E}_p$, $\hat{E}_q$, $\hat{E}_r$ (or $\hat{E}_{\bar{p}}$, $\hat{E}_{\bar{q}}$, $\hat{E}_{\bar{r}}$). The corresponding reconstructed surfaces without (i.e. $\hat{S}^{o}_{L_{2a}}$) and with (i.e. $\hat{S}^{not(o)}_{L_{2a}}$) outlier removal modifications obtained by 2D-Leap-Frog (after 6-th iterations) are presented in Fig. 13 (for distant illuminations) and in Fig. 14 (for non-distant illuminations). □

## 4   Conclusions

In this paper non-linear optimization schemes to recover the unknown Lambertian surface from three noisy images (with non-distant illuminations) are introduced. The latter is set up to be either insensitive or sensitive (see (12) or (13)) to the outliers contaminating reconstructed surface (see Sect. 2). The computational scheme called 2D-Leap-Frog is used here to perform numerical calculations. The experiments confirm the suitability of (12) and (13) to model noisy photometric stereo with non-distant illuminations as well as indicate improvement in outliers' removal with the aid of (13). 2D-Leap-Frog Algorithm is also proved here to be a feasible computational scheme dealing with (12) and (13) (as well as for distant illuminations) – see Sect. 3.

Noticeably, Leap-Frog structure makes it a versatile tool to any opimization depending on large number of variables not necessarily occurring only in computer vision (see e.g. [26, 31, 32]). Future programming work includes parallelization of 2D-Leap-Frog scheme for noisy images with non-distant illuminations as well as incorporation of shadows into algorithm in question. A similar theoretical analysis to [21] is needed to analyze the nature of the optimization schemes (12) and (13) including an appropriate choice of initial guess. More work related on the topic of outlier removal with the aid of median filtering can also be found in [33].

## References

1. Horn, B.K.P.: Robot Vision. McGraw-Hill, New York (1986)
2. Luneburg, R.K.: Mathematical Theory of Optics. University of California Press, Berkeley (1964)
3. Hurt, N.E.: Mathematical methods in shape-from-shading: a review of recent results. Acta Appl. Math. **23**, 163–188 (1991)
4. Kozera, R.: Uniqueness in shape from shading revisited. J. Math. Imag. Vis. **7**, 123–138 (1997)
5. Kozera, R.: On complete integrals and uniqueness in shape from shading. Appl. Math. Comput. **73**(1), 1–37 (1995)
6. Brooks, M.J., Chojnacki, W., Kozera, R.: Impossible and ambiguous shading patterns. Int. J. Comp. Vis. **7**(2), 119–126 (1992)
7. Oliensis, J.: Uniqueness in shape from shading. Int. J. Comp. Vis. **6**(2), 75–104 (1991)
8. Brooks, M.J., Chojnacki, W., Kozera, R.: Circularly symmetrical eikonal equations and non-uniqueness in computer vision. J. Math. Anal. Appl. **165**(1), 192–215 (1992)

9. Brooks, M.J., Chojnacki, W., Kozera, R.: Shading without shape. Quart. Appl. Maths. **50**(1), 27–38 (1992)
10. Brooks, M.J., Chojnacki, W.: Direct computation of shape-from-shading. In: 12th International Conference Pattern Recognition Jerusalem, Israel, pp. 114–119. IEEE Computer Society Press, Los Alamitos, CA (1994)
11. Horn, B.K.P., Brooks, M.J.: Shape from Shading. MIT Press, Cambridge (1989)
12. Woodham, R.J.: Photometric method for determining surface orientation from multiple images. Opt. Eng. **19**(1), 139–144 (1980)
13. Kozera, R.: Existence and uniqueness in photometric stereo. Appl. Math. Comput. **44**(1), 1–104 (1991)
14. Kozera, R.: On shape recovery from two shading patterns. Int. J. Patt. Rec. Art. Intel. **6**(4), 673–698 (1992)
15. Onn, R., Bruckstein, A.: Integrability disambiguates surface recovery in two image photometric stereo. Int. J. Comp. Vis. **5**(1), 105–113 (1990)
16. do Carmo, M.P.: Differential Forms and Applications. Springer, Heidelberg (1994)
17. Horn, B.K.P.: Height and gradient from shading. Int. J. Comp. Vis. **5**(1), 37–75 (1990)
18. Wei, T., Klette, R.: On depth recovery from gradient vector field. In: Bhattacharaya, B.B., et al. (eds.) Algorithms, Architectures and Information Systems Security, pp. 765–797. World Scientific Publishing Co., Private Ltd., Singapore (2009)
19. Simchony, T., Chellappa, R., Shao, M.: Direct analytic methods for solving poisson equations in computer vision problems. IEEE Trans. Patt. Rec. Mach. Intell. **12**(5), 435–446 (1990)
20. Frankot, R.T., Chellappa, R.: A method of enforcing integrability in shape from shading algorithms. IEEE Trans. Patt. Rec. Mach. Intell. **10**(4), 439–451 (1988)
21. Noakes, L., Kozera, R.: The 2-D Leap-Frog: integrability, noise, and digitization. In: Bertrand, G., Imiya, A., Klette, R. (eds.) Digital and Image Geometry. LNCS, vol. 2243, pp. 352–364. Springer, Heidelberg (2001). doi:10.1007/3-540-45576-0_21
22. Noakes, L., Kozera, R.: The lawn-mowing algorithm for noisy gradient vector fields. In: Latecki, L.J. (ed.) Vision Geometry VIII, Proceedings of SPIE, vol. 3811, pp. 305–316, Denver, CO, USA (1999)
23. Noakes, L., Kozera, R.: The 2-D Leap-Frog Algorithm for optimal surface reconstruction. In: Latecki, L.J. (ed.) Vision Geometry VIII, Proceedings of SPIE, vol. 3811, pp. 317–328, Denver, CO, USA (1999)
24. Noakes, L., Kozera, R.: Nonlinearities and noise reduction in 3-source photometric stereo. J. Math. Imag. Vis. **18**(3), 119–127 (2003)
25. Noakes, L., Kozera, R.: Denoising images: non-linear leap-frog for shape and light-source recovery. In: Asano, T., Klette, R., Ronse, C. (eds.) Geometry, Morphology, and Computational Imaging. LNCS, vol. 2616, pp. 419–436. Springer, Heidelberg (2003)
26. Noakes, L.: A global algorithm for geodesics. J. Math. Austral. Soc. Ser. A **64**, 37–50 (1999)
27. Kozera, R., Okulicka-Dłużewska, F., Noakes, L.: Integrated parallel 2D-Leap-Frog algorithm for noisy three image photometric stereo. In: Huang, F., Sugimoto, A. (eds.) PSIVT 2015. LNCS, vol. 9555, pp. 73–87. Springer, Heidelberg (2016). doi:10.1007/978-3-319-30285-0_7
28. Cameron, T., Kozera, R., Datta, A.: A parallel Leap-Frog algorithm for 3-source photometric stereo. In: Wojciechowski, K., et al. (eds.) Computer Vision and Graphics. Computational Imaging and Vision, vol. 32, pp. 95–102. Springer, Dordrecht (2006)

29. Castelán, M., Hancock, E.R.: Imposing integrability in geometric shape-from-shading. In: Sanfeliu, A., Ruiz-Shulcloper, J. (eds.) CIARP 2003. LNCS, vol. 2905, pp. 196–203. Springer, Heidelberg (2003)

30. Kozera, R., Okulicka-Dłużewska, F.: Conjugate gradient in noisy photometric stereo. In: Chmielewski, L.J., Kozera, R., Shin, B.-S., Wojciechowski, K. (eds.) ICCVG 2014. LNCS, vol. 8671, pp. 338–346. Springer, Heidelberg (2014)

31. Kozera, R., Noakes, L.: Optimal knots selection for sparse reduced data. In: Huang, F., Sugimoto, A. (eds.) PSIVT 2015. LNCS, vol. 9555, pp. 3–14. Springer, Heidelberg (2016). doi:10.1007/978-3-319-30285-0_1

32. Wöhler, C.: 3D Computer Vision: Efficient Methods and Applications. Springer-Verlag, Heidelberg (2009)

33. Kozera, R., Tchórzewski, J.: Outlier removal in 2D Leap Frog algorithm. In: Cortesi, A., Chaki, N., Saeed, K., Wierzchoń, S. (eds.) CISIM 2012. LNCS, vol. 7564, pp. 146–157. Springer, Heidelberg (2012)

# The Use of Interpolation Methods for Nonlinear Mapping

Evgeny Myasnikov[(✉)]

Samara University, 34 Moskovskoye Shosse, Samara 443086, Russia
mevg@geosamara.ru

**Abstract.** In this paper we consider the possibility of using several multivariate interpolation methods as a supplement to existing dimensionality reduction techniques. Analyzed methods including nearest neighbor interpolation, inverse distance weighting, radial basis functions, and data mapping error minimization are evaluated using well-known datasets. Conducted experiments showed that radial basis functions and interpolation by the data mapping error minimization outperformed other considered methods in terms of the data mapping error yielding slightly worse quality then using stochastic gradient descent method for the whole data sets without interpolation.

## 1  Introduction

Nonlinear dimensionality reduction techniques operating on the principle of preserving the data structure are widely used in scientific research, and in production activities in many areas. Researchers use nonlinear dimensionality reduction methods for multivariate data analysis and visualization. In signal and image analysis such methods have been applied in creation of browsing systems for image and multimedia databases. In multi- and hyperspectral image analysis nonlinear dimensionality reduction methods have been applied for segmentation, thematic classification, and visualization of such images.

In all considered applications, dimensionality reduction techniques map data points (multivariate vectors) from some multidimensional space into low- dimensional space. Let $N$ be the number of data points, $x_i$ be the coordinates of points in the multidimensional space $R^M$, $y_i$ be the coordinates of the corresponding points in the lower dimensional space $R^L$, $d(\cdot)$ be the Euclidean distance function. In this paper we assume that the data mapping error can be estimated by the following equation:

$$\varepsilon_0 = \mu \cdot \sum_{i,j=1,i<j}^{N} \left( \rho_{i,j} \cdot (d(x_i, x_j) - d(y_i, y_j))^2 \right) \tag{1}$$

that for some values of the constants $\mu$, $\rho_{i,j}$ leads to the Kruskal stress $\mu = 1/\sum_{i<j} d^2(x_i, x_j)$, $\rho_{i,j} = 1$ [6], or for values $\mu = 1/\sum_{i<j} d(x_i, x_j)$, $\rho_{i,j} = (d(x_i, x_j))^{-1}$ leads to Sammon data mapping error [11].

© Springer International Publishing AG 2016
L.J. Chmielewski et al. (Eds.): ICCVG 2016, LNCS 9972, pp. 649–655, 2016.
DOI: 10.1007/978-3-319-46418-3_58

This data mapping error can be minimized using a number of numerical techniques but the most widely used is the gradient descent approach. It leads us to the following iterative procedure:

$$y_i(t+1) = y_i(t) + 2\alpha\mu \sum_{j=1; i \neq j}^{N} \rho_{i,j} \cdot \frac{d(x_i, x_j) - d(y_i, y_j)}{d(y_i, y_j)} \cdot (y_i(t) - y_j(t)) \quad (2)$$

Here $t$ is the number of iteration, and $\alpha$ is the coefficient of the gradient descent.

Well-known drawbacks of this method are high computational complexity ($O(N^2)$ per iteration), memory requirements ($O(N^2)$ to store precomputed distances, otherwise the optimization process becomes even more time consuming and dependent on the dimensionality of the input space), impossibility to add new data. Several approaches to reduce the computational complexity have been proposed: tringulation [7], linear transformation [10], stochastic gradient descent methods, methods based on the hierarchical partitioning of the space [9], methods based on neural networks [3,8], and others.

At the same time the drawbacks mentioned above can be partially eliminated using interpolation. The idea of interpolation has already been applied for non-linear dimensionality reduction. For example in [4] a vector quantization is performed first, and base iterative optimization procedure is applied only to centroids obtained from quantization. Then full set of points is mapped into output space using interpolation-extrapolation algorithm based on the same optimization criterion that was used in the base algorithm. Another example is the paper [13] where radial basis function interpolation is used.

In this paper we evaluate and compare several multivariate interpolation methods as a supplement to the described nonlinear mapping technique. It is expected that considered methods will be used not as an alternative to existing nonlinear mapping approaches but to extend the limits of applicability of such techniques.

## 2   Methods

In this section we assume that the given set of known points $x_i, i = 1...K$ in multidimensional space $R^M$ has been successfully mapped into corresponding points $y_i$ in the lower dimensional space $R^L$, and it is required to obtain the interpolated value $y$ of the previously unknown point $x$.

### 2.1   Nearest neighbour interpolation

The nearest neighbour (NN) interpolation is the most simple and fast method, which takes into account only the nearest point:

$$y = y_k, x_k = argmin_{x_i} d(x, x_i) \quad (3)$$

## 2.2  Inverse Distance Weighting

Inverse distance weighting (IDW, Shepard Interpolation) [12] calculates the weighted sum of the values at the known points to obtain an interpolated value:

$$y = \frac{\sum_{i=1}^{K} w_i(x) y_i}{\sum_{i=1}^{K} w_i(x)} \tag{4}$$

Here weights $w_i(x)$ are defined by the inverse distance weighting function $w_i(x) = 1/d(x, x_i)^p$ where $p$ is the parameter (power) of the algorithm.

## 2.3  Radial Basis Functions

Radial Basis Function (RBF) interpolation is based on linear combination of radial kernels, placed at the known points $x_i$ [1]:

$$y = \sum_{i=1}^{K} w_i \phi(||x - x_i||) \tag{5}$$

Here kernel $\phi(\cdot)$ may be any fixed radial basis function and $w_i, i = 1..K$ are real valued coefficients. We use Euclidean distance $d(\cdot)$ as the most common choice for the norm $|| \cdot ||$. Some examples of kernel include multiquadric $\phi_m(r) = (r^2 + r_0^2)^{1/2}$, inverse multiquadric $\phi_{im}(r) = (r^2 + r_0^2)^{-1/2}$, thin plate spline $\phi_{tps}(r) = r^2 log(r/r_0)$ (a special case of poliharmonic spline), etc. Here $r_0$ is tunable parameter.

To calculate weights we form the following system of linear equations:

$$\sum_{i=1}^{K} w_i \phi(d(x_j, x_i)) - y_j = 0, j = 1..K \tag{6}$$

The solution gives us known values $y_j$ at known points $x_j$, and allows to get interpolated values according to the above expression at other points.

## 2.4  Interpolation by Data Mapping Error Minimization

The described above interpolation methods are generic methods of multivariate interpolation. Another approach consists in minimizing given error function to find an interpolated value. In the context of the considered task iterative interpolation algorithm takes the form:

$$y(t+1) = y(t) + 2\alpha\mu \sum_{i=1}^{K} \rho_{i,idx(x)} \left( \frac{d(x, x_i)}{d(y(t), y_i)} - 1 \right)(y(t) - y_i) \tag{7}$$

Here we assume that the positions $y_i$ of the known points $x_i$ remain constant and only position of interpolated point is refined.

## 2.5  Computational Complexity

The computational complexity of the NN and IDW interpolation can be estimated as $O(K)$ per one interpolated point. For the RBF case one interpolation requires $O(K)$ operations but besides that it is required $O(K^3)$ operations to solve a system of linear equations. Interpolation by iterative data mapping error minimization requires $O(TK)$ operations per one interpolated point, where $T$ is the number of iterations.

# 3    Experiments

To evaluate the described above algorithms the following well-known data sets were used:

- color moments (CM) from Corel Image Features Data Set [2] (dimensionality $M = 9$),
- texture features based on co-occurrence matrices (CT) from Corel Image Features Data Set [2] (dimensionality $M = 16$),
- pixels from Indian Pines Test Site 3 hyperspectral satellite image (IP) [5] (dimensionality $M = 220$).

At the first stage of experiments samples containing $N = 5000$ points were selected from above data sets. After that subsets $x_i, i = 1..K$ containing $K = 100, 500, 1000$ points were selected from the samples of size N. Then the base dimensionality reduction algorithm (gradient descent) was applied to reduce the dimensionality for the selected subsets to $L = 2$ (2D mapping) and to compute coordinates $y_i, i = 1..K$ of data points in the low-dimensional space. After that,

**Table 1.** Experimental results

| K | Base | NN | IDW | RBF | ErM | SGD |
|---|------|------|------|------|------|------|
| Feature Set: CT M = 16 | | | | | | |
| 100 | 0.009802 | 0.04389 | 0.04202 | 0.01387 | 0.01681 | 0.01059 |
| 500 | 0.01005 | 0.02314 | 0.02239 | 0.01221 | 0.01035 | 0.01059 |
| 1000 | 0.01062 | 0.01834 | 0.01779 | 0.01119 | 0.01020 | 0.01060 |
| Feature Set: CM M = 9 | | | | | | |
| 100 | 0.05733 | 0,1265 | 0,1253 | 0,078423 | 0.08077 | 0.06251 |
| 500 | 0.06281 | 0,09463 | 0,09388 | 0,073737 | 0.06416 | 0.06250 |
| 1000 | 0.06334 | 0,08388 | 0,08327 | 0,068599 | 0.06337 | 0.06250 |
| Feature Set: IP M = 220 | | | | | | |
| 100 | 0.001883 | 0.02039 | 0.01947 | 0.002819 | 0.005982 | 0.002197 |
| 500 | 0.002409 | 0.008402 | 0.007992 | 0.002817 | 0.002302 | 0.002198 |
| 1000 | 0.002338 | 0.005975 | 0.005710 | 0.002585 | 0.002230 | 0.002198 |

multidimensional coordinates $x_i$ and corresponding low-dimensional coordinates $y_i, i = 1..K$ were used to obtain the solution for the rest (N-K) data points using considered above interpolation methods.

The following table shows the results of the experiment (Table 1).

Data mapping error after reducing dimensionality using the base gradient descent approach for subsets containing K data points is shown in the Base column. Data mapping errors for samples containing N = 5000 data points after interpolation using nearest neighbor (NN), Shepard (IDW), radial basis functions (RBF) with multiquadric kernel, and data mapping error minimization (ErM) are shown in the corresponding columns. SGD column shows data mapping error after applying stochastic gradient descent method for samples containing N = 5000 data points without interpolation for comparison.

In the first series of experiments, the best parameters of the considered methods were determined. Thereafter, experiments were conducted for samples containing N = 10000 data points. The results are shown in Figs. 1, 2 and 3 with timings. It is worth noting that the time is shown on a logarithmic scale.

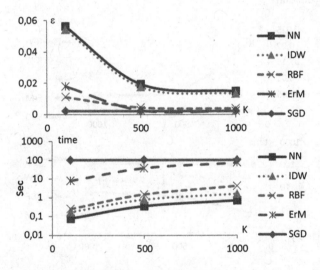

**Fig. 1.** Experimental results for texture features based on co-occurrence matrices. Data mapping error (top) with timings (bottom)

As it can be seen from the results of the experiments the nearest neighbour interpolation and inverse distance weighting provide higher error values but perform faster than the other methods.

Radial basis functions and interpolation by error minimization provide quite low error values compared to nearest neighbour and Shepard interpolation. In several cases RBF interpolation outperformed interpolation by error minimization when the number of base points was low (K = 100). For larger values of K the preference should be given to interpolation by error minimization.

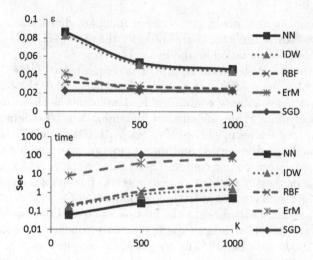

**Fig. 2.** Experimental results for color moments features. Data mapping error (top) with timings (bottom)

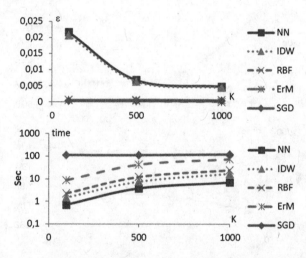

**Fig. 3.** Experimental results for Indian Pines Test Site 3 hyperspectral satellite image. Data mapping error (top) with timings (bottom)

At the same time latter method was significantly slower due to its iterative nature. Thus when the number of base and extra points was large the overall runtime was about the same as for stochastic gradient descent approach. Interpolation by radial basis functions was significantly faster.

# 4   Conclusion

Several multivariate interpolation methods have been applied in this paper to map extra data points to existing nonlinear mappings. Experiments showed that RBF and interpolation by the data mapping error minimization outperformed other considered methods in terms of the data mapping error yielding slightly worse quality then using stochastic gradient descent method for the whole datasets without interpolation. It is worth noting that data mapping using interpolation is faster and requires much less memory than using only conventional techniques. Therefore interpolation methods can be useful when working with large amounts of data, such as hyperspectral images.

**Acknowledgments.** This work is supported by Russian Foundation for Basic Research, projects no. $15 - 07 - 01164 - a$, $16 - 37 - 00202$ mol_a.

# References

1. Broomhead, D.H., Lowe, D.: Multivariable functional interpolation and adaptive networks. Complex Syst. **2**, 321–355 (1988)
2. Corel image features dataset. https://archive.ics.uci.edu/ml/datasets/Corel+Image+Features
3. Ridder, D., Duin, R.P.W.: Sammon's mapping using neural networks: a comparison. Pattern Recogn. Lett. **18**(1113), 1307–1316 (1997)
4. Demartines, P., Hrault, J.: CCA: curvilinear component analysis. In: Proceedings of 15th Workshop GRETSI (1995)
5. Indian Pines Test Site 3 hypersectral image. https://engineering.purdue.edu/biehl/MultiSpec/hyperspectral.html
6. Kruskal, J.B.: Multidimensional scaling by optimizing goodness of fit to a nonmetric hypothesis. Psychometrika **29**, 1–27 (1964)
7. Lee, R.C.T., Slagle, J.R., Blum, H.: A triangulation method for the sequential mapping of points from N-Space to two-space. IEEE Trans. Comput. **26**(3), 288–292 (1977)
8. Mao, J., Jain, A.K.: Artificial neural networks for feature extraction and multivariate data projection. IEEE Trans. Neural Netw. **6**(2), 296–317 (1995)
9. Myasnikov, E.V.: Nonlinear mapping methods with adjustable computational complexity for hyperspectral image analysis. In: Proceedings of SPIE 9875, 987508–987508-6 (2015)
10. Pekalska, E., de Ridder, D., Duin, R.P.W., Kraaijveld, M.A.: A new method of generalizing Sammon mapping with application to algorithm speed-up. In: Proceedings of 5th Annual Conference of the Advanced School for Computing and Imaging, ASCI 1999, pp. 221–228 (1999)
11. Sammon Jr., J.W.: A nonlinear mapping for data structure analysis. IEEE Trans. Comput. **C–18**(5), 401–409 (1969)
12. Shepard, D.: A two-dimensional interpolation function for irregularly-spaced data. In: Proceedings of the 1968 ACM National Conference, pp. 517–524 (1968)
13. Webb, A.R.: Multidimensional scaling by iterative majorization using radial basis functions. Pattern Recogn. **28**(5), 753–759 (1995)

# Author Index